Cambridge Companion to

The Cambridge Companion to Homer is a guide to the essential aspects of
Homeric criticism and scholarship, i
ancient and modern times. Written b
intended to be the first port of call for
to important subjects and suggestions
tional topics like the Homeric questio
formulas, the characters and the archa
discussions of similes, speeches, the p
both within Greece and worldwide. Th
of ancient Greek and Roman readings as well as selected modern interpretations from the eighteenth century to the present day. Chapters on Homer in English translation and 'Homer' in the history of ideas round out the collection.

Mattia Preti, *Homer*. Gallerie dell' Accademia, Venice

THE CAMBRIDGE COMPANION TO HOMER

EDITED BY

ROBERT FOWLER

Henry Overton Wills Professor of Greek in the University of Bristol

CAMBRIDGE UNIVERSITY PRESS
Cambridge, New York, Melbourne, Madrid, Cape Town, Singapore, São Paulo, Delhi

Cambridge University Press
The Edinburgh Building, Cambridge, CB2 8RU, UK

Published in the United States of America by Cambridge University Press, New York

www.cambridge.org
Information on this title: www.cambridge.org/9780521012461

First published 2004
Fourth printing 2008

Printed in the United Kingdom at the University Press, Cambridge

A catalogue record for this publication is available from the British Library

Library of Congress Cataloguing in Publication data

ISBN 978-0-521-81302-0 hardback
ISBN 978-0-521-01246-1 paperback

CONTENTS

ILLUSTRATIONS

Frontispiece

Plates

CONTRIBUTORS

RICHARD BUXTON is Professor of Greek Language and Literature at the University of Bristol. Among his books are *Persuasion in Greek Tragedy* (1982) and *Imaginary Greece* (1994). He has also edited *From Myth to Reason?* and *Oxford Readings in Greek Religion*. His book *The Complete World of Greek Mythology* was published by Thames and Hudson in 2004. He is currently researching a work on Greek metamorphosis stories.

MATTHEW CLARK is an Associate Professor in the Division of Humanities at York University in Toronto, Canada. He is the author of *Out of Line: Homeric Composition Beyond the Hexameter*, as well as various articles on the Homeric epics. His most recent book is *A Matter of Style: Writing and Technique* (2002), and he is now working on a study of persuasion in the *Iliad* as well as a book about the representation of the self in narrative.

MICHAEL CLARKE studied at Trinity College Dublin and Oxford University, and since 1999 he has been Lecturer in Ancient Classics at the National University of Ireland, Maynooth. He is the author of *Flesh and Spirit in the Songs of Homer* (1999), and he is currently working on a study of historical semantics and linguistic change, using materials from Greek and other Indo-European languages.

KEN DOWDEN is Professor of Classics in the Institute of Archaeology and Antiquity at the University of Birmingham. He is well known for his work in mythology (*Death and the Maiden* (1989); *Uses of Greek Mythology* (1992); but has also published more widely on religion *European Paganism* (2000), *Religion and the Romans* (1992), *Zeus* (forthcoming), and has written a variety of periodical articles on Greek and Roman literature, particularly the ancient novel.

JOSEPH FARRELL is Professor of Classical Studies in the University of Pennsylvania. He is the author of *Vergil's Georgics and the Traditions of*

Ancient Epic (New York 1991) and of *Latin Language and Latin Culture* (2001).

NANCY FELSON is Professor of Classics at the University of Georgia. She has published *Regarding Penelope: From Character to Poetics* (1994) and, as guest editor of *Arethusa*, 'Semiotics and classical studies' (1983) and 'Deixis and Greek choral lyric' (forthcoming, *Arethusa* 37, 2004). She has also edited *Symbols in Ancient Greek Poetry and Myth* (1980), and co-edited (with T. M. Falkner and D. Konstan) *Contextualizing Classics: Ideology, Performance, Dialogue* (2000). Her articles and book chapters include publications on story patterns and deictics in Pindaric epinicia and on constructions of gender in epinicia and epic, most recently with an emphasis on boyhood and masculinity.

JOHN MILES FOLEY is a specialist in the world's oral traditions, with particular emphasis on ancient Greek, medieval English, and contemporary South Slavic traditions. He serves as Curators' Professor of Classical Studies and English, as W. H. Byler Distinguished Chair in the Humanities, and as the founding Director of the Center for Studies in Oral Tradition at the University of Missouri–Columbia, USA, where he edits the journal *Oral Tradition*, the *Blackwell Companion to Ancient Epic*, and two series of books. He has published many volumes and articles on Homer and worldwide oral poetry, most recently *How To Read an Oral Poem* (2002), which is complemented by the website *www.oraltradition.org*.

ROBERT FOWLER is Henry Overton Wills Professor of Greek and Dean of Arts in the University of Bristol. He is author of *The Nature of Early Greek Lyric: Three Preliminary Studies* (Toronto 1987), *Early Greek Mythography I: Text and Introduction* (Oxford 2000), and articles on early Greek poetry and prose and the history of scholarship. He is preparing *Early Greek Mythography II: Commentary*.

JASPER GRIFFIN is Professor of Classical Literature at Oxford University, where he is also a Fellow of Balliol College. His publications include *Homer on Life and Death* (1980), *Homer: The Odyssey* (Cambridge, 1987) and *Homer: Iliad IX* (1995). He has also published extensively on Attic tragedy, Virgil, and Latin prose, especially Cicero.

LORNA HARDWICK teaches in the Department of Classical Studies at the Open University, where she is Professor of Classical Studies and Director of the Research Project on the Reception of Greek Texts and Images in Modern Drama and Poetry (see *http://www2.open.ac.uk/ClassicalStudies/GreekPlays*). Recent publications also include *Translating Words, Translating*

Cultures (2000) and *New Surveys in the Classics: Reception Studies* (2003). She is currently working on the relationships between classical texts and their receptions in post-colonial drama and poetry.

RICHARD HUNTER is Regius Professor of Greek at the University of Cambridge and a Fellow of Trinity College. His most recent books are *Plato's Symposium* (New York 2004), *Theocritus, Encomium of Ptolemy Philadelphus* (Berkeley 2003) and (with Marco Fantuzzi) *Muse e modelli. La poesia ellenistica da Alessandro Magno ad Augusto* (Bari 2002). An English-language version of *Muse e modelli, Tradition and Innovation in Hellenistic Poetry*, is forthcoming from Cambridge University Press.

EMILY KEARNS teaches classical languages and literature at St Hilda's College, Oxford. She is author of *The Heroes of Attica* (London 1989) and has edited with Simon Price *The Oxford Dictionary of Classical Myth and Religion* (2003).

DONALD LATEINER teaches humanities and classics courses at Ohio Wesleyan University in Delaware, Ohio (USA). His research includes non-verbal behaviours in ancient literature, Homeric and Ovidian epic poetry, the Roman novels, and the historiography of Herodotus and Thucydides. His published books are *The Historical Method of Herodotus* (1989) and *Sardonic Smile: Nonverbal Behavior in Homeric Epic* (Ann Arbor 1995). He is currently working on a study of insult and humiliation in Homer and classical Athens based on texts from epic, pottery, comedy, philosophy and oratory.

ROBIN OSBORNE is Professor of Ancient History in the University of Cambridge and a Fellow of King's College. He is the author of *Greece in the Making, 1200–479 BC* (1996) and *Archaic and Classical Greek Art* (1998) and editor of *Classical Greece* (2000) and, with P. J. Rhodes, of *Greek Historical Inscriptions 404–323 BC* (Oxford 2003).

JAMES I. PORTER is Professor of Classical Studies and Comparative Literature at the University of Michigan. He is the author of *Nietzsche and the Philology of the Future* (2000) and *The Invention of Dionysus: An Essay on The Birth of Tragedy* (2000), and is editor of *Constructions of the Classical Body* (1999). His current projects include a collection of essays, *Classical Pasts: The Classical Traditions of Greece and Rome*, a book entitled *The Material Sublime in Greek and Roman Aesthetics*, and a study on the reception of Homer from Greece to the present (*Homer: The Very Idea*).

RUTH SCODEL is Professor of Greek and Latin at the University of Michigan. She is the author of *Credible Impossibilities: Conventions and*

Strategies of Verisimilitude in Homer and Greek Tragedy (1999) and *Listening to Homer* (2002).

MICHAEL SILK is Professor of Greek Language and Literature at King's College in the University of London and, at the time of writing, Visiting Professor of Greek and Comparative Literature at Boston University. His books include *Homer, The Iliad* (2nd edn, 2003) and *Aristophanes and the Definition of Comedy* (2000).

LAURA M. SLATKIN teaches classical studies at New York University (Gallatin School) and the University of Chicago. She has published *The Power of Thetis: Allusion and Interpretation in the Iliad* (1992) and articles on Greek epic poetry and drama. She co-edited (with Nicole Loraux and Gregory Nagy) *Histories of Post-War French Thought*, vol. 2, *Antiquities: Rewriting the Past, Rethinking the Present* (2001).

GEORGE STEINER is Emeritus Professor of English and Comparative Literature, University of Geneva, and a Fellow of Churchill College, Cambridge. He is author of some fifteen books including *The Death of Tragedy* (1961), *Antigones* (1984), *Real Presences* (1989), and *Lessons of the Masters* (2003).

TIMOTHY WEBB is Winterstoke Professor in the Department of English at the University of Bristol. His books include *The Violet in the Crucible: Shelley and Translation* (1976), and editions and critical studies of a wide range of authors and topics including Shelley, Byron, Keats, Leigh Hunt, Romantic Hellenism, Romantic perceptions of Ireland, Yeats and Joyce.

PENELOPE WILSON is a Fellow and College Lecturer in English Literature at New Hall, Cambridge, and has published mainly on eighteenth-century literature and on the classical tradition. She is currently working on the history of translation and on a study of English commentary on classical poetry from the seventeenth to the early nineteenth centuries.

VANDA ZAJKO is Lecturer in Classics at the University of Bristol. She has wide-ranging interests in the reception of Greek and Latin literature. Her most recent essay is '"Petruchio is Kated": *The Taming of the Shrew* and Ovid', in C. Martindale and A. B. Taylor, eds., *Shakespeare and the Classics* (2004).

PREFACE

Extremely pleased though I was at the Press's invitation to edit this volume, the enormity of its subject induced an unusually acute sense of apprehension. No one could ever do it complete justice. It is also a subject which arouses the greatest passions – as is only right, for Homer is an author whose stature in the Western tradition is approached only by Virgil and Plato, and surpassed only by the Bible. Everything is at stake in him. But apprehension was balanced by the many pleasures of the task, not least that of being able to spend more time in the company of the supreme bard and so many insightful readers. The authors here assembled hope to have done him at least a worthy service; and Homer is surely sublime enough to forgive the inevitable injustice.

I have been fortunate at every stage to have excellent advice from the Press's readers and its Classics Editor, and from my fellow contributors. There was much discussion at the very beginning about the design of the volume, from which I benefited greatly. Perhaps the most noticeable feature of this design is the devotion of much space to Homer's reception. Some of the reasons for this I have sought to make clear in the Introduction. In general, reception of Classics is increasingly seen as part of the subject itself. There is a world of work to be done, and new vistas of interpretation are constantly opening up. Further on in the process of production, drafts were circulated, so that we could take account of each others' views and add appropriate cross-references. The result is a more cohesive and useful book, but not one with a uniform critical perspective: that was never the idea. My warmest thanks to all involved.

Some practical notes for readers: abbreviations in the volume follow standard lists such as those in the *Oxford Classical Dictionary* (3rd edn, 1996) or the ninth edition of Liddell, Scott and Jones' *Greek–English Lexicon* (with Supplement, Oxford 1968), and throughout, books of the *Iliad* are cited in Arabic numerals, of the *Odyssey* in Roman. In the matter of Latinisation of names, we have allowed contributors their preferences, so that you will find 'Patroklos' in one chapter, 'Patroclus' in the next. Citations of Homer's Greek follow Martin West's edition of the *Iliad* (Stuttgart 1998–2000) and Helmut van Thiel's edition of the *Odyssey* (Hildesheim 1991). Translations of Homer are by contributors, unless acknowledged.

R. L. F.
7 November 2003

MAPS

Mt Olympus
R. Peneus
EPIRUS
R. Peneus
Larisa
Dodona
THESSALIAN PLAIN
MAGNESIA
THESPROTIA
Corcyra
R. Achelous
PHTHIA
R. Spercheus
Scyros
R. Achelous
ACARNANIA
Leucas
LOCRIS
Euboea
AETOLIA
Hyampolis
PHOCIS
R. Cephisus
Orchomenus
Mt Parnassus
Chalcis
Ithaca
Calydon
W. LOCRIS
Delphi
Aulis
Eretria
L. Copais
BOEOTIA
Thebes
Cephallenia
ACHAEA

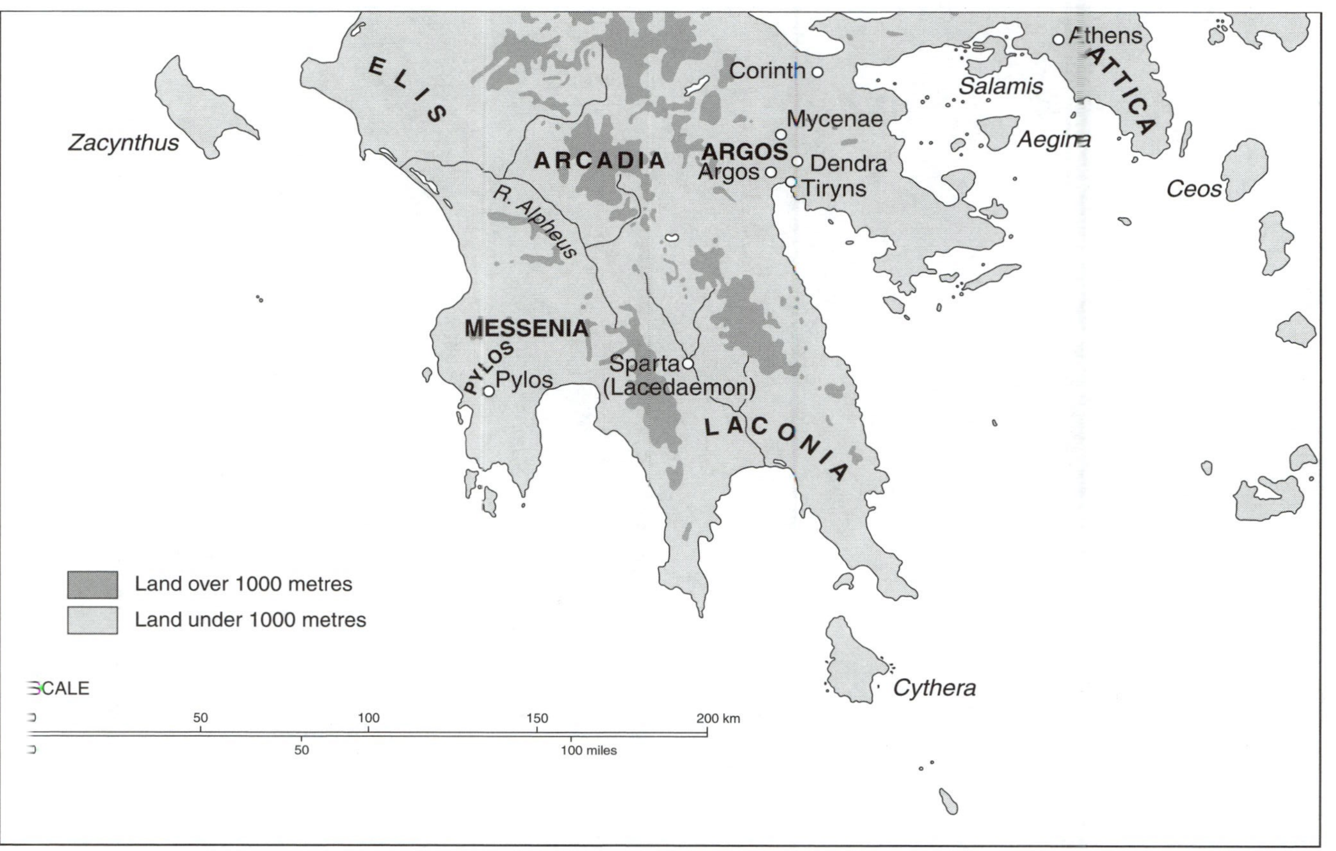

Map 1. Mainland Greece

Map 2. Eastern Aegean

1

ROBERT L. FOWLER

Introduction

The portrait of Homer that forms the frontispiece of this volume hangs in the Gallerie dell' Accademia, Venice. It is generally thought to be an early work of Mattia Preti (1613–1699), from a period when the influence of Caravaggio on him was strong. As a rendering of the bard, considered retrospectively from the twenty-first century, it offers much to ponder. The general appearance – closed, useless eyes upon a gaunt and bearded face – follows the ancient type.[1] The upward turn of the head, however, evokes ancient portraits of Alexander of Macedon, that great dreamer, and the painting's dark and brooding atmosphere, like many other portraits of the *seicento*, seems already to evoke the spirit of Romanticism. Proto-Romantic too is the stress on the inspiration of the lonely genius. The principal light in the picture streams from heaven, abode of the Muses, the source of this inspiration. It falls full on the unseeing eyes, underscoring the paradox that the blind poet sees more than the sighted. Yet the poet is no mere passive receptacle. Above his eyes, Homer's deep brows are obscured by Apollo's laurels; this is a learned poet, like the *docti poetae* of Hellenistic Alexandria or Catullan Rome. The doctor's robes reinforce the point: medieval, of course. The wreath too more probably springs from medieval conceptions of the poet's garb[2] or from the famous close of the third book of Horace's *Odes* – *sume superbiam | quaesitam meritis, et mihi Delphica | lauro cinge volens, Melpomene, comam*[3] – than from close knowledge of Greek cultic practice. The most splendid anachronism of the picture, however, is obviously the violin. Certainly Preti would have known that Homer's instrument, if indeed he sang (rather than chanting, with the rhapsode's staff in

[1] Ancient portraits of Homer are discussed most recently by Graziosi (2002) 128–32.

[2] Blech (1982) 312–16.

[3] 'Assume the pride you have earned, Melpomene, and be pleased to entwine the Delphic laurel in my locks.'

hand),[4] was a lyre. Apparently he did not care about that kind of historical accuracy. Instead, like most of us, he sought to create a Homer who, though indescribably ancient, could plausibly sing forth in his own day.

Preti's Homer is at once both modern and primitive. This in itself represents a familiar dynamic of interpretation. From a twenty-first century point of view, it sits halfway between us and antiquity, not in terms of years, but in a middle position between ancient realities and the various critical approaches which, arising since the eighteenth century, have fundamentally shaped our understanding of Homer – enhancing, distorting, or neither according to one's convictions. As such, the painting is a fitting emblem for a volume devoted both to Homer in his original context, so far as it can be recovered, and to his reception.

This tension between primitive and modern, difference and sameness, has dogged Homer since antiquity, and is perhaps at its most acute in our own day. Preti's violin, for instance, immediately raises the issue of performance. No less thought-provoking to me is the photograph of Avdo Međedović cradling his *gusle* on the cover of the new edition of Albert Lord's *The Singer of Tales*.[5] For the historicist, the context of the original performance lies right at the heart of the Homeric Question, unavoidable and unsettled even after two centuries of debate. There is no doubt that the discoveries of Lord's mentor Milman Parry, based on his observations of the South Slavic singers, have allowed us to reconstruct with some confidence the nature of poetic tradition and performance in Homer's day. But when I listen to recordings of the *guslars* I hear sounds from a culture so different from my own that I wonder how, if this really is the closest thing to Homer available to our experience, I can ever pretend to understand him. Perhaps I do deceive myself in this pretence. The gap between me and Homer must be ten times, a hundred times bigger than the gap between me and the *guslars*, already difficult to bridge except by patient, hard work. One could dismiss the South Slavic analogy – many people do – but that is too facile a solution to the present problem. The fear is that Homer belongs to an altogether different era of human history, the other side of some evolutionary and psychological divide. Scholars who write Greek literary history in terms of developments (not all yet extinct) have difficulty not thinking of Homer in this way. Other, more recent and cosmopolitan critics make the same claim from a quite different, postmodernist perspective.

[4] Probably he did sing; see West (1997b) 218, (1992a) 42–3. For a discussion of the rhapsodes' art see most recently Graziosi (2002) 18–40; Powell (2002) 134–45; Pelliccia (2003), taking issue with Nagy (1996a), (1996b).

[5] Lord (2000), with CD of recorded performances by various singers.

But then there are the texts themselves: however incomprehensible in this or that particular (can anyone really pretend to understand, for example, the scene in *Iliad* 1 where Athena yanks Achilles' hair?), for centuries these poems have stirred the emotions, enlightened the minds and ennobled the spirits of their readers who, however much their interpretations differ, all recognise their fellow human beings, hear and comprehend a sublime voice, and feel the redemptive power of civilisation. This cannot be an illusion. However easily contradicted any particular account of sameness is in its details, some quality as yet imperfectly understood – or less perfectly understood than it used to be – in the work of the *poeta sovrano* reaches across time, to achieve the same immediately arresting effect upon its listeners that Athena had on Achilles. The *Iliad*'s profoundly sophisticated voice transcends the bounds of age. Like countless others, there are moments when I think that this stupendous masterpiece, produced the better part of 3,000 years ago, fountainhead of Western literature and in many people's view still its greatest work, is simply a miracle, a serious argument for divine intervention in human history.

Yet even as one feels the way towards a transhistorical perspective, one realises that both these views of Homer – unrecoverably primitive or miraculously present – are demonstrably modern views, or more precisely Romantic. After two hundred years this tremendous movement still shapes our consciousness and interpretation, despite the wrench of the twentieth century. Let anyone who doubts it consider this opinion from an earlier age:

> To works, however, of which the excellence is not absolute and definite, but gradual and comparative; to works not raised upon principles demonstrative and scientific, but appealing wholly to observation and experience, no other test can be applied than length of duration and continuance of esteem. What mankind have long possessed they have often examined and compared, and if they persist to value the possession, it is because frequent comparisons have confirmed the opinion in its favour. As among the works of nature no man can properly call a river deep or a mountain high, without the knowledge of many mountains and many rivers; so in the productions of genius, nothing can be styled excellent till it has been compared with other works of the same kind. Demonstration immediately displays its power, and has nothing to hope or fear from the flux of years; but works tentative and experimental must be estimated by their proportion to the general and collective ability of man, as it is discovered in a long succession of endeavours. Of the first building that was raised, it might be with certainty determined that it was round or square, but whether it was spacious or lofty must have been referred to time. The Pythagorean scale of numbers was at once discovered to be perfect; but the poems of Homer we yet know not to transcend the common limits of

> human intelligence, but by remarking, that nation after nation, and century after century, has been able to do little more than transpose his incidents, new name his characters, and paraphrase his sentiments.
>
> The reverence due to writings that have long subsisted arises therefore not from any credulous confidence in the superior wisdom of past ages, or gloomy persuasion of the degeneracy of mankind, but is the consequence of acknowledged and indubitable positions, that what has been longest known has been most considered, and what is most considered is best understood.

Johnson here, in his *Preface to Shakespeare* (1765), argues that though Homer is a genius, he is a genius who in principle might be produced by any age. (Shakespeare was another.) He allows no veneration simply on grounds of antiquity. A Romantic, so far from resisting the tendency, would actively embrace the mystique of the very old and especially the wonder of being in its immediate presence – a cult of antiquity that has its uncritical side and sits quite well with Romantic melancholy, but is much more complicated than simple credulity or curmudgeonly gloom. Most remarkable, however, is Johnson's totally unthinking confidence that there is no essential difference in the world observed and experienced by Homer and that observed and experienced by the eighteenth century. It does not even cross his mind that mentalities might differ. In the wake of Herder such a view became problematic and increasingly rare. In the postmodern age it has disappeared altogether.

While Johnson could read Homer without mediation, Romanticism pretends to be able to read him without mediation, but knows that it cannot really do so without undermining its enterprise. Romantic feeling about the very old depends upon simultaneously keeping the sense of distance and difference – the *frisson* of getting close to Homer is not the same if you actually are one of his contemporaries – and nurturing the hope that, through an effort of imagination, one can bridge the gap. Romanticism is thus concerned to recreate original historical contexts. There have been, above all, the battles over the Homeric question itself. In its older form, analysis assigned different layers of the poems to precise dates, erroneously in most cases; with much greater probability, philology has laid bare the historical layers of the dialect. The modern study of oral poetry is an avatar of nineteenth-century study of folk tradition. Inspired particularly by Nietzsche, scholars have sought to see Greek gods through Greek rather than Roman or Christian eyes, a project which could not have started before artists and thinkers, in the wake of the Enlightenment, began to resurrect paganism as a serious way of looking at the world. By the end of the nineteenth century archaeology had added enormous impetus to the search for the original Homer (following on arch-Romantic Schliemann's discovery of Troy itself).[6] Continuing efforts throughout the twentieth century have brought huge gains in knowledge. The picture of early Greece has become much more detailed, sharper in focus. We are getting closer even to the Bronze Age itself. The excavations at Hisarlik have begun anew. Recent work makes it all but certain that the *Ahhiyawa* of Hittite texts is the land of Homer's Achaeans, and that *Wilus(s)a*/*Wilusiya* is Ilios, Troy. A seal found in 1995 shows that Priam's name is Luwian.[7]

Yet such advances cannot (thankfully) remove the mystery. Even if we could accumulate an infinity of facts, some of it would remain. Homer was already a mystery to the archaic Greeks. The ancient biographies, with their plenitude of specious detail, are entirely fictitious, depending on inferences from the poems themselves, plausible conjecture and outright invention (the bard Phemius plays a prominent role in the *Odyssey*: therefore such a bard must have been important in the poet's life: perhaps this was his stepfather?). This is the first stage of Homer's reception, in fact. The difficulty was, first, that he gave no real clue in his poems about his person (enabling seven different cities to claim him as their own), and second, that the individuality of an author was a concept only beginning to emerge (partly, one might think, through the efforts of this very singer). The unique symbiosis of tradition and individual talent operative in the context of oral poetry meant that, by the time tradition took the form of a finite number of fixed texts with authors' names attached, the Homer legend was already firmly entrenched.[8] Should the sands of Egypt yield up all the epics of the Cycle, we would undoubtedly acquire a wealth of new information and insight, but Homer himself would still remain just beyond reach. Even if we could invent a time machine, and take Parry-like recordings of the bard – if he existed as an individual – this would remain the case. The sophistication of the traditional art instantiated in Homer implies a wealth of contemporary performance practically beyond imagination; we must think that Homer's songs represent a tiny fraction of what was on offer in his day, all over the Greek world (*ipso facto* a far more sophisticated civilisation than most students of oral poetry, besotted by Romantic notions of bards, actually realise). Because of the quality of the poems, Homer cannot be demythologised as just one singer among many – either because, on one view of the phenomenon, the individual is only a hypostasis of tradition: 'just one singer among many' *constitutes* the mythical

[6] On Schliemann see in general Traill (1995), Allen (1999).

[7] Latacz (2001), (2002); Janko in Montanari and Ascheri (2002) 664.

[8] On the ancient lives of Homer see Lefkowitz (1981b) ch. 2; Latacz (1996) 24–30; Graziosi (2002).

dimensions of the situation; or because, on another view, this individual has transcended the tradition through his genius. The approach to Homer remains tinged with a delicious longing for the inaccessible not found with any modern author, nor even with most ancient ones.

Johnson displays no such feeling, and reads Homer with the same aesthetic filters as he reads Shakespeare. But even before his time things were changing. The advance of science precipitated the Quarrel of the Ancients and Moderns in the seventeenth and early eighteenth centuries, when Moderns turned their backs on Homer and other antique sages. Of course the illusion of superiority could never last; Homer could hardly be suppressed. The late eighteenth and early nineteenth centuries, rediscovering their own true, sublime Homer, resolved the Quarrel by putting the inspiration of the ancients at the service of a progressive, forward-looking world. This rapprochement continued until the cataclysm of another Modernism, which, on a superficial reading, turned its back even more decisively on the past; yet it could not really do so without engaging in a dialogue with antiquity, as most practitioners were ready enough to admit.

Throughout the twentieth century classical antiquity seemed, again on a superficial assessment, ever farther to seek, finally left behind by a world changed beyond all recognition. Yet, just as in the eighteenth century, there were still legions of people reading Homer, and at the turn of the millennium his fortunes have never seemed better. Classics as a discipline flourishes. Numbers of pupils rise once more in the schools. Popular and highbrow culture alike cannot get enough of antiquity. The Quarrel, it seems, is reaching a new stage of rapprochement. Looking back on the story since about 1770, with its essential Romantic continuity in spite of much superficial change, and contemplating the 'aesthetic turn' said to lie on the horizon of the humanities after centuries of historicism and decades of increasingly homogenised cultural studies, one might prophesy a return to a style of criticism such as Milton or Pope might have recognised. Certainly many interesting readings would result from such a move. But somehow I doubt it will happen, at least not soon. Homer, like most Greek authors before Callimachus, is just alien enough to justify, even force, the historicising bent that has come naturally to every Homerist since Bentley discovered the digamma.[9]

The oscillating dialectic of past and present, immanence and distance, is as unstable for us as it was for Preti. We are more aware of it now, though one may wonder whether that is a gain. The myth of progress dies hard; believers in it have a vested interest in sharpening the lines of controversy.

[9] On this relic of prehistoric Greek in the Homeric dialect see Dowden in this volume p. 192; on Bentley see Pfeiffer (1976) ch. 11 and Brink (1985).

As a matter of fact, historicists have always recognised, if insufficiently, the ephemeral nature of their findings, and their entanglement in their own perspectives, long before postmodernism made the point with all force. Conversely, receptionists do not argue that all readings are equally valid. Any defensible reading of Homer must depend both upon the soundest contextualisation philology can offer, and an informed appreciation of the contingencies of interpretation both past and present.

Hence the general plan of this volume. In the case of Homer, however, the vastness of his scholarship exacerbates the usual problems facing the contributors to a Cambridge Companion, whose remit is both to provide essential advice for the novice and to suggest future directions for research. Editor and contributors alike are bound to be selective. This being a book primarily for English speakers, non-English receptions have hardly been touched on, important though they are; ideally, too, much more space would have been devoted to the interpretation of Homer by artists. Separate treatments of the Middle Ages and the Renaissance would have yielded valuable results. The periods I have chosen, however, arguably represent the most formative moments in the long story of Homeric reading. Certainly they raise issues of fundamental concern. Perusal of the studies in this volume suggests a provisional list: text and original context; the preference of the *Iliad* over the *Odyssey*, and vice-versa, at different times for different reasons; what to make of the violence in the poems, and the status of war; how to assess Homer's religion; Homer as modern or ancient, sophisticated or primitive; the status of myth; gender issues; stylistic issues (have we even now devised a new 'oral poetics'?); how to translate Homer (a translation, we ought not to forget, is everyone's first experience of reception); how to translate cultures; Homer as an authority and as a guide to life; Homer's place in the history of ideas; Hellenism.

Many of these issues have their roots in antiquity, of course, and therefore also find expression in those chapters which seek to communicate and extend the best insights of scholars working within the more familiar boundaries of Homeric scholarship. The list of topics is deliberately literary in bias, though obviously the prehistoric and historical background, or the perennial Homeric question, were not to be overlooked. One can quibble about the balance, and there will always be topics whose inclusion or exclusion this or that reader might query. For myself, I could not have conceived of the volume without chapters on the human and divine characters, without studies of the plots and their narration, or without treatments of the poet's stunning craft, from the minutiae of his formulas to the splendours of his similes – no mere ornaments – and his unsurpassed oratory. In confronting similar issues on the level of their several topics, contributors were asked to identify particular ideas or passages for paradigmatic treatment and relegate others to brief mention, possibly only in footnotes. While this seemed the right policy to yield the best results for the greatest number of readers, it can leave gaps. Editor and contributors alike have looked out for these and attempted to fill them wherever possible; it is hoped that, in cases where extended discussion has not been possible, the needs of readers will have been met by references to appropriate bibliography.

It will not surprise readers to find different perspectives and styles of scholarship throughout the volume, not to say outright disagreements. The plan was always to bring in as many kinds of voice as possible. Homer is too good to be left to any one person or group. He is also too good to think that he needs us to rescue him; whatever we might do or not do with him, he will continue to speak forcefully for himself. In talking about Homer, however, we do well to remember how very heterogeneous and numerous are those who wish to claim him as part of their heritage, and to bring as many of these heirs into the conversation as we can. The demolition of intellectual boundaries in recent decades, while entailing many risks and terrors, brings also exhilaration, liberation and reward. Whatever new understanding of humanity might emerge from this tumult, Homer is certain to be part of it.[10]

[10] My thanks to Michael Liversidge and John Foley for comments on this Introduction.

I

THE POEMS AND THEIR NARRATOR

2

DONALD LATEINER

The *Iliad*: an unpredictable classic

Can the oldest text of European literature be the greatest ever composed? An epic of killing, unprecedented and *sui generis* in myriad ways, was perhaps completed before ink and stylus were (re-)introduced to a savage European continent, long after the crash or whimpers of the Bronze Age, citadel-dominated civilisation that in some way the poem celebrates. This narrative of and meditation on death, loss and individual decisiveness became and remains fundamental for Mediterranean, European and even transatlantic literature. In the third, computerised millennium, when many still endorse Christian ethics of 'turn the other cheek' but otherwise rigorously forget former canons of honour, beauty and truth, conscientious readers anxiously confront this complex, inexplicable colossus, the *Iliad*. A provoked but fiercely introspective and precisely responsive young man becomes angry, and this anger trumps his community's desperate need for help. The consequences of Akhilleus' decisions for himself, his friends and his enemies constitute the *Iliad*, a uniquely long and uniquely coherent poem by some one or many called 'Homer'.[1] This synoptic consideration of its plot hopes to orient new readers to the story and provoke returning ones to consider afresh the terrifying subject, the various nature of the narrative with its inimitable pacing and episodic units, the characters, and their social and personal values nigh incomprehensible today.

Subject and themes

Forty days' interrupted fierce fighting for a few prime Anatolian acres around Troy town between overseas, mostly Balkan Greeks (Homer collectively calls them Akhaians, Danaans and Argives) and local Trojans seems a strange, even weird subject for any poem. Fifty or more Hellenic bards over five

[1] I employ this convenient term for the last creator of the available *Iliad* text, all that we can read today; cf. Parry (1966).

hundred years or more on two continents perhaps composed this epic that can surprise Sokrates and us. So much killing – 240 named battle dead and many others anonymously dispatched; Homer knows sixty ways to say 'X died' (Garland (1981) 52–3, 50). The savage slaughter provides a background for the *Iliad*'s other conflicts, those that mere strength, agility and military power cannot solve. A determined West Aegean[2] expeditionary group's problems with a tactless but indispensable commander, and the epic protagonist's struggle to maintain honour, rank and self-esteem while fighting a war that he cannot win or even survive provide the skeletons of two, intertwined plots. Akhilleus' wars pit him against a greedy and sometimes incompetent bully, his own closest friends, the powerful enemy, and sometimes even against the gods, in hand-to-hand and even post-mortem exchanges (with dead Patroklos' spirit and Thetis over Hektor's dead body).

The narrator of heavenly and earthly events collapses a massive ten-year siege in an allied war of revenge and retaliation, many generations past, into less than seven weeks, the duration of an internal dispute between Agamemnon the Akhaian leader and Akhilleus his best warrior. Events of only fourteen days are narrated, most of them within a three-day span (Taplin (1992) 14–22), a blink of the Olympian eye. No city or hamlet is sacked, only two or three major heroes die (Sarpedon, Patroklos, Hektor), the poem's story begins and also stops in the midst of mutilated histories – a few long days in the war's tenth year, certainly much closer to the end than the beginning. Nevertheless, already the Akhaians have been nearly pushed back into the sea, while Hektor's death (Book 22) marks Troy's doom. The plot recounts crises (those of Akhilleus, Agamemnon, and the Akhaians; of Hektor, the Trojans, and Priam) in the extended tale of legendary Troy. Homer expands the severely circumscribed and truncated time and scene – a confused Bronze and Iron Age battlefield and its two fortified camps – in various ways. He provides vignettes of other heroic myths, allusions to the divine and natural cosmic order, and sharp cuts to other worlds in the similes and in the ecphrasis or description of Akhilleus' divinely wrought shield. These pauses in the killing, short as a line or longer than a hundred, sketch the noisy city and the quiet countryside of other days and better ways.

[2] The anti-Trojan coalition shares no one constant name. Akhaians, Danaans and Argives (*pars pro toto*), used indifferently, illustrate their lack of unity and absence of any sense of shared nationality. At the time of composition, here assumed to be *c.* 700 BCE, 'Hellenic' denoted a very limited territory in southeast Thessaly. 'Greek' is a Roman ethnic name yet to be invented and later incorrectly extended!

Iliadic warfare beyond the duel is hard to visualise and 'highly unrealistic'.[3] The poet follows aristocratic individuals, not lines (?) or masses of infantry, into combat to a degree that one wonders why the latter groups are there at all. Logistics are largely ignored: where do Akhaians get horses, iron and wine?[4] How do Trojans sneak cattle for barbecues into the fortified cities after a siege of ten years? Noncombatant slaves and battle-attendants barely appear; chariots are war-taxis more than battle-platforms or moving weapons. The one-on-one heroic conflicts are highly ritualised: narrative patterns of attack and defence and the lethal results are usually clear-cut and oft repeated.[5] 'No walking wounded' and few words at death. Most of the pathophysiological causes of death are precisely recorded and medically sound; many are delightfully gruesome.

References to the distant past and the equi-distant future[6] frame furious action in battle and infuriating inaction *chez* Akhilleus in three venues only: Troy town, the Akhaian shore entrenchment, and the battle-plain between. The narrator swiftly moves between east of the Aegean and west to Mt Olympos, between Anatolian city and Akhaian troop-camp, between present Ilion and far-off Lykia and Sparta. He also unexpectedly spirits away the audience to anonymous Balkan, Anatolian and unspecified homely locales of the similes.[7] We observe – often through the eyes of solitary witnesses on the spot, but at a distance – a peaceful snowy forest, a threatened midnight farmstead, stormy Aegean seas, and unpoliced upland pastures – but also working women and playing children (e.g. dyer and weaver, 4.141–5, 23.760–3; sandcastle and wasps' nest destroyers, 15.362–4, 16.259–65).

The omniscient Ionian narrator knows this Troy story well, and inserts other local and alien legends embedded with similar patterns of heroic deeds and losses. He knows its numberless cast and contingents but requests, by

[3] Rutherford (1996) 37–9 surveys some of these problems and provides entrée into the vast bibliography.

[4] Raiding expeditions gain occasional mention, e.g. 6.414–28 (Kilikian Thebe), 9.129, 328–32, 19.296. Book 7.467–75 provides a scene of barter and gifts between Lemnians and Akhaians.

[5] The battle narratives, vaunting and taunting, tactics, grisly wounds (fatal or not; cf. Rutherford (1996) 39, 43), and quick deaths (or healings) are wonderfully diverse. See Fenik (1968), Lohmann (1970), Latacz (1977), van Wees (1992), also Garland (1981), Rutherford (1996), and Morrison (1999) on Homeric inventiveness in wound placement (catalogue: 143–4).

[6] Past: Thetis' prehistoric assistance to Zeus, 1.396–406; mythic paradigms of Herakles, Bellerophon, etc.; building of Troy, 21.443–7, 5.638–51. Future: destruction of Argos, 4.51–2; Troy, 7.461–3, 12.15–35; relative weakness of men now: 5.304 = 12.445 = 20.287 (boulder-heavers – a future *topos* for epic parodies).

[7] Edwards in Kirk *et al.* ([illegible]) vol. v: [illegible] compactly discusses forms, subjects, and distribution of the similes. See also Redfield's (1975) useful categories and Buxton in this volume.

prayerful invocation, supernatural assistance for the whole and special parts such as big battles and catalogues (1.1, 2.484, 14.508, etc.). He injects other tellers (e.g. Nestor, Phoinix, Akhilleus, Thetis, Hephaistos and Zeus) into the *Iliad* to recount their own deeds and those of yet others (such as Lykourgos, Bellerophon, Tydeus, Eëtion, and Akhilleus' unique lays noted at 9.189). Many dynamic mini-narratives vary the tactics of persuasive speech and pepper dialogues between friends and enemies.

The tale of 15,693 verses develops rapidly for an audience presumed already familiar with the characters from the ocean of existing legend faintly known to us from later references to the 'epic cycle'. The protagonist absents himself early from the central battle action, 1.295 to 20.42, 68 per cent of the text. This unexpected deferment of the central character's engagement provides one of many ways that the poet obstructs and delays, and so enlarges, his story.[8] Book 9 envisages various outcomes for Akhilleus – none of them to happen. Another example of retardation: Hypnos, a minor divinity or *daimon*, says (14.258 ff.): 'And [Zeus] would have sunk me [Sleep] out of sight . . . | had not Night . . . rescued me.' Or, a crucial example anticipates the fall of Troy itself (16.698–701). Homer's 'winged words' delight in misdirection, bold miscues, fumbled prayers,[9] Zeus's weighing of odds, and other such contrafactual hypotheticals. Oral story-tellers succeed by both frustrating and fulfilling face-to-face audience expectations. Homer has a formula for junctures forbidden but delightful to imagine: 'And now, X would have happened, if Y had not . . .'[10] The bard at the dawn of the Western literary tradition betrays the anxiety of centuries of influential shorter, less ambitious epics that had been created, disseminated, recited and perhaps already transcribed.

Anger is thematic and problematic in the monumental text. Akhilleus, Agamemnon, Apollo above and Khryses below experience and explain it. Phoinix, Zeus, Patroklos, Akhilleus, Priam and others meditate on and discuss anger: its justifications, damage, limits, placation and cessation. Humans oscillate here between passion and reason, caught in a bewildering mesh of circumstance, duty, loyalties, fate and choices. The heroes speak differently of honour, love, desire, respect, and responsibility. Homer presents many points of view (from horses' to gods'), but rarely his own *in propria persona*.

[8] Owen (1946) well describes retardation, amplification, postponement, interludes, etc. See also Richardson (1990), and Scodel in this volume.

[9] See Lang (1975), Lateiner (1997), and Pulleyn (1997) on prayers and their literary uses.

[10] Lang (1989), Morrison (1992a) and (1992b), Nesselrath (1992), Louden (1993). The gods appear in half of these non-events (e.g. 3.373–5, 5.311–17, 20.288–91). These potential violations of the tradition are not fulfilled. Homer is working with and against traditions, amplifying and altering, fulfilling and frustrating audience expectation.

Insult and unjustified humiliation (*lōbē*) in intricate varieties keep the plot afloat. Responsive anger and limited self-restraint ground the touchy cast of characters. The *Iliad* is initiated and repeatedly refueled by insult and humiliation, public and private, on both the human and divine level. Akhaians and Trojans duel with words as well as with spears, swords and arrows. The pleasing *klea andrōn* ('famous deeds of men')[11] that Akhilleus sings to himself and Patroklos while briefly dormant from the battles raging near him have an opposite side: harsh words that inflict permanent damage on their targets and attract advantage in status for the aggressors. Flyting is verbal fighting: competitive creatures that the heroes are, they compare genealogies, estates and previous kills. They smartly vaunt their own statistics and taunt their enemies with stylised abuse while observing careful limits for their verbal aggression. The habit naturally and culturally extends even to one's own allies, subordinates and family. Enemies on the battlefield ritually criticise their opponents' lineage, courage, strength and skill.[12] Flyting infects both men and gods' conflicts and competitions. Stripping the defeated, mutilation, and gloating caps many a victory (e.g. 13.414–16, 22.371–4; Athene, 21.410–14, 428–33; see below on 'social complexity').

The big chief Agamemnon seizes the indispensable lesser chief Akhilleus' dearest prize – at first something that was only a major prize, a woman he was allotted, but in the crisis no less than a person that he has come to cherish, someone with a name, Briseis. The humiliating public outrage (*lōbē*) of forceful deprivation causes the invincible warrior to withdraw from the brutal military contest (Book 1). The Akhaian ranks split, disconcerting the general staff, while the Trojan forces, the hometown community's army and its Anatolian allies, remain strong. The Trojan host, with Zeus's nod, devastates the discouraged invaders and eventually reaches their ships (3–8). When annihilation is imminent, the somewhat chastened commander-in-chief offers vast material compensation for his strategic and personal error, but Akhilleus penetrates the ruse and refuses the 'king's ransom' (9). Thus he confounds heroes trained keenly to scent booty (which presumably confers most of the desired honour) and at least eighty-one generations of critics. The absent presence shapes more than half the poem (end of Book 1 to 19). The Trojans, on the very next day, advance a cross the plain, penetrate the Akhaian barricades, and reach the invaders' ships, one of which Hektor torches (11–16). Not cash, land, sex or half-hearted apology moves Akhilleus to don armour, but the death of his dearest friend and companion Patroklos

11 The poem sings the achievement of men, so Homer is slyly metatextual, making Akhilleus here this poem's only character to sing of heroes.

12 Hektor unwisely mocks Akhilleus: 'You missed' (22.279; cf. 5.287, 16.336). Cf. Parks (1990).

(16–17). This unexpected outcome produces a guilty and furious grief and, then, Akhilleus' return to battle with explicit rejection of all the previous life-saving and dignity-enhancing conventions of war such as ransom for Lykaon and non-mutilation of Hektor's corpse (18–23). Sarpedon, Patroklos and finally Hektor kill heroically and die the same way. Akhilleus becomes trapped again in another of the troubling codes of the heroic world: the corpse of the Trojan hero Hektor can be neither kept nor returned. The gods and his enemy's father, Priam, are needed for him to understand the morality of mortality. Priam delivers much more than mere ransom. Agency, responsibility, habits and eccentric choices become clearer – even to clear-headed Akhilleus – along with their unintended consequences (22–4).

Heroes need great hearts and anger nourishes that mysterious centre of vitality (*megathumos*, 9.561, cf. 18.109). Akhilleus' heart and self-definition strike many a reader as catastrophic, ruinous, indigestible, even when a reader today admires his almost existential acuity in Book 9. From his Archimedean, if not Olympian, vantage point, this massive, opportunistic raid of retaliation for wife-stealing comes to seem an inappropriate response.[13] This battler's moral vision of humanity's proper business leads him to enforce a physical and spiritual isolation from his gung-ho, macho warrior community – deracinated men represented by Diomedes and Sthenelos. Diomedes' speeches expressing his eagerness to kill or even be killed heroically frame the thoughtful yet passionate exchange in Book 9 between Akhilleus and Agamemnon's proxies, Odysseus, Phoinix and Aias. Akhilleus' worthy opponent Hektor similarly finds himself separated in situation from his family (Book 6) and then literally cut off from his city (22). Both have impressive prowess to protect their people from destruction; both are doomed by their essential yet ruinous heroic honour.[14] Both intermittently possess longer vision than most or all of their companions and dependents. Nevertheless, both are trapped by personal obligations and issues beyond right and wrong (Redfield (1975)). Both face and accept death, Akhilleus welcoming it whenever, Hektor acknowledging it as its hulk looms before him (Books 1, 9, 18–21 and 22). They transcend the merely heroic warriors like Diomedes, Aias, and Homer's Aineias with their *aristeiai* or berserker battle-glory, and thus become tragic. Having been positioned by the poet at an angle to their warrior culture's horizons, they learn too late, they concede too late.

[13] Adam Parry, before the United States fought a messy and long war overseas in Vietnam, discovered anti-war sentiment in Akhilleus and persuaded much of a generation or two (Parry (1956)).

[14] *Timē*, *geras* and *aidōs*; see Sarpedon's deceptively unproblematic definition: 12.310–28. Cf. Cairns (1993a) on appropriate senses of shame, *aidōs*.

As soon as anyone can, however, they contemplate the grim limits of human influence on events swirling around them, on their lives, and on their gods.

After Patroklos has been killed, Akhilleus is subsequently more bitter, yet more reflective. He wishes that competitiveness over *timē* and *geras* (recognition and material reward) among both men and gods would vanish. Alongside competition for honour, anger (*cholos*, 18.109) should vanish. He describes anger, unexpectedly but incisively, as 'sweeter than honey'. The champion of invective, insult and injury has tired of heroic competitiveness. Power and many forms of vulnerability provide pervasive themes on earth and Olympos. Never as primitive as post-Virgilian readers may deem it, the *Iliad* continues to perplex readers with the complex moral questions that Hektor, Akhilleus, evasive Agamemnon and Priam address and answer.

Narrative structures

Khryses' supplication of Agamemnon, the occupier of local territory, opens the action and King Priam's supplication of invader Akhilleus closes it. Patterns of acts and responses (external more than internal) alert audiences to appropriate expectations and thematic resonances. Khryseis' ransom rebuffed and accepted, the traffic in Briseis held up in gendered heroic customs, Hektor's body abused and gently swaddled, failure and success bracket arguments and combats. Such decisive events are ringed and framed by formulaic verses, similes and rituals.[15] They propel one city's final crisis to ripple outwards to a disastrous close. This gridlocked stand-off at the same time offers a compressed segment, artfully yet unexpectedly chosen, from the extended cycle of the Troy tale.[16] Khryses' public plea, one almost unanimously approved by the invading troopers,[17] miniaturises as it foreshadows the main plot (namely a sequence of dishonour, divine displeasure, disaster and atonement by restoration and uneasy 'reconciliation'). Elderly Priam's nocturnal odyssey, a divinely pre-approved secret, takes him and Hermes through danger to Akhilleus' bivouac. Their colloquy affirms Akhilleus' generous understanding of compassion while echoing his earlier grasp of the

[15] Ring composition, geometric structure, chiastic arrangement, Chinese-box techniques describe the structural analyses of Sheppard (1922), Myres (1932), van Otterlo (1944), Whitman (1958), Stanley (1993); all reviewed by N. Richardson in Kirk *et al.* (1993) vol. 6, 4–14. Heiden (2000c) examines how parallelism and symmetrical rings reinforce each other. Segal (1971b) elegantly analyses the secular or magical rituals of mutilations of corpses.

[16] Griffin (1977) contextualises our only two surviving epics among the many that we hear once existed. Aristotle (*Poet.* 1459a29–b7) reassures us that the two survivors are the most deserving.

[17] The armed Akhaian host, Apollo, Akhilleus, Nestor and Zeus, at least, oppose Agamemnon's actions and rationale. Agamemnon eventually but clumsily confesses his error.

protocols for heroic gifts. The two enemy chieftains' parley confirms the wisdom of heeding divine warnings. By contrast, their rapprochement confirms the folly of Agamemnon's refusal, his disastrous plague-producing fault, termed here moral blindness (*atē*), and then his mis-steps in ignoring the pleas of his men and chieftains after the prophet's clear explanation. These framing books 1 and 24 contain unusually varied (e.g. involving many changes of scene) and compressed actions that decisively define the plot of the *Iliad.* Two kinds of structure shape this epic: the visual and static principle of balance and the aural and temporal principle of dynamic change.[18] Repeating moments of significant human activities (sacrifice, feast, arming, *aristeia*, supplication, killing one enemy grimly or butchering bunches of opponents, etc.) are first sketched, then elaborated, often with significant differences. Thus the mirror scenes anticipate or 'reverse forward' major developments: a magnanimous Akhilleus of enlarged sympathies (in 23 and 24) publicly reconciles antagonists and gives lavish gifts even to the earlier antagonistic and agonistic Agamemnon of Book 1 – items that the bully never thought to ask for. Soon after, in private, he fulfils a harder request from his 'enemy' Priam than the one he had rejected from his best friends, Odysseus and Aias, and that cuddly surrogate for his absent father Peleus, Phoinix. He who has rejected food and fellowship repeatedly for blood-lust (e.g. 19.213–14) eventually provides nurture to another mortal while he justifies human fellowship and companionship even in dreadful circumstances. Similarly, although – as always – with different (because never fatal) consequences, the gods quarrel over Troy in Book 1 but come to agreement in 24 about Hektor's violated corpse.

Episodes segment the poem and its events into sections of varying length, some few of them matching the Alexandrian book divisions.[19] Some scenes last much longer (one day of battle extends from 11 through 18), but most are far shorter.[20] Oral formulaic phrases neatly divide Homer's rendition (both when it was delivered orally to ears and written to eyes): 'so she said in winged words', or 'they sat still for a long time and in silence'. The

[18] N. Richardson in Kirk *et al.* (1993) vol. VI and Heiden (2000c) both note that the correspondences are strongest in the first six and last six books.

[19] See *inter alios*, Edwards (1991), Taplin (1992), Heiden (2000c), and also Fowler in this volume. No two readers pick the same (23 or other) divisions. Some mark a break in the action; others seem arbitrary, as the alphabetical division into 24 chunks suggests. Book lengths vary from 424 verses in Book 19 to 909 in 5, a fact that prevents our imagining the divisions to be only a convenience of the book trade. The 15,693 verses on average would run to books of 654 verses. See Fingerle (1939) 68–9 for useful book-by-book verse counts, speech counts and speech percentages.

[20] Cf. the death vignettes of Lykaon's son Pandaros and of ambidextrous Asteropaios to Lykaon's (5.290–6, 21.171–99, 21.68–135).

repeating formulae remind us of the ritualisation of everyday experience. Speech appears both directly and (more rarely) indirectly, the former closer to 'real time' than summaries or syncopated narrations can be. With rare narratorial intrusions, speakers[21] and their urgent gestures are left to reveal character. Directness contributes to Homer's appeal. Scenes and speeches expand according to significance (e.g. the extended embassy to Akhilleus of 9.192–657, his speeches therein, Nestor's encounters with Patroklos in 11.643–804, and the pursuit, duel and death of Hektor in 22).[22]

Ecphrases (extended descriptions of objects: for spectacular example, Akhilleus' divine new shield), genealogies (for heroes, gods, sceptres, cups and other objects), and similes suspend the principal narration. So do para-narratives such as analogous earlier battles and cautionary tales (e.g. Nestor, Meleagros, Niobe and the Centaurs).[23] References backwards and forwards are less common in the *Iliad* than in the *Odyssey* or in the *Aeneid*, but they supply a horizon of normality, parallels and anticipations such as Andromakhe's and Briseis' captures or Eëtion's death and burial (6.413–20).[24] Little incidents or examples of type-scenes anticipate and echo in advance their chief exemplar, as in arming, fighting or feasting scenes or consolations (Thetis in Books 1 and 18). Single-combat encounters (e.g. Diomedes and then later Akhilleus attack gods; Sarpedon, Patroklos, and then later Hektor die) and strippings and mutilations of corpses (e.g. Patroklos, Hektor) prepare, indeed train, the reader for the rhythm of heroic events. These events provide another technique in the Homeric aesthetics of enticing retardation and reinforcement. Repetition structures all experiences of body and mind: pain in war and the pleasures of shared food, sex and solitary sleep.[25]

Characters

The people of Troy show us what men fight for, what consolations for life's sorrows peace would have offered, what violations the vulnerable children,

[21] Of the *Iliad*'s verses, 45 per cent occur in direct speech; 83 per cent of verses in Book 9.

[22] Austin (1966) and Martin (1989) illuminate Akhilleus' speeches. The 'expansion aesthetic' works hand in glove with retardation to tease and thus please a knowing audience. See also Griffin in this volume.

[23] See Willcock (1964), Austin (1966), Alden (2000).

[24] The 'cyclic' epics were less nimble and profuse in their references to the rest of the Trojan War.

[25] Clark, following Milman Parry and others, in this volume examines Homeric repetitions, echoing incidents, parallel formulae and iterated verses – both those occurring singly and those clumped in type-scenes.

women and the elderly dread and risk daily. Andromakhe, Hekabe and even Helen express the dread of victimisation in words and weaving (3.125–8). Astyanax's screaming fear of his own father in armour represents the misery accurately anticipated by his parents (6.466–74). Andromakhe, Briseis, Hekabe and Astyanax provide paradigms for all non-combatant women and children raped and rubbed out in retaliation (2.354–6), killed *en masse* or enslaved in war.[26] Akhaians and Trojans anticipate the city's fall in identical words (4.163–5 = 6.447–9; cf. 24.410–11, etc.). This epic is not nationalistic, and 'Homer', once cognisant of the opportunities for different focalisation and attendant pathos (Sale (1989); de Jong (1987)), may well have expanded the sympathetic attention paid to the Trojans as opponents. Hektor is strategically inadequate (12.60 and 210 ff.; 13.726 ff., 18.254 ff.) but clearly Troy's last best hope.

Having suffered the ultimate violation of hospitality (*xeniē*) because of the abduction of Helen, the Akhaians hold the moral high ground.[27] Agamemnon's genocidal fury (6.57–60: 'kill the baby in the Trojan womb'), however, and Nestor's 'gentler' expression demanding retaliation and vengeance (2.355–6: 'let every Akhaian rape ["bed down", *katakoimēthēnai*] a [captive] Trojan wife') affect and alienate audience sympathies – certainly ours and, I would guess, Homer's audiences'. Paris and Helen are guilty but not villains. All characters receive sympathetic portraits. Even Thersites, the disrespectful Danaan 'grunt' of Book 2 speaks truth to power, focalising the point of view of the men in the bivouacs and echoing Akhilleus. Akhilleus' predicaments demand that we ask what a man should be and what he owes others.

Paris, Helen, Hektor and Agamemnon prefer to blame gods in self-defence rather than accept full responsibility for their faults. The Akhaian soldiers struggle to maintain their military foothold, their military status with each other, and their self-respect in a fragile environment. Ten years camped on a cold and windy shore take a toll on tempers. The people not at Ilion (farmers, shepherds and hunters), the animals (of land, air and sea), and the weather events that populate the breath-taking extended similes provide

[26] Gender issues are more salient in the *Odyssey* (see Lateiner (1995)), but women signify the prime trafficked commodities. (Chryseis and Briseis share value and scansion; thus they provide character 'doublets'. Note also the ransom of Andromakhe's mother, 6.425–8). Women are active agents (Helen, Thetis, Athene), not only paradigms of victims. See also Felson and Slatkin in this volume.

[27] Homer fudges the mythic question of whether she went willingly, although 3.173–5, 241–2, and 6.344–50 encourage belief in the mortal's personal choice. However, 3.396–412, Aphrodite's epiphany for and to Helen, suggests the other story. The question presents another difficult case of Homeric psychological motivation.

picture-windows on a contrastive peaceful civilisation set in a still violent nature. The similes affirm another life where organised Iliadic killing fields are not the only reality.

Homer treats the human (and animal) victims and the vignettes of their unknowing survivor families with sympathy (e.g. 3.236–44, 5.148–58, 21.78–96). War and death were facts of life, even if this war's extreme savagery becomes abnormal. The war had long since seemed hopeless – if not absurd – to many of the warriors and their wives. We hear the misery in Akhaian troops in 2, in the shamed Trojans who wish to return Helen, the *casus belli*, in 3.50–1, 112, 160, 173, 6.328, 356–8, in Akhilleus in 9, and in Akhilleus and Priam in 24.[28] The poem's finale portrays all parties as exhausted (9.337–9, 406–9, 24.540–8).

The Homeric gods and their daily rituals provide an unsettling (and entertaining) counterpoint to mortal life-and-death struggles. They involuntarily comment on their own mental and emotional foibles and fallibility in their horseplay and interplay with the ephemeral bodies of human toys and pets. Their irresponsible Unlimit defines the Iliadic human condition. Their crude amusements shape human sorrow. The narrative's account of their favouritism (1.195–8, 16.788–93, 24.66–70), indifference, hostility (6.311–12, Athene reacts to Trojan prayer), capriciousness and even limitations (16.433–52, Sarpedon's death) pathetically contradicts human expressions of vain but touching confidence in divine anxiety for justice (4.157–62, Agamemnon on oath-breakers).

These gods – like men, especially chieftains – are terrifying, unpredictable, cruel and occasionally ludicrous. They provide (internal) audiences for mortal combats and contests and offer comments (sometimes perhaps shared by the poet) on dilemmas and duels. They cheer and fight alongside their favourites, prophesy the future of this past (and thus foreshadow the poet's plot), natter amongst themselves, and affect the main plot in material ways (Apollo's plague, Thetis' supplication, Hephaistos' smithing, Xanthos' combat and Zeus's exciting the slaughter). Their (near and far) perspectives multiply Homeric ironies: false hopes (2.35–40, 16.46–7, 11.193–4), misunderstandings (18.6–14), and humans as mere gaming-tokens and goads (4.5–29, 51–4). But Zeus can also show pity.[29]

[28] Akhilleus and Hektor race in combat past the double springs of whirling Skamander (22.145–60) where 'lovely Trojan wives and daughters always washed clothes, long before the Akhaians came, in days of peace'. Does the wistful recollection belong to the poet, or the runners, or those frozen spectators watching them?

[29] 16.458–61; cf. Griffin (1980), Rutherford (1996) 44–7, Lateiner (2002).

Social complexity

Homer captures personal and social entanglements without overtly psychologising them. Eschewing more recent fictional (and non-fictional) literature's penchant for authors' and characters' psychological analysis of moods and motives (to phrase the matter anachronistically), Homer's heroes speak aloud their feelings, even when alone.[30] Iliadic men and women confront insoluble dilemmas – not here the Odyssean black and white heroes and villains, fairy-tale reunions and happy endings. Comic and tragic at once, this amalgam of late Bronze Age-early Iron Age life furnished unexpected behavioural paradigms for the Hellenes – but perhaps no odder a collection of fallible mortals than the warriors-chiefs of the Hebrew Bible like Samson. All values – material, mental, social and moral – are contested. Antitheses between characters, choices and worlds – no easy questions or happy answers – present themselves until the poem's end, which is an end only in part.

Homer's poems provide Hellenic textbooks of social protocols: courtesy but more often slights, abusive looks and words, and put-down gestures and acts.[31] Homeric conflicts have few non-combative modes of resolution. Vaunts, taunts, dark looks, smiles and condescending arm-stroking illustrate both competition with peers and efforts to control subordinates and slippery superiors. Several memorable epic moments feature verbal, gestural

[30] Soliloquy: 'But why does my mind (*thumos*) debate thus', e.g. Menelaos (17.90–112), a formula appearing in 'stand or retreat' situations that Fenik (1978) and Scully (1984) investigate. The Homeric mental apparatus does not resemble ours in any simple way (other than lack of clarity); divisions in one's spirit can paralyse one's limbs. Homeric psychology has been fiercely debated since Snell's provocative 1946 book; see in response, *inter alios*, Dodds (1951) esp. 13–18; Lesky (1961); Griffin (1980) esp. 70–6; Schein (1984), Sullivan (1988), Gaskin (1990), Pelliccia (1995) and Clarke (1999).

[31] In the *Odyssey*, the bully Kyklops mocks and taunts his helpless and unheroic vagrant victims trapped in his cave, but Odysseus, once he has escaped, returns the abuse, infantilising the one-eyed oaf, telling him to summon his 'Daddy'. On Ithaka, the aristocratic suitors enjoy mocking the disguised beggar's age, lack of hair and poverty. Their varied strategic repertoire polices hospitality at the princely table. Their lackey Melanthios unimaginatively kicks the beggar, but his betters have a carefully calibrated armoury of insulting names and gestures. They also throw objects at him: e.g. stools and an ox-hoof (XVII.462, XVIII.396, XX.300). They cheerfully threaten him with mutilation and castration. The two Homeric epics provide admirable and shameful forms of impoliteness with Agamemnon's acts as 'host' and the suitors' activities as guests certainly occupying the bottom of the scale. The question of the rightness or wrongness of Akhilleus' behaviour towards the sons of Atreus and their allies remains contested. The quandary secures an open reading for the *Iliad*, but I think Homer endorses his every move against them. Akhilleus errs, and hugely, in his flawed advice to Patroklos in Book 16 and his abuse of Hektor's corpse in 22–4, but these flaws are as essential to the plot as is his justified earlier withdrawal from Agamemnon's battalions.

and physical degradation: nasty sneers, subtle insults of social timing, social orientation and/or elevation, and calm beating or kicking of unco-operative inferiors. Odysseus assaults and batters Thersites with the big stick of authority (the chiefly sceptre, 2.265) when the trooper objects to Agamemnon's greed for gold, women and other prizes of honour as well as to his humiliation of Akhilleus and his fellow troopers' flaccid acceptance of all these outrages (2.225–42). Helen reviles her personal goddess Aphrodite and also scolds her beloved Paris as a coward in Book 3. In 6, his brother Hektor treats him similarly. Akhaian and Trojan commanders repeatedly chastise and rebuke their own commanders, lieutenants and troops when things go wrong (e.g. 'most chieftainly' (1.69: *basileutatos*) and cheerful Agamemnon, 4.223–420; Sarpedon, 5.471–93; Glaukos, 16.537–53; cf. Fenik (1978)). Lykian Sarpedon, one of those Trojan allies, effectively chides Hektor himself as a shirker and skulker. God Apollo also taunts Hektor, the most attractive Trojan hero (15.244–62). Agamemnon's vilification of his loyal commanders as scared animals and cowards (Martin (1989)), may motivate the other 'big men' to fight, but his ineptitude in substance, venue, timing and target catastrophically alienates the admittedly 'mightiest' man of all (1.146, 178; 9.116–18).

Iliad 1 contains thirty-six separate speeches (Fingerle (1939)), largely taunts, threats and insults. Issues of political leadership and just obedience pepper decisions on both sides. Agamemnon's first words sadistically and gratuitously taunt the politely supplicating coastal East Aegean priest of Apollo, Khryses. The Argive chief (*basileus*) asserts, insultingly and gratuitously, that he will have sex with the neutral priest's (possibly virgin) daughter, 'meeting her' across his kingly bed (31, a unique sexual euphemism). He next insults the justifiably nervous Akhaian seer Kalkhas (and his own wife Klytaimestre, incidentally) after the mantic guide explains the divine cause of the plague afflicting the invaders (74–83). The commander demands a replacement prize if he must give up his status-enhancing, beloved badge of honour (1.118–20). The seer's protector, Akhilleus, in return, points out the dearth of spare booty but promises multiples of lovely prizes for the chief, after the Akhaians take Troy. Once called an intending cheat by his 'superior', Akhilleus publicly insults Agamemnon before the entire Akhaian army. He calls the commander-in-chief 'greediest of men' and 'shameless profiteer'. Then he escalates his attack to aggravated, ritualised name-calling (122–7, 158–9): 'shameless deer-heart' and 'dog-eyed' (the last evoking a cloud of negative Iliadic dog metaphors).

Agamemnon taunts him in return as an abusive underling and unneeded fighter, indeed a potential runaway. He has escalated the conflict when he threatens to seize his nominal subordinate's war-booty – a serious loss of face and status (173–87) – in order to demonstrate one punishment available for insubordinates. Akhilleus has suffered a 'conspicuous slight' in the Akhaian assembly and is literally ready to kill him (1.194). Agamemnon's acts constitute the paradigm case of *hubris* in the *Iliad* (203, 214, 9.368: 3/5 of all actual occurrences in the *Iliad*). The irascible but notably dextrous hero of heroes Akhilleus must devise a way to recover his prizes, his damaged honour and status. Although Athene advises him (211) to limit his present response to further abuse of Agamemnon, his 'chiefliest' leader, his counter-attacking rebukes (e.g. 1.225) scarcely right Akhilleus' perceived deep wrong. He therefore deserts his warrior comrades after threatening to kill Agamemnon himself – if he ever tries to lift anything else (303). Power has been asserted, rebutted, ridiculed, trumped and threatened with force. Intentional infliction of dishonour and inadequate means to manage and channel anger fuel the plot of the Greeks' foundational narrative of manly honour.

Mortal fury and warrior insults are quickly echoed on Olympus. Hera jeers at her husband Zeus and accuses him of plotting 'dirty tricks'. Zeus refuses to divulge his plans and threatens to beat up his sister, wife and queen, and strike her down, if she does not shut her mouth – a hint of Hellenic gender hierarchy and policing. Hephaistos confirms the likelihood of Zeus's actual infliction of such shocking violence, mentioning his own past experience (590–3; cf. 399–406, 15.160–7). Book 1 offers this wide spectrum of insult and humiliation.

Agamemnon's damaging of Khryses and then of Akhilleus creates the plot's essential quarrel. Disconcertingly fragile alliances on both sides explain Homeric society's inherent political instability. In literary terms, the quarrel motif repeats itself within and outside the invaders' ranks. The division leads to Akhilleus' decisive 'departure'. Akhilleus elects to abandon this nastily manipulated and fluid system that establishes and disestablishes his worth and his fellow commanders' illegitimately legitimated hierarchy. The insult is perceived as non-negotiable. It is such, because procedures adequate to defuse the dispute do not exist.[32] Agamemnon later (9) 'reasonably' offers seven lovely Lesbian women, land, his own daughter and restoration of the undamaged goods in dispute, Briseis. Nestor, Odysseus, Phoinix and Aias – each rational and sympathetic in his own way – fret in frustration over Akhilleus' immovability. Because they mistake or disapprove of

[32] The mirroring dispute described on Akhilleus' shield (18.497–508) never reaches resolution. Elder Akhaians claim that an obligation to accept compensation exists (Nestor, 9.110–13; Phoinix, 9.496–524; Aias, 9.630–42), but the best argument, Phoinix's, recoils on itself. See Wilson's (1999) case for the failure of the proferred analogies to match the unique crimes of Lord Agamemnon, his faulty forms of compensation and his moral ambush. Van Wees (1992) and Cairns (1993a) offer further insight into the social complexities.

Akhilleus' issues of inadequate concessions improperly extended, Odysseus inadequately hears and slanderously reports only the first of his progressively modulated responses (9.676–92). Their own interests trump their natural heroic sympathies.

Bluntly put, any audience that does not comprehend the justice of Akhilleus' grand refusal (or Odysseus' slaughter of the west-coast suitors one and all) will not understand the system of honour and its negotiations that Homer painstakingly constructs.[33] Akhilleus' self had been publicly humiliated and Akhilleus' friends painfully failed to support him immediately – as they owed it to him to do (9.105–11). Akhilleus answers the delegates' points, admits Phoinix's and Aias' better arguments and appeals to sympathy (9.612, 645–8), and actually softens and modifies his initially uncompromising response. His motivation is not selfishness, much less materialism, but the little that remains to him planted in this barren, now blasted landscape: his status and honour.[34]

His unconventional rejection of the warlord's materially generous offer responds to Agamemnon's utter lack of visible contrition (e.g. personal appearance to apologise and offer compensation) and his hidden hook of permanent subordination by marital affiliation – marriage to one of his antagonist's daughters. The bargain's severely disadvantageous conditionality (9.158–61)[35] is ably understood by Akhilleus, even if he has not

33 One eminent, helpful Homerist here commented 'But Achilles is *wrong* (18.97 ff.)'. T. S. Eliot, president in 1944 of the British Virgil Society, also thought him a 'ruffian', or a spoiled teenager. I don't claim that he was perfect, or even that he was like us in his reasoning or morality (his heel is not mentioned by Homer). In the passage that my critic cited, however, the Phthian hero acknowledges correctly his responsibility for Patroklos' death, not his obligation to become Agamemon's son-in-law, liege and vassal. Every reader can, if she wants, construct six scenarios for Akhilleus to honour and protect Patroklos without accepting Agamemnon's corrupt and corrupting offer.

34 Patriotism is an anachronistic objection to Akhilleus' actions, of course. Akhilleus' obligations to his fellow warriors (*aidōs*) cease when they allowed Agamemnon without objection to violate divine law and heroic conventions for gifts. Akhaians need to learn consequences. Redfield (1975), Scodel (1989), and Cairns (1993b) usefully discuss social obligations on both sides. For the contrast of battlefield to domestic chores and bliss at Troy in days of yore see 22.152–61, 442–6.

35 Donlan (1993) explains Agamemnon's strategic plan in this 'dueling with gifts'. Agamemnon would subordinate Akhilleus to him by the proposed marriage to his daughter. Agamemnon is not incapable at negotiation (his plan fools or persuades his wily commanders (who in fact would benefit from any success) as well as most of my teachers and students), but his Machiavellian tactics are transparent enough for Akhilleus to penetrate. Wilson perceives the careful justice of Akhilleus' rejection of the inappropriate if emphatically 'limitless ransom' (*apeiresia apoina*), which is not the recompense (*poinē*) that he requires and deserves. He has experienced, in Donlan's phrase, Agamemnon's 'gift attack'.

overheard – as we have, Agamemnon's concluding demand in distant conclave (9.158–61: 'let him stand below me'). Akhilleus' touchy superiority in war needs recognition. Briseis is the delicate, diminutive honour that he had received from the host and its war leader (1.354, 507, 9.332–6). His prize visibly embodied his status and becomes the instrument of his keen disgrace. Briseis' removal (a rape ironically echoing Helen's removal – as Akhilleus notes, 9.336–45) means war and reprisal. Athene admonishes against homicide (1.210–14), as she endorses his self-demobilisation and that of his Myrmidons. Patroklos' own conflict of loyalties, cleverly played on by sympathetic Nestor, as the Akhaians collapse and fall back (11.640–805), echoes Akhilleus' own in a disharmonious, nearly single-sex society suffering continual conflict. Akhilleus' wrath ceases (16.53–61), however, even before the death of Patroklos and well before Agamemnon's faulty verbal amends and material restitution in 19.

Patroklos' dreadful death and despoliation at Apollo's and Hektor's hands (16.793–17.197) radically redirects Akhilleus' attention and thereby the *Iliad*'s plot.[36] Only Akhilleus sees that the strategic and moral backdrop of Ilion's great stage has changed. Patroklos' killing – he now understands – is partly Akhilleus' fault, since he had assigned him an impossibly limited mission, one that contravenes heroic imperatives in the heat of battle. Since he is partly responsible for Patroklos' death (16.46–95, 17.406–11, 18.12–14, 24.5–12),[37] Akhilleus gets something he somehow deserves.[38] But this deadening campaign has also repeatedly seen his considerable compassion – accepting supplication, ransoming captives, burying the dead – as well as his inimitable achievement in war (*aretē*). Knowing how to reach agreement peacefully – the skills of persuasion and mollification – are rare in the disrupted, not fully monarchical but only 'chiefly', world that Homer paints in the crucial, powerfully agitating, and plot-obstructing Book 19. The manipulative overlord never can rise to the occasion (19.77), but the impatient warrior Akhilleus is by this point indifferent. He waves off

[36] 18.6–14, 80–93, 98–100; 19.65–8, 145–8, 200–10, 319–25: one contribution that many attribute to the 'final poet' known as 'Homer'. See Clay (2002) on extended scenes of death.

[37] In a notable case of multiple determination, Homer has moribund Patroklos list *Moira* (Destiny), Apollo and Euphorbos as his killers before mentioning Hektor now coming in for the kill (16.849–50). However, as we sort out the narrower than expected differences between gods and men, we observe that Father Zeus has cruelly given Akhilleus half his wish, while answering all his selfish, ignorant, all-too-human prayer (16.233–50). Akhilleus comes to realise lucidly his excessive egotism and admit his fault (18.6–14, 98–104).

[38] If we employ Phoinix's problematic theology in the central speech of 9, namely the parable of the *Litai* or 'Prayerful Supplications' and the sometimes parallel, sometimes oppositional para-narrative of Meleager's disaster.

restitution and the 'free gifts',[39] the commander's half-hearted, excuse-laden and self-aggrandising apology (comparison of Agamemnon's fault to Zeus's!), and Agamemnon's oaths denying that he has sexually enjoyed his replacement prize, svelte Briseis, commandeered from Akhilleus' bivouac some days before by herald-proxies (19.258–65). Gold and girls could never buy intransigent Akhilleus. Agamemnon never restores his own or his best warrior's prestige, assuming he somehow could have, not in Book 1, nor 9, nor 19. The sun will never shine the same again, although the Akhaian contests at Patroklos' funeral in 23 show Akhilleus making progress in his own status-restoration by granting, from his own store, prizes to Agamemnon himself.

Akhilleus' rage at Hektor replaces and surpasses his rage at Agamemnon because it builds on it and on his greater love for Patroklos (cf. 19.56–62). He discovers, however, that Hektor's death, like Agamemnon's ransom offer, cannot satisfy his anger and grief. But Priam's heroic supplication approaches the impossible, because he appeals to different and deeper sources of human grounding: sons and fathers, home and vulnerable mortality.

Evaluations

Homer is neither objective nor partisan. Apollonius, Virgil and Ovid convey more moods, more subjectivity, but – short of Shakespeare and Tolstoi – no poet presents a richer canvas of human experience. But Akhilleus! Can we empathise with the hero of impossible wishes (16.99–100)? He is both right and wrong to his fellow-fighters – although mostly the latter to new readers. If you seek moral satisfaction, like T. S. Eliot you will prefer the *Odyssey*. Akhilleus' own feelings, thoughts and choices oscillate. The justice of his position rises and falls with the working out of his disengagement, re-engagement and new vision – the issues and themes that embody the plot. In the end, he has all the respect and all the tokens of status imaginable: no one else has won, but Akhilleus still has lost the most. Least of all winners is the man partly guilty for the death of his *therapon*, companion, alter ego and best friend – and also for the deaths of so many others. He has nothing to live for except death. He in the poem best appreciates how little we can do, how irresponsible or at least unpredictable are the gift-giving gods. The story remains always one of loss and noble failures.

Any just evaluation of this eccentric centre of Western consciousness must examine its different, but not inconceivable, aesthetic. Oral traditional

[39] At 19.172–80, Odysseus is still pointlessly enumerating them, because he can never understand so fine a spirit as Akhilleus'. Alles (1990) discusses Homer's heroic ideology.

features starkly shape it, such as the need for and delight in repetitions, subtle variations, and disciplined spontaneity in the units of utterance: formula, verse and type-scene (such as supplication, welcome and feast). Repetition in particular functions in ways unknown in later, more 'sophisticated' literary forms. Fathers and sons, royal women and slaves, enemies and friends, humans and gods, men and beasts face the same threats and spearpoints expressed in the same phrases. Such typical elements, however, always resurface in new ways.[40] The diverse characters, the homely and the unique similes, the parallel scenes placed distant from each other that awaken recollection unbidden, the speeches and inserted tales that retard the main plot, and the astonishing expansions offer unexpected pleasures.[41] Post-antique readers and patient audiences still experience the joy and the grief even through translations. The beat of the flexible hexameter rhythm, however, the music of Greek dactyls, the continuous archaic metre with uncontracted vowel sounds, and the verbal echoes rarely survive when others translate for us into modern tongues. The very nature of the experience of literature today – reading alone, interrupting for snacks and experiencing in silence – differs from hearing together aloud, without interruption, and sensing your neighbour's absorption. Further, paratextual elements – such as book divisions, paragraphing, quotation marks, punctuation, italics and word-division – necessarily cause any modern reader's Homeric experience to differ from an ancient man or woman's.

Unique elements, whether oral or literate, include the monumental length, spiritual depth and sympathetic human breadth of Akhilleus' conflicts at Troy. Often taken for granted, the size itself of the poem prevents us from feeling that we have all the persons and events 'under control' in imagination. The music of rare and obsolete words and their order, the power of end-stopped and enjambed verses, simple yet so inimitable (as his close reader Virgil recognised), invite awe twenty-seven centuries later. The

[40] Familiar elements repeatedly appear in unfamiliar contexts, applied as never before or again. One example is the parallel between old Nestor's welcome of his ally, young Patroklos, and young Akhilleus' welcome of his enemy old Priam (11 and 24). 'Soft Parryists' such as Fenik or Segal, seeking anticipatory enrichment in these doubled scenes, use such elements to modify 'hard Parryist' conclusions. These reverberations are arguably central to Homer's unlikely 'genius'.

[41] For example, Sarpedon's near-death in battle and the real thing in 5 and 16, Akhilleus' gift of new armour in 18, and the gods joining the mêlée from 20.23–30 to 21. Fenik (1978) examines selected battle-scene expansions. Morrison (1999) notes that these same battlers (namely, Sarpedon, Patroklos and Hektor) are the only ones to speak after suffering a fatal wound. They also share an otherwise unique common verse of closure (16.502 = 16.855 = 22.361)

individuality of Helen, Paris, Andromakhe, Nestor, or even briefly Lykaon, or, more briefly yet, pathetic Tros, Ekheklos, Antiphos and Iphidamas who left an expensive young wife behind, etc., compel presumptuous praise. The scrupulous listener and reader discover in every rereading, whatever his or her filter, some exciting new analogy or glimmering foreshadow or meaningful repetition. Homer imperceptibly adumbrates details of the past and future for and through his story's heroic sondage of human intractability and loneliness. Homer values strength, strategic intelligence, cunning, generosity and courage, of course, but he esteems more highly quieter, yet still heroic, qualities such as respect for one's enemy, compassion and appreciation of every human's limitations. Indeed, this is why we reread the *Iliad*: its sublime, perhaps definitive – certainly unpredictably beautiful – description of human strength and incapacity.[42]

FURTHER READING

Owen (1946) sensitively follows the meanders of the story as it unfolds on earth and in heaven – *alpha* to *beta* and on to *omega*. Lowe (2000) analyses the plot with the help (?) of game theory and further describes the vast influence of the two Homeric paradigms of Story. Fenik (1968), Segal (1971b) and Thornton (1984) provide good introductions to type-scenes, themes and motifs such as battles, death and defilement of the enemy, and supplications. These are traditional formulaic elements on narrative levels beyond Milman Parry's path-breaking field research on formulaic epithets and individual verses. Parry's difficult research into oral traditional epic (see the comprehensive 1971 volume) can be partly digested in consequential studies on Homeric speech, the predominant event in the epics, e.g. Adam Parry (1956) and Martin (1989). Partly in response to bean-counting, Parryistical scholarship, Griffin (1980) produced a rich, brief appreciation of the aboriginal classic, also helpfully comparing the *Iliad* to unrelated epic traditions.

De Jong has written essential and rewarding narratological studies of both the *Iliad* (1987) and the *Odyssey* (2001, in commentary form). Before narratology was given a name, Sheppard (1922), Myres (1932), van Otterlo (1944) and Whitman (1958) discussed unexpected symmetrical structures, such as ring composition, in the organisation of archaic narrative and art. Willcock (1964), Morrison (1992b) and Alden (2000) introduce students to readers' plot expectations and their satisfaction or surprising divagations, but this complex of issues trenches on compositional problems of Unitarianism, Analysis and Neo-Analysis (see Fowler in this volume).

The 'psychology' of decision-making (and thus plot-propelling) among Homeric figures (humans, gods, perhaps dogs) remains hotly contested since Snell's seminal, if surprisingly reductive, essay on self and psyche (Snell 1953, 1–22). Dodds (1951), Adkins (1960), B. Williams (1993) and Zanker (1994), among too many, intelligently discuss both their mental processes and ethical considerations. Anthropological and sociological parallels illuminate 'give-and-take' expectations and violations,

[42] Jenny Clay especially, and also Robert Fowler, Jasper Griffin and Ruth Scodel improved this chapter, when permitted to do so.

the nature of heroic hierarchies and of their protocols (getting angry and getting even) and etiquettes (looking darkly, throwing objects at or before others). Dodds (1951) followed in the footsteps of Cook, Harrison and others here. His study and Marcel Mauss' monumental *The Gift* (1954) have been fruitfully applied in the work of Donlan (1980, 1993) on various issues of rank, status in 'Big Man' societies and gifting. The plot of the *Iliad* hinges repeatedly on insult, humiliation, lethal revenge, and the repair of fragile alliances in a world with few dependable institutions. One can profitably consult the pioneering Redfield (1975), van Wees (1992), Cairns (1993a) and, recently, Wilson (1999, 2002) on social power and prestige management.

3

MICHAEL SILK

The *Odyssey* and its explorations

Where the *Iliad* deals with one short phase of the Trojan War, the *Odyssey* tells the drawn-out story of the Achaean hero Odysseus after the sack of Troy: his enforced wanderings, his return to his homeland Ithaca, his struggle to regain his kingdom and Penelope, his queen, who has spent the best part of twenty years resisting the advances of the local princes.

The *Odyssey* has long been regarded as a poem like, but not like, the *Iliad*. For 'Longinus', in the first century AD, the poem is 'an epilogue' to the Trojan epic, and in support of this proposition the critic cites old Nestor's recollections of the Trojan battlefield, as told to Odysseus' son Telemachus in Book III:[1]

> There lies warlike Ajax; there lies Achilles;
> There lies Patroclus, peer of the gods in counsel;
> There lies mine own son.

The *Iliad* celebrates a ritualised way of living and dying and, complementary to it, practises a ritualised way of describing that living and dying – which is the aesthetic rationale of its formulaic alternations and repetitions.[2] It celebrates also a human striving for heroism and an agreed, if elusive, harmony of human striving and divine facilitation.[3] The *Odyssey* is different. Though its formulaic idiom, its ritualism and its heroic ideal are similar, the Odyssean universe, by comparison, seems restless and less assured of any ultimate correspondence than concerned to achieve one. Even before the action of the poem is under way, the *Odyssey* foregrounds the issue of disharmony of the spheres. Mankind reads life one way, the gods (apparently) another – or so Zeus would have us believe (1.32–5):

[1] [illegible] [Longinus] *Subl.* [illegible]
[2] See Silk (2004) 47–61, 88–92, and below, p. 39.
[3] See below, p. 40.

Look at the way we gods are blamed by mortals.
Evil comes from us, they say, yet the truth is
They suffer all too much through their own blind folly,
Even as now Aegisthus . . .

and there follows the case history of Agamemnon. Agamemnon comes back, victorious, from Troy; his wife's lover Aegisthus murders him; his son Orestes kills Aegisthus in revenge. How very different, then, from the fate of Odysseus – which, in narrative terms, is precisely the point. As far as Zeus is concerned, though, the point is what it sounds like: Agamemnon and the problem of evil. It is as if Zeus has been brooding on Agamemnon's 'apology' in the *Iliad* (19.78–144). 'Well', says Agamemnon there, 'I did rob Achilles of his prize (89), but actually I am not to blame (86): Zeus took my wits away (137).'

The Odyssean Athena is only interested in Agamemnon and Aegisthus as a parallel, contrasting case to Odysseus. 'Yes', says Athena, 'Aegisthus has suffered his deserts, but . . .' (I.48–50) –

my heart is smitten in two for smart Odysseus,
Hapless man, suffering far from his dear ones
Out on a sea-swept island –

and, from this point on, the Agamemnon theme recurs, again and again, as a parallel case to Odysseus',[4] while Odysseus himself becomes and remains the central figure of the poem. This centrality is, indeed, marked out by the opening words of Book I:

Tell me about that man, the ingenious one . . .

Odysseus here is *polutropos*, 'man of many turns', therefore 'ingenious'. The *Odyssey* is essentially the tale of one man (not so predictable, this: the *Iliad* is not), and a man with a particular, defining quality, his ingenuity, which ensures his survival in a world of unpredictable challenges and temptations. Odysseus' ingenuity is proclaimed in I.1 by the unique epithet *polutropos*, as it is elsewhere by his 'stock' epithet, *polumētis*, 'man of many wiles';[5] and

[4] The theme is articulated, in all, by Zeus (I.35–43), Athena (I.298–302), Nestor (III.193–200, 301–12), Proteus, reported by Menelaus (IV.512–37), Agamemnon in the Underworld, reported by Odysseus (XI.405–61), Odysseus himself (XIII.383–6), Agamemnon again (XXIV.191–202). See further Hölscher (1967) 1–16.

[5] Odyssean epithets with a similar sense include *daïphrōn* (below, p. 33). The meaning of *polutropos* – 'much-travelled' or (like *polumētis*) 'versatile' – has been debated since antiquity: see Heubeck *et al.* (1988–92) *ad loc.* Odysseus is also, among other things, *polutlas*, 'much-enduring'. On Homeric stock-epithets, see below, ch. 8.

it is borne out by all his personal history: wanderings, escapes, disguises, triumphs against the odds.

Humanity reads life one way, divinity (according to Zeus) another. The horizons of the human poem, indeed, already go beyond Zeus and his apparent preoccupations. It is not that we doubt the wisdom of Zeus, however – if only because his moralising view of humanity is borne out by the poet–narrator's passing comment in the opening lines. Ingenious Odysseus wandered much, learned much, suffered much, as he strove to win his life and his comrades' return (I.2–5). The comrades, however, perished 'through their own blind folly' (I.7) – and the word used is the word Zeus uses of human folly in his denunciation of Aegisthus (I.34): *atasthaliai*. Even so . . . there is an odd relativising about the presentation of Zeus here.

'*Smitten* for *smart* Odysseus' (I.48): in Greek, *daïphroni daietai*.[6] Unlike the *Iliad*, the *Odyssey* favours wordplay.[7] The play here marks off Athena's first reference to Odysseus in this, her first, speech, while her closing words in the same speech work in a comparable way. Odysseus is trapped on a paradise island by the nymph Calypso (meaning 'Cover': her name, like many others, is significant), but despite the obvious temptations he longs to be home. 'What' (asks Athena) 'has he done wrong? *Odysseus*? – sounds like *misuse*, *Zeus*', where the featured sequence echoes and interprets the hero's name as a sentence of cosmic ill-treatment.[8] The guile of ingenious Odysseus will be operative on this same stylistic level when he meets the giant Cyclops, Polyphemus (meaning 'Famous'), and tricks him by giving his own name as 'No-man' (*Outis*: IX.187–414). Athena's foregrounding of wordplay at the outset establishes the technique as an Odyssean mode in its own right. It also serves to anticipate a special relationship between herself and Odysseus. When Odysseus finally reaches Ithaca, Athena, in disguise, meets him, and Odysseus, true to his ingenious self, seeks to conceal his identity and outwit the stranger (XIII.221–310). Athena's revelation of her real identity, and identification of his, is as charming as it is indicative. 'Enough of this: we are both experts in trickery – you among men, I myself among the gods' (XIII.296–9). Athena is both Odysseus' divine protectress and his poetic–creative exemplar. She is also, like Zeus and the poet–narrator, one of the main carriers of the poem's overt morality. Throughout, her protection of Odysseus, his family and his cause is coloured by her indignation

6 ἀλλά μοι ἀμφ' Ὀδυσῆι δαΐφρονι δαίεται ἦτορ. The striking use of δαίεται here is unparalleled, whether as the passive of δαίω, 'kindle' or of δαίω, 'divide'.

7 Stanford (1939) 98–106.

8 I.62: τί νύ οἱ τόσον ὠδύσαο, Ζεῦ; (literally, 'why have you so hated him, Zeus?', with the implicit equation of *ōdusao*, *Zeu* and *Odusseus*). This Homeric 'etymology' is picked up by Sophocles, fr. 965 Radt.

against Penelope's 'shameless suitors' (I.254 etc.), who, in his absence, lay claim to his wife, feast in his palace, use the palace women and consume his wealth. She too is one of the articulators of the Agamemnon theme ('be like Orestes', she tells Telemachus, 'who won fame by avenging his father', I.298–300), and clearly that theme sustains the same large moral lesson.

The *Odyssey* is a poem of remarkable diversity, not least in technique and in mood. At the end of Book V, the shipwrecked hero is washed up on the coast of Phaeacia. Alone and close to death, he finds shelter in a bed of fallen leaves (V.488–91):

> Like a farmer hiding a burning log in the ashes
> Right at the edge of his land, a man with no neighbours,
> Saving a seed of fire, lest he have to rekindle from somewhere,
> So Odysseus covered himself in the leaves.

As when a farmer, on the edge of his land, keeps a fire going, even so Odysseus, on the edge of life, keeps himself going. The simile articulates the apprehension of bare life, and, with its stress on remoteness ('right at the edge', 'no neighbours', 'lest . . . from somewhere'), the precariousness of Odysseus' solitary condition. Remarkably, the simile contains a metaphor, 'seed of fire' (*sperma puros*). There are few demonstrable metaphors in Homer (formulaic idiom hardly encourages that kind of linguistic experiment), and this is one of the clearest examples.[9] Remarkably, too, the vehicle of the metaphor (*sperma*, 'seed') interacts with the vehicle of the simile – the *farmer*, now sowing a special kind of 'seed'. Striking moment of individual crisis: striking stylistic intensification, opening up a whole new landscape of poetic expression.

What follows, in Book VI, represents a complete contrast. The young Phaeacian princess Nausicaa decides to do the family washing, as a pretext to freshen up her clothes for a prospective suitor. Off she goes, with permission from her father (and 'though she was too shy to mention marriage, he understood', VI.66–7). The washing is duly done in the river, near where our hero is still asleep; while the clothes are drying, Nausicaa and her maids (with their veils off, 100) play ball; she throws one of them a catch, misses her target, and the ball ends up in the water, 'in a deep eddy' (116); the girls 'shriek out loud' – and noble Odysseus wakes up (117).

[9] I.e. new, live, deviant, defamiliarising metaphor (as opposed to 'dead metaphor', cliché etc.); see e.g. Silk (2003) 116–18, 122–4.

To 'Longinus' the *Odyssey* seemed to anticipate comedy of manners,[10] and here, certainly, are some of its characteristic ingredients: slice of ordinary life, comic coincidence, humorous appreciation of gender stereotypes (beautifully understated) – from the father who 'understood' to the girls, who (being girls) can't throw straight and cry when it all goes wrong. The disparity, now, between these fluttery innocents and the unkempt and appalled hero ('oh no, where am I *this* time?', 119) is obvious, and what enormously accentuates the disparity is a collision of fictional affiliations. He is an Achaean warlord; they come from a kind of other-worldly paradise.[11] Odysseus has stepped out of a heroic myth; Nausicaa seems to belong to a fairy-tale. And indeed, in the Phaeacian episode as a whole (Books VI–VIII), the fairy-tale elements are striking: young princess in faraway land dreaming of husband meets mysterious stranger . . . Everything is there, even the frog turned into a handsome prince – because Odysseus makes his entrance like an unappealing amphibian ('fouled with brine', 137), but (thanks to Athena) re-emerges, after a bath, taller, broader, with hair curled and 'grace on his head and shoulders' (229–35), so that with good reason Nausicaa can say to her maids, 'if only a man like this could be my husband' (238–45).[12]

Eventually, it dawns on the Phaeacian royal household that the stranger has a wife at home and yearns to get back to her,[13] and that their role is to help him do it. Meanwhile, Homer lingers over the extraordinary moment of meeting. Odysseus hears female voices (122): who and what are they? Emerging naked from his thicket, he comes out to see – 'breaking off a leafy branch with his strong hand to keep his embarrassments covered' (127–9).[14] 'Forth he came like a mountain lion' (130) – like an Iliadic hero, therefore – and the maids run off in terror (138). Nausicaa alone stands her ground, and, sizing up the situation, Odysseus 'pondered' (141). He needs help from a vulnerable-looking young person of unknown provenance, taken by surprise and not wearing her veil. *Question*: should he (a) take hold of her knees (normal suppliant's etiquette) (142) or (b) try and explain himself at a

[10] *Subl.* 9.15. Likewise, to the nineteenth century, the *Odyssey* prefigures the novel. 'Farrar declared that the *Odyssey* was the best novel ever written', Jenkyns (1980) 209. ('Farrar' is F. W. Farrar; the 'declaration' comes in ch. 18 of his 1859 novel, *Julian Home*.) Cf. Steiner, p. 365 below.

[11] See below, p. 40.

[12] On Odyssean folk-tale/fairy-tale, see Peradotto (1990) 32–93; Schein (1996) 20–6; Reinhardt (1996) 63–132.

[13] This is apparent to the Phaeacians by VIII.243: cf. Hainsworth in Heubeck (1988–92) *ad loc.*

[14] 'Embarrassments': μήδεα. The tone of this rare euphemism (cf. Hainsworth in Heubeck *et al.* (1988–92) *ad loc.*) is elusive.

distance (143–4)? Preserving one's dignity (and concealing one's 'embarrassments') while manoeuvring with knees, branches and leaves might be tricky. He chooses (b), wins her confidence and, shortly, her heart: *right answer*.

The whole imagined scene is bizarre and in its complex tone – romantic, pathetic, comic – as charming as its psychology is delicate. In a celebrated essay, Erich Auerbach laid emphasis on the external realism of Homeric description.[15] Strange realism here: collision of fictional realms; haunting, elusive tone – and all finely calculated to help set up a romance that (we *know*) can never happen. Transient Nausicaa is a foil for durable Penelope, as murdered Agamemnon is for surviving Odysseus, and playful romantic interlude for sombre heroic return.

As the *Odyssey* proceeds, its range enlarges and the contrasts with the *Iliad* multiply. These are apparent even within the martial heroics that the two epics have in common. Iliadic fighting involves warfare between massed armies or duels between select pairs of heroes. The *Odyssey*'s fighting (much more restricted in scale) is almost all Odysseus, whether coping with aliens, like the Cyclops, or confronting the suitors (Book XXII) and their kin (XXIV). In both cases our hero relies, in part, on his proverbial guile. The Cyclops is tricked, and so are the suitors. Back in Ithaca, Odysseus must re-enter his own palace in a beggar's disguise and plan his campaign with the aid, eventually, of a few confidants – chiefly, his son Telemachus and (surprisingly in this aristocratic ambience) two out-house servants, a pig-handler Eumaeus and a cowman Philoetius, who make up his fighting force, as against the much more numerous suitors. The unequal arithmetic of the rival groupings is underlined (XXII.203–4) –

> Breathing might, they took their stand, there at the threshold:
> Four, against many fine men inside the palace –

though, as always, somewhere nearby is Odysseus' divine protectress (XXII.204–5):

> Four, against many fine men inside the palace.
> But now they were joined by the daughter of Zeus, Athena.

After the battle is over, Odysseus offers his considered view of the 'many fine men' of Ithaca (XXII.413–16):

> Heavenly Fate and their own iniquitous actions
> Undid these men. No living soul did they honour,
> Evil or good, who found his way among them.
> Thus by their own blind folly their end has been shameful.

[15] Auerbach (1953) 3–23.

The 'blind folly' is that same *atasthaliai* which Zeus and the poet–narrator ascribed to mankind at the very start of the poem. The coherence of the poem's insistence on this moral lesson is impressive – and yet . . . 'No living soul did they honour.' Really? This is false, as we know from the case of the suitor Amphinomus, who was respected by Penelope (XVI.397–8) and who paid public 'honour' to the beggar Odysseus himself (XVIII.119–57), and again from the case of the Ithacan soothsayer Leodes.

We meet Leodes twice. In Book XXI, on Penelope's initiative, a contest for her hand is set up: whoever can string Odysseus' bow and shoot an arrow 'through twelve axes' can have her. The unkempt stranger Odysseus, his identity revealed now to his son and to the loyal few, but not to Penelope herself, will duly win the contest, but first the suitors try, among them Leodes (XXI.144–74). The narrator's description of him is startling: 'to him alone deeds of blind folly were hateful' and 'he hated the suitors' (146–7). 'Blind folly' is once again *atasthaliai*, and 'the suitors' means the *other* suitors, since Leodes himself, by virtue of both his participation in the contest and his own words in the event (152–6), is evidently one. Our second meeting with Leodes is his death scene (XXII.310–29). The Ithacan nobility lie dying or dead in the palace halls, and Leodes rushes forward in supplication to Odysseus: the other suitors (as he calls them, 314–15) have met a shameful end through (once more) their *atasthaliai* (317); he has done no wrong himself (318).[16] To Odysseus the fact that Leodes wanted Penelope is enough; he kills the soothsayer 'while he was still speaking' (329).

There are obvious issues of cultural difference here. Odysseus is a returned husband, long missing and plausibly presumed dead; Leodes, among many others, desired his wife. Few of Homer's modern readers would condone revenge killing in such a context, let alone acclaim it, but the *Odyssey* does – or does it . . . ? The modern reader, certainly, is left to ponder the grossness of the overstatement in Odysseus' triumphant words, a hundred verses later: '*no* living soul did they honour'.[17]

As a moral problematic, one gathers, the rights and wrongs of revenge killing are not in themselves at issue (this is not yet the world of Aeschylus' *Oresteia*), but a (problematically?) high value is put on loyalty. This is the lesson of the Agamemnon theme ('my wife had me killed, yours knows better': Agamemnon, in Hades, to Odysseus, XI.409–46), and as the poem proceeds,

[16] Leodes specifies his consistent opposition to the way the other suitors used the palace women, which was a particular offence to Odysseus (XVI.108–9).

[17] Not the only time Odysseus' moralising is clearly overstated. Cf. his unqualified assertion that the palace women were forcibly taken (XXII.37), against the clear evidence of XX.6–8 (and, later, XXII.420–5, 443–5).

the importance of loyalty in Odysseus' cause becomes ever clearer. He wins out because, and only because, a small group centred on his immediate family stands by him or keeps faith in him: wife Penelope, fobbing off the suitors, year after year, on the pretext of having to finish weaving a shroud for Odysseus' aged father Laertes (II.93–110); son Telemachus, who goes in search of news of his father and assists him when the two eventually meet in Ithaca; loyal servants and functionaries (among them the two warriors and the minstrel Phemius); then also Laertes, proved loyal after protracted testing (XXIV.216–355); Odysseus' old dog Argos, even, doggedly living on until he sees his master (XVII.291–327); and Athena, active on behalf of Odysseus and his family, from start (I.44–50) to finish (XXIV.541–8).

Even the great romantic climax of the epic, the reunion of Odysseus and Penelope in Book XXIII, centres on loyalty. Old nurse Eurycleia (*loyal* servant) wakes up her mistress, who has slept through the battle, knowing nothing yet of her husband's return. The nurse's message is simple: Odysseus has come, has come at last and killed the suitors (XXIII.7–8) – and the repeated 'has come' is fraught with emotional significance.[18] Confronted with the thought that the unkempt stranger is really Odysseus, Penelope is incredulous. Soon, she is prepared to accept the killing, but, still, not the return of her man: no, one of the gods must have killed them – but Odysseus has *lost* his return home and is *lost* (dead) himself (XXIII.63–8). The plangent repetition of 'lost'[19] echoes the nurse's repeated 'has come' and enforces the sharp psychological insight: Penelope finds it easier to accept the miraculous than the long-awaited.

The recognition scene is delicately observed and exquisitely paced. Downstairs, in awkward silence, Penelope sits 'opposite Odysseus in the light of the fire against the other wall' (89–90). Telemachus, also present, is impatient. His father calmly plans ahead. Everyone bathes and dresses, including Odysseus himself, who re-emerges, at last, properly dressed and (with Athena's aid) taller, broader and . . . precisely as he was to Nausicaa in the playful young-love episode to which this husband-wife reunion is the grown-up counterpart.[20] Odysseus is the great trickster and tester, but now Penelope begins to test *him*. Seemingly losing patience, like his son before him, he asks for his bed to be made up. 'His' bed, we soon learn, is special, designed and constructed by Odysseus himself as a fixture in the royal bedroom: a symbol, then, of marriage and its permanence. Penelope instructs

[18] ἦλθ' . . . ὀψέ περ ἐλθών. By the fifth century, such phraseology is definitively associated with the return, and perhaps recognition, of an absent lover or protector: Silk (1988) 98–100. Odysseus is both.

[19] XXIII.68: ὤλεσε/ὤλετο.

[20] XXIII.156–63: VI.229–35.

the nurse to make up the bed 'outside the well-built chamber' (XXIII.178), provoking her startled husband to reveal the secret of the bed's construction which, as she knows, no other man could know. In tears she embraces him, while he weeps in turn, as he 'takes in his arms his beloved, true-hearted wife' (232), and (233–9) –

> Welcome as land, coming into view, to swimmers
> Whose well-wrought ship on the open sea Poseidon
> Shattered, by wind and solid wave driven –
> Few of them made an escape to the shore by swimming
> Against the gray water, and thick brine's stuck to their bodies,
> And stepping on land they welcome their salvation:
> Just so, welcome to her, as she looked at him, was her husband.

High-climactic moment; another extraordinary simile. Two special features stand out: first, the vehicle of the simile – Poseidon, shipwreck, swimming, land – is drawn directly from the tenor of the poem, in fact from Odysseus' own painful adventures themselves;[21] second, the tenor of the simile, at the start seemingly *his* feelings about *her*, switches at the end to *her* feelings about *him*. The cumulative effect is of reciprocity and harmonious resolution – between the husband's return now and his whole painful past, and between, more immediately, husband and wife themselves. The technical brilliance of the moment is remarkable; no less so, the poise between psychological realism and a remorseless symbolic logic which requires the loyalty of wife to husband, as of husband to wife, to be proved, and celebrated, almost ritually. The *Odyssey*, after all, has its ceremonial affirmations.

In the most literal sense, the *Odyssey* is the story of a wanderer, even an explorer. 'Many men's cities he saw, many men's minds he discovered' (I.3). The wanderings have been read as explorations of Odysseus himself.[22] The hero whose name *he* once gives as No-man, and the meaning of which the gods debate, now becomes an explorer in search of identity: perhaps a war-lord who becomes a moral man; perhaps a man who becomes a discoverer of, even, existential value. How far Odysseus can be said to *become* anything (not a normal Homeric propensity)[23] is debatable. Beyond dispute, though, is the range of experience – realms of experience, even – that his explorations encompass: from heroic Troy to the various provinces of fairyland, from the mythical Underworld which he visits in Book XI to Ithaca itself, which, in

[21] Note also the evocation of an earlier simile, V.394–8, and the threefold stress on 'welcome' (ἀσπασ-) in both (XXIII.233, 238, 239; V.394, 397, 398).

[22] Among the very different attempts to read the poem along such lines: Dimock (1956), Rutherford (1986), Pucci (1987).

[23] Silk (2004) 75–6, 83–4.

relative terms, is a credible and unglamorised world. In particular, the Ithaca where Odysseus first finds refuge in his beggar's disguise is a world of poor people, humble food, modest dwellings and menaces from lords and masters, in marked contrast to his two previous venues, the wonderlands of Phaeacia and Calypso's Ogygia. Phaeacia is a place where fruit grows all the year round (VII.117–21), ships never sink (VIII.557–63), and peace rules (VI.201–5). Ogygia is all vines, violets and parsley, where 'even a god who came that way would gaze in wonder and pleasure' (V.73–4). Phaeacia, of course, also offers marriage with the young Nausicaa and Calypso's isle, for its part, sex with the goddess and immortality too (V.203–27). Even by itself, Odysseus' choice of his own Ithaca over such glamorous alternatives represents a clear affirmation of moral purpose: one, indeed, that resonates down the millennia of Western fiction, high and low, from Virgil's *Aeneid* (whose Aeneas, driven from Troy, must spurn even Dido to found a new resurgent Troy in Italy)[24] to *The Wizard of Oz*: 'Oh, Auntie Em', says Dorothy, 'there's *no* place like home'.[25]

Counterpointed against the overt straightforwardness, both of Odysseus' quest and of the moral values associated with it, is the behavioural quirkiness of a whole series of characters in the poem. Quite unlike the *Iliad*, the *Odyssey* abounds in striking female characters,[26] whose actions are frequently devious or unpredictable or both. Athena is the archetypal cunning goddess. Circe (who, like Calypso, detains Odysseus in Wonderland) is a witch and a sorceress. Beautiful Helen, visited by Telemachus on his travels, is all we might expect of an Iliadic *grande dame* – except that, uniquely, she takes drugs to obliterate the pain of living (IV.219–34).[27] Even Nausicaa tries to outwit her father. And Penelope too has her devious side (the testing of Odysseus, the shroud-trick) and her inexplicable behaviour, when she flaunts herself in front of the suitors ('with a meaningless laugh', XVIII.163), and then sets up the contest. In both cases the decision is presented as Athena's idea (XVIII.158–60, XXI.1–4); but, by the rules of 'double determination', divine initiative in such cases should be divine prompting for human impulse – so that Penelope's behaviour remains as inexplicable as ever.[28]

[24] *illic fas regna resurgere Troiae*: *Aeneid*, I.206.

[25] Judy Garland's closing words in the 1939 film.

[26] See e.g. Cohen (1995) and Felson and Slatkin, ch. 7 below.

[27] Circe has 'drugs' that are magical, rather than merely mind-altering: X.212–13, 235–40, 290–3, 316–28. Odysseus' men in IX are given lotus, with evident narcotic properties, but none become regular users (IX.91–104). Contrast Tennyson's 'Lotos-Eaters' (1832).

[28] Double determination: see below, p. 59. Critics tend to ignore the general point about females in favour of specific 'explanations' of Penelope. See e.g. Clay (1984) 73–6 on her laugh, Peradotto (1990) 82–5 on the contest; Katz (1991) 77–113, 192–5, and Felson-Rubin in Schein (1996) 168–75 on both.

In this context, the deviousness of Odysseus himself – validated by Athena's endorsement and Penelope's emulation – seems open to interpretation as an essentially feminine quality, and alien indeed to the manly simplicities of the *Iliad*.[29] 'Hateful as the gates of Hades is the man who says one thing and hides another' is the representative statement of the Iliadic Achilles (to the Iliadic Odysseus, no less: 9.312–13). The *Odyssey* as triumph of the feminine, then? Up to a point, maybe – but then again, its defining figure Odysseus is in all other respects utterly masculine, and in the end proves himself, as he evidently must, by a man's physical prowess.[30]

In an important sense, the *Odyssey* as achieved epic poem is devious too, not least by repeated allusions to the working in words and the fashioning of narratives which constitute the medium of epic poetry itself. This is a poem of overt wordplay. Above all, it is a poem of stories and story-telling within its own narrative.[31] Telemachus hears stories – mostly about Odysseus – from Nestor in Pylos (Book III), from Menelaus and Helen in Sparta (IV); Odysseus recounts his own adventures to the Phaeacians (IX–XII), and in the Underworld, for instance, others (from his mother to Agamemnon) recount theirs to him (XII); Athena, in human form, tells stories, part-false, part-true, about her personae and Odysseus (first to Telemachus, I.179–212); Odysseus in his beggar's disguise tells false tales – sometimes about Odysseus himself – to a series of attentive listeners, from Athena (XIII.256–86) to his father (XXIV.266–79, 304–14). And stories are told by *aoidoi* – minstrels, bards. In Ithaca, Phemius sings of the return of the Achaeans (I.325–7), and in Phaeacia, his counterpart, Demodocus, of the Trojan horse (VIII.499–520) and the love of Ares and Aphrodite (VIII.266–366): two, then, of the many evocations of the Trojan heroics that (as 'Longinus' noted) give an Iliadic perspective to the poem,[32] together with a cautionary tale of infidelity that points up the marital commitment of Penelope and Odysseus.

[29] The association of cunning and the female, though almost ignored in the classic study of 'cunning intelligence' by Detienne and Vernant (1978) (at 321 n. 78), is a feature of Greek thought from Homer and Hesiod (*Op.* 67) to Plato (*Leg.* 781ab) and beyond. Odysseus' epithet *polumētis* and his relationship with Athena evoke the *female* power embodied in the goddess Metis ('Cunning'), who is Zeus's first wife and Athena's mother.

[30] A characteristic, ever since, of epic poetry and, more recently, the Western film, where a relevant motif involves a reluctant fighter proving himself by fighting. Two classic instances: James Stewart in *Destry Rides Again* (1939) and Alan Ladd in *Shane* (1953).

[31] On the *Odyssey* and tale-telling: Goldhill (1991) 37–68; Pucci (1998) 131–77.

[32] The full list includes the recollections (and mere presence) of Nestor in Book III, Menelaus and Helen in IV, Agamemnon and Achilles (from the Underworld) in XI, together with the Agamemnon theme itself (p. 32 n. 4 above).

In the *Iliad* a disillusioned Achilles sings unspecified 'heroic tales' to himself and a silent Patroclus (9.186–91). It is richly symptomatic of the *Odyssey*, not just that 'tales' should be more frequent, or that we actually hear most of them, but that tale-telling itself is presented as something special. The two court singers are honoured and respected: even the unruly suitors behave when Phemius starts singing (I.325–6). Odysseus as tale-teller is himself likened to a tale-telling minstrel (XI.368, XVII.518) and his triumphant stringing of the bow to a minstrel stringing his instrument (XXI.404–9), while the climactic recognition scene of husband and wife reaches its appropriate fulfilment, first with an act of love-making (XXIII.300), then with an exchange of personal histories, duly recapitulated for our information (XXIII.301–30).

The fact that so many of the tales told in the *Odyssey* are false and deceptive, or else 'tall stories' by any standard, has a deeper significance. Odysseus' narrow scrapes and escapes; the uncertainties about how he will, in the end, be victorious; and the unforeseeable developments *en route*, of which Penelope's decision to hold a contest is one: all of these signify an aesthetic of surprise rather than suspense. The *Iliad*'s power depends on a profound commitment to an inexorable working-out of conflict and its consequences. The *Odyssey*, though committed to the eventual triumph of Odysseus, is – like its own twisted tales – all twists and turns, with Odysseus supreme *polutropos*, 'man of many turns' (I.1), himself.

In the range and configuration of its basic material, the *Odyssey* has a distinctive complexity. The *Iliad*'s characters are mostly adult fighting men in their prime. The *Odyssey* offers something like a cross-section of humanity, male and female: from aristocrats to slaves, from country to town, from vagrants to court professionals. There are characters caught and psychologised, as if in vignette, at particular ages: old Laertes, digging his vines in shin-guards and gardening gloves (XXIV.226–30); young Nausicaa, touched by her first love; young Telemachus, asserting himself, seemingly for the first time, to his mother ('you go upstairs: I'll do the talking', I.356–62). Unlike the Iliadic Achilles, reacting to a short series of related crises on, and off, the battlefield, the Odyssean Odysseus is on display in every imaginable environment, home and away, natural and supernatural, ennobling and degrading, physical and intellectual, desperate, humorous, romantic and workaday. For the first four books, he is presented *in absentia* (a brilliant technical device) – by the gap he has left, by his reputation, by eye-witness accounts; only then by his own actions and his own version of his actions.

Yet if its human cast-list is longer and more varied, and (in the case of Odysseus) its fullness of presentation considerably greater, the *Odyssey* has a significantly simpler equivalent of that parallel realm of essentially amoral gods and goddesses who inform the warrior world of the *Iliad*, competing and lamenting the human outcome. Our epic features a series of minor superhumans and, on the divine level proper, a miniature and morally schematic heaven. Somewhere in the background, Poseidon, like an Iliadic god, maintains a personal hostility to Odysseus (the 'offence' was the blinding of the Cyclops, Poseidon's son), while his eventual triumph is guaranteed by the assumed rightness of his cause, as validated by Athena with the authority of Zeus; most of the Olympian pantheon is irrelevant. The defeat of the Ithacans engenders no dispute or regret in heaven, even if the Zeus who denounces mankind's 'blind folly' in Book I (32–43) is back at the end to call for peace between Odysseus and the slain suitors' vengeful kin (XXIV.481–6, 542–4). And yet . . . ends stay open. In the Underworld, the prophet Tiresias foretells a strange sequel, involving more travel for Odysseus and some kind of propitiation of Poseidon (XI.119–37). The reconciliation in the last book is itself perfunctory. Has the Homer of the *Odyssey*, like the Tolstoy of *Anna Karenina*, problems with closures? – or, like the later Tolstoy, even, moral–theological preoccupations at odds with his own art?[33]

In the most fundamental sense, too, the contours of the action in the *Odyssey* are distinctive. Where the *Iliad* takes place over a few weeks in one setting, the *Odyssey* travels backwards and forwards in place and in time. Its temporal range, in fact (essentially the ten years since the end of the Trojan War), is only exceeded by its topographical coverage (from Troy to Ithaca, Pylos to Sparta, Hades to Phaeacia, the land of the Lotus-Eaters to Calypso's isle). The *Iliad*, furthermore is constructed on a simple, powerful linear sequence (*ABC* . . .). The *Odyssey*, more artfully, begins in present time in Ithaca (Books I–II), follows Telemachus on his travels to Pylos and Sparta (III–IV), then (ostensibly, still, in present sequence, though effectively in flashback to the start of I),[34] turns to Odysseus' escape from Ogygia to Phaeacia (V) and his meetings there with Nausicaa and her parents (VI–VIII), then gives, in flashback, Odysseus' account (to the Phaeacians) of his wanderings, from Troy to Ogygia (IX–XII), before narrating (in the present, again) his return to Ithaca (in XIII), where the action remains until the end. The second half of the poem, therefore, is like the whole of the *Iliad*, in that its action takes place on a single site and over a short space of time (seemingly, about a week). In these terms, though, the overall difference is obvious. If the *Iliad* is *ABC* . . . , the *Odyssey* is *BAC* . . . , and a complicated

[33] The end of the *Odyssey* – from XXIII.297 – has been regarded as compositionally problematic since the Alexandrian age (see p. 221 below). In terms of poetic efficacy, what matters is that the end, though broadly necessary, is less than satisfying. The same goes for some less necessary sequences, notably the catalogues of heroines and heroes in XI.[illegible] and [illegible]–631.

[34] Cf. Hainsworth in Heubeck *et al.* (1988–92) *ad loc.*

sort of *BAC* . . . too, where the *A* is the flashback in Books IX–XII, and the *B* is the two separate sequences involving Telemachus (I–IV) and Odysseus (V–VIII). The major reversal of time here has a disconcerting effect, heightened by the switching between relative normality and Wonderland exotica.

The shape, like the scope, of the Odyssean epic enforces its restless, exploratory character: ends are opened, questions raised, alternative voices let loose.[35]

FURTHER READING

For general introductions to the *Odyssey*, see Griffin (2003) and Rutherford (1996). The standard edition of the Greek text is by van Thiel (1991). Widely read modern translations include those by Fitzgerald (1961) and Shewring (1980). Commentaries on the Greek text, in whole or part, include those by Stanford (1958–9), Heubeck *et al.* (1988–92), Rutherford (1992), Garvie (1994). A range of recent interpretation, not necessarily in line with the present author's positions, is offered by Cohen (1995), Katz (1991), Peradotto (1990), Pucci (1987), Schein (1996).

[35] In Bakhtinian terms – but *pace* Bakhtin (1981) himself – the *Odyssey* is thus more of a dialogical novel than a monological epic: cf. Peradotto (1990) 53–4.

4

RUTH SCODEL

The story-teller and his audience

Narrative method has long been a central issue in Homeric scholarship, since Analysts relied on narrative difficulties to identify earlier levels, while Unitarians responded by claiming that an understanding of Homer's narrative rules would explain inconsistencies.[1] More recently, oral poetry and structuralist narratology have contributed to more understanding of Homer's narrative techniques.[2] Yet even while scholars have treated Homeric narrative as problematic, readers have been moved by the poems.

To the Greeks of the eighth century, epic presented a remote, splendid, shared past. Heroic stories were a valuable cultural resource; they provided entertainment, historical continuity and a method of ethical thought. Epic performance was an especially important vehicle for transmitting these tales: at a successful performance, everyone shared in excitement, sorrow and admiration, making the occasion a source of social cohesion. The familiarity of the main characters and stories, reinforced by epic's conservative language and style, offered stability in a changing world, while the flexibility of performance meant that the stories could be adapted to their immediate contexts.

However our epics were written down, their first audiences typically heard them performed. Hearers could not go back and check a detail, or skip ahead to see what happened. Homer learned how to perform from earlier performers, and his poems reflect practical experience in story-telling and the particular characters of this tradition.[3] The basic stories had been told many times already and were believed to be true. The tradition provided a style fitting the importance of the tales. The story-teller's task lay not in inventing

[1] For Unitarians and Analysts, see Fowler in this volume ch. 14. Among the finest Unitarian studies of Homer's narrative are Rothe (1910) and Bassett (1938); more recently Fenik (1974) and Erbse (1972).

[2] For example, Edwards (1987), de Jong (1987) and (2001) and Richardson (1990).

[3] For 'Homer', see Introduction, pp. 2, 5.

a tale and telling it with originality, but in selecting his story, telling it at the level of detail appropriate to the occasion, and deploying the familiar epic language to make it vivid.

Clearly, however, these poems are not routine products of this once-thriving tradition. The return from war of a long-delayed hero is a familiar theme of tales around the world: why is the *Odyssey* special? The answer lies in two different strengths of these poems. First, the epics define their plots and control narrative tension with exceptional sophistication. The *Odyssey*, for example, begins by following not Odysseus, but Telemachus. We have the pleasurable frustration of waiting for the hero to appear, and we quickly realise that he is not the only character worth caring about, and that his world is not a simple one, as we watch Telemachus learn to manoeuvre in it. Both epics are much longer than an ordinary performance could be, but their length is not the result of simple elaboration of standard material. They vary the relation between narrative and story time over the fullest possible range: some events are fully dramatised, others briefly summarised. They concentrate on particular spaces – Odysseus' house, the plain of Troy – yet see these places within the entire panorama of earth, heaven and Hades.[4] Second, they are thematically powerful. In their original context, the political problems of the army at Troy and of Ithaca were immediately relevant.[5] Yet it is easy for readers in very different cultures to find meaning in them. Their central concern is the mortal individual embedded in complex social relations. Though the *Iliad* and *Odyssey* are very different, they are both about deciding what one's life is worth, and about connecting an understanding of one's own life with the demands of communities, friends and family. Homeric characters seek goals with which the hearer sympathises – to satisfy injured honour, to drive away invaders, to protect a home and son – under conditions of extreme risk and usually with insufficient knowledge. They make mistakes, because their world is realistically complicated. Homer was an exceptionally strong tradition-bearer, who combined a vision of the meaning of inherited stories with the ambition to organise narrative on an extraordinary scale.[6]

The poet could choose where in the immense saga an episode started and ended. The *Iliad* follows its hero's estrangement from his community through its disastrous consequences for both the army and Achilles himself, until his reconciliation with the army and his moment of human closeness to Priam.

[4] On space and duration, and on the classical plot, see Lowe (2000) 103–56.

[5] See Osborne in this volume.

[6] For the 'strong tradition-bearer', and the social function of story-telling, see Niles (1999) 66–188, 173, 193.

Ending with Hector's funeral, not Achilles' death, and with the laments of the Trojan women, the *Iliad* defines itself as concerned with both the social and personal costs of the pursuit of warrior honour. The *Odyssey* begins with the gods' decision to bring Odysseus home, a decision prompted by Zeus's reflections on the parallel story of Aegisthus and Orestes. The decision leads to two divine interventions: Athena goes to Ithaca to rouse Telemachus, Hermes to free Odysseus from Calypso. So from the start, the poem proclaims that it is about divine order and about the hero's family and social world. Each epic reaches a decisive closure, with the initial conflicts settled, the wider questions explored but not answered.

The Homeric poems are relatively self-contained. In many epic traditions, knowledge of the 'whole story' provides a context for performance of any episode, even though nobody ever tells the whole tale.[7] Such a tale is a 'notional epic'; it may become a text when a collector asks for a complete performance. In this way, the Trojan War and its aftermath clearly formed a recognised, unified, story. However, the *Iliad* and *Odyssey* are not typical episodes from a notional epic. Our epics are too ambitious to be episodes, but they do not tell the long series of famous events in order, either. Instead, each epic immensely expands a single incident – the Quarrel and the Return.

However, the poems do not define their themes narrowly, but incorporate a wide range of narrative material. The *Iliad* transposes events that should have taken place early in the Trojan War, such as the single combat of Menelaus and Paris, or Helen's description of the Greek heroes to Priam, to the first day of fighting after Achilles' quarrel with Agamemnon.[8] The *Odyssey* includes the travels of Telemachus in search of his father, repeated summaries and allusions to the fates of the other heroes of the war, and Odysseus' narrative of his adventures.

All this story material is of very different kinds. The Greek epic tradition was voracious, and singers knew not only the stories of the great wars of Thebes and Troy, but many others. Indeed, the epics borrowed material from other stories to expand their own tales.[9] Both *Iliad* and *Odyssey* include comic anecdotes of quarrels and sex on Olympus. Odysseus tells several lies in which he is an adventurous Cretan: these play variations on the 'real' adventures of Odysseus, but take place in the real fringes of the contemporary world, Egypt and Epirus, rather than in the imaginary world of the 'real' adventures. The adventures combine folk-tale themes – one-eyed giants, witches who transform men to swine – with the 'travellers' tales'

7 See Foley (1999a) 42, and in this volume, pp. 170–[illegible]. 8 Whitman (1958) 265.

9 See Dowden in this volume. For the *Odyssey*, Danek (1998) meticulously discusses possible sources.

that circulate in times of exploration and colonisation.[10] Some of Odysseus' adventures open with brief descriptions of the land and customs of the place he visits. These may exceed what Odysseus could plausibly have learned, and they are irrelevant to the following adventures. The epic made room for the contemporary fascination with exotic places.

Perhaps because the poet knew how diverse his material was, and how complicated his presentation is, he does not rely too much on his audience's knowledge of specific stories. The more familiarity the hearer has with heroic tales, the richer Homer's version is, but the poet demands only basic familiarity with the Trojan War and other epic traditions. His narrative makes sense without extensive prior knowledge. Homer provides extensive exposition, typically placed in speeches by characters or otherwise naturalised. Telemachus, for example, explains to the disguised Athena who the suitors are (I.245–51), even though it is hard to believe that the audience would not know. Hence, the epics are in many ways still accessible.

Some Homeric techniques work directly for us. The *Iliad* draws the audience in with a small mystery: having asked what god began the quarrel, and named Apollo, the narrator moves backward instead of forward, through a chain of causally linked events to the real beginning. This is a dramatic, pathetic scene, as the old priest Chryses tries to ransom his daughter and Agamemnon cruelly rejects him. The narrator wastes no time with explanations. Instead we are rapidly placed in a situation that encapsulates much of the experience of the whole epic. The hearer must sympathise with Chryses, yet the plague that answers his prayer is horrifying.[11] From the start, Homer shows his power and unpredictability, in the vision of Apollo's descent 'like night', and the odd detail that the plague first attacks the mules and dogs. Homer is not a realistic author (on his battlefield, grisly though it is, nobody dies slowly). Yet he often achieves powerful realistic effects by including precise-looking details, and powerful emotional effects by moving from the heroes to a broader world of women, slaves, even animals. Famous examples are Hector's little son, frightened by his father's helmet (6.466–71), and Odysseus' faithful dog (XVII.291–327).

However, many aspects of Homeric technique rely on audience familiarity with the generic rules. Everyone understood that the variants of 'type-scenes' mark meaning.[12] Where the poet meticulously describes a sacrifice, social order is secure. When the narrator carefully describes how the sacrifice at Pylos is organised (III.4–9), the audience knows that this city is prospering. The poet never describes the sacrifices of Penelope's suitors, because their

[10] Page (1973). [11] It is thus a parallel for Achilles' anger; see Rabel (1997) 37–56.
[12] See Clark in this volume, pp. 134–6.

feasting does not express proper order, but corrupts it.[13] When Odysseus' companions slaughter the Cattle of the Sun, their attempt to conduct the sacrilege as a sacrifice is both pathetic and frightening (XII.353–65). In the *Iliad*, the poet extensively describes the Greeks' return of Chryseis to her father, especially the sacrificial ritual (I.430–87). This re-establishment of order stands in contrast to the disruption that will soon arise again.

Repetition with variation is the poet's most important method of pointing to meaning. At a general level, the *Odyssey* is organised around the hero's repeated arrival on an island where he confronts both hostile men and a potentially dangerous woman.[14] The main plot of the *Odyssey* follows a familiar folk-tale pattern: the hero, absent so long that he is assumed to be dead, returns in disguise just in time to prevent his wife's remarriage.[15] The poet expands the basic story of the disguised hero in a number of ways. The Ithacan section of the *Odyssey* develops through variants on the theme of the beggar well or badly treated. The beggar's reception by the swineherd Eumaeus gives the poet ample opportunity to develop the theme. There are three attacks by suitors, and insults from the paired Melanthius and his sister Melantho.[16] An entire episode is built around the suitors' staging of a fight between the established local beggar, Iros, and the new beggar. The fight sustains the story by providing the disguised Odysseus with a right to remain in the house, despite the suitors' hostility. Thematically it offers the suitors yet another warning that the old man is more than he seems, and displays their bad behaviour. More abstractly, it offers almost a parody of Odysseus' final battle with the suitors – a mock-epic would turn the fight to regain control of one's home and kingdom into a fistfight whose prize is a sausage. Homer also parodies Odysseus' wanderings in those of Menelaus: Odysseus hides his men under sheep in order to escape the Cyclops' cave, while Menelaus, in order to catch Proteus, hides his men under seal-skins, and emphasises how badly they smell (IV.435–48). The poet varies the same themes, allowing the audience to draws its conclusions through comparison and contrast.

Homer's listeners knew how to pay attention to significant variation. They knew other rules, too. Homer rarely presents simultaneous actions, but puts events in sequence, even when the result is unrealistic.[17] Many stories told by characters are compressed and are told through 'ring composition': they start in the middle, go back in time, and then go forward again (XX.66–78). The audience knew, however, that such stories would reflect on the main

[13] Said (1979). [14] Louden (1999). [15] Hölscher (1989) 40–55.
[16] On repetitions in the *Odyssey*, see Fenik (1974) 173–232.
[17] 'Zielinski's rule'; see Krischer (1971) 91–129.

action, and could look for their meanings without worrying too much about their internal coherence.[18] Everyone knew that a digression marks the significance of the main action. When Penelope fetches Odysseus' bow, the poet carefully explains how Odysseus acquired this bow (XXI.13–38). The story itself has broad thematic relevance, with Heracles' violation of the laws of hospitality and Odysseus' unfulfilled friendship with Iphitus, but it is told at this moment because the poet has just revealed that the bow is 'the beginning of slaughter' (XXI.4). The narrator moves away from the main action precisely at momentous points in that action.[19] The bow, like other important objects, is not introduced in advance. In modern narrative, if the hero's scar is to be significant in the plot, the scar needs to be mentioned well before it serves its important function. Introducing such narrative elements when needed is easier for both poet and audience.

Such techniques are foreign to modern readers. Sometimes the narrative preparation seems out of proportion to the outcome. Both Nausicaa and Athena lead Odysseus to think that it is very important that Queen Arete favour him when he supplicates the Phaeacians, yet she initially takes no part. Later she asks him his identity, and especially where he obtained his clothes (VII.237–9); this is surely an important test, but it is brief compared to the preparation. Still later, she takes the lead in soliciting more gifts for Odysseus (XI.336–41).[20] The theme of Odysseus' possible marriage to Nausicaa is richly developed. Yet the end of this theme, when Odysseus says farewell to Nausicaa (VIII.457–68), seems truncated, though touching. Again, Telemachus meets on his way home the prophet Theoclymenus, who seeks his help fleeing the family of a man he has killed (XV.223–81). When Telemachus reaches Ithaca, he plans to send Theoclymenus to stay with a friend, but decides that, despite the difficulties, he wants him in his own house, after Theoclymenus interprets a bird-sign favourably for Telemachus (XV.508–46). Yet all this preparation concludes in Theoclymenus' giving a prediction of Odysseus' return to Penelope – she does not believe it – and delivering an eerie prophetic vision to the suitors (XVII.151–61, XX.345–72). Thereupon Theoclymenus disappears from the story.[21]

The audience could fit these characters into familiar narrative types – the powerful, dangerous queen; the possible bride; the prophet ignored. The poet does not need to emphasise an expectation fulfilled or overturned. Hearers may have thought that the prophecy to Penelope fulfilled Theoclymenus'

[18] Frequently such stories allow differing interpretations; Alden (2000) is useful but too insistent on a single, 'correct' interpretation. On invention in such stories, see Willcock (1964) and Andersen (1990); on audience competence, Scodel (2002) 62–4.

[19] Austin (1966). [20] Fenik (1974) 105–30. [21] See de Jong (2001) 372–3.

function. So his ecstatic prophecy was a surprise, like Arete's intervention with more gifts.[22]

The poet often manipulates the audience through tricky preparation. The reader must learn that disappointed narrative expectations often point to events later. For example, Polydamas warns Hector against taking horses across the ditch in attacking the Achaean camp. Polydamas' warnings are crucial to the narrative progression of the poem. Hector listens this time, but he is scornful when Polydamas tells him of a hostile bird-omen. He accepts Polydamas' advice once more, but rejects his warning not to keep the Trojans in the field after Achilles returns to battle (12.60–79; 12.210–50; 13.725–53; 18.249–309). The bird-omen actually predicts only the long-term outcome, and Hector's response has no immediate consequence. It prepares for his last, fatal rejection of Polydamas' advice. Asius rejects Polydamas' advice about the horses, and is killed – but his failure to heed Polydamas is irrelevant to his death. On the other hand, the Trojans later take their horses across the ditch, and the outcome is disastrous (16.367–93). Circe warns Odysseus that any attempt to fight Scylla is futile, but he forgets, and prepares for battle (XII.116–36, 226–30). This action makes no difference, but reminds the audience of how difficult Odysseus finds it not to fight when attacked – precisely the challenge he will face in disguise at home. Events that seem to have little point are often smaller-scale versions of later, crucial moments.

The narrator can also be tricky about characterisation. He clearly defines what kind of people the characters are, and invites the audience to imagine that they have psychological complexity. He then leaves many details of motivation opaque, so that the audience must infer or guess (especially in the *Odyssey*).[23] Why does Odysseus ask to have his feet washed by an old woman, when this request leads to the dangerous recognition by Eurycleia?[24] What is going through Penelope's mind when she appears before the suitors?[25] The narrator is omniscient, but sometimes stingy with his knowledge.

At the same time, the narrator invites the audience to feel broad sympathies with his characters. The *Iliad* directs the audience to pity the Trojans both by showing the Trojans in both private and political settings, as well as on the field, and by having Zeus express his pity for them even as he acquiesces in Troy's destruction. There is reason to think that this was not a feature of the older tradition: there are few regular epithets for the Trojans,

[22] One might also compare the *Odyssey*'s re-use of props, discussed by Lowe (2000) 149–50.

[23] Griffin (1980) 50–80.

[24] Köhnken (1991) suggests that Odysseus assumes that Eurynome, who is close to Penelope [illegible] Odysseus, will perform the task.

[25] See Murnaghan (1995) 70–1. For bibliography on this scene, see Byre (1988), Katz (1991), 78–93.

their hostile epithets ('war-loving') seem underutilised, and the formulaic language for being 'in Troy' or coming 'from Troy' is less developed than that for going 'toward Troy'.[26] The older tradition probably made the Trojans bad guys; Homer, in contrast, sees them as flawed, unable to overcome the corruption of some of their leaders, and perhaps justly doomed, but sympathetic nonetheless. The Homeric epics show an astonishing range of sympathy. Even the *Odyssey*, which makes it clear that the suitors deserve to die, invites pity for a few of them. The poet has a habit of momentarily shifting the centre of attention to a minor figure. When Briseis, for example, is taken away from Achilles' hut, the narrator tells us that she is unwilling (1.348): just for an instant, the pawn is a person, and we are reminded that she could have a story too (she tells it at 19.286–300).

The narrator occasionally adapts emotionally coloured language from a character. In the extreme case, Nausicaa's mules eat 'honey-sweet' grass. When moral judgments appear in such passages, it is impossible to know exactly whose they are. Agamemnon convinces Menelaus not to spare the lives of any Trojans, 'persuading him in accordance with how it should be' (6.62): this is Menelaus' reaction, but by giving his voice to Menelaus' feelings, the poet hints that for Menelaus, the victim of Trojan outrage, this reaction is appropriate. Zeus waits for Hector to fire a Greek ship as the fulfilment of Thetis' 'excessive' prayer (15.598), inviting the hearer's agreement. When Achilles 'cruelly' sacrifices Trojan prisoners on Patroclus' pyre, the poet almost merges their viewpoint with his own. The technique is surprisingly modern.[27]

This sympathy for the characters is central to Homeric narrative tension. Perhaps the most common misconception about traditional stories is that they do not allow for suspense. This is not true – a good story-teller can create suspense even when the audience knows the outcome.[28] In Homeric epic, the situation is especially complicated, since many details of a traditional story could vary among different versions. So the audience could never know just how the end would be reached. The poet carefully keeps the audience aware of how the plot will turn out in general, but uncertain about specifics, combining extensive foreshadowing of events with misdirection about others. Reliable prophecies occur, but they are limited and imprecise.[29] Beside them appear human guesses about the future, sometimes right and often not. The audience already knows some of what must happen, but can still be drawn into action that tends the 'wrong way'. The poet makes the threat that the Trojans will burn the Greeks' ships real.[30]

[26] Sale (1987) 21–50; (1994) 5–9. [27] de Jong (1987). [28] Gerrig (1989).
[29] Schadewaldt (1966) 10–11, 110 n. 3, 140. [30] Morrison (1992b).

The audience, who knows that Troy will fall, can share Hector's anticipation of the catastrophe, and be pained by his blindness when his success makes him optimistic. The combination of foreshadowing and misdirection can have powerful thematic force. At the beginning of the *Iliad*, Zeus is unwilling to yield to Thetis' plea to honour Achilles, because Hera will be annoyed. Yet in anger against Hera (8.469–77), he predicts that Patroclus will enter battle, as is fated, and later he predicts Patroclus' death (15.59–71). Patroclus is a 'fool' at 16.46–7 when he pleads to enter battle, where he will die. Yet the audience knows that Patroclus cannot know what will happen. Even for the audience, the Plan of Zeus in response to Thetis at first seems to be the controlling structure of the plot. However, it gradually becomes clear that Zeus has more complex plans, and that Achilles, though closer to the gods than other mortals, is still far from being in charge. The poet does not elucidate when or why Zeus devised this way of making the *Iliad*-plot, with its Greek defeat, conform to the overall outline of the tradition, which requires that the Trojans lose. This very ambiguity contributes powerfully to the tragic effect.

The *Odyssey* works somewhat differently.[31] Here the poet repeatedly makes it clear that Odysseus will be successful: Athena will not let him down. However, in the Ithacan books, the audience is not told where the plot is going except in general terms. Odysseus' actual plan does not even begin to appear until Penelope announces her intention of holding the bow-contest (XIX.571–81). Instead he plans a simple surprise attack. By not telling the audience too much about Odysseus' plans, and emphasising instead his struggles to control his emotions, the narrator both keeps the audience wondering what will happen and shows Odysseus as a brilliant improviser.[32]

To balance this misdirection, there are firm narrative structures. The *Iliad* is organised around scenes of pleading: Chryses for his daughter, the ambassadors for Achilles' return to battle, Priam for Hector's body. In Odysseus' narrative of his wanderings, the adventures are in groups of three, one in each group more elaborated than the others (Cyclops, Circe/Underworld, Cattle of the Sun). There are three dominant dangers in the Wanderings: being eaten, forgetting one's return, and bringing disaster on oneself through lack of self-control. One episode in each group emphasises each of the dangers, and the three elaborated sections each develop a different one.[33]

This pointed order is obvious to the modern reader, but the epics themselves tend to deny it. Homeric poetics sharply distinguish poetic storytelling, which offers an uncontaminated, disinterested truth directly provided

[31] On exposition, see Sternberg (1978) 56–128.

[32] Olson (1995) 145–8. [33] Most (1989b).

by the Muses, from the story-telling of everyday life, where the teller selects details to meet his audience's needs or to make a point. By placing the source of its authority outside the social world, Homeric epic gives itself room to manoeuvre. This breathing room is both political and a matter of practical narrative. Amid different versions of stories, the Muse allows the poet to recombine familiar elements in new ways.

By stressing some details and ignoring others, a story-teller can impose a moral on his tale. However, a telling that is directed towards a particular message lacks the impartiality that the tradition identifies with truth. Homer associates truth with the catalogue or simple chronological narrative, and the poems seem almost uneasy with their own chronological and narrative complexity.[34] In the *Iliad*, incidents are simply placed in the ninth year of the war, as if they belonged there. The *Odyssey* has its hero tell the most fantastic part of its story: his tale is reliable, but it also serves both as a defence of Odysseus' failure to save his men, and as a disguised sermon on good hospitality. Characters summarise events and tell stories about earlier heroes, but also tell about antecedents of the story itself, allowing the poet to frame his narrative without openly abandoning a straightforward movement through time or pointing a moral. The *Odyssey* uses the parallel stories of Nestor, Menelaus, the lesser Ajax and especially Agamemnon both to create suspense about Odysseus' story and to direct the audience's judgement – but not in the narrator's own voice. Similarly, the poet uses characters' guesses about the future as well as authoritative prophecies to extend the narrative to events beyond its conclusion, such as Achilles' death and the fall of Troy in the *Iliad*. Although he directs the audience's sympathies and judgements, he does not force a single interpretation, and his guidance is usually unobtrusive.

The narrator also moderates tendencies to be overly schematic. The experience of hearing the story is not as neat as a chart of Odysseus' adventures. The Underworld is subordinate to Circe and its dangers are not the same as those of the other adventures. Sometimes Odysseus is self-controlled in contrast to his men, especially on Thrinacia, where they perish because they eat the cattle, but he survives because he does not. Odysseus cannot convince his men to take their plunder from the Cicones and flee (IX.43–4). Yet in the Cyclops episode, this pattern is reversed: the companions unsuccessfully try to convince Odysseus to steal some food and flee (IX.224–9). They try to stop him from boasting afterwards (IX.494–500), and they remind him that he has stayed too long with Circe (X.471–4).

Though he pretends to be a neutral reporter, Homer manages his material ruthlessly. He summarises: 'as long as Hector was alive, and Achilles was

34 Finkelberg (1998).

angry, and the city of lord Priam was unsacked . . . but when all the best of the Trojans were dead, and of Argives some had been killed, while others survived, and Priam's city was sacked in the tenth year, and the Argives sailed to their dear home' (12.10–16). Such a passage presupposes that the audience knows the larger story, but it also asks them to forget all that happened between Hector's death and the fall of Troy, so that they may feel the pathos in equating Hector's death with Troy's end. The scope of Homer's narratives gives them immense authority. They reinvent their own antecedents and sequels. Even for modern readers, their claims are hard to resist.

FURTHER READING

For the application of structuralist narratology to Homer, the essential works are de Jong (1987) and (2001). The earlier, *Narrators and Focalizers*, is concerned especially with who speaks and whose experience filters the narrative, while the narrative commentary addresses a variety of questions, including focalisation, type-scenes, the treatment of time and characterisation. Also helpful from the structuralist side is Richardson (1990). For Homer's techniques for manipulating his audience for suspense, see Morrison (1992b), and Olson (1995), and for the plot development as the audience follows the early books of the *Odyssey*, Sternberg (1978). Lowe (2000) looks at the plotting of both epics; this and Sternberg are especially interesting because they study Homer in wider contexts of Western fiction. Very valuable on narrative pattern and the technique of repetition with variation is Fenik (1974). Danek (1998) discusses every passage in the *Odyssey* that implies another version of the tale or an outside source, and has rich bibliography. 'Originality' of narrative material in Homer is extremely controversial; see Scodel (2002) and L. Edmunds, 'Myth in Homer', in Morris and Powell (1997) 415–41. Two older, general books on Homeric narrative methods that are very much worth reading are Bassett (1938) (reprinted 2003), and the insightful Rothe (1910) (neglected, probably in part because of its Gothic script).

2

THE CHARACTERS

5

EMILY KEARNS

The Gods in the Homeric epics

A popular, somewhat pretentious, party game in certain circles not so long ago was to summarise a famous work of literature as briefly as possible: give the plot of Proust in one sentence, and so on. If we were thus to reduce the storylines of the *Iliad* and the *Odyssey* to the bare essentials, the Gods would not have to feature at all. Zeus's co-operation is not necessary, given the hero's larger-than-life status, to explain the disastrous effects of Achilles' withdrawal from battle, and neither do Poseidon or the Sun need to be invoked to account for misadventures at sea and the effect of twenty years' absence on a man's home. The party game was of course intended to provoke amusement by making the summary factually accurate but also entirely incongruous with the spirit of the original. Similarly, without the Gods the epics would be quite different from the *Iliad* and the *Odyssey* that we have, and surely also from the tradition that produced the poems. The (slightly longer) summaries given by the poems themselves, after all, give divine action a certain prominence: 'the plan of Zeus was accomplished', 'he took away from them the day of their return'; and the action of the *Iliad* begins with the question 'Which God caused them to quarrel?'[1] The words of the characters reflect a pervasive view that significant ideas, emotions and events are in some way caused by the intervention of a God.[2] Insofar as some concept of cause and effect is inherent in narrative, then, the divine must make its appearance; arguably it is not until Thucydides that the idea of a sustained narrative without the divine is born.

This causal function is not of course the only role of the Gods in the epic, and as we shall see it doesn't explain many of the distinctive features of

[1] 1.5, 1.9, 1.8.

[2] Although this concept of causation does not, or does not always, let mortals off the hook. It is one of the most conspicuous, and most discussed, features of the interaction between humans and gods that the same event has frequently both a divine and a human cause: so called 'double motivation' or 'over-determination'. The fullest treatment is still Lesky (1961); standard and very clear presentations also in Dodds (1951) 1–18 and Willcock (1970).

the epic Gods. For all the Homeric resonances of Herodotus' *Histories*, the contrast between his 'the God', or 'the divine', equally a key player in human affairs, and the individualised, highly personal Gods of Homer, could hardly be greater.[3] The Gods may perfectly well be implicated in the working-out of human affairs without making a personal appearance. But such appearances are a central and characteristic feature of the Homeric Gods, so that they are presented as characters in a sense equipollent to the human actors. So deeply embedded in the narrative style is that personal presentation that it occurs even when it causes logical difficulties. In *Odyssey* XII, when Odysseus' men have eaten the herds of the Sun, their guardian Lampetie informs their owner, her father Helios, and he in turn complains to Zeus, who agrees to destroy Odysseus' ship in vengeance. But all this is part of Odysseus' own narrative – how can he possibly know this? It is as though the poet suddenly realised the problem, pulled himself up with a start, and quickly found an explanation: 'I heard this later from Calypso, who was told it by Hermes' (XII.374–90). This highlights the singularity of the poet's own perspective, which goes far beyond the 'some God must have guided me' of his characters, or Herodotus' axiom that the divine principle acts by nature to upset things, and claims a knowledge of the Gods which – surely – no human being can possess. The audacity of this claim is somewhat softened by the introduction of the Muse or Muses as intermediary,[4] but it can still hardly be taken literally.

The Gods of the *Iliad*: who and where?

Book I of the *Iliad* introduces us not only to a world of divine causation and interaction, but to a whole society of Gods. Apollo, Athena, Hera, Zeus and Hephaestus make their appearance, and there are clearly other Gods who spend much of their time together, but also have separate homes, on the peaks of Olympus. The Gods indeed can be characterised as 'having Olympian homes' (I.18 and often). But there are also Gods such as Thetis who are able to travel to Olympus but who normally live elsewhere – 'in the depths of the sea, beside her aged father' (I.358). The picture is rounded out in subsequent books with the addition of further players: Ares, Aphrodite, Dione, Leto, Artemis, Hermes, and the messenger Iris all seem to have their homes on Olympus, while Poseidon, though at home in the depths of the sea which he rules, seems also to spend a good deal of his time with the other Gods on Olympus or on earth, presumably because as a son of Kronos and

[3] The Herodotean usage is present sporadically in the speech of human characters in Homer, e.g. XVII.218 ('*theos* (god) always brings like to like', clearly proverbial).

[4] See especially 2.484–5.

brother of Zeus his status is rather higher than most of the non-Olympian Gods; he is even unwilling to accept Zeus's overall authority, though in the end he submits, grumbling (15.184–217).

Other Gods are mentioned in the *Iliad*, but they are scarcely or not at all characters in the action. There is Enyo, a female counterpart of Ares, who features in one battle scene but never on Olympus; there is Charis or Pasithea, the wife of Hephaestus (18.382–3). Of the Gods who are prominent elsewhere in literature and in cult, Hades and Persephone (mentioned, e.g. in 9.569) may be presumed to be out of the action because they are effectively confined to their own sphere, the Underworld. This is the final destination of the heroes, but as it marks the end it is never explored itself; even the other Gods would shudder if Tartarus were laid open (20.62–5). But the absence of Demeter and Dionysus is harder to explain. Since they are both mentioned in the text, it seems very unlikely that they were unfamiliar to Homer's audience, and the most likely explanation is that these deities were difficult to treat convincingly in a way appropriate to the story. Hera, Athena, Poseidon, were all prominent as patrons of Greek cities, *poliouchoi*: Apollo, and therefore, it could be assumed, his mother Leto and sister Artemis had strong connections with the Asiatic mainland.[5] It made sense, therefore, to show them as passionately involved in the action on behalf of their favoured human communities. Dionysus, on the other hand, though sometimes thought of as Asian, was by human descent Theban and thus Greek, and both he and Demeter spent most of their mythological time travelling from city to city teaching the benefits of agriculture and viticulture and establishing their own worship.[6] This did not always occur without trauma, but essentially these deities were benefactors of humanity in general, rather than partisans of one group or the other. To show them favouring Achaeans or Trojans would involve too radical a shift in their essential nature, so they can have no part in the story.

There are other differences between the Iliadic pantheon and those we know from other sources, differences which seem unlikely to be solely or even primarily chronological. Hephaestus is prominent in other early Greek literature, but only in a few Greek cities did he have a significant cult presence (one of these cities was Athens, which is why this fact is not always realised).[7] Iris was even less of a cult figure, though she too appears quite often in literary mythology.[8] But perhaps the most general and far-reaching distinction

[5] Although the view that he originated from here is too simple: see Burkert (1985) 144.

[6] See Flueckiger-Guggenheim (1983). [7] Burkert (1985) 167–8.

[8] The sum of her known cult appears to be one Delian sacrifice recorded in Semos of Delos, *FGrHist* 396 F5.

between the Gods as they appear in the *Iliad* and the Gods as they were actually worshipped is the Iliadic conception of the Gods as precisely defined individuals, in the manner of human beings. Zeus, Hera, Aphrodite are individual characters as are Agamemnon, Odysseus and Diomedes, and you can no more speak of two Apollos than you could speak of two Achilleses. But where cult was concerned, it was demonstrably normal to speak of 'a God' meaning the God of a particular sanctuary, so that we would have the Apollo of this place and of that place, each with different qualities and traditions and yet still Apollo. This has continued as an ordinary way of thinking in some systems. In South India, Meenakshi at Madurai, Sivakami at Chidambaram, are different, but they are both Devi, the Goddess. In the Aegean, the Megalochari of Tinos and the Ekatontapyliani of Paros are different, but they are both the Panayia (the Virgin Mary). This double perspective is missing in Homer, as indeed in most of our literary sources or those that deal with panhellenic mythology. To be sure, each Homeric deity has his or her own array of favoured places; thus, for instance, Chryses prays to Apollo as frequenting Killa, ruler of Tenedos (1.38) and later Apollo deposits Aeneas in his temple on the Trojan acropolis (5.445–6). But here there are no ambiguities – whichever way you look at it, it is the same character who moves between the two places. This is a rather obvious point in regard to the narrative, but it is none the less important in differentiating the Homeric (or more broadly, epic/literary) Gods from those of other contexts.

There is a similar ambiguity affecting the location of the Gods, but here the epic is itself less definite. Our first impression, that the Gods live as an extended family, perhaps a rather unusual one, on Olympus, is to an extent modified in the course of the epic. They spend a lot of time in other places. They visit the Ethiopians en masse to attend sacrifices on a huge scale, but they may also attend any other place on earth where sacrifices are offered. They come to Troy and its environs to intervene in the action. Even Zeus, though he never comes to earth (or at least sea level),[9] moves from Olympus to Ida to get a better view. In fact, he is presented as worshipped on Mt Ida – he has a temenos and an altar there (8.47–8), and the human characters often address him as 'ruling from Ida' just as Chryses calls on Apollo 'ruling Tenedos', and Achilles, more remarkably, addresses Zeus as 'you who live far off and rule over wintry Dodona' (16.233).[10] They think of particular

[9] Although this is clearly implied by stories of his sexual union with mortal women, of which the poet is well aware, e.g. 14.323.

[10] Dodona is a very long way from Troy, but somewhat less far from Achilles' homeland of Phthiotis.

Gods as living in particular earthly locations; it is the Gods as a group who 'have their homes on Olympus'.

But can the Gods really be in a place at all, in the sense that human beings are? The whole concept of prayer implies that the Gods can be present anywhere at will, or at least that they can hear and attend to their worshippers over vast stretches of space. When Achilles prays to the Zeus of Dodona, he is using a *modus operandi* which is quite different from his communications with him in Book 1, where he speaks to Thetis and Thetis intercedes with Zeus on his behalf, a procedure which suggests only a quantitative, not a qualitative, difference between Gods and humans. Since the characters of the *Iliad* pray and sacrifice quite a lot, the real-life assumption that the Gods are not subject to spatial limitations is certainly implied in the *Iliad*. But in keeping with the humanising depiction of the Gods, they are also sometimes shown as constrained by space, though to a lesser extent than are mortals. They must move from one place to another, but far more quickly and efficiently than humans can. Thus they may use the quickest means of transport known to humans, the chariot – but their horses and chariots can travel at high speed through air and sea. They can swoop down from mountain peaks like birds. Or, more plausibly perhaps, they can simply go as quickly as a man can think 'I wish I were in such-and-such a place' (15.79–83). It is hard to see why one method of transport is chosen over another. They can, however, all be taken as emphasising the superiority of Gods over mortals in their relative freedom from normal limitations.

Other passages seem to lay emphasis on the restrictions. Some places are far away even for the Gods. Thetis cannot contact Zeus until he comes back from visiting the Ethiopians with the other Olympians (and similarly, at the beginning of the *Odyssey*, Athena can act when she does because Poseidon is away in Ethiopia). Even when they are relatively near, the Gods do not always perceive everything. Zeus on Ida is notoriously distracted from the battle below by the seductive wiles of Hera (14.159–355), but even before this he has turned his attention away from Troy to study the affairs of the Thracians, Mysians and others (13.3–6), allowing Poseidon to interfere on behalf of the Achaeans. There is no sense that a God is different from a human, able to deal with many things at once – and yet this must be at least a passive, background hope of those who pray.

The Gods of the *Iliad*: interaction with humans

I have suggested that the Iliadic Gods are seen somewhat inconsistently as both like and unlike humans in the limitations imposed by locality. A parallel phenomenon is seen in the two types of divine–human interaction observable in the epic. On the one hand, there are the normal channels of communication between humans and Gods – prayer, sacrifice, dreams, oracles and so on – and on the other, there are modes which seem less plausible, more fantastic, and which at the same time evoke Gods who are more like humans – sexual and parental relations, for instance. The epiphany stands somewhere between the two groups, because Greeks of the historical period did experience divine epiphanies, yet not so frequently nor so – almost – routinely as do the heroes of the *Iliad*. These two types of interaction show not only a dichotomy in conceptions of the Gods, but also indicate something about humans: the heroes of the epic were men of another age, privileged to hold converse with Gods at a much lesser distance or a much more nearly equal level than is possible for us now. Divine limitations and human excellence go together; perhaps the famous dictum of 'Longinus',[11] that Homer made his men Gods and his Gods men, is not so far from the mark.

The heroes of the *Iliad* pray frequently, and in ways as far as we can tell that are strikingly similar to those of the Greeks of later times and 'real-life' situations. They pray with some special request in mind, they remind the Gods of their past benefits and promise gifts for the future if their prayer is granted. Very often they perform animal sacrifice, whether to bolster up their request or to make good a promise, or even as a pious preliminary to eating. The centrality of animal sacrifice to Greek religious practice is abundantly clear from other sources, and in the epic it is indicated from an Olympian perspective by the keenness of the Gods to receive sacrifice, wherever it may be performed and – other things being equal – their regard for those who offer it: Hector's generous offerings are the main reason given by Zeus for his favour towards the chief Trojan fighter (24.66–70). Nonetheless, it is also clear that in real life and less heroic situations, there were many less elaborate, less expensive and more usual offerings made to the Gods; but the characters of the *Iliad* are heroes of a past age, and offer only the grandest, most splendid gifts to the Gods. We miss, too, in the *Iliad* the regularly recurring ritual, the monthly or annual sacrifice so much a part of polis life. This must be due to the more purely narrative demands of a war story, describing dislocated communities; the Achaeans are far from their ancestral sanctuaries, and even for the Trojans, city life is hardly normal. The scene (6.297–312) where the Trojan women attempt to propitiate Athena, in response to a communication of the seer Helenus, has a dramatic urgency and relevance which would be lacking in more routine sanctuary scenes.

Helenus here represents another facet of communication with the divine which reflects more normal experience, the realm of the oracular and

[11] *Subl.* 9.7.

prophetic. The oracular shrine is known to the *Iliad* (see Achilles' prayer to Zeus of Dodona, above), but the nature of the story demands that more prominence be given to the (mobile) individual who is skilled in *manteia*, the interpretation of signs and portents sent by the Gods. Here the Gods communicate at a distance, because the message that is conveyed is seldom of direct concern and relevance to the prophet, its first human recipient. However, sometimes signs are more obvious and can be interpreted by anyone – for instance, at 10.274–6 Athena sends a heron to the right of Odysseus and Diomedes, which they recognise as indicating her favour.

Direct communication with the Gods through a waking or sleeping vision was not uncommon during the historical period, but the waking form especially appears much more frequently in the *Iliad*. As ever, the Iliadic heroes were that much more privileged, that much closer to the Gods. For all that, when they do appear to humans the Gods very often put on a human disguise, typically for instance when they are encouraging their protégés or their favoured side. There is no consistency, though: in the most often cited of all these appearances, Athena is instantly recognisable to Achilles (1.199–200). As well as the frequency, it is the authorial perspective, the claim to knowledge about the Gods, which differentiates the Homeric accounts from any real-life experience. Athena appears to Achilles because she has been sent by Hera, who cares for both Achilles and Agamemnon and wishes to avert a fatal outcome. Typically, in fact, an epiphany scene is preceded by some narrative or description of the God who appears, an exposition of his or her motives, and often a communication with another divine figure. A further not uncommon feature of the Homeric epiphany is physical intervention, not to be found (one supposes) in real-life events: Aphrodite removes Paris from the battlefield in a cloud of mist (3.380–2), Apollo snatches Aeneas from Diomedes and takes him to recover in his temple on the acropolis (5.438–50). The importance of such episodes to the plot should make one rather sceptical about the claim that magical and supernatural elements are lacking in the *Iliad*.

Sometimes Gods intervene in human affairs without actually appearing to the humans involved. Hera puts it into Agamemnon's mind to encourage the Achaeans (8.218–9), or, more physically, Apollo destroys the Achaean wall like a child kicking a sandcastle to pieces (15.361–6). This is very much in line with expectations of the Gods' behaviour elsewhere, and has a close relation to their function as cause and explanation. What is distinctive is the attribution of clear personal motives to an individual deity, and even more so, the all-knowing perspective from which the narrative is told.

A notable feature not just of the epic but of Greek mythology in general, is the extent of sexual relations between divine and human characters. This and the consequent birth of heroes is the theme of the Hesiodic *Ehoiai*; the storyline of the Homeric epics does not suggest a particular prominence for the motif, and indeed most of the main heroes have human fathers, even grandfathers. But the propensity of the male deities to take human lovers and beget human offspring is nevertheless an important part of the divine background, from Sarpedon, son of Zeus and Laodameia (6.198–9), to charming vignettes such as that describing the birth of the Myrmidon Eudorus:

> . . . a maiden's son, borne by the lovely dancer Polymele, daughter of Phylas; the powerful slayer of Argos desired her when he saw her among the group of girls dancing for clear-voiced Artemis of the golden spindle. Straight away guileless(?) Hermes took her secretly to an upper room and lay with her, and she bore him a fine son Eudorus, exceedingly fast of foot and a good fighter. But when Eileithyia of the birthpangs brought him into the light and he saw the rays of the sun, strong Echeklus son of Actor offered countless gifts and took Polymele to his house, while the old man Phylas brought up and cherished the child well, loving him as though he were his own son. (16.180–91)

Such affairs and entanglements are not presented in any way as problematic. Much more difficult, and less common, are the affairs of Goddesses with mortal men. Since sex, to the Greek mind, normally implies the domination of the woman by the man, such relationships subvert the proper order of things and threaten the superiority of the Gods, which is why Calypso in the *Odyssey* claims that the male Gods always want to put an end to them (V.118–29), and why the immortal Thetis was reluctant to marry the mortal Peleus (18.432–4), and eventually left him. It is one more sign of the specialness of Achilles that he is the result of such a rare and paradoxical union. And of course there is implicit in the poems the awareness that divine parenthood was a feature of the age of heroes, a time when human beings were greater and somehow closer to the gods; such claims were made only very rarely (and with what degree of conviction?) for contemporaries.

The strangely omniscient standpoint of the epic narrator allows us to witness, not merely infer, certain things about the attitude of the Gods to the human beings who so preoccupy them. First, they are interested in mortals, and not just those of the Achaean cities and the Trojan plain; they visit the Ethiopians, they observe the affairs of the Thracians and Mysians (1.423–4, 13.3–6). Each deity has his or her favourites (and often un-favourites) among cities and individuals. They may give them special gifts, as Apollo gives a bow to Pandarus (2.826–7), or they may bargain with each other about their mortal preferences, as Hera notoriously would allow Zeus to destroy her favourite Achaian cities in return for the fall of Troy (4.50–4). Being passionately involved in promoting the interests of their protégés, they often come into conflict with each other. On one level, then, human affairs are an arena in which each God can act competitively against the others. But when this threatens to get out of hand, peace can be restored by getting things in perspective; it is not worth getting worked up over mere humans, after all (1.573–6, 21.462–7). This near contempt can be modified or varied with pity, especially by Zeus, who feels pity not only for his favourites like Sarpedon and Hector, but for the human condition in general: μέλουσί μοι ὀλλύμενοί περ, 'I care for them, mortal though they are' (20.21). Seeing the mistreatment of Hector's body, all the Gods except the most staunchly pro-Achaian feel pity (24.23–6). These two attitudes, pity and disregard, spring from an unquestioned superiority in strength, status and durability – almost everything, in fact, except ethical considerations, which though not absent from the *Iliad* are not a major concern of its Gods.

The Gods in the *Odyssey*: differences between the epics

When we think of the Gods of Homer, and especially of their relations with each other and the glamorous yet strangely uncomfortable world that they inhabit, it is mainly episodes from the *Iliad* that come to mind and form our picture. The one major exception, the story sung by the minstrel Demodocus of the adultery of Ares and Aphrodite and the vengeance of Hephaestus (VIII.266–366), has been convincingly interpreted as a sophisticated pastiche of Iliadic motifs.[12] Otherwise, though many similarities remain, the Gods of the *Iliad* seem to have been toned down in the *Odyssey*, to have become less colourful and less clearly individualised. Even the number of deities involved is diminished: Zeus, Athena and Poseidon alone are the main actors, with a few appearances from Hermes, and a number of non-Olympian Goddesses, immortal yet very specifically localised on earth (or, in the case of Ino-Leucothea, in the sea).

This last point is clearly related to the different focus of the *Odyssey* story, for although Odysseus is presented as a superhero, no doubt, he is still only one individual, and his affairs are not of such overwhelming importance that we could expect all the Olympians to take sides on the issue. Those Gods who do have an interest, however, are depicted along clearly Iliadic lines – in fact, the favour of Athena towards Odysseus is already shown and remarked on in the *Iliad* (10.245, 23.782–3). The hatred of Poseidon is a new motif, deriving from an episode in the *Odyssey* itself, but the type of relationship, originating in a personal affront, is entirely consonant with the motives for

[12] Burkert (1960).

the Gods' enmities in the *Iliad*. Even within this framework, however, less play is made with the relationships of the Gods than we might expect if we took the *Iliad* as model. There are plenty of scenes between Athena and Zeus, with the Goddess pleading for help to be given to her favourite, but whereas Poseidon clearly hampers Athena's efforts (e.g. VI.325–6, 329–30) the opportunity for a full-scale quarrel between the two is passed over; rather, it is Poseidon's absence which gives the plot its impetus. It is as though the most spectacular elements of the Olympian scenes of the *Iliad* have been separated off and relocated, the fantastic into the sub-Olympian world of magic and monsters through which Odysseus travels, and the emotionally charged into the arena of human relations and human–divine relations. With the single exception of the Ares and Aphrodite story (which is, after all, only a song sung by a court entertainer), there is much less to offend and scandalise in the behaviour of the Odyssean Gods. True, they hardly satisfy Homer's critic Xenophanes' alternative conception of 'one God, greatest among Gods and men . . . neither in form nor in thought like human beings' (21 B23 DK), but though their behaviour is human, it is not spectacularly bad behaviour, nor, for the most part, are they made to look ridiculous. Where the function of the Gods of the *Iliad* often seems to be to contrast with the serious, heroic and tragic human characters, these Gods, though obviously more powerful than humans, at the same time form much more of a continuity of character with them. This is true both on a general level and more specifically in the main characters: it is in the *Odyssey* that the reason for Athena's favour towards Odysseus becomes explicit – she finds him appealing because he is like her, intelligent and devious (XIII.296–9).

'Gods behaving badly' is not then a theme prominent in the *Odyssey*, and this facilitates the much greater concern with human morality that they display in this epic. In the *Iliad*, there is some human expectation that Zeus, at least, will act to punish wrongdoing – but this is a view we hear only occasionally, mainly from Menelaus (3.351–3) and Agamemnon (4.155 ff.), who regard themselves as aggrieved parties. It has occasionally been denied that there is any real difference between the epics in this regard, because in the *Odyssey* also the bulk of the evidence for the Gods' interest in morality comes from the opinions of the human characters.[13] It is, however, an overwhelmingly more prominent theme among Odyssean characters, and in view of the clearly programmatic statement of Zeus at the poem's outset (I.32–43), that mortals' sufferings are due to their presumptuous folly (*atasthaliai*), it seems impossible to deny that the Gods think in moralistic terms. It is true that Zeus does not state '*We* punished Aegisthus', but the

[13] See Winterbottom (1989), Yamagata (1994).

whole tone of the speech suggests his attempt to direct human beings in the proper ways of behaviour – a radical shift from the divine attitudes displayed in the *Iliad*.[14] Of course, the shift is not complete – we have already remarked that the motives of both Athena and Poseidon are essentially personal. But this point is not emphasised equally throughout the poem. Poseidon's anger is the motive force behind the first part of the story, the delayed and difficult return from Troy, but in the second half of the poem he fades out of the picture entirely. Nowhere does he appear encouraging the suitors in their insolent behaviour – indeed, it is Athena who makes them yet more overbearing and arrogant, so that Odysseus may be all the more angry and their punishment more certain (XVIII.346–8). The view of the Gods presented in this second half of the poem has moved still further from the Iliadic presentation of individuals in conflict. Now the Gods form a united front, rooting for the success of Odysseus, with Zeus at their head and Athena as active participant in the detailed working out of the plan. And this unity, it is strongly implied, is founded on a moral basis: personal favouritism apart, it is simply right that Odysseus should triumph over his enemies and be reinstated as ruler of Ithaca. The suitors are wicked men who deserve their punishment; it is not just the characters who tell us this, but the author himself: 'There would be no more unpleasant supper than this, which the Goddess and the strong man were about to place before them, for they had previously devised [or, they were the first to devise] unfitting things' (XX.392–5). It is Athena who leads the action, but she has the full and willing support of Zeus and, it seems, the Gods in general. Her Iliadic-style personal championship of Odysseus blends effortlessly into the more moralistic concept in which the Gods (eventually) restore the upright and punish the wicked.

'Homer's Gods' between epic and religion

Apart from a few Linear B documents naming individual deities, the Homeric poems are chronologically the first testimony we have to Greek perceptions of the Gods.[15] They also seem to have been formative; Herodotus' statement, that Hesiod and Homer 'made a theogony for the Greeks and gave

[14] A clear exception here is Zeus's anger with 'crooked judgements' in 16.384–88 – but this is a simile, not part of the main narrative. Within the main story itself, the bare facts might seem to support a 'justice of Zeus' interpretation (Lloyd-Jones (1983)). Paris is to blame, a Trojan broke the truce, Troy will fall, as Agamemnon predicts (4.160–8) – but although both offences are very specifically against areas of concern to Zeus (hospitality and oaths) we, unlike Agamemnon, can see Zeus's 'real' attitude. When this Zeus brings about the fall of Troy it will be with sorrow and not with righteous indignation.

[15] Unless with M. L. West we date the *Theogony* earlier (West (1966) 40–8).

the Gods their eponyms and divided up their honours and crafts, and indicated their appearances'[16] is well known. Yet in some ways they seem to be unlike what we know of the Gods from later sources. Their interaction with humans, their relations with each other, though they have points of contact with what we know from elsewhere, are importantly different. This prompts us to ask at what level of seriousness or acceptance the Homeric deities were understood. Did the Greeks believe in the Gods of these myths?[17]

'Literal' belief is perhaps an impossibility. All talk about the divine is to a degree metaphorical, because it is necessarily beyond our everyday experience, and certainly beyond the closely related constraints of language. This is as true of the Greece in which the Homeric poems took shape as it is of the settings of the most sophisticated theological systems. That said, there are different kinds of metaphors and different reactions to them, different degrees of acceptance. If we talk about the divine as 'father' or 'mother', we are using a familiar relationship and experience to try to say something about the less clear and less familiar. If we tell a story such as that of the child Krishna making the whole universe appear in his mouth, we are making a statement, among other things, about the divine in human form. In the same way, we could understand, for instance, the aerial chariots of the Homeric gods as a way of saying that their users are not subject to ordinary spatial limits. But what are we to make of their quarrels with each other and their partisanship in human affairs? The quarrel scenes seem to be designed largely for entertainment, while the partisanship, if it is a metaphor, might seem to be telling us about the chanciness of human affairs rather than saying anything about the Gods; the Gods would themselves be part of the metaphor, not something to be explained or clarified. So here a metaphorical presentation of the Gods will have been built on and elaborated by other elements. On the other hand, if we do try to take quarrels and partisanship as statements about the Gods – as has been done in various contexts from antiquity onwards – their literal application is obtrusive and disturbing. Hence from a relatively early date Homer's depiction of the Gods was seen as problematic: in the late sixth or early fifth century, Xenophanes was famously blaming Homer and Hesiod for 'ascribing to the Gods all things that are shame and disgrace among mortals',[18] and proposing further that the divine is not like this, indeed not like human beings at all. Simple rejection of the 'miserable tales of poets',[19] not least by the poets themselves, was a popular strategy in the fifth century. After all, the Muses know how to tell many things that merely

[16] Hdt. 2.53.2. [17] Cf. Veyne (1988). [18] 21 B11 DK. [19] Eur. *Her.* 1,346.

seem like the truth.[20] The alternative, promoted rather enthusiastically in the Hellenistic period and later, was to maintain that Homer's depictions of the Gods were not only metaphorical, they were also allegorical. In these systems, Homer's versions of the Gods were actually statements about the physical universe (Hera = air, Hephaestus = fire) or about ethical and psychological matters (Athena preventing Achilles from killing Agamemnon represents wisdom, argued at length in Heraclitus' *Homeric Allegories* of perhaps the first century AD).[21] This method involves radical rereadings of the whole texts of the epics, which then become puzzles to be read only with the help of a key. The problem of the Gods is solved at the expense of the poems.

The poems themselves – at least as it appears to us today – do the opposite. They pursue their vision of human heroism, glory and suffering at the expense of a plausible and satisfying treatment of the divine.[22] I said at the beginning that the outline stories of both poems could be told without reference to the Gods; these are not poems about Gods, but about human beings. These human beings inhabit a world of which the Gods are an unquestioned part, but still, within each epic, the Gods are there to illuminate, comment on and contrast with the depiction of human actions and the human condition. Of course in the process they bear more than a passing resemblance to the Gods as the Greeks knew them in other contexts. Consider for instance this scene from the Homeric *Hymn to Demeter* (275–80), where the disguised Goddess reveals herself as divine to the amazed family which has given her hospitality:

> Saying this, the Goddess changed in stature and appearance, casting off old age and putting on beauty all around. A lovely perfume diffused from her fragrant clothes, and radiance shone far about from the deathless flesh of the Goddess, her fair hair flowed down her shoulders, and the close-built house was filled with light as bright as lightning.

All of this is entirely compatible with the epiphanies of the *Iliad*, but the effect is quite different. Demeter's changed appearance is described in attentive and loving detail, quite unlike the fast-paced description of the appearance of Athena to Achilles in *Iliad* 1:

[20] Hes. *Theog.* 27, cf. XIX.203.

[21] On these interpretations, see Lamberton (1986).

[22] I should perhaps clarify that by this I mean a version of the divine which (although not necessarily problem-free) can reasonably be the object of relationship and belief. Modern readers who find plausibility and satisfaction in Homer's Gods are quite legitimately appreciating them as a way of saying something about the world that humans inhabit. They are not, I think, proposing to start worshipping these deities.

> Athena came from the sky, for white-armed Goddess Hera had sent her, loving and caring for them both [Achilles and Agamemnon]. She stood behind him, and took hold of his fair hair, appearing to him alone; none of the others saw her. Achilles was amazed, and turned round. Straightway he recognised Pallas Athena – her terrible eyes shone. . . .

Here the shining of the eyes might be regarded as a very abbreviated form of the physical signs of divinity in the *Hymn* passage, and the amazement of Achilles certainly parallels that of Metaneira and her family. But the emphasis is firmly on Athena as a player in the (human-based) action, on what she does rather than how she is or how she appears.

The point comes through even more clearly when we consider the words that are spoken and the purpose of the epiphany. In line with what we have already been told, Athena tells Achilles not to kill Agamemnon but to withdraw from the fighting, thus creating the main plot-line of the *Iliad*. Demeter has been searching for her abducted daughter, and her interest in mortal affairs is tangential to this: she wishes to reward the family who have been kind to her, then rebuke them for their lack of understanding. She reveals her divine form in order to explain – too late – the real situation, and to announce what will happen next – the establishment of certain rites at Eleusis. A religious matter, in other words; something that relates to the following generations as well as those of the story itself,[23] and one in which human–divine relations are centred on, and move towards, the divine rather than the human. This is obviously not the intent of the epics. The account of Demeter in the *Hymn* is a compelling one, whereas the central figure in *Iliad* 1 is Achilles, and we get only a side-glimpse of what might make Athena compelling. Even Achilles recovers quickly enough from his astonishment to ask Athena why she has come – is it to witness the insolence of Agamemnon? But the family of Metaneira, and with them the poem's audience, are focused entirely on the Goddess; the child Demophon, the original stimulus for the whole episode, lies forgotten on the floor.

In this way, the Gods of epic have been subordinated as a central concern to human beings, and yet within the world of the poems, for the characters themselves, they remain superior. Even Achilles could not defeat the river-god: θεοὶ δέ τε φέρτεροι ἀνδρῶν, Gods are stronger than, or superior to, men.[24] The result is a double perspective. As long as we focus on the main

[23] Cf. *Hymn* 265–8, 274–5.

[24] 21.264. Diomedes wounds and so overcomes Aphrodite in *Iliad* 5 – so an individual mortal may excel an individual God in one particular field, especially when encouraged by another God. But we are told that those who try to subvert the hierarchy by attacking a God are not long-lived.

drift of the poem, and what human–divine relations tell us about the human condition, we have a vision that is at once heroic and (especially in the case of the *Iliad*) tragic. If we allow the focus to shift to the Gods themselves – and the poet of the *Iliad* seems sometimes to encourage this, with his frequent scene-setting on Olympus – the result is entertaining, intriguing, but ultimately problematic. Certainly the Greeks tended to scepticism about the knowability of the divine, but that did not necessarily mean that any picture was as likely to be 'correct' as any other. In Homer, a way of speaking about the Gods which is properly metaphorical has been made literal, elaborated on and pushed to its limits. This is why 'belief' in the Gods of Homer could never be fully given and yet could not exactly be withheld either.

FURTHER READING

A very great deal has been written about the subject of the Homeric Gods; this note is extremely selective. On the religious background, a marvellous compendium of information and interpretation is Burkert (1985); pp. 119–25 deal specifically with the place of Homer. A very influential and largely persuasive overview of the Gods in Homer, especially in the *Iliad*, is to be found in Griffin (1980), especially 144–204. Although his main interest is in the literary function of the Gods, Griffin argues strongly for their 'reality'; so, from a different perspective, does Emlyn-Jones (1992). Among those who incline to the opposite view are Tsagarakis (1977) and Erbse (1986). Other perspectives on Gods and mortals are to be found in Thalmann (1984) and Kullmann (1992). Of the modern works cited in the notes to this chapter, Dodds (1951), Lloyd-Jones (1983), Willcock (1970), Winterbottom (1989) and Yamagata (1994) may be particularly mentioned.

6

MICHAEL CLARKE

Manhood and heroism[1]

The opening crisis of the *Iliad* drives Achilles to send uncounted hosts of his own comrades to death, merely in order to prove what folly it was for Agamemnon to belittle him in the assembly of his peers (1.1–5, 240–4, 407–12). By any standards this is a bizarrely exaggerated response to an insult:[2] but as the story develops the moral problem of Achilles' behaviour looms less large than its unsought consequences. When he reveals his plan to his mother Thetis, she responds not with praise or blame but with lamentation for Achilles himself:[3]

> ὤιμοι τέκνον ἐμόν, τί νύ σ' ἔτρεφον αἰνὰ τεκοῦσα;
> αἴθ' ὄφελες παρὰ νηυσὶν ἀδάκρυτος καὶ ἀπήμων
> ἧσθαι, ἐπεί νύ τοι αἶσα μίνυνθά περ, οὔ τι μάλα δήν.
> νῦν δ' ἅμα τ' ὠκύμορος καὶ ὀϊζυρὸς περὶ πάντων
> ἔπλεο· τώ σε κακῆι αἴσηι τέκον ἐν μεγάροισιν.
> (1.414–18)

> Alas my child, why did I conceive you, bringing miseries to birth? If only you had remained sitting beside the ships without tears and without troubles: for your portion of life is short, it is not abundant. But now instead you are to be both swift-fated and also wretched beyond all men; indeed it was for an evil portion that I gave birth to you in the house.

These words of prophecy or foreboding introduce the central sorrow of the *Iliad*: the vengeful anger of the greatest of all warriors will not only 'send many sinewy ghosts to Hades' (1.3) but will also lead to his own untimely

[1] I am grateful to Jasper Griffin for comments and corrections in response to the first draft of this chapter and to Michael Crudden for permission to quote from his translation of the *Homeric Hymns*.

[2] Cf. Lateiner in this volume, p. 15.

[3] On Thetis and the death of Achilles see Slatkin (1991) esp. ch. 1.

self-destruction. From the start, then, heroism and death are tied together in a bond that is as certain as it is mysterious.[4]

Why does Zeus nod assent (1.528–30)? Perhaps his agreement is part of a higher plan that needs no justification beyond itself;[5] but Homer does not say so, and among the gods this is just another stage in the intrigues of family politics. Zeus's main concern is to repay an old debt to Thetis (1.393–412) without excessively offending Hera (1.518–27), and the ensuing squabbling ends only when Hephaestus complains that it will spoil the pleasure of their feast (1.573–6). So the party begins. To general laughter Hephaestus, lame and fumbling, plays wine-bearer with cups of *nectar*, the immortalising drink whose name – originally 'that which overcomes death'[6] – is a reminder of the gods' freedom from the misery of mortality. Apollo makes music, the Muses sing and dance: the god whose arrows have sent plague and death to the Greeks now bends his lyre, instead of his bow,[7] for the entertainment of his fellow revellers. Homer does not tell us the subject-matter of the song; but food for thought comes from the *Homeric Hymn to Apollo*, in a description of Apollo at the feast of the gods which is closely akin to this scene of the *Iliad*:

> And then he goes to Olympus, speeding like thought from the earth,
> To the house of Zeus, and enters the concourse of other gods;
> At once the minds of immortals turn to the lyre and song.
> All the Muses with beautiful voices together responsively hymn
> The gods' undying gifts, and those pains that humans endure
> At the hands of immortal gods as they live without wits or resource,
> And can find no cure for death or defence against old age.
>
> (*Hymn. Hom. Ap.* 186–93, tr. Crudden 2001, 29)

The theme of the god's song is the wretchedness of the human condition: the Olympians' gifts to mortals – which bring woe as well as joy (cf. e.g. 3.64–6) – are the essence of our suffering in a life which will culminate in decrepitude and death. Because the gods have no fear of the bonds of death, *olethrou peirata* (7.402, XXII.33, etc.), our toils need have no meaning for them: they are a trivial matter, a foil to the cheerful ease that allows the gods

[4] Cf. Griffin (1980) 103–43.

[5] We cannot be certain which myths and theological explanations were known to Homer and his audience. In the cyclic epic *Cypria* (see Dowden in this volume, ch. 12 for discussion of epic cycle), Zeus's purpose in causing the Trojan War was to lighten his grandmother Earth of the physical burden of the human race (cf. 18.104). The *Cypria* referred to this in the formula 'the plan of Zeus was coming to pass' (*Cypria*, fr. 1.7), which appears also in the Proem of the *Iliad* (1.5) but is there tantalisingly vague. See further Mayer (1996).

[6] Watkins (1995) 391–7.

[7] On the parallelism of lyre and bow see esp. XXI. 404–11.

to be frivolous and petty-minded and to use mortals as tools in their private schemes.[8]

This may seem grotesque or absurd to modern readers, reared as we are on the assumption that if any god exists he ought to be kind and caring. But we must listen to the poem as the expression of a conception of mankind that is remote from our norms and assumptions, rooted in the world-picture of the single great culture-area that stretched in the early first millennium BC from the Aegean Sea across what is now Turkey and as far east as Iraq.[9] From Greece itself we have nothing to guide us more ancient than the Homeric poems themselves: but there is much illumination in the *Epic of Gilgamesh*, the foremost narrative poem surviving from the eastern side of that culture-area in the centuries before Homer. In this poem Gilgamesh, struck after the death of his friend Enkidu by a horrified awareness of mortality, travels to the ends of the earth to seek out the truth about human life. The answer is summed up in a stark aphorism:

> The life that you seek you will never find:
> when the gods created mankind,
> death they dispensed to mankind,
> life they kept for themselves.[10]

This unrelievedly pessimistic idea is fundamental to the traditional wisdom of the Greeks no less than of Mesopotamia: as Achilles puts it when briefly united with Priam in the shared experience of grief, 'So have the gods woven their web for wretched mortals, to live in misery while they themselves are without care' (24.525–6). The same wisdom underlies Hesiod's teaching on the right way for a farmer to live his life: κρύψαντες γὰρ ἔχουσι θεοὶ βίον ἀνθρώποισιν (*Op.* 42), 'the gods keep life[11] hidden from mankind'. For Hesiod this motivates an ethic of hard work and restraint: win a livelihood with sweat and prudence, avoid debt and greed and overreaching ambition, live in accordance with the ordinances of Zeus (*Op.* 42–326 *passim*).[12] In the first book of the *Iliad*, the jarring disjuncture between the divine and human planes is a narrative enactment of this fundamental principle: life is overshadowed by inevitable wretchedness and certain death, and it can be

[8] See Griffin (1980) 179–204; Clay (1983) 133–48; Edwards (1987) 131–42; Clay (1989) 55–6; Pucci (2002).

[9] See in general Burkert (1992), West (1997a).

[10] George (1999) 124. This text is from a library tablet of the eighteenth or seventeenth century BC; the same ideas are expounded in more elaborate form by Uta-napishti in Tablet X of the Standard Version of the epic (pp. 86–7).

[11] Or 'livelihood': the Greek *bios* spans both meanings.

[12] For summary analyses see Tandy and Neale (1996), Nelson (1998) 59–81.

fully understood only through the contrast with the carefree existence of the gods.

How does this help us to understand the social and psychological patterns of the poems, above all in the context of war? The Homeric warrior is driven to action by a need for social validation: status, respect, honour in the eyes of other men.[13] At first sight this suggests a sense of human identity which is social rather than existential; but it turns out that mortality is the cornerstone of this ethic, because the most urgent need of all is to perpetuate one's status in the form of continuing fame after death. In these terms Sarpedon of Lycia urges his friend Glaucus to excel in combat:

> τῶ νῦν χρὴ Λυκίοισι μέτα πρώτοισιν ἐόντας
> ἑστάμεν ἠδὲ μάχης καυστειρῆς ἀντιβολῆσαι,
> ὄφρα τις ὧδ' εἴπηι Λυκίων πύκα θωρηκτάων·
> "οὐ μὰν ἀκληεῖς Λυκίην κάτα κοιρανέουσιν
> ἡμέτεροι βασιλῆες ἔδουσί τε πίονα μῆλα
> οἶνόν τ' ἔξαιτον μελιηδέα· ἀλλ' ἄρα καὶ ἴς
> ἐσθλή, ἐπεὶ Λυκίοισι μέτα πρώτοισι μάχονται."
> ὦ πέπον, εἰ μὲν γὰρ πόλεμον περὶ τόνδε φυγόντε
> αἰεὶ δὴ μέλλοιμεν ἀγήρω τ' ἀθανάτω τε
> ἔσσεσθ', οὔτε κεν αὐτὸς ἐνὶ πρώτοισι μαχοίμην
> οὔτέ κε σὲ στέλλοιμι μάχην ἐς κυδιάνειραν·
> νῦν δ' ἔμπης γὰρ κῆρες ἐφεστᾶσιν θανάτοιο
> μυρίαι, ἃς οὐκ ἔστι φυγεῖν βροτὸν οὐδ' ὑπαλύξαι,
> ἴομεν, ἠέ τωι εὖχος ὀρέξομεν, ἠέ τις ἡμῖν.
> (12.315–28)

> That is why it is right for us to stand amongst the foremost of the Lycians and confront blazing battle, so that someone among the close-armoured Lycians may say: 'Not without fame do our chieftains rule over Lycia and consume the fat herds and honey-sweet wine: there is noble fibre in them too, for they fight amongst the foremost of the Lycians.' Dear friend, if by escaping this war we could go on to live ageless and immortal forever, I would not fight myself in the front rank, nor would I send you out to the battle where men win glory; but since in truth the demons of death stand around us innumerable, whom no man can flee or elude, let us go forth, whether we give some other man cause to boast, or he give it to us.

Here as elsewhere martial excellence is part of a reciprocal contract: the noblemen are honoured by their people because they achieve fame (*kleos*, implied by *aklēeis* in 318) and thus glorify the Lycian people as a whole, and this in turn encourages the warriors to continue their display of prowess and

[13] See van Wees (1992) 25–166; Zanker (1994) 1–71; and cf. Seaford (1994) 1–29.

maintain their good name. But notice the further twist in his discourse. If we were like the Olympian gods there would be no need to behave admirably and so risk death among the front-fighters (*prōtoi, promachoi*): but because the end of life is inevitable, the call to perpetuate our glory beyond the grave becomes imperative. Fame, then, is a kind of surrogate immortality:[14] just as the warrior's greatness in battle ensures his continued prestige during his life, so by implication the tale of his deeds will ensure that his identity persists among future generations.

It is significant that these words are said by Sarpedon, who is Zeus's own son and so especially close to divine status: his mortality is doubly pathetic because of the contrast with what might have been.[15] When the day of his death comes Zeus looks down in pity and is tempted to save him, until Hera reminds him that Sarpedon must accept his fate like anyone else: his only concession is an especially gentle end at the hands of the gods Sleep and Death in person (16.431–61), but he will rot in the grave like the rest of us. The men of the *Iliad* have only the bleakest of prospects in the afterlife: Hades is a place of darkness and decay (*zophos, erebos, eurōs*),[16] and there is no Heaven, no Valhalla, no reward beyond the grave in the Isles of the Blest or Elysium.[17] Likewise, the *Iliad* never mentions the possibility that after death a hero might attain to an especially privileged status through cultic veneration. There is no telling whether this portrayal of death as an absolute and bitter certainty is a deliberate choice by Homer, or whether it simply reflects the shared assumptions of the time the poem was composed.[18] Either way, the inevitability of death means that the challenge facing the Homeric warrior is precisely equivalent to that facing any member of the poem's audience: the driving force behind manhood is the need for praise and admiration, such as will enable one to face death with equanimity and to see that a soldier's death in war is not necessarily worse than disgrace.[19]

Nonetheless, the Homeric warriors are not the same as later men; and it is vital to appreciate the factor that determines the contrast. Here we must beware of the peculiar semantics of the English word *hero*, which suggests several conflicting images – often no more than the central character of a story, but sometimes a man characterised by heightened courage and sense

[14] In this sense the poet himself, passing on the reputation of the hero into future times, ensures that his name does not die among men (cf. 6.355–8, VIII.579–80).

[15] Cf. Janko (1992a) 370–3.

[16] Sourvinou-Inwood (1995) 10–107.

[17] In the *Odyssey* Menelaus is bound for Elysium not as a favourable afterlife but as an alternative to death; and he is given this gift because he is Zeus's son-in-law, with no suggestion that other men might have the same prospect (IV.561–9).

[18] Cf. Griffin (1977), and see Osborne in this volume, pp. 211, 216–18.

[19] See further Loraux (1995) 63–100; Vernant (1991).

of duty, or specifically a male warrior in the vague universal category of 'heroic literature'.[20] The way out of the confusion is to see that the Homeric hero is defined as such by one thing alone: his membership of a specific generation or race of men, belonging at a particular point along the scale of human history. The most illuminating evocation of this concept is the place of the heroes in Hesiod's explanation of the life of disease, hard labour and poverty to which modern man has been committed by Zeus. This state of affairs is the end-product of a long decline in vitality, represented by the sequence of five stages of the human race: from the godlike and carefree lives of the Golden Race, when the earth bore fruit unasked-for and the horror of old age was unknown, up to the present Race of Iron, which is characterised by bodily and spiritual weakness and disarray (*Op.* 106–201). In this succession the Race of Heroes is an interlude of virtue and strength, interrupting the sequence of decline just before the coming of the present age:

> But when the earth had covered over this race [sc. the Race of Bronze], Zeus, Kronos' son, made a fourth race on the earth that feeds many, more just and better, the godly race of hero men, who are called half-gods, the race before [our own] along the boundless earth. Evil war and bitter battle destroyed them: some before seven-gated Thebes, in Cadmus' land, fighting over the flocks of Oedipus, others when it had brought them in ships over the great gulf of the sea to Troy for the sake of Helen of the beautiful hair. (*Op.* 156–65)

Although Homer never contextualises the heroic generation in such a schematic way, his portrayal reflects the same sense of their place in the decline of mankind.[21] For Homer as for Hesiod these warriors are *hēmitheōn genos andrōn*, 'the race of men who are half-gods' (12.23), often by the literal fact of divine parentage but more generally because they stand at an intermediate stage between the gods' infinite vitality and the sickly feebleness of modern man. Because of this, they are open to the accusation that they represent a decline from earlier and still more godlike greatness, including that of their own fathers (see e.g. 1.260–72, 4.370–4); but the more

[20] It is doubly confusing that scholars writing about Homer tend to use the word indeterminately either in the second and third senses or to signify the range of reference of the Greek word *hērōs*. But *hērōs* is highly problematic: in post-Homeric Greek it is overwhelmingly a religious term, referring to the great men of the past as the objects of veneration, while within the poems the word is used almost as an equivalent for 'man', labelling any of the poems' characters without overt connotation of praise or admiration.

[21] Van Wees (1992) 6–18. On the complexities of interpreting the Myth of the Races and the heroes' place within it, see Vernant (1983) 3–72; Nagy (1979) 151–73; Most (1997), Sourvinou-Inwood (1997).

potent contrast is with the weaker race that has come after them. Just as the gods' defining characteristic is their abundance of life, which involves both immortality and superhuman power, so the basic difference between the heroic generation and our own is their greater capacity for self-propelled vigour, which is the essence of excellence in both physical and mental life. This is what Homeric Greek calls *menos*, the force of onrushing energy that is manifested in swift physical and mental movement and embodied in fluid essences like blood and semen.[22] The heroes wield weapons too large and heavy for modern men to carry; one alone can hurl a boulder that nowadays three men could not lift (e.g. 5.302–4, 12.381–3, 12.445–9, 20.285–7); they reach heights of action, thought and emotion that approach the level of gods, just as the gods walk among them as parents or friends or rivals. The key characteristic of the heroes' behaviour – perhaps, indeed, the nearest Homeric equivalent to our word 'heroism' – is *agēnoriē*, the abstract noun corresponding to the adjective *agēnōr*, literally 'having abundant or excessive manhood'.[23] The key to understanding the heroic personality is its extreme level of male energy, a level which the lesser men of later times can never reach.[24]

Seen in this light, the exalted version of human nature represented by the Homeric warrior becomes fraught with half-hidden tensions. The men of the heroic race command wonder because of their strength, their fierceness, their superhuman force, in some cases their heightened wisdom or skill in the arts of speech: to that extent they are models to be imitated by young men, especially young soldiers, and praise is part of what the epic poet communicates to his audience. By the same token, however, the energy that underlies such excellence is liable to push the hero to dangerous extremes of anger, passion and recklessness: so that his exalted status makes him deeply problematic if one tries to take him as a model of moral excellence. Here the forms of the poetic language require careful negotiation. The most striking single characteristic of Homeric style is the tendency for ornamental adjectives or epithets to cluster around proper names: *bright Odysseus, glorious Hector, blameless Menelaus, Achilles dear to Zeus*.[25] Because these epithets are so prominent and tend to survive in translations where other features of the diction are

[22] See Padel (1992) 23–30; Clarke (1995a), (1999) 106–15.

[23] See Chantraine (1968–80) *s.v.* It is possible that the word originally meant 'leading men', the first element being equivalent to the verb *agô*; but the Homeric usage shows that in practice the first element was understood as the compounding element *aga-*, indeterminately 'exceedingly' or 'excessively'. The adverb *agan* (not found in Homer) incorporates the same ambiguity. See further Graziosi and Haubold (2003).

[24] Cf. Weil (1999).

[25] The literature on epithets and formulas is vast. See Clark in this volume, ch. 8.

ironed out, it is easy to read them as if they implied an attitude of unequivocal praise and exaltation on the poet's part. But the linguistic reality is more complex: it is enough to cite the famous example *amumōn*, conventionally translated 'blameless', which is in fact so far from moral approbation that it can be applied to the arch-villain Aegisthus (1.29) as well as to innumerable other characters. Few would now go so far as to claim (as was formerly the standard view) that the epithets are empty of meaning and serve as mere metrical fillers; nonetheless, their expressive role is definitely different from what we would expect of adjectives in modern English. Perhaps their cumulative function is to articulate a contrast: they suggest a simple and univalent image of the heroic generation, which acts as a foil to the complexities, problems and equivocations of the behaviour-patterns that are brought to the fore in the narrative.

Against this background, the tension in the heroic condition becomes a focal point in Homeric discourse. At its furthest extreme, 'excessive manhood' can drive the hero to a volatile and perilous level of warlike passion. The paradox is tellingly expressed when Diomedes is surging across the battlefield under the influence of special *menos* that has been breathed into him by Athena (5.1–6, cf. 5.125–6, 134–43). Helenus, the Trojan prophet, warns his comrades against trying to face one in such a state:

> ἀλλ' ὅδε λίην
> μαίνεται, οὐδέ τίς οἱ δύναται μένος ἰσοφαρίζειν.
> (6.100–1)

> But this man is raging [*mainetai*] too much, and no one can draw equal with him in *menos*.

There is a revealing figure of speech here. The verb *mainetai* derives from the same root as *menos*, so that the two words chime with each other in derivational class as well as meaning: but *mainetai* carries the additional implication of madness, frenzied and self-destructive behaviour, implying that the excessive *menos* of the hero is pushing him towards what would nowadays be labelled insanity.[26] More-than-human *menos* is characteristic in different ways of gods and of wild beasts: in this sense the raging warrior is poised between two extremes, and (as we will see in detail below) his movement can be articulated either as an impossible aspiration to divine glory or as a descent towards the reckless and self-destructive fury of a flesh-eating animal.[27]

[26] See Hershkowitz (1998) 125–60, and cf. Schein (1984) 67–88.

[27] Schnapp-Gourbeillon (1981), Clarke (1995b).

The *Iliad* can be seen as an exploration of the responses of two men, Hector and Achilles, to the challenge of heroic excellence and its inherent perils.[28] Thus we return to the problem with which this chapter began, the extraordinary vindictiveness of Achilles' anger against Agamemnon and all the Greeks. No one on the plain of Troy is more agonisingly close to divinity than Achilles: son of a goddess, great-grandson of Zeus, greatest of the Achaeans,[29] bred to greatness as speaker of words and doer of deeds (9.443): but the special favour granted to him by Zeus is tied to the shortness of his life (1.352–4, 505–6). It is Achilles' godlike and passionate nature that drives him to such extreme anger at Agamemnon's insult: thematically it is vital that his rage is called *mēnis*, 'remembering wrath' (1.1, etc.), a word elsewhere overwhelmingly associated with the anger of gods against mortals who have neglected to pay them due respect.[30] In Book 9, after Achilles has rejected Agamemnon's offer of conciliation communicated by the 'embassy', Diomedes captures the essence of the problem in his response to the news: '[Achilles] has always been *agēnōr*; but now you have pushed him to still further *agēnoriē*' (9.699–700). We miss the point if we ask whether Diomedes means to attack Achilles for his stubbornness, or to praise him for his uncompromising sense of his own worth: the point is rather that the source of Achilles' implacable anger is precisely his unparalleled level of vitality, which has made him unable to 'conquer his mighty spirit' (9.496).[31]

Achilles responds to his comrades' pleas by rejecting the warrior's way of life altogether: he will go home and grow old in peace, abandoning the 'imperishable fame' that will be his due if he accepts death at Troy (9.308–429). Maybe this seems like wisdom, a rejection of the high and perilous life of the hero for simpler and lowlier values: it is the same choice as the Chorus of Aeschylus' *Agamemnon* make when they reflect on the glory and horror of war – μήτ' εἴην πτολιπόρθης, 'let me not be a sacker of cities' (*Ag.* 472). But the death foreseen by Thetis at the outset is inevitably fulfilled. After Hector kills Patroclus, the internalised need for vengeance (*tisis*) replaces Achilles' socially determined need for honour (*timē*); he must fight till he kills Hector, and if his own death is waiting straight after Hector's, then so be it: without that vengeance life would be unbearable (18.79–126). From

[28] Outstanding essays around this theme include Whitman (1958) 181–220; Redfield (1975); Schein (1984) 89–196; Zanker (1994).

[29] On the deeper implications of this phrase see esp. Nagy (1979) 26–41.

[30] See Muellner (1996) with Kahane (1994) 43–79. It is possible that *mēnis* is etymologically as well as thematically linked to *menos* and *mainomai*: see Considine (1985), with Muellner (1996) 177–94.

[31] Hainsworth (1993) 149; Gill (1996) 191–204; Clarke (1999) 92–7.

the moment that he rises up to pursue Hector, his death is certain: and it is from this knowledge that he enters a state that stretches the limits of human nature:

> αὐτὰρ Ἀχιλλεὺς ὦρτο διίφιλος· ἀμφὶ δ᾽ Ἀθήνη
> ὤμοις ἰφθίμοισι βάλ᾽ αἰγίδα θυσανόεσσαν,
> ἀμφὶ δέ οἱ κεφαλῆι νέφος ἔστεφε δῖα θεάων
> χρύσεον, ἐκ δ᾽ αὐτοῦ δαῖε φλόγα παμφανόωσαν.
> ὡς δ᾽ ὅτε καπνὸς ἰὼν ἐξ ἄστεος αἰθέρ᾽ ἵκηται,
> τηλόθεν ἐκ νήσου, τὴν δήϊοι ἀμφιμάχωνται,
> οἳ δὲ πανημέριοι στυγερῶι κρίνωνται ἄρηϊ
> ἄστεος ἐκ σφετέρου· ἅμα δ᾽ ἠελίωι καταδύντι
> πυρσοί τε φλεγέθουσιν ἐπήτριμοι, ὑψόσε δ᾽ αὐγή
> γίγνεται ἀΐσσουσα περικτιόνεσσιν ἰδέσθαι,
> αἴ κέν πως σὺν νηυσὶν ἄρεω ἀλκτῆρες ἵκωνται,
> ὣς ἀπ᾽ Ἀχιλλῆος κεφαλῆς σέλας αἰθέρ᾽ ἵκανεν.
> (18.203–14)

But Achilles rose up, dear to Zeus; and Athene cast the tasselled aegis around his sinewy shoulders, and around his head the bright goddess set a golden cloud, and from it she kindled a flame shining all around. As when smoke reaches the high air, rising from a city, far away on an island, round which its enemies are fighting, who are making division in bitter war from their own city; and at the hour of sunset pyres burn in succession, and the gleam appears, shooting high above, so that those who dwell round about can see it, so that perhaps they will come with their ships to help in the war: so from Achilles' head the gleam reached the high air.

Achilles is transfigured, superhuman, blazing;[32] his voice alone when he cries out is enough to make twelve men fall dead (18.228–31). Achilles' wild career in pursuit of Hector unfolds the implications of his exaltation above the limitations of mortal nature; but as he moves closer to Hector's death and his own it is not the divine but the bestial articulation that becomes paramount. Achilles refuses mercy to suppliants, wishing all men to die because Patroclus died (21.106–13); he refuses to make a civilised compact with Hector 'because there are no oaths to be trusted between lions and mere men' (22.261–66); he drills holes in the dead Hector's heels and drags him behind his chariot; and finally he lets him rot in the sun unburied, abandoning the laws of human restraint. Apollo complains that his nature has become that of a savage beast:

[32] On fire as a symbol of warlike fury see Whitman (1958) 128–53.

[sc. Ἀχιλῆϊ] οὔτ' ἄρ φρένες εἰσὶν ἐναίσιμοι οὔτε νόημα
γναμπτὸν ἐνὶ στήθεσσι, λέων δ' ὣς ἄγρια οἶδεν,
ὅς τ' ἐπεὶ ἄρ μεγάληι τε βίηι καὶ ἀγήνορι θυμῶι
εἴξας εἶσ' ἐπὶ μῆλα βροτῶν, ἵνα δαῖτα λάβηισιν.
ὣς Ἀχιλεὺς ἔλεον μὲν ἀπώλεσεν, οὐδέ οἱ αἰδὼς
γίνεται . . . (24.39–45)

Achilles' mind is unbalanced, nor is his thought kept in check in his breast; his thoughts are wild, like a lion who gives in to his great force and overmanly [*agēnōr*] heart and goes against the flocks of mortals, to seize his feast: so Achilles has lost pity, and there is no abashment [*aidōs*] in him.

If anything in Greek epic is a description of madness, it is this passage: yet still Achilles is the epitome of heroism, the mightiest and most glorious of all his race. Here lies the most difficult problem posed by the *Iliad*: is Achilles' heroic excellence fulfilled or undone by his wildness as he moves towards death? The poem forbids us to frame an easy answer. Perhaps, however, there is no more authentic response to the crux than the interpretation of Achilles which Plato puts in Socrates' mouth in the *Apology*. Addressing a jury of everyday fifth-century Athenians, Socrates invokes Achilles as a model for his own decision to die for the sake of his philosophical ideals, not because of the hero's moral or military prowess but because of the unflinching determination with which he accepts that death will be the price of avenging Patroclus.[33] On balance, perhaps, if the *Iliad* vindicates Achilles it does so through his sheer defiance of mortality: 'Well I know that it is my fate to die here, far from my dear father and mother: but I will not yield before I have driven the Trojans to the utmost limit of war' (19.421–3).

It is in this willingness to look death in the face that we find the common ground between the responses of Hector and Achilles to the challenge of heroism. At first sight the two are very different, above all because Hector is a more ordinary man, remote from divine ancestry, driven less by the conviction of his own worth than by his practical duty towards city and family. But for him, too, the need for validation in the eyes of others puts him on a path to military glory which also propels him towards the blessedness of gods and the self-destructive fury of beasts. The theme is set out in his meeting with Andromache on the walls of the city. For Andromache, prudent strategy dictates that Hector should fight a rearguard action, avoiding risks in order to live to fight another day (6.431–9); but he answers that the need for status is paramount, he cannot let it be said that he hung back from the fighting (441–65). Andromache sums up the fundamental problem of the heroic

[33] *Ap.* 28b-d; cf. *Crit.* 44b.

condition: δαιμόνιε, φθίσει σε τὸ σὸν μένος (6.407), 'your own vital energy will destroy you'.[34] A parallel formulation appears when Hector, urging his men to cross into the Achaean camp to burn their ships, is compared to a wild boar at bay that hurls itself on its attackers: 'its own *agēnoriē* kills it' (12.46; cf. 16.753). The theme of self-destructive excess comes to the fore in a still more uncanny way as Hector's fury grows on him in the battle by the ships:

μαίνετο δ' ὡς ὅτ' Ἄρης ἐγχέσπαλος ἢ ὀλοὸν πῦρ
οὔρεσι μαίνηται, βαθέης ἐν τάρφεσιν ὕλης·
ἀφλοισμὸς δὲ περὶ στόμα γίνετο, τὼ δέ οἱ ὄσσε
λαμπέσθην βλοσυρῇισιν ὑπ' ὀφρύσιν· ἀμφὶ δὲ πήληξ
σμερδαλέον κροτάφοισι τινάσσετο μαρναμένοιο
Ἕκτορος . . . (15.605–10)

He raged [*maineto*] like shield-shaking Ares, or like ruinous fire that rages in the mountains, in the thickets of a deep wood; foam appeared round his mouth, and his eyes blazed under his bristling eyebrows, and his helmet rang out terribly around Hector's temples as he fought . . .

The foam on his lips, the raging of fire, the wild gleam in the eye: this is *lussa*, wolf-madness,[35] the descent of the hero to the reckless and bestial fury that we know by the Northern name of *berserkr*. His brief triumph has been granted by Zeus because Athene is already preparing his death at the hands of Achilles (15.610–14): and this makes it all the more pathetic that Hector, as if in a mirror image of his descent to the level of an animal, has also been moving towards the belief or aspiration that he might become a god:[36]

. . . εἰ γὰρ ἐγὼν ὥς
εἴην ἀθάνατος καὶ ἀγήρως ἤματα πάντα,
τιοίμην δ' ὡς τίετ' Ἀθηναίη καὶ Ἀπόλλων,
ὡς νῦν ἡμέρη ἥδε κακὸν φέρει Ἀργείοισιν
(8.538–41; cf. 13.54, 13.825–9)

If only I were immortal and ageless down all the days, and I would be honoured as Athene and Apollo are honoured, as surely as this day now is bringing evil on the Argives.

We know that his hour of glory is a delusion, and his life and self-belief are mere instruments in Zeus's game with Thetis. But if Hector is less high

34 See further 22.457–9, where Andromache attributes Hector's self-destructive decision to *agēnoriē* and excessive *menos*.

35 See also 13.53, with 8.299, 9.237–9; similarly Achilles, 21.542; and see Padel (1995) 17–21, 141–3.

36 Nagy (1979) 142–51.

than Achilles he is also less remote and incalculable: which makes it all the more significant that he accepts the same inevitable death despite his human weakness. He takes his stand despite the sure knowledge that his city will fall (6.448); and when the final test comes, his wavering and indecision – even, eventually, his realisation of the strategic mistake, which makes it unthinkable that he should ever return to the city and face shame there (22.99–130) – do not prevent him from continuing the struggle to the end, even at the moment when he realises that he has been tricked by Athena into facing impossible odds (22.297–305). It is his resolution to accept the fact of mortality that constitutes his final act of courage: 'Let me not die without an effort, without fame, but after doing some great deed that future men will still hear of' (22.304–5).[37]

In this way the *Iliad* looks back along the succession of mythical time, with the challenges and agonies of the heroic race defined both by their elevation above normal human limitations and by their exile from the immortals' carefree ease. In a corresponding sense the *Odyssey* looks forward, setting the heroic way of life in opposition to the folly and feebleness of the contemporary world.[38] Ithaca seems to have moved closer to the world of the poet's own time, exiled from concourse with the gods and from the ethical certainties of the Iliadic battlefield. Telemachus is an ordinary youth, unsure of his manhood and unsure that Odysseus is really his father at all (I.215–16); the suitors' greed and laziness (I.106–12, XVI.105–11, etc.), and their lack of regard for the watchful anger of Zeus (*opis*, XIV.80–4), represent the same seediness as Hesiod sees around him in crooked rulers and petty-minded farmers (*Op.* 185–201). In Odysseus' absence the political situation in Ithaca seems confused and ridden with strife.[39] Consequently, his vengeance can be seen as the heroic race asserting supremacy over later and lesser men. This is indeed how Homer depicts the homecoming in distant prospect, when Menelaus looks to the return of Odysseus as that of a lion returning to its den:

> ὡς δ᾽ ὁπότ᾽ ἐν ξυλόχωι ἔλαφος κρατεροῖο λέοντος
> νεβροὺς κοιμήσασα νεηγενέας γαλαθηνοὺς
> κνημοὺς ἐξερέῃσι καὶ ἄγκεα ποιήεντα
> βοσκομένη, ὁ δ᾽ ἔπειτα ἑὴν εἰσήλυθεν εὐνήν,
> ἀμφοτέροισι δὲ τοῖσιν ἀεικέα πότμον ἐφῆκεν,
> ὣς Ὀδυσεὺς κείνοισιν ἀεικέα πότμον ἐφήσει
> (IV.335–40; repeated by Telemachus, XVII.126–31)

[37] Redfield (1975) 153–9. [38] Cf. Rutherford (1991–3).

[39] For suggestions of social strife in Ithaca see esp. II.26–34, II.229–41, III.214–5, XVI.95–6, with Haubold (2000) 110–24.

> Like when a deer puts its fawns, newborn nurslings, to sleep in the den of a fierce lion, and goes out to search for grass to feed on in the hill-slopes and grassy glens, and the lion then returns to its own den, and sends miserable doom on both [fawns] together: so Odysseus will send miserable doom on those men.

The imagery is unmistakeably that of the Iliadic warrior, driven by the force and violence of his nature to seize what is his due. But Odysseus, vitally, is more than one of the heroes of the Trojan War by the time he returns. In his wanderings he has been reduced to the barest common level of humanity, and his return can be seen as a symbolic rebirth.[40] He has rejected the immortality offered by his union with Calypso (V.135–6, VII.255–8, XXIII.334–6);[41] he has experienced to the full the inexplicable fickleness of the gods (see esp. XIII.314–28); he has heard the dead Achilles' evocation of the misery of death (XI.488–91); he has been alone and nameless among the ashes while a minstrel sang of his own famous deeds at Troy (VIII.73–92, 485–531). So it is that when he enters his palace in disguise he must depend on his own resourcefulness (*mētis*) and his existential identity, 'my own dear heart', as he lies among the disgrace to which his home has been reduced (see esp. XX.5–30). When he slaughters the suitors, the act of vengeance brings his heroic self to the fore once again, and for a moment he is revealed in unbridled ferocity:

> εὗρεν ἔπειτ' Ὀδυσῆα μετὰ κταμένοισι νέκυσσιν,
> αἵματι καὶ λύθρωι πεπαλαγμένον ὥς τε λέοντα,
> ὅς ῥά τε βεβρωκὼς βοὸς ἔρχεται ἀγραύλοιο·
> πᾶν δ' ἄρα οἱ στῆθός τε παρήϊα τ' ἀμφοτέρωθεν
> αἱματόεντα πέλει, δεινὸς δ' εἰς ὦπα ἰδέσθαι·
> ὣς Ὀδυσεὺς πεπάλακτο πόδας καὶ χεῖρας ὕπερθεν.
> (XXII.401–6)

> Then [Eurycleia] found Odysseus among the slain corpses, spattered with blood and gore like a lion, who is going away after devouring a wild ox: all his breast and his jowls on both sides are covered in blood, and he is a terrible sight to see: so Odysseus' feet and hands above were spattered with blood.

The picture is sinister, recalling the lion-like Achilles denounced by Apollo in the *Iliad*. But Odysseus immediately checks himself: when Eurycleia begins

[40] This theme has produced many interpretations based on speculative reconstruction and cross cultural comparison: outstanding examples are Carpenter (1946) 90–156 and Frame (1978) 34–80. For more cautious approaches see Reinhardt (1996); Clay (1983) 54–132; Segal (1994) 3–109.

[41] Crane (1988) ch. 1.

to crow in exultation over the slaughter, he warns her that it would be an unholy thing (*ouch hosiē*, XXII.412) to take vainglorious pleasure in the suitors' deaths, because the true cause of their downfall has been their own folly and disrespect for gods and men (XXII.413–16). It is in this moment, more than any other, that the depth of Odysseus' humanity is revealed. His heroic prowess, his skill as warrior and as master of wiles and stratagems, is only part of the wisdom that has enabled him to regain his home and his kingship: it is as if his manhood has been confirmed and deepened by his experience of thoroughly inglorious degradation, of the instability of good fortune and of the gods' remote and unpredictable power.

Against this background the punishment of the suitors is more than an example of reciprocal vengeance: it is an enactment of absolute and timeless justice.[42] It is only part of their crime that they have tried to exploit Penelope's anomalous status to bully her into marriage. More fundamentally, they have abandoned the laws of due restraint – feasting and gaming and living in idleness on another man's wealth, mocking and bullying beggars and strangers, living without fear of the watchfulness of Zeus or the dismay of their fellow men (see esp. I.368–80, XV.326–34, XVI.418–33, XVIII.274–80, XXII.35–41). Their error is their false sense of security in trusting that they can flout the laws of Zeus and man with impunity, seizing what they want without recompense. Just as they are physically feeble, unable to string the great bow of Odysseus as he and Telemachus can do (XXI.124–9, 321–9, 409), so they lack understanding of the ways of the gods and the proper order of things, *dikē* and *themis* and *thesmos*. It is significant that the pigman Eumaeus, whose piety and respect for strangers make him the antithesis of the suitors (see esp. XIV.5–108, 420–4), was born a king's son and became a slave through ill-luck (XV.390–492): he has direct experience of the instability of fortune,[43] and wisdom has come through suffering. Similarly, when the disguised Odysseus takes pity on one of the suitors and warns him of his peril, he does so by reminding him of the wretchedness of mankind:[44]

τοὔνεκά τοι ἐρέω, σὺ δὲ σύνθεο καί μευ ἄκουσον·
οὐδὲν ἀκιδνότερον γαῖα τρέφει ἀνθρώποιο
πάντων, ὅσσα γαῖαν ἔπι πνείει τε καὶ ἕρπει.
οὐ μὲν γάρ ποτέ φησι κακὸν πείσεσθαι ὀπίσσω,
ὄφρ' ἀρετὴν παρέχωσι θεοὶ καὶ γούνατ' ὀρώρηι·
ἀλλ' ὅτε δὴ καὶ λυγρὰ θεοὶ μάκαρες τελέωσι,
καὶ τὰ φέρει ἀεκαζόμενος τετληότι θυμῶι.
τοῖος γὰρ νόος ἐστὶν ἐπιχθονίων ἀνθρώπων,

[42] See Clay (1983) 213–39; Rutherford (1986).

[43] Segal (1994) 164–83.

[44] See Rutherford (1986) 157–8.

οἷον ἐπ' ἦμαρ ἄγῃσι πατὴρ ἀνδρῶν τε θεῶν τε.
καὶ γὰρ ἐγώ ποτ' ἔμελλον ἐν ἀνδράσιν ὄλβιος εἶναι,
πολλὰ δ' ἀτάσθαλ' ἔρεξα βίηι καὶ κάρτεϊ εἴκων,
πατρί τ' ἐμῶι πίσυνος καὶ ἐμοῖσι κασιγνήτοισι.
τῶ μή τίς ποτε πάμπαν ἀνὴρ ἀθεμίστιος εἴη,
ἀλλ' ὅ γε σιγῆι δῶρα θεῶν ἔχοι, ὅττι διδοῖεν.
(XVIII.129–42)

Therefore I will tell you: take heed and listen to me: the earth nurtures nothing more feeble than mankind, of all that breathes and creeps about on the earth. For a man never expects to suffer evil in the future, as long as the gods give him prowess and he can move his limbs. But when the blessed gods bring misery to fulfilment, this too in degradation he must bear in his suffering heart. Men who dwell on the earth have no more expectation than whatever Zeus will bring on them from day to day. I too had the prospect of secure prosperity among men, and I did many foolish things, indulging in force and violence, trusting in my father and brothers. Therefore no man should be entirely without regard for divine law [*athemistios*], but he should bear the gods' gifts in silence, whatever they give.

This reminder of man's feebleness and insecurity implies a warning not only against idleness and greed but also against complacency in the face of the gods. The suitors ignore their peril, despite the voice of prophecy (XX.345–58) and even despite having acknowledged that the beggar among them may be a god come to make trial of their virtue (XVII.483–7).[45] Their folly, which is sufficient justification for their wholesale destruction (XVII.360–4, XVIII.155–6), is to disregard the facts of the human condition and to forget the simple wisdom of the world: do not go too far, do not trust in easy money, do not swell beyond your proper sphere: lightning strikes the highest trees, the gods are jealous, human vitality is slight and feeble.[46] Where the *Iliad* problematises heroic excellence and explores its underlying bitterness, the *Odyssey* moves below and beyond the glamour of heroism to a more fundamental level of the human condition, where the hero succeeds only by accepting the inevitability of his lowliness:

Since you are human, you cannot say what will happen tomorrow,
and when you see a man prospering you cannot say how long he will last:
for his death comes more swiftly than a slender-winged mayfly swept away.[47]

This bleak and uncompromising wisdom is at the centre of the world-view that motivates the Homeric poems. On the surface, of course, the brilliance of the heroic generation offers consolation to their lowlier successors; but in

45 See Kearns (1982).
46 Hdt. *Histories* 7.10, 7.46.
47 Simonides, fr. 521 *PMG*.

their different ways the two epics also move on a deeper and more universal level, on which the miseries and exaltations of heroic experience become a device for exploring the universal realities of man's struggle for self-validation under the immortal and carefree gods.

FURTHER READING

The quarrel in *Iliad* 1: Wilson (2002), Slatkin (1991). *Gilgamesh* and the Near Eastern background to Greek heroism: accessible version by George (1999), and the full edition, George (2003); Haubold (2002). Mortal pain versus divine ease: Griffin (1980), Pucci (2002). Hesiod's world-view: Clay (2003), Nelson (1998), Tandy and Neale (1996), Most (1997). Fame and status among Homeric warriors: Zanker (1994), van Wees (1992). Hector and his death: Redfield (1975). Achilles and his death: Muellner (1996), Schein (1984), Crotty (1994). Fury in Homeric warfare: Whitman (1958), Padel (1995), Clarke (1995b), Loraux (1995). Vengeance and justice in the *Odyssey*: Rutherford (1986) and (1991–3); Clay (1983), Kearns (1982).

7

NANCY FELSON AND LAURA SLATKIN

Gender and Homeric epic

We are never outside what the anthropologist Gayle Rubin has taught us to call a 'sex/gender system': it is the task of cultural critics – anthropologists, literary scholars, classicists, archaeologists – to specify the components and dynamics of such systems as they take cultural form, whether in societies or in artefacts like poems.[1] Sex, sexuality, gender, reproduction, production and ideas about all of these are structurally linked in any society; consider, for example, Lévi-Strauss's meditation on exogamy – the exchange or 'traffic in women' between social groups, fundamental to human communities thus far – as the foundational requirement for any human traffic, for society itself. Over the last thirty years scholars and activists have greatly refined our understanding about sex, sexuality and gender: a sex-gender system is not simply about men and women, nor even about 'masculinity' vs. 'femininity', or 'homosexuality' vs. 'heterosexuality'. Each of these categories has a history and a cultural specificity; it is a truism worth repeating that sexuality, gender and ideas thereof are culturally variable. Yet just as the linguist Émile Benveniste observed that nowhere do we find a human society without language, so we might also say that nowhere do we find a human society without a sex-gender system (however debated, brittle or fragile) – some way of organising sexual dimorphism, reproduction and child-rearing.

The *Iliad* and the *Odyssey* are informed by the same sex-gender system that structures the entire Greek mythological tradition. Yet each epic represents aspects of this system with differential specificity. The two Homeric epics diverge from one another in the roles they assign, for example, to conjugal harmony or disharmony within their respective plots. The *Iliad* moves from

1 Rubin (1975) and Butler (1990) give crucial, far-reaching analyses of gender as an institution. Rubin's essay, in particular, provides an astute reading of Lévi-Strauss's influential argument, in *The Elementary Structures of Kinship*, that the exchange of women between social groups organises the interactions necessary for the creation of culture.

a quarrel over a woman to an unexpected resolution of a quarrel between two men over a (male) corpse. In addition, the *Iliad* makes vivid the devastation that war wreaks on communities – on warrior brotherhoods and on households, both inside Troy and, implicitly, back home, for Achaeans and Trojan allies alike. Inside Troy, Hector, Andromache and Astyanax epitomise the household that the war will soon utterly destroy, in a sense representing all the families to be fractured by the Trojan War. The *Odyssey* moves in the opposite direction, reconstituting the family unit, as wife, husband and son overcome diverse obstacles and reunite in Ithaca. Penelope at the palace surmounts the pressures brought upon her by the suitors during her husband's long absence; Odysseus triumphs over a series of impediments and challenges on his journey; and Telemachus overcomes his stagnation by completing his voyage to the Peloponnese and back. For the marital couple at Ithaca, the resumption of marriage provides closure, albeit provisional, to each of their tales.

When dealing with epics such as the *Iliad* and the *Odyssey*, we find ourselves in the world of the cultural imaginary, a zone of representation both profound and complex. We should note that genre – epic, for example – refers both to a socio-historical form and is a relational term: the properties of ancient epic are thrown into relief, for example, when juxtaposed with those of lyric or of tragedy. So too 'gender' is a term that evokes both the socialisation of sexual difference and the relational binaries that typically get installed in the name of that socialisation (e.g. male vs. female, masculine vs. feminine, active vs. passive). Despite their efforts, scholars have been unable to mine the *Iliad* or the *Odyssey* in any easy way for historical evidence of the way of life of the early Greeks; what the poems do offer, however, are elaborate, powerful representations of communities at war, of individuals at risk – men, women, gods and goddesses, working out their very different fortunes in a universe in which *kleos* (glory) is the highest value, competition the norm, strife ever-present, like-minded marriage an ideal for the *oikos* (household), male solidarity the ideal for the warrior class, and desire ever beckoning, ever disturbing.

It is of course an act of strategic but, we hope, illuminating artifice to explore ancient epic in terms of gender. Inasmuch as Homeric epic conjures up a total world, the gendering of its conflicts, contradictions and values informs both the social order represented (and disturbed) within the poems and the metaphysical – indeed ideological – orders there limned. A complete reading of Homeric epic in light of its sex-gender system necessarily exceeds the bounds of this essay: in the following pages we confine our discussion to epic representations of gender roles in the *human* domain, briefly touching on the way the gods both shape and analogically reproduce the human experience of this system.[2] We will explore, among other matters, the paradigmatic structure of triangulation that results when two or more men contend over one woman; the significance of the bonds of alliance among men, especially as foregrounded in the *Iliad*; and the apparently alternative, complementary sphere of the *oikos*, with its idealised marital bond embodied in the notion of *homophrosynē*.

Gender and the *Iliad*

Not Helen but another woman is the contended prize between two men as the *Iliad* opens. Not the Trojans fighting Achaeans but Achaeans fighting among themselves: this is, in the first instance, the context for Achilles' wrath. The catastrophic conflict that initiates and propels the *Iliad*'s narrative until the point at which Patroclus dies is not the Trojan War but the strife between two allies, Agamemnon and Achilles, both of whom lay claim – on different grounds – to the same woman, Briseis. As each hero asserts the legitimacy of his competing prerogative, the terms of their dispute outline fundamental tensions at the heart of the social structure depicted in the epic. A struggle over honour, the opening struggle also alerts us to the interaction between the institution of war and the institution of gender – a dynamic that drives the poem's unfolding.

The fatal conflict over Briseis is provoked by an even earlier dispute over a woman we never meet, as it were, face to face. Of Chryseis, the priest's daughter – whose father pleads unsuccessfully for her, then invokes Apollo to compel her return – we see nothing but her receding back, as Agamemnon finally, grudgingly, is obliged to return her. But shadowy – almost anonymous[3] – as she is, contention over her sets in motion at the outset of the poem a dazzling and disastrous chain of events. Agamemnon speaks to Achilles before the assembled warriors:[4]

> Now once more you make divination to the Danaans, argue
> forth your reason why he who strikes from afar afflicts them,
> because I for the sake of the girl Chryseis would not take
> the shining ransom; and indeed I wish greatly to have her

[2] Gender relations among divinities differ markedly, though they occasionally reflect and comment upon human relations and gender roles. Characterised as the gods are by endogamy and (in some cases) by parthenogenesis, they serve to highlight the rules (such as the prohibition against incest) that regulate human social interactions.

[3] The name Chryseis means simply 'daughter of Chryses'.

[4] All translations of Homer are from R. Lattimore, *The Iliad of Homer* (Chicago 1961) and *The Odyssey of Homer* (New York 1967).

in my own house; since I like her better than Klytaimestra
my own wife, for in truth she is no way inferior,
neither in build nor stature nor wit, nor in accomplishment.
Still I am willing to give her back, if such is the best way.
I myself desire that my people be safe, not perish.
Find me then some prize that shall be my own, lest I only
among the Argives go without, since that were unfitting;
you are all witnesses to this thing, that my prize goes elsewhere.
(1.109–20)

Agamemnon declares that his position as supreme commander of the Achaeans means that he must not remain without a *geras* – prize – and requires that he find a replacement, now that he is constrained to return Chryseis to her father. His expression not only of his reluctance to relinquish Chryseis, but of his preference for her over his own wife initiates a crucial epic motif – that of the instability of marriage and of the *oikos*. Agamemnon's explicit, provocative juxtaposition of Chryseis with Clytemnestra raises the spectre of infidelity and of the uneasy co-existence of concubinage and married domesticity[5] – perils that reverberate from the prehistory of the *Iliad*'s plot to its distant aftermath. Equally far-reaching, the leader's assumption of the overriding privilege of his supremacy threatens to undermine the bonds among allies, the communal spirit of the interdependent collectivity of fighting men – their ethos of structural equality – and to redirect the forces of competition within the cohort. Instead of mobilising against Trojans, these contending Achaeans are on the verge of unleashing calamitous forces of competition and strife against themselves.

At the opening of the *Iliad*, then, Agamemnon fatally disturbs a fragile economy of reciprocal battlefield honours and benefits, as he lays pre-emptive claim to yet another share or portion. He also upsets, and by upsetting lays bare, a precariously balanced set of relations among *philoi* – warrior comrades. To Achilles' objection that all the prizes have been shared out and that Agamemnon must now defer his until Troy has been sacked, Agamemnon replies:

I take no account of your anger. But here is my threat to you.
Even as Phoibos Apollo is taking away my Chryseis.
I shall convey her back in my own ship, with my own
followers; but I shall take the fair-cheeked Briseis,
your prize, I myself going to your shelter, that you may learn well

[5] On Clytemnestra's regular association with the theme of infidelity, see n. 51 below. For a dramatic example of the disastrous presence of a *pallakē* – concubine – within the household, see Phoenix's autobiography at *Iliad* 9.447–77.

how much greater I am than you, and another man may shrink back
from likening himself to me and contending against me.
(1.181–7)

The confluence of desire, strife and gender signalled here – the competition between men conducted through women – recapitulates the aetiology of the Trojan War; at the same time it dramatically rehearses just how this endless repetition is enacted. The struggle over Chryseis entails the struggle over Briseis, both of which follow upon the struggle over Helen.[6] Structurally speaking, then, we see that disputes among men – whether allies or enemies – entail disputed traffic in women. If marriage is the peaceful exchange of women among men, war is its violent counterpart.[7]

These serial contests over women early in the poem all converge in the climactic speech in Book 9, in which Achilles articulates the structural relationship among them as he refuses Agamemnon's propitiating gifts:

But I say that I have stormed from my ships twelve cities
of men, and by land eleven more through the generous Troad.
From all these we took forth treasures, goodly and numerous,
and we would bring them back, and give them to Agamemnon,
Atreus' son; while he, waiting back beside the swift ships,
would take them, and distribute them little by little, and keep many.
All the other prizes of honour he gave the great men and the princes
are held fast by them, but from me alone of all the Achaians
he has taken and keeps the bride of my heart. Let him lie beside her
and be happy. Yet why must the Argives fight with the Trojans?
And why was it the son of Atreus assembled and led here
these people? Was it not for the sake of lovely-haired Helen?
Are the sons of Atreus alone among mortal men the ones
who love their wives? Since any who is a good man, and careful,
loves her who is his own and cares for her, even as I now
loved this one from my heart, though it was my spear that won her.
(9.328–43)

Here Achilles collapses the categories of wife and war prize, in favour of a claim to Briseis based not on power (like Agamemnon's) but on affection. He frames his account through a series of questions whose logic encompasses an implicit as well as an explicit critique: first, if the abduction of Helen was an outrage, how is the seizing of Briseis any different? and second, if the

[6] Note the parallel phrasing: *Helenēs henek'* (9.339), *heineka kourēs* (19.58), underscoring the structural iteration.

[7] For example, when Achilles proposes to abandon the war and return to Phthia, marriage appears as the alternative: Peleus will find a wife for him (9.394–7).

Atreides' love of their wives justifies starting a war to retrieve them, and if Agamemnon prefers his war prize to his wife, then if Achilles loves *his* war prize, isn't Achilles entitled to keep her? Implicitly challenged here as well is the value system by which Agamemnon's offence in appropriating Briseis can be remedied by offering Achilles *more* women. At the same time, Achilles foregrounds affection as the basis for prizing a woman – a value that does not submit easily to the logic of equivalence, to substitution.

In this crucial speech Achilles does more than argue the legitimacy of his claim to Briseis; he offers as well a critique of the broader exchange-logic animating war and a meditation on its apparent cause – traffic in women as a medium of contended honour among men. What, ostensibly, is being protected or defended in this war? Marriage, aristocratic honour, civilised behaviour? Not *woman* (the ideological phantasm) nor *women* (the diverse assortment of female humans) but the gendered institution that secures patriliny: *marriage*.

Yet if war announces itself as a defence of marriage and the broader aristocratic arrangements it supports, paradoxically war also destroys households and annihilates families. The heroes whom the *Iliad* celebrates have committed themselves to activity that is thus simultaneously social and anti-social, at once allied with the professed values and institutions of warring communities and deeply destructive of them.[8] Preoccupied not only with war but with contending explanations and evaluations of war, the *Iliad* encourages us to see war both as the noblest venture and the most destructive endeavour, as – in more contemporary terms – a masculinist tragedy inflicted on both sexes. Even more remarkable, the poem bestows upon its hero this critical consciousness of war, its costs and its glories. Undertaken by men, organised by sworn oaths, war nevertheless implicates the larger social order, its institutions, its values – not least its gendered norms.

The core impetus for epic conflict, as Achilles' speech discloses, is Helen – the 'originally' contended woman – the cynosure for this conflict, the gendered nucleus of strife par excellence. What in fact is Helen the paradigm for?[9] As justification for why men should wage war for a decade, her erotic aura is so overwhelming that even the Trojan elders acknowledge its irresistibility; yet she herself makes an effort to resist *erōs*. On the one hand, then, she is the contended object, the prize whose seizure prompts battle, according to the warriors' own ideological representations; on the other hand, she

[8] See the valuable discussion of the death of Simoeisios in Schein (1984) 73–5.

[9] In the Hesiodic *Catalogue of Women*, the courtship of Helen sorts out the Achaean heroes and forms the basis for their allegiance to the Atreidae in the expedition against Troy. On the logic of wooing as a volatile, agonistic practice, see Slatkin (2006).

is in Iliadic representation a speaking subject, a human being given voice in the epic, a woman who exceeds the meanings men have made of her, even as her sisters in captivity (Briseis) and marriage (Andromache) are given epic voice.[10] Representing both the alienated condition of a Briseis and the assimilated condition of an Andromache, Helen's speech is introspective, questioning, critical and self-critical, regretful, realistic.[11]

Chryseis, a contested figure moved by male agents among her various roles – daughter, concubine, slave, protégée of Apollo – enters and departs the poem wordlessly; yet a significant number of female characters in the poem, even apart from the ever-loquacious female deities, speak eloquently and at length. Their speech most often takes the form of mourning. To women is traditionally assigned the ritual care of the dead, and in particular the performance of funeral lament, one of the few sanctioned modes of women's speech in antiquity.[12] In the context of lament, Andromache, Hecuba and even Briseis – in addition to Helen – each recounts her particular share of the ordeals of war and her disappointed hopes.[13] For each, these hopes are defined by husband and children; and only in Helen's case is there any sense – even if fraught with ambiguity – of autonomous agency in relation to her expectations.[14] The sorrows of bereaved women and the grief of warriors at the loss of their comrades and brothers are similarly expressed in tears and groans,[15] but the heroes' mourning is regularly accompanied by active responses of anger and vengefulness, as well as pity, and often by an acknowledgement of responsibility.[16]

The conversion of emotion into action seems to be the proper prerogative, but also the obligation, of men. If men's anger is channelled into (even as it is called forth by) warrior activity (just as *mēnis* launches this epic song), women's anger is so foreign to Iliadic representation that it almost never appears, as if it were, or should be, unimaginable. The anger of various goddesses, however, is a potent threat (as are, later, the infuriated women

[10] On the idea of a contested woman who nevertheless has a voice and a subjectivity, see the insightful discussion by King (2001); also Wohl (1998) xiii–xxxvi and Dué (2002).

[11] On Helen's discourse of self-reproach, see Worman (2001) 19.

[12] On female lament, see Vermeule (1979) 14–17; Loraux (1990); Easterling (1991); Holst-Warhaft (1992); Alexiou (2002).

[13] It is with the laments of Andromache, Hecuba and Helen for the dead Hector that the poem closes, at 24.723–75. On Briseis' mourning see King (2001).

[14] On the ambiguity of Helen's options and her relationship to Aphrodite, see Suzuki (1989) 36–40.

[15] See the discussion in Monsacré (1984) 158–96.

[16] On pity necessarily involving action on the part of Iliadic warriors, see the helpful analysis in Kim (2000) esp. 35–67.

in tragic drama);[17] yet while women and goddesses share certain predicaments as female beings, they are not identically situated vis-à-vis their male peers.[18] To state the obvious: while Athena (for example) may exercise her various divine prerogatives, with the exception of Hecuba in Book 24, there are no angry, active women in the *Iliad* – although there is mention of Amazons (3.189; 6.186), a female warrior population that implicitly shadows and inverts Iliadic structures and norms.

How entirely the lives of Iliadic women are circumscribed by the fortunes of their families and defined by their husbands is expressed with particular lucidity by Andromache, whose affective bonds are all encompassed by her relationship to her husband:

> Hektor, thus you are father to me, and my honoured mother,
> you are my brother, and you it is who are my young husband.
> (6.429–30)

Here Andromache collapses category distinctions – in a sense even more radically than Achilles in Book 9 – as she characterises the completeness of her dependence on Hector, anticipating and attempting to forestall his death and its irremediable consequences for her. But unlike Achilles, she has no recourse in her distress – apart from Hector, the defender of his city. Hector envisages for his son a future as an admired warrior at 6.475–81; Andromache more realistically paints a darker picture.[19] She delivers her lament for her husband, as it were, in stages – beginning even before he dies.[20]

[17] Aphrodite, for example, is enraged at Helen at 3.413–17; Hera's anger, directed sometimes at the Trojans, sometimes at their divine supporters (and shared by Athena), menaces Olympian harmony, but only in the human realm are its effects potentially disastrous, as when she is willing to offer up even the cities under her protection – her favourites – in order to see the Trojans destroyed, at 4.51–6.

[18] Zeus's claim at 4.34–6 that Hera would eat the Trojans raw, so enraged is she at them, is echoed by Hecuba's wish at 24.212–14, that she could sink her teeth into Achilles' liver for what he has done to her son – an extraordinary expression of fury on the part of a (mortal) female. See Loraux's crucial account of the connection between maternal anger and grief (1990).

[19] See Segal (1971a) on Andromache's understanding of her situation.

[20] Andromache's prediction of what both she and Astyanax will have to undergo, once Hector has been killed, takes the form of the lament delivered by a female relative after a hero's death; and the poem explicitly acknowledges her proleptic mourning, although Hector is still alive:

> So *they mourned in his house over Hektor while he was living*
> *still*, for they thought he would never again come back from fighting
> alive, escaping the Achaian hands and their violence.
> (6.500–2)

Confronted with Andromache's grief and her diction of radical dependence, Hector responds with an acknowledgment of their 'divided world':[21]

> Poor Andromache! Why does your heart sorrow so much for me?
> No man is going to hurl me to Hades, unless it is fated,
> but as for fate, I think that no man yet has escaped it
> once it has taken its first form, neither brave man nor coward.
> Go therefore back to our house, and take up your own work,
> the loom and the distaff, and see to it that your handmaidens
> ply their work also; but the men must see to the fighting,
> all men who are the people of Ilion, but I beyond others.
>
> (6.486–93)

A divided world is divided along many axes, not least gender: the dream of marital harmony, of good union between the sexes, breaks precisely along the fault-lines of sexual strife that the *Iliad* everywhere takes as its background mythic understanding. Yet as much as the *Iliad* locates its origins in the violation of an *oikos*,[22] it devotes many lines to the representation of a loving marriage put under duress by the war designed to defend marriages. Through its portrayal of the family of Hector – aged parents, brothers and sisters, but above all, wife and child – the poem demonstrates the costs of the larger cultural system of which Hector is at the same time champion and victim.

The intimate conversation, or *homilia*,[23] between Hector and Andromache in Book 6 – all the more precious for its unlikeliness[24] – adds increased poignancy to the emblematic rendering, later in that book, of Andromache as the wife who prepares to welcome her husband home, not knowing that she is already a widow. It is a mark of Iliadic strength and complexity that it imagines the counter-spirit to its own reigning value, *kleos*: with Hector and Andromache the poem develops a countercurrent, imagining an alternative

21 See Katz (1981) on the 'divided world' – a discussion that nuances, even as it describes, the gendered division of roles and attributes in the poem. Note the structural obstacles to *homophrosunē* between Hector and Andromache. Although Andromache actually ventures strategic military advice, her counsel is ignored or dismissed by Hector, who directs her to return to 'women's work' (6.490–3). Note, too, that after the sack of a city, the destinies of men and women remain divided, despite Andromache's claim at 22.477–81 that she and Hector 'were born to a single destiny' (*aisa*).

22 I.e. the household of Helen and Menelaus, violated by Paris.

23 This conversation is re-evoked in Hector's own self-ironising fantasy of an *oaristus*, a private 'chat' with Achilles at 22.122–30.

24 As Christian Wolff observed (oral communication), the poem underscores the exceptional quality of the encounter between Hector and Andromache by narrating it as a meeting that almost did not take place: neither is where the other expects her/him to be; they meet at the ultimate moment, just as Hector is about to walk through the Scaean gates for the last time.

universe of sustained adult relations and of continuity; its destruction is equally at the heart of the poem's pathos, and its powerful residue is carried into the *Odyssey*.

Hector's speech to Andromache in Book 6 foresees the destruction of Troy but also, with great tenderness, the endless grief of his widowed wife:

> For I know this thing well in my heart, and my mind knows it:
> there will come a day when sacred Ilion shall perish,
> and Priam, and the people of Priam of the strong ash spear.
> But it is not so much the pain to come of the Trojans
> that troubles me, not even of Priam the king nor Hekabe,
> not the thought of my brothers who in their numbers and valour
> shall drop in the dust under the hands of men who hate them,
> as troubles me the thought of you, when some bronze-armoured
> Achaian leads you off, taking away your day of liberty,
> in tears; and in Argos you must work at the loom of another,
> and carry water from the spring Messeis or Hypereia,
> all unwilling, but strong will be the necessity upon you;
> and some day seeing you shedding tears a man will say of you:
> 'This is the wife of Hektor, who was ever the bravest fighter
> of the Trojans, breakers of horses, in the days when they fought about Ilion.'
> So will one speak of you; and for you it will be yet a fresh grief,
> to be widowed of such a man who could fight off the day of your slavery.
> But may I be dead and the piled earth hide me under before I
> hear you crying and know by this that they drag you captive.
>
> (6.447–65)

In his sympathetic imagining of Andromache's grievous future, Hector gives priority to marital devotion over even filial or warrior bonds. Yet that sympathy is conditioned by loss and grief, and the oddly contorted temporality of its expression – alternately prospective and retrospective – seems to elide any hope of its enjoyment in the present. In the *Iliad*, male and female domains and fates are profoundly separate, however much individuals may care for each other. Although Helen anticipates attaining (negative) renown among future generations,[25] the poem's cherished value, *kleos*, is something Iliadic women cannot earn, given their limited agency, and this disparity

[25] Weaving her tapestry, Helen generates a competing vision of epic as a 'battle fought over me', thus shifting attention to herself as maker and subject – not just object – of epic song and the fame it confers. Her weaving thus commemorates the woman of many men, the woman who generates a second bride-contest for the sake of her: the Trojan War.

renders men and women mutually unknowable,[26] their portions fundamentally incommensurate.

The *Iliad* privileges cohesiveness among the fighting men above other lateral ties. In the situation of Achilles – and the countless young warriors who will never return to reciprocate the care of parents and dear ones – the *Iliad* highlights the radiance and charisma of the hero who gives his all and dies in the bloom of youth; the trope of the 'beautiful death', still ideologically powerful in the classical period, is fully developed here.[27] The battlefield creates its own community among those whose valour and loyalty earn them *kleos*.[28] Warriors on the battlefield are united in a bond created not by a common cause but by their dependence on each other for their very lives; it is their *philoi* (friends) who must rally them, protect them, avenge them, and – far away from loved ones – give their bodies to the funeral pyre.[29] Achilles and Patroclus epitomise that bond; theirs is the most fully elaborated in the poem, but is by no means unique.[30] In the battle books in particular, we are introduced to numerous pairs of friends (or actual brothers, like Ajax and Teucer, or more distant relatives like Glaucus and Sarpedon) whose devotion to each other is the specific occasion for their heroic attainments. The *Iliad* narrates countless instances of fighters entering the fray specifically on behalf of their companions-in-arms; this is in fact the primary motivation for entry into battle in any given, local moment of the fighting.[31]

In a sense, we might say that the fighting cohort celebrated in the *Iliad* represents an alternative paradigm of social relations, parallel to the *oikos* in importance, and more stable. The *Männerbund* formed by the solidarity of the fighting host, the warriors' fidelity to their imperilled comrades, offers a model of allegiance free from the frailties and vulnerabilities of the domestic household:[32] no fighter in the *Iliad* displays the inconstancy of a Helen or the treachery of a Clytemnestra. The only scene in the poem in which a warrior

26 As an example of intersubjective impasse, at 6.473–81 Hector imagines that Andromache would be pleased to think of Astyanax as a fighter, risking his life to bring back bloody spoils.

27 Loraux (1977); Vermeule (1979) 145–63; Vernant (1982).

28 Haubold (2000) 100–43.

29 The rhetoric of encouragement is often a dare that takes the form of a gendered taunt: e.g. 15.561–661. Such exhortations, regularly accompanied by the battle cry 'Shame!', derive the courage of warriors from a contrast to the implied cowardice of women; cf. 2.235. On the conventions of battlefield exhortations see Latacz (1977) and Irwin (2000).

30 On Iliadic *philotēs*, see Sinos (1980), Nagy (1979) 103–11 and Kim (2000) 56–67.

31 See the indispensable analysis of Fenik (1968).

32 On the ideology of the *Männerbund*, see Sinos (1980), Murray ([illegible]) and now especially Ferrari (2002) 113–14, with bibliography.

is betrayed on the field of battle is in Book 22, when Athena, leading Hector on to his death at Achilles' hands, masquerades as his brother Deiphobus; at the moment Hector realises that he has been abandoned, he knows it could only have been by a god. He has been tricked, so to speak, by his faith in the *Männerbund*. Yet among its bitter paradoxes, the social code that unites the warriors both creates and subverts the powerful attachments between *philoi*; thus the quarrel between Agamemnon and Achilles (who asserts in Book 1 that the war is about loyalty and reciprocal obligations) sends many noble heroes to Hades, including, finally, Patroclus.

Only after Patroclus' death do the Achaeans re-constitute themselves as allied brothers-in-arms. It is striking that the resumption of the bonds among *philoi* seems structurally to require the expulsion and rhetorically imagined elimination of a woman. Unsettling to modern readers has been Achilles' seeming renunciation of Briseis in his speech of reconciliation with Agamemnon:[33]

> But now, when all the Achaians were in one body together,
> Achilleus of the swift feet stood up before them and spoke to them:
> 'Son of Atreus, was this after all the better way for
> both, for you and me, that we, for all our hearts' sorrow,
> quarrelled together for the sake of a girl in soul-perishing hatred?
> I wish Artemis had killed her beside the ships with an arrow
> on the day when I destroyed Lyrnessos and took her.
> For thus not all these too many Achaians would have bitten
> the dust, by enemy hands, when I was away in my anger.
> This was better for the Trojans and Hektor; yet I think
> the Achaians will long remember the quarrel between us.'
>
> (19.54–64)

Just as Achilles identifies Helen, at 9.339, as the source of the conflict between Trojans and Achaeans, here he specifies Briseis (although he never speaks her name) as the cause of the discord between himself and Agamemnon. His repudiation of her is equally and at the same time a repudiation of that quarrel, and marks his relinquishing of the wrath that created the poem's primary subject.[34] Yet if Achilles' wrath has ended, that of the Danaan fighting force is re-fueled, as the poem proceeds to narrate, carrying us through the death of Hector to the imminent destruction of Troy. As Achilles had predicted, the poem enacts the remembrance not only of his wrath but also of the terrible allotment of death and glory that is the song of *kleos*.

[33] On this passage, see Suzuki (1989) 24–7.

[34] See Nagy (1979) 79–81 on the '*transfert du mal*', as Achilles' enmity shifts from Agamemnon to Hector.

Under the sign of *nostos* (return), however, Homeric epic offers an alternative vision in which the divergent shares and divergent experiences of men and women can be reconciled. The *Odyssey*'s theme of successful *nostos* gains force from the many failed, thwarted or renounced homecomings that are the groundwork of the *Iliad*.

Gender and the *Odyssey*

The *Odyssey* moves in the opposite direction from the *Iliad* and exists in a complementary relationship to it. As a poem of recuperation, it privileges as its overarching categories the *oikos* and the institution of marriage, which are secured by the hero's *nostos*. A husband and a wife reunite in a marriage that is symbolised by their steadfast marriage-bed, its construction a reliable and private sign between them.[35] The poem attributes their attainment of reunion to their individual *mētis* (ingenuity), a trait that the resourceful patron goddess Athena both fosters in them and herself embodies.[36] With a comparable ingenuity, the poem guides its audiences towards fervently desiring that reunion, which will restore order in Ithaca and also recover for the Ithacan household, at least in part, the losses exacted by the Trojan War. Thus the *Odyssey* performs a kind of reclamation of the *oikos* that requires the wife's sexual fidelity but also the husband's successful return and successful elimination of all competitors for his wife.

A poem that celebrates ingenuity, the *Odyssey* might be read as a series of ingenious plans, their collisions and their unfolding: from Odysseus' outwitting of the Cyclops, to Circe's provisional ensnaring of the hero to Odysseus' test with the bow, to Penelope's bed-test, the *Odyssey* presents male and female figures scheming, thinking, collaborating and outwitting. Odysseus and Penelope, in particular, as consummate schemers, overcome every obstacle to reunion – a horde of unruly young suitors (for Penelope) and (for Odysseus) a series of female 'detainers' (along with other threats to his return) as well as the challenge, once home, of ridding his household of the suitors and winning Penelope over.

The *Odyssey*, as if in conversation with the *Iliad*, invites reflection upon the impact of the war and the warrior's absence on the wife left behind. The poem asks: Who will take charge of the *oikos* and *polis* in his absence?

35 On the bed's immovability and indissolubility see especially Zeitlin (1996) 19–52 and the scholiast *ad* XXIII.288, ed. Dindorf. On the reunion itself see Murnaghan (1987), Winkler (1990) 129–62, Katz (1991), Doherty (1995) and Felson (1987) and (1994), with additional bibliography. Russo (1982), Pedrick (1988) and Wohl (1993) are helpful on specific aspects of the reunion.

36 Slatkin (1996) esp. 234–37.

How will the patriarchal domestic economy work, or not work, when the patriarch is gone, perhaps never to return? Will it survive? What are the obligations of the wife? Perhaps in response to the catastrophes associated with the Trojan War, the *Odyssey* minimises the importance of the *Männerbund*. There is no viable cohort of men in the entire poem. Odysseus has arrived home alone, moreover, having lost every single member of his crew: he did not sustain solidarity with them, did not succeed in protecting their homecoming, and was (in short) not a successful leader.[37] Ironically, the collectivity of unruly suitors forms the only cohesive cohort in the epic. They have banded together for unheroic purposes, however: to deplete Odysseus' household, court Penelope, ambush Telemachus and finally to defend themselves at the bow-contest. The violence that Odysseus perpetrates against them ends up eliminating the aristocratic princes; moreover, Odysseus and his small band of four 'would have killed them all, and given none of them | homecoming' (thus devastating his own populace), had not Athena, backed by Zeus, intervened with both sides (XXIV.528–48). Athena's intervention in Ithaca recalls her staying of Achilles' hand at *Iliad* I.193–222 in a comparable case of strife over a woman, like the strife that launched the Trojan War.

The *Odyssey*, far from providing a competing paradigm of social relations, as discussed above, or questioning marital relations as the basis of order and stability, puts marriage at the centre – for its human characters at least[38] – and idealises it. The poem proposes the kind of reciprocal marriage that Odysseus sets before Nausicaa when he asks the gods to grant the Phaeacian princess

> a husband and a house and sweet agreement
> in all things, for nothing is better than this, more steadfast
> than when two people, a man and his wife, keep a harmonious
> household; a thing that brings much distress to the people who hate them
> and pleasure to their well-wishers, and for them the best reputation.
> (VI.181–4)

Such a marriage based on sweet agreement – *homophrosunē* (like-mindedness) – and on keeping a harmonious household *homophroneonte* (both being like-minded') is tested and amplified in the course of the *Odyssey* before it is ultimately secured in Book XXIII. Its differential impact on enemies and well-wishers coincides with Odysseus' vision of an ideal kingdom

[37] Haubold (2000) 100–43.

[38] On gender in the Song of Aphrodite's Adultery (VIII.266–366), see esp. Newton (1987); for further bibliography, Felson (1994) 134–5.

as he sets it forth in his 'reverse simile' when he later compares Penelope to a just and pious king whose people prosper under him (XIX.107–14).

The presence of 'reverse similes' invites audiences to imagine permeable (even interchangeable) gender roles and spheres of activity as an alternative to the traditional 'divided world', which these similes invert and indeed interrogate.[39] They exist in tension with the assertive directives of certain male speakers, in both poems, who invoke the divided world by ordering a woman to go into the house and take up her own work of weaving and to leave to men such activities as warfare, story-telling, escort of the bow.[40] In comparing Penelope's fame to that of a blameless and god-fearing king (XIX.107–14), Odysseus envisions the sort of flourishing kingdom he has just encountered in Scheria, his last stop before arriving at home. There his guide (Athena in the form of a young girl) gives an elaborate description of Arete that anticipates what Odysseus will find in Ithaca when he shortly returns. Athena describes the Phaeacian queen as remarkable in status and versatile in pursuits, by virtue (in large part) of the way 'Alcinoos . . . gave her such pride of place | as no other woman on earth is given | of such women as are now alive and keep house for husbands'.[41] This singling out of Queen Arete raises the question of whether Odysseus will bestow a comparable honour on Penelope, and whether Penelope will turn out to be equally, or even more, remarkable.

The *Odyssey* explores the edges of its paradigm of reciprocal marriage by presenting divine and immortal females who pursue Odysseus and openly express the desire to wed him. This subset of the Adventures introduces into the text the tale-type of divine lovers and their mortal consorts who, traditionally, pay dearly for their pleasures. Odysseus not only survives the danger/pleasure of sleeping for a year with Circe and for seven with Calypso,[42] and of listening to the Sirens, whose song is fatally seductive for mariners, but he even incorporates these adventures into his triumphant survivor's tale. Significantly, he never loses his *menos* (life-force) – unlike the emasculated mortal lover of the love goddess in traditional stories of this

39 Foley (1978) 7–26. Examples include VIII.523–31, where Odysseus is like a woman weeping over the body of a husband lost in war, and XXIII.233–40, where Odysseus is as welcome to Penelope as land to ship-wrecked men.

40 Three male characters invoke the divided world in this way, using slight variants of the same formulaic language: Hector to Andromache at 6.490–3, Telemachus to Penelope at I.356–9 and XXI.350–3; and Alcinous to Arete at XI.352–3.

41 At VII.66–74 Athena presents Queen Arete as a paragon of womanhood who ventures into the world of men.

42 At V.14–15 and 153–5 the text calls attention to Odysseus' reluctance to be Calypso's bedmate – even before he rejects her final proposal, at V.206–10, to be 'lord of this household | and be an immortal'.

type.[43] Nor does he express the accompanying misogyny of the mortal lover evident, for example, in other traditions, as in Gilgamesh's rebuke and rejection of Ishtar. In fact, because he declines Calypso's repeated proposals of 'marriage' and yet (unlike Gilgamesh) does not incite her rage, Odysseus will escape the disasters that typically befall such lovers.[44] He ultimately rejects, after experiencing it, the quintessential male fantasy of sharing a bed, and a life of luxury, with a goddess. Far from refuting Calypso's claim to surpass Penelope in build and stature, Odysseus concedes it, saying Penelope is 'mortal after all, and you are deathless and ageless' (v.218). Nevertheless, he tactfully insists on 'his day of homecoming, whatever suffering may lie ahead' (v.215–24).

Odysseus' choice of a mortal wife is a choice to be mortal and a choice not to abandon epic heroism and sacrifice immortal acclaim.[45] And Odysseus formulates his belief in like-minded marriage among equals only after his years with Calypso. Disenchantment with an unequal partner precedes (and implicitly shapes) the conversation in which he politely communicates to Nausicaa that he is not her equal and not her match.

Through these potent and dread goddesses, the poem represents forms of female desire filtered through the ideological requirements of *nostos*, examining the nature of that desire and the consequences of its denial or provisional fulfilment. Both Circe and Calypso manage their lives independently of husbands: a mortal consort, should they acquire one, is more erotic object than partner, and they have no offspring. Despite much dissimilarity, their independence resonates with Penelope's involuntary self-reliance over the twenty years of Odysseus' absence.

The human version of the 'detaining goddess' is the Phaeacian princess – nubile, desirous of a husband, and savvy like her mother, perhaps even a younger version of Penelope herself.[46] But the hero has just declined Calypso's offer, and the life of ease on Scheria carries a similar threat to his return and to the preservation of his *oikos*. Odysseus' refusal to remain on Scheria and marry the princess attests to his determination, and readiness, to return to Penelope. By not pursuing Nausicaa or her maidens, by not behaving like the ravenous lion to which he is compared (v.130–8), Odysseus reassures the maiden that she and her companions are safe. His civility

43 See Giacomelli (1980) on the semantics of *menos* in Greek poetry.

44 Calypso herself cites three couples – Dawn and Orion, Demeter and Iasion, and herself and Odysseus – in her complaint at v.118–28; cf. *Hymn. Ven.* 202–38 for a similar catalogue. In a humorous precursor the Akkadian Gilgamesh catalogues at length Ishtar's discarded and ruined lovers (*Gilgamesh*, Tablet 60).

45 On the refusal of Odysseus, see Vernant (1996) esp. 187–8, and Schein (1996) 3–31.

46 Van Nortwick (1979); also Wohl (1993) and Felson (1994) 46–8.

contributes to the mutual respect and admiration in their eventual parting exchange at VIII.457–68, which itself exhibits a measure of *homophrosunē*.

As with Queen Arete (a thoroughly domesticated yet empowered human female), these figures illuminate aspects of Penelope as the eventual idealised partner of Odysseus. The exposition of their subjectivities resonates with the query of Odysseus to his mother's shade in the Underworld: 'What does Penelope want? What is she thinking?' (XI.76–9).

While Odysseus is pondering the state of Penelope's *noos* (intention), Homer's audiences know that she is at a critical juncture. She has, strictly speaking, returned to the liminal phase of courtship, to the threshold of womanhood. But her situation is complicated and problematic. It is ten years since the fall of Troy, and though the destinies of other warriors have become the topic of song (I.325–7), no one knows whether her husband is alive or dead. At home in Ithaca, moreover, several events have recently converged: Telemachus is grown, enabling her to remarry (according to Odysseus' parting words at XVIII.269–70),[47] and her 108 suitors, who have been wooing her for more than three years, have caught her in a delaying tactic – the famous ruse of the loom – and are pressing her all the more urgently. The uncertainty about Penelope's marital status intensifies this moment of crisis even as it multiplies her options: she might remarry and either commit adultery (if Odysseus is alive) or wed an inferior man (if she is a widow). If she holds out and waits, she might either contrive a successful reunion (if Odysseus returns) or might (if he is dead or lost or permanently detained) further antagonise her spurned suitors. Already, they violate her household and are attempting, without success, to ambush and murder her son.[48] For Penelope, then, the stakes are high and timing is all-important: a false move on her part will endanger not only her own status and reputation but her husband's safety as well, should he come back. At jeopardy is the very integrity of the *oikos* to which her warrior-husband hopes to return and which it is her responsibility, as a wife, to safeguard.[49] Everything depends, then, on what she does and on what type of wife she turns out to be.

The poem places Penelope's dilemma within a set of comparable scenarios that help define the sex-gender system within which she operates. The governing situation of the *Odyssey* draws on wartime stories familiar to

[47] On the question of who will be the guardian of Penelope once Telemachus comes of age, see Katz (1991) esp. 35–9.

[48] On the set of narrative options for Penelope, see Felson (1994) 7 and Katz (1991). An additional ambiguity as to where home will be if she remarries arises from the [illegible] of various suitors (e.g. at I.275–8 and 292).

[49] See Katz (1981) 19–44 and n. 21 above.

Homeric audiences, from the *Iliad* and from the surrounding mythological tradition, in which the wives of absent warriors are vulnerable, their lives volatile. The poem introduces two wives – Helen and Clytemnestra – who highlight the challenges and choices Penelope faces by modelling the fundamental question: 'Could she turn out to be like either of them?'[50] Their stories, as depicted within the poem, set forth a range of possibilities for the wife who has been left to her own resources: still married, still desiring, besieged by others who desire her, sometimes the woman succumbs. The choices of Helen to run off with Paris and of Clytemnestra to yield to the persuasion of Aegisthus[51] (each in the absence of her husband) throw into sharp relief Penelope's decision to remain faithful. Like these two notorious adulteresses, Penelope is a much-desired bride.[52] Like them, she has no male guardian nearby. Yet of the three – who are all objects of desire and, to different degrees, desiring subjects as well – only she staves off ruinous *atē* (folly). She alone is *periphrōn* (circumspect), *ekhephrōn* (of enduring mind) and can be self-protectively *apistos* (untrusting) (XXIII.72) and hard-hearted (XXIII.97), in ways that protect her from self-deception and make her effective in her schemes and plans.[53]

The other problematic triangles have both been resolved, in one fashion or another, by the time the story of the *Odyssey* begins: Helen is retrieved and returned to Sparta[54] and all members of the Argive triangle – Clytemnestra, Aegisthus and Agamemnon – are dead. At Ithaca, however, the courtship by 108 suitors continues to threaten the marital reunion once Odysseus is home, until he annihilates every one of them at the contest. The courtship not only tests Penelope's intelligence and steadfastness but also orients her toward (re)marriage by relocating her in the sphere of Aphrodite tempered by Artemis.[55] This aligns her with all the *parthenoi* who are wooed by suitors and at the same time with her desired and long absent husband, who as her

50 On paradigms for the epic bride see Slatkin (2005).

51 Clytemnestra represents the extreme case of the wife who will not wait but instead beds her husband's enemy. Always associated with the theme of infidelity in mythic tradition, she is notoriously transgressive in every Odyssean account of her actions.

52 As her suitor Eurymachus tells her: 'you surpass all women | for beauty and stature and for the mind well balanced within you' (XVIII.248–9).

53 At III.266 Nestor attributes 'virtuous thoughts' to Clytemnestra before Aegisthus seduces her. On Helen's ways of knowing, see esp. Bergren (1981) 201–14.

54 The tensions in the reconstituted Spartan *oikos* are revealed by the juxtaposition of dissonant Trojan War stories; see especially Bergren (1981) 201–14, Olson (1989b) 387–94, Katz (1991) and Worman (2001) 119–37.

55 On the interplay of Artemis and Aphrodite in the character of Penelope, as at XIX.53–4, see Felson (1994) 36–7.

109th suitor will win her (and win her over), first in a contest and then in a test that she devises.[56]

The *Odyssey* draws on mythic tradition and engages dialectically with the *Iliad* in its portrayal of its characters. In the case of the 'polytropic' Odysseus of epic tradition, the poem selectively highlights his skills as a warrior, an orator in the assembly and a crafty trickster but makes all these traits serve a domesticated and socialised Odysseus who heads his own *oikos* in Ithaca. His self-designation in the *Iliad* as 'father of Telemachus' (2.260; cf. 4.354) and characters' recollection of him as *epios* ('gentle')[57] provide materials for the Odysseus of the *Odyssey*, whose drive to return home competes with his curiosity to learn about the minds of men (1.3) through risky adventures. In his orientation to family and fatherhood Odysseus differs from Agamemnon, who returned from Troy with Cassandra, and brought her as a *pallakē* (concubine) into the household.[58] Odysseus, in contrast, has affairs but always elsewhere and always with goddesses – affairs he does not bring home.[59] As a result, his sexual adventures do not disrupt the *oikos*: the fact that he narrates these escapades to Penelope (as earlier to the Phaeacians) indicates that they do not constitute a violation of societal norms and in this poem they threaten neither patriarchy nor patriliny.

The poem distances Odysseus from his erotic liaisons through the intervening 'reunion' with the goddess Athena – always, in myth, a compelling alternative to the goddess/mortal lover paradigm (see above, pp. 00). It times the hero's first open encounter with his patron goddess (who has played such a pivotal role in plotting out his return) after the Adventures, upon his arrival at home, transported by the Phaeacian sailors. It situates the meeting at the boundary between 'over there' and 'here at Ithaca'. Athena's acknowledgement of their affinity and like-mindedness has the impact of securing Odysseus' identity as a hero of *mētis*: their meeting looks backward to his survival on his journeys and forward to his new challenge, namely to resolve

56 Woodhouse (1969) discusses the *Odyssey*'s adaptation of several traditional folk-tales. See also Page (1955) 1–2, with references, on the folk-tale of the returning hero.

57 Evidence for a traditional 'domestic' Odysseus comes from a story in the *Cypria* (summarised in Phot. *Bibl.* 319a21): a reluctant warrior, he tried not to join up in the expedition to Troy by feigning madness, but he revealed his sanity when, on the advice of Palamedes, the embassy threatened to harm his infant son. At 2.260 and 3.354 Odysseus calls attention to himself as 'Telemachus' father'. Moreover, several characters remember him as 'a king gentle as a father' (II.47 and 234 and V.12) or as having gentle ways (XI.202–3).

58 Laertes, in contrast, 'for fear of his wife's anger', refrained from sleeping with Eurycleia, whom he 'favored in his house as much as his own devoted | wife' (I.429–33).

59 Alternate traditions assign offspring by Odysseus to both Calypso and Circe and later to the Thesprotian Callidike; see Phot. *Bibl.* 319a21 for the *Telegony* and Hes. *Theog.* 1,101–13.

the triangle that threatens his *oikos* and his safe *nostos*. As such, she can provide a bridge for Odysseus between his erotic liaisons, which seem to occur outside of human time, and his very human erotic encounter with Penelope.

Once back in Ithaca, Odysseus makes trial of his wife, investigating and asking questions (XIII.333–6), instead of immediately making her his confidante. In this, he follows the advice of Agamemnon's shade but also of Athena,[60] who reinforces Agamemnon's warning with her emphatic command (XIII.306–10) to 'tell no one of all the men and women | that you have come back from your wanderings', including Penelope. Odysseus' secrecy with Penelope, as he maintains his disguise, gives him a strategic advantage over her: he can observe her, incognito, as she interacts with the suitors, and in this way play a role in her tale. This enables him, an eyewitness, to interpret her actions from the vantage point of a self-confident suitor and to assume, as he watches her solicit gifts from the suitors, that 'her mind has other intentions' (XVIII.272–80).

At the pair's first face-to-face encounter[61] – a climactic moment in their renewal of contact – Penelope announces her plan to hold a bride-contest (570–80) and essentially to give herself away in marriage.[62] This decision has every appearance of a new *mētis* (plan): it comes upon her suddenly, like the ruse of the loom (a 'brainstorm' she has just related to the stranger). It indicates, moreover, that she is in charge of herself, not subject to any male guardian, and that she is indeed being won over by the stranger/Odysseus,[63] who seizes upon the proposal as an opportunity not only to win her from the suitors and reclaim his *oikos* but to engage them in a heroic battle and prove, once again, his manhood and his entitlement to Penelope. Yet at

[60] The shade of Agamemnon stereotypes all women as treacherous on the basis of the special case of Clytemnestra (XI.432–4). Hearing of the adultery of Clytemnestra, Odysseus associates the two sisters as schemers and causes of destruction, but he resists the generalisation to 'all women' (XI.436–9).

[61] This *homilia*, in contrast to the one between Hector and Andromache (see above, pp. 99–100, takes place indoors and at a location that symbolises all that is sacrosanct within the *oikos* and fundamental to its continuation.

[62] Note the untraditional nature of this move. In the mythic tradition, a maiden (or her father) who determines the rules of the contest for her hand often seems to be trying to avoid marriage by making the contest an 'impossible task'.

[63] By obscuring Penelope's degree of certitude about the stranger's identity and by postponing any actual contact between Odysseus and Penelope until the conversation (*homilia*) at the hearth in Book XIX, the poem practises on its audiences the same *mētis* it ascribes to its leading characters. On the *mētis* of the poem see Slatkin (1996); on the strategy of teasing its external audience about the crucial topic of what Penelope knows and when, see Felson (1994) 3–5, 16 and 18.

that contest Penelope is the one who places the event before her suitors (XXI.67–79), intervenes in their wrangling (312–19) and bids them give the stranger the bow (336). In fact, until she departs at XXI.354, sent back to her quarters by Telemachus, Penelope is a major force in implementing the restoration of her marriage. She remains in charge until the close of the second interview: there, after telling her impatient son (XXIII.109–10: 'we have signs that we know of | between the two of us only, but they are secret from others'), she inflicts her test on Odysseus. This final *mētis* – a seemingly casual order to a servant to move outside for the beggar 'the very bed that he himself | built' (XXIII.177–80) – provokes Odysseus to retrace the steps of its making and to prove (to her satisfaction) that he is indeed her husband. The trick may be read as Penelope's (playful) retaliation for Odysseus' prolonged secrecy.

Reunited within their *oikos*, the couple enacts *homophrosunē* not only in their love-making in the steadfast marriage bed but in the mutuality of their exchange of tales, which the poem summarises at XXIII.300–41. Each of them has narrated a partial epic, an eyewitness account of personal experiences. The summary that interweaves their separate stories recapitulates (and re-enacts, as it were) the entire *Odyssey*, an epic that includes both adventure tales. In Penelope's segment of 'all she had endured | in the palace' she is the contested bride-prize, the woman over whom the suitors vie first among themselves and then in unwitting competition with Odysseus; she is won by Odysseus after she proves that she stands out for virtue and intelligence; but she also endorses her choice of him, and is won over by him, after she tests him with a *mētis* that allows her to outshine even Queen Arete of Scheria.[64] Indeed, all the other females that Odysseus has encountered pale by comparison, finally, with Penelope, who fits Athena's very description of a sharp and stealthy figure at XIII.291–2: 'It would be a sharp one, and a stealthy one, who would ever get past you | in any contriving; even if it were a god against you.' Penelope does 'get past' Odysseus with her ruse of the marriage bed. And in the end Odysseus – survivor, adventurer, world traveller, who returns home alone and without his comrades – stands out as much for having an exemplary wife as for being *polumētis* ('devious') and *polutropos* ('versatile').

In retrospect, Penelope comments on the dilemma of a wife left at home, on the precariousness of her virtue. In her 'apology for Helen', and for herself, she reframes her own reluctance to embrace Odysseus as a virtuous act, and one which might have saved her from the plight of adultery had he been

[64] Odysseus (as the intimate listener) equates their trials at XXIII.350–3.

someone other than Odysseus. She excuses her hesitation by citing Helen's cognitive error and folly in 'lying in love with an outlander from another country', which Helen would not have done, 'if she had known that the warlike sons of the Achaeans would bring her | home again to the beloved land of her fathers' (XXIII.215–24). This strange apology for Helen reveals that she, Penelope, a wife left at home, realises that she too could have ended up (like Helen and Clytemnestra) as a woman of many men, with two lovers/husbands, or been deluded, perhaps by a god in disguise.

Coincidence of desire allows Penelope and Odysseus to embody the marital ideal of the *Odyssey* as they reclaim their marriage. Their success at reuniting affirms the principle that this husband and wife both maintain their separate spheres and roles, traditionally configured, and (at times) seem to identify across gender boundaries. In this, they match the poem's 'reverse similes' discussed above, which liken Odysseus to a woman 'lying over the body of her dear husband, who fell fighting for her city and people' (VIII.522–30) and Penelope to 'some king who, as a blameless man and god-fearing . . . upholds the role of good government . . . and the people prosper under him' (XIX.108–14). For audiences receptive to the ideal of marriage with *homophrosunē*, the poem represents a husband and a wife who, having survived individually, now thrive as a couple, keeping 'a harmonious | household; a thing that brings much distress to the people who hate them | and pleasure to their well-wishers, and for them the best reputation'.

When the shade of Agamemnon invokes a song of praise for Penelope for fulfilling the traditional expectations of a virtuous wife at XXIV.192–8, the poem celebrates her *mētis* in the service of the *oikos*. This emphatic bestowal of *kleos* on Penelope, alongside Odysseus, suggests that the *Odyssey* has a dialectical relation to the *Iliad* in terms of the sex-gender system in which they both participate, the system that permeates the tradition to which both these epics belong. Where the *Iliad* celebrates the beautiful death of the warrior and the bonds between men that emerge in the face of war, with all its casualties, the *Odyssey* highlights the efficacy (along with the subjectivity) of the stalwart and non-adulterous wife left behind. To her the poem assigns ingenuity and a capacity to plan. She sustains the *oikos* and protects the continuity of her husband's patriliny and at the same time follows a pathway she actively chooses from among the alternatives laid out before her. In one sense, the poem represents her as no less trafficked than the other women of epic, in another, as herself taking charge of her own trafficking and exhibiting astounding agency, within cultural limits. In the end, the voice of Penelope is the voice of a wife reinstated in an idealised marriage based on *homophrosunē*, a wife at once traditional and full of ingenuity and certainly the match of her polytropic husband.

Although the *Odyssey* might be seen to offer a kind of 'comedy of remarriage',[65] it also intermittently posits ominous narrative alternatives – its own shadows. The narrative continues beyond the culminating fairy-tale reunion between a mature bride and bridegroom, as the men of the *oikos* join in a second battle – the three-generational combat against the suitors' relatives. Laertes, reinvigorated, rejoices to fight alongside his son and his son's son, all three 'contending over their courage' (XXIV.514–15). His rehabilitation places the continuity of their lineage (*genos*) in the centre; his pleasure sets civic harmony momentarily aside. Just as the three fighters are proving their mettle as Iliadic heroes who heartlessly dispatch their enemies, Athena (backed by Zeus) intervenes. Her very preclusion of further strife and bloodshed, as she instils peace and tranquillity in Ithaca (XXIV.528–48), highlights the even darker, more violent pathway that the epic chose not to take. The shadow comes from what might have happened in Ithaca, had strife been left for the men to resolve. Another detail that radically qualifies the happy ending is the final voyage foretold by Tiresias (XI.119–34) and retold by Odysseus to Penelope (XXIII.267–81). It evokes a number of variant tales in which Odysseus has additional liaisons and fathers additional offspring: traces of these appear in the *Telegony* and the *Cypria* of the Epic Cycle.[66]

Just as the *Iliad* makes a point of acknowledging the values and domestic spaces war will destroy, as when Andromache laments and Achilles longs for home, so too the *Odyssey* resists a simply triumphant closure. The *oikos* is, after all, a political space in which debate mediates difference. In Ithaca the political economy of sex here has left blood on the floor, carnage in the palace. The epic makes plain that the ongoing sustaining of human arrangements and institutions, such as marriage, will require vigilance and violence as well as *homophrosunē*.

Conclusion

Beyond their provisional endings, the *Iliad* and the *Odyssey* continue to resonate in our classrooms, theatres, memories and political lives. It is not surprising that these epics, and their divergent, powerful articulations of gender and society, should have proved a rich resource for critics, artists and political theorists interested in thinking gender both historically and in its contemporary configurations. It was Simone Weil who famously called the *Iliad* 'the poem of force': the gendered logic of that force is something

[65] The term is from Cavell (1981).
[66] See Sacks (1996).

now drawn into sharp relief. The sexual revolution and the rise of gender studies and social theory – very different phenomena yet not unrelated – have had their impact on our readings of epic: how could they not? Perhaps because these poems are such rich, dialogic and even dialectical works, the *Iliad* and the *Odyssey* have continued to engage the imagination of artists, particularly those interested in the interface of desire, gender, social roles and social narrative. When Louise Glück wished to explore a contemporary American marriage as it fell apart in her book of poems, *Meadowlands*, she turned to Odyssean personae: Penelope, Telemachus, Circe. Odyssean personae have proven to be extremely versatile in their late twentieth-century incarnations: the Cohen brothers' film, 'O Brother, Where Art Thou?', for example, or Derek Walcott's post-colonial epic, *Omeros*. The *Iliad* has long served as an exemplary text on war: it is no accident that scholars of Vietnam and the first Persian Gulf War looked to the ancient epic as a template for their thinking.

The examples could go on, of course. The point we wish to make is this: inasmuch as these are 'our' epics, or 'your' epics, the *Iliad* and the *Odyssey*, and their respective explorations of gender, will continue to influence the ways we imagine ourselves, our pasts, our communities and our gendered fates. Our sense of the difference of epic difference necessarily reveals, among many other things, our sense of the difference gender makes, 'then' and now.[67]

FURTHER READING

On sexuality and gender in ancient Greece, see Arthur (1973) and (1998); Bergren (1983); DuBois (1988); Ferrari (2002); Foucault (1985); Halperin, Winkler and Zeitlin (1990); Hawley and Levick (1995); Hubbard (2003); King (1998); Loraux (1993) and (1995); McClure (2002); Stewart (1997); Winkler (1990).

Among the vast literature on gender theory two seminal works are Butler (1990) and Rubin (1975); see also the essays collected in Rosaldo and Lamphere (1974).

On sexuality and gender in Homeric epic, see Cohen (1995); Doherty (1995); Felson (1994); Foley (2001); Katz (1981) and (1991); Monsacré (1984); Suzuki (1989); and Zeitlin (1996).

Finally, modern/postmodern engagements with this topic include: Bidart (1997); Glück (1996); H. D. (1961); and Walcott (1990), (1993b).

[67] We are profoundly grateful to several colleagues and friends who read earlier versions of this collaborative effort. In particular, Maureen McLane's invaluable critiques helped to shape and sharpen our thinking about gender theory and its applications to the Homeric poems. Seth Schein, as so often, generously provided sound readings of our interpretations of texts he knows so well. We thank, in addition, Erika Thorgerson Hermanowicz, Sara Bershtel and Carolyn Dewald for their timely and constructive suggestions. In addition, each of us thanks her co-author for an invigorating, illuminating, and enjoyable collaboration.

3

THE POET'S CRAFT

8

MATTHEW CLARK

Formulas, metre and type-scenes

Repetition in Homer

The idea that Homer was an oral poet composing in a tradition of formulaic language is one of the seminal concepts of twentieth-century scholarship. The major figure in the development of this idea was Milman Parry (1902–1935), though many other scholars have contributed to the theory. Parry built on earlier work, and it is fair to say that many elements of his theory had been stated previously; what was new was his way of combining these elements – and also the persuasiveness of his research, both in his close analysis of the texts of the Homeric poems and in his fieldwork with living South Slavic oral epic poets.[1] The work of Parry and his followers has been supplemented by analysis of recurring type-scenes, begun by Walter Arend in 1933 and continued by many scholars since.[2] The implications of these ideas have been felt not only in Homeric studies, and not only in classics, but in other fields as well, such as folk-lore, anthropology, medieval studies and the study of orality and literacy.[3] Thus an account of oral-formulaic theory is essential for those interested in understanding modern Homeric scholarship, and also important for those generally interested in the development of twentieth-century thought in the humanities.

Many students of literature, even those who do not read Greek, know that the Homeric epics are very repetitive; they know, for example, that Agamemnon is King of Men (ἄναξ ἀνδρῶν Ἀγαμέμνων, used thirty-seven times in the

[1] Milman Parry's writings have been collected in M. Parry (1971), edited by Adam Parry; I cite Parry's writings by the abbreviations in the Table of Contents to that volume, with page references. Lord (2000) gives an account of fieldwork among oral poets in the former Yugoslavia, with comparison to the Homeric epics.

[2] The basic work on type-scenes is Arend (1933), for discussion of type-scenes see section, 'Composition with type-scenes', below.

[3] For work directly influenced by Parry see among many others Havelock (1982); Foley (1988); Goody (1977) and (2000); Whallon (1969); Magoun (1953); Duggan (1973); McLuhan (1965); Ong (1982).

two epics) and that Achilles is Swift-footed (πόδας ὠκὺς Ἀχιλλεύς, thirty-one times).[4] Repetitions of this kind – a noun with modifiers – are common and important, but they are only part of the story. Close examination of the poems reveals many repetitions of various kinds. If an individual word is repeated, it may always or nearly always occur in the same place in the line; the names of many characters or the words for common objects are repeatedly linked with particular adjectives or modifying expressions; whole lines are repeated; many passages of several lines (such as messages) may be repeated word for word; and frequently recurring situations, such as putting on armour or performing a sacrifice, are described over and over in very similar language.

Some scholars, both ancient and modern, have been troubled by the repetitions in Homer. Often the argument has been made that a repeated line or passage is Homer's original in one place, but in other places it has been inserted by someone after Homer; the job of the editor is to find these illegitimate repetitions and mark them as interpolations or even remove them from the text.[5] Suspicion of repeated passages, however, may raise problems. First, critics often disagree about which passage is the original. Second, scholars will question instances of certain repeated phrases, but other repeated phrases are accepted as necessary to the story or to the business of narration. Third, because repetition is so frequent in the poems, a consistent excision of repeated passages would leave only a skeleton of the epic, with greatly reduced interest and value.

Already by the early twentieth century a number of scholars had rejected the idea that repetition in Homer necessarily implied imitation,[6] but it was not until the work of Milman Parry in the 1920s and 1930s that the role of repetition in the composition of the epics was fully understood. Parry demonstrated that the repeated phrases in the epics are neither faults nor stylistic eccentricities, but essential tools of composition in the tradition of Greek oral epic poetry. This conclusion was then bolstered by fieldwork

[4] The bibliography on repetition in Homer is large. For general discussion, see Calhoun (1933); also Lowenstam (1993).

[5] A few examples must do for many. In the Hellenistic period, Zenodotus questioned 16.141–4 partly on the grounds that it was a copy of 19.388–91; Aristarchus, however, argued the reverse. Leaf (1960) questioned 1.430–92, and made particular note of 1.463, which appeared 'more at home' as III.460. (But see Kirk (1985) 102 who defends the passage against Leaf's critique.) Leaf also questioned the repetition of a famous simile, used to describe Paris (6.506–11) and Hector (15.263–68). For discussion, see Calhoun (1933) 2; also Fenik (1974) 133–5. Repetition is, of course, only one ground for suspicion, and not the most important. See the chapter on the Homeric question in this volume.

[6] See, for example, Scott (1911) 321 and Shewan (1913) 234.

among living oral poets, carried out by Parry and, after Parry's death, by his student, Albert Lord. The result of these studies was a far-reaching change in the way we think of Homeric poetry.[7]

The theory of oral-formulaic composition is complex and still developing; moreover, scholars do not agree about some of the fundamental definitions and concepts of the theory. It is not possible to give a complete account of the theory in this chapter, but the works cited in the footnotes will offer direction to those interested in pursuing the arguments further.

At the centre of Parry's theory is his conception of the formula. Before Parry, the term had been used in a rather vague way, but he offered a clear definition: 'the formula can be defined as an expression regularly used, under the same metrical conditions, to express an essential idea'.[8] Three points stand out in this definition. First, a formula must be 'regularly used': here we see that the theory first derives from repetitions found in the text; Parry later noted that repetition of the individual formulaic expression is not strictly speaking necessary, as we shall see when we look at formula systems. Second, the formulas are defined in terms of their relation to the metrical structure of Homeric verse. This point will be the topic of the next section of this chapter. And third, the formula expresses 'an essential idea'. This point raises the very important question of meaning in oral-formulaic poetry, a topic which we will examine in a later section of this chapter.

Homeric metre

Homeric metre can be analysed from two different perspectives, which can be called *outer metrics* and *inner metrics*.[9] Outer metrics is the traditional scanning of long and short syllables, not unlike the scanning of strong and weak syllables in English verse. But whereas English verse is qualitative – that is, based on patterns of strong and weak syllables – ancient Greek verse is quantitative – what counts is the length of the syllable, rather than stress. A syllable is long if it contains a long vowel or a diphthong, or if the vowel of the syllable is followed by two consonants; otherwise it is short. The vowels eta (η) and omega (ω) are always long; the vowels epsilon (ε) and omicron (ο) are always short (though they may occur in a long syllable, if followed by two consonants); the vowels alpha, iota and upsilon (α, ι and υ)

7 Whether or not the Homeric poems as we have them are the direct product of oral composition is impossible to establish finally to everyone's satisfaction. In my opinion, the debate is not now very fruitful. In any case, the style of the poems is marked by the techniques of oral composition, and we can say with some confidence that the poems are oral-based.

8 Parry (1971) TE: 13.

9 These terms are taken from O'Neill (1942).

may be either long or short; the consonants zeta (ζ), ksi (ξ), and psi (ψ) count as double. Word boundaries are irrelevant; what matters is simply the succession of sounds. Homeric verse also allows a variety of licences, such as the lengthening of a short syllable or the shortening of a long syllable in certain circumstances.[10]

The basic unit of Homeric verse is the line, and the basic structure of all the lines is the same.[11] From the perspective of outer metrics, the Homeric line is divided into six feet. The first five feet are dactyls – a dactyl is one long syllable followed by two short syllables, but the two short syllables can be replaced by a single long syllable; this substitution is not common in the fifth foot. The sixth foot consists of two syllables, the first long, and the second either long or short. A line of this metrical form is called a dactylic hexameter, and schematically it is represented as follows:

— ∪∪ | — ∪∪ | — ∪∪ | — ∪∪ | — ∪∪ | — x

Here is the scansion of the first three lines of the sixth book of the *Odyssey*:

— ∪ ∪ | — ∪ ∪ | — ∪ ∪ | — — | — ∪ ∪ | — x
ὣς ὁ μὲν ἔνθα καθεῦδε πολύτλας δῖος Ὀδυσσεὺς
— — | — ∪ ∪ | — — | — ∪∪ | — ∪∪ | — x
ὕπνωι καὶ καμάτωι ἀρημένος· αὐτὰρ Ἀθήνη
— — | — — | — — | — — | — ∪∪ | — x
βῆ ῥ᾽ ἐς Φαιήκων ἀνδρῶν δῆμόν τε πόλιν τε·
(VI.1–3)

Inner metrics, in contrast to outer metrics, is fundamentally concerned with word boundaries and with the way words and phrases are deployed in the line.[12] From the perspective of inner metrics, the Homeric hexameter strongly tends to divide into four sections, called *cola* (singular: *colon*). These sections are determined by word and sense boundaries within the line. A word boundary within a foot is called a caesura, a word boundary at the end of a foot is called a dieresis (or diaeresis). Technically speaking, every word

[10] For those interested in the details of Homeric scansion there are many good accounts, such as Maas (1962), Raven (1962), West (1982) or (1987).

[11] That is, Homeric verse is stichic; some epics, however, such as Spenser's *Fairy Queen*, are stanzaic rather than stichic.

[12] Among those scholars who have contributed to the analysis of inner metrics are Fränkel (1926), O'Neill (1942), Porter (1951), and Peabody (1975). My account necessarily excludes discussion of different versions of inner metrics. In particular, though there is general agreement about the two B caesuras and the Bucolic Dieresis, there is some disagreement about the first C caesura and the A caesuras. For a good discussion of the topic, see Foley (1990) 73–84.

boundary in the line creates either a caesura, or a dieresis, but some of these breaks are more frequent and more important than others. In particular, the important breaks combine a word break with a break in the sense. What is important, however, is not the breaks, but the word groups; the breaks are simply the points of division. According to the theory of inner metrics, the Homeric hexameter tends to have three breaks, which form four cola.

The B caesura

In about 99 lines out of 100, there is a word break near the middle of the line, either after the first long syllable of the third foot (the B1 or penthemimeral caesura) or after the first short syllable of the third foot (the B2 or trochaic caesura), and this break divides the line into two unequal halves. Very often there is a clear division in the sense and the syntax in the middle of the line; this division is most easily seen when this sense division is strong enough to deserve punctuation:

B1 or penthemimeral caesura:

— ⏑⏑ | — ⏑⏑ | — || — | — — | — ⏑⏑ | — x
αἰνότατε Κρονίδη, ποῖον τὸν μῦθον ἔειπες;
(1.552, etc.)

Most dread son of Kronos, | what sort of word have you spoken?

B2 or trochaic caesura:

— ⏑ ⏑ | — ⏑⏑ | — ⏑ || ⏑ | — ⏑⏑ | — ⏑⏑ | — x
καὶ γὰρ ἐγὼ θεός εἰμι, γένος δέ μοι ἔνθεν ὅθεν σοί
(4.58)

For I am likewise a god, | and my descent is even what yours is

Even when there is no punctuation, it is often possible to feel a division in the sense:[13]

— ⏑⏑ | — ⏑ ⏑ | — || ⏑ ⏑ | — — | — ⏑ ⏑ | — x
τὸν δ' ἀπαμειβόμενος προσέφη κρείων Ἀγαμέμνων
(1.130)

And him answering | lordly Agamemnon spoke

[13] Greek allows the object and main verb of the sentence to be in the first half of the line, while the subject is in the second half; my translations rather awkwardly attempt to keep this order to show the structure of the line.

— — | — ∪ ∪ | — ∪ ‖ ∪ | — | — ∪ ∪ | — x
τὸν δ' ἠμείβετ' ἔπειτα ποδάρκης δῖος Ἀχιλλεύς
(I.121)

And him answered then | swift-footed brilliant Achilles

The C caesura and dieresis

In addition to this break at the middle of the line, in about nine lines out of ten there is a word break either after the first long syllable of the fourth foot (the C1 or hephthemimeral caesura) or between the end of the fourth and the beginning of the fifth foot (the C2 or bucolic dieresis):

C1 or hephthemimeral caesura:

— ∪ ∪ | — ∪∪ | — ∪ ∪ | — ‖ — | — ∪ ∪ | — x
τὸν δ' ἀπαμειβόμενος προσέφη πολύμητις Ὀδυσσεύς
(VIII.412, etc.)

And him answering spoke | Odysseus of many counsels

C2 (or bucolic dieresis):

— — | — — | — ∪ ∪ | — ∪∪ ‖ — ∪ ∪ | — x
ὣς εἰπὼν δμώεσσιν ἐκέκλετο, τοὶ δ' ἐπίθοντο
(VI.71)

Having spoken thus, she commanded the maids, | and they obeyed her.

The A caesura

Some scholars (but not all) have also postulated a break near the beginning of the line, either between the end of the first foot and the beginning of the second (the A1 dieresis) or after the first long syllable of the second foot (the A2 caesura):[14]

A1 dieresis:

— ∪ ∪ ‖ — ∪ ∪ | — — | — — | — ∪ ∪ | — x
ἀλλὰ δότ', ἀμφίπολοι, ξείνῳ βρῶσίν τε πόσιν τε
(VI.209)

But give, | servant maids, to the stranger food and drink

[14] Kirk (1966) 103 argues that the A caesura 'is due primarily to the average lengths of Greek words available in the poetical vocabulary'; one must also take into account the effect of run-over enjambement, as I discuss below.

A2 caesura:

— — | — || ⏑ ⏑ | — — | — ⏑ ⏑ | —⏑⏑ | — x
Ἀρήτη, θύγατερ Ῥηξήνορος ἀντιθέοιο
(VII.146)

Arete, | daughter of godlike Rhexenor

Most lines have more than one break, and many have all three, as in the following lines:

— ⏑ ⏑ ||— — | — ⏑ || ⏑ | — || ⏑⏑ | —⏑ ⏑ | — x
ἀλλ᾽ ὁ μὲν ἤδη κηρὶ || δαμεὶς Ἄϊδόσδε βεβήκει,
— ⏑⏑ | —|| ⏑ ⏑ | — ⏑ || ⏑ | — ⏑ ⏑ || — ⏑⏑ | — x
Ἀλκίνοος δὲ τότ᾽ ἦρχε, θεῶν ἄπο μήδεα εἰδώς.
(VI.11–12)

But he [Nausithous] | already by fate | mastered | to Hades went,
Alcinous | then ruled | from the gods | having counsels.

According to this account of inner metrics, the Homeric hexameter is composed of the following cola, depending on exactly where the divisions fall:

1.	2.	3.	4.
— ⏑⏑	⏑⏑ —	⏑ —	— ⏑⏑ | — x
— ⏑⏑ —	⏑⏑ — ⏑	⏑⏑ —	⏑⏑ — ⏑⏑ | — x
	— ⏑⏑ —	⏑ — ⏑⏑	
	— ⏑⏑ — ⏑	⏑⏑ — ⏑⏑	

Metre and formulas

At this point the connection between inner metrics and formulaic composition becomes clear: there is a strong tendency for the repeated words and phrases in Homeric verse to take just these metrical forms and to fall in just these positions in the line.[15] If we examine combinations of a name and an adjective or epithet – these were analysed in Parry's first publication – we find that these formulas fall into the cola of the hexameter. One group consists of name and epithet formulas which extend from the B2 caesura to the end of the line: (with the form ⏑ — ⏑⏑ — ⏑⏑ | — x: e.g. ποδάρκης δῖος Ἀχιλλεύς, θεὰ γλαυκῶπις Ἀθήνη, and fourteen more); another group consists of name and epithet formulas which extend from the C1 caesura to the end of the line (with the form ⏑⏑ – ⏑⏑ – x: e.g. κρείων Ἀγαμέμνων, πολύμητις Ὀδυσσεύς, and

[15] This point was already implicit in Parry's initial definition of the formula, quoted above, which requires that the formular phrases be used 'under the same metrical conditions'.

fifteen more) and so on. These naming formulas can then be combined with predicate formulas which fill the rest of the verse. For example, five times in the epics we find the naming formula 'Agamemnon, king of men' (ἄναξ ἀνδρῶν Ἀγαμέμνων) in this whole line formula:

τὸν [or τὴν] δ' αὖτε προσέειπε ἄναξ ἀνδρῶν Ἀγαμέμνων

and him [or her] in turn answered Agamemnon, king of men

Here the predicate takes up the first half of the line, up to the B2 caesura, and the naming formula ἄναξ ἀνδρῶν Ἀγαμέμνων runs from the B2 caesura to the end of the line. The same predicate can then be combined with any naming formula of the appropriate metrical shape. Thus the following line, identical except for the naming formula, is found eight times in the epics:

τὸν [or τὴν] δ' αὖτε προσέειπε πολύτλας δῖος 'Οδυσσεύς

and him [or her] in turn answered much-suffering brilliant Odysseus

And there are twenty-four additional naming formulas which appear with this same predicate, and similar patterns can be found for other predicates and other naming formulas.[16]

Thus these formulas conform to the colon structure of inner metrics. The complications of oral compositions would be impossible if the formulas had to fit randomly varying parts of the line; but because the line tends to fall into regular parts, formulas are needed to fit only those metrical shapes. Moreover, the systems of name and epithet formulas are characterised by extension (all or almost all needed formulas are found) and thrift (there is rarely more than one metrically equivalent formula for a particular name).[17] The system is efficient and economical.

Moreover, these naming-formulas form systems: the system of all naming formulas from the B2 to the end of the line, the system of all naming formulas beginning at the bucolic dieresis, and so on. It is not the individual repeated phrase which is fundamental, but rather the system of related formulas.[18] Even a phrase which is found only once in the epics can be considered a formula if it belongs to a system: the phrase Διώνη, δῖα θεάων occurs only once (τὴν δ' ἠμείβετ' ἔπειτα Διώνη, δῖα θεάων, 5.381), but it counts as a formula

[16] See the tables at Parry (1971) TE: 10 and TE: 11 for complete details.

[17] See, for example, the list in Parry (1971) HS: 277–8, fn. 2.

[18] Parry's emphasis on the role of system is consistent with developments at that time in linguistics; see, for example, Saussure (1969). It might be useful to keep the word *formula* for phrases which are in fact repeated, and the word *formulaic* for phrases which are formed by analogy to formulas or which fit into formula systems, but scholars have not been consistent in their use of these terms.

because it belongs to the system of name and epithet formulas extending from the B2 caesura to the end of the line, along with ποδάρκης δῖος Ἀχιλλεύς, θεὰ γλαυκῶπις Ἀθήνη, etc.

Some scholars have feared that the implication of this account of formulaic composition amounts to a severe limitation on what the poet can choose to say, if the poet is bound to use only those formulas which fit the metrical cola of the hexameter. A more extended discussion of meaning in the epics follows in a later section of this chapter, but a few comments are in place here.

On the one hand, it is probably true that once the metrical form of the hexameter became firmly established, it did to some extent control the phrases which could be used; but this kind of constraint occurs in almost all forms of art, and in principle it need be of no great concern. On the other hand, it is possible that the hexameter itself was gradually formed through the repetition of certain traditionally valued phrases.[19] Such repeated formulas are most likely to have occurred in ritual contexts, and ritual language tends to be formulaic. As John D. Niles points out

> Like the prayers and incantations of ritual, the voiced speech of myth and heroic poetry is linguistically distinguishable from ordinary language by its forceful rhythm, its formulaic or archaic diction, its use of rhetorical parallelism, antithesis or other special syntactic features, its sheer amplitude (including a degree of pleonasm or redundancy that would be excruciating in ordinary speech), and its special vocal range or timbre.[20]

If the phraseology of the epics is to some extent rooted in tradition, the meanings of the epics are also traditional (though tradition need not be static or unchanging, either in form or in meaning).

This account of formulaic composition is powerful and persuasive, and without doubt it accounts for many features of the Homeric epics. It is, however, neither complete nor completely correct, and it must be modified in several ways. First, not all lines fall naturally into four sections; even the central caesura can be bridged, as in 9.145: Χρυσόθεμις καὶ Λαοδίκη καὶ

[19] See Nagy (1998b) 500: 'From a diachronic point of view meter is a result rather than a cause of traditional phraseology . . . traditional phraseology contains rhythms that evolve into meters (diachronic perspective), and meters contain traditional phraseology that we call formulas (synchronic perspective). Some of these formulas may preserve rhythmical patterns that had shaped the meters that now contain the formulas.' See also Peabody (1975) 312–13.

[20] Niles (1999) 122. For discussion of Homeric epic as ritual, see Sale (2001) 75–7 and Seaford (1994). Bertolín Cebrián (forthcoming) argues that Greek epic poetry derives from funerary ritual. For discussion of formulaic composition and ritual language in another tradition, see the articles in Fox (1988).

Ἰφιάνασσα ('Chrysothemis and Laodice and Iphianassa'). And in some lines a break is possible, but seems unnatural, as in VI.101, τῇσι δὲ Ναυσικάα λευκώλενος ἤρχετο μολπῆς ('and white-armed Nausicaa led the dance for them'), where the central caesura divides the formula Ναυσικάα λευκώλενος (cf. VI.186, VI.251, VII.12, VII.233, VII.335, XI.335).

Second, this account works best for name and epithet formulas, but there are formulas of many other kinds: common noun and adjective phrases (such as ὑγρὸν ἔλαιον, 'fluid oil', 23.281, VI.79, etc.), prepositional phrases (such as παρὰ θῖνα, 'beside the shore', 1.34, etc.), as well as complete clauses and sentences. As one investigates other kinds of formulas, it becomes clear that they do not all behave quite the way the name and epithet formulas do. In particular, many of these formulas can be found in more than one metrical position in the line. Thus the phrase ἐπὶ θῖνα θαλασσης is found the end of the line, as in

> Τηλέμαχος δ' ἀπάνευθεν ἰὼν ἐπὶ θῖνα θαλασσης
> (II.260)
>
> And Telemachus going apart along the shore of the sea[21]

but also in the middle of the line, as in

> οἳ δὲ Πύλον, Νηλῆος ἐυκτίμενον πτολίεθρον,
> ἷξον· τοὶ δ' ἐπὶ θινὶ θαλάσσης ἱερὰ ῥέζον
> (III.4–5)
>
> They to Pylos, Neleus' well-built city,
> came; and the people along the shore of the sea were making sacrifice[22]

If the compositional techniques typical of the name and epithet formulas were typical of Homeric style as a whole, the oral-formulaic manner of composition would be a mechanical process of simply fitting pre-existing phrases into predetermined slots in the line. But in fact Homeric style is quite flexible; it allows for the rearrangement of the word-order in a formula, the separation of the words, and the expansion of a formula by the addition of other terms.[23]

[21] Compare VI.236, X.154, X.402, X.407=XII.367, X.569, XI.75, XIII.65, XV.205, XVI.358.

[22] Compare also IV.432, XIV.347.

[23] See Hainsworth (1968) 38–9 and *passim* for these and other aspects of the flexibility of the Homeric formula. Some scholars, such as Austin and Shive, have thought that this flexibility counts as a fatal counter-objection to the whole theory; in my opinion, however, their studies are useful additions to our knowledge of the techniques of oral composition.

Definitions of the formula

As the complexity and flexibility of Homeric composition became more evident, it became necessary to re-examine the concept of the formula.[24] A first view of the formula might suggest that the formula is simply like a compound word or an idiom: this conception lies behind the frequent statements that the oral poet composes with formulas in the way a literate poet composes with words. This set-phrase model of the formula does not easily explain the systems of related formulas, such as the name and epithet systems. These formulas seem to be composite – composed of slots which can be filled by any appropriate member of the proper grammatical and metrical class. A system of this kind is sometimes called a slot-class or chain-and-choice grammar. This model accounts for name and epithet formula and also for some whole-line formulas, such as speech introductions.

A slot-class system, however, does not easily account for the flexibility of formulas in Homeric verse. In order to explain these, we must assume that the words of the formula are somehow associated in the mind of the poet without a predetermined metrical shape or position. This model of the formula is in some ways similar to a generative grammar; it assumes a level of deep structure, where the formulas are stored in an abstract form, and then a surface level, where they are variously deployed as the context of the verse demands.[25] This model moves away from a description of the text towards an attempt to understand the cognitive psychology of the poet.

Some recent accounts of Homeric composition attempt to define the formula by function, rather than structure, or even to bypass the formula entirely.[26] According to one such model, the words in a line are positioned within the metrical scheme of the hexameter through a sort of hierarchy of selection: the most important elements find their place in the line first, and then other elements needed to complete the meaning of the line are chosen to fit the metrical positions not yet filled.[27] By moving away from exclusive attention on the formula, which is only one part of Homeric technique, these models encourage a broader understanding of oral composition;

[24] For a fuller discussion of the models of the formula, see Clark (1997) 5–19; for a good general bibliography on the formula, see Edwards (1986) and (1988).

[25] See Russo (1963), Nagler (1967), and Hainsworth (1968) for analyses leading towards a generative model of the formula.

[26] See Bakker (1988) 189: 'Phrases are not to be called formulas because of what they are but because of what their function is. Accordingly there is no qualitative difference between formular and non-formular language use.'

[27] See Visser (1988); also Bakker and Fabricotti (1991); Bakker (1997).

nonetheless, the formulas, however they are defined, remain an important part of Homeric style.

These different models seem to fit different aspects of Homeric composition; perhaps each is partly true. As our understanding of oral-formulaic composition improves, it may be necessary to develop new models in addition to these.

Meaning in formulaic composition

One of the oldest and most persistent problems in Homeric criticism is the question of the meaning of the epithets. Ancient scholars had noted that many of the epithets seem irrelevant to their context, and some even seem to be misapplied. Thus, in *Odyssey* VI the dirty laundry which Nausikaa takes to wash is 'glossy' (σιγαλόεντα, 26) and 'shining' (φαεινήν, 74); in *Odyssey* XVIII the mother of the beggar Iros is 'queenly' (5–6), and so on. Various strategies have been developed to resolve these problems: in some cases the text of the passage has been questioned; or it has been suggested that an epithet may be correct in general even if it is inappropriate in the specific context; sometimes a seemingly inappropriate epithet may be used for wit; the epithet may in fact be appropriate if the passage is interpreted correctly; the meaning of the epithet may have been misunderstood; and last, the epithet may be ornamental, that is, it may be used not because of its meaning but because it is metrically useful for the construction of the verse.[28]

The last of these strategies (which can be traced as far back as Aristarchus) fits particularly well with Parry's concept of formulaic composition.[29] As he says, the function of the fixed epithet is simply to accommodate a particular name to a particular metrical position in the line. When we see, for example, that the epithet δῖος is applied to thirty-two different heroes (Parry (1971) 146–7) we must conclude that this epithet has at best only a very general meaning, and perhaps it has very little meaning at all. Furthermore, if Odysseus is πολύτλας δῖος Ὀδυσσεύς in one line and πολύμητις Ὀδυσσεύς in another, the reason for the difference is not to be found in the meaning of the passages, but only their metrical structure. Parry concluded that some epithets, at least, were only ornamental; that is, such epithets were used simply to accommodate a noun to the metrical requirements of the verse,

[28] This list is adapted from Lowenstam (1993) 14–17.

[29] See 'The meaning of the epithet in epic poetry', 118–72; also 'About winged words', 414–18, both in Parry (1971).

and therefore these epithets really had no meaning. Thus the phrase θεὰ γλαυκῶπις Ἀθήνη really means no more than 'Athena'.[30]

This explanation accounts for certain words and phrases which seem odd or inappropriate. One of the most famous examples of an inappropriate epithet comes from the first book of the *Odyssey*, when Zeus is talking about Aegisthus, the seducer of Clytemnestra:

> μνήσατο γὰρ κατὰ θυμὸν ἀμύμονος Αἰγίσθοιο (I.29)
>
> For he was thinking in his heart of blameless Aegisthus.

If the word ἀμύμων means 'blameless', as it is often taken, it is applied to Aegisthus most inappropriately. But if the epithet is purely ornamental, that is, if it has only a metrical function, with no particular meaning, if ἀμύμονος Αἰγίσθοιο means only 'Aegisthus', then the problem disappears.[31]

Although Parry's account of ornamental epithets seemed to solve this problem and others like it, it did so at a great cost, a cost which not all critics have been willing to pay. In this understanding of oral poetics, the epithets were merely metrical filler, and the poet was merely the slave of his formulas. Some critics simply concluded that the oral-formulaic theory had nothing to offer the interpretation of the epics.[32] Some scholars have wanted to save the literary interpretation of the poems by arguing that the importance of the formulas has been much exaggerated.[33]

[30] See Parry (1971) 272 for this example. Parry makes the point repeatedly; see also Parry (1971) 266 where he says that an ornamental epithet 'has no bearing on the idea of the sentence'. Nor is this argument restricted to simple noun and epithet formulas: 'The essential part of the idea is that which remains after one has counted out everything in the expression which is purely for the sake of style. Thus, the essential idea in the word group ἦμος δ' ἠριγένεια φάνη ῥοδοδάκτυλος Ἠώς is 'when it was morning. . . .' (Parry (1971) 272). But Parry does not suggest that all epithets are ornamental: see Parry (1971) 153–65. Sale (2001) 65 argues that the concept of the formula as expressing an 'essential idea' should be replaced by the concept of the 'context free' formula.

[31] Compare the position and function of the word at 1.423; 2.674; 5.247; 6.155; 11.835; 20.236; IV.187; XIII.117.

[32] According to Griffin (1980) xiii–xiv, 'the whole conception of oral poetry as in its nature quite different from written poetry is coming to seem less and less tenable'; Homeric criticism has to 'go on with aesthetic methods not essentially or radically new'.

[33] Thus, according to Austin (1975) 24, 'We can see that the name-epithet formulas are not as essential as Parry believed, nor as useful, and that their selection is governed by various contextual forces.' See also Shive (1987) 17, 'Homer's repetitions have received much attention; failure to repeat is also Homeric and deserves much attention.' Thus the original problem of repetition has oddly become turned on its head: what needs to be explained now is lack of repetition.

Some other scholars grant the validity of Parry's formulaic analyses but attempt to show that some seemingly inappropriate epithets have simply been misunderstood. Thus Anne Amory Parry argued that the epithet ἀμύμων did not in fact mean 'blameless', but rather 'handsome', and by extension 'strong' and 'excellent' in general; the epithet applied to Aegisthus is not inappropriate; rather, it 'implies one cause of Aegisthus' misfortunes'.[34]

More recently, some scholars have argued that a proper understanding of oral poetics does not detract from the meaning of the poems but in fact adds to it. This approach develops the idea, already suggested in ancient criticism, that the meaning of a word may refer beyond its context to the rest of the poem or even to the rest of the epic tradition. Thus the Homeric epics make no direct reference to the myth of succession of supreme sky-gods (as found, for example, in Hesiod's *Theogony*), but the phrase 'Zeus, son of Kronos' implies that the myth was available to the Homeric audience and could be activated by any appropriate context.[35] Our interpretations should attempt to revive the traditional associations of the epithets and of other allusions in the poems. In some way this model is like the Saussurian view of language: the tradition is *langue*, while each performance within the tradition is *parole*; thus at the level of tradition, everything is formulaic, but at the level of performance, everything is individual. This approach to meaning in Homer seems to be one of the most promising developments in recent Homeric criticism.[36]

Composition beyond the hexameter

The colon theory of the formula suggests that formulas are parts of lines or at most a whole-line. Many lines in the epics can be seen as combinations of colon-length formulas, and many of these whole lines are themselves repeated; these lines, if they are repeated often enough, may have been thought of as unitary formulas, rather than as combinations of shorter

[34] See Anne Amory Parry (1973) 112, 124 and *passim*. Lowenstam (1993) 48–51 argues that the epithet means 'cunning' or 'crafty'; he also considers other examples of seemingly inappropriate epithets.

[35] See Slatkin (1991) 14 for this example. According to Slatkin (1991) xv, 'The poet, it appears, constructs his narrative using myths that are not related in full, but only in part . . . For an audience that knows the mythological range of each character, divine or human – not only through this epic song but through other songs, epic and non-epic – the poet does not spell out the myth in its entirety but locates a character within it through allusion or oblique reference.'

[36] In addition to Slatkin (1991), see also Foley (1991) and Nagy (1992a). See Nagy (1979) for important formulations of this approach to Homeric interpretation.

formulas. Sometimes several whole-line formulas will follow each other in succession, in what can be called a chain of formulas.[37] Parry argued that 'the easiest formula for the oral poet to handle is that which is both a whole sentence and a whole verse', and he concludes that 'the art of the oral poet is largely that of grouping together whole fixed verses'.[38] As a consequence, Parry argues, oral epic verse, both Homeric and South Slavic, has a strong tendency to end-stopped lines, with very little enjambement.

Homeric style does, however, allow for some enjambement, and these enjambements must be explained. Often an enjambed line in the epics is simply added on to a whole-line which would have been complete without the addition. At the beginning of the *Iliad*, for example, the adjective οὐλομένην ('destructive') merely adds to a sentence which is complete in itself:

> μῆνιν ἄειδε, θεά, Πηληϊάδεω Ἀχιλῆος
> **οὐλομένην**, ἣ μυρί' Ἀχαιοῖς ἄλγε' ἔθηκεν,
> (1.1–2)
>
> Sing, goddess, the anger of Peleus' son Achilles,
> destructive [anger], which brought myriad pains to the Achaeans,

Enjambement of this kind, adding enjambement, is very common in Homeric verse.[39] But sometimes an enjambed line is required to complete the sense of the preceding line:

> ἦ γάρ μ' Ἀτρεΐδης εὐρὺ κρείων Ἀγαμέμνων
> **ἠτίμησεν**, ἑλὼν γὰρ ἔχει γέρας αὐτὸς ἀπούρας.
> (1.355–6)
>
> For me the son of Atreus, wide ruling Agamemnon,
> dishonoured; for he took away my prize and keeps her.

Here the verb in the second line is needed to complete the grammar of the clause which begins in the first line. This kind of enjambement – necessary enjambement – is relatively rare in Homer, compared to poets such as Apollonius or Virgil. According to Parry, adding enjambement is more common in Homeric style because it is easy for an oral poet, while necessary enjambement is less common because it is hard: the oral poet 'must order his

[37] See, e.g. XXI.269–76, for a passage of eight whole-line formulas.

[38] Both of these statements are in Parry (1971) WF: 389. See also Nagy (1990) 27; Kirk (1966) 106; Peabody (1975) 4 and Higbie (1990) 67 and 76.

[39] I follow the terminology of Higbie (1990), which is now the standard work on the subject. For statistics comparing Homeric practice with that of Apollonius or Virgil, see Higbie (1990) 82.

words in such a way that they leave him much freedom to end the sentence or draw it out as the story and the needs of the verse demand'.[40]

Most discussions of oral composition have concentrated on the combination of formulas within the line or the concatenation of whole-line formulas. The Homeric style, however, also includes formulaic associations beyond the boundaries of the line. In some passages, for example, the meaning of a line is completed in the next line by a single word or short phrase in adding or necessary enjambement; these short enjambements are called 'runovers'.[41] As it happens, a runover often shows an association either with the words in the previous line, to which it is grammatically linked, or to the following words in its own line, with which it has no grammatical connection. In the following passages, for example, the runover verb τιμήσηις/τιμήσηι in the second line is associated both with the phrase ὡς Ἀχιλῆα in the preceding line and also with the phrase ὀλέσηις/ὀλέσηι δὲ πολὺς ἐπὶ νηυσὶν Ἀχαιῶν in its own line:

τῆι σ' ὀΐω κατανεῦσαι ἐτήτυμον, ὡς Ἀχιλῆα
τιμήσηις, ὀλέσηις δὲ πολὺς ἐπὶ νηυσὶν Ἀχαιῶν.
(1.558–59)

I think you bowed your head in assent that Achilles
you would honour, and destroy many beside the Achaean ships.

ἀλλ' ὅ γε μερμήριζε κατὰ φρένα, ὡς Ἀχιλῆα
τιμήσηι, ὀλέσηι δὲ πολὺς ἐπὶ νηυσὶν Ἀχαιῶν.
(2.3–4)

But he was pondering in his heart how Achilles
he would honour, and destroy many beside the Achaean ships.

This use of runover enjambement contributes to rhythmic variety in the construction of larger formulaic passages. The following passage, found twice in the *Odyssey*, has a mixture of end-stopped lines and enjambements:

ὅσσοι γὰρ νήσοισιν ἐπικρατέουσιν ἄριστοι,
Δουλιχίωι τε Σάμηι τε καὶ ὑλήεντι Ζακύνθωι,
ἠδ' ὅσσοι κραναὴν Ἰθάκην κάτα κοιρανέουσι,
τόσσοι μητέρ' ἐμὴν μνῶνται, τρύχουσι δὲ οἶκον.
ἡ δ' οὔτ' ἀρνεῖται στυγερὸν γάμον οὔτε τελευτὴν

[40] Parry (1987) DE: 261; see also Lord (1948). For a dissenting account of Homeric enjambement, see Friedrich (2000).

[41] See, for example, Bassett (1926). Corresponding to runovers we find anticipations, when a sentence begins towards the end of the line (often at the bucolic dieresis) and continues into the next line. For discussion of anticipations, see Clark (1997) 107–58.

ποιῆσαι δύναται· τοὶ δὲ φθινύθουσιν ἔδοντες
οἶκον ἐμόν· τάχα δή με διαρραίσουσι καὶ αὐτόν.
(I.245–51 = XVI.122–8)

For all the greatest men who have the power in the islands,
in Doulichion and Same and in wooded Zacynthus,
and all who rule throughout rocky Ithaca,
all these are wooing my mother, and they are consuming my household.
And she does not refuse the hateful marriage nor an end
is she able to make, and they eat and waste
my house; soon they will break me myself to pieces.

Sometimes, as in this example, the runovers and anticipations are embedded in a passage which is in effect a compositional unit (as here the whole passage can be considered a repeated formula). But enjambements can also be used as hooks to connect passages. Thus the runover ἔξοχον ἡρώων ('conspicuous among heroes') is found twice in Book 18 of the *Iliad:*

ὤι μοι ἐγὼ δειλή, ὤι μοι δυσαριστοτόκεια,
ἥ τ' ἐπεὶ ἂρ τέκον υἱὸν ἀμύμονά τε κρατερόν τε,
ἔξοχον ἡρώων, ὃ δ' ἀνέδραμεν ἔρνεϊ ἶσος·
(18.54–6)

Ah me, my sorrow, ah the bitterness of this best of child-bearing,
since I gave birth to a son without fault and powerful,
conspicuous among heroes; and he shot up like a young tree;

υἱὸν ἐπεί μοι δῶκε γενέσθαί τε τραφέμεν τε
ἔξοχον ἡρώων, ὃ δ' ἀνέδραμεν ἔρνεϊ ἶσος·
(18.436–7)

since he gave to me a son to bear and to raise up,
conspicuous among heroes; and he shot up like a young tree;

The two passages then continue identically for six more lines; thus the runover has hooked two different beginnings onto a chain of formulas.

Runovers and anticipations can be used in a variety of ways in the construction of long passages: they can simply be embedded within a more or less stable chain of formulas (as in I.245–51 = XVI.122–8); they can be used as hooks (as in 18.54–6 and 18.436–7); in addition, they can be used in the construction of long passages, up to fifty lines or more, through the combination of formulaic sequences, sometimes one directly after another, sometimes with a line or more connecting formulaic sequences to each other.[42] Only

[42] For analysis of long sequences, see Clark (1997) 189–211.

through a close analysis of long passages is it possible to appreciate the power and flexibility of the Homeric technique of formulaic composition.

Composition with type-scenes

The techniques of oral composition are not restricted to the use of formulas within the line, or even to the construction of longer sequences by adding formulas into blocks and chains. One of the most important aspects of the Homeric epics is the use of type-scenes; that is, recurring situations which are narrated according to a more or less fixed pattern.[43] For example, four times in the *Iliad* we find an extended description of a warrior's arming himself (Paris, 3.328–38; Agamemnon, 11.15–44; Patroclus, 16.130–54; Achilles, 19.364–424).[44] None of these is exactly like any of the others, and although they include much formulaic repetition, they do not feature the sort of exact repetition that we find, for example, in the repeated description of Penelope's trick of the loom (II.93, XXIV.128). Nonetheless, they all clearly have the same structure, and many of the same formulaic elements are used in their construction.[45]

Each scene begins with a line or two of introduction (3.328–9, 11.15–16, 16.130, 19.364), followed by a three-line description of the greaves and breastplate (3.330–2 = 11.17–19 = 16.131–3 = 19.369–71). In three of the four scenes, there follows an explanatory account of the breastplate (3.333, 11.20–8, 16.134), but in the fourth this explanation is missing: there is no need here to explain how Achilles got his arms. All four scenes now move on to the sword (ἀμφὶ δ' ἄρ ὤμοισιν βάλετο ξίφος: 'and around his shoulders he threw a sword' in 3.334, 11.29, 16.135 and 19.372). Three of the scenes then complete the line with a descriptive adjective and then continue with a second adjective in runover enjambement in the next line (ἀργυρόηλον/χάλκεον 'with silver nails/bronze'); at 11.29, however, a new clause beginning at the bucolic dieresis gives a somewhat expanded description of the sword

43 The foundational work on type-scenes is Arend (1933); Arend has been called the Milman Parry of the type-scene (see Edwards (1975) 52). Lord (1951) and (2000) calls the recurrent scenes in oral epic 'themes', but since the word 'theme' has other meanings, the terms 'type-scene' or 'typical scene' are better. For discussion of terminological difficulties, see Edwards (1975) 52.

44 For discussion of arming scenes, see Arend (1933) 92–7, Armstrong (1958), Russo (1968) 282–5 and Hainsworth (1993) 215–23.

45 Armstrong (1958) 344. Arend (1933) 93 argues that this sequence is simply realistic, but other typical scenes show the same reliance on a consistent sequence of events. Minchin (2001) argues that type-scenes are like the 'scripts' or 'schemas' of cognitive psychology; since scripts are typically stored as sequences, so too would type-scenes.

(11.29–31). In all four passages, the shield is described next; three of the four have the same wording here (3.334–5 = 16.135–6 = 19.372–3), but the expanded description of the sword at 11.29–31 then leads to a different description of the shield. Moreover, the description of Achilles' shield begins with the formula found in Books 3 and 16, but there follows an elaborate continuation, including a simile (19.374–80). The helmet comes next; three of the four passages continue with a two-line formula (3. 336–7 = 11.41–2 = 16.137–8), but Achilles' helmet is also described with more detail. The final element of these arming scenes is the spear: Paris picks up a single spear that fits his grip (3.338), Agamemnon picks up two spears, and the light from their bronze heads flashes to heaven (11.43–4); Patroclus picks up two spears that fit his grip, but he does not use Achilles' spear, which only Achilles could wield (16.139–44); this, however, is the spear with which Achilles arms himself (19.387–91; note that 16.141–4 = 19.388–91).[46]

The sequence of arming in each scene is the same – greaves, breastplate, sword, shield, helmet and spear – but each scene has been developed in its own way. It is surely meaningful that Patroclus cannot wield Achilles' spear; and the great development of Achilles' arming is certainly appropriate to the great hero of the story. The particularities of the scenes are as important as the similarity of their overall structure. The technique of the type-scene offers the poet a basic scaffolding, but it also allows the poet to adapt each scene for specific purposes.[47]

Arend's original study of type-scenes included discussion of arrivals, sacrifice and meals, journeys by ship and chariot, arming and dressing, sleep, pondering before a decision, assembly, oaths and bathing. Mark Edwards has divided type-scenes into five broad categories (battle, social intercourse, travel, ritual, speeches and deliberation) with many subcategories. Ritual, for example, includes sacrifice, prayer, funeral rites, omens, libation, oath-taking and purification. Clearly type-scenes make up a large part of the Homeric narratives.[48]

There is some debate about exactly what constitutes a type-scene; Edwards includes battle scenes in his list of type-scenes, but others find them too

[46] The scenes in Books 16 and 19 continue with the preparation of the chariot, a new type-scene.

[47] These comments perhaps privilege the particular written text which has been preserved; a tradition of oral performance would be likely to include various versions of these scenes, and these versions might present different details in different performances.

[48] See the bibliographic discussion in Edwards (1992) for the division into broad categories. Edwards (1980) 1 argues that the narrative of the epics 'is carried forward almost entirely by a succession of type-scenes, with only occasional use of short passages of description, similes, or apostrophes by the poet'. He then illustrates this claim by dividing almost the whole of *Iliad* 1 into type-scenes.

various to be included in the category.[49] In any case, Homeric battles clearly show a high degree of structure; for example, five times in the *Iliad* we find a battle with the following pattern: '(1) a Trojan sees an enemy wreaking havoc among his men; (2) he goes to a friend and suggests they make a joint attack; (3) the second Trojan agrees and they charge; (4) the Greek, either alone or with a friend, sees them coming, expresses fear, but holds his ground just the same; (5) he may call for help; (6) the Trojans are beaten off.'[50] The battle scenes are complex and various, but analysis shows clear patterns of structure; these patterns would have been very useful for an oral poet.[51]

The search for patterns in the Homeric epics extends beyond formulas and beyond type-scenes to larger narrative components. Thus Fenik argues that certain interpretive problems about the role of Arete in Book VII of the *Odyssey* can be clarified by a comparison with similar incidents from other parts of the story.[52] In addition, Fenik notes that composition of doublets is characteristic of the *Odyssey*; these include doublets within a single passage or episode, doublets of episodes or situations, and character doublets.

More recently, Bruce Louden has argued that the overall plot of the *Odyssey* is composed of an extended narrative pattern which occurs three times in the poem, in Aeaea, in Phaeacia, and in Ithaca. Odysseus arrives at an island. A divine helper appears, advising him to approach a powerful female figure. This female figure imposes a test, which Odysseus passes. Odysseus is now offered sexual union and/or marriage with the female. However, a band of young men abuse Odysseus and violate a divine interdiction. The band's consequent death is demanded by a wrathful god, but a divine consultation limits the extent of death and destruction.[53] Louden's structural description leads to interpretation; he argues, for example, that Elpenor in the Aeaean sequence is parallel to Leodes in the Ithacan sequence, and therefore 'Elpenor should no longer be seen as an "addition" to or "intrusion" upon the poem'. On the other hand, Louden's analysis emphasises the differences between Circe and Calypso, 'characters often seen as virtually indistinguishable'.[54]

Large-scale structural patterns have been found in the *Iliad* as well. According to Steven Lowenstam, for example, 'Agamemnon's refusal of a

[49] Fenik (1968) 2 says that battle scenes are among those 'which do not fall into the categories of type scenes and themes and which do not therefore bear any immediate or obvious similarity to dictional formulae in structure or in use'.

[50] Fenik (1968) 3; see also Foley (1990) 241.

[51] See Fenik (1968) 229–30.

[52] See Fenik (1974) 6–7 and 48–53 for general discussion of the use of parallel passages in interpreting Homer. Part 1 of Fenik (1974) is devoted to discussion of the role of Arete in particular; part 2 is devoted to a more general discussion of doublets in the *Odyssey*.

[53] This summary is adapted from Louden (1999) 2.

[54] The citations are from Louden (1999) 130 and 132.

ransom in Book 1 will be seen to foreshadow the similar action of Achilleus in Book 9, but the depiction of a legal case on Achilleus' shield in Book 18 will permit us to judge the propriety of both refusals.' In general, 'particular scenes inform upon each other, not solely in a linear progression but in a retroactive fashion. That is, scenes in one part of the poem are constantly affecting the reading of scenes in other parts.'[55]

Patterns at this level can be found in most long narratives, oral, oral-based or written. In *The Portrait of a Lady*, for example, Henry James has constructed a plot in which the heroine, Isabel Archer, is courted by three different suitors; James must have expected readers to draw comparisons. But even if such repetition can be found in written fiction, the pervasiveness of repetition at all levels in oral epic is of a different order. These repetitions are partly a matter of facilitating performance, but they have been turned to advantage by generations of poets, who used patterns of metre, vocabulary, phraseology, symbol and action in their creation of richly layered and profound works of art.

The fundamental conceptions of the theory of oral formulaic composition have proved to be both robust and fruitful. A good theory, however, does not settle all questions forever, like some perpetual dictator. A good theory stimulates new work, which leads to new questions and new findings, which in turn may modify the original theory. Scholars since Parry and Arend have modified and added to the theory, and we may expect that new work will continue to lead to new understandings of the composition of the Homeric epics, perhaps in quite unexpected ways.

FURTHER READING

The bibliography on formulaic composition and composition in type scenes is enormous, and any suggestions for futher reading will necessarily omit much valuable work. The essential starting point for understanding the formulaic theory and its history is the work of Milman Parry, now conveniently collected in Parry (1971). These papers are somewhat technical; Lord (2000) offers a somewhat easier introduction to the theory, along with comparative data from his and Parry's fieldwork among twentieth-century South Slavic oral poets (as well as discussion of composition in type-scenes, which Lord calls 'themes'). For interesting critiques of the theory of formulaic composition see Austin (1975) and Shive (1987). Explorations of the wider implications of oral theory can be found in Havelock (1986), Goody (1977), and Ong (1982). Important developments of the theory can be found in Russo (1963) and (1966), Edwards (1966), Kirk (1966), Hainsworth (1968) and Nagler (1967), which formed the basis for his later book, *Spontaneity and Tradition*. The many books and articles by John Miles Foley give good accounts of oral theory and its

[55] Lowenstam (1993) 60. See also Heiden (1996) and (2000c) for discussion of large-scale patterns in the *Iliad*.

application to literature outside classics. Recent developments include the application of discourse theory and cognitive psychology; see, for example, Bakker (1997) and Minchin (2001).

Enjambement in Homeric verse is a rather technical issue, but it has been an interesting test-case for the theory of oral composition. See, for example, M. Parry, 'The distinctive character of enjambement in Homeric verse', in Parry (1971) 251–65; Lord (1948), Bakker (1990), Higbie (1990) and Clark (1997).

The fundamental work on type-scenes is Arend (1933); this has not been translated into English, but the ideas and methods of type-scene analysis may be found in many books and articles, including Lord (1951), Armstrong (1958), Edwards (1975), Fenik (1968) and (1974), and more recently Louden (1999).

Bibliography on formulaic composition and composition with type-scenes up to the late 1980s can be found in Edwards (1986), (1988) and (1992).

9

RICHARD BUXTON

Similes and other likenesses

In the last thirty years a great deal of sophisticated work has been done on the notion of metaphor: linguisticians, philosophers, scientists and archaeologists, amongst others, have all joined in the debate.[1] At the centre of the discussion has been the 'location' of metaphor: is it a distortion of ordinary (= 'degree zero') language, or is it, on the contrary, at the very centre of linguistic usage? Far less attention, however, has been devoted to the closely related linguistic-rhetorical figure of the simile. In the recently published *Encyclopedia of Rhetoric*, for instance, the entry on 'simile' receives 30 lines, as against 258 for 'metaphor'.[2] Yet there are certain forms of literature in which similes forge well ahead of metaphors as regards the insistence of their claims upon readers' attention. A prime example of such a form is Homeric epic.

Before approaching Homer directly, however, I want to ask a preliminary and very basic question. Is there anything to be gained, in spite of all the theoretical elaborations in recent criticism,[3] by retaining an elementary, formal, linguistically based distinction between metaphor and simile, according to which a metaphor is a comparison which does *not* contain a word signifying 'like' or 'as', whereas a simile is a comparison which – however short or long – *does* contain such a term? To describe the ocean as 'like an unfingered harp' will be, on that formal definition, to use a simile; whereas to observe, with Stephen Spender, that 'afternoon burns upon the wires of the sea', will be to employ a metaphor.[4] Put more formally, the distinction may be expressed like this (the words are those of Stephen Ullmann): 'In the final analysis . . . metaphor is an abridged simile. Rather than explicitly spelling

[1] For orientation one may consult Ortony (1993). See also Black (1962), Hawkes (1972), Ricoeur (1975), Mooij (1976), Tilley (1999). Some splendid remarks in Nowottny (1962) esp. chs. 3 and 4.

[2] Sloane (2001).

[3] Few treatments have been more theoretical, or more elaborate, than that in Derrida (1972).

[4] See the fine analysis of Spender in Nowottny (1962) 58–60.

out analogies, one compresses them into an image that has the air of an identification.'[5] Such a distinction[6] has been attacked on the grounds that it seems to imply that the resemblances expressed by similes are psychologically prior to those expressed by metaphors, whereas in fact metaphors tend (it is argued) to *create* resemblances rather than just compressing already perceived ones.[7] If we set aside the fruitless question about which of the two, metaphor or simile, can claim priority, we may more profitably note that there are *some* circumstances where the 'simple' metaphor/simile contrast can indisputably be made to serve a very useful heuristic purpose.[8] A good instance of such circumstances arises when we are trying to distinguish between different kinds of poetic language, and different kinds of poet.

I would like to illustrate this point by contrasting the poetic strategy of Homer with that of Aeschylus. About halfway through Aeschylus' *Agamemnon*, the chorus of old Argive men recalls the fateful arrival, long ago, of Helen at the city of Troy. Seduced and then abducted by Paris, Helen brought in her wake destruction for the city which took her in, and ruin for its people. The chorus often turns its mind to those ruinous consequences, but at line 737 the elders briefly muse upon another side of Helen: her heart-stopping beauty, the stillness at the eye of the hurricane:

πάραυτα δ' ἐλθεῖν ἐς Ἰλίου πόλιν
λέγοιμ' ἂν φρόνημα μὲν
   νηνέμου γαλάνας,
ἀκασκαῖον <δ'> ἄγαλμα πλούτου,
μαλθακὸν ὀμμάτων βέλος,
δηξίθυμον ἔρωτος ἄνθος.

At first, I would say, there came to the city of Ilion a temper of windless calm and a gentle delight of wealth, a soft arrow of the eyes, a heart-stinging flower of desire. [trans. E. Fraenkel]

This is language at its most allusive, intense, compressed. Helen is, or perhaps produces, a temper of windless calm; a soft but piercing glance; a flower. So much for Aeschylus' evocation of Helen's arrival. What of Homer's?

ὡς δ' ὅτ' ἐν οὐρανῷ ἄστρα φαεινὴν ἀμφὶ σελήνην
φαίνετ' ἀριπρεπέα, ὅτε τ' ἔπλετο νήνεμος αἰθήρ·

[5] Ullmann (1975) 277.

[6] Cf. Sloane (2001) 716, *s.v.* 'simile': 'metaphor, which is often defined as a simile in an elliptic form'.

[7] Black (1962) 37. Ricoeur (1975) 152–3 attacks the 'psychologising semantics' which, in his opinion, underlies the 'metaphor-as-condensed-simile' view.

[8] So, rightly, Silk (1974) 14 n. 4.

ἔκ τ᾽ ἔφανεν πᾶσαι σκοπιαὶ καὶ πρώονες ἄκροι
καὶ νάπαι· οὐρανόθεν δ᾽ ἄρ᾽ ὑπερράγη ἄσπετος αἰθήρ,
πάντα δὲ εἴδεται ἄστρα, γέγηθε δέ τε φρένα ποιμήν·
ὣς θυμῶι γήθησεν Ἀλέξανδρος θεοειδής
Ἀργείην Ἑλένην προτὶ Ἴλιον ἠνεμόεσσαν
νηυσὶν ἐνὶ γλαφυρῆισιν ἄγων· αἰνῶς δ᾽ ἀπέλαμπεν
κάλλος ἀπ᾽ ὀφθαλμῶν Ἑλένης. κείνη δ᾽ ἄρ᾽ ἔμελλεν
ὠκυμόροις Τρώεσσι γόον, καλή περ ἐοῦσα,
θησέμεναι . . .

As when in the heavens the stars shine brilliantly around the shining moon, when the air is a windless calm; and all the hill-tops and sharp headlands and glens spring clear into sight, and from the sky brightness bursts down infinite; and every star is visible, and the shepherd's heart is glad; just so was the heart of godlike Paris glad, as he brought Argive Helen to windy Troy in his hollow ships; and beauty shone out terribly from the eyes of Helen. That woman, lovely though she was, would put woe upon the Trojans, who were soon to die . . .

This is not a hitherto unknown piece of Homeric epic: I composed these lines myself.[9] But they suggest the kind of approach which would, I believe, have been adopted in the Homeric poems: not an intensive strategy, but an extensive one. Whereas Aeschylus fuses imagery into a single amalgam, Homer holds the terms of the comparison side-by-side.

I do not apologise for inventing 'Homeric' verses. It has become a commonplace of reception-oriented criticism that every generation re-invents Homer; and I might mischievously add that it is of the nature of poetry with a strongly oral dimension to its composition that there should be a fundamental doubt about which verses can be called authentic. But it is time to abandon my impoverished fantasy and to turn instead to the text which tradition has canonised as Homeric.

Modern scholars have approached Homeric similes from diverse angles. For some, the interest has been *rhetorical–thematic*: what is the function of a given simile within its immediate context, and then within the poem as a whole?[10] One insistent concern within this approach – a concern already exemplified by certain comments of ancient scholiasts and their medieval successors – has been to ask whether a given simile relates to the narrative

[9] For the record, the first five lines are lifted verbatim from *Il.* 8.555–9; the rest I wrote in (more or less) the style of Homer. The translation of the first five lines is adapted from the version by Martin Hammond.

[10] See Coffey (1957), Porter (1972–3), Moulton (1977). The articles by Coffey and Porter, and an extract from the work by Moulton, can be found in de Jong (1999).

at just one point or at several.[11] This somewhat *pointilliste* perspective has been balanced by those, above all H. Fränkel, who have sought to classify and analyse the kinds of subject-matter evoked in the similes.[12] Another approach has been that of critics seeking to *date* the similes. It has been suggested that certain linguistic features found in the similes mark them out as 'late' compared to the rest of Homer's text; one way of interpreting this has been to identify the similes closely with the 'contemporary' world of the Homeric composer.[13] Against this, it has been persuasively argued that there is no reason to deny the quality of traditionality to epic similes.[14] Others, again, have focused on *performance*, highlighting, for instance, the role of similes in prolonging 'the pleasure of a selected narrative moment . . . for its listening audience'.[15] It has also been maintained that the similes occur at moments of significant transition ('performance shifts'), and that their language may reflect the incorporation into epic of material from other, non-epic modes of song.[16] My own approach will be closest to the rhetorical–thematic perspective, and I too shall make generalisations about the kinds of activity which go on in the 'world' of the similes; but in particular I shall be drawing attention to the relationship between similes and other Homeric strategies for highlighting *likenesses*. I shall hope to demonstrate that what is at stake is much more than a question of 'technique'; rather, the issue goes to the heart of poetic meaning.

We need to establish at the outset some sense of what we are to understand by 'Homeric simile', a notion which is not always so easy to isolate as my discussion so far might have suggested. Two different types of passage will exemplify some definitional edges which are potentially fuzzy.

There is, first, a group of passages in both epics in which the Homeric narrator presents gods in the form of – or, alternatively, as simply 'like' – birds. Athena and Apollo, 'assuming the likenesses of birds, of vultures', settle high in a great oak tree (7.58–61); Sleep sits in a pine tree 'in the likeness of a singing bird' (14.290); Apollo comes down from Mt Ida 'like a swift hawk, dove-killer, fastest of all winged creatures' (15.237–8); Hermes speeds over the waves 'in the likeness of a sheerwater' (v. 51); the sea goddess Leucothea slips into the heaving sea 'in the likeness of a gannet' (v. 353); Athena, in the

[11] See Edwards (1991) 30–4. For one example of a medieval commentator who makes observations about a simile's single or multiple anchoring in the main narrative, see Eustathius on 24.480 (cf. p. 153 below). For a lucid, general discussion of the attitudes of scholiasts towards the similes, see Snipes (1988).

[12] Fränkel (1921).

[13] Shipp (1972) 208–22; Hainsworth (1989) 22; cf. Rutherford (1996) 103 n. 45.

[14] Muellner (1990) esp. 97–8.

[15] Minchin (2001) 160.

[16] Martin (1997).

midst of the battle against the suitors, 'shot up high aloft and perched on a beam of the smoky palace, likening herself to a swallow in their sight' (XXII. 239–40). Scholars have disagreed as to whether what is at issue in these passages is the *metamorphosis* of a deity into a bird, or the *comparison* of a deity to a bird.[17] Often the argument has been linguistic – whether there might be significant distinctions between the various words for 'in the likeness of' (e.g. εἰδόμενος, ἐναλίγκιος, ἴκελος); such arguments have been inconclusive. Alternatively, commentators have invoked arguments about what it is plausible or appropriate to find depicted in Homer (Heyne considered it 'ridiculous' if Athena and Apollo are turned into vultures).[18] In my view the most persuasive solution is that in some of these cases what is implied is metamorphosis, in others comparison, while in yet others the text leaves the matter in doubt; after all, since one of the attributes of a Greek divinity can be mystery, why should a poet not register that mystery by means of textual ambiguity? The case of Hermes at V. 50–4 is a perfect example, since there is no internal audience to witness his descent from Olympus to visit Calypso – an audience whose reaction might have clarified whether or not we are to imagine a 'real' transformation; this is quite unlike, say, I.319–24 and III.371–9, where Athena's instantaneous departures in the likeness of a bird cause wonder and amazement amongst onlookers. In terms of a general enquiry into the religio-poetic aspects of Homer, these passages are part of a larger pattern: the possibility of change-of-form is, above all in the *Odyssey*, but in the *Iliad* too, a fundamental dimension of the poems.[19] For our present purpose, however, the relevant point is that the edges of the definition of 'the Homeric simile' must be imprecise. Mere 'linguistic' comparisons fall within, and merge into, a wider set of likenesses, some of which the gods alone have power to effect.

A second example of potential definitional imprecision concerns comparisons which, though meeting the formal requirement of incorporating a Greek word for 'like' or 'as', nevertheless approximate very closely to the status of metaphor by virtue of their brevity or concentration or intensiveness. (Ancient scholiasts did not regard such comparisons as *parabolai*, a term which they reserved for longer or elaborated comparisons.[20]) A wonderful

[17] Dirlmeier (1967), Bannert (1978), Erbse (1980). Dirlmeier tries to deny that any of these is a depiction of metamorphosis; Bannert and Erbse disagree with him. De Jong (1987) 134–5 attempts to distinguish between metamorphosis and 'resemblance'.

[18] Heyne (1802) n. on 7.59; cf. Dirlmeier (1967) 5.

[19] I propose to explore these issues in much more detail in the context of a book-length study, whose provisional title is *Greek Metamorphoses: Myths, Religion and Belief*.

[20] See Snipes (1988) 205–8.

example is to be found in Book 6 of the *Iliad*, when Hector has temporarily left the battlefield in search of his wife Andromache and their baby son.

> [Andromache] came to him there, and beside her went an attendant carrying
> the boy in the fold of her bosom, a little child, only a baby,
> Hector's son, the adored, like a lovely star,
> whom Hector called Scamandrius, but all of the others
> Astyanax ['lord of the city']; since Hector alone protected Ilion.[21]
>
> (6.399–403)

So dense and unelaborated is the comparison of the baby boy to 'a lovely star' that its meaning is left wide open. Is the child 'radiant' (in some sense), as a star can be radiant? This is by no means the only possible interpretation. A quite different – or additional – implication has been detected by some critics. A few lines earlier (293–5) there occurred another comparison to a star; this time, what is said to shine like a star is the robe which Hector's mother Hecuba offered to Athena. But that offering was made in connection with a prayer, which Athena rejected (311); does a 'negative charge' therefore adhere to the comparison with a star, a negative charge which, by implication, portends disaster for the baby boy?[22] However we answer that question, what I want to emphasise is the considerable degree of Aeschylean metaphoricity of what is, in formal terms, unambiguously a simile.[23] Nor is Astyanax-as-star the only Homeric instance of the phenomenon: when angry Apollo descends on the Greeks 'like night' (1.47), or when Hector goes on his way 'like a snowy mountain' (13.754), we are not far from the Aeschylean linguistic world in which Helen 'is' a windless calm.

The preceding discussion of two types of definitional fuzzy edges illustrates the care needed in generalising about Homeric similes. However, neither of the two sorts of likeness which we have just discussed has quite the characteristics which have been regarded since antiquity as typical of the fully fledged Homeric simile. For a first example of the kind of elaborated and extensive comparison which does meet those requirements, I cite the following extract (which does, this time, come from the transmitted Homeric text):

> They found Odysseus beloved of Zeus, and around him
> the Trojans crowded, as bloody scavengers in the mountains

21 Here I have adapted the translation from Richmond Lattimore's magnificent version. Elsewhere, unless otherwise indicated, I again reproduce (or adapt) Lattimore.

22 Moulton (1977) 25–6; cf. Kirk (1990) on 6.400–1, who regards the negative charge as 'just possible'.

23 When Achilles' helmet shines like a star (19.381–2), this is in a context in which there is already an association between Achilles' armour and light/fire; there is none of the enigmaticness of the Astyanax-as-star image.

crowd on a horned stag who is stricken, one whom a hunter
shot with an arrow from the string, and the stag has escaped him, running
with his feet, while the blood stayed warm, and his knees were springing
beneath him.
But when the pain of the flying arrow has beaten him, then
the rending scavengers begin to feast on him in the mountains
and the shaded glen. But some spirit leads that way a dangerous
lion, and the scavengers run in terror, and the lion eats it;
so about wise much-devising Odysseus the Trojans
crowded now, valiant and numerous, but the hero
with rapid play of his spear beat off the pitiless death-day.

(11.473–84)

There are many dozens of other examples, from both poems, of similes which draw their comparisons from the world of living nature: as well as lions and stags we find wolves, dogs, boars, flies, donkeys, mules, bulls, cicadas, wasps, locusts, swarms of clustering bees, an octopus, a dolphin, eagles, hawks, vultures, snakes, goats, and oxen, not to mention poplars, immovable mountain oaks, and a solitary poppy.[24] Occasionally one part of the natural world is used to illustrate another: Eumelus' mares are 'swift-moving like birds' (2.764); Hector will, mocks Ajax, soon be praying that his horses 'might be swifter than hawks are' (13.819). More usually the natural world is invoked to illustrate the human.[25]

A second common source of comparison is the landscape, usually in vigorous or violent motion:

As when a swollen river hurls its water, big with rain,
down the mountains to the flat land following rain from the sky god,
and sweeps down with it numbers of dry oaks and of pine trees,
until it hurls its huge driftwood into the salt sea;
so now glittering Ajax swept over the plain as he chased them . . .

(11.492–6)

Alongside rivers in spate there are snowstorms, ferocious gales, tempestuous seas, forest fires, as well as occasional moments of ethereal, Mediterranean stillness:

As when in the sky the stars about the moon's shining
are seen in all their glory, when the air has fallen to stillness,
and all the high places of the hills are clear, and the shoulders out-jutting,
and the deep ravines, as endless bright air spills from the heavens

[24] For animals see Schnapp-Gourbeillon (1981) and Lonsdale (1990). One may also with profit go back to Fränkel (1921).

[25] On which theme see, for example, Mason (1972) 61–112.

> and all the stars are seen, to make glad the heart of the shepherd;
> such in their numbers blazed the watchfires the Trojans were burning . . .[26]
> (8.555–61)

A third major source of comparison derives from the ordinary, productive activities of humans when not involved in warfare. Here is part of the evocation of the furious battle over Patroclus' corpse:

> As when a man gives the hide of a great ox, a bullock,
> drenched first deep in fat, to all his people to stretch out;
> the people take it from him and stand in a circle about it
> and pull, and presently the moisture goes and the fat sinks
> in, with so many pulling, and the bull's hide is stretched out level;
> so the men of both sides in a cramped space tugged at the body
> in both directions . . .
> (17.389–95)

To this we may add a long and varied list, including the Maeonian or Carian woman who stains ivory with purple to make a cheek-piece for a horse (4.141–7); two lines of reapers (11.67–71); beans and chickpeas bouncing on a threshing floor (13.588–92); a shipwright boring a ship's timber (IX.384–8); the smith who tempers an axe (IX.391–4).

What is remarkable is the sheer diversity of these similes. Rarely is there any repetition;[27] even in the numerous comparisons in which heroes are likened to lions, there are countless tiny variations (contrast, for instance, the two lion-similes at 11.113–21 and 172–8). Nor are our three main categories of simile by any means exhaustive: we could add the mother brushing a fly away from her slumbering child (4.130–1), the little boy making sandcastles and knocking them down again (15.361–6), and many others. Purely in terms of the number of lines dedicated to these comparisons, it is clear that they make a major contribution towards shaping the epics' meaning. But how do we evaluate that contribution?

Elaborated, extensive similes are four times more frequent in the *Iliad* than in the *Odyssey*. Different scholars go about the counting differently, depending on how they define 'simile', and on how they discriminate between 'long' and 'short' similes. One method is to count as 'long' (or 'full' or 'elaborated') those comparisons which contain a verb ('as when a man gives the hide of a great ox . . .'), and as 'short' those which do not ('like a lovely

[26] The reader will recall these lines from my earlier 'composition' (this time the translation is Lattimore's); as can be seen, in its Homeric context the simile is used to illustrate the number of the watchfires.

[27] A few exceptions are noted by Edwards (1991) 24 n. 29.

star . . .'). On that basis, one scholar finds 197 'long' similes in the *Iliad*, as against 45 in the *Odyssey*; as for 'short' similes, he finds 153 as against 87.[28] In themselves these statistics might not be decisive; but in fact the disparity points to fundamental differences between the two epics. We must therefore take the two works separately.

The principal narrative of the *Odyssey* covers a vast and diverse geographical range – Ithaca, Sparta, the island of Circe, the home of the Cyclops, the kingdom of the Phaeacians, the land of the Dead – and a broad social sweep – from kings and princesses to beggars and swineherds. Built into this principal narrative are numerous features also found in 'typical' Homeric similes. From Polyphemus' favourite ram to the enchanted lions and wolves on Circe's island, to the ill-fated cattle of the Sun, to the dog Argos which at its last gasp recognises its returning master, animals figure repeatedly and prominently in the story of Odysseus' wanderings and return home. The same goes for plants and trees, from the eerie grove of Calypso, with its alder, black poplar and cypress, to the orchard of Laertes, not to mention the olive, whose centrality to Greek culture is repeatedly expressed in the poem. Storms and competing winds figure in the episode of Aeolus, and in the several scenes in which Poseidon vents his wrath on Odysseus' ships and raft. As for craftsmanship and productive labour, we meet everything from the herding by the Laestrygonians, by the Cyclops, and by the stalwart Eumaeus, to the clothes washed by Nausicaa, to the skill which enabled Odysseus to construct his bed from living (olive) wood.

Within this already complex and richly diversified world, what scope is there for the constructing of fresh likenesses, in order to extend still further a sense of the equivalence between the narrated phenomena? The answer is threefold.

One group of characters possesses the power to effect changes of physical likeness: the gods. The gods habitually make one thing seem like another. Proteus metamorphoses into a lion, a serpent, a leopard, a boar, water and a tree (IV.456–8). Circe can transform humans into beasts, and back again. Athena regularly changes Odysseus' form, whether from outcast beggar to near-divinity, or vice-versa. And of course, when they visit mortals, the gods transform themselves: a common pattern is for them to appear in the shape of a specific and 'persuasive' human, and later to leave as a bird. Within the world of the *Odyssey*, change-of-form is fundamental, central, pervasive.

A second agency for the multiplying of likenesses is human story-telling. In the mouth of, above all, Odysseus, human speech becomes a medium

[28] Lee (1964) 3–4. The statistics are reviewed by Edwards (1991) 24.

for the representation of possible worlds. After yet another in the series of Odysseus' self-concealments ('Deucalion had two sons, myself and the lord Idomeneus . . . My glorious name is Aethon . . .', XIX.181–4) the poet observes:

> He knew how to say many false things that were like true sayings.
>
> (XIX.203)

All the various, more or less convincing versions of the past told by Odysseus to Polyphemus and Eumaeus and Penelope and Laertes, create a kaleidoscopic surface of jostling plausibilities.

Third: the Homeric narrator himself intervenes in order to point out likenesses through the medium of similes. He does so, as we have said, less frequently than in the *Iliad*, but when they do occur the interventions are often brilliantly effective, in both a local and a broader context. One classic example of 'local' graphicness is the octopus simile:

> As when an octopus is dragged away from its shelter
> the thickly-clustered pebbles stick in the cups of the tentacles,
> so in contact with the rock the skin from his bold hands
> was torn away . . .
>
> (V.432–5)

Another is the description of the pitiless dispatching of the unfaithful maidservants. Strung up in a line and hanged with a ship's cable, they resemble

> thrushes, who spread their wings, or pigeons, who have
> flown into a snare set up for them in a thicket, trying
> to find a resting place, but the sleep given them was hateful . . .
>
> (XXII.468–70)

Of broader significance are similes which explore the feelings of the poem's principal figures. When Telemachus embraces his father, the two of them cry like ospreys or vultures who have had their offspring taken from them (XVI.216–19) – a far-from-casual comparison which implies that the pain of prolonged separation cannot be easily assuaged. Equally evocative is the simile which likens Eumaeus' embracing of Telemachus to the emotions of a father for his only, long-absent son (XVI.17–21); the social divide between the two characters is effortlessly elided, through an image which, by implication, assimilates Eumaeus to Odysseus himself.

But even these two similes pale beside the most powerful comparison in the entire work. After Demodocus' song about the sacking of the city of Troy, the disguised and unrecognised Odysseus breaks down amongst his Phaeacian hosts.

> So the famous singer sang his tale, but Odysseus melted,
> and from under his eyes the tears ran down, drenching
> his cheeks. As a woman weeps, lying over the body
> of her dear husband, who fell fighting for her city and people
> as he tried to beat off the pitiless day from city and children;
> she sees him dying and gasping for breath, and winding her body
> about him she cries high and shrill, while the men behind her,
> hitting her with their spear butts on the back and the shoulders,
> force her up and lead her away into slavery, to have
> hard work and sorrow, and her cheeks are wracked with pitiful weeping.
> Such were the pitiful tears Odysseus shed . . .
>
> (VIII.521–31)

With a reciprocity of pathos worthy of the *Iliad* (and there can be no higher praise), this simile refuses to allow Odysseus any escape from his memory of the Trojan past; it locks him into an image in which, as one of the victors, he is obliged to relive the emotions of one of the humiliated vanquished. Not only that: the simile also depicts a widow grieving for her husband and oppressed by enemies – a situation both uncomfortably resembling and subtly different from Penelope's own state, which is of course less catastrophic than that of the widow, but is, for all that, characterised by another sort of anguish, that of not knowing whether or not her husband is still alive. The power of this utterly 'untypical' simile derives from its shock value: for once, the usual, introductory 'as'-word leads not into an image *parallel* to the main narrative, but into an image which stands in a relationship of complicatedly ironical *inversion* of that main narrative. Its only peer is to be found, as we shall shortly see, at the very climax of the *Iliad*.

When all is said and done, and without denying any of the impact made by individual comparisons, we must concede that the Odyssean similes do not construct a dimension which the poem would otherwise lack. They *supplement* the main narrative's virtuoso exploitation of variable possibility and equivalence and multiplicity of form, but do not carve out for themselves a truly central role in the constitution of the epic's meaning. In this as in many other respects, the *Iliad* tells a different story.

The principal narrative of the *Iliad* is tightly concentrated. It is concentrated geographically: the action takes place in a small part of the Troad. It is concentrated socially: the human dimension of the plot concerns Achaean and Trojan nobles, the role of their social inferiors being relatively marginalised. And it is concentrated temporally: even though there are aspects of the plot (the duel between Paris and Menelaus; the Catalogue of Ships) which are appropriate to the opening of an epic on the theme of, quite simply, 'The

Trojan War', the action is in fact narrowed into a few days of unblinking battle in the middle of the war. How is this relentless intensity made to yield meanings which reach far beyond one corner of the Troad, one group of heroes, a few days? There are many kinds of answer to this question, but the one which is relevant here concerns the way in which the poem exploits likenesses.

The first respect in which it does so relates (as with the *Odyssey*) to the gods. Occasionally – though far less commonly than in the *Odyssey* – divinities intervene to control *human* likenesses, as when Apollo, having whisked Aeneas away to safety in Troy, fabricates a simulacrum of the hero about which Greeks and Trojans then fight (5.449–53). But more often the gods change *their own* likenesses. We noted earlier some passages in which the Iliadic gods, when they are present among humans, metamorphose into birds. Another common motif is a god's shape-shifting into the likeness of a particular human: Athena as a herald or as the Trojan Laodocus (2.279–80, 4.86–7), Iris as a son of Priam or as Helen's sister-in-law (2.791, 3.121–4), Aphrodite as an aged Spartan wool-dresser (3.386–9), Hera as Stentor (5.784–6), Poseidon as Calchas or as Thoas (13.45, 216) – the examples can easily be multiplied. In a poem in which epithets so often cast heroes as 'like the gods' (within a few lines in Book 2, Euryalus is 'godlike' (565), Meges is 'equal to Ares' (627), and Odysseus is 'equal to Zeus in counsel' (636)), and in which heroes can exceptionally venture, as Diomedes does in Book 5, to attack the gods themselves with impunity, the gods' power to change shapes is one of the qualities which actually does distinguish immortals from mortals.

To find the second respect in which the *Iliad* exploits likenesses we need to turn (again as we did with the *Odyssey*) to the speeches. Given that the broad context of the plot is a war, and that on each side there are powerful internal antagonisms (Agamemnon versus Achilles; Hector versus Paris, or Priam versus his sons), it is hardly surprising that many of the dialogues are verbal duels. The weapons used are, as often as not, insults, which is where the likenesses come in – not, usually, as similes, but as metaphors. To Achilles, Agamemnon has a dog's eyes and a deer's heart (1.225); Menelaus calls the Trojans 'wretched dogs' (13.623); to Achilles, Hector too is a 'dog' (20.449). The characteristics which these and other insults inferentially attribute to this or that animal have their counterparts in some of the vignettes developed in the similes; but the likenesses of insult tend to privilege aggressive directness over elaboration of detail.

Finally we come to the similes, whose poetic significance greatly outweighs that of the second and even the first of our other two types of likeness. By far the commonest Iliadic location for similes is in what have been described as the 'battle-scenes': in the *Iliad*, roughly 164 in such scenes as against 38 elsewhere.[29] On the basis of these imbalances, one critical voice expresses an opinion which many have echoed, even if not necessarily in such bald terms: '[the similes] are needed to relieve the monotony',[30] a statement which is, in effect, simply giving a negative spin to the comment of an ancient scholiast on 15.362–4 (the boy making sandcastles): 'the similes provide relief from the suffering/struggle [of warfare]'.[31] Let us see whether a more nuanced attitude can pay dividends.

In a work where such overriding emphasis is placed on the interpretation of death, the poet goes to enormous lengths to individualise the fates of even the most minor of heroes. One way in which he does so is to make their death-wounds unique: Hippothous' brains run out of his head (17.297–8); Harpalion is pierced through the bladder (13.651–2); the variations are virtually endless. The other principal way of conferring uniqueness is through a simile. The effect varies: sometimes we might be tempted to talk of grotesqueness, sometimes of sheer beauty and pathos, sometimes of something in between. When Agamemnon has killed Hippolochus, he lops his victim's arms off at the shoulder, sending his body 'spinning like a log' (11.147). Patroclus' slaying of Thestor – he spears him and drags him out of his chariot – is likened to the action of a fisherman hooking a fish (16.406–10). Harpalion collapses 'like a worm extended along the ground' (13.654–5). Having speared Harpalion through the eyeball, Peneleus decapitates him and holds up the head, which remains impaled on the spear 'like the head of a poppy' (14.499). When Cebriones, his skull smashed, vaults to earth 'like a diver' (16.742–3), strictly speaking this is not, in terms of the simile used, a *unique* death – because the death of Epicles too, a few books earlier, had been described in the same words (12.385–6); but it *becomes* unique when Patroclus mockingly elaborates the simile by invoking the image of a somersaulting acrobat (16.745–50). The death of Imbrius demonstrates how it is sometimes impossible to separate the beautiful-pathetic from the grotesque: he falls like an ash tree on a mountain (13.178–81), yet (202–5) Ajax the son of Oileus decapitates him and sends the head spinning along through the dust, till it rolls to a halt at the feet of Hector. Sometimes there is no other word but 'beautiful' to describe the evocation of the death of an otherwise insignificant warrior. Euphorbus, slain by Menelaus, is like a slender young olive tree: isolated, trembling, laid low by a tempest (17.53–60). Gorgythion's death is even more poignant:

[29] This time the figures come from Wace and Stubbings (1962) 70.

[30] Ibid.

[31] διαναπαύουσι δὲ τὸν πόνον αἱ παραβολαί (Erbse, *Scholia Graeca in Homeri Iliadem*, ad loc.)

> He bent drooping his head to one side, as a garden poppy
> bends beneath the weight of its yield and the rains of springtime;
> so his head bent slack to one side beneath the helm's weight.
>
> (8.306–8)

Simoeisius, for his part, drops like a felled black poplar,

> which in the land low-lying about a great marsh grows
> smooth trimmed yet with branches growing at the uttermost tree-top;
> one whom a man, a maker of chariots, fells with the shining
> iron, to bend it into a wheel for a fine-wrought chariot,
> and the tree lies hardening by the banks of a river.
> Such was Anthemion's son Simoeisius, whom illustrious Ajax killed.
>
> (4.483–9)

The magic of the comparison is to make it seem as if this young man's death achieves something absolutely worthwhile – the construction of a fine and useful object. Even here, though, there is irony: the chariot-maker's skill has enabled many a warrior to reach this very battlefield with speed and efficiency, never to return home again. I can think of only one analogy for the virtuosity with which Homer evokes the uniqueness of each one of these deaths through an individually crafted simile. That analogy is with Dante's seemingly inexhaustible ability to find, in the manifold and idiosyncratic fates undergone by the souls of the dead in *Inferno*, equivalents for the characteristics which each of those individual men and women had in life.

As if all this were not enough, the Iliadic similes have a more fundamental role within the poem: that of locating the action within the wider rhythms of nature, of the weather and landscape, of production and craftsmanship. In the course of this chapter we have seen many examples; more need not be added here. What needs to be emphasised, rather, is the cumulative effect of these comparisons, which is to build up a picture of a world outside, a world alongside, a world which will exist when all the bloodied dust has settled, all the lamentations have ceased, and all the booty has been distributed. Unlike the world of the main narrative – a world whose economics are those of 'consumption and exchange but not of productivity'[32] – the parallel world of the similes is not entropic: its rhythms are there to stay. It is not an *ideal* world: it has its own violence and its own disputes, as when a hard-fought military encounter is likened to a bitter altercation between two men with measuring rods at the boundary between two plots of land (12.421–4) – very much as the Shield of Achilles (Book 18), which is in many ways a simile writ large, figures disputation and even warfare amongst its imagery. It has even

[32] Redfield (1975) 186.

been argued that the majority of Iliadic similes contain 'recurrent subject-matter depicting mankind *in a losing struggle with nature*'.[33] Nevertheless, it remains true that the parallel world of the similes offers alternatives, a set of possibilities on which to gaze if the traumas of the battlefield become overwhelming.

And yet, even this is not quite the end of the story. The greater the distance between main narrative and simile, the more sense it makes to talk of a parallel world established by the poet to frame and act as a foil for the main action. But conversely, the more closely a simile approximates to the main action – for example, by departing from natural regularities and social rhythms in order to evoke the *unusual*, especially the unusual within the sphere of human action – the more the world of the simile and that of the action threaten to collapse into one another. We saw a memorable example in *Odyssey* Book VIII. In the final Iliadic simile which I wish to consider, a simile which occurs at the very climax of the emotional intensity of the epic, we find an identical example of this kind of threatened collapse.

We are in Book 24. Thanks to Hermes, Priam has managed to reach Achilles' tent unseen by the Greek army; but now Priam is alone.

> Tall Priam
> came in unseen by the other men and stood close beside him
> and caught the knees of Achilles in his arms, and kissed the hands
> that were dangerous and manslaughtering and had killed so many
> of his sons. *As when dense ruin seizes a man who in [his] fatherland,*
> *having killed a man, has come to the country of others,*
> *to a rich man's dwelling, and wonder seizes on those who behold,*
> *so Achilles wondered as he looked on Priam, a godlike*
> *man, and the rest of them wondered also, and looked at each other.*
> (24.477–84)

That the complex power of this simile resides in its embodiment of the notion of *reversal* has often been noticed; the point was made already in the commentary on 24.480 by the twelfth-century bishop of Thessalonica, Eustathius, who observed that in the main narrative, unlike in the simile, it is the supplicated rather than the suppliant who is the murderer.[34] A more subtle aspect of reversal relates to the circumstance, recalled by the dead Patroclus at 23.85–90, that it was through an act of involuntary murder that he had first come to the home of Achilles' father Peleus, a home in which

33 Edwards (1991) 35 (my italics). Against this, cf. Porter (1972–3), who stresses the stark juxtapositions – peaceful vs warlike, gentle vs violent – characteristic of many Iliadic comparisons.

34 See Richardson (1993) on 24.480–4.

he, Patroclus, had been offered care and protection; the simile thus forges an implicit link between Priam and Patroclus, in that both have been obliged to seek protection in a place where Achilles is at home.[35] But the point which I want to emphasise is slightly different. It concerns a seemingly small detail: the onlookers' reaction.

Since the linguistic texture, and in particular the order of the words, is vital for a proper appreciation of the effect, I cite the original Greek of the section italicised above:

> ὡς δ' ὅτ' ἂν ἄνδρ' ἄτη πυκινὴ λάβηι, ὅς τ' ἐνὶ πάτρηι
> φῶτα κατακτείνας ἄλλων ἐξίκετο δῆμον,
> ἀνδρὸς ἐς ἀφνειοῦ, θάμβος δ' ἔχει εἰσορόωντας,
> ὣς Ἀχιλεὺς θάμβησεν ἰδὼν Πρίαμον θεοειδέα·
> θάμβησαν δὲ καὶ ἄλλοι, ἐς ἀλλήλους δὲ ἴδοντο.

As when dense ruin seizes a man. . . . [ὡς δ' ὅτ' ἂν ἄνδρ' ἄτη πυκινὴ λάβηι . . .] At this stage in the development of the simile, the image of a man seized by ruin must predominantly evoke Priam: bereft of his son, Priam has taken a 'ruinous' decision to expose himself to the likelihood of immediate death. And yet 'ruin' has seized Achilles too: having lost his dear friend, he has turned to an action (dragging the corpse of Hector) of an insensate recklessness. The simile continues: . . . *who in [his] fatherland* . . . [ὅς τ' ἐνὶ πάτρηι . . .] Who is the principal referent here? In a sense it is still Priam: the Troad, after all, is his own kingdom, his father's land. But this tent, lying as it does within the Greek camp, has for all the long years of the war been effectively *Greek* territory; in this tent it is Achilles, not Priam, who is at home. The simile proceeds: . . . *having killed a man* . . . [φῶτα κατακτείνας . . .] Achilles, there can be no doubt, is a killer. . . . *has come to the country of others* . . . [ἄλλων ἐξίκετο δῆμον . . .] This time, the reference is perfectly ambiguous: Achilles has come to a foreign land, for sure – to the land of Troy; but so, in this episode, has Priam – to a little piece of Greece. . . . *to a rich man's dwelling* . . . [ἀνδρὸς ἐς ἀφνειοῦ . . .] Who, Priam or Achilles, is (like) the rich man? Priam's Troy is a place of wealth; but Achilles is rich too – in booty, of course, but most of all symbolically. He has the one thing which Priam wants but does not have: Hector's body.

And then comes the amazement, *thambos*, repeated thrice in the text: the amazement of onlookers, of Achilles, of onlookers again. The effect of the extraordinary simile is to enact, through language, the alternation between

[35] See Moulton (1977) 115–16. The minor character Epeigeus too fled to Peleus after committing murder (16.570–6), cf. Fenik (1968) 206–7. But the relevance of this to 24.480–4 is surely distant.

the two principals, as the spotlight falls at one moment upon Achilles, at the next upon Priam, and consequently upon the likeness between the two. This last point is crucial to the meaning of, not just Book 24, but the whole *Iliad*. In the final analysis, in all the matters which the poem presents as important, Priam and Achilles resemble each other. As anger and pity struggle for supremacy in this climactic scene, a simile allows the reader/hearer, for once, no distance, no luxuriant pause, no parallel 'other world' from whose vantage-point the action can be viewed. Readers and hearers have no choice but to follow the example of the onlookers in Achilles' tent, who turn their eyes now this way, now that way, and now, finally, look at each other: astonished.[36]

FURTHER READING

The encyclopaedia entries on 'Metaphor' and 'Simile' in Sloane (2001) provide basic orientation. Fränkel (1921) remains, in spite of its age, a thorough and very sensitive treatment, but it is accessible only to those who read German. A more recent general treatment is that of Moulton (1977); see also Coffey (1957) and Porter (1972–3), reprinted in de Jong (1999). Especially (but not exclusively) for those reading Homer in the original Greek, an excellent starting point for further research, particularly in relation to the *Iliad*, is Edwards (1991) 24–41, with helpful references to earlier scholarship.

One other, more specialised interpretative approach is worth highlighting. By insightfully contrasting Homer's text with the august (and Augustan) 'translation' by Alexander Pope, Mason (1972) not only makes a strong case for the individuality of the Homeric perception of animal nature, but also exemplifies a revealing aspect of the 'reception' of the Homeric simile.

[36] A preliminary sketch of the Iliadic sections of this chapter appeared in French under the title 'Deux mondes de l'*Iliade*', in *Europe* 79, no. 865 (May 2001) 48–58; the comments of Bernard Mezzadri were extremely useful to me. For valuable advice on the present version I would like to thank James Diggle, Jasper Griffin, Antonis Rengakos, Martin West and the editor of this volume.

10

JASPER GRIFFIN

The speeches

> Is it that Homer talks about different things from all other poets? Doesn't he talk mostly about war and the dealings of men with one another: good men and bad, laymen and craftsmen; and the dealings of gods with men?
>
> (Plato, *Ion* 531c)

More than half of the Homeric epics consists of speech by characters, not narrative by the narrator.[1] That is a very high proportion, and the speeches, with their scope, variety, and vividness, are a striking feature of the poems. That was to have momentous consequences. Homer is, as Plato says, the first and greatest of the tragic poets;[2] and without the example of Homer, showing the heroes and heroines of myth conversing in dialogue in a high style, Attic tragedy would never have come into existence in the form that it did.[3] That would have had grave implications for the plays of Seneca, and consequently for all European verse drama, including Shakespeare. It was the Homeric epics which showed how it was possible to present great figures, participants in elevated and significant action, conversing in a manner which was at once dignified and true to convincing human psychology. From Homer the line runs to Aeschylus' *Agamemnon* and Shakespeare's *Antony and Cleopatra*. By contrast Virgil, who took so much from Homer, does not excel at dialogue and never has extended conversations. Dialogue in the *Aeneid* is normally just statement and reply, and a famous scene with Dido is broken off with Aeneas 'still having much to say'.[4]

Plato did not intend a compliment. He objected, first, that the 'pretence', as he calls it, that the words and gestures are those, not of the poet, but of the

[1] *Iliad*, 15,690 lines: direct speech, 7,018. *Odyssey*, 12,103 lines: direct speech, 8,225. Direct speech thus amounts to some 55 per cent of the total of the two epics (figures: Schmid and Stählin (1929) 92).

[2] Plato, *Republic* 10.607a.

[3] To put it another way, Homer is much more important in the origins of tragedy than the satyrs, Silenuses, padded dancers, and the rest of the zoo who loom so large in such books as Webster (1962).

[4] Virgil, *Aeneid* 4.390, cf. 4.283–6, 6.467–76; Feeney (1983). Aeneas' inarticulate response to Dido in *Aeneid* Book 4 is in mortifying contrast to the tact with which Odysseus handles Calypso in *Odyssey* Book v.

speaking characters themselves, was immoral. Second, Homer damaged the self-control of the audience by making his characters express their feelings so freely. The spectators felt licensed to weep and wail, when they saw kings and heroes lamenting, and men were drawn to imitate the emotional and uncontrolled women of drama: of amorous Phaedra or heart-broken Hecuba.[5] Plato therefore banishes Homer from his ideal city. He has rewritten some of the first book of the *Iliad* in plain narrative, getting rid of the seductive appeal of personal speech,[6] to show how Homer should have avoided all this slippery imitation of speakers and of emotions, regardless of their moral goodness or badness. He should simply have said that Chryses came to the Achaean camp to ransom his daughter and supplicated the army, and especially the kings – 'saying all this in his own person as Homer, not speaking as if he were Chryses' –

> the priest came and prayed to the gods that they would succeed in taking Troy, and begged them to accept the ransom and give him back his daughter, showing respect for the god. But Agamemnon in anger told him to go away and not come back, or his staff and his priestly head-dress would not protect him; as for his daughter, Agamemnon said that before he would let her go she would grow old with him. He told the priest not to struggle but to be off, while he could still get home unscathed. Hearing this, the old man was intimidated and went away in silence; but when he had got clear of the camp he prayed to Apollo, invoking him by his cult titles and reminding him of his own services, calling on Apollo, if he had ever given anything that pleased the god, either by building shrines or making offerings, in return to punish the Achaeans and make them pay for Chryses' tears with his arrows . . .[7]

When we compare this with what Homer actually gives us at *Iliad* 1.8–42, we see that the loss is, in literary terms, very great.[8] Homer carries us into the action and makes us witnesses of an intense and memorable scene; Plato's rewriting is by contrast lifeless. That was indeed his intention: to dethrone Homer from his central position in Greek life and education. Poetry is to cease to be a rival to Platonic philosophy. It is, in fact, precisely in its departure from Platonic correctness that the Homeric style achieves greatness as literature.

After forcing us into the headlong rush of events that forms the first half of Book 1 – the appeal of Chryses and his brutal rebuff, his prayer to Apollo, the sinister coming of the god, the plague, the assembly, and the carefully

[5] *Republic* 3.392c ff. [6] *Republic* 3.393c7–398b4. [7] Plato, *Republic* 3.393c11–394b1.

[8] Homer does in fact often give the gist of a speech without reporting it directly: cf. the discussion in Richardson (1990) ch. 3, 'The speeches', who shows how the choice of the poet depends on the pace of the episode being narrated.

orchestrated quarrel of Achilles and Agamemnon – the poet of the *Iliad* does actually give a résumé, in narrative form, of events so far. The device has a specific function. It gives the audience a breathing space to catch up with all these exciting events. They have gone past at an exceptionally rapid pace, intended to get the audience into the story immediately. Also the résumé is put into the mouth of Achilles, recounting his grievance to his mother. Such a context colours the narrative with emotion; and Achilles naturally omits his own role in enraging the king and forcing the disastrous outcome.[9]

Plato's objection is, among other things, to the range of Homeric characterisation. Not only gods and heroes speak, but also women, servants, and people not fit to be imitated by a gentleman; while even the heroes do not limit themselves to edifying and up-beat utterances, but complain, squabble, tell lies, insult one another, criticise the gods, and lament their fate. The poet has ambitious aims: his subject-matter is the actions and utterances of gods and mighty heroes of the past, when 'men were far greater than they are nowadays'. And he has his own standards of decorum. We do not find in the *Iliad* or *Odyssey* low or indecent language,[10] any more than they admit to the heroic world such human themes as homosexual love, or bribery, or treachery, or even buying and selling;[11] but Homeric decorum is much less anxious and restrictive than that of the *Aeneid* or of *Paradise Lost*. It admits the free expression of a wide range of emotions, and a convincing cast of female speakers. Not all heroic literature is as woman-free as *Beowulf*,[12] or *Moby Dick*, or Ernest Hemingway's significantly titled *Men Without Women*. The great Mesopotamian epic *Gilgamesh* had already featured female speakers.[13] They are not, however, presented with such full or subtle characterisation as in Homer.

Plato's disapproving comments also confirm that the performers who recited the poems did not have a straightforward and uniform delivery. Speeches uttered by different characters, by women, or gods, or heroes in angry confrontation, were delivered so as to bring out the emotion and the individuality of the speaker. That contributed to the power of the performance over its hearers. In the epics themselves, the audience of a singer

9 1.364–92. The narrated and enacted versions are well compared by Bethe (1914) 23–7.

10 'Homer is, in point of purity, a most blameless writer': William Cowper, Letter to Rev. J.Newton, 3 December 1785. 'Weitere Lücken des homerischen Wortschatzes sind durch die Vornehmheit des Epos, das Anstandsgefühl der epischen Dichter bedingt', Wackernagel (1916) 224, with following discussion.

11 For example, Athenaeus 8e–17c, on Homeric eating and its stylisation; Fränkel (1962) 38 f.

12 One hardly counts Grendel's mother.

13 The harlot who ensnared Enkidu, Gilgamesh's mother, the angry goddess Ishtar, and the 'ale-wife' at the end of the world.

is regularly described as 'silent, held by enchantment'; and in Plato's dialogue *Ion* the Homeric rhapsode Ion describes how, when he performs some pathetic passage involving Andromache or Hecuba or Priam, his eyes fill with tears, while the audience gaze at him with weeping eyes and expressions that show how completely they are carried away by emotion.[14] We are indeed on the way to drama. The speeches have a great range: defiant challenges in battle, 'political' harangues in public debate, scenes of domestic intimacy and even of seduction (*Iliad* 14), exhortations to demoralised troops, reminiscences of the past (especially associated with Nestor), episodes of teasing (*Iliad* 5, on Olympus), begging for one's life, praying to gods, and a wide range of other forms.

Thus the speeches are important in creating variety. A central theme of the *Iliad* is that of the heroic duel and the death of heroes.[15] The supreme spectacle is that of the hero, vital and splendid, facing imminent death at the hands of a heroic opponent, and the recital of deadly wounds inflicted and suffered is a vital part. But the poet also provides us with scenes of contrast, which include lively episodes of conversation, conflict and mirth among the gods, on Olympus and elsewhere,[16] while human episodes, very various in atmosphere, are set in Troy and in the Achaean camp.[17] Among the benefits of these scenes is the vivid presence in this martial poem of non-combatants – old men, women, the baby Astyanax – and of the gods.

In the *Odyssey*, the more fantastic adventures of the hero – the Laestrygonian ogres 'the size of a mountain', the Cyclops Polyphemus, the enchantress Circe, the Sirens – are distanced from us by being narrated in detail by Odysseus, rather than being vouched for by the poet himself.[18] These are sailors' stories; who knows how much truth they contain?[19] That has consequences. We follow such episodes as the entry into Polyphemus' cave or the encounter with Circe, both of which lead from apparently peaceful openings

[14] Plato, *Ion* 535b–e.

[15] That is announced at once, at 1.1–5. Cf. Griffin (1980) ch. 3; Friedrich (1956).

[16] For instance, the visit of Thetis to Hephaestus in 18.369–617: a variant on the 'typical' type-scene, in that the visitor is feminine; cf. Arend (1933) 34 ff., and cf. 14.133–223, Hera's visit to Aphrodite. The feminine ethos looks forward to such episodes as the visit of Hera and Athena to Aphrodite in Apollonius of Rhodes, *Argonautica* 3.25–111, and that of Juno to Venus in Virgil, *Aeneid* 4.90–128.

[17] In Books 1, 3, 6, 9, 10, 11, 16, 18, 19, 22, 23 and 24.

[18] The point was made by Aristotle, *fr.* 163 Rose = A-Scholion on *Iliad* 19.108. Homer has not achieved quite complete consistency: there is a mention of the Cyclops in his own narration at II.19, and one of Circe at VIII.448. These are slips and tell us little: not that Circe was an enchantress, or that the Cyclops had one eye.

[19] Suerbaum (1968b), on the special effects, and some difficulties, so created; also Effe (1975) 142 ff.

to sudden horrors, in the same way as the characters experienced them. In these stories, too, we are told less of the activities of the gods, and less also of the psychology of the characters Odysseus meets. Thus Calypso and Circe retain for us the opaqueness which they possessed – as goddesses, as females – for Odysseus himself. Interesting work has been done on the complexities of the presentation of events in the light of the different perspectives from which speakers perceive them.[20]

Equally important is the conception of heroism which is implied for the poems. In the late Romantic period in which we live, it is conventional that a hero, or a man of action, should be inarticulate. The stiff upper lip of the British Raj, succeeded by the laconic manner which Ernest Hemingway bequeathed to John Wayne and Clint Eastwood: that is the form of rhetoric to which we have had to grow accustomed, and which perhaps we nowadays accept as 'natural' or 'true to life'. It is not hard to imagine how the death of Patroclus and its avenging in the death of Hector might be described in that convention: the curt utterances, the significant silences, the lump in the throat which never finds explicit or eloquent expression.

The *Iliad*, by contrast, takes nearly 4,000 lines over those events, with many emotional and elaborate speeches; and Homeric heroism is utterly unlike that tongue-tied tradition. When warriors meet on the battlefield, they often have both time and inclination to talk before they fight,[21] and the scene may be as long, articulate, and moving, as that of Diomedes and Glaucus (6.119–236). It is in debate, in the *agorē*, as well as in battle, that men win glory, and Achilles' father ensured that he should be trained to be 'a maker of speeches and a doer of deeds'.[22] Both are necessary to the man who wants to excel, and the greatest heroes – Achilles in the *Iliad*, Odysseus in the *Odyssey* – are the most eloquent.[23]

The poet expects his audience to delight in Nestor, too old to fight effectively, but always ready with a tale of his heroic youth. That lets the poem include some good stories from outside the Trojan Cycle,[24] as the presence at Troy of Diomedes, son of Tydeus, makes possible the inclusion of exciting stories about Tydeus and the Theban War,[25] and as Glaucus tells the tale of his ancestor Bellerophon;[26] but Nestor is more than a peg to hang stories on. In Book 23 he showers his son Antilochus with advice about chariot racing,

[20] Cf. especially the work of Irene de Jong (1987).

[21] Cf. Fenik (1968) 20, 32, and index *s.v.*'threats and taunts'; Parks (1990).

[22] 9.438–43; *agorē kudianeira*, 1.490.

[23] It is of Nestor, old but eloquent, that Agamemnon says that with ten such men he would soon take Troy: 2.370–4.

[24] 1.259–74, 7.132–160, 11.655–803: 'If only I were young and strong, as I was when . . .'

[25] 4.370–410, 5.800–8. [26] 6.145–211.

advice which his son, in the event, completely disregards.[27] Nestor, that is, has been brought in for his own sake.

In the *Odyssey*, where so many of the fascinating people of the *Iliad* are allowed to reappear and speak (part of the point of *Odyssey* XI is to permit the reappearance of Iliadic favourites who are already dead), Nestor retails to young Telemachus his memories of the Trojan War,[28] and the poet allows himself the self-conscious touch of making Telemachus avoid a second instalment on his return journey from Sparta, by plotting with Nestor's son to pass the old man's place under cover of darkness. The son agrees, but with some reluctance: 'I know what his temper is like, how peremptory . . . he will be very angry'.[29] The 'peremptory temper' is precisely what the poem ascribes to the wicked suitors; here, with a witty declension into social comedy, a son applies it to his father's determination to bore all comers with his reminiscences.

The great hero Odysseus is a polished and effective orator.[30] In the *Odyssey* he sets out his adventures with magical eloquence to the Phaeacians, holding them spell-bound in the shadowy halls, and receiving the compliment that 'Your speech has shape, you have your wits about you, and your story is told with all the art of a professional singer' (XI.362–9).[31] The swine-herd Eumaeus, to whom he spins yarns in his hut, says to Penelope that his stories melt the heart and are irresistible to listen to (XVII.513–21).

That idea receives extraordinarily subtle and elaborate development in the last books of the *Odyssey*. The atmosphere is heavily charged when the disguised Odysseus finally gets to talk to his wife, without revealing his identity. She tells him of her loneliness and her desperate position, resorting to tricks to keep the importunate suitors at bay. He tells her that he is a Cretan who entertained Odysseus in Crete years ago, on the way to Troy; he describes what his guest was wearing. Penelope's tears flow like melting snow, and Odysseus sits beside her, feeling pity, but keeping his own eyes tearless, as dry as horn (XIX.100–212).

A sort of intimacy grows up between the pair as they talk – old Eurycleia remarks on the resemblance of this stranger to Odysseus (XIX.378–81) – and it seems natural to Penelope to tell him her dream (XIX.508–53). When they

[27] 23.304–48. [28] III.102–200, 218–24, 253–328. [29] XV.195–214.

[30] 2.238–335, where he is shown as effective; 3.213–24, where his style is described and praised; n. also his role in Books 9 and 19.

[31] As the audience listened to a singer telling the story, and here doing so in the role of the hero himself, the compliment opened up wonderful vistas of identification: the singer is, in a sense, Odysseus, and his audience are one with the fabulous Phaeacians who listen to the recital in the poem, as they are listening in reality.

are bedded down in adjoining rooms, Penelope has a vivid dream that her husband is sleeping by her side, just as he was when he left home for Troy twenty years earlier (XX.88–90); she has recently heard him described as he looked then (XIX.224–34). Odysseus hears her speak, 'and it seemed to him that she was standing beside the head of his bed' (XX.91–3). The married couple, after their conversation, somehow feel each other's presence. With subtle psychology of this kind the epic comes close to the novel,[32] of which it is one of the ancestors. When the suitors are dead, Odysseus' recital to Penelope of his adventures and perils follows their reunion and 'the renewal of the old ritual of their bed'; only after that can the couple go to sleep together (XXIII.310–43).

The still greater hero Achilles says, in a moment of despair, that he is great in battle, 'but in debate there are others who are better' (18.105–6); but it is he who makes the most powerful speech in the whole *Iliad*, expressing his passionate rejection of Agamemnon's overtures,[33] and placing his own life in the perspective of heroic endeavour and death. At the end, again, he rises to nobility of feeling and utterance, as he shares that perspective, now even more profoundly experienced in the light of Patroclus' death and his own imminent fate, with his broken enemy Priam. Together they contemplate the doom of humanity, what it is to be a man and not a god (24.513–51). In the *Odyssey* Achilles' ghost tells Odysseus, in the underworld, how bitter a lot death is: Better to be the lowest of the low among the living, than to be king of all the dead! (XI.483–503).[34]

Memorable scenes of conversation help to give vital structure to the poems.[35] Both epics open with scenes of conversation. The *Iliad* gets under way[36] with the momentous quarrel of Achilles and Agamemnon, but we have already had two scenes, powerful but highly compressed. The appeal of Chryses and its rejection are disposed of in two speeches, respectively of five and seven lines; and the old man is immediately off by himself, praying

[32] On these passages see Russo (1982).

[33] 9.307–431. For two rather different views of this speech see Martin (1989) and Griffin (1995) 109–27.

[34] Cf. Edwards (1985) 51 n. 17 and refs. there.

[35] See on this Lohmann (1970). Thus, the supplication of old Chryses in *Iliad* 1 is echoed in striking detail by the supplication of old Priam in Book 24 – with, of course, expansion both in scale and in intensity, and with crucial reversal of outcome: at last, after the vain appeal of Chryses in Book 1, and of Phoenix in 9, the appeal of the helpless to the man of power is allowed to prevail. The dialogue of the dying Patroclus with his slayer Hector (16.330–61) is echoed, with devastating irony, in the exchange between Hector and his slayer Achilles (22.31–66). Other examples are numerous.

[36] Cf. Griffin and Hammond (1982).

to his god, in an utterance of only six lines.[37] The quarrel itself, now that the audience is hooked, is on an altogether fuller scale. In this extensive and elaborate scene there will be no less than fifteen speeches, some short but some much longer, not only from the two angry heroes but also from Calchas, Nestor, and Athena.

It is Achilles who summons the assembly; that means that he will naturally do the talking, and he will be the one to anger the king. The scene is composed with care, and the poet is masterly in the depiction of character. Each speech goes a little further than the one before, until suddenly the two men are at the point of murder.

At first the prophet Calchas is reluctant to speak out. He asks for protection; naturally it is Achilles who offers it. It is not unnatural, but it is unfortunate, that he adds, 'I shall protect you, even if you mean Agamemnon, who claims to be the best of the Achaeans.'[38] When Calchas' verdict is given, naturally Agamemnon is enraged and demands recompense for the loss of prize and of face. Agamemnon's utterances in the poem will develop his character as an alternation of bluster and bullying with uncertainty and sudden collapses.[39]

Here his reaction is natural but not right, and Achilles is ready to protest: 'You will have to wait!' But Agamemnon's emotion will not let him accept such a solution, especially from Achilles, whom (the poet lets us infer) he already regards with hostility. 'Good fighting man that you are, you shan't trick or deceive me' (1.131–2), is not a logical thing to say, unless it is Achilles' all too formidable prowess which has already made Agamemnon uneasy about him; and soon Agamemnon is telling Achilles, 'I dislike you more than any other captain; you always love rows; if you are strong, that's just a gift – nothing to boast of!' (1.176–8). But his immediate response is to say that if the Achaeans will not give him compensation for his loss, he will take it, from one or another of the chiefs: 'Either from you, or from Ajax, or from Odysseus.' No need, though, to settle all that now; now we must send the girl back to her father in Chryse, and one of the chiefs will need to escort her: 'Either Ajax, or Idomeneus, or shining Odysseus, or you, son of Peleus, most high-handed of men' (1.130–47).

How are we to interpret this speech? In real life[40] we should be inclined to see it as bluster: the threat is made, but immediately shelved; and the

37 Cf. Kakridis (1971) 125–37. Schadewaldt (1943) 147 observes that the Chryses scene strikingly foreshadows in miniature the themes of the main plot of the *Iliad*.

38 1.90 f. See Lohmann (1970) [illegible]

39 4.133–82, 336–418; 9.9 ff.; 14.42–134; 19.74–144.

40 An interesting discussion of this question in Kakridis (1970).

chiefs whose pride might be wounded by the thought of losing their prize are instantly mollified by the prospect of being singled out for a nice little trip to Chryse. Unfortunately, it does not work. Achilles is too touchy – too heroic – for that. An insult to him cannot be simply passed over. A parallel shows how different things might have been. In Book 4 Agamemnon insults Diomedes, telling him he is not the man his heroic father was. Diomedes' second-in-command, Sthenelus, is quick to resent the insult, but Diomedes silences him and refuses to rise to it: 'I don't quarrel with Agamemnon for his anxiety: the commander in chief has most at stake' (4.364–418). So far, so good; but Diomedes is a great hero, and he will not let the matter pass so simply. At the beginning of Book 9 Agamemnon, in one of his moments of collapse, declares that all is lost: they should run for home while they still can. It is Diomedes who breaks the gloomy silence produced by this speech. 'Son of Atreus, do not resent what I am about to say. You slighted my courage publicly, saying I was no fighter. Everybody heard you. Now let me tell you what I think of you: you have the supreme sceptre, but you don't have courage. How can you make such a proposal . . .?' (9.9–49).

Achilles, too, might have bided his time and waited for satisfaction. Instead, he forces Agamemnon's hand by an explosion of rage. 'Why am I here? The Trojans have never done anything to me. It's all for your sake, you shameless wretch; you never play fair about the division of the spoils, anyway; and now I'm going home' (1.148–71). Provoked and insecure, Agamemnon replies 'Go on, then, run away! I hate you; I don't respect you or your temper; and as I am losing Chryseis, I'll take lovely Briseis, going to your hut in person, your prize, to show you how far I outrank you, and to stop anyone else claiming equality and openly opposing me' (1.172–87). The next step must be violence, and Achilles has his sword half out, when Athena intervenes to prevent the ruin of the expedition and the deliverance of Troy. A little dialogue scene follows between goddess and hero, which strikes a quite different note, one of seriousness and a kind of intimacy, but which allows the tension to remain acute: what will Achilles do (194–222)? In the event he will settle for a stormy speech, attacking Agamemnon and withdrawing his labour from the war (225–44).

The poet economically suggests a background of bad feeling between the two heroes: on one side 'You *always* like a row'; on the other, 'You *never* do your share of fighting, and you are *always* unfair about the prizes.' That makes the quarrel convincing, and the steps by which it became deadly are skilfully arranged. The psychology of the two men is brought out by the way they speak. Agamemnon told Chryses that his beloved daughter would not be returned to him: 'I will not let her go. Old age will come on her first, in my house, in Argos, far from her home, working at the loom and coming to my bed.'[41] To Achilles he uses the same wounding style, rubbing his nose in the details of what he says: 'I will take lovely Briseis – going to your hut myself – your prize.'

Achilles, in contrast, opens up a wide and sudden vista of the world: 'The Trojans have never done anything to me; they have never driven away my cattle or my horses, nor in Phthia of the deep nurturing soil have they ever ravaged the crops; since there are between us many shadowy mountains and much echoing sea.' This is the Achilles who will tell Agamemnon's envoys in Book 9 that he would not accept his offered gifts,

> not even if he gave me ten times as much, or twenty; all that he has, and all that he could get; even if he gave me all the wealth that enters Orchomenus, or Thebes, Thebes in Egypt, where the vastest treasures are stored: the city has a hundred gates, and at each one two hundred men sally forth with horses and chariots; even if what he offered me were as numerous as the sands and the dust: even then Agamemnon would not prevail on my will, before he has paid me back for all my grief and heartfelt pain. (9.380–7)

Even when killing a man in battle, Achilles may say 'You are down, son of Otryntes, most high-handed of men; here is your death, but your birth was by the Gygean Lake: there is your ancestral land, on the Hyllus with its fish and the Hermus with its whirlpools' (20.389–92).

The Achilles who opens up these far distant vistas, where in the midst of the *Iliad*'s violence the poem for a moment stands still, is the same man, the audience is to feel, who bears on his shield an image of the whole world, with stars and sea and all the activities of men, and who will share with Priam a vision of the fragility of all human life.[42] Agamemnon, no less suitably, arms himself only with images of death, the head of the Gorgon on his shield, and serpents on his shield belt and his breastplate, one of them with three heads (11.26–40); if he had known of Priam's touching scene with Achilles, his response would have been to charge Priam's sons three-fold ransom for their father's release (24.685–8).

The rest of the great quarrel scene would repay fuller discussion than is possible here. The high point, at which Achilles flings down the sceptre which is the symbol of civilised discourse and withdraws from co-operation with his fellows, threatening that 'All the Achaeans are going to miss Achilles, when they are mown down by man-slaying Hector', is followed by a speech in strongly contrasting ethos, old Nestor trying to calm the situation. In

41 1.29–31. 'By emphasising step by step the distance between them he wounds the old man's feelings', is the comment of an ancient commentator (A Scholion on 1.30)

42 The shield, 18.478–617; on it, see Marg (1957), Taplin (1980), Stanley (1993). The scene with Priam, 24.468–691; on it, see Macleod (1982).

vain; the sulking heroes snarl at each other (285–91, 292–303), and the assembly breaks up. Agamemnon's envoys fetch Briseis from Achilles' hut; he receives them, to our relief, with courtesy. His next scene is with his goddess mother: Achilles weeps, but his speech is much less emotional than the quarrel scene (364–412). The return of Chryseis to her father is charming, but unstressed: Odysseus and Chryses each say what is appropriate (430–74). Then intensity returns as Thetis finds Zeus alone on the mountain top and by the insistence of her prayers forces him to grant them, nodding his head in majestic assent (493–530). There follows a lively scene on Olympus, as Hera protests and Zeus threatens her, his violent speech producing a general chill, until Hephaestus restores good humour by an adroit speech and a bit of clowning. That brings out, too, the insignificance in the divine perspective of even the greatest of humans.

The first book[43] thus exemplifies the range of Homeric speech, all the way from very short utterances to lengthy and unhurried ones, and from threats of violence to prayers, supplications and attempts to make peace, both mortal (Nestor) and divine (Hephaestus), and from human squabbles to the most sublime utterance of the father of gods and men (1.524–7). We see the different settings: in the Achaean camp or alone on the sea-shore, on an isolated mountain peak or in the crowded house of Zeus. We see too the effects which speech can produce: Agamemnon enraged by Calchas and infuriated by Achilles; Achilles provoked into a passion which unleashes his hoarded bitterness, or speaking with tenderness and hope to his mother; Thetis weeping at her son's lamentation and persisting with Zeus despite his initial silence; Zeus intimidating the gods, and Hephaestus reviving and delighting them.

It is suggestive that it is in Book 9 that a great series of speeches marks the next turning point in the plot. Agamemnon sends three envoys to Achilles, and each of them makes a powerful speech, strongly contrasting in style: Odysseus competently sets out a very attractive set of offers: he evokes a passionate outburst, a torrent of resentment and refusal: 'And in the morning, if you are interested, you can watch my ships sailing home!' Old Phoenix makes an emotional appeal: he loves Achilles, the son he never had. Achilles replies with affection, half withdrawing his refusal: 'We'll decide in the morning whether to stay or go.' Ajax can only make a blunt address, man to man: 'We thought we were your comrades!' Achilles replies with a further concession: 'When Hector reaches my ships, he'll find he has his hands full.' This scene, like the quarrel in Book 1, is vital to the Achilles-centred plot of our *Iliad*. Both must have been created by the poet we call Homer, who would

[43] Cf. the discussion of Book 1 by Edwards (1980).

not have found the sort of pre-existing material for it which existed, say, for a standard battle scene. Both times we find direct speech deployed with great power: eloquent utterance defines the characters, as well as directing the action. Books 16, 18, 22 and 24, all centring on Achilles and crucial to the plot, are also all marked by intense scenes of dialogue.

The work of Milman Parry and others has shown that the Homeric poems are composed in a formulaic language of essentially unchanging phrases which fit given metrical positions. That truth is sometimes overstated. Our *Iliad* and *Odyssey* were not produced by singers obsessed with merely getting their verses to scan; many forms of artistry are unmistakably visible. One is that the speeches use an importantly different style and vocabulary from the narrative.[44] In the mouths of Homer's people we find expressions of moral judgment – words like *arrogant, bad, ill-fated, just, unjust, ought, poor, violent, wretched, evil Troy not to be named*; the emotional words for *anger*; words for *gentleness, kindness, restraint*; abstract nouns expressing mental and moral qualities; superlative epithets (*dearest, most hateful, mightiest*, etc.); even little words of emphasis with meanings like *very, indeed, excessively, all the same* (with nuance of defiance). The speakers use bolder metaphors than the poet sees fit to use in his own utterance, which reproduces the words of the Muse herself. They speak with more open emotion.

Above all, they express strong and clear moral judgments, which the narration does not.[45] Thus the speeches play a vital role in guiding the mind of the audience, while the poet reserves for his own narration that serene and dispassionate style which presents horrors, crimes, heroism, domestic scenes, and the workings of heaven, with the same almost superhuman objectivity. We are meant to judge, but not to be bullied into judgment by the poet; his people, more human than the Muse, help us to do it.

FURTHER READING

On the range of types of speech, direct and indirect, see Richardson (1990) 70–88. Devices of the construction of speeches, especially ring composition, are discussed by D. Lohmann in Wright and Jones (1997) 71–102. Griffin (1986b) discusses the individuality of different speakers in the epics; see also Griffin (1980) 50–80, which deals with the creation of characters by this means. Narratology is well applied by de Jong (1987); shorter version in Morris and Powell (1997) 305–25.

44 Griffin (1986b).

45 The second half of the *Odyssey* is to some extent an exception; here we do find more moral comment from the narrator himself.

4

TEXT AND CONTEXT

11

JOHN MILES FOLEY

Epic as genre

> “Φήμιε, πολλὰ γὰρ ἄλλα βροτῶν ϑελκτήρια οἶδας,
> ἔργ' ἀνδρῶν τε ϑεῶν τε, τά τε κλείουσιν ἀοιδοί.
> (*Odyssey* 1.337–38)

> ‘Phemios, you know many other enchantments of mortals,
> deeds of men and of gods, those things that the singers memorialize.’

With these words Penelope attempts to steer the Ithacan bard Phemios away from his ongoing saga of the Achaeans’ homecoming and toward what would be for her a far less painful tale. In the process she offers precious testimony that his repertoire contains many other enchanting stories, accounts of human and divine actions that singers keep alive by celebration in epic performance. But Penelope’s words could also serve as a first approximation for epic, and not only in the Homeric context. As an international genre, epic always involves stories that enchant; it often features both humans and gods; and, most centrally, it memorialises the events that singers celebrate.

Beyond Penelope’s working definition, however, lies a world of variety, a world we have not always seen fit to explore or, having glimpsed its unfamiliar territory, actively taken into account. Does ‘the epic’ exist as one in a series of chapters constituting an overall cycle, or is it best understood as a singular and freestanding work? The answer will depend on whether we choose the Turkic and Mongolian epics of *Manas* and *Gesar*, for example, or the medieval Spanish *Poema de mio Cid*. Does ‘the epic’ involve performance features such as musical accompaniment and dancing? Is it situated in a ritual context? Once again, no absolute set of features conveniently characterises the west African *Son-Jara*, Altai narrative from central Asia and the *Iliad*. Can the story behind ‘the epic’ be told or referenced through any other genres by different performers? Certainly the mythology behind the south Indian *Siri Epic* can take alternate forms, but not every epic story worldwide is available in different generic media. Length versus terseness, poetry versus mixed prose and poetry, tales of heroic combat versus stories of origin and descent – all these and many more commonly applied distinctions simply are not diagnostic of epic, which refuses to be pigeonholed according to the dictates of any single culture, time or place. Thus the first goal of this chapter is to sketch the fundamental diversity of epic, to show by example how this master-genre takes many different shapes internationally and through time.[1]

Paired with this aim is a second goal: to examine those features that scholars have identified as emblematic of or intimately related to the genre of epic *as we know it from Homer's poems*. For this purpose we will be concerned with many of the characteristics and topics previewed in part one of the chapter, such as length, omnibus genre (the epic's appropriation of other genres), diction and narrative pattern, the role of prologues, catalogues, and similes, national character, heroic attitudes and actions and the 'author' Homer. Which if any of these much-discussed features truly help us understand the *Iliad* and *Odyssey* as members of an international category of verbal art? On the other hand, which of them assist us in seeing and hearing the ancient Greek epics as something unique? It is well to remember that the profile of Homeric epic has had far-reaching influence outside its immediate context; the search for epic around the world has very often been focused – and sometimes severely constrained – by the unexamined assumption that 'the epic' is a universal, archetypal form identical or extremely similar to the *Iliad* and *Odyssey*. Scholars have not seldom tried to discover Homeric epic where it does not (and cannot) exist, and therein lies a cautionary tale of the need for diversity in frame of reference.[2]

One final preliminary matter should be addressed. In the interest of fairness and full disclosure, I should preface our discussion with a disclaimer. 'Epic' is of course an invented concept, a Western imposition on the natural heterogeneity of long narrative forms from cultures around the world. Stemming ultimately from ancient Greek *epos*, which spans the field from 'word' to 'tale' in Homer, and the popular term *epopoiia* ('verse composition'), ancient

[1] For additional resources on the heterogeneity of the epic genre, see esp. Oinas (1978), Hatto (1980), Beissinger *et al.* (1999), and McCarthy (2001). Limitations of space make it impossible to cover more than a few examples of worldwide epic within this chapter; I especially regret not treating such major traditions as Arabic (Connelly (1986), Reynolds (1995)), Russian (Bailey and Ivanova (1998)), and Old French (Brault (1978a, b)). It has even been claimed that Native America produced a heroic epic in Inyo-kutavêre's *Mohave Epic* (Hatto (1999)). I leave aside here the question of Hesiod's and later Greek poets' epic and non-epic poetry, as well as the *Homeric Hymns* that are in some respects so closely related to the *Iliad* and *Odyssey*; see further Dowden in this volume, as well as Clay (1989) and Foley (1995) 136–80 on the *Hymns*.

[2] As recently as 1980, John William Johnson had to counter the conventional wisdom by showing that 'Yes, Virginia, There is an Epic in Africa'. Since that time, numerous editions, translations and studies of African epics have appeared; see esp. Johnson (1992), Johnson *et al.* (1997), Hale (1998), Belcher (1999), and, more generally, Okpewho (1975), (1992) 202–3.

Greek epic has been described as a genre in some depth since Aristotle;[3] once canonised, it became a literary tool of unquestioned usefulness and applicability worldwide, primarily on the cultural and ideological strength of its Greco-Roman origins. Like all genre labels, 'epic' can help focus our vision, creating categories that facilitate comparison and contrast as well as filling in a background against which individual tales can be understood. In that sense it can function as an effective organising principle, and generic identity can certainly serve as a tool for effective reading. But, as already adumbrated, neither 'the epic' nor any other genre is an archetype. The nations and individuals who produce 'epics' have no uniform code of generic requirements; indeed, even their internal systems of nomenclature for various kinds of verbal art prove radically divergent.[4] The fact is that – everywhere in the myriad traditions outside ancient Greek – 'the epic' is an analytic rather than an indigenous concept and label, and in applying it uncritically to long narrative forms from other cultures we run the risk of unintentionally colonizing their verbal art. Any gains we register by using this well established label should thus be weighed against its endemic shortcomings. What I attempt below is offered in that spirit.

Epic as cornucopia

Although any survey of international epics will inevitably present only a partial view of their richness and complexity, I have chosen traditions from India, North Asia, Africa, the Former Yugoslavia, Finland and England that in their variety begin to reflect the larger world in which the Homeric poems exist. In the order that we will examine them, the witnesses are: the *Siri Epic* from the Tulu people, the Gesar and Janggar traditions from Mongolia and Tibet, the *Mwindo Epic* from the Banyanga and the *Son-Jara* from Mali, the South Slavic epics from Bosnia, Croatia and Serbia, the Finnish *Kalevala* as collected and edited by Elias Lönnrot, and *Beowulf* from Anglo-Saxon England. This mix of contemporary and older epics, of living traditions and manuscript works, will provide points of both convergence and divergence from the *Iliad* and *Odyssey*, as well as assist us in framing problems in ancient Greek epic that the paucity of direct evidence leaves insoluble. Again, I make no pretence whatsoever to thoroughgoing or even absolutely representative

[3] On the origins and ancient use of this terminology, see Ford (1997) 396–99. Martin (1989) esp. 10–14 contrasts *epos* and *muthos* within Homer.

[4] On local, ethnic labels created and used by each culture to name its verbal arts versus the analytic conception of 'epic' applied externally from Western scholarship, see Honko (1998) 205–6.

coverage, but bring these examples forward simply to sketch a fuller, more natural context for the Homeric epics that are our primary focus. Hopefully, these very brief remarks on international epic will set the stage for highlighting Homer's shared qualities and his uniqueness in part two of this chapter.

In December 1990 a team of Finnish and Indian fieldworkers responded to a request by the Tulu singer and possession priest Gopala Naika to record his performance of the *Siri Epic*, which in the event totalled some 15,683 lines of sung narrative.[5] The story concerns the exemplary female character Siri and three generations of her descendants in a matrilineal society, and belongs to the Tulu people living in Karnataka province in southern India. Its mythology is not held at arm's length or treated merely as entertainment; the story of Siri informs people's everyday lives as a group charter of religious and ethnic identity. In addition to the long narrative, the Siri mythology also takes the separate forms of ancestor worship, pre-wedding celebrations, and work songs sung by people engaged in palm-tree tapping and plucking seedlings from rice paddies. This is to say nothing of the lengthy rituals that may last all night, in which different individuals are possessed by Siri and her son Kumara. Within the ecology of genres that serve as vehicles for various aspects of the story, Gopala Naika's narrative performance is a remarkable species, to be sure. But it is just one species in a complex, interactive ecosystem, and the critical act of singling it out and textualising it begins to detach his poem from its cultural and expressive environment.

Even these few observations highlight both similarities to and differences from the Homeric poems. The *Siri Epic* is only five lines shorter than the *Iliad*; were we to inquire further into its composite structure, we would find constituent parts not unlike the *Odyssey*'s main narrative, the Telemacheia (Books II–IV), and the Apologia (Books IX–XII). But in the Tulu epic we encounter a female hero, together with a general deprecation of male figures and a virtual absence of violence, none of which the Western model of epic leads us to expect. And in addition to the common epic trait of serving as a digest of smaller genres, it soon becomes clear that the *Siri Epic* is in active symbiosis with other genres, apparently because of the broadly and deeply functional role of the Siri-Kumara mythology in social life. More thorough examination would also uncover the building blocks of narrative composition typical of the *Iliad* and *Odyssey*, that is, the formulas and typical

[5] For the original text and English translation, see Honko *et al.* (1998a), (1998b); for context, Honko (1998) and Honko and Honko (2000). For additional sources on other Indian epics, see esp. Blackburn *et al.* (1989), Richman (1991) and Smith (1991).

scenes that have become familiar to readers of Homer.[6] But, as common sense would suggest, the Tulu epic's building blocks have their own size, shape and flexibility, as well as their own set of idiomatic implications. Based on only this single analogy, we can already see 'the epic' resisting any neat definition by recipe. Penelope's description still holds, of course, but we might wonder how much further it is prudent to go.

That impression deepens as one looks across the vast expanse of North Asia, in particular at the enormous epic cycles featuring the heroes Gesar and Janggar.[7] Sung in numerous different societies in a broad range of Turkic languages as well as Mongolian and Tibetan, these epics can run to literally hundreds of thousands of lines, dwarfing European epics. Depending on the region, singers may employ instruments for musical accompaniment or sing *a cappella*; they may depend on the magical resources of certain implements or on particular costumes; and their stories may be grounded in indigenous or foreign religions. Over time pre-performance rituals such as prayers have become part of the epics themselves, while detached performances have found their way into printed volumes and wood-block representations. Among Tibetan composers of epic (*sgrungmkhan*) are found bards who are also sorcerers, shamans, and even an associate professor; as in much of the rest of the world, the supposed boundary between orality and literacy is hardly absolute.[8] But perhaps the most intriguing of the *sgrungmkhan* are the so-called 'paper-singers', illiterate bards who gaze intently at a sheet of white paper as they perform. Contrary to our expectation, the sheet contains no text, not even notes; it is completely blank. And if no blank paper is available, this kind of singer simply resorts to some newsprint; since he can't read, it hardly matters. As he explains, looking at the paper brings the epic's action to his mind in visual form, and that is what he sings.[9]

Modelled after the North Asian epics, and especially the performances of the Tibetan paper-singers, our definition has to make room for a host of unfamiliar phenomena. First is the criterion of length: no Western epic can match the Gesar and Janggar stories, one of which was published in Beijing in a version of more than one million verses. Apart from their sheer size, these epics also present the riddle of the *cycle*, a loosely confederated series of episodes in which a main hero like the Mongolian Janggar presides

[6] On these traditional units, see Clark in this volume, as well as Foley (1990) chs. 4, 7; (1991) chs. 1, 2, 5; (1999a) chs. 5–7.

[7] On the Turkic epic tradition, see Reichl (1992), (2000); on Uzbek, Reichl (2001); on Mongolian, Heissig (1987), Chogjin (1997), Chogjin and Foley (2002); on Tibetan, Yang (1998).

[8] See further Yang (1998); on the interaction of orality and literacy more generally, Finnegan (1992).

[9] For more on the paper-singer, see Foley (2002a) Four Scenarios.

over a troop of subsidiary heroes to whom he (and the poetic tradition) delegate many of the individual adventures. Whether the most basic unit of such epics is the so-called 'canto', which may itself cover many thousands of verses, or the larger superstructure, which is always imminent but almost never performed as a sequenced whole, is a problem created by imposing the Western notion of an epic text complete in itself.[10] As for the structural and expressive units of North Asian epic, once again research has shown that singers do employ building blocks of diction and narrative to make and remake their epics, but that these constituent materials little resemble the formulas and typical scenes in Homer's compositional repertoire. The paper-singer – and each of his counterparts in proximate, related epic traditions – is *sui generis* in more ways than one.

The *Mwindo Epic* of the Banyanga and the *Son-Jara* from Mali provide us with additional points of discrimination on the international spectrum of epic. The former of these long African narratives recounts the mythical history of its focal character, Mwindo, from his family background and miraculous birth through celestial and subterranean journeys and a dragon hunt. The version collected and translated by Daniel Biebuyck (1969) was performed by Shé-Kárisi Candi Rureke, fifty years old at the time and the last great local bard in a tradition that stems from three cultural traditions – the Pygmies, Bahimbi and Nyanga. According to conventional practice, bards perform with the assistance of relatives who provide musical instrumentation and who themselves know extensive passages from the epic in question (13): 'Episode by episode, the epic is first sung, then narrated. While singing and narrating, the bard dances, mimes, and dramatically represents the main peripeties of the story. In this dramatic representation, the bard takes the role of the hero.' The multimedia presentation also incorporates most of the smaller genres of verbal art in the Nyanga repertoire, and reflects in its content the major institutions, values, behaviour patterns and cultural artefacts of the society.

The epic of *Son-Jara*, as performed by the Mande bard Fa-Digi Sisòkò, offers a complementary perspective on heroic epic from this continent.[11] Narrated entirely in poetic verse through three subsidiary channels – the narrative, song and praise-poetry modes – it demonstrates a number of familiar characteristics: substantial length (thousands of lines), heroic content, multi-generic makeup and social embedding. Interestingly, the epic also 'plays a

[10] This point also bears on the nature of the shadowy remains of now-lost Homeric-era poems we call the Epic Cycle. See further Dowden in this volume; also Holmberg (1998), Foley (1999b) and Burgess (2001).

[11] See Johnson (1992).

definitive role in building a sense of national identity, in spite of the fact that political boundaries drawn by French and British colonial powers persist in dividing these peoples' (Johnson (1992) 11). Bards or *jeli* serve a complex set of social functions, including chronicler and analyser of the group's history, entertainer, preserver of social customs, and seer or mediator. Their performances employ a specialised language of episodes, typical scenes and smaller increments, a metrically complex idiom that requires years to master. At origin a historical figure whose actual reign predated modern collection by seven centuries and more, the focal character Son-Jara has attracted to himself a whole constellation of heroic deeds and become a composite culture hero.

By themselves these two vital and multidimensional traditions settle the once-debated question of whether epic exists in Africa, and numerous publications over the last two decades have closed the case.[12] But the vast panorama of African epic holds some surprises for Homeric scholarship. For example, Mr Rureke, narrator of the *Mwindo Epic*, was mystified by fieldworkers' requests that he perform the entire epic, claiming that bards always told a part or parts of the whole; indeed, Biebuyck reports, he 'repeatedly asserted that never before had he performed the whole story within a continuous span of days' ((1969) 14). Were we to conduct a thorough survey of the world's epic traditions, we would find that this 'immanent' approach to epic performance – letting the part stand for the implied whole – is in fact a very common strategy that reflects the traditional, non-textual nature of composition and reception.[13] Likewise, the variety among published versions of the Son-Jara story – some of them telegraphically told with a great deal left implicit and others augmented by their translators with the kind of detail that makes outsiders' reading easier – shows the same dependence on understood, inexplicit context.[14] Among many other things, the African narratives teach us that 'the epic' lives beyond the borders of any single performance or text, although it idiomatically informs each one of them. Audiences are crucial partners in the transaction of epic.

Because of Milman Parry's and Albert Lord's comparative research,[15] South Slavic epic may be more familiar than the other traditions so far cited,

[12] See n. 2 above.

[13] See esp. Foley (1991) chs. 1–2; (2002a) Fifth Word.

[14] For example, compare Johnson's (1992) translation of an actual performance, which depends upon an implicit context, with the reconstructed, filled-out version published by Niane (1989). The latter is easier (for the outsider) to follow, but at what cost?

[15] See Parry (1971), Lord (2000), and Foley (1988) (history of the method), (1985) (bibliography with updates available online at *www.oraltradition.org*). The first fruits of their collecting are published in *SCHS*; for a digest of South Slavic epic in the Milman Parry Collection, see Kay (1995).

although most readers are probably better acquainted with structural profiles and measurements than with the epics themselves. Two major subgenres comprise this tradition: the longer Moslem epic, which can reach tens of thousands of lines and stems chiefly from present-day Bosnia and Croatia, and the much shorter Christian epic found largely in Serbia. Parry and Lord concentrated on recording the Moslem songs because of their similarity to Homer's works in length and elaboration, and they especially favoured those with story patterns like Return (strikingly similar to the *Odyssey*), Wedding and Siege of a City. Their analyses turned up units of expression that seemed cognate with Homeric formulas, typical scenes and larger narrative sequences, and on that basis they posited an oral tradition for Homer. Moreover, South Slavic epic's apparent congruency with the *Iliad* and *Odyssey* suggested the hypothesis of oral epic as an archetypal form, a sweeping concept that both promoted and hindered further research.

Addressed on its own terms, the extremely well collected tradition of the *guslari* offers a great deal more than tangible ballast for hypotheses drawn from the Homeric texts. Through the systemic variety of songs and song-types with overlapping and interlocking heroes and events, we can begin to see how epic lives and develops on a grand scale. Of course, we can manufacture well ordered cycles from what is actually a loose confederation of stories by aggressive and selective textualising, by converting a living organism into a museum exhibit. But in reality every performance samples an implied whole, a context that supplies 'missing' content as part of the idiomatic process of composition and reception. South Slavic epic also furnishes us with a helpful perspective on the identity of legendary singers, those larger-than-life figures who bear such a close resemblance to the mysterious Homer.[16]

Authorship presents a different set of issues for the Finnish *Kalevala*. This massive epic poem, collected and assembled from Karelian oral fragments by the physician-scholar Elias Lönnrot, stands as one prominent and far-reaching instance of the nineteenth-century European quest for ethnic identity in the verbal arts of the folk. In this ideological respect it mirrors the Christian subgenre of epic collected from Serbian singers during the same period by Vuk Stefanović Karadžić.[17] Scholarship has established the dimensions of the *Kalevala*'s specialised language, from its recurrent phraseology

[16] See further part two, 'Homer's epics', below.

[17] On the *Kalevala*, see esp. DuBois (1995), Honko (1998) 169–76, Branch (1994) and Harvilahti (1994). On the Christian subgenre of South Slavic epic, see, e.g. the selected translations by Holton and Mihailovich (1997) and commentary in Foley (1991) ch. 4 and (2002a) Eighth Word.

through larger scenic patterns. Additionally, there is no doubt that the poem reflects social realities and acts as a mythological digest, and we would be hard pressed to find an epic anywhere in the world that has had a greater effect on the literary and visual arts, music and group identity of its inheritors. As far as the measure of mere size (the 1849 edition contains 22,795 lines), the presence of features such as catalogues, and the inclusion of other genres (especially charms), the *Kalevala* certainly qualifies as epic and furnishes numerous parallels to Homer.

But, like the other works and traditions surveyed here, the Finnish epic also presents us with some idiosyncratic qualities and features. Foremost is the role of Lönnrot, who, in addition to having served as collector and editor, was also an active contributor to the poem as we have it. A series of field trips provided 'real' materials, to be sure, but he reshaped the rather short poems he recorded by arranging them into a long narrative and creating his own lines (about 3 per cent of the entire poem) to fill out individual passages and interstices. The result is effectively an invented epic, or at least a composite form for which no separate, bona fide evidence survives.[18] And this in turn begs the question of genesis and transmission more generally. In how many other cases worldwide and throughout time have editors learned the language of composition well and thoroughly enough to intercede in the making and remaking of epic? What is to prevent this kind of 'traditional editing' as part of the process of transmission, even after an oral epic reaches written form, and how does that possibility affect our understanding of ancient works (like the Homeric poems) whose early history is shrouded in doubt?[19] As we have seen with other epics, the *Kalevala* demands that we open up the genre of 'the epic' even further, that we continue to pluralise the model.

At first sight *Beowulf* may appear to be a near-perfect generic fit with the *Iliad* and *Odyssey*.[20] We recognise many familiar ingredients in this Anglo-Saxon poem: a tale of heroic accomplishment in the face of overwhelming odds, a specialised diction and narrative style, national character (though ultimately Danish and Swedish, rather than properly English), a prologue and catalogues, and multiple constituent genres. The fact that it reaches to only 3,182 lines, rather than the nearly 16,000 of the *Iliad* or the hundreds of thousands of *Gesar* or *Janggar* epic, still leaves it the longest poem in

[18] As Honko puts it (1998) 176 'the patches may be identical with oral poems, but the patchwork as a whole is Lönnrot's vision of a long epic'.

[19] Cf. the report of 'formulaic reading' by Anglo-Saxon scribes who recreated poetic works as they copied them (O'Keeffe (1990) esp. 23–46).

[20] For various perspectives on *Beowulf*, see Bjork and Niles (1997).

the surviving canon of Old English poetry. Once we make adjustments for the idiosyncratic metrical makeup of Anglo-Saxon verse, the units of formula and typical scene reveal their presence and function. Even the internal descriptions of bards or *scopas* – Hrothgar's court singer and the minstrel-on-horseback are two – resemble the idealised portraits of the Ithacan Phemios and Phaeacian Demodokos. Small wonder, then, that *Beowulf* has often been summoned as an analogy for the Homeric poems.

Even this close-kin European epic, however, strains the first impression of close equivalence. For one thing, *Beowulf* is unique: we have just one epic, just one version, just one manuscript. No alternative tellings or even alternative readings survive; we know of no tradition of scholia or other textual commentary from pre-modern times. The 32,000 lines of Old English poetry harbour saints' lives, elegies and other lyrics, biblical paraphrases, riddles, maxims, charms and other genres, and many of these smaller forms help to constitute *Beowulf* itself.[21] But there is no other epic (besides the fragmentary *Waldere*), and this fact alone leaves us at somewhat of a loss in formulating a secure generic classification that would help us understand *Beowulf* in relation to other Old English poetry as well as to comparative epic. Fortunately, however, the uniform system of language and implication across the Anglo-Saxon poetic spectrum – qualified only by the different roles of individual genres in the overall ecology – means that the implied context we have seen as a characteristic of other epic traditions also plays a part here. Phrases that occur in *Beowulf* echo against recurrences in the hagiographic *Andreas*, for example, while typical scenes like Exile and the Beasts of Battle ramify throughout the corpus.[22] Complementarily, within *Beowulf* itself we can glimpse the poet's immanent art in the telegraphic references made to other tales from the Germanic story-hoard. As with other epic traditions, mere intelligibility can hinge on information or perspectives that the composing poet assumes to be available to the audience and thus does not explicitly rehearse in the present performance or text. As with so many other epics, but of course in its own fashion, *Beowulf* is much more than the sum of its (literal) parts.

If these few examples illustrate anything, they reveal the necessity for an open-ended model of 'the epic'. Although strategic choice of a few different traditions can lend credence to a more restricted concept of the genre, a fair evaluation of evidence from international sources and throughout history points in the other direction. This larger world in which Homeric epic

[21] On the composite generic nature of *Beowulf*, see esp. Harris (1982).

[22] On this phenomenon of 'leakage' among genres in Old English, ancient Greek, and South Slavic oral and oral-derived poetry, see Foley (2002b).

exists is more diverse than we have usually acknowledged. For such reasons Lauri Honko proposed a functional definition, claiming that 'epics are great narratives about exemplars, originally performed by specialised singers as superstories which excel in length, power of expression and significance of content over other narratives and function as a source of identity representations in the traditional community or group receiving the epic' ((1998) 28). This perspective fits the witnesses examined above rather comfortably, from the *Siri Epic* and North Asian cycles of Gesar and Janggar through the African masterworks celebrating Mwindo and Son-Jara and the songs of the South Slavic *guslar* and Anglo-Saxon *scop*; even the *Kalevala*, refracted through its collector-editor-'singer' Lönnrot, squares with this idea, at least to a degree. But that after all is the point – even so wide-ranging a definition as Honko's cannot ever perfectly capture the manysidedness of 'the epic'. In the end, I advocate a two-part procedure: first, giving each epic its due by adopting Penelope's non-parochial concept of 'those things that the singers memorialise'; and, second, providing realistic comparisons by placing Homer's epics against the background of as informed and diverse a model as we can muster.

Homer's epics

In this second section we reverse our procedure, working outward from features customarily cited as characteristics of Homeric epic toward the wider international context sketched in part one. Our purpose here is twofold: to identify often-cited generic symptoms of Homeric epic (even if they are derived only or primarily from that source) and to inquire whether a comparative perspective sheds any light on their centrality and function. Towards that end we will be considering – very briefly, due to limitations of space – the parameters of length, omnibus genre, diction and narrative pattern, the role of prologues, catalogues, and similes, national character, heroic attitudes and action, and the 'author' Homer.

As the North Asian epics have taught us, the *Iliad* and *Odyssey* are actually of middling length on an international scale. The epics of *Janggar* and *Manas* can run to ten times their size, while the *Siri Epic* from southern India about matches the *Iliad* and the South Slavic songs vary from a few hundred to many thousands of verses. Given this range, we may conclude that length is a property of the individual tradition. Relatively few epics are smaller in extent than the Homeric poems – *Beowulf* at 3,182 lines and the hundred-odd medieval French *chansons de geste* at about the same or lesser length are examples – but many are far longer. A more dependable characteristic of epic across cultures is the often-cited feature of 'omnibus genre', that is, the extent to which the epic absorbs or is in conversation with other poetic genres in the cultural repertoire. Critics have identified prayers, laments, proverbs, catalogues and inset stories within the *Iliad* and *Odyssey*, though of course the generic inventory is hard to assess from the shards of ancient poetry that survive to us. What we can say, however, is that all of these forms and more are found in living, well-documented traditions, and further that they act as cues with special indexical force. Thus, whether we are speaking of the elegiac passages in *Beowulf* or the catalogues of the *Kalevala* or the proverbs embedded in South Slavic epic, the general theorem is clear: the master-genre of epic uses the poetic resources of other genres as part of its overall expressive program.

Closely related to these issues is the trademark diction and narrative patterning of Homeric epic, about which an enormous amount of research has been published. The presence of formulas, such as 'swift-footed Achilles' or 'wine-dark sea', has often been cited as an indication of the Homeric poems' debt to an ancient Greek oral tradition, as has the recurrence of typical scenes like Arming the Hero or Feasting. However we envision the relationship of our texts of the *Iliad* and *Odyssey* to their origins, this special 'register' or way of speaking has long been counted as an important aspect of Homer's epic style. In addition to their structural contribution, these strategies have expressive implications: formulas, typical scenes, and story patterns can contribute idiomatically as well as tectonically. The phrase 'green fear' (*chlōron deos*), for instance, constitutes a 'large word' in itself and means 'supernatural fear' in Homer, although neither of its elements has anything to do with divinity. When Andromache pleads with Hector in *Iliad* 6 to remain inside Troy with her and Astyanax, her use of the traditional scene of Lament – customarily a vehicle for actually mourning the dead – suggests the inevitability of her husband's demise. The Return story pattern of the *Odyssey*, mirrored in a host of Indo-European epic traditions, accounts for the order and sequence of the poem (which starts not 'in the middle', but at the traditionally prescribed beginning), for Penelope's trademark intransigence (ambiguity is a powerful weapon for this sort of heroine), and for the closure of the poem after Book XXIII, line 296. Homer's specialised language is useful not only structurally but also idiomatically.[23]

As reported in part one of the chapter, traditional phraseology and narrative patterning seem to be characteristic of oral and oral-derived epics around the world and throughout history, with one crucial caveat. Each tradition moulds its register according to a different set of rules, which are in

[23] For discussion of these and dozens more examples of what I call 'traditional referentiality' in Homer, see Foley (1991), (1999a).

turn based on the natural characteristics of the given language. That is, we will find formulas and typical scenes throughout the African *Son-Jara*, the medieval Spanish *Poema de mio Cid*, and other epics that bear some relation to oral tradition, but they will not match Homer's traditional units exactly. For instance, formulas in Mongolian epic, which must obey a complex regimen of head-rhyme and vowel harmony and can stretch to as many as six verses in length, will not answer the same definition as the Homeric formula, which takes shape within a hexameter medium and is usually limited to a line or part-line. Likewise, and predictably, the idiomatic yield of phrases, scenes and story patterns will always be a function of the particular tradition to which an epic belongs. Once again, the watchword is diversity, even in regard to parallel features.[24]

Homeric epic has drawn definition from other stylistic features as well, very prominently from its prologues, catalogues and similes. The *Iliad* begins with an appeal to the Muse and a sketch of the mythic background to the action that follows, and the *Odyssey* starts similarly, with particular attention to Odysseus' striving and an exhortation to the Muse to 'speak also to us' (*eipe kai hēmin*). Correspondingly, the *Siri Epic* begins with an extensive series of invocations (not unlike the Hymns, which some scholars believe may have preceded ancient Greek epic performance[25]), while South Slavic songs also make use of *pripjevi*, or prologues, to start up the narrative action. The difference is that neither the Tulu incantations nor the South Slavic proems have any direct, necessary connection to the subsequent action; in the latter case, a *guslar* can and does use the same initiatory passage with different stories. *Beowulf*'s prologue, even briefer at only three lines, seems to fall between these poles in its relationship to the narrative that follows, attached in general to the story-hoard of Germanic heroic mythology. Unattached to either Beowulf or the eponymous hero Scyld Scefing, it sounds very much like proems to other Old English poems (of different genres) like the saint's life *Andreas* or even the lyric *Dream of the Rood*. The opening lines of *Son-Jara* create an arena for what follows with nested references to praise-names, cosmology and performance. Across the epic spectrum we usually find some sort of cue that announces what Dell Hymes has called a 'breakthrough into performance',[26] but once again the nature of the cue is tradition-dependent.

24 Very importantly, other genres besides epic demonstrate this same characteristic of an expressive register, usually quite different from epic and from each other.

25 See further Foley (1995) 144–9.

26 See Hymes (1975) (1981). Note also that the Parry Collection abounds with South Slavic epic performances embedded in conversations with singers, who announce the change in speech-act – from interview to epic – via traditional *pripjevi*, or 'prologues'.

The same is true for catalogues and similes. The famous Catalogue of Ships and Men in Book 2 of the *Iliad* and the how-to manual for building a raft in Book v of the *Odyssey* have many analogues in international epic. African epics codify history, for example, and the *Kalevala* includes ethnobotanical and aetiological catalogues as part of its presentation. In the South Slavic Moslem epic, muster-lists of combatants for a great war are virtually required if the song is to be sung at any length, and *Beowulf* certainly presents us with genealogies that fit a similar expressive slot. Homeric similes, on the other hand, have fewer true analogues elsewhere. While many epics make use of elegant comparisons, often – like Homer's poems – aligning the hurly-burly of the present narrative moment with quieter scenes from the untroubled world of nature, the multiline structure that stretches majestically from 'As' to 'So' seems uniquely Greek.[27] While Homer's catalogues are of a sort and texture we find in other epic traditions, his similes seem to be distinctive.

National character – the epic as a charter of group identity, myth in the service of indigenous social history – is an aspect of many scholars' concept of the genre. The two epics that survive from ancient Greece fit this idea clearly enough: the *Iliad* glorifies Achaean achievement in battle and the *Odyssey* memorialises the post-Troy return to one's homeland with all the dangers and challenges such a journey and homecoming pose. In this respect the Mongolian and Tibetan *Janggar* epics offer an interesting lesson. Each group's epic tradition is attuned to its ethnic history and serves as a sort of living heritage for its owners; in the Tibetan case the image of Janggar's heroism is refracted through the lens of Buddhist values, while in Inner Mongolia the heritage lives even beyond the arena of epic, with people citing the actions of Janggar and other heroes and quoting famous singers' words in everyday speech. Likewise, both Mwindo and Son-Jara function as culture heroes, as do Beowulf and the *Kalevala*'s Väinämöinen; the fact that these are larger-than-life or wholly invented characters only increases their power in the arena of epic. They embody ethnic and national values suprahistorically, by idealisation, and though their actions trace a culture's self-concept in hyperbole and metaphor, they contain more than a grain of truth. Thus the South Slavic Prince Marko, famous for his outwitting of the Ottoman Turks who employ him as an unwilling mercenary, reflects the reality of what it was to be a Serb under the imposed control of the Ottoman Empire. Thus the hero-kings of *Beowulf* are praised for their ability to maintain political order in a world fraught with incursions by enemies and the accidents of fate. The relative transparency of modern tales and traditions makes it evident that the 'epic ethos' reaches far beyond its most immediate context, and well

[27] See further Buxton in this volume.

beyond where document-based history can go: the *Kalevala* has long fuelled the emergence of the Finns as an individual nation, as well as the discipline of folk-lore studies and the music of Sibelius. For national identity, epic is a foundational genre.

National character and group identity are often encoded in heroic actions, with a central focus on martial achievement, but there are other sorts of epic vehicles as well. Indeed, if we watch our generalisations carefully, we discover that heroism in the *Iliad* – the acts of war and winning of *kleos* on the battlefield, irrespective of whether one lives or dies – is not entirely coincident with heroism in the *Odyssey*, which consists of winning survival, return and re-establishment of the social order.[28] Just so, the *Siri Epic* portrays a long line of courageous women whose feats include surviving under difficult conditions, weaving together the social fabric and providing for succeeding generations. Simply because we find no battlefield glory in this remarkable epic narrative, we cannot refuse it membership in the larger international genre. Siri and her sisters are heroes of a different sort, as is the Finnish Lemminkäinen, whose very rashness and taste for wooing and adventure contribute to the *Kalevala*'s overall heroic and mythic dynamics. Even champions who in many ways parallel Achilles, Hector, Diomedes and Patroclus sometimes achieve their heroic ends by what we would call trickery, as when the South Slavic *junak* ('hero') Tale of Orašac wins the day when all others fail. Never mind that with his swayback horse, tattered peasant clothes and backwards-mounted standardbearer he looks the part of a foolish impostor; the fact is, as the epic itself puts it, 'Tamo bez njeg' hoda neimade' ('There's no going there [to war] without him').[29] Heroism can usually stand as a dependable indicator of epic, but only if we adjust its nature to each tradition's values and perspectives.

Finally, we reach the long-disputed question of Homer's identity as the epic poet of the *Iliad* and *Odyssey*. Whatever perspective we select must deal with the often contradictory ancient testimony on his place of origin, parentage, historical provenance, repertoire and the like.[30] The nineteenth- and early twentieth-century Analysts imagined one or more master-editors who assembled our texts from constituent shorter songs, while the Unitarians insisted on a single genius author for both works. As a matter of habit we continue to refer to 'Homer' as if we could be confident of a historical bard

[28] See further Clarke in this volume.

[29] On this fascinating trickster figure, see Foley (1995) 32–41. On epic heroes more generally, see Miller (2000).

[30] See further the Introduction to this volume. For a full presentation of the argument made here, see Foley (1999a) 51–62.

at least chiefly responsible for the *Iliad* and *Odyssey* that have survived to us. But what if the Homeric question, as it is commonly called, amounted to a misconstrual of epic authorship? What if the terms in which we frame our investigation of his identity have imposed a false menu of possibilities?

The very multiformity of 'Homer the epic poet' as represented in the ancient sources – from the various lives of Homer through accounts from Herodotus, Plutarch and Proclus – argues for a legendary rather than a real, documentary figure. Instead of seeking to determine which of the disparate histories is true, or trying to reduce their obvious inconsistencies to one archetypal story from which others must have evolved, we would do better to understand Homer as an anthropomorphisation of the epic tradition, a name for the art and practice of epic poetry. Comparative evidence for this phenomenon is abundant. Interviews with South Slavic *guslari*, for example, turned up recurrent reference to a master-bard (called Isak, Huso, or Ćor Huso, among other names) who lived for decades beyond the normal life cycle, was born in many different locales, plied his trade over an extremely wide region (uncharacteristically for this tradition), accomplished heroic feats of epic performance, and was credited with an impossibly large repertoire (its specific contents varying from witness to witness, but always including 'the best songs'). Most telling of all, none of the singers who describe this paragon ever actually met him: he was always one or two villages too far away or lived one too many generations back or in some other fashion existed just beyond the reach of time and place. Singers of Mongolian epic tell a similar kind of tale about the famous Choibang, again best understood as a legendary bard, a figure who far exceeded conventional human abilities in language, athletics, longevity, miraculous feats of performance and so forth. Even if a real figure stands somewhere behind one or more of these idealisations, the process of legend-making – so closely akin to the morphology and transmission of a traditional epic – has had its way with that historical kernel. Given the fit between the diverse ancient evidence on Homer and this model of the multiform epic bard, we should keep in mind that the most realistic answer to the Homeric question is not an individual *aoidos* but the collective epic tradition.

Conclusion

In summary, the early twenty-first century is an exciting time for epic studies, most immediately for the *Iliad* and *Odyssey* but also for their ever-widening international context. As the world continues to open up its treasure-house of long narrative forms, we will come to appreciate both the overall genre and the Homeric poems even more deeply. Epics from six continents already illustrate how much the ancient Greek tradition shares with various other traditions, how parallels and analogues from other times and places can help us grasp the excellence of Homer. Complementarily, the comparative perspective also clarifies the uniqueness of the *Iliad* and *Odyssey*, the ways in which they are finally their own poems, with their own distinct, inimitable genius. Let me close, then, with Homer's own definition of epic poets, which we can profitably extend to all bards who practice the genre of epic (VIII.479–81):

> πᾶσι γὰρ ἀνθρώποισιν ἐπιχθονίοισιν ἀοιδοὶ
> τιμῆς ἔμμοροί εἰσι καὶ αἰδοῦς, οὕνεκ' ἄρα σφέας
> οἴμας Μοῦσ' ἐδίδαξε, φίλησε δὲ φῦλον ἀοιδῶν.

> For among all people of the earth the singers
> are due honor and reverence, because it is them
> the Muse has taught the pathways, for she loves the tribe of singers.

FURTHER READING

The special nature of Homeric epic is best appreciated by consulting as wide a variety of international analogues as possible. Strong comparisons and contrasts include, for example, the epic traditions of Africa (Johnson (1992) on the *Son-Jara* from Mali, Biebuyck and Mateene (1969) on the *Mwindo Epic* from the Banyanga, and Johnson *et al.* (1997) with selections from many different African areas); Arabic regions (Connelly (1986), Reynolds (1995)); Asia (Honko *et al.* (1998a, b) on the *Siri Epic* from southern India, Richman (1991) on the *Ramayana*, Reichl (1992), (2000) on Turkic traditions of central Asia); the Former Yugoslavia (*SCHS*); and Finland (DuBois (1995)). Comparative perspectives on these and other epics are available in several overviews of the world's epic traditions (Oinas (1978), Hatto (1980), Beissinger *et al.* (1999), McCarthy (2001)), and a thorough history of collecting oral epic in modern cultures can be found in Honko (1998) 169–218. On structure and meaning in epics from oral tradition, see Foley (1990), (1991), (1995), (2002a); for direct comparison of Homer to South Slavic oral epic, see Foley (1999a).

12

KEN DOWDEN

The epic tradition in Greece

Introduction: contexts

The later twentieth century saw a trend in the study of classical authors from a historical ('diachronic') approach to one that focused more on the author's own times (a 'synchronic' approach) and on the text itself. Nowhere is this more true than in the case of Homer, where the identification of Homer as an oral poet turned critics inward on his text and its special character. This Homer newly created, or 're-created', each instance of epic for each performance[1] and his work was accordingly part of a largely irrecoverable performance tradition, rather than one in a history of interacting texts.

Nevertheless, we cannot really understand Homer, or the emergence of Greek literature, if we have no idea of the tradition that preceded him and of the different uses made of that tradition by poets of his time. And we should not exaggerate the fluidity of these poems: our *Iliad* and *Odyssey* were relatively fixed texts, which could be badged 'Homer', as far back as the sixth century BC and probably a good deal earlier.[2] It is credible that the poems of his contemporaries were fixed to a similar extent, making after all a family of 'texts', with a recognisable intertextuality. Depending on our views of what was fixed and what was improvised, we may differ on the nature of this intertextuality: perhaps it will be easier to accept the recognition of the argument between Achilles and Agamemnon as a typical motif, 'argument between heroes',[3] than to see in the sudden appearance of Thetis to lead the lament over Achilles (23.14), the footprint of a specific epic that depicted Thetis mourning the dead Achilles.

In any case, Homer continues a tradition of epic poetry (solo performance of narrative) that goes back at least to the fourth millennium BC, or whenever we date 'Proto-Indo-Europeans', the hypothesised linguistic ancestors of the

[1] This develops a view presented by Nagler (1974) 199. On Lord and 're-creation' rather than 'improvisation', see Russo (1997) 248.

[2] See Fowler in this volume. [3] Burgess (2001) 63.

speakers of most of the languages of Europe, of the Indo-Iranian languages and some others. Looking in a different direction, Greek culture was not quarantined – its vibrancy is a product of fertile interaction with other cultures, especially those of the Near East (West (1997a)). Traditional poetry was highly characteristic of these societies, and their poetry, like the alphabet, had a profound influence on Greece. Finally, looking forward in history, Homer stands at the beginning of the slow crystallisation of the genres of literature and has a special canonical, practically super-generic, influence over them. In addition, his realism and anthropomorphism are part of a change in the conceptual world that also underlies the development of Greek sculpture and painting, to which he was to provide so many specific themes.

Origins

Indo-European society, such as we can envisage and reconstruct it (say, around 3500 BC), certainly had myths and public poetry.[4] It would appear, from the traditions in societies that derive significantly from it, such as the Norse (in Scandinavia and Iceland) and the Sanskrit (in India), that this epic embraced issues of traditional history and genealogy, of world-order, of values, and above all of fighting men who had done notable deeds in the past and who inspired, or worried, men in the present. Very rarely, a story or cluster of themes in one tradition so resembles one in another tradition that we conclude that this may be more than coincidence and that there may well have been an Indo-European original story.[5] Some individual characters, or components of them, may go back to these times too: there are some strong points of contact between Herakles and the warrior-god Indra,[6] and between Achilles and one of the heroes of the ancient Sanskrit epic, the Mahābhārata, Arjuna.[7] And the whole story of Agamemnon and Menelaos' retrieval of Helen seems to replay Indo-European myth, evidenced in various forms – for instance in tales of the Aśvins (the Sanskrit equivalent of the Dioscuri)[8] or in the plot structure of the Mahābhārata where the hero-brothers, the Pandavas, must recover their joint wife Draupadī.

The ways in which Greek epic talks also sound like the Sanskrit epic and earlier Vedic hymns. A number of stereotype phrases, 'formulas', match in the two traditions, sometimes using not just the same concepts but what are

4 Dowden (1992) 57–9.

5 Puhvel (1987) 88–9 gives two examples of common material in Norse and Sanskrit tradition.

6 Dumézil (1970), esp. section II

7 Puhvel (1987) 84, for one aspect of this (cross-dressing).

8 Dowden (1992) 59; Puhvel (1987) 59–60, 141–3.

in origin the very same words: 'immortal gods', 'all the immortals', gods who are 'givers of good things', 'broad earth', 'untiring fire', 'boundless sea', '*hieron/iṣirá* might' (Indo-European **iseros* was evidently something like 'active, vigorous, sacred'), 'name-famous', 'unperishing fame', 'ageless and deathless'.[9] On its own it is no surprise to see 'swift horses' in both traditions, but this is part of a total vocabulary which is so cumulatively compelling that we can rule out coincidence. To this stratum also may belong the description of Agamemnon as 'shepherd of the people', mirrored in other cultures.[10] Indeed, these formulaic concepts influence the distinctively Indo-European two-part personal names, like the Greek Onomaklytos ('name-famous') or Eurykles ('broad-fame'). Such names, in a Germanic context, have even been described as mini-poems.[11]

There are also similarities between Greek and Vedic verse and West has reasonably speculated that the metre employed for Greek epic, the dactylic hexameter, with its unusually long lines, has evolved from pairs of lines similar to the Vedic patterns that in turn evolved into the sixteen-syllable verses (*ślókas*) of Sanskrit epic.[12] So, the distant origins of Greek epic seem to lie in the epic of the common society of the linguistic ancestors of the Greeks and Sanskrit-speakers.

As this tradition was unbroken, it also existed in Mycenaean times. Here it presumably transmuted in the economic environment of the great palaces. This was a key stage: as Greek mythology is largely written on a Mycenaean geographical map,[13] the obvious conclusion is that this was a specially creative age which laid the groundwork for the Greekness of our

[9] Durante (1968) 297–309; (1974) ch. 2; West (1988) 154–6. The identity of the Sanskrit and Greek versions of *awesome might* (frequent in Homer) and *unperishing fame* (once only in Homer, 9.413) was first noted, as an etymological fact, by A. Kuhn, *Zeitschrift für Vergleichende Sprachforschung* 2 (1853) 274, 467 respectively. It took longer to realise that this equation implied an Indo-European poetry. Metre led to this conclusion faster, particularly in the work of A. Meillet, culminating in *Les origines indo-européennes des mètres grecs* (Paris 1923). Poetic phrases attracted attention intermittently, e.g. from J. Wackernagel in a 1932 lecture, 'Indogermanische Dichtersprache' (repr., e.g., in Schmitt (1968)), but only received full-scale treatment in the compendious and thoroughgoing work of Schmitt (1967) and in the work of Durante (1971–4). On the metrical side, Nagy (1974), West (1988) are notable in modern times. Watkins (1995) gives the best sketch of the history of this subject and himself has contributed much to its study.

[10] Schmitt (1967) §§582–4, including Sanskrit, Old English (*Beowulf* 610 etc.: *folces hyrde*) and . . . non-Indo-European Akkadian, as Puhvel (1956) 204 had pointed out, on which more below.

[11] By Andreas Heusler ('wie ein kleines Gedicht nach Inhalt und Klang' – see Schmitt (1973) 5); see also West (1988) 153.

[12] West (1997b) 235–6; cf. Janko (1992a) 9–12; Haug and Welo (2001).

[13] Nilsson (1932), Dowden (1992) 60–2.

Greek mythology and for the epic that embodied it. Before then, poets may have been members of the entourage of aristocratic warriors, like the bards that accompanied and praised Celtic warriors.[14] The poetic tradition may also have been preserved by the efforts of leaders themselves, as by Achilles (below) – or in our own times by Radovan Karadjić, himself an exponent of the Bosnian Serb tradition. But the integration of this society into a palace society allowed a new professionalisation of this leisure activity. Association with heroic achievement, and entertainment at lavish dinners, could magnify the status of a palace-based *wanax*. And the courts of Homer's *Odyssey*, which occupy the place in his history where Mycenaean society should be, regularly employ bards: Demodokos amongst the Phaeacians and Phemios in Ithaca. Iliadic heroes do not have bards with them, perhaps because they haven't performed the deeds yet – it is left for Achilles, with Homeric irony, to be found idle in his tent singing the *fames of men* (*klea andrōn*, 9.189).[15] Demodokos, like Homer, is singing of the Trojan War, though its alarming status as a contemporary event ensures the remarkable scene of Odysseus' reaction to the mythology in which he participates.

Sometimes details of Homer's language seem to go back to a dactylic poetry just like Homer's but which cannot be later than Mycenaean times, e.g. when lines can only be made metrically correct by assuming forms that were already obsolete in our late Mycenaean (Linear B) texts.[16] Another sign may be the *phorminx*, an instrument rather like a lyre and specially[17] associated with the epic. Depicted on the Hagia Triada sarcophagus, it may have come from the Near East in Minoan-Mycenaean times and perhaps this was when it became attached to the singing of epic, technologically overhauling inherited oral tradition.[18]

[14] Poseidonios, *FGrHist* 87 F116 (Diodoros, 5.31.2).

[15] There is of course nothing in itself wrong with upper-class composers, like Eumelos of Corinth from the clan of the Bacchiads (on whose work see West (2002)), and Herodotos' uncle Panyassis (see below, p. 204).

[16] (1) All Greek loses *s* before and between vowels (apparent counter-examples are later developments) but there are instances in the epic where there is still a trace of the lost *s*, which means that they originated in at least early Mycenaean times (West (1997b) 228). (2) Sometimes the metre requires *r* to be used as a *vowel*: *androteta* (e.g. 16.857) is really **ănṛtāta* and *ambrote* (14.78) **ămṛtā*; Linear B already has *-ro-* and the intrusive *-d-* in *-ndr-* patterns (West (1997b) 226–30; Horrocks (1997) esp. 201–3). (3) Prepositional prefixes to verbs can still be separable (*apo- thymon -olessen*), a feature lost in Linear B (Horrocks (1980) and (1997) 201-3; West (1988) 156).

[17] It accompanies the *linos* song at 18.569.

[18] Stella (1978) [illegible]; NB the claim at [illegible] that Indo European cultures do not have stringed instruments, only wind and percussion (but Gauls had instruments 'similar to lyres' – see Poseidonios below). See also West (1997a) 612.

The so-called 'Dark Age' that followed the collapse of Mycenaean power was actually a period of sustained economic growth in which trading and cultural links with the East were developed, and the colonisation of Asia Minor intensified. This too was when the shared Greek epic tradition took shape. Language again is an important tool for the Homeric detective: the epic language had passed through a stage when it incorporated features of the Aeolic dialect, some of which could not for metrical reasons be transformed into the Ionic Greek in which we have it. Aeolic Greek was spoken in historical times in the northern part of the west coast of Asia Minor, on Lesbos, and on the mainland in Thessaly and Boeotia (though here it was substantially influenced by West Greek dialects). Its precursors had once been spoken more widely on the mainland and it is part of the route back to Mycenaean society.[19] The Doric dialect, however, which came into mainland Greece (or came into prominence there) after the fall of Mycenaean society, has no part in the formation of the epic language.

The influence of the Near East continued to be powerful after Mycenaean times. Some places had a special importance in the transmission of culture: the bilingualism of Cyprus makes it seem an ideal point for literary form and expression to jump language;[20] and the island of Euboea (so close to the Boeotian home of the orientalising poet Hesiod) was a key point in trade with the East.

As a result, Greek epic reflects not only the long, ultimately Indo-European, epic tradition, but also the generally Semitic traditions of the Near East, embracing such texts as the Gilgamesh epic. The extent of this influence has

[19] Thus there are five stages possibly traceable in the linguistic history of the epic: (1) Indo-European (pp. 189–90 above); (2) pre-Mycenean Greek (see n. 16 above); (3) Mycenaean Greek ('Achaean', see Ruijgh (1957) and n. 57 below for an instance – *autar*); (4) Aeolic Greek; (5) Ionic Greek. The Aeolic stage was already observed by Dikaiarchos in the fourth century BC (fr. 90 Wehrli); it was accounted for in various ways in nineteenth- and twentieth-century scholarship (Ruijgh (1957) 1–3) and may not be different from a northern Mycenaean stage (Palmer (1962) 102–3), but the easiest explanation, if often resisted (cf. Hainsworth (1988) 24 n. 2), is that the Ionic epic tradition continued an earlier Aeolic tradition. Janko (1982) 89–92 demonstrates this anew, suggesting Lesbos as its home (on the Mycenaean colonisation of Lesbos and the embedding of Achilles in Aeolic traditions, see Dowden (1989) ch. 3, e.g. 56); the view is worked out forcefully, with less stress on Lesbos, maybe wisely, by West (1988) 161–5. Detailed studies of the Greek dialects: C. D. Buck, *The Greek Dialects*, 2nd edn (Chicago 1955); Schmitt (1977). Homer's Greek: Palmer (1962), concise update in Palmer (1980) ch. 4.1. Aeolic dialect in Homer: P. Wathelet, *Les Traits éoliens dans la langue de l'épopée grecque* (Rome 1970) and G. Hinrichs, *De homericae elocutionis vestigiis aeolicis* (Berlin 1875). Ionic Greek evolved too: the lost digamma at the beginning of words (*w*-), without which lines would not scan, may belong to an Ionic dialect much older than Homer's – ninth/eighth century, thinks West (1997b) 228.

[20] West (1997a) 621–9.

been copiously displayed by West.[21] It is striking that some of the specific comparisons we use are the same for both Indo-European tradition and for Semitic tradition – for example, the 'broad earth' and the 'shepherd of the people'.[22] Unless such phrases are banal and obvious,[23] we must suppose that epic poetry did not respect linguistic boundaries but was truly international from the earliest times. Oral poetic tradition was both conservative in its assertion of pasts and at the same time responsive and fashionable. Most cultures possessed it, in the same way that most cultures practised animal sacrifice, and Homer represents a culmination of inheritances and influences at a moment when a new chapter was being written in the story of the movement from performance to the literary book.

Contemporary generic contexts

'Epic' is our word for a genre, inheriting the generic distinctions that were consolidated in the Hellenistic age. It may have looked rather different in the time of Homer.[24] Occasions laid the foundation for genre – however freely that genre might then be developed.[25] One prominent model was that of participatory songs, with their lead singer and responding group. These included those sung at the vintage (the *Linos* song, 18.565–72), as well as 'Paeans' (hymns of social solidarity sung to Apollo-Paian as healer, 1.473, 22.391),[26] and laments (*threnoi*, 24.719–76).[27] Similarly participatory were dithyrambs, songs involving Dionysos – sung by groups of fifty in historical times. Weddings too had their special song, the *hymenaios* (18.493) and doubtless so did other occasions.

Epic operates a different model (Ford (1997) 401): it is sung by a soloist before a non-participating audience, whose ideal response is to 'sit listening in silence' (1.325–6). As times changed, performance would no longer use the *cithara* and the 'singing' became a metaphorical posture: rather, the performer, known in historical times as a 'rhapsode',[28] marked his demand for

21 West (1997a) ch. 5. See also S. Morris (1997) esp. 616–23.

22 See West (1997a) 226 f. for this problem.

23 The expressions are not actually identical: Schmitt (1967) §584; the Sanskrit literally means *cowherd of the race*, the Greek *shepherd of the peoples*.

24 On genre, see Ford (1997) and Foley in this volume.

25 Ford (1997) 400; Fowler (1987a) ch. 3 esp. 90, viewing lyric poetry as primarily determined by occasion but hexameter poetry including epic as being already in effect more literary.

26 The definitive work on paeans is Rutherford (2001).

27 West (1997a) 43–4; Ford (1997) 400–1.

28 Càssola (1975) xxvi; first explicitly in Hdt. *Hist.* 5.67; implied in Pindar, *Nem.* 2.1–3, and 'Hesiod', fr. 357.

attention to his solo by his staff, in just the same way as speakers in Homeric assemblies claim their right to be heard by holding the sceptre, a grand staff. Hesiod's sceptre at *Theogony* 30 is the staff, I think, of a non-singing performer.[29] Homer may keep quiet about the rhapsode's staff, because he maintains his archaic tone so consistently and meticulously.

In this light, we should not overlook the collection of solo texts known as the *Homeric Hymns* – which, though they cannot, by their language, actually have been composed by 'Homer' deserve some space in a book devoted to him. They are typically said to range from the eighth century to the second (Clay (1997) 489), though the great majority are archaic products. Apart from the misplaced *Hymn to Ares* and the hymns to Sun and Moon, probably none is older than the seventh century BC (it depends on the date of Homer) or later than the fifth (the *Hymn to Pan* must be at least that late).[30] The main collection was assembled by the third century when Kallimachos wrote *Hymns* presuming it.

The *Hymns* are elusive works, whose flavour and interest it is difficult to apprehend. The basis for their survival is not always literary merit as we understand it, though 'charm, humour and pathos' are more apparent in the longer, ambitious pieces.[31] Rather, they variously enshrine a religious sentiment, if distant from most modern conceptions of religion. They constitute hymns in that they are addressed to a god, and capture his or her distinctive features, sometimes referring to, or even telling, a story or two. But these hymns are not restricted narrowly to ritual – they could have been performed wherever there was an audience ready to hear the praises of a god. Strictly, paeans and dithyrambs were hymns too;[32] these *Homeric Hymns* are something distinct from that, a particular type of hymn composed in the hexameter metre of the epic. Recognised as distinct, they were collected together and seem internally to recognise their own coherence: some of them conclude with the formula, 'beginning with you I will pass to

[29] Pausanias, 9.30.3 (cf. Nikokrates, *FGrHist* 376 F8); West (1966) 163–4; Càssola (1975) xxiv.

[30] Janko (1982) is the most detailed attempt at dating, though his statistical method means that only the long texts can be dated – and only relatively to other texts, *Iliad*, *Odyssey*, *Theogony*, *Cypria*. Inasmuch as he has a sense of absolute dates, the *Hymn to Aphrodite* may come around 675, *Apollo (Delian)* around 660 and *Demeter* around 640. But there are mighty arguments (West (1995)) for down-dating Homer to the 670s/660s anyway, perhaps even the 650s, and that would bring down other dates with it.

[31] Kirk (1985) tries to inscribe the long hymns in the history of literature; 'charm etc.' comes from Clay (1997) 499. No one has much to say about the numerous short hymns.

[32] Fowler (1987a) 129 n. 31. Fowler 94–5 also observes the 'semantic shifts' in the word *hymnos* from archaic to classical times from praise of a god to praise of men to almost any song which is sufficiently formal and festive.

another hymn', which sounds more like a speaking book than an evening's hymnathon.

Thucydides (3.104) refers to the *Delian Hymn to Apollo* as a *prooimion*, 'prelude', which may point to a typical occasion for hexameter hymns. Such works of pagan piety or propriety could serve as preludes to an epic performance (this idea goes back to Wolf in 1795),[33] much as inscriptions often begin with the word GODS as a pious authentication of the decisions they record. Hesiod's hymn to the Muses that begins his *Theogony* may offer an integrated example,[34] and some ancient copies of the *Iliad* even had a hymn to Apollo and the Muses at the start.[35] A different hymn to Apollo and the Muses is found in our collection as no. 25, as though performance of the *Iliad* typically began with a hymnic 'cadenza' – but Hesiod, like Beethoven, had written his own 'cadenza'. Conversely, if we are to take seriously a line like 'we the bards sing you as we begin and as we end' (*1 Hymn Dionysus* 17–18), these pieces could also round off a performance. This might be a factor in the otherwise poor closure of epic texts, the way they just peter out ('so they handled the burial of Hector tamer of horses').

The *Hymns* differ markedly in length: they are long (4 of them, 293–580 lines), or they are short (29 of them, 3–59 lines).[36] One possible way of viewing this is that, as a beginning, such a hymn need be no more than our saying of grace before a meal, if with 'attitude' and atmosphere. Some, however, use this performance opportunity to build up something large and ambitious, much as Homer did with the epic itself, and include extended narrative – a feature which distinguishes this genre from the hymnic traditions of Egypt and the Near East.[37]

Homer's epic was only one type of solo performance for entertainment and for negotiating the values of the community. The works ascribed to Hesiod present a large variety of subject-matter in hexameters and are arguably designed for the same sort of performance environment as the epic, something mythicised in the legend of a poetic competition between Homer and Hesiod. We know best his piece of 'Wisdom Literature', the *Works and Days*, and his *Theogony* ('births of the gods'), a subject that was already known to Homer (14.201) and would blossom in the age following him.[38] Another extensive and influential work that went under his name, the *Catalogue of*

33 Strictly Wolf saw them as preludes to performances of *Homer* (Clay (1997) 495).

34 Càssola (1975) xxi.

35 Càssola (1975) lviii–lix; cf. West (1966) 150.

36 Figures compiled by Kirk (1985).

37 For narrative as distinctive, see Rutherford (2001) 74. For difficulties concerning how to view the variation in the length of the hymns, see Clay (1997) 49[illegible]. Nonetheless, it [illegible] *long* hymn that Thucydides characterises as a prelude.

38 West (1966) 12: 'In the archaic period the genre was as actively cultivated as heroic narrative.'

Women, listed and organised mythological women and was a key work in giving shape to Greek mythology (this sort of poetry is conjured up at XI.225–329). As the oral tradition had existed in an illiterate society, it also enshrined memory (the Muse is properly a goddess-resource of memory) and therefore at times rightly proceeded by catalogue, a style preserved in the Catalogue of Ships (*Iliad* 2). Other Hesiodic poems explored a variety of mythic subjects, such as the prophet Melampous (known to XV.225 – and prophets clearly have their niche, as the Kalchas of the *Iliad* or the Teiresias of the *Odyssey* show) or the ancestral king of the Dorian Greeks, Aigimios. And that is not to mention the Instructions of Cheiron (who trained Achilles and Peleus and was 'justest of the Centaurs', 11.832, 16.143–4) or the *Astronomy* (myths about the origins of constellations). Thus, amidst what may have been an increasingly innovative use of solo performance, Homer both affirmed and remodelled the traditional warrior-epic.

Cyclic and other epic

He was not, however, alone. We know of a range of epics, now lost, and whatever the uncertainties of dating, most of them must have been composed within the following century. Furthermore, they generally continued the traditional themes and subjects which had been expressed in earlier epics, which would have been amongst the influences on Homer.

Some epics he knew dealt with Herakles (5.638, 14.323–4; XI.267–8, 601–26)[39] and we know of a *Sack of Oichalia* (cf. 2.596, 730, VIII.224). In Theban mythology there was an *Oidipodeia* ('Oedipus-epic', cf. 23.679, XI.271), a *Thebaid* about the Seven against Thebes, and an *Epigonoi* about the attack on Thebes by the descendants of the Seven. Diomedes, one of these descendants, talks about the *Epigonoi* (4.406) and lives in the shadow of Tydeus, the father that he barely knew, who died in the *Thebaid* (6.222, 14.113–32). Teiresias, consulted by Odysseus, belongs in a Theban world too. On the other hand, Achilles' suggestion that Thetis should mention the hundred-handed monster Briareus in her application to Zeus for support (1.403), seems to draw on a specific kingship-in-heaven narrative – one looking rather like what we know of the *Titanomachy* attributed to the Corinthian poet Eumelos, of which there are other echoes too. This poem may account for one of only two appearances of Dionysos in the *Iliad* (6.132, 135) and for

[39] A story of Herakles on Kos (14.255) may presuppose an epic like the *Meropis* (Bernabé (1987) 131–5).

the division of the universe between Zeus, Poseidon and Hades (15.187–95).[40]

There must also have been an *Argonautika* if the ship Argo is 'famous to all' (XII.69), and that must be where our *Odyssey* got the Clashing Rocks and even the whole Circe story. The descent of Odysseus to the Underworld depends on other heroes such as Herakles performing a *katabasis* ('descent') – Herakles tells Odysseus briefly about it at XI.617–26. Other themes, such as cattle-rustling and wife-winning, were clearly worked up in poems whose flavour he borrowed for his own purposes. This is particularly visible when wise elders, Nestor and Phoinix, draw lessons from history, which in the oral tradition can only mean epic, the *klea andrōn hērōōn*, 'fames of hero men' (9.524–5).[41] Cattle raids at Pylos and the magical destruction of the hero Meleager evoke poetry such as we find in the Old Irish tradition.

Homer knows a whole range of Trojan material which was told more straightforwardly in other epics now lost. At least one possible author is named for each of these poems, with Lesches and Eugammon perhaps being more credible than the earlier authors.[42] Our knowledge of the poems is due above all to a summary of their plots by Proclus (perhaps the fifth-century AD Neoplatonic philosopher). It has generally been thought that these epics were designed all along to fill in the story around Homer and to divide up the job amongst themselves. This is certainly the impression given by the collected version of them which Proclus knew, the *Epic Cycle* as it had been known since the Hellenistic age.[43] This *Cycle* appears also to have included the *Titanomachy* (battle of Zeus and his Olympian gods against the Titans) and possibly a *Theogony*, but not the Theban epics, though they were contemporary with some of the epics in the *Cycle* and similar in style. Truth to tell, we do not know exactly why this was called the *Kyklos* ('Wheel') or what coherence the term implied,[44] but it is increasingly recognised that there is something suspect about it. This has been brought to a head by

40 West (2002) 110–18.

41 Nestor at 1.260–72, 4.319–21, esp. 11.670–761, 23.629–42. Phoinix at 9.524–99.

42 Burgess (2001) 8–9; 11 (*Telegony* and Cyrene); for Lesches see Bravo (2001) *passim*. The traditional Greek chronology in absolute terms rests on guesswork, but it does put the activity of Lesches around 658 and Eugammon around 567, as against 760/735 for other authors; they may therefore be more historical, cf. Bravo (2001) 84 n. 42.

43 First in this sense in Alexandrian commentators, though the term first appears in Aristotle, *Posterior Analytics* 1.12: see Davies (2001) 1–2. Burgess (2001) 15 also discusses early usage of the term.

44 Nagy ([illegible]) [illegible] term first used to express the perfect craftsmanship of the large poem. Perhaps the cyclic epics are the spokes of the super-poem?

Burgess ((2001) 18–33, 135–48), who argues convincingly that the way the story is divided between the poems, and occasional citations of the poems for events that should be beyond their scope, suggest that the *Epic Cycle* was formed by taking originally independent, and overlapping, poems and 'cropping' a number of books from beginning and end of them to achieve reasonable fit.[45] He thinks this was done early in the Hellenistic age, though it could have been earlier.

One conclusion from this cropping is that, though the *Iliad* and *Odyssey* are still unusually long epics, the cyclic epics will not originally have been as short as we have usually imagined. Another is that they were not as slavishly dependent on Homer as they might have been if they had been designed simply to tell the rest of the story around him.

In any case, the content (which I paraphrase) and number of the books which Proclus summarised was as follows:

The eleven books of, or from, the ***Cypria* of Stasinos** or Hegesias (in either case a Cypriot) begin with the marriage of Peleus and Thetis, the dispute between the three goddesses, the Judgment of Paris and Paris eloping with Menelaos' wife Helen. Her brothers, the Dioscuri, become 'immortal on alternate days'. The expeditionary force is put together: Palamedes reveals that Odysseus is only pretending to be mad in order to avoid the war. Now they are at Aulis, and Kalchas interprets the portent of the snake and the sparrows. Having set out, they sack Troy, only to discover they have sacked the wrong city – Teuthrania. Achilles marries on Skyros (so that his son Neoptolemos may be conceived?) and heals Telephos, whom he had wounded at Teuthrania. Now Telephos will guide them to Troy. Back at Aulis, Agamemnon while hunting offends Artemis and must sacrifice his daughter Iphigeneia, but Artemis takes her from the altar to make her immortal amongst the Taurians. At Tenedos, Philoktetes is bitten by a snake; and the suppurating wound stinks so much that they abandon him on Lemnos. They land at Troy, and Protesilaos is the first to be killed. An embassy seeks restitution of Helen and property from the Trojans, but is rebuffed. The siege begins and the surrounding cities are sacked. Achilles, fuelled by desire to set eyes upon Helen, has an expedition into Troy, and then sacks a few cities, and kills Troilos. He gains Briseis amidst these spoils. Odysseus brings about the death of Palamedes. And finally there is a catalogue of the Trojan allies.[46] Now the *Iliad* may

45 There remains a problem with the contents of the *Cypria*, on which see Burgess (1996) and especially Finkelberg (2000) 11 who argues that contradictory ancient references show that the *Cypria* reflected 'in the written form the multiformity of the oral tradition', unlike the more standardised *Iliad*. However, the text was surely fixed by the time of Herodotos, as Burgess (2001) 20 points out, and Bravo (2001) 53 destroys the key piece of evidence if Herodotos, 2.117, is a careless later interpolation.

46 Given that there is already such a catalogue in the *Iliad* (2.786–877), this supports the view that the *Cypria* was not originally meant to introduce the *Iliad* (Burgess (1996) 85–7; (2001) 135, 138). A further possibility is that the *Iliad* originally lacked this catalogue (Davies (2001)

begin and tell its idiosyncratically selected story of fifty-two days in the penultimate year of the war.

In the five books of the ***Aithiopis* of Arktinos of Miletos**, the Amazon Penthesileia arrives to help the Trojans, but is slain by Achilles; Thersites taunts Achilles with loving Penthesileia – and is killed by him; Achilles is purified of the murder, on Lesbos. Now Memnon the Aethiopian arrives with armour made by Hephaistos, and Thetis warns Achilles about Memnon (and what follows from his death). Memnon kills Antilochos, Achilles kills Memnon. Memnon's mother Dawn begs Zeus for immortality for him, and is successful. Meanwhile Achilles swoops into the city with Trojans on whom he is wreaking havoc, but is shot down by Paris and Apollo. There is a mighty battle as Ajax drags the body back and Odysseus covers him. Thetis arrives with the Muses and laments her son, then takes him up from the pyre to immortality on Leuke ('White' Island). At the burial games occurs the dispute of Odysseus and Ajax over the arms of Achilles.

The four books of the ***Little Iliad* of Lesches of Mytilene** begin with Odysseus gaining the arms of Achilles; Ajax commits suicide and dies. Odysseus kidnaps Helenos the Trojan prophet and discovers that Philoktetes must be brought back from Lemnos. Diomedes fetches him, he is healed and slays Paris in single combat; Menelaos mutilates the body. Now Deiphobos marries Helen. Odysseus brings Neoptolemos from Skyros, gives him the arms of Achilles, and Achilles appears in person to him. He now kills Eurypylos, the last ally to arrive to help Troy. To break the siege, the Wooden Horse is built. Odysseus disfigures himself and slips into Troy; he is recognised by Helen and plots with her. Later, he and Diomedes steal the Palladion (the powerful statue of Athene that protected Troy). The Greeks burn their camp, sail away to Tenedos and the Trojans take in the Wooden Horse and hold a victory feast.

In the two books of the ***Sack of Troy* (*Iliou Persis*) of Arktinos**, the Trojans debate what to do with the Wooden Horse, decide to dedicate it to Athene, and feast (which, NB, has already happened in the previous poem). Two snakes appear and destroy Laocoon and one of his sons. Aeneas and his followers take the portent to heart and withdraw to Mt Ida. Sinon lights beacons for the Achaean fleet, and the Greeks take Troy. This is when Neoptolemos kills Priam at the altar of Zeus Herkeios and Menelaos recovers Helen, slaughtering Deiphobos. Ajax son of Oileus drags Cassandra away and, tangled with her, the ancient wooden statue of Athene. The Greeks want to stone him, but he seeks refuge at the altar of Athene. They burn down the city and slaughter Polyxena at Achilles' tomb; Odysseus kills Astyanax; and Neoptolemos gets Andromache. Now the Greeks are sailing away from Troy, but Athene is planning destruction at sea.

48–9) and that the *Cypria*'s catalogue has found its way into the *Iliad*. ('T[illegible] in the *Cypria* and the *Iliad* were very similar, if Apollodorus has based his version on the *Cypria*', Burgess (1996) 85–6 referring to Apollodorus, *Ep*. 3.34–5.) Book 2 is rather long.

As the five books from the ***Returns*** (***Nostoi***) **by Hagias of Troezen** begin, Agamemnon and Menelaos quarrel about the return, and people go their separate ways. Agamemnon stays behind to placate the wrath of Athene. Diomedes and Nestor get home safe. Then Menelaos reaches Egypt with his five surviving ships. Kalchas, Leontes and Polypoites get to Kolophon, and Kalchas dies there.[47] Despite warnings from the ghost of Achilles, Agamemnon sets out. Ajax son of Oileus is killed in a great storm. Neoptolemos, on Thetis' advice, goes home on foot, meeting Odysseus at Maroneia in Thrace, presently burying Phoinix, and finally being recognised by Peleus. Agamemnon is murdered, and Orestes and Pylades take revenge. And Menelaos gets home. Which is where the *Odyssey* slots in.

The *Odyssey* leads to two books of the ***Telegony*** **of Eugammon of Cyrene**. The suitors are buried. Odysseus prays to the Nymphs and goes to Elis to inspect his herds; entertained there by Polyxenos, he is given a mixing-bowl richly decorated in mythological themes. He then goes back to Ithaca, does the sacrifices Teiresias had told him to, goes to the Thesprotians and marries Kallidike their queen; he fights a war for them and in the course of it Apollo has to break up a battle between Athene and Ares. Kallidike dies, and Odysseus' son Polypoites takes over. He himself returns to Ithaca, where Telegonos (his son by Circe) is looking for him and ravaging the land; Odysseus goes out to defend the land and is killed by his son. Telegonos realises his mistake, buries his father, takes Telemachos and Penelope back to Circe, who makes them immortal; thenceforth, he cohabits with Penelope and Telemachos with Circe.

If the *Telegony* seems aberrant, it may be struggling to reconcile varying local traditions.[48] But otherwise these Trojan poems are best viewed as representing a standard tradition independently of Homer[49] and predecessors of such poems will have been reflected by him. This point is not always fully appreciated, since the specific cyclic epics we know about have been negatively viewed since Aristotle in order to magnify Homer.[50] It does not help either that they are lost or that they have been believed, probably wrongly as

[47] The text says they bury Teiresias (where had he come from?). I have followed those who correct the text in the light of Hesiod, fr. 278 M.-W. (Strabo, 14.1.27).

[48] I am grateful to Ruth Scodel for the reminder that Thesprotians too, or the Greeks that met them, had their traditions. These were presumably enshrined in a predecessor of the *Telegony*, the *Thesprotis* – which Clement says he plagiarised (Clem. Alex., *Strom.* 6.2.25.1 (*Telegony* T3 Bernabé), Pausanias, 8.12.5). If Teiresias promised 'death (far) from the sea' (XI.134–5), then death amongst the Thesprotians provides it – see Davies (2001) 88 – unless we take seriously the version of the *Telegony* (fr. 4 Bernabé, with Burgess (2001) 153) that Telegonos killed him with a spear made from a poisonous stingray!

[49] As Burgess (2001) esp. 134–5, though perhaps Burgess' poems have become too isolated from each other.

[50] Burgess (2001) 18–19: structure condemned by Aristotle (*Poetics* 23); literary quality deplored since Aristarchos.

we have seen, simply to fill in the story around Homer (answering, e.g. the question 'Where did Briseis come from?'). Finally, concentration on the oral aspects of Homer's tradition has sat uneasily with the search for intertextuality in Homer. Yet those who have explored intertextuality, the largely German tradition of 'Neoanalysts',[51] have made some telling inferences about Homer's method and meaning by comparing the *Iliad* with cyclic epic and exploring ways in which his audience may be meant to recall specific incidents as related in these poems.

The *Aithiopis* above all casts interesting light on the *Iliad*. Here, the role of Antilochos has seemed specially important. In the *Aithiopis* he is Achilles' closest friend, and his death is the catalyst for the death of Achilles, which looms over the *Iliad* and is anticipated by it, particularly in the area of Books 16–23. Antilochos suddenly and unexpectedly acquires significance as Patroklos is faded out: *Antilochos* (17.653) must tell Achilles the news of Patroklos' death (which on this view foreshadows Antilochos' own imminent death) and *he* is treated with special consideration in the funeral games. Achilles responds to Patroklos' death by lying 'hugely' on the ground, intertextually anticipating his own death,[52] and Thetis arrives awkwardly in a sort of dress rehearsal for the real lament for her son (esp. 18.70–2). If Patroklos is stopped from taking Troy by Apollo, that would be rather odd, but for the fact that its purpose is to anticipate *Achilles'* final onslaught on Troy where *he* is halted by Apollo (whom he reviles at 22.15) and shot by Paris – rather than by Paris' avatar Euphorbos (16.849–50). It looks as though Homer has constructed the later books of the *Iliad* with powerful resonances and anticipations of an epic plot very similar to that of the *Aithiopis* – possibly an earlier version of that poem, or (why not?) his own.

The reminiscence of Aulis (2.303–32) and the Catalogue of Ships (2.484–760) reach out to tellings of the departure for Troy. Helen on the wall (Book 3) recalls the arrival. The *Doloneia* (Book 11) anticipates Odysseus and Diomedes' theft of the Palladion, the almost magical statue of Athene (*Little Iliad*), and Achilles and Priam's discussion of their fathers in Achilles' hut (Book 24) has a non-coincidental relationship with Achilles' son

[51] Scholars such as W. Kullmann, notable e.g. for Kullmann (1960); see M. E. Clark, 'Neoanalysis: a bibliographical review', *CW* 79 (1986) 379–94; Willcock (1997); Dowden (1996) esp. 47 n. 1. On the quest for reconciliation between oral poetics and Neoanalysis, see Burgess (2001) 240 n. 4; on intertextuality and oral poetics, *ibid*. 134; Fowler in this volume pp. 228–30.

[52] This distinctive Greek phrase describes the dead Achilles at xxiv. 40 and is on this hypothesis drawn originally from a poem which, like the *Aithiopis*, contained the death of Achilles. See Dowden (1996) 59 and n. 63 for bibliography and discussion.

Neoptolemos slaughtering Priam at an altar in his home (*Sack of Troy*).[53] We can of course argue about which episode presupposes which, but the impact is greater if we credit Homer with a sophisticated intertextuality.[54] The funeral games in *Iliad* 23 anticipate subsequent stories: they prepare the dynamics for the dispute of Odysseus and Ajax over the weapons of Achilles (23.708–35); they also prepare the ground for the conflict between Locrian Ajax and Athene (23.774, 782). Less specifically, the *Odyssey* is just one *Nostos* ('Return') of a hero. And we never really discover why Odysseus is 'city-sacker' or indeed Achilles 'swift-footed'. In the latter case he may keep up with Hektor in Book 22, but there was a cyclic story of how he caught and murdered Priam's son Troilos even though the latter was galloping away on horseback (his death was in the *Cypria*).

Homer had a distinctive style in comparison with the cyclic and similar epics, as Jasper Griffin once showed.[55] Except for Odysseus' first-person narrative to Alkinoos (Books IX–XII), Homer adopts a realism that excludes the magical and the fantastic – not for him the seventeen oracles and prophecies of the cyclic epics. The fantastic is not a new decadence in the tradition after Homer, but rather, as Griffin demonstrates, is something that Homer opts out of. Ajax and Achilles may be invulnerable in the cyclic epics, and Memnon may gain immortality in the *Aithiopis* and Achilles the Lordship of the White Island. Tydeus too in a Theban epic might have gained the immortality that Athene was bringing down from heaven, had he not disgusted her by eating his enemy Melanippos' brain. Lynkeus can have superhuman sight, and Achilles superhuman speed. But in the *Iliad* Achilles is brought up by a man (Phoinix), not a monster (Cheiron the Centaur only leaves traces at 11.832) and Homer leaves aside the marital difficulties of Peleus and Thetis, in particular her capacity for changing shape. Only for a moment is this image broken when Achilles' horse gives voice (19.404–23), a strange and incongruous episode. The hints of a sexual desire of Achilles for the Amazon Penthesileia as he killed her, or the cowardice of Odysseus as he sows salt, pretending to be mad to avoid the danger of war, or the sheer blasphemy of Kapaneus, despiser of the gods blown away by Zeus's thunderbolt at Thebes – these things are cyclic, unsuitable for Homer's chosen style.

53 Virgil perhaps reverses the flow at *Aeneid* 2.540–1.

54 For this sort of intertextuality, cf. John Foley's discussion of a process in the *Mwindo Epic* of 'part standing for the implied whole' (p. 177): the *Iliad* may usually, or always, have been performed in part (cf. Dowden (1996) 50–1) and itself is situated within an implied Troy story (cf. Burgess (2001) 147), which in turn is part of the corpus (intertext) of Greek myth. However, this is not to say that the *Iliad* and *Odyssey* are simply the episodic ingredients of a super-epic; cf. Ruth Scodel (p. 47) on 'episodes from a notional epic'.

55 Griffin (1977) esp. 48–52.

In what little survives of the text of these epics, Griffin evokes some stylistic differences. Their swift pace seems to have led to their being blunter and more pedestrian.[56] A later poet expresses loathing for 'these Cyclic poets who say *autar epeita* ('and next')',[57] a feature which Griffin illustrates from a fragment of the *Thebaid*:

> and he, Zeus-born hero, blond Polynices
> first set a fine table beside Oedipus
> a silver one of divinely intelligent Kadmos; *and next*
> he filled a fine gold cup with sweet wine;
> but when (Oedipus) noticed beside him his father's
> valuable prizes, great evil fell upon his heart,
> and straightaway upon his own sons both of them he
> prayed grievous curses, not unnoticed by the Erinys of the gods . . .

Nevertheless, for all Griffin's ingenuity and good taste, it is hard to judge a poem's style from such fragmentary remains (as admitted, if countered, by Griffin (1977) 52) and the danger of subjectivity is always present. Griffin's comment on a passage of the *Cypria* that 'the list of flowers is too long'[58] is worrying and might cause problems with the Catalogue of Ships or the listing of nymphs at 18.39–48:[59]

> The clothes she put over her skin were those the Graces and Seasons
> had made for her and dyed in spring flowers
> such as the Seasons bear, in crocus and hyacinth
> and vigorous violet and the fine flower of rose,
> sweet and nectarine, and in ambrosial buds,
> ablaze,[60] of streaming narcissus; such were the clothes that Aphrodite
> put on, fragranced with every type of season.
>
> (*Cypria*, bk 1, fr. 4 Bernabé)

These authors made different choices and, if perhaps they were not as great as Homer, they were not therefore without value, style or imagination, and their basic narrative style may even have led to the simple character of early Greek prose books (Bravo (2001) 84–9). It may indeed have been from

56 See Burgess (2001) 146; Griffin (1977) 51; Bravo (2001) 79 – who sees the *Little Iliad* as especially rapid.

57 *Autar* for 'and' is deeply archaic, belonging to the 'Achaean' strand in the epic vocabulary. In fairness, Homer does use it a lot – seventy-eight times (Ruijgh (1957) 37).

58 Griffin (1977) 50. Burgess (2001) 158 equates Griffin's approach with that of Aristarchos: later than Homer, worse than Homer.

59 This is [illegible] problem passage, denounced by Alexandrian critics and thought by West (1995) 208 to be based (by Homer) on Hesiod, *Theogony* 240–62.

60 'Ablaze' (*aithesi*) is Ludwich's correction of the manuscripts' 'flowers' (*anthesi*).

them rather than from the overpowering example of Homer that the epic tradition developed. To give some examples, there would be an epic on Theseus in the late sixth century BC, a fourteen-book epic on Herakles by Herodotos' uncle Panyassis (around 490), and Antimachos' *Thebaid* (early 300s). For Kallimachos, Antimachos' poetry was bloated, but this was a tradition that could not be repressed and would lead via the *Thebaid* of Antagoras in the early 200s and the *Argonautika* of Apollonios of Rhodes (*c.* 250) on to many more examples, culminating in the Roman tradition with such masterpieces as the *Aeneid* of Virgil and the *Thebaid* of Statius, and in the Greek tradition with a work building on the popularity of epic in late imperial Egypt, the fifth-century magniloquence of Nonnos' 48-book *Dionysiaka*.[61] And this is simply to consider mythological epic as opposed to the epics based on local history and military and political subjects, or with the whole range of artistic production that Homer and his tradition influenced. Aeschylus after all acknowledged that his tragedies were just 'slices of Homer'.

Conclusion

So, Homer's epics stand in a tradition which recedes through Mycenaean courts and Indo-European warriors into the mists of history. In the context of his own times, his working environment is likely to have been amongst the aristocrats at leisure and the religious festivals that between them represented the ways in which the archaic *polis* had moved on from the Mycenaean world.[62] At the same time, the influence of performers from the Near East, their manners and their repertoire, was felt, however indirectly.

Homer had his place in a rich context of poetry and song, some solo, some with responding chorus. All of it was part of his world of reference and had its influence on him. But more particularly and specially, he drew on the work of his competitors and recent predecessors in the epic in order to heighten the significance and scope of his own work. More than that, he adopted a distinct and somewhat austere tone, which formed part of the special intensity of his work. As he began his hymn for that evening, perhaps to the god under whose auspices the festival was held, the audience knew that this composer was about to open a distinctive window on the epic tradition which he had inherited. What they could not know was the impact on the rest of European literature.

[61] Bravo (2001) 52 calls attention to the numerous third- and fourth-century papyri (including a scrap from the *Little Iliad*!).

[62] Cf. de Polignac (1995) esp. 150–4.

FURTHER READING

On the hypothesised poetry of the Proto-Indo-Europeans English readers should read Watkins (1995) (more detail in n. 9). Arguably the best sense of the contents and scope of the *Mahābhārata* and other Indo-European epic traditions is given by Jaan Puhvel, *Comparative Mythology* (Baltimore and London 1987), e.g. ch. 5. The best translation of the *Mahābhārata*, a superb edition altogether, is that begun by the late J. A. B. van Buitenen, e.g. vol. 1, *The Mahābhārata, I, The Book of the Beginning* (Chicago 1973) (see too James L. Fitzgerald's pages at *http://web.utk.edu/~jftzgrld/MBh1Home.html*). The influence of the East on Greek epic and literature of all sorts is bountifully illustrated or suggested by West (1997a). On the forms of Greek that Homer uses, you need to go back to Palmer (1962) or (1980). On the cyclic epics the classic article was Griffin (1977), now accessibly reprinted (see bibliography), but Burgess (2001) is a huge step forward. The *Homeric Hymns* are now easily available in the Oxford World's Classics series: M. Crudden (trs.), *The Homeric Hymns* (Oxford 2001). Fragments of the cyclic and other early epics (Greek text and English translation) are now conveniently available in M. West, *Greek Epic Fragments* (Loeb Classical Library, Cambridge Mass. and London 2003). Willcock has been the English scholar who has given (judicious) house-room to Neoanalysis; his (1997) piece is the best starting point.

13

ROBIN OSBORNE

Homer's society

Introduction

What sort of a world did Homer live in? What sort of a world does Homer create? If we allow that 'Homer' in these questions stands not for the text in the form we have it but for the whole tradition that created that text, the difficulty of answering these questions becomes plain. This chapter endeavours to explain what we know about the societies in which the epic tradition was shaped, to describe the social and political arrangements implied or alluded to in the *Iliad* and the *Odyssey*, and to examine the relationship between the worlds in which 'Homer' lived and the worlds which 'Homer' created.[1]

Greek society in the Late Bronze Age and Early Iron Age

The epic tradition which lies behind the *Iliad* and *Odyssey* was already flourishing in the late Bronze Age. Some of the evidence for that proposition is linguistic, some of it archaeological: words and objects (e.g. a boar's tusk helmet, 10.261–5) appear in the poem whose presence cannot easily be explained by their survival or people remembering them into the time that the *Iliad* and *Odyssey* as we have them were put together.[2] Any reading of the *Iliad* or *Odyssey* needs to be informed by an appreciation that the epic tradition had been formed and shaped through successive very different social arrangements and material cultures.

What we know best in the late Bronze Age are the palace societies.[3] The citadels of Mycenae and Tiryns in the north-east Peloponnese have been extensively excavated; the palaces of Pylos, in the south-west Peloponnese, and Knossos, in Crete, have yielded extensive records written on clay tablets, as well as rich architectural remains. Although many details will be long

[1] I am grateful to the editor for comments on an earlier draft.

[2] See ch. 12 above, Horrocks (1980), West (1988), Sherratt (1990), Bennet (1996).

[3] For an introduction to the Bronze Age generally see Dickinson (1994).

debated, the broad outlines of palace societies seem clear. From the end of the early Bronze Age onwards (i.e. end of third millennium BC), population throughout the Aegean world shows tendencies to cluster in nucleated settlements; these settlements grow in size and sophistication during the first half of the second millennium. With street plans exhibiting some regularity, houses with two storeys and many rooms, and some grouping of major facilities around squares, these towns suggest a high degree of community organisation. Contemporary with this growth of towns is the emergence of the first of the palaces, at Knossos. But the major development of palaces on the mainland begins towards the middle of the second millennium and reaches its height around 1300 BC.

Architecturally the mainland palaces are distinguished by units comprising a large hall, its roof supported by columns, approached from a court, often via an anteroom, flanked by corridors leading to further small rooms. Construction of the main floor employs timber framing, with an additional mud-brick storey above. The main rooms often show signs of painted fresco decoration; other rooms can be identified as places of storage or craft activity.

The evidence of the clay tablets, which survive only when accidental fire has baked them, increases our confidence that the palaces were administrative centres concerned to collect and record the production and movement of a wide range of agricultural and other goods.[4] The hierarchy of administrators visible in the tablets emphasises the bureaucratic nature of the society. The Pylos tablets reveal the existence at the top of the hierarchy of a 'leader of the people' (*lawagetas*) and a *wanax*; the former has military responsibilities, the latter religious responsibilities, and the respective shares of land that they have suggest that it is the *wanax* who has the paramount position.[5]

More general insight into rulership within the palaces is afforded by the evidence of burials and of iconography. The iconography of frescoes, both in Minoan Crete and at Mycenae and Pylos, reinforces the impression that religious rituals played a central role in palace societies and that religious authority was crucial.[6] Ritual scenes are also frequently found on seals, although outnumbered there by scenes of animals. Most late Bronze Age tomb types – chamber tombs, shaft graves and the 'beehive' or tholos tombs – are used for group burial.[7] This fact, along with the richness of the tombs, in particular at Mycenae where the grave goods include the gold masks that caused Schliemann to claim that he had looked upon the face of Agamemnon, indicate that kinship was important in claims to authority. The care taken at Mycenae to preserve and indeed pick out the earlier Grave Circle 'A'

4 Bennet (1996). 5 See Rehak (1995), especially the paper by Palaima.

6 On frescoes generally see Immerwahr (1990). 7 On burial generally see Laffineur (1987).

when citadel walls were built suggests that claims to particular ancestors were an important part of asserting status among the elite. Painted clay coffins (*larnakes*) show groups of women involved in ritual lamentation, and the standard ritual seems to have involved placing the body in the tomb, surrounding it with grave goods, and then engaging in a ceremony involving drinking and/or pouring libations. Cremation is attested but is a minority rite limited to certain particular places. The wealth of the richest burials suggests that the elite also competed in access to exotic goods and materials, and the extent to which vessel forms, in metal and in pottery, are dominated by shapes associated with drinking suggests that much of social life and social competition focused upon feasting, and more particularly drinking, and that not just among the elite.

Competition within the elite is also apparent from the very elaborate treatment that weapons receive: from Dendra in the north-east Peloponnese elaborate body armour, greaves and a boar's tusk helmet survive, evidence of sophisticated craftsmanship, and spears and swords and daggers are found in highly decorated versions, above all the 'Lion Hunt Dagger' from Mycenae. But it is in competition between elites that such arms were employed. That competition is apparent from the fortification of citadel sites, above all at Mycenae itself, and from scenes of warfare in frescoes and on pottery. A miniature frieze from Akrotiri on Thera shows warriors with body-length shields. Chariots are also known, their design apparently specially adapted for Greek conditions, and the Mycenaean road system may have been developed primarily for chariot use.[8] But of their use in war we have no evidence.

Around 1200 BC Mycenaean palace society collapsed.[9] For reasons which are still the subject of much speculation, the whole edifice, with its complex administration, high degree of specialisation, and extensive contacts both east and west in the Mediterranean, crumbled. The twelfth-century post-palatial period saw changes in settlement pattern and population distribution as people moved to coastal sites and then out of the southern Greek mainland altogether, to Ionia, Cyprus and elsewhere. Not only were specialisms such as scribal literacy, figurative drawing and metallurgical skills lost, but the common culture was replaced by highly localised variation, seen above all in the vast range of local burial customs to be found in the eleventh and tenth centuries.

The contrast with the late Bronze Age has caused the period from 1100 to 800 BC to be dubbed the 'Dark Age'. Our knowledge of the period is increasing, and it is now clear that in some areas of Greece, and in particular

[8] Crouwel (1981), Jansen (2001).

[9] For a general survey of 'Dark Age' Greece see Snodgrass (1971).

in central Greece, there was quite a flourishing population, but the cultural contrasts remain.[10] Archaeologists remain divided over whether the evidence is best accounted for by supposing an invasion of 'Dorians' from the north or supposing internal developments. Continuities are few, but they include some religious continuity: Linear B tablets mention the names of Olympian gods, including Dionysus, and continuity of cult activity is clear at the important site of Kalapodi (classical Hyampolis) in Phocis. They also include the epic tradition.

What we know most about during the eleventh to ninth centuries is burial customs. Group burial ceased to be the predominant custom during the twelfth century, and outside Crete those dead that receive archaeologically visible burial generally continue to be disposed of individually. Inhumation and cremation are both attested, sometimes as contemporary alternatives within a single community, more normally as alternatives at different times. The methods of inhumation (cist graves, pit graves, inhumation in pots) and cremation (on a pyre or within the tomb) vary from time to time, place to place, and with the status of the deceased. The quantity and nature of grave goods similarly varies; ninth-century graves are generally richer than eleventh- or tenth-century graves, but while in Argos graves continue to get richer in the eighth century, elsewhere the eighth century sees grave goods decreasing. Similarly, in general weapons are most common in tenth- and ninth-century graves, but at Argos they are rare in those centuries and become common in the eighth century.[11] Some changes may be by-products of technological change. In particular bronze is gradually replaced by iron, which does not survive well, as the working metal; this cannot but have had an impact on the real and symbolic value of both metals. Nevertheless, changes in burial goods allow us to say something about the nature of the community, and not just about its technologies.

Two sorts of inference can be made from grave goods. The very presence of certain sorts of goods indicates something about the communities' concerns and connections. Weapons suggest that value was put upon prowess in war, spits (associated with the cooking of sacrificed animals and prominent in burials in late eighth-century Argos) may point towards the prestige to be gained from contributing to the communal feasting that marked religious festivals. Similarly, imported goods in graves indicate both the extent to which a community was part of the wider exchange networks that seem to have opened up, in particular in the ninth century, and the possibility of marking status by depositing exotic goods to which not everyone had access.

[10] For a brief, up-to-date surveys see Morris (2000) ch. 6; Whitley (2001) ch. 5.

[11] Whitley (1991).

It is precisely the differential distribution of goods, both across different graves in the same period and across periods that enables the second sort of inference: about social structure. Women's graves can be distinguished from men's graves not by the quantity of grave goods (there are some very rich women's graves) but by their type (and in Athens also the manner of burying). From the fact that in the Ceramicus cemetery at Athens both vases and more particularly metal goods are less evenly distributed in the tenth and ninth centuries than in the eighth archaeologists have inferred that an increasingly hierarchical society became distinctly more egalitarian.[12] Throughout the period and in all regions, children are treated in a quite different way from adults.

Support for the view that at least some Greek communities in the Dark Age were extremely hierarchical has come from the dramatic discovery at Lefkandi, between Chalcis and Eretria on Euboea, of a massive building, employing dressed stone as well as mud brick, dating to around 1000 BC and housing elaborate burials of a man and a woman, with gold jewellery, exotic items and associated horse burials.[13] Built on the edge of the cemetery area, this building testifies to the ability of someone within that community to command enormous labour resources, as well as the incomparable wealth represented by the grave goods. Much remains unclear about this building, including whether the burials came before or after the building, but it offers material evidence for elaborate funerary ritual and makes clear how important the treatment of the dead was in the social construction of the community.

By contrast, those who stress the continuing egalitarianism of the period point to the best known of all settlements, that at Zagora on Andros.[14] Here in the eighth century co-ordinated single-roomed houses were built of extreme regularity. Even when these houses were enlarged after a generation by the construction of additional rooms, this was done in a remarkably uniform way. At least as excavated, this is a settlement quite without exceptional dwellings (the cemetery has not been discovered).

The eighth century has sometimes been termed a 'renaissance'.[15] Various marked cultural changes occur: sanctuaries, both new and old, receive massively increased quantities of dedications, the first substantial temple buildings are constructed, and in certain areas offerings begin to be deposited at old tombs; figure scenes, involving both humans and animals, reappear on painted pottery; writing, employing a new alphabet derived from Phoenician practice, spreads very rapidly round the Greek world, with communities

[12] See in particular Morris (1987).
[13] Popham *et al.* (1993).
[14] Cambitoglou *et al.* (1971), (1988).
[15] Cf. Hägg (1983).

developing their own local letter forms; settlement numbers increase substantially, and, from the middle of the century onwards, Greek communities set themselves up outside the traditional Greek homeland, and in particular in Italy and Sicily.[16] These developments all imply social complexity and a whole range of new choices and possibilities for individuals.

It is notable that many of these developments involve new means of communication; it is not simply writing itself that is important here, though it opened up momentous possibilities for communication at a distance, but the communicative powers of iconography, the sanctuary as an arena for communication between the living independent of the presence of the dead, and the tomb as a place of communication with the (often distant) past. That new means of communication should become attractive itself implies that human relations now needed to be conducted differently, and on a new scale, perhaps both because of burgeoning links with a wider world and because a higher proportion of community members were coming to play an active role in local societies.

These developments in communication impinged on the epic tradition. Scholars dispute whether any figures on geometric pottery are to be identified with figures from epic, but from the first half of the seventh century there can be no doubt that episodes of epic, some of which relate closely to the *Iliad* and *Odyssey* and some of which do not, attracted the attention of artists.[17] Epic allusions are certain, too, in early writing, most notably on the late eighth-century Rhodian cup found at Pithecusae in the bay of Naples which proclaims itself to be 'the cup of Nestor'.[18] Whether the rise in tomb cult should be associated with the circulation of epic poetry has been disputed, but there can be no doubt that the interest in the past that it manifests is parallel to the interests of the Homeric poems.[19] Certainly in the late eighth century, as not before, the artefacts known to archaeology and their disposition suggest that epic poetry and its concerns are 'in the air'. But how far does Homeric epic itself reflect back this material world?

Politics and society in the Homeric poems

Homeric epic is highly political. The *Iliad* explores relations between paramount chiefs in the context of a rather exceptional form of inter-city

[16] On all this see generally Snodgrass (1980), Osborne (1996) ch. 4.

[17] Burgess (2001) ch. 2 for a recent discussion.

[18] For the most far-reaching claims about the relationship between the invention of writing and the Homeric poems see Powell (1991) who discusses 'Nestor's cup' at 163–[illegible]) (cf. Powell (1997)).

[19] Morris (2000) 267–73, Whitley (2001) 150–56, Boehringer (2001) for recent discussions.

warfare. The *Odyssey* examines issues of political succession in an extreme situation of political vacuum and uncertainty. The desirability of self-government, and the importance to individuals of status and power within the community, go without question. But the formal structures and institutions of the communities involved are never more than lightly sketched.[20]

The fullest description of a political community in action is that of Ithaca in the *Odyssey*. Business is transacted at meetings of an assembly of the people (II.6–257; cf. XXIV.420–66) which may be called by any one of a number of people (how great a number is not clear). Elders among the people appear to have priority in speaking, and affairs are regulated by a herald who puts a sceptre into the hands of the person who will contribute. Debates occur, and men are listened to who have something at stake in those debates or who have specialised knowledge (e.g. Halitherses, the interpreter of portents). The people gathered are not so much expected to reach a collective decision as to hear reports of what individuals have decided and to be guided in their own actions by the information disseminated.

The delicate balance between conventional rules, individual authority and community participation found in the Ithacan assembly is not peculiar to the unusual situation there. It is a mark of civilised society to have laws and councils (cf. IX.105–15) and we find similar assemblies and councils in the army at Troy (2.84–394, 9.9–79, 14.109–27; cf. Trojan assembly of 7.345–79) and indeed among the gods (esp. 4.1–72). In all cases, status, whether ascribed by birth or achieved, is not without influence, but it creates only a presumption of authority that has to be confirmed by the quality of advice. High birth, wealth, prowess in battle, are all factors that are put into the balance, but ability to give good advice on a particular occasion may outweigh them all.[21] The delicacy in the position of leader is mirrored in the difficulty scholars have in defining the position of Agamemnon with regard to the other Greek leaders, or working out the succession system on Ithaca: these are the worries of a world with written constitutions; the epic world is a world of charismatic power.

How a world of this sort can run itself day-to-day is revealed on the shield made for Achilles by Hephaestus (18.490–606). Here we are shown both a city at war and a city at peace, and in the latter there are both weddings and banquets and also an act of litigation. The dispute concerns an act of homicide and the refusal of the relative of the deceased to accept compensation. The community is divided and in uproar, but both sides agree

[20] Among many discussions of politics in the Homeric poems note especially Calhoun (1962), Raaflaub (1993) esp. 46–59, and Hölkeskamp (2002).

[21] Schofield (1986).

that the case should be decided by a third party; the elders are gathered and a large reward is offered to the one among them who pronounces justice 'most straightly'. Here dispute settlement is in the hands neither of a single designated individual nor of a group who have to agree; rather, it is in the hands of whichever member of a select group can convince those who listen to his words that he has best reconciled the claims of justice in the particular circumstances at issue.

The always provisional nature of authority is a fundamental feature of both Homeric poems. It lies behind both the dispute between Achilles and Agamemnon in the *Iliad*, and also the implicit approval bestowed upon Odysseus' ability to extricate himself from potentially threatening situations by tricks and deceit. Odysseus' ability to adapt himself to the needs of the moment contrasts strongly with the intransigence of Achilles, and one major theme that the two epics explore is the moral limitations of both positions.

Material goods are important markers of status within epic society (note the two-talent reward offered to the elder on Achilles' shield). Negotiation of position by material exchange is omnipresent, in private as well as public contexts.[22] The items exchanged are chiefly of metal (gold, silver, iron) or cloth: Glaucus and Diomedes exchange gold and bronze armour (6.230–36); Achilles gives as prizes at the funeral games of Patroclus tripods, cauldrons, mixing bowls, talents of gold, unworked iron, axes, armour and weapons, but also animals (a mare, an ox) and female slaves (23.257–897). Menelaus offers Telemachus horses and a chariot as well as a fine cup and in the end gives him a silver mixing bowl, while Helen gives him a garment to be stored up for his future wife (IV.589–619, XV.99–129). Helen herself had made the garment, but the silver bowl had been a gift to Menelaus from the king of the Sidonians, just as the silver bowl that Achilles gives as a prize (23.741–7) started off life in Sidon and then passed through the hands of Phoenician men who gave it to Thoas, from whom it passed into the hands of Euneus who gave it to Patroclus. Other objects identified by origin include a silver wool-basket and silver bathtubs from Egypt (IV.125–9), and a silver-studded dagger from Thrace (23.807–8). Where something (or someone, in the case of slaves) came from, and who previously owned it, matters: value is created in multiple ways.

For the Greeks at Troy trade by ship is a source of necessities: Lemnian ships bring wine which the warriors acquire in exchange for bronze, iron, hides and slaves (7.467–75). It is a mark of the oddity of the Cyclopes that they have no ships (IX.125–9), but those whom we meet sailing the sea to sell goods are non-Greeks who deal in luxury, or at least semi-luxury, goods and

[22] The classic discussion of Homeric gift-exchange is Finley (1954). See also Donlan (1997).

some of them clearly do not expect to visit the same place more than once.[23] Eumaeus remembers the Phoenicians who kidnapped him (xv.415–84) for the pretty things, and in particular the gold necklace strung with amber, that they brought. Eumaeus' kidnap is masterminded by his Sidonian nurse, noted for her craft skills, who had herself been kidnapped by Taphians who deal in bronze and iron (i.183–4, xiv.452, xvi.426) and whose relationship to the real world is uncertain. The circle of evil represented by the kidnap and counter-kidnap is of a piece with the general presentation of slavery in epic: Eumaeus avers that slavery takes away half the goodness of a man (xvii.322–3), and the hanging of the maidservants caught up with the suitors is flagged up, by the simile used to describe it, as the most ethically questionable part of Odysseus' revenge (xxii.465–72).[24]

Wives, as well as slaves, are regularly acquired from foreign parts.[25] Persons of status do not marry locally: Menelaus' son by a slave woman is indeed married to a local wife, but his daughter by Helen, Hermione, is married to Neoptolemus from Thessaly (iv.1–19). Wives usually migrate to live with their husbands (as Penelope to Ithaca), but Bellerophon moves to Lycia on marriage. Bellerophon is one of a number of bridegrooms who receive gifts from their bride's father (6.191–5; cf. Priam, 22.49–51, Odysseus, ii.132–3 and Agamemnon's offer to Achilles, 9.144–57). More frequently the bride's father receives rather than gives gifts, as Peleus does for Polydore and Phyleus for Polymele (16.175–8, 190–2) or Laertes for Odysseus' sister Ctimene (xv.367). Scholars disagree as to whether any historical society can have known both dowry and bride-price, particularly since some anthropological work suggests that they are to be associated with quite different economic and social organisation.[26] There is some reason to think that in the poems bride-price is a 'marked signifier': in almost all cases the situation in which it is given is peculiar or 'foreign'.

By taking a wife and acquiring slaves a man builds up his household. In the *Iliad* we get only glimpses of the 'normal' *oikos* (Priam's polygamy is exceptional), but the *Odyssey* presents a series of households – Odysseus' own, Laertes', Alcinous' in Phaeacia, Menelaus' at Sparta. Although all but Laertes inhabit extensive palaces, the scale of the household is in no case great. Laertes himself works in his orchard, Alcinous' daughter Nausicaa is

[23] On the importance of 'semi-luxuries' see Foxhall (1998) who draws attention to the fact that Isaiah's Sidonians (23.2–3) trade in grain.

[24] On slavery and the *Odyssey* see Thalmann (1998).

[25] See generally Leduc (1992) esp. 235–54.

[26] The impossibility of combining bride-price and dowry is central to Snodgrass' arguments against there being a single historical model for Homeric society: Snodgrass (1974). The conflict is denied by Morris (1986).

not exempt from involvement in household laundry duties, and Helen and Penelope engage in textile manufacture. In Ithaca, at least, the economic base is agricultural: the households have specialists devoted to breeding pigs and goats, and Laertes appears to command a large agricultural workforce. Although phratry organisation is alluded to (*Iliad* 2.362, 9.63), no unit larger than the *oikos* is available in the *Odyssey* to co-ordinate action.

The activities that unite communities in epic are warfare, sacrifices to the gods (cf. the cities on Achilles' shield), burial of a great hero, and the feasting that generally follows both sacrifices and burials. That relations with the gods matter to men is crucial to the plot of the *Iliad*. Only at Troy do we meet temples (of Apollo and Athene) and a procession to present a new garment to a cult statue (6.269–73, 293–311). Sacrifices, however, are frequently encountered, both at the level of the household and for larger gatherings (2.402–31, 7.313–18, 9.772–4, III.418–463, XIII.24–27, XXII.334–6), and the Greeks have altars at the centre of their camp (11.807–8). Relations with the dead matter too: both Patroclus and Elpenor intervene to remind their companions that they need burial, and Priam dares to journey to Achilles' tent in order to recover the body of Hector for burial. For all three and for other heroes the funerary ritual is essentially alike: the body is burned on a pyre (cf. XI.218–22), the pyre is quenched with wine, the white bones are collected and buried and the burial marked. Patroclus' funeral is further elaborated, particularly by the slaughter of both animals and humans (23.166–82), the latter signalled by authorial voice as an evil deed, and by the addition of funeral games.

Warfare required co-ordinated action, whether at the level of families (as in the final battle on Ithaca), at the level of cities, or at the level of the Greek alliance against Troy. But the description of warfare in epic concentrates on the exploits of the individual warrior, and the question of how Homeric battles are to be envisaged has occasioned great scholarly dispute.[27] But if the overall organisation of warfare is not discussed, the individual warrior, his role and his armour are. Arming is a 'stock scene', and although details vary (as with Agamemnon's remarkable Gorgon shield at 11.32–40) the elements are consistent – greaves, cuirass, sword, shield and crested helmet. Both major heroes and the mass of the army are heavily armed (cf. e.g. 14.340–3), and armour is sufficiently part of a warrior's identity that even minor figures such as Elpenor are cremated in it. Only major champions, however, travel about the battlefield in chariots. The primary offensive move is the throwing of spears; hand to hand fighting develops only occasionally, and the overall impression is of open formation conflict, with warriors moving

[27] See van Wees (1997).

together only to protect a fallen comrade or rescue his body (cf. the fight over the body of Patroclus, 17.352–65).

Situating Homeric society

For many aspects of the world portrayed in the *Iliad* and *Odyssey* archaeology offers no correlates. The social obligations, so vaguely defined but so central to human relations in both poems, cannot be measured against the archaeological record.[28] But there are also many aspects that do relate to the material record: archaeology gives us good evidence not only for settlements, sanctuaries and architecture, for burial, warfare and for the exchange of non-perishable goods, but also, if more speculatively, for social organisation and the distribution of wealth and power. Schliemann's success in using the *Iliad* to locate major Bronze Age sites at Troy, Mycenae and Tiryns, and the possibility of identifying most, if not all, of the places mentioned in the 'Catalogue of Ships' (2.494–759) with sites with late Bronze Age remains, led to the assumption that the Homeric epics would relate directly to other aspects of the late Bronze Age material record.[29] That assumption was crucially questioned when the decipherment of Linear B revealed a palace organisation very different from that implied by the Homeric poems.[30] In the 1950s M. I. Finley argued that the Homeric world was a picture of the Greek Dark Ages.[31] Anthony Snodgrass, in the wake of his major study of the Dark Ages, denied that the world of the poems mapped onto any particular historical society.[32] More recently a number of scholars have argued both that oral traditions must always relate primarily to the world of those that hear them and that the material world of the poems aligns with that of eighth-century Greece.[33] The descriptions given above of the world created by archaeology and the world created in the poem are offered as the basis on which the reader can begin to assess the contours of this debate. In this final section I offer a balance sheet and ask what is at stake in this argument for the reading of the poems.

Much in the *Iliad* and *Odyssey* would certainly have been more or less familiar to an inhabitant of the Greek world of the late eighth century. Burning the dead and burying their bones in individual graves was familiar, if not universal, practice in contrast to the group inhumations of the late Bronze

28 On these see Gould, 'The idea of Society in the *Iliad*', in Gould (2001) 335–58.

29 Hope Simpson and Lazenby (1970), Visser (1997). Giovannini (1969) argues that the Catalogue fits seventh-century BC geography better, and this is supported on philological grounds by Visser (1997).

30 Finley (1957). 31 Finley (1954). 32 Snodgrass (1974).

33 Morris (1986), Crielaard (1995) and (2002).

Age. Members of the elite had long marked themselves out for their military contribution; heavy bronze armour was certainly worn by some before the end of the eighth century, and eighth-century painted pottery regularly shows warriors with two spears, suggesting that at least one was thrown. Mycenaean contacts with Italy and the eastern Mediterranean were extensive, and no doubt resulted in travellers' tales worthy of Odysseus, but it was only from *c.* 1000 onwards that Phoenicians will have been encountered, whether as visitors to Greek waters or in other parts of the Mediterranean. Exotic goods, above all vessels and jewellery in precious metal, were a much more important means of asserting and displaying social distinction within early Iron Age communities than earlier, and some good archaeological cases can be made for the pedigree of an object contributing to its value in eighth-century Greece.[34] If religious cult activity was long the major factor in bringing a community together, the devotion of high levels of communal expenditure to cult and cult buildings not closely associated with a ruling group is peculiar to the eighth century.

But much in the world of epic would have brought an eighth-century audience up short. The palaces, the silver bath tubs, the chariots of war, the exotic armour, the treatment of iron as a precious metal, the existence of bride-price as well as dowry, the domination of the labour force by slaves: all of these will have served to distance the world described in the poems from that experienced by an eighth- or early seventh-century audience. And almost all of these find close correlates in the late Bronze Age archaeological record.

Anachronism is a familiar literary technique, and should cause no surprise.[35] Defamiliarisation ensures audience attention. The epic tradition inevitably provided a rich source of material whose status had been changed by the passage of time; but not always enough. Slaughtering animals at human funerals was familiar, slaughtering enemy prisoners was not. As with the institution of bride-price, discussed above, so with silver bath tubs, epic heroes inhabit a world that is distinct in both material and actions.[36] Chariots, tower shields and the exchange of speeches and of armour in the midst of battle are all ways in which the field of war is made a field in which the individual is tested and status and value negotiated. In real-life battles survival and victory are what count. But readers of epic have far less investment in the result: for them war is good for revealing personal and social values. What the audience hears needs to be broadly credible, but it does not need to mimic all the details.

If allusions to objects and practices both familiar and unfamiliar to the audience are the poet's means, what is the end? What ensures the success

[34] Coldstream (1983). [35] Cf. Easterling (1985). [36] Griffin (1986a).

and survival of the poems is that the issues which they raise engage the audience. Much is at issue in the *Iliad* and *Odyssey* on moral and theological fronts, but the core issues are political. The diffusion of authority which Linear B tablets suggest for the late Bronze Age palaces makes it possible that poetic exploration of how authority was established, sustained and handed on would have been appropriate there. The basis of political authority was certainly an issue in the Greek world of the late eighth and early seventh centuries: the rapid changes seen in the archaeological record indicate that old ways of asserting status and authority (e.g. by what one deposited in tombs) were challenged, and new ways (making dedications in sanctuaries and at old tombs) both devised and themselves countered (as whole communities reshaped their sacred landscape and increased the emphasis on temple and cult statue). Painted pottery shows artists developing figurative decoration first to suggest general storylines and then to suggest particular, mythical, stories.[37] So the tradition of oral hexameter poetry was developed to produce not only *Iliad* and *Odyssey* but *Theogony* and *Works and Days*, poems which also display a strong interest in authority and succession.

Bronze Age as well as early Iron Age archaeology can help us understand the resources out of which Homer's society is created. But the Homeric poems show an awareness of particular material circumstances not found before the later eighth or early seventh centuries: writing (6.168–70); narrative art in general and Gorgon shield devices in particular, settlement overseas and knowledge of a world that extends from Phoenicia, Egypt and the Black Sea to the east to Sicily in the west, temples and cult statues.[38] They also show a concern with social and political circumstances peculiarly apposite for eighth- and seventh-century Greeks as they began to assert community identities and devise, in part in connection with settlement abroad, rules for communal living.[39] Knowledge of the past requires the possibility of social memory, and that seems ensured by the demonstrable epic tradition; knowledge of the future would be far harder to account for, and for that reason it makes sense to ascribe the creation of the *Iliad* and *Odyssey*, in the form in which they have come down to us, to somewhere around, or shortly after 700.[40]

[37] Osborne (1996) 129–36, 161–7; Osborne (1998) 29–41, 53–67.

[38] For a clear recent discussion see Crielaard (1995).

[39] Much recent work has tried to assess Homer's 'class' sympathies: see Qviller (1981), Geddes (1984), Halverson (1985), Morris (1986), Thalmann (1988), Scully (1990), van Wees (1992), Rose (1997), Thalmann (1998), Haubold (2000).

[40] See Fowler (ch. 14) in this volume for the implications of this for the Homeric question.

FURTHER READING

The archaeology of the Bronze Age is well surveyed in Dickinson (1994). For the archaeology of the Dark Ages see Snodgrass (1971, 2000), and for the eighth century Coldstream (1977, 2003). Part four of Morris and Powell (1997) contains chapters on Homer's relationship to the archaeology of the Bronze and Iron Ages, and also on Homeric society, the Homeric economy, Homeric warfare and Homer and the Near East.

Exactly what the political implications are of the stories told in Homeric epic and the way in which those stories are told has been much debated: see variously Geddes (1984), Morris (1986), van Wees (1992), Rose (1997), Thalmann (1998), Haubold (2000).

For attempts to date elements within the Homeric epics see Sherratt (1990). For attempts to give dates on archaeological and historical grounds for the poems in the form that we have them see Crielaard (1995).

14

ROBERT FOWLER

The Homeric question

How and by whom were the *Iliad* and *Odyssey* composed and preserved?

Certain anticipations apart,[1] the modern debate began in 1788 with the publication by Villoison of the scholia in the tenth-century manuscript of the *Iliad*, Venetus Marcianus Graecus 454.[2] These marginal notes preserve substantial remnants of ancient scholarship on the poems, going back as far as third-century BC Alexandria and permitting inferences about the earlier state of the text. Starting from the premise that Homer lived in an illiterate age (a premise which, ironically enough, we now know to be false), and using the new evidence, F. A. Wolf in 1795 argued that the poems as we have them were put together by a compiler living long after Homer, who had been a simple singer of heroic lays.[3] The game was then to detect by analysis of the poems which bits derived from the original Homer, and which bits from later bards or editors; of these epigoni most scholars working in the analytical tradition (Wolf himself excepted) had a low opinion. Their handiwork was betrayed by inconcinnities, inconsistencies and repetitions in the poems, allowing the scholar to determine which parts had been composed independently of each other and in what order; by these means a wonderful variety of theories emerged, dividing the poems up in different ways and placing 'Homer' at various points in their evolution.[4] Nowadays critics tend to explain most of these irregularities by reference to the exigencies of oral performance. In the *Odyssey*, for instance, to start the second strand of the narrative – the instruction to Calypso that she release Odysseus – after

[1] In the first century AD Josephus, *Ap.* 1.2.12, in a highly polemical context, claimed that Homer was illiterate; cf. schol. Dion. Thrax, *Gramm. Gr.* 1.3.179. For discussions in the seventeenth and eighteenth centuries see Davison (1962) 242–5, Clarke (1981) and Wilson in this volume pp. 271, 284.

[2] On Villoison see Rossi (1999). [3] Wolf (1985) with commentary.

[4] See Myres (1958), Davison (1962), Heubeck (1974) 1–39, 87–98; A. Parry (1971) x–xxi; Turner (1997). Some scholars continue to work in this tradition.

Athena has seen to matters in Ithaca (I–IV, the so-called 'Telemachy'), the poet simply resumes the divine assembly scene of Book I at the beginning of Book V. A brief cross-reference would presume the ability of a puzzled reader to turn back the pages. There is no need to assume that two poems, a *Telemachy* and an *Odyssey*, have been patched together.[5] But although many difficulties can be so explained, some remain. Many scholars still think that Book 10 of the *Iliad* (the 'Doloneia'),[6] some parts of *Odyssey* XI (the 'Nekyia'),[7] and the ending of the *Odyssey* (everything after XXIII.296)[8] are interpolations. Anyone entertaining a view of the epic tradition involving at least partly fixed (non-oral) texts might find room for this or that analytical tenet. The Analysts' research into Homer's poetic dialect, which sought to distinguish its various historical strands, produced lasting results, and formed the background to Milman Parry's work.

Arrayed against the Analysts were the Unitarians, who stressed the planful design and artistic quality of the poems, which argued for a great poet's involvement at a late stage in their evolution; these scholars have made many excellent observations on Homer's literary art, which no student of the poems can ignore.[9] The whole nature of the debate changed, however, with Milman Parry's discovery that the poems' many formulas combine in extensive and economical[10] systems, in origin explicable only as aids to oral composition-in-performance; moreover, they had to be the creation of tradition, not of any one bard. Parry subsequently observed and recorded poets using just such a method of composition in Yugoslavia. It became clear that archaisms and neologisms could exist side by side as bards employed formulas originating at different times in the tradition. Scholars' attention gradually turned to the study of oral and traditional poetry, shedding light on typical scenes, performative aspects, narrative technique and much else. It took time for Parry's discoveries to take hold, and even now some scholars stubbornly declare their scepticism. One can debate how far Homer might have moved

[5] The 'Telemachy' could hardly have functioned as a separate poem in any case (M. Parry (1971) 454). On the second assembly see e.g. Rengakos (1998) responding to Olson (1995).

[6] Danek (1988), Hainsworth (1993) 151–5.

[7] Specifically, XI.225–332 and 565–627 (the view that the whole of XI is adventitious is no longer popular). Within the latter section, however, one would have to suppose awkwardly that 602–4 were a *subsequent* interpolation no earlier than the late sixth century: Cassio (2002) 116 n. 52.

[8] Discussion in West (1989); Russo in Heubeck *et al.* (1988–92) 3.342–5; Sourvinou-Inwood (1995) ch. 2; Rutherford (1996) 81 with n. 69.

[9] E.g. Bowra (1930), Schadewaldt (1943), (1944), Reinhardt (1961), (1996), Erbse (1972), Griffin (1980), Hölscher (1988), Di Benedetto (1994); within an oralist framework, Tuplin (1992).

[10] For the details on formulas and their systems see Clark in this volume.

away from the oral background, but it is retrograde to argue that we can go on reading him like Virgil or Shakespeare.

In the early, dogmatic days of these researches, scholars tended to believe that there were only two alternatives for a poem, written or oral; Parry enthusiasts claimed Homer for the oral camp, while others seized on imperfections in the South Slavic analogy (and the manifest superiority of Homer) either to ignore Parry or to argue that, whatever lay in Homer's background, he had left it far behind. Further work on the cognitive aspects of formularity, the mechanics of composition-in-performance, and oral literature worldwide has produced a more sophisticated picture. But certainty remains as elusive as ever. Our understanding of the formula has been much improved, but even if all scholars were to agree on its definition, and by implication on the extent of formularity in Homer, it is not clear how much formularity one needs in order to be oral. Study of oral traditions has shown that they all have their own character, and interact with contemporary literacy in various ways;[11] the notion of a 'transitional text', one partly oral and partly written, produced by an 'oral-derived' poet, one who can write but who has not lost his ability to compose-in-performance, has much to recommend it.[12] But it would be a mistake to think that the dichotomy oral/written has been transcended. The oral background explains much about the style and puts paid to many of the older analytical theories which, if true, would have a fundamental effect on our assessment of Greek literary history. Textual critics will invoke formulaic technique in making their decisions, and many literary judgments turn on an appreciation of the oral environment. Even within the mixed oral/written framework there are radically different descriptions of the text's evolution and qualities. So one must at least confront the issues, even if certainty is unattainable on many points.

Parry's original thesis has been subjected to intense criticism, both for the apparent rigidity of the formulas and for his vapid notion of their content: the 'essential idea' of a formula like 'godlike Achilles' was merely 'Achilles', he said, and the poet was obliged to say 'godlike' if the metre dictated. Subsequent studies showed that the formulas were a good deal more flexible than Parry at first thought; the poet can be seen to adapt his formulas to suit particular contexts, so that more of the text turns out to be formular. Better understanding of composition-in-performance shows that it could make possible much that appears to be non-formular; it is also wrong to think that all formular stretches were produced off the cuff, as premeditation is quite

[11] See e.g. Niles (1999) ch. 4 and Foley (1999a) 39–45.

[12] See e.g. Foley (1999) 16; Lord (1995) 212–37 (who does not however agree that Homer is transitional).

possible in an oral context. Furthermore, without the whole of the Greek tradition before us, our ability to measure formularity in any one composition is limited. But one suspects that there remains a stubborn percentage of non-formularity, particularly in the similes and speeches (the latter accounting for a large part of the text), which are among the glories of the poems and may be thought to contain the best of Homer's art. At this point one asks, where does the onus of proof lie (if proof were possible)? If the text is at least oral-derived, as most people admit, should we require those who say the text is written to prove that the non-formular aspects exceed the capacity of the oral poet, or should we require those who say it is oral to prove that the non-formular aspects lie within his capacity?

Unknowable too is the limit of quality in oral poetry. It is an old canard that Homer is simply too good to be oral. 'Quality' might have various meanings: style, on the level of individual words and lines, or in the similes and speeches again; perhaps complexity of overall conception; often the presence of large-scale structures spanning thousands of verses.[13] Challenged to cite comparable examples from oral traditions, oralists have picked out some of the more impressive bits of the Parry archive, particularly the songs of Avdo Međedović, the 'Yugoslav Homer', which have received high praise.[14] Judgments will differ about Međedović; but he need hardly be Homer's equal for the comparative case to be made. If oral poets can produce works of considerable subtlety and sophistication, the way lies open to maintaining that a poet of Homer's genius could have produced songs like his in an oral environment. At bottom, the argument 'these poems are so good they must be written' simply begs the question.

Another argument appeals to quantity. The poems are so big – 'monumental' is the usual word – that we must be dealing with something new in kind. Raised in an oral tradition, Homer transcended its limits. Only writing could have afforded him the opportunity. It is hard to imagine an occasion on which such long poems could have been recited; so one infers they were not composed to be recited in their entirety. In response, it is pointed out that under favourable conditions oral poets can produce very long poems. Examples from Africa and Asia are cited as well as from the South Slavic tradition. As for the occasion of recitation, the tolerance and appetite of public audiences at archaic Greek festivals can hardly be known (three days would

[13] Reinhardt (1961), Lesky (1967) 698–709 and elsewhere; Lohmann (1970), A. Parry (1971) lxi n. 1; Schadewaldt (1975), Lloyd-Jones (1981), Macleod (1982), Schwabl (1990) 107–9; Stanley (1993), Garvie (1994) 1–18; cf. Heiden (1996), (2000c). *Contra* Nagler (1974), Martin (1989) and Taplin ([illegible]). On the [illegible] song composition see Minchin ([illegible]) ch. 6.

[14] Lord (2000) with CD.

suffice). Alternatively, it has been suggested that the stimulus to produce the poems came from some outside source, some admirer of Homer's public performances who induced him to produce special poems for dictation, like the *guslars* who performed for Parry. In this case the *guslars*' attitude to the experience is instructive. The recorded texts do not replace the sung version; the next time they perform the song, it will be the 'same song' in their terms, though quite different in ours. The recorded version, though good, is not a fixed point of reference for the future, the definitive version to which all who would learn the song should turn. Within a century of their composition, Homer's poems were such a point of reference. Can we trace this aspect of their reception back as far as their origin? Before exploring this trail further, let us look at more uncertainties.

The texts were written down, or we would not have them; how, then, was the transformation from oral to written effected? The quantity of text of the Homeric epics has also been used as an argument, oddly enough, against their being written down at the time of their first composition. We are told that the technical problems of writing down poems so long *c.* 700 BC were simply too great. Writing material was too scarce and expensive. Consequently, the poems must have been transmitted by oral means – which is to say, they remained polymorphous[15] – until they were finally written down. The moment at which this is usually said to have happened is sixth-century Athens in the context of the Panathenaic festival: the so-called 'Peisistratid redaction', after the family of tyrants who turned the festival into an international cultural showcase. There are at least two problems with this view. One is that, though the evidence suffices to show that a text was produced for the Athenian festival, it does not show that this was the first such text; indeed it rather suggests the opposite. Who or what was the 'Homer' of which the Peisistratids wished to ensure the authentic version? The story implies that liberties were being taken, not that there was no text; it implies an interesting textual awareness of oral vagaries, which indeed continued to work their mischief for a long time afterwards, and which had already left some indelible marks on our text, but it does not imply the birth of the text it sought to control.[16] An even greater problem is that, were the

[15] G. S. Kirk's special theory that the poems, though oral, were somehow preserved with minimal alteration until recorded in writing in Athens, has been sufficiently refuted by A. Parry (1966).

[16] The main authorities are [Plato], *Hipparch.* 228b; Dieuchidas, *FGrHist* 452 F6; Lycurg. *Leoc.* 102; Isoc. *Paneg.* 159; Cic. *De Or.* 3.137. It is a real question, however, whether later writers do not retroject the conditions of their own day. For concise discussion and full references see now Cairns (2001) 1–7; Scodel (2002) 54–5. That an Athenian text has contaminated the tradition is clear from its Atticisms, which are not however deeply embedded.

texts still essentially oral, constantly being recomposed in performance until fixed in the sixth century, their formulaic diction would betray the fact. The formulas continued to evolve, and one can establish the relative dates of texts by analysing their neologisms. Richard Janko's important book applies this dictum to archaic Greek epic, taking into consideration a whole range of linguistic phenomena and applying proper statistical techniques.[17] The method establishes the chronological sequence *Iliad*, *Odyssey*, *Theogony*, *Works and Days*. The poems were therefore written down at different times, in that order; and this is fatal to the Peisistratid theory.[18]

The difficulty-of-finding-papyrus argument is, in truth, singularly weak.[19] Was the technology so much easier in sixth-century Athens? Was no papyrus available before the emporium of Naucratis was established in Egypt? Byblos, the Phoenician source of papyrus, provided the Greek word for 'book' (and our 'Bible'). Parchment was also available (Hdt. 5.78); the number of skins required to write down the Homeric poems was hardly beyond the resources of the late eighth century. And besides Homer, there is Hesiod. Almost everyone accepts that his *Theogony* was preserved at the time of its creation; the view that he wrote the poem for the funeral games of Amphidamas, and refers to it in the *Works and Days*, has found general assent.[20] Hesiod wrote thousands of verses; clearly a critical point on the scale of literacy, and preservation, had been passed. The lyric poets were the same. The sudden preservation of so many literary texts soon after writing re-enters the Greek world is not accidental, and a 'hard' oralist view cannot explain why there are no texts from any earlier period.[21]

If the poems emanate from the time of their authors, either they wrote them down themselves, or they dictated them to others.[22] Some Homerists, not wishing to acquiesce in the dogma that oral poets cannot write, have argued on the basis of wide-ranging comparisons that there is a spectrum of possibilities between purely oral and purely verbal, and that Homer, although

[17] Janko (1982), building on Hoekstra (1969) and Edwards (1971). I do not think his essential findings have been successfully challenged.

[18] Nagy's evolutionary theory (Nagy (1992a), (1996a), (1996b), (1997), (1999) etc.) faces this and other serious objections. Criticism in Janko (1998) 12 nn. 63–4; Haslam (1997) 81 n. 68; Powell (1997) 30 n. 54; Finkelberg (2000); West (2001) 159 n. 2; Pelliccia (2003).

[19] Parry (1966) 183–5; Heubeck (1979) 152–6; Powell (1997) 30.

[20] *Op.* 654–9; West (1966) 44–5 after Wade-Gery (1958) 8.

[21] Latacz (1996) 18. The earliest Greek inscription dates to about 770 BC: Powell (1997) 23.

[22] For the dictation theory see Lord (1991) 38–48, 98, 109 f.; Jensen (1980) 89–92; Janko (1990), (1992b), (1994), (1998), West (1990), Powell (1991), (1997). For the absolute date of the poems, see Andersen and Dickie (1995) with Papadopoulos (1996); Dowden in this volume p. 194; Osborne in this volume p. 218. I believe myself that the *Iliad* dates from about 700 BC.

trained in oral methods, was able to take advantage of the new skill to create a new kind of work, at once more precise and more extended.[23] The text is, then, transitional. To look no further than Greece for analogies, consider Herodotus. Here is someone who gave oral performances up and down the Greek world. It is unlikely that he performed the whole of his text on any one occasion. The master text, the great template, was in his head; based upon it he gave performances suited to the particular audience and venue in which he found himself. Ultimately he decided to record his findings for posterity. There is no doubt that the text is literate; one need only mention the constant use of the verb γράφω, 'I write'. Yet even while writing, Herodotus continues to use parataxis, deixis, ring-composition, anaphora and all the familiar devices of oral delivery.

In Herodotus' case we assume he is aiming to provide the best and definitive version, because he knows it will last. We do not so readily assume the same of Homer, two and a half centuries earlier. We might do so if we knew that he was his own amanuensis. If he conceived the desire himself to write down poems of this size, he would have been conscious of working in a new medium (the thought, indeed, would have preceded the wish); whereas he could have dictated his songs – even dictated them very carefully, as comparison shows is apt to happen under such circumstances – to a keen admirer, without entertaining revolutionary thoughts about the nature of the written version (cf. above p. 224). So here is a potentially serious difference between the implications of the two views of contemporary redaction.

Several aspects of Homer's text might possibly help us in this regard. One is the bard's relation to the Muse. Ostensibly, the epic singers regard themselves as her mouthpiece and submerge their personal identity in hers. In terms of oral poetics, one could say that the individual singer does not regard himself as anything but the latest instantiation of tradition.[24] Though there are good and bad singers, who to that extent are individuals, what distinguishes good ones is not their originality or distinctiveness, but their ability to sing accurately, not to make mistakes, not to leave anything out or make illegitimate additions. This is how Parry's singers constantly put the matter, and the singers in Homer's poems too win praise for accuracy.[25] Yet the Muse is one half of a relationship. As various passages show, Homer is perfectly aware that his heroes' fame, their *kleos*, lives on because of his

[23] See e.g. Bowra (1930) 48–52 (contrast Bowra (1961) ch. 9); Parry (1966) 190, 210–16; Rossi (1978), Lloyd-Jones (1981) 19–20. Finnegan (1992) is regularly cited in this regard; criticism in Jensen (1980) 22–5; Janko (1998) 5.

[24] On the notion of an 'author' in an oral tradition see Niles (1999) 24.

[25] Cf. Finkelberg (1990) 294; VIII.489, 496; *Homeric Hymn to Mercury* 433.

singing.[26] It is not long before the poets are stressing their part of the work a little more clearly than the Muse's. Sappho, for instance, says (fr. 55 Voigt) that a rival will be forgotten because she has no share in the Muses (whereas, of course, Sappho does). Perhaps she means only the power of oral tradition, but the fact that she wrote her poems down for posterity adds a fillip to the argument. Somewhat later, Ibycus says that Polycrates will have fame for ever, 'as my song and my fame can bestow it'. We have the poem (*PMGF* S151). In the same tradition of praise poetry is Pindar, about whom there can be no doubt; for all the local colour of the poems, Pindar has one eye always on a pan-Hellenic and future readership. He looks on himself as a kind of Homer, and it is fair to say that this attitude is in Homer at least *in nuce*. Very interesting in this regard is the proem to the *Theogony*. Hesiod tells the story of his encounter with the Muses, who place the staff in his hand and give him the power of poetry, so that he might render famous – *kleioimi* – 'what is to come, and what went before' (32). And he names himself. As already mentioned, we can infer on other grounds that this is a fixed text. So far from suppressing the poet's individuality, the Muse actually raises his profile. And on closer examination one realises that she is not easily equated with our notion of oral tradition.[27] Both the Muse and the emergence of poetic personality are distinctive features of the Greek milieu. Arguments about authenticity and ownership were rife already in the archaic period, and guilds like the Homeridae and the Creophylii heroised their putative founders.[28]

Another clue may lie in Homer's many allusions to other stories, i.e. other songs. We hear about the wars at Thebes, about Heracles, Meleager,

[26] 6.358, 9.189, I.338, III.204, VIII.73, VIII.580, and the many passages where heroes express their desire for glory (a reflex of the epic tradition). Cf. Macleod (1983).

[27] Finkelberg (1990), Scodel (1998), (2001), (2002). Also relevant here are the poems' concern with memory, monuments and posterity, variously treated by Ford (1992) and Lynn-George (1988).

[28] I grant that we first hear of these arguments in the late sixth century, when attitudes to literary history were changing, but the poets were individualised, and the Homeridae active, before then. Against the tendency of these remarks, some scholars see 'Homer' as a projection of the tradition or a creation of the Homeridae: Foley (1998), (1999a) 49–62 and in this volume; West (1999). If already Callinus cited 'Homer' as the author of the *Thebaid* (details in West (1999) 377), the likelihood of his legendary status is increased; in that case the *Iliad* and *Odyssey*, as the creative products of particular individuals, were foisted upon him like other poems on Orpheus, or oracles on Bakis (though the same thing can happen to historical figures: the laws of Athens were all ascribed to Solon). West (1999) revives Durante's interesting argument that the name 'Homer' derives from an archaic word for 'festival', where epics were performed. In itself this does not negate the poet's historicity; one recalls Stesichorus' wonderfully apt name ('he who sets up the chorus'). See further below n. 46.

the Argonauts and others.[29] Together these references add up to an encyclopaedic awareness of Greek myth. Some references are less than explicit. Many scholars have identified similarities between events in Homer's poems and events in the cyclic epics, and have argued that although the versions of these epics known to us are later than the *Iliad* and the *Odyssey*, their predecessors are in Homer's background. Whatever one may think of the details of these Neoanalytical claims, everyone will agree that behind Homer there is the traditional body of myth which has a presence in his poems.[30] How does intertextuality work in an oral tradition? An intertext implies a text in the first place; if the songs aren't fixed texts, then their interrelation must work in some other way. Foley has coined the term 'traditional referentiality' and suggests that the presence of other songs in the song of the moment is a matter of 'resonance'.[31] The story of Troy as Homer tells it gains its depth from the audience's knowledge of the whole tale. As soon as the poet names any of the major characters a whole set of associations is brought to mind. Astyanax, for instance: the Hector and Andromache scene is pathetic because we know what will happen to the boy, although the event is not related in the *Iliad*. When the singers in Homer's poems are asked to perform, they tell a story which is an excerpt from a much longer tale, in outline well known to the audience; their knowledge provides the context. At every level, from formula to plot, this kind of resonance is at work. It can be extraordinarily rich, and poets will play on its effects.[32] But in cases where we suspect Homer of major mythological innovation, 'resonance' does not seem a wholly adequate term. Rather than offering a novel take on a familiar story, he is offering a new story. In offering such personal revisions, Homer is behaving like every other Greek poet after him; it would be very odd were he the only exception. One of the most egregious examples is the addition of Phoenix in the embassy to Achilles in *Iliad* 9, together with the tale of Meleager which has been adapted to suit Achilles' circumstances.[33] That Phoenix is intrusive is an inference from the duals in lines 182–98, apparently a survival from an earlier version in which the only ambassadors were Ajax and Odysseus.[34] One explanation among many of this notorious inconcinnity is that, like some other oddities in the text, it is a mark of oral dictation, explicable as a momentary lapse under the pressure of composition-in-performance, which a writer would have revised out of his text.[35] This is quite possible, though

[29] See the list in Cairns (2001) 36–8; cf. Burgess (2001) 209 n. 1.

[30] See Dowden in this volume.

[31] Foley (1991), (1997), (1999a).

[32] Schein (2002). Against this, Andersen (1990), (1998) argues that the allusive capacity of an oral text is more limited than we think.

[33] Willcock (1964).

[34] Hainsworth (1993) 85–7; Griffin (1995) 22–4, 51–3, 96.

[35] Janko (1998) 8, with other examples; see also Burkert (1995a).

given the vast length of the poems one might expect the number of such inconcinnities to be greater. Moreover, we can hardly know what the threshold of tolerance might have been. Herodotus' apparently finished text contains three unfulfilled promises (1.106, 1.184, 7.213). The duals of *Iliad* 9 are unique on any reckoning. Scodel, for one, has argued that Homer used them deliberately in order to enhance the mystery surrounding Phoenix; if so, the text overtly signals its relation with tradition, and asserts its own innovation.[36]

On the basis of such problematic passages one is reluctant to build too much, of course. Some scholars would argue that such interplay with tradition can still be analysed in oral terms. The basic facts of the familiar stories are fixed – there was an unsuccessful embassy to Achilles – but considerable licence might be granted an individual poet (perhaps more in the Greek tradition than in others) to adapt the tale using other traditional material, like the figure of the wise advisor. The tale being adapted could even be represented for poet and audience by particular songs, which they regarded as fixed (in oral terms). Perhaps this is how one should assess the attitude of the *Odyssey* to the *Iliad*.[37] Scholars have noted various ways in which the later poem seems to betray awareness of its predecessor, in its structure, themes and characterisation; that it builds upon, yet avoids duplicating, Iliadic material is also a kind of recognition.[38] All such allusions could be possible in an oral tradition of story-telling, working with famous stories and legendary characters, possibly with extraordinary subtlety. Yet the more innovation one finds, the more the whole notion of traditional poetry is weakened. Indeed the basic conception of the *Iliad* and *Odyssey* mark them out as untraditional: they are astonishingly innovative in design and aim, reacting to and pondering tradition rather than promulgating it.[39]

Some scholars would claim the poems make allusions on the level of specific words; the claim is very difficult to sustain in a formular environment, but if upheld bespeaks the beginning of true intertexts, which assume fixity on the level of diction. One possible example is the phrase 'and the will of Zeus was fulfilled' in the proem of the *Iliad* (a highly marked context). The same formula at the beginning of the cyclic *Cypria* referred to Zeus's plan to decrease the earth's population by means of war; if its predecessor is in the

36 Scodel (1997), (2002), though she would keep the passage within the bounds of what she terms the 'rhetoric of traditionality'. The general rule is that innovation is never admitted; but in this passage one may think the pretence is beginning to show.

37 Danek (1998).

38 See Heubeck in Heubeck *et al.* (1988–92) I.12–23; the discussions cited by Rutherford (1996) 78 n. 2; Jones (1997) 34–8.

39 E.g. Bowra (1930), Heubeck (1974) 148; Dowden (1996b).

background here, Homer's much profounder application of the formula is a very significant, and distancing, innovation, lying close to the heart of his poetic conception.[40] Some of the other links claimed by Neoanalysis might be turned to similar advantage.[41] The whole question of archaic intertextuality needs further work, and could throw much light on the character of these texts at the time of their recording.[42]

In sum, with due regard to the unknowables, I would argue that the *Iliad* and *Odyssey* were conceived as new kinds of text by their oral poet(s).[43] The notion that they wrote and lovingly revised their texts with pen in hand seems anachronistic, but it is possible that large portions of the songs, through premeditation, came to be fixed. Their contemporary recording in writing cannot be coincidental; but which is cause, and which effect? The pairs 'unfixed/fixed' and 'oral/written' are not exactly synonymous. Perhaps one could describe the progression thus: (1) non-fixed, because oral; (2) oral, with many consciously fixed passages; (3) mostly fixed, and therefore written; (4) written to start with, and therefore fixed. In Homer's day, I suggest, Greek epic moved through (2) to (3). Does one put the historical entrance of writing before, after, or at the same time as (2)? The answer will differ from society

40 Against this, the recurrence of the phrase at XI.297 (after the story of Pero) makes one suspect it is a traditional equivalent to 'the plot of this epic'.

41 Neoanalysts have plausibly argued that Thetis' sudden appearance at 15.35 derives from the *Aethiopis*; accordingly, the phrase μέγας μεγαλωστί at 16.775, 18.26 and XXIV.39 might count as an allusion/quotation, in a strong sense. Cf. Danek (1998) 468; (2002).

42 It is difficult to reconcile Neoanalysis with an oral perspective, as the former thinks in terms of interrelations between fixed, if not written, texts. If oral is becoming written in Homer, such relationships must be starting to form; but one would not wish to assume any excessively mechanical model of production. Any solution to these problems implies a view on Homer's sense of text. Nagy, for instance, who stakes out an extreme oralist position, denies mythological innovation in Homer ((1996a) 130 ff., (1998a), (1999a), cf. (1979) ch. 3) and offers a complicated analysis of the duals involving the interplay of traditional elements. Conversely, Goold (1977) 10 and others think that Homer revised his own already written text over a period of time, in the case of *Iliad* 9 less than carefully; cf. West (2000), who urges VII.103 ff. as a similar case (unconvincing). For pertinent theoretical considerations and discussion see also Pucci (1987), though I would describe most of his examples as traditional referentiality; Pucci (1998) xi speaks of the poems' 'conscious textuality'. Most (1993) argues the case that Hesiod's *Works and Days* presumes his *Theogony* fixed in writing.

43 Those scholars (called '*chorizontes*' in antiquity) who hold that the *Iliad* and *Odyssey* stem from different authors appeal to 'the many differences of narrative manner, theology, ethics, vocabulary, and geographical perspective, and [to] the apparently imitative character of certain passages of the *Odyssey* in relation to the *Iliad*' (West (1999) 364): all inconclusive, as ever, though the cumulative case is hard to resist. See Garvie (1994) 2–3; Heubeck in Heubeck *et al.* (1988–92) I.7. Perhaps Homer wrote the *Iliad*, one of the Homeridae the *Odyssey* (Scodel (2002) 58).

to society, as the cognitive shift between (1) and (2) will depend on a variety of factors, one of which might, but need not, be literacy.

It is reasonable to claim, at any rate, that the reception of the poems as monumental, fixed texts is grounded in the poems themselves. Regrettably, the fortunes of the texts immediately after their fixation are no less obscure, as it is highly contentious whether any clear allusion (once again) exists in either the art or the literature of the seventh century.[44] The failure of the poems to impose themselves immediately in spite of their quality is perhaps unsurprising; the traditional style of composition-in-performance did not vanish overnight. Most scholars agree that the texts were in general circulation by the mid-sixth century, when the poems' influence on art is also much clearer. Some imponderable combination of factors enabled the 'man from Chios'[45] suddenly, or finally, to secure his dominant position in Greek culture, never to be ousted. The Homeridae, a guild of rhapsodes claiming actual descent from Homer, were probably instrumental in preserving the precious texts up to then.[46] Even after its fixation, the text was subject to additions and alterations, as is demonstrated by early quotations and papyri; but the variations are plainly controlled by a firm point of reference, and their extent has caused needless alarm.[47] A stable vulgate text eventually emerged under the influence of Alexandrian scholarship, especially that of Aristarchus in the second century BC; in particular, the number of verses in his edition was decisive. He omitted very poorly attested lines (possibly omitting some genuine ones in the process), but merely recorded his suspicions about others

44 Thorough discussion in Burgess (2001) ch. 2, supporting the sceptical view.

45 So Simonides (late sixth or early fifth century), fr. 19 West, calls the poet of the *Iliad*; the relationship between this figure and the blind Chian who composed *Homeric Hymn to Apollo* 172–3 (perhaps 523/2 BC), identified by Thuc. 3.104.5 as Homer, is one of Homeric scholarship's tastiest problems. See the works cited in the next note, and Janko (1982) 112–15, 258–62.

46 Their name implies belief in a single author of (at least) the two great poems, as would the provision for recitation of the *Iliad* and *Odyssey* alone at the Panathenaea, could we be sure that this was the case. In the archaic period most of the Cycle and the *Hymns* were also ascribed to Homer; Thucydides (3.104.4–6) quotes the *Hymn to Apollo* as Homer's, but Herodotus signals his doubt about the *Cypria* and the *Epigoni* (2.117, 4.32). For all archaic poets ancient biographers had little evidence to draw on except the poems themselves; the conventions of epic requiring anonymity on the part of the poet, the uncertainty among the ancients about basic facts is unsurprising. On the Homeridae see Burkert (1972), (1987), West (1999), Graziosi (2002) 201–17, 220–7; Scodel (2002) 58–61. The division of our text into books possibly occurred at this time (though other views assign them to Homer at one extreme, and the Alexandrians at the other): see Hägg (1999), Heiden (2000a), (2000b).

47 The type of variation is Lord's category B, recitations influenced by fixed texts (Lord (1991) 170–85). Relevant here is Rossi's (1997) interesting diagnosis of alternative versions of oral performances in Hesiod's *Works and Days*.

in his commentary ('athetesis', a practice originating with Zenodotus in the early third century). Oddly, his readings in individual lines achieved much less success, implying that the readings in his edition as published were not those he recommended in his commentary (some of which had manuscript authority, some of which were conjectures).[48] The reason for this situation, in turn, is probably that the 'edition' was originally a preferred manuscript, judged by Aristarchus to be of superior quality and then linked to the commentary by critical signs, rather than a text freshly created from scratch in the manner of modern editions.[49]

It is sometimes said that modern scholarship cannot hope to get beyond Aristarchus in establishing Homer's text. The judgment is too pessimistic. The extra verses, whether in medieval manuscripts or the pre-Alexandrian 'wild' or 'eccentric' papyri, are usually easy to spot, and we have reasonable criteria for distinguishing variant readings in authentic verses. Within the limits created by early oral variation and contamination, we can be modestly confident of reconstructing the earliest text. The best modern editions are M. L. West's of the *Iliad* and H. van Thiel's of the *Odyssey*.[50]

FURTHER READING

Davison's earlier treatment of the topic (1962) is still valuable for its history of the scholarship. Rutherford (1996) provides a concise overview. The foundational work is that of Milman Parry (1971), developed by Albert Lord (1995), (2000); see also Kirk (1962). Adam Parry (1971), Lloyd-Jones (1981) and Janko (1998) are important for the general issues. The most vigorous discussion at the time of writing revolves around the work of Gregory Nagy, who has proposed a radical new answer to the Homeric question; he has met with both enthusiastic assent and heavy criticism. The work of John Miles Foley is an excellent guide to the worldwide perspective of oral literature; see for a start his chapter in this volume. Also in this volume, the contributions of Clark and Dowden are most pertinent. Discussions of the history of the text are given in my last footnote; for the early reception of Homer, see Burgess (2001) and Graziosi (2002); on writing in early Greece see Powell (1997). An introduction to the great tradition of German scholarship is available to those without German in Wright and Jones (1997).

48 The issue is endlessly discussed. With others, I would argue that when an Aristarchean reading has little support in early MSS or papyri, it is probably a conjecture; where it *also* springs from a concern about propriety or some other such criterion, it is almost certainly a conjecture.

49 Montanari (2002).

50 The latter, however, deliberately edits the vulgate. For authoritative discussions of the history of the text see S. West (1967), (1988), Apthorp (1980), Janko (1992a) 20–38, Haslam (1997), M. West (2001), Rengakos (2002) and Montanari (2002).

5
HOMERIC RECEPTIONS

15

RICHARD HUNTER

Homer and Greek literature

> From the very earliest infancy young children are nursed in their learning by Homer, and swaddled in his verses we water our souls with them as though they were nourishing milk. He stands beside each of us as we start out and gradually grow into men, he blossoms as we do, and until old age we never grow tired of him, for as soon as we set him aside we thirst for him again; it may be said that the same limit is set to both Homer and life.
>
> ('Heraclitus', *Homeric Problems* 1.5–7)

Father Homer

In antiquity the relationship between Homer and subsequent Greek literature was figured through a series of (often overlapping) images: Homer was the 'source' from which all subsequent writers were irrigated, the fountainhead of both subject and style,[1] and also the 'father' of all later literature (cf. Nonnus, *Dionysiaca* 25.265).[2] On a famous late Hellenistic relief by Archelaos of Priene (Plate 1)[3] the enthroned poet is acclaimed by (among others) History, Poetry, Tragedy and Comedy, and crowned by Time and 'Oikoumene' (the inhabited world) as being, in Thucydides' hopeful words about his own work, not only 'a possession for all time', but also one for everyone; no one 'owns' Homer.[4] As both the *Iliad* and the *Odyssey*, which kneel beside Homer on the relief, as well as the post-Homeric literary genres are Homer's 'children', so the same relief also depicts Zeus and his children,

[1] Cf. 'Longinus', *Subl.* 13.3 on Plato (in D. Russell, *Longinus: On the Sublime* (Oxford 1964), with Russell's note); Brink (1972) 553–6; Williams (1978) 98–9. Galaton's painting of Homer vomiting and 'all other poets' collecting up the vomit deserves special mention (Aelian, *VH* 13.22).

[2] For Homer and Nonnus cf. Hopkinson (1994) with further bibliography.

[3] Cf. Pinkwart (1965a) and (1965b), Brink (1972) 549–52, Zeitlin (2001) 197–200 with further bibliography. The relief is commonly dated to the late second century, but Ridgway (1990) 257–66 has suggested that it may be appreciably later.

[4] This does not, of course, mean that many different cities did not try to claim him as their own (cf. e.g. 'The contest of Homer and Hesiod' 6–7 Allen); Ptolemy Philopator built a shrine of Homer in which his image was encircled by all the cities which claimed him (Aelian, *VH* 13.22). For ancient cults of Homer cf. Pinkwart (1965a) 169–73.

1. Archelaos of Priene, Hellenistic relief depicting the apotheosis of Homer

Apollo and the Muses; the clear iconographic parallelism between Homer and Zeus, the 'father of gods and men', points to the two key origins of all human culture.[5]

The idea of Homer as 'father' is of particular importance when meaning depends crucially upon an overt sense of rewriting the past.[6] In Sophocles' *Philoctetes*, for example, Neoptolemus is first addressed as 'son of Achilles' (4), in a play in which not only will the abandoned hero be undone by his devotion to the memory of the central figure of the *Iliad*, but Neoptolemus, sent with Odysseus to fetch Philoctetes, as Achilles was fetched by Odysseus and Nestor (11.767–70), will deceive Philoctetes by 'replaying' the experience of his father: he pretends that he has withdrawn in anger after being deprived of what was rightly his and is sailing home, as Achilles had said he would, but never did (*Phil.* 363–84; cf. *Il.* 9.356–63).[7] Neoptolemus' false tale, like those of Odysseus in the *Odyssey*, is 'like truth' (cf. XIX.203); the audience know the tale to be false, but it is their knowledge of Homer which allows them to appreciate the powerful plausibility of the tale and its effect upon Philoctetes. It is in fact Neoptolemus who must (reluctantly) act out the part of Odysseus from *Iliad* 9 in trying to persuade a stubborn and self-willed man upon whom the Greek cause depends, whereas it is Philoctetes who remains, like Achilles, impervious to the buffetings of rhetoric. More broadly, the descent of Neoptolemus from Achilles and the emphasis upon the passing of an entire heroic generation (*Phil.* 410–52), but for the inevitable wicked survivors, marks Sophocles' play as the 'child' of Homer. It is, however, in the figure of one of these cross-generational survivors, Odysseus, that the meaning of this descent is most potently expressed: Odysseus' amoral devotion to ends rather than means, which evokes in part the *Realpolitik* of the late fifth century, sets the present in counterpoint to the (idealised) past and raises disturbing questions about both. Neoptolemus' ambiguous role, and the fact that so much of the Homeric texture of the play is focused through Philoctetes' memories of a now distant past, remind us that 'Homer' is already an idea whose significance is always contextually determined. Recourse to the Homeric text and/or ideas about Homer has become a way of constructing and seeking to understand the present.

This procreative and genealogical fashioning of literary descent, whose influence is powerfully visible in Aristotle's account of the development of

5 On the relief, the mice at Homer's feet perhaps pick up the eagle which waits beneath Zeus's sceptre.

6 Cf. further below pp. 250–2 on Heliodorus, *Aethiopica*.

7 For discussion and bibliography on the use of Homer in the *Philoctetes* cf. Perysinakis (1992).

tragedy and comedy (*Poetics* ch. 5),[8] may particularly appeal to modern readers who find considerable suggestive power in Harold Bloom's psychological model of the strategies by which later writers seek to overcome the 'anxiety of influence',[9] but other ways of figuring the Homeric heritage may be equally attractive: Homer as a migrating soul,[10] a permanently haunting spectre, a more-or-less absent presence,[11] whose textual traces may be either barely discernible or clear and easy to read when the palimpsest of Greek literature is carefully examined.[12] One part of this palimpsest, however, is particularly marked as both easy to read and difficult to interpret. The traditional language of epic is the basis of the language of all subsequent hexameter and elegiac poetry,[13] as well as a vital component of the language of tragedy,[14] and so Homer is immanently present in a special way in the very fabric of much Greek poetry; the language of the great lyric narratives of Stesichorus (early sixth century), for example, is remarkably Homeric in colour.[15] Poets, of course, allusively exploit the fact that the very language with which they are working is 'used', and hence all *poiesis* is in one sense repetition: Theocritus' young and lovesick Cyclops (*Idyll* 11) is a prisoner not just of the future which Homer has written for him, but of the fact that he is forced to express himself in the language of hexameters, which is inevitably the language of the Homeric enemy.[16] Nevertheless, the conservatism of poetic language over time, combined with the 'formulaic' character of Homeric language itself,[17] can place particular obstacles in the way of identifying *significant* re-use of Homeric language by later (particularly hexameter) poets; the broader shaping of scenes and characters, which works together with linguistic evocation, is central to the interpretative process, particularly in epics, such as Apollonius of Rhodes' *Argonautica* (third century BC) and the narrative poems of later antiquity (Triphiodorus, Quintus of Smyrna, Nonnus), which demand that readers constantly consider similarity and difference from the Homeric 'source'.[18] In other poetic forms, however, such as the thousands of literary

[8] Here drama does not 'descend from' Homer – it develops from 'improvisations' – but (to shift the metaphor) the *Iliad* and the *Odyssey* foreshadow tragedy, as the *Margites* foreshadows comedy.

[9] Cf. Hardie (1993) on post-Virgilian epic.

[10] Cf. Antipater, *Anth. Pal.* 7.75 (= LXXIV Gow–Page *GP*) on Homer and Stesichorus.

[11] Cf. Hardie (2002) on illusion and allusion in Ovid.

[12] For the idea of literature as a palimpsest cf. esp. Genette (1982).

[13] For the Hellenistic period cf. especially Fantuzzi in Fantuzzi and Hunter (2004) ch. 6.

[14] Cf. Goldhill in Easterling (1997) 129–30.

[15] Cf. 'Longinus', *Subl.* 13.3; Burkert (1987).

[16] Cf. Hunter (1999) 219.

[17] Cf. above ch. 8.

[18] For Apollonius and Homer cf. Carspecken (1952), Campbell (1981), Knight (1995), Rengakos (1993) and (1994).

epigrams, most of them in elegiacs, which were written between the high Hellenistic period and the end of pagan antiquity, levels of significance in 'echoes' of Homer may be very difficult to distinguish. These echoes are, however, rarely just background music, designed not to be heard. From very early on, indeed from Homer himself, Greek poets and prose-writers are very conscious of the traditions in which they are sited, and it is in the texture of the language that this sense of tradition is worn as a badge of belonging; 'significance' is thus not limited to 'intentional allusion'. 'Homeric' language in early inscribed epitaphs (both 'literary' and 'non literary')[19] is not simply determined by metre, but conveys something of what the living feel for the dead; Homer is the 'natural' language of suffering and strong emotion, as also the 'natural' language of *kleos*, the perpetuation of one's name. Moreover, the later we proceed, for example in the history of Greek epigram, it is the cumulative significance of a growing corpus of poems which takes over, and individual epigrams are often composed as small contributions to an overarching, common project.

How early we should listen for echoes of Homer in Greek literature is a matter of great dispute, for this depends in part upon how soon we wish to separate (the idea of) 'Homer' from the rest of the epic tradition[20] and upon how 'intertextuality' itself is to be conceived as operating within a predominantly oral culture. For 'Longinus', Archilochus and Stesichorus were 'very Homeric' (*Subl.* 13.3), but there is little modern agreement about, say, the extent to which Archilochus' picture of an unprepossessing but brave general (fr. 114 West) reacts against the masculine beauty of Homeric heroes or the specific debt which the seduction scene of the 'Cologne Epode' (fr. 196A West) owes to Hera's seduction of Zeus in *Iliad* 14.[21] Sappho's poetry evokes a world of female experience and emotion, a world in which Aphrodite reigns and to which she is summoned (fr. 1), rather than the martial world of epic from which she is banished (*Iliad* 5), but to what extent that female world is constructed through the appropriation and rewriting of 'male' epic and its values (e.g. the apparently positive evaluation of Helen in fr. 16 and the erotic 'death' of fr. 31) is disputed.[22] 'Echoes' of Homer are particularly difficult to identify in early elegy for the linguistic reasons outlined above, but as Simonides (late sixth–early fifth century) explicitly quotes *Iliad* 6.146, 'as

[19] Cf. Mickey (1981). On 'epigrammatic funerary topoi' in the *Iliad* see Scodel (1992), Thomas (1998) 205–7.

[20] Cf. above pp. 228–31.

[21] For sceptical surveys of alleged 'echoes' of Homer cf. Davison (1968) 70–85, Fowler (1987a) [illegible] (with further bibliography), [illegible]

[22] For the strong case cf. (with very different approaches) Rissman (1983), Winkler (1990) 162–87; Rosenmeyer (1997).

are the generations of leaves, so are those of men', and ascribes it to 'a man of Chios' (fr. eleg. 19 West), it is at least tempting to think that Mimnermus' use (second half of the seventh century) of the same image (fr. 2.1–2 W) also alludes to these verses of Homer;[23] whereas, however, Homer's Glaucus uses the image to denote the ceaseless passing of successive generations, Mimnermus refocuses it as an expression of the brevity of each man's youth before the onset of the miseries of old age. The historical and commemorative function of epic is here replaced (as often) by the sympotic and personal focus of elegy.

By the fifth century, the outlines of the Homeric presence in Greek literature are clear. In particular, the monumentality of the epic poems offered not just a rich store of narrative material, but also both a challenge to the apparently evanescent fragility of the present and a way of representing (and saving) it through parallel and analogy with the past. Thus, Simonides (fr. eleg. 11 W) sets the Greek victory at Troy in parallel to the Spartan victory over the Persians at Plataea,[24] and Pindar can use analogy with the *kleos* of Homer and past heroes to glorify both his patrons and himself;[25] such a technique was to have a long history in the Greek and Latin literature of patronage. Links and analogies between the past and the present need not, of course, be made explicit. The Peloponnesian War hovers over many tragic dramatisations of the Trojan War and its aftermath (Euripides' *Trojan Women* is perhaps the most familiar example), and comedy could fuse past and present to rewrite both (cf., e.g. Cratinus, *Dionysalexandros*). Thucydides' intellectualising stress on 'historical' explanation must then be seen as a powerful rejection of this contemporary mode of representation: for Thucydides, the Homeric poems merely provide evidence about the past which requires (like all such testimony) evaluation, whereas the size and importance of the Trojan War itself are easily surpassed by the contemporary war which Thucydides narrates.[26] In making Pericles proclaim that Athens does not need a Homer to celebrate it (2.41.4), Thucydides offers himself and his history as a replacement for Homer and epic.

Thucydides, of course, had his eye on more than just Homer. History's debt to Homer, depicted on the relief by Archelaos (above p. 235), is a commonplace of modern scholarship,[27] and antiquity acknowledged in particular,

[23] Cf. Allen (1993) 41 with further bibliography. West (1995) 206–7 rejects Homeric echo here; for him, Alcaeus fr. 44.6–8 (Achilles, Thetis and Zeus) is the earliest certain allusion to our *Iliad*.

[24] On this poem see Boedeker and Sider (2001).

[25] Cf. Nagy (1990), Sotiriou (1998).

[26] Cf. 1.1.1, with its echoes at 1.10.3 and 1.11.2. For Thucydides' attitude to Homer cf. also Graziosi (2002) 120–3.

[27] Strasburger (1972) is still fundamental.

as modern readers have also confirmed, the relationship between the epic poet and the Ionic writer who, for later generations, stood at the head of the tradition of stylistic prose, Herodotus, 'the prose Homer'.[28] The 'father of history' himself acknowledges his literary paternity in staking out in his proem the epic magnitude of his project as he also explains its purpose, 'so that the great and marvellous deeds of both Greeks and barbarians should not lack *kleos*, and in particular the cause of their war with each other'.[29] Against this 'epic' conception, Thucydides begins his history with an intense focus upon his own activity as an historian, what motivated him, and the intellectual processes by which he operates, thus constructing his predecessor, Herodotus, as part of the unexamined tradition which went before.[30]

Homer and Attic drama

The whole fabric of Attic tragedy (and much of comedy) is washed in Homeric dye, though the staining is not uniformly visible. It was not just that the world of epic poetry offered tragedy the grandeur of that crucial distance between 'now' and 'then' upon which much of its emotional power depended, and which Old Comedy set out to destabilise, but the Homeric poems already contained within themselves the regretful sense of loss of a larger and paradigmatic past; Homer's repeated contrast between the heroes of the *Iliad* and 'men of the present day' and the idea of a past to which only the Muse had access was now translated into the intensity of the tragic experience, enclosed and finished in its narratives but also open and suggestive in its meaning for the audience. Most familiar perhaps is how tragedy exploits the analogy which Homer himself had already established between the return and revenge of Odysseus and his son and the return and revenge of Orestes, with the associated contrasting models of wifely behaviour, Penelope and Clytemnestra.[31]

[28] The phrase occurs in the (? late Hellenistic) so-called 'Pride of Halicarnassus' poem (Merkelbach and Stauber (1998) 01/12/02), cf. Isager (1998), Lloyd-Jones (1999). Lloyd-Jones (11) rightly observes that 'it seems unlikely that this poet was the first author to call Herodotus "the prose Homer"'; the style of the 'judgement' recalls Polemon's alleged saying that 'Homer was an epic Sophocles, and Sophocles a tragic Homer' (Soph. *Test.* 115 Radt) or Antipater's designation of Sappho as 'the female Homer' (*Anth. Pal.* 9.26.3 = XIX.3 Gow-Page *GP*).

[29] Herodotus' allusion to Homer here has been very much discussed: cf., e.g. Goldhill (2002) 11–13.

[30] This is, of course, not necessarily how Herodotus is viewed today: cf. Thomas (2000) with earlier bibliography.

[31] How tragedy uses Homer here is already of concern to the scholiasts, cf., e.g. scholia to Soph. *El.* 1 ff. (interesting comparison with Athena's revelation of Ithaca to Odysseus in

The relationship between epic and drama is not one of simple allusiveness, for later literature appropriates and subsumes the past, so that the past is made in the image of the present. Thus, for example, in Aristophanes' *Acharnians* (425 BC) the comic poet satirises the state of democratic politics by likening it to the hierarchical structures depicted in martial epic. When the comic hero Dicaeopolis tries to get the Athenian assembly to talk about peace, he gets no further than does the loud shouting of the ugly Thersites in *Iliad* 2, 'who would say whatever he thought would amuse the Greeks' (2.215), when he urges the Greeks to abandon the war against Troy; both are silenced by force. In representing 'democracy', Aristophanes takes over the implied social distinctions of the Homeric text to depict a world in which Dicaeopolis, dressed as 'the poor nobody' (πτωχός), has to yield before the privileges and greed of self-important generals like 'the hero' Lamachus (cf. 595–7, 619).[32] In the *Iliad*, only real 'heroes' are given rights of speech, however 'fair' what others have to say might be (thus Thersites' words echo the charges of Achilles against Agamemnon in *Iliad* 1); in democratic Athens all male citizens were supposed to enjoy 'freedom of speech', παρρησία (cf. *Ach.* 45), but 'big shot' politicians like Lamachus seek to limit such rights to their own kind (cf. *Ach.* 578, 593). So too, Dicaeopolis' pretended terror before Lamachus' absurd shield, and the subsequent farcical skit in which he uses a feather from the general's helmet to make himself vomit into the upturned shield (*Ach.* 581–7), seem to turn the child Astyanax's fright before the plumed helmet of his father Hector (*Iliad* 6.466–70) into a very Aristophanic dramatisation of the appallingness of war. If Homeric heroes, most notably Achilles and Hector, are the direct ancestors of the central figures of *tragoidia*, it is the anti-Achilles, Thersites, who is made to foreshadow the *trugoidia* ('wine-lees song') of Dicaeopolis.[33]

If the *Acharnians* assimilates the present to the past, much of Attic tragedy gains its depth from intimations of the present in dramatisations of the epic past.[34] The inestimable debt of Attic tragedy to the Homeric heritage was

Odyssey XIII); 1137 (Electra's 'urn speech' compared to Penelope's lament for her husband who is in fact sitting beside her).

32 For Thersites and Dicaeopolis cf. Whitman (1964) 46–8; Hunter (2000) 273–4.

33 For *trugoidia* cf. Taplin (1983). For the very rich tradition of Thersites in post-Homeric Greek literature cf. Gebhard in *RE* 5A.2463–8; of particular interest is a Stoic representation of Epicurus as both more outrageous and a worse stylist than Thersites (Cleomedes, *Met.* 2.1 (pp. 60–1 Todd)).

34 On the whole subject cf. Rutherford (1982), Easterling (1985), both with further bibliography. On tragedy's self-conscious placement of itself 'against' epic see (from very different perspectives) Herington (1985) ch. 6; Goldhill (1986) ch. 6; Garner (1990), Davidson (1999–2000).

probably already a commonplace in the fifth century.[35] When in the *Phoenissae* Euripides replaces one of the 'scouts and observers' who tell Eteocles of the encircling Seven in Aeschylus' *Seven against Thebes* (cf. 36–68) with a dramatic version of the *teichoskopia* of *Iliad* 3, with Helen and Priam replaced by the young Antigone and her aged escort and the male now instructing the female, this is not simply a virtuoso piece of theatrical fun, but it constructs the 'descent' of tragedy from epic by a return to the founding text; such a concern for literary history, which we may also think of as a proclamation of generic identity, is of a kind which was to become very familiar in Hellenistic and Roman literature, and it is of a piece with the wholesale sense of 'belatedness' from which the *Phoinissai* derives such dramatic power. There is here an important contrast with Aeschylus' *Persians*, in which the 'puzzling ignorance'[36] of the Persian queen concerning Athens (230–45) is, in part, an earlier borrowing from the *teichoskopia*, but this time without 'literary critical' intent. In both Homer and Aeschylus, enquiries about the enemy mark the beginning of climactic events; in Aeschylus, however, the climax consists in the revelation and understanding of events which have already occurred.[37] The menace and foreboding of the Aeschylean scene arise from the fact that, whereas in Homer (and in the *Phoenissae*), the enemy is right before the eyes of the characters – a device which, of course, is a powerful tool of *enargeia*: we the audience 'see' what and as the characters see – in Aeschylus the enemy is invisibly 'far away' (232), and, in an extraordinarily bold dramatic experiment, the audience *is* the enemy.

Euripides' concern with the descent of dramatic poetry from Homer is shared, unsurprisingly, by Aristophanes' *Frogs*. In shaping his Aeschylus as an angry Achilles, Aristophanes does not merely assimilate the tragedian to his own presentation of the epic hero in the lost *Myrmidons*, but also forges a close alliance between epic poetry and the 'real' tragedy of Aeschylus, which had now been replaced by Euripides' word-games and low melodrama (cf. esp. *Frogs* 1013–44). So too the scene of the weighing of verses

35 Some later passages are collected at Gudeman (1934) 109; Rutherford (1982) 145 n. 3; cf. also Cantarella (1926). Beyond the famous anecdote (Aesch. test. 112 Radt) that Aeschylus called his tragedies 'cuts from Homer's banquets', particularly striking is the account of Sophocles' debt to Homer in the extant *Life* of the tragic poet (test. 1.80–9 Radt, *TrGF* 4.39).

36 Hall (1996) 127.

37 The queen's enquiries about the size of the Athenian army and the Athenian 'political' system acquire particular point against the background of Helen's revelations about Greek *basileis* and the Homeric stress on the huge numbers involved. The literary exploration of the analogy between the Greek expedition against Troy and the Persian expedition against Greece has, of course, a very long history.

(*Frogs* 1365–1410) is a comic version of Aeschylus' *Psychostasia*, in which Zeus weighed the souls of Achilles and Memnon while their respective mothers pleaded on their sons' behalf; as throughout the comic contest, then, the dice are here loaded against Euripides because it is Aeschylus who is 'Achilles' and the whole game is conducted on Aeschylean terms. Aeschylus' play, at least in the view of ancient literary critics,[38] was derived from the Iliadic image of Zeus weighing the souls of Achilles and Hector (22.209–13), and this literary history too fits the repeated pattern of the contest of the *Frogs*.

If tragedy, in its exploration of the significance of the Homeric heritage, has a particular fondness for dramatising 'cyclic' stories set after the events of the Homeric poems (e.g. Aeschylus, *Oresteia*, Sophocles, *Ajax*, Euripides, *Andromache*, *Hecuba*, *Trojan Women*), whole episodes from Homer were, nevertheless, frequently dramatised on both the tragic and the comic stages – one would give much to have some idea of how Sophocles himself impersonated Nausicaa.[39] Of plays devoted wholly to the dramatisation of episodes from the *Iliad* or the *Odyssey*, however, only the *Rhesus* ascribed to Euripides and based on events of *Iliad* 10, and Euripides' satyr-play *Cyclops* (? late fifth century), one of many ancient dramatisations of the story of *Odyssey* IX, survive. There are many different intertextual games which the *Cyclops* plays with the Homeric text, from the allusive re-use of individual motifs to very self-conscious exploitation of the differences between narrative and drama,[40] but it is the modern reading which is given to the character of the Cyclops himself which attracts particular attention. The fashioning of Polyphemus' inebriation as a refusal to participate in the civilised Athenian pleasures of the communal symposium and *komos* (530–40), the last in the series of his rejections of Dionysus,[41] builds upon Homer's juxtaposition of the Cyclops' violation of all rules of civilised behaviour (including the drinking of wine mixed with water, IX.208–11) to Odysseus' famous praise of the delights of the feast at which 'the wine pourer draws wine from the mixing-bowl and pours it into the cups' (IX.9–10).[42] Most striking of all perhaps are the obvious echoes of contemporary intellectual ideas, often today (though not always with proper discrimination) associated with 'the sophists', in the Cyclops' defence of his way of life in vv. 316–46:[43] the distance between Homeric and sophistic *anomia* is again blurred, as the asocial solitude and

[38] See the testimonia gathered by Radt (*TrGF* 3.374–6).

[39] Cf. Soph. test. 28–30 Radt.

[40] Wetzel (1965) is only of limited use here; the subject deserves further work.

[41] Cf. Rossi (1971).

[42] For a later example of the Cyclops used in this way cf. Callimachus fr. 178 Pfeiffer with Hunter (1996).

[43] Cf., e.g. Paganelli (1979) 21–60, Seaford (1984) 51–5. Euripides here is probably specifically influenced by contemporary Homeric interpretation, for which see Richardson (1975).

self-sufficiency of the Homeric Cyclopes (IX.106–15, cf. *Cycl.* 113–20) is read in the light of fifth-century views about primitive man and the fashioning power of *nomos* (law/custom). Giving protective help to suppliants was presented by the Homeric Odysseus as enjoined by Zeus's sanction (IX.270–1); for his Euripidean descendant this becomes rather a '*nomos* for mortals' (299), which the Cyclops can then reject in favour of a purely self-willed hedonism (336–41), in which cannibalism (even if accompanied by a certain culinary refinement) is on a par, say, with the anti-social activities advocated by the newly educated Pheidippides in Aristophanes' *Clouds*.[44]

In Homer the only authority which the Cyclops recognises is his own appetite, θυμός (cf. IX.278). In turning this into a blasphemous 'cult' of his own belly (334–5), the Euripidean Cyclops not only produces 'a parody of contemporary redefinitions of deity',[45] but also throws back at Odysseus the personification of that organ which Odysseus used in another context at the court of Alcinous (VII.216–21):

> There is nothing as shameless as the hateful belly, which compels men to think of it, even when they are worn out and grieving in their hearts, as I too now grieve; but my belly ever bids me eat and drink, and makes me forget all that I have suffered, as it demands to be filled full.

The grim Odyssean recognition of the constraints, *anankai*, which bind our lives, becomes a celebratory devotion to those constraints, and the Cyclops' cannibal appetites are rewritten as an amoral 'right of the stronger', different only in its savagery from the views of Thrasymachus in Book 1 of Plato's *Republic* or of Callicles in the *Gorgias*. In shaping the confrontation of Odysseus and the Cyclops as a battle between *metis*, which is not just 'cunning' but covers the whole field of reasoning and the application of intelligence,[46] and brute, unreasoning force, Homer stands at the head of much later Greek psychology, most notably that of Plato.[47] The behaviour of human beings is determined by a battle between their irrational desires and their wiser understanding, and if Odysseus and the Cyclops offer a paradigmatic contrast of the two, Odysseus himself is an example of a man who must learn to control his *thumos* (cf. IX.500, XI.105).[48]

44 Thus τοῖσι σώφροσιν at *Cyclops* 337 mockingly appropriates the language of 'the opposition' (cf. *Clouds* 1071–2, and Seaford's note *ad loc.*).

45 Seaford *ad loc.*

46 Cf. Detienne and Vernant (1978).

47 As the allegorising 'Heraclitus' triumphantly points out (*Homeric Problems* 17–18); cf. [illegible]

48 For the Cyclops embodying the *thumos* opposed to *logismos* cf., e.g. 'Heraclitus', *Homeric Problems* 70.4–5.

Homer and Plato

The Homeric poems held not merely a central place at great public festivals, such as the Athenian Panathenaea, but were, throughout antiquity, the basis of literate education: through Homer one learned Greek and Greekness.[49] The *Iliad* and the *Odyssey* offered powerful patterns of behaviour and moral judgment which could easily be moulded to the shapes required by different didactic and rhetorical situations. Thus, for example, Agamemnon, whose behaviour as 'commander-in-chief' in the early books of the *Iliad* has not always seemed to modern readers a model of good judgment, was regularly held up in antiquity as a paradigm of 'the great leader'. Here, for example, is an extract from Isocrates' eulogy of him, which forms part of a demonstration of the wickedness of the Spartans in 'destroying' Argos, Agamemnon's birthplace:

> He commanded an army which had come together from every city, a host whose size may be imagined since it contained many of the descendants of the gods and of the direct sons of gods – men who were not of the same temper as the majority of mankind nor on the same plane of thinking, but full of spirit and passion and envy and ambition – and yet he held that army together for ten years, not by great bribes nor by outlays of money, by which means all leaders nowadays maintain their power, but by the supremacy of his intelligence (*phronesis*), by his ability to provide from the enemy subsistence for his soldiers, and most of all by his reputation of being better advised in the interest of others than others in their own interest.
>
> (*Panathenaicus* 81–2, trans. Norlin, adapted)

If such a 'reading' of Homer is determined by the contextual demands of a particular rhetorical situation, it is nevertheless of a piece with antiquity's predominantly positive and normative readings of Homer. Attic tragedy had indeed persistently questioned the certainty of such readings, but it was Plato who was to argue that Homer himself should be displaced from his enthroned cultural authority. Plato repeatedly calls Homer 'a tragic poet'[50] because he lumps epic and tragedy together as the most powerful source of moral education in Athens, and one to which, despite the obvious influence of

[49] For Homer as a didactic text and Homer in educational practice much information and bibliography can be traced through, e.g. Morgan (1998), Sluiter (1999), Horsley (2000), Cribiore (2001). For some cautionary remarks concerning the classical period cf. Ford (2002) 201–8.

[50] Cf. *Rep.* 10.607a2 ('Homer is the most poetic and first of the tragic poets', though the context is ironic), *Theaet.* 152e4–6. For Homeric quotations in Plato cf. Howes (1895) and Labarbe (1949).

Homer on the dialogues,[51] Platonic philosophy is to offer an alternative. When Homer is finally banished from the ideal state, because he is a mere 'imitator' with no 'knowledge' of what he describes, Socrates ascribes to the poet's admirers the view 'that this poet has been the educator of Greece, and that for the management and education of men's affairs one should take up his works and learn them, and organise and lead the whole of one's life in accordance with this poet's work' (*Rep.* 10.606e2–5, trans. Halliwell); whatever ironic exaggeration is involved here, Homeric cultural authority is certainly not merely a rhetorical construction of Plato's own devising. That the sophists had made Homeric exposition and interpretation an important tool of their own teaching made things worse (in Plato's eyes).[52] In the *Hippias Minor* Socrates questions the famous sophist who has been declaiming ('giving an *epideixis*') about Homer, and observes that the problem with Homer is that one cannot ask him 'with what intention he composed his verses' (365d1), a remark which immediately recalls the critique of written texts in the *Phaedrus*. As the *Ion* also makes clear, the Homeric texts offer an unexamined (and, to some extent, unexaminable) body of 'knowledge', which can only be used, whether by rhapsode or sophist, in a 'display' (*epideixis*), and this is no path to real 'knowledge'. So too, the *Laches*, which is to become a discussion of the nature of 'bravery' (*andreia*), begins as a consideration of whether 'hoplomachy', i.e. armed single combat, should form part of a young man's education.[53] Though such training is intended as preparation for hoplite fighting (cf. 182a), the great duels of the *Iliad* clearly hover over this consideration of the educational value of such 'display'. The point is made by the story of the ludicrous 'hoplomachos' Stesilaos, who gave marvellous *epideixeis* of his skill, but when real warfare came made a complete fool of himself. If the implicit message seems to be that reading the *Iliad* will not make you brave, what gives the whole discussion its pointed edge is that no less is at stake than how young citizens should be educated, and this loomed very large indeed in Plato's concerns. Even the eschatological 'myth of Er' at the end of the *Republic*, whose mode is so far removed from dialectic, is introduced by Socrates as 'not a tale told to Alcinous, but the tale of a brave (*alkimos*) man' (*Rep.* 10.614b2–3), thus directly challenging not just Odysseus' account of the Underworld and the fate of

[51] Already a commonplace in antiquity, cf. Russell on 'Longinus', 13.3 (Russell (1964)).

[52] Cf., e.g. Richardson (1975), Morgan (2000) ch. 4. The Pre-Socratics are also involved: of particular interest for Plato's concern with Homer is the claim of Favorinus that 'Anaxagoras was the first to show that the poems of Homer concerned virtue (*aretē*) and justice ([illegible])' ([illegible])

[53] On the *Laches* cf. von Reden and Goldhill (1999) 267–77; Hobbs (2000) 76–112.

souls in *Odyssey* XI, but the whole story of Odysseus' encounters, which probably already carried for Plato's society the weight of a parable of moral endurance.[54]

Plato himself could, of course, use Homeric paradigms for his own purposes. In a very striking passage of the *Apology* Socrates illustrates his assertion that one should give attention to nothing other than 'whether one is acting justly or unjustly, and whether one's deeds are those of a good (*agathos*) or a bad (*kakos*) man' by the case of Achilles who, when told by his mother that Hector's death would lead to his own, 'had no thought of death and risk, but was rather afraid to live as a *kakos* and not to avenge his dear ones – "May I die as soon as I have imposed punishment (*dikē*) upon the wrongdoer (*adikounti*) . . ."' (*Apol.* 28b–d). The Homeric Achilles had not, of course, used the words *kakos* or *dikē/adikein* in the passage to which Socrates refers (18.94–106), but Socrates follows already well established practice in 'reading' Homer as he requires him to be read. Modern scholarship has rightly pointed out that there are considerable difficulties in the way, not just of reconciling the Homeric Achilles with Socratic morality, but of seeing how the analogy works in the *Apology* itself.[55] The appeal to the paradigm of Achilles, repeated in the *Crito* (44a5–b2), always carries a powerful emotional and rhetorical charge, but here Socrates uses the hero as the model of someone who did what *he* thought was right, regardless of the views of the majority (cf. *Apol.* 28d7), not just in the matter of Hector and Patroclus, but throughout Homer's account of him; neither the Homeric Achilles nor the

[54] Xenophon reports Socrates as joking that Circe turned men into swine by the lavishness of her entertainment and that Odysseus resisted both because of Hermes' warning and because he himself was self-controlled (*enkratēs*) (*Mem.* 1.3.7); this 'jest' foreshadows an important stream of Homeric criticism of later antiquity, cf. Kaiser (1964) 197–213. It is a great pity that we do not know more of Antisthenes' Homeric works, particularly in this regard the *On Circe* and *Cyclops or On Odysseus* (D.L. 6.17–18), with which such moralising criticism has often been associated. For different aspects of how Greek literature used the idea of Odysseus as 'enquirer' cf. Marincola (1997), on Odysseus and the historians; Hunter (1996), on Odysseus and the 'learned' writers of the Hellenistic age; and Montiglio (2000) on 'wandering philosophers'. At the very end of Plato's *Republic* there is perhaps an ironic contrast between Odysseus who in the Underworld chooses the very opposite of his famous *ponoi* (620c–d), i.e. does not wish to live the same life over again, and the eternal pursuit of philosophy, expressed through Socrates' conviction that 'the soul is immortal and capable of enduring many evils and many blessings [cf. Odysseus]' and that therefore 'we shall always stick to the path upwards, and shall use every means to practise justice and wisdom, in order that we may be at peace with ourselves and the gods' [unlike Odysseus?].

[55] Cf., e.g. Stokes (1997) 142–3, Hobbs (2000) 178–86. For the tradition of Achilles in post-Homeric literature generally cf. King (1987), Michelakis (2002).

Platonic Socrates ever saw virtue, any more than the Sophoclean Antigone did,[56] in taking important decisions by simply counting votes.

If Plato elsewhere uses Achilles as a negative model of uncontrolled *thumos*,[57] we should not be surprised; as we have already seen, Homeric paradigms were there to be exploited as varying contexts demanded. Achilles was a great figure of the past about whom stories, with powerful ramifications for the present, were told. So too, as Plato's *Symposium* (above all) and, in a different way, Xenophon's *Memorabilia* make clear, was Socrates; to that extent at least, both were mythic heroes.

Homer as classic

If Attic tragedy depends in part upon a sense of distance and of the broader implications of very particular events which comes with that distance, it also depends upon a sense of continuity, upon the audience's identification of itself as part of the future of the heroes of whom Homer sings; Homeric characters were an essential part of the civic fabric and iconography, and Homeric values had been subsumed into, rather than erased by, the values of the polis. With much of what survives of post-classical Greek literature, however, this sense of continuity is placed under very great strain; the past and its poetry must now be actively recovered. At Alexandria, the new city at the mouth of the Nile founded by Alexander and ruled over by the family of Alexander's general, Ptolemy, from where much of what survives of third-century poetry derives, that past was indeed assembled in monumental form for the purposes of recovery and restoration in the unparalleled collection of the texts of the Royal Library. Into this new city the poetry of Homer was of course imported, not only because of Homer's traditional place in education and society, but also as a self-conscious sign of identity, a talismanic assertion of continuity in a distinctly changed world.[58] At the political level, Homer carried a powerful charge through the traditionally cultivated closeness of the Macedonian elite to the epic world, best known through the many tales of Alexander's fascination with the figure of Achilles, and it is in Homeric terms that poets regularly depicted their royal patrons (e.g. Theocritus, *Idylls* 15 and 17).[59] Many Alexandrian poets, most notably Callimachus

[56] For the influence of the Homeric Achilles in shaping the 'Sophoclean hero' cf. esp. Knox (1964) 50–3 and Index *s.v.* Achilles. For Socrates as hero cf. also Fowler (1987b) 33–4.

[57] Cf. Hobbs (2000) 199–219 on the *Republic*.

[58] Important considerations in Bing (1988) and Selden (1998).

[59] Cf. Hunter (2003). On Homer and Theocritus' bucolic poems cf. esp. Halperin (1983).

and Apollonius, were also professionally engaged with the study and interpretation of Homer's text and their poetry reacts to that of Homer at every turn;[60] the scholastic mode fashions allusion to Homer as a shared code which binds the poet to his audience: if the comic and tragic poets spoke to 'fellow Athenians', Callimachus speaks to 'fellow readers of Homer', for whom intellectual identity is crucial to the sense of self.

Similar things could be said of the high Greek literature of the Roman Empire, but as with the sophists and Plato, it is now Homer's cultural power, rather than the detailed interpretation of his verses, which holds the attention. Greek culture of this period is, as is well known, obsessively concerned with its debt to Homer and with ways of escaping from the bondage of that debt.[61] In the now much broader context of the Roman Empire, Homer's iconic power, and the uses to which it was put, differed greatly from the sophisticated understatement of Alexandrian poetry. Homer is now a 'fact of life', a cultural *lingua franca* and the instrument of the spread of Hellenisation to the remotest parts of the world (cf. Dio Chrys. 53.6–8), a staggering monument to be satirised, denied and reinvented. Intimate knowledge of the textual detail of Homer, outside a fairly small circle of the learned, is however not to be assumed; it is clear that already, as in later antiquity,[62] some parts of the poems were much more widely read (and taught) than others. Nevertheless, perhaps the most striking testimony to Homer's pervasive presence is indeed the epideictic 'literature of denial' which erects alternative stories and accounts of the war at Troy to that given by Homer (Dio Chrysostom's *Trojan Discourse*, Philostratus' *Heroicus*); the particular ironic mode of such 'thought experiments' derives from the implicitly acknowledged hopelessness of the task – to deny Homer is merely to recognise the power of the icon.

It is unsurprising that Homer had a particular importance for the narrative literature of the period, particularly the Greek novel.[63] The *Odyssey* offered the paradigmatic founding text for tales of separation and travel and, with greater or less explicitness and with varying degrees of sophistication, all extant novels align themselves with the Homeric tradition. This is not merely a generic claim, nor just a nod to 'literary history' in an attempt to magnify the importance of the stories told; in Chariton's *Callirhoe*, extensive use of

[60] For Apollonius and Homer cf. above n. 18. For Callimachus and Homer cf. (in addition to the standard commentaries) Herter (1929), Rengakos (1992) and (1993).

[61] There is a large bibliography, but helpful guidance can be found through Kindstrand (1973) and Zeitlin (2001). For more general considerations Bowie (1970) remains a fundamental starting-point.

[62] Cf., e.g. Lamberton (1986) 193–4.

[63] Basic orientation in Fusillo (1989) 26–33 [= (1991) 24–31].

Homeric quotation and explicit parallels between the characters and those of Homer are a guide to reading, they tell us what the narrative 'means'. Such a novel exploits (and constructs) Homer as a text of universally agreed significance, particularly in the fields of personal emotion and inter-cultural contact, which can, by its very familiarity, bind the story to the audience's own emotional and imaginative lives.

The novel which most elaborately lays claim to the Homeric mantle is the *Aethiopica* of Heliodorus (third or fourth century AD).[64] This extraordinary story of the return (*nostos*) from Greece and recognition of Charikleia, an Ethiopian princess, together with Theagenes, the man she loves, is (over-) 'Homerically' structured: i.e. it begins, without narrative explanation, *in mediis rebus*, much of the action is related in flashback, and Homeric quotation and allusion abound. Theagenes is explicitly a latter-day Achilles, as Charikleia's devotion to chastity is clearly an interpretation both of Homer's Penelope and of how the figure of Penelope had been constructed in the intervening centuries (cf. 5.22.3). The central books are narrated by Kalasiris, an Egyptian holy-man (and Homeric scholar), who masterminds the return of the lovers to Ethiopia; although his role as story-teller inevitably casts him as something of an Odysseus, his own life story (2.24–6) resembles that of Homer himself, who we learn (through a 'shaggy thigh' story which Kalasiris tells) was an Egyptian, a fact found 'completely convincing, on the basis of the typically Egyptian mixture of riddling meaning and pure pleasure in his poetry' by the (rather gullible) Athenian to whom Kalasiris tells his story (3.14–15).[65] Kalasiris' double role as philological exegete (cf. esp. 3.12–13) and priest – a guide, in fact, into two related kinds of mystery – is most fully played out in 5.22. Here Odysseus appears to him on Kephallenia in a dream and threatens dire consequences, because Kalasiris has not travelled to nearby Ithaca to pay his respects to the Ithacan hero *par excellence*; Odysseus himself has now become the angry deity of the narrative patterns which Poseidon's anger against him first bequeathed to Greek literature, and the punishment he imposes upon Kalasiris is precisely to become an Odysseus, finding 'enemies on sea and land' (5.22.3). Kalasiris thus enjoys (or claims to have enjoyed) a privilege of which all scholars quite literally 'dreamed', namely direct contact with, and inspired revelation

[64] The standard edition is the Budé of R. M. Rattenbury and T. W. Lumb (Paris 1935–43); the most convenient translation is that of John Morgan in Reardon (1989).

[65] On this account of Homer cf. Winkler (1982) 102–3; Dowden (1996a) 281–2; Whitmarsh (1998) 104–6. 'Riddling meaning' (τὸ ᾐνιγμένον, 3.15.1) refers not merely to the specific context, but also to the whole tradition of 'allegorical' [illegible]; for guidance in this area cf. Buffière (1956), Lamberton (1986), Lamberton and Keaney (1992) and, with particular reference to Kalasiris, Sandy (1982) and Telò (1999).

from, Odysseus.[66] There is clearly here also an explicit generic resonance to Kalasiris' dream. As Homer appeared to Ennius in a dream to inform him that his spirit had passed to the younger poet (frr. ii–x Skutsch), and Callimachus' sense of the debt of the *Aitia* to Hesiod is expressed through a dream experience in which the Hesiodic Muses appear to him, so Kalasiris' vision of Odysseus marks the descent of the novel from Homer[67] and of Kalasiris himself from Odysseus. The Odyssean motif of divine anger had long been at home in the novel (cf. Chariton, 8.1.3, Petr. *Sat.* 139), and so the texture of literary history is here palpable: despite (or because of) his closeness to Homer himself, Kalasiris has failed to give due recognition to the origins of the story he himself is constructing.

A related confrontation between the Homeric text and its offspring occurs in the following book. Kalasiris and Charikleia are travelling through Egypt when they come upon the aftermath of a battle, with corpses strewn everywhere. They find an old woman who tells them what has happened and offers to guide them safely into the nearby town, once she has conducted certain rites with the dead. What follows is a consultation, of a kind 'common among Egyptian women' (6.14.2), between the woman and her dead son, one of the corpses on the field, who proves very talkative indeed.[68] The necromancy is very clearly modelled upon that of Odysseus in *Odyssey* XI, though the old woman's witchcraft owes as much to contemporary (beliefs about) magical practice as to Homer. Here too there is a complex play with the reception of Homer. Homeric and other hexameter verses are a very regular feature of magical texts, and it is clear from the extant corpus of 'magical papyri' from Roman Egypt that *Odyssey* XI was an important formative influence upon actual magical practice: the division between 'literature' and 'life' is far messier than is often imagined. In forcing Kalasiris to wake up to witness the necromancy (6.14.5), in which the dead son plays the role of Teiresias, Charikleia makes this latter-day cross between Homer and Odysseus confront the use to which the great tradition has been put. Kalasiris can protest all he likes about the unclean vulgarity of such practices (6.14.7), but the Homeric texture from which he is woven, and our knowledge of the cultural significance of Homer, prevent us from taking those protests at face value.

The almost obsessive concern of the *Aethiopica* with hermeneutics and interpretation[69] forms a narrative counterpart to the reading practices of the

[66] Cf., e.g. Protesilaus' story of Homer's necromantic consultation of Odysseus (Philostratus, *Heroicus* 43.13–14) and Lucian's 'true' meeting with the shade of Homer (*VH* 2.20); the latter fantasy is at least as old as Plato, *Apol.* 41a (and cf. 41c1 for a meeting with Odysseus).

[67] For Heliodorus' use of the genealogical trope cf. esp. Whitmarsh (1998).

[68] On this scene cf. further Hunter (1998) 56–7.

[69] Cf. Winkler (1982), Lamberton (1986) 150–5; Hunter (1998) with further bibliography.

Neoplatonists, who found their view – and what they took to be Plato's view – of the world already in Homer, and, in particular, to the complex structures of the Homeric exegesis of Proclus, who was Head of the Academy at Athens in the middle of the fifth century AD.[70] Thus as pagan antiquity draws to a close, Homer's monumental poems continued to be read, as they had been for more than a millenium, as a way of making sense of the world and its governance,[71] and that, after all, is not a bad reading strategy.

FURTHER READING

Almost any book on Greek literature will be concerned with the heritage of Homer, and the following is no more than a list of works which will direct readers to some of the main issues. For the archaic period: Fowler (1987a), Nagy (1990), Rissmann (1983), Sotiriou (1998); Attic drama: Garner (1990), Goldhill (1986), Herington (1985); Hellenistic poetry: Carspecken (1952), Fantuzzi and Hunter (2004), Herter (1929), Knight (1995); the literature of the Roman empire and late antiquity: Buffière (1956), Hopkinson (1994), Kindstrand (1973), Lamberton (1986), Zeitlin (2001).

70 Cf. Lamberton (1986), (1992).

71 For the particular place of the Shield of Achilles in the earlier history of such readings cf. Hardie (1985).

16

JOSEPH FARRELL

Roman Homer

Latinists are accustomed to measuring Homer's presence in Rome by his impact on Roman poetry. Epic looms largest in this regard, but most poetic genres can be regarded to some extent as derivatives of Homer. And even outside of poetry, Homer's impact on Latin letters is not small. But the reception of Homer by Roman culture is a very widespread phenomenon that is hardly confined to literature. Homerising literature in Latin needs to be understood as part of a much broader and more pervasive Homeric presence in material culture and social practice. Abundant evidence from the material and social spheres shows that elite Romans lived in a world pervaded by Homer, and would have done whether Roman poets had interested themselves in Homer or not. That the poets did so should be regarded as an outgrowth of material and social considerations rather than as their source. This is not to challenge traditional ideas about the importance of literary–historical engagements with Homer by Livius Andronicus, Ennius, Virgil and others. Such ideas have been voiced many times, and each of these important authors is in his own way justified to claim the title of 'the Roman Homer'. But habitual celebration of poetic achievement without due attention to the broader cultural milieu in which the poets worked has produced a very partial picture of Homer's presence throughout Roman culture. Accordingly, in part one of this essay I will survey the nonliterary presence of Homer in Rome and elsewhere in Italy as a context for understanding Homeric elements in the realm of Roman literature. In the second half of the essay, I will proceed to literary evidence, but will focus on those aspects that look to the circulation of Homer in Roman social life, again as a context for more belletristic performances of Homer. In following this procedure, I do not mean to give short shrift to such monuments of Homeric culture as Ennius' *Annales* and Virgil's *Aeneid*. Rather, I hope to redress an imbalance between the use of literary and nonliterary evidence in assessing Homer's impact at Rome.

Italy as a Homeric landscape

It was very early that ancient Italy became mythologised by the Greeks. Hesiod's *Theogony* ends with a reference to the sons of Odysseus and Circe – Latinus and Agrius, who ruled over the Tyrsenoi (Etruscans), and perhaps Telegonus, who is elsewhere credited with the foundation of Praeneste.[1] The Etruscans, like many other peoples who came into contact with Greek colonists, seem to have accepted their place in the Greek system of heroic genealogy by about the seventh century. Within about two hundred years, Odysseus in particular, known in Etruscan as Utuse, was credited with the founding of Cortona and even with leading the Etruscan migration from Lydia to Italy.[2] By the late sixth or early fifth century, a tradition existed that Odysseus and Aeneas had journeyed to Italy together and jointly founded the city of Rome.[3] The Romans themselves were responsible for insisting on Aeneas as their sole founder, apparently to distinguish themselves decisively from the Greeks. But although they rejected Greek ancestry, by adopting as their progenitor the Trojan Aeneas, they stayed within the Greek system of heroic genealogy.

To say 'Greek mythology' is of course not the same as saying 'Homer'. But the historical Greek colonists of the eighth and seventh centuries brought with them stories of a heroic colonisation that was the direct result of the Greco-Trojan diaspora set in motion by the fall of Priam's city. The authoritative source to which these stories were traced was naturally Homer, which means not only the *Iliad* and *Odyssey* but also the epic cycle and Homer's followers in other poetic genres, such as Stesichorus and the tragic poets of Athens, as well as a rich artistic tradition that developed in intertextual relation to the Homeric poems and their literary descendants. This dispersion of authority prevents us from making facile assumptions about what is and is not 'Homeric'. But even if one takes a conservative approach, adopting a limited purview in order to concentrate on evidence that points to Homer specifically, a conviction emerges that the settling of Italy took place within a Homeric frame of reference.

The earliest Greek colonists brought to Italy a culture that was every bit as Homeric as the ones they left behind, if not a bit more so. Important aspects of this culture were adopted by the Etruscans and adapted to their

[1] Latinus and Agrius: Hesiod, *Th.* 1,011–13. Telegonus is mentioned in the following line, which may be a late interpolation. But Telegonus was known in Roman times as founder of Praeneste and Tusculum: see Dion. Hal. *Ant. Rom.* 4.45, Festus *s.v. Mamiliorum*, Horace, *Odes* 3.29.8, Ovid, *Fasti* 3.92.

[2] Utuse: Colonna (1973–4) 132–50; Cortona: Malkin (1998) 173–5 with further references.

[3] Analysed by Solmsen (1986) 93–110.

own practices. For the period of about 750 to 350 BC these developments are clearly illustrated by a series of monumental burials, one Greek and two Etruscan, in which Homeric elements play a central role.

In about 730 BC, a family of Euboean colonists living in Pithecoussae on the Bay of Naples buried their twelve-year-old son with a number of artefacts that, for us, attest a cultural milieu of material comfort, social sophistication and a traditionally Hellenic cultural identity. One of the objects is a cup inscribed with three lines of Greek. The form of the first line is uncertain, but the second and third are dactyllic hexameters that read, 'I am the cup of Nestor, a joy to drink from, but anyone drinking from this cup will be struck immediately with desire for lovely-crowned Aphrodite'. The cup of Nestor, of course, is the star of a brief ecphrastic passage in the *Iliad*:

> πὰρ δὲ δέπας περικαλλές, ὃ οἴκοθεν ἦγ' ὁ γεραιός,
> χρυσείοις ἥλοισι πεπαρμένον· οὔατα δ' αὐτοῦ
> τέσσαρ' ἔσαν, δοιαὶ δὲ πελειάδες ἀμφὶς ἕκαστον
> χρύσειαι νεμέθοντο, δύω δ' ὑπὸ πυθμένες ἦσαν.
> ἄλλος μὲν μογέων ἀποκινήσασκε τραπέζης
> πλεῖον ἐόν, Νέστωρ δ' ὁ γέρων ἀμογητεὶ ἄειρεν.
> (11.632–7)

> . . . and a very beautiful cup, which the old man had brought from home, studded with golden nails. It had four handles, and two golden doves were feeding about the sides of each, and there were two bases underneath. Another man with effort might lift it from the table when it was full, but Nestor, an old man, could raise it without effort.

Irad Malkin brings out the contextual meaning of this artifact.[4] The inscription, the vessel itself, and the other materials found in the grave (mixing bowls, for example), allude to the social context of the symposium, a cultural institution devoted to connoisseurship especially in the realms of wine, poetry and song, the visual arts and the pleasures of the body. It was an occasion for performing the aristocratic self as it had been formed, to no small degree, in the school of Homer. The symposiast, lifting his 'Nestor's cup' with ease, playfully demonstrates his 'heroic strength'. He might display his learning as well by quoting the lines of the *Iliad* cited above. An artefact of this type would be at home in any part of the ancient Greek world. Indeed, the ecphrasis of 'Nestor's cup' acquired a life of its own, in both the ancient exegetical and artistic traditions.[5]

[4] Malkin (1998) 156–60.

[5] Athenaeus, 11.433b–d, 461d, 466e, 477b, 487f–493d, 781d; Eustathius *ad* 11.635.

Our second burial, the François Tomb at Vulci, dates to the late fourth century BC and is also Iliadic. The central chamber of this tomb is laid out in the form of an inverted T. The room that one enters first, which represents the cross of the T, is decorated with a series of frescoes depicting various Greek mythological scenes – mostly Trojan and mostly Homeric – on the left and events from Etruscan history on the right. The twin programs are brought into focus in the next, smaller room, in which two scenes on the left, depicting Achilles as he sacrifices Trojan victims to the shade of Patroclus (cf. *Iliad* 23.175–7), face two scenes on the right of specific Etruscan warriors, Mastarna and the brothers Vibenna, defeating their enemies.[6] The clear implication of this spatial relationship is that the Etruscan soldiers are engaged not in routine warfare, but in a heroic pursuit that casts them in the role of Homer's Achilles. This is perhaps curious: in light of those ancient traditions that regarded the Etruscans as Lydian in origin, and of the fact that the Lydians are in Homer allies of the Trojans, one might have expected a different typological alignment. Equally intriguing is the identity of the enemy in the historical panel: his name is given as Cneves Tarchunies Rumach, or none other than Gnaeus Tarquinius of Rome. The Tarquins, of course, were themselves traditionally Etruscan, but in this program they are treated as a foreign enemy and thus, according to the Homeric prototype, identified with the Trojans, while those who commissioned the monument assume the role of the Greeks. This inversion anticipates by several centuries the celebrated role-reversal that occurs between Trojan Aeneas (who plays the role of the victorious Greek hero Achilles) and Italian Turnus (who becomes the defeated Trojan hero Hector) in Virgil's treatment. Thus the Homeric pattern of victory and defeat trumps genealogy in determining how Etruscans and Romans understand their own myth and history.[7]

From Nestor's cup to the François tomb is in some ways a small step, but it is laden with cultural significance. The Pithecoussae burial is a Greek expression of the Greek ideals that a group of Euboean settlers brought with them to the Italian peninsula. To be sure, the implied equation between Nestor, the eldest of Homer's heroes, and a twelve-year-old boy who died before his time, between the still-heroic strength with which the old man lifted his cup and the unfulfilled manhood of the lamented youngster, requires a prior leap of imagination sufficient to connect eighth-century colonists in Italy with the heroic past and with the Greek mainland. The paintings of the

[6] On the tomb and its pictorial program see Brilliant (1984) 30–4 with further references.

[7] In a narrower sense, since gladiatorial contests originated among the Etruscans in a context of ritual sacrifice, the visual comparison of Etruscan soldiers to the greatest of Greek heroes in a most atypical moment may contain an element of tendentious self-justification as well.

François tomb draw a similar analogy – indeed, one that is in some ways closer, since both the tenor and the vehicle of this comparison involve the military exploits of grown men. But this time, although the vehicle remains Homeric, the tenor is not Greek, but Etruscan. The procedure as well deserves notice. By placing the deeds of Etruscan warriors in a spatial composition that invites comparison with the deeds of Achilles, the designer of the tomb creates a distinctly typological relationship between the recent Etruscan past and distant but definite Homeric antecedents. This is a pattern that we shall see repeated again and again.

Our third burial – the Tomba dell'Orco at Tarquinia, also from the fourth century BC – is again decorated with frescoes, this time pointing to the Homeric *Odyssey*.[8] As one enters the tomb, the first chamber is undecorated; but the second contains, on the right, a recessed area representing the cave of Polyphemus. Within this area is depicted the blinding of the Cyclops. Several details of this fresco indicate an especially close relationship with Homer's telling of the story.[9] An adjacent room is more amply decorated with scenes representing the Greek world of the dead. The decorative program incorporates traditional but non-Homeric denizens of the Underworld, such as Geryon, but corresponds in large measure to the Homeric *nekyia*, beginning with Odysseus' sacrifice of a black ram and a black sheep (XI.20–33) and concluding with Theseus and Perithous (631).[10]

Monumental productions such as the François Tomb and the Tomba dell'Orco are not the only evidence of Homeric culture in early Italy. The material record contains many examples of bowls and cups, mirrors, burial urns, and other small-scale artefacts that bear representations of individual Homeric scenes.[11] A series of cinerary urns produced between about 250 and 25 BC depicts a variety of mythological topics, with dramatic moments from

[8] On the Tomba dell'Orco in general, see Weber-Lehmann (1995) 71–100 with further references.

[9] Here I follow the analysis of Weber-Lehmann (1995).

[10] The addition not only of Geryon but of the Lernaean Hydra as well anticipates the appearance of these creatures in Virgil's Underworld (*Aen.* 6.289, 287). Weber-Lehmann's (1995) positing of a specific common source for the Tomba dell'Orco painter and for Virgil is too reductive. What is notable about this parallelism is that the Etruscan artist and the Roman poet allowed themselves similar licences in following their respective Homeric programs. The verse that names Theseus and Perithous (631) was suspected in antiquity (Plut. *Thes.* 20), but this very information suggests that, authentic or not, it was a commonly attested ancient reading and thus probably known to whoever was responsible for designing the pictorial program of the tomb.

[11] See for example Robert (1890), Weitzmann (1959) 31–51 and (1970) 14–17; Hausmann (1959), Moret (1975), Sinn (1979).

the *Odyssey* prominent among them.[12] In one type, used for the burial of a woman, Odysseus' victory over Penelope's suitors presumably praises the woman's fidelity to her husband.[13] Episodes from Odysseus' career outside of Homer also figure in this genre: more than one urn depicts Odysseus' retrieval of Philoctetes, perhaps representing the death of the man whose ashes it contained as liberation from a debilitating disease.[14] But especially common are representations of adventures – with Circe, with the Sirens, with Polyphemus – that have no obvious connection with the life or character of the deceased, or none that we can readily suggest.[15] What these episodes all have in common, however, is the fact that the rationalising exegetical tradition placed them in Italy and Sicily. That is to say, the *Odyssey* itself, on this view, attests Odysseus' travels in the region where the people honoured by these burials had lived their lives. And, as was mentioned above, the Etruscans by the fifth century – at least 150 years before the earliest of these urns – had accepted Odysseus as the hero who brought their people to Italy. It seems quite likely, therefore, that among the purposes of depositing the ashes of the deceased in urns bearing such scenes was to assert a continuity of cultural identity between the Greek hero and his Etruscan 'descendants'. The prevalence of the urns may thus indicate that the heroic identification of an older warrior class with Iliadic ideals was gradually replaced by a more general sense of 'ownership' of Homeric mythology and a preference for Odyssean motifs among the well-to-do.

Like the Etruscans, the Romans lived with Homer on familiar terms from an early date. Some part of their Homeric culture was acquired from the Etruscans, some from direct contact with the Greek colonies of southern Italy and Sicily as well as with the mother cities of the Greek mainland. The smaller artefacts that dominate the record from about 250–25 BC are, as has been said, often difficult to tie closely to Homer rather than to a drama or some other type of literary work, not to speak of an independent tradition of visual representation. But they do attest a continuity of interest, throughout the various cultures of Italy from archaic to classical times, in Homeric stories. What is more interesting is that among the Romans as well as the Etruscans there existed a powerful tradition of representing not merely Homeric episodes, but Homeric narrative as well.

[12] Van der Meer (1977–8). For bibliography on workshops and favoured scenes see Brilliant (1984) 44 n.

[13] Brilliant (1984), pl. 1.5.

[14] Brilliant (1984), pl. 1.3.

[15] A connection, of course, there may be. By the mid third century, and certainly by the end of the first century BC, there is no reason to doubt that the choice of episode may be governed by allegoresis. On allegorical interpretation of the Homeric poems, see further below, n. 45.

This interest in visual Homeric narratives on a small scale is represented as well by a series of twenty small marble tablets known collectively as *tabulae Iliacae*.[16] These were produced in Rome and its environs between the first century BC and the middle of the second century AD. Eleven of the tablets represent scenes from the *Iliad*, six concern the sack of Troy, and the others combine scenes from the rest of the Trojan cycle, including the *Odyssey*. What was the audience for these tablets? Nicholas Horsfall plausibly suggests that they were produced for a vulgar clientele, one with no real literary education, but with enough money, perhaps new money, to have acquired pretensions.[17] However this may be, visual Homeric narratives on a grand scale eventually make their return among the Romans. In his treatise on architecture, Vitruvius mentions Homeric wall paintings as a traditional subject to adorn a fine home:

> Ceteris conclavibus, id est vernis, autumnalibus, estivis, etiam atriis et peristylis, constitutae sunt ab antiquis ex certis rebus certae rationes picturarum . . . nonnulli locis item signorum megalographiam habentes; deorum simulacra seu fabularum dispositas explicationes, non minus Troianas pugnas seu Vlixis errationes per topia (7.5.1–2).
>
> In all other [kinds of rooms] – whether used in spring, fall, or summer, and even in courtyards and colonnades, particular cycles of painting dealing with particular subjects have traditionally been used . . . Some rooms have paintings on a large scale where sculpture is usually found: images of the gods or narrative tableaux, even the Trojan War or the wanderings of Ulysses from place to place.

A good example of what Vitruvius means is found in the famous cycle of Odyssean landscapes from the Esquiline.[18] The panels, which were painted in about 30 BC, present generous vistas of varied landscapes, including beaches backed by wide expanses of ocean; mountainous hinterlands; a few, but significantly placed, trees; and at least one architectural complex. At first sight it is the scenery itself that is the hero of this composition; but on closer inspection, one notices the figures that inhabit this landscape, and realises that they are telling a story. The first panel has been lost, but those that survive depict a sequence of episodes from the *Odyssey*: the adventure with the Laestrygonians (1–3); Odysseus' encounter with Circe (5; an additional panel, 6, has probably been lost); and the *nekyia* (7–8). A further fragment appears to contain the adventure of the Sirens, and is thought to have contained as

16 Sadurska (1964), Horsfall (1979); Weitzmann (1959) 34–49, 107, 131; Schefold (1975) 125–8.

17 Horsfall (1979) 34–35, endorsed by Brilliant (1984) 57; Sadurska (1964) 18.

18 Andreae (1962) 106–17; von Blankenhagn (1963) 100–46; Weitzmann (1970) 19; Schefold (1952) 81.

well the struggle with Scylla. Looking back over this sequence, it seems certain that the lost first panel contained Polyphemus, and that the cycle was devoted to those adventures that occupy the central books of the *Odyssey*.

What is immediately obvious is the similarity between the pictorial program of the Tomba dell'Orco and that of the Esquiline house. To be sure, differences exist as well: not all of the Esquiline scenes are present in the tomb; the domestic setting of the landscapes differs from the funereal setting of the tomb (even if ritual banqueting did take place at the burial site); the styles of the two sequences differ radically, as one would expect in view of the three hundred years that separate them. Nevertheless, the fact that both programs focus on the central books of the *Odyssey*, and that they supplement the Homeric text in similar ways, remains striking. There seem to be three possibilities: (1) the similarity is pure, meaningless accident; (2) the plan of the Etruscan tomb was the more or less direct model for the Roman triclinium; (3) the program represented in both places was of a type that was familiar throughout Italy from at least the fourth century BC onward.

The last of these possibilities seems likeliest, even if examples of large-scale compositions between the fourth and first centuries are not plentiful. But in any case, the kind of Homeric program embodied in the the Esquiline frescoes remained a feature of domestic decoration for generations. In the via dell'Abbondanza of Pompeii there are two houses that exhibit such programs, all involving not the *Odyssey*, but the *Iliad*. The House of D. Octavius Quartio contains a cycle of fifteen or more episodes from the *Iliad*, subordinated to a different Trojan cycle representing Hercules and Laomedon.[19] A second house, called the House of the Cryptoporticus, shows in one room about 300 feet of Iliadic material culminating in the flight of Aeneas, Anchises and Ascanius under the protection of Hermes.[20]

As a final example of this tradition – and undoubtedly the most spectacular – let us briefly consider the remarkable sculpture garden of Sperlonga. This litoral town, known in antiquity as Spelunca, was the site of a villa owned by the emperor Tiberius.[21] The town was aptly named. Excavations in 1957 revealed a seaside cave that served as a nympheum and also, it is thought, as a summer triclinium.[22] The main feature of the complex is, however, a spectacular sculptural program. The centrepieces are two

[19] Spinazzola (1954), Kemp-Lindemann (1975).

[20] Discussed by Brilliant (1984) 63–4. For the relationship between the Iliadic material and Aeneas' flight, cf. the *tabulae Iliacae*.

[21] Suetonius, *Tib.* 39; Tacitus, *Ann.* 4.59.1.

[22] On the investigation of the place and the discovery and reconstruction of the statuary, see Jacopi (1958) and (1967). The form and purpose of the complex are lucidly discussed by Viscogliosi (1996).

monumental recreations of scenes from the *Odyssey*, one of Scylla attacking Odysseus' ship and the other of the blinding of Polyphemus. Additional subjects are drawn from the *Iliad* and the Trojan cycle, including Ganymede, Menelaus and Patroclus, the body of Achilles, Diomedes and the Palladium.[23] The significance of this design has been widely discussed and variously interpreted in specific details. What is unmistakable is that it incorporates crucial episodes from both the *Iliad* and the *Odyssey* into its design. The *Odyssey*, which is represented by the two colossal sculpture groups of Polyphemus and Scylla, assumes by far the larger share of importance, as is not uncommon in ancient Italian art over the centuries. In particular, the central books of the poem and the adventures that were thought to have taken place on or near Italian soil are the focus – just as was true centuries before in Etruscan tomb painting. The Iliadic material focuses on Achilles and Patroclus, like the climax of the typological program in the François Tomb. The cyclic elements contribute thematic associations that are absent from the *Iliad* and *Odyssey* proper, but that establish an important reference for the intended audience: Ganymede, for example, is a common symbol of apotheosis – a motif of pointed significance within a Roman imperial setting – and the Palladium, of course, represents the transferal of Trojan cult to Rome. Much has changed between the arrival of Homeric stories in seventh-century Italy and the design of this astonishing masterpiece, but the main forces that govern the reception of Homer in a context of cultural identification and appropriation have remained amazingly constant.

This partial survey shows that elite Romans, like the Etruscans before them, surrounded themselves with visual *Iliads* and, especially, *Odysseys*. The interest in such scenes both in Rome and in provincial cities like Pompeii and the habit of constructing narratives that link the heroic past of Greece to the Italian present hark back to the monumental burials of the seventh to the fourth centuries; and the procedure of focusing on sequences rather than on individual episodes implies an interest not in detachable stories but in monumental narrative structures. Furthermore, the structures in question are undoubtedly Homer's masterpieces, and not popular treatments of this or that story in tragedy or any other, less expansive genre.[24] The popularity of Odyssean cycles seems to have been connected with the idea that

[23] The sculptures are evidently from the same workshop that produced the famous Laocoon: see Conticello, Andreae and Bol (1974).

[24] Confining the inquiry to evidence that depends on larger narrative structures than tragedy typically avoids questions about whether Homer or tragedy is the 'real' source of the scenes being depicted. In view of the thoroughly Homeric character of tragedy in general, however, paying homage to this false antithesis may be felt unnecessarily to limit one's field of vision. On Homer and tragedy see the remarks of Hunter in this volume. On the 'theatrical mentality'

Odysseus was an Italian culture hero and even the ancestor of some peoples. Also notable in at least some of these examples is a typological relationship between Homeric mythology and the deeds of the Italian patrons who sponsored the creation of the monuments. These relationships remain relatively constant from the time that they first appear in classical Etruscan culture down to the Roman imperial period. With this background in mind, let us turn to the literary evidence for Homer's impact on Roman culture.

Living with Homer

As the artistic evidence suggests, Homer was an important element of elite Roman ideology. His texts defined a world of aristocratic epistemology and stood as the paradigm against which to measure one's own experience. And if artistic representation suggests a typological relationship between the Homeric poems and ancient perceptions of contemporary events, no less is true of the literary record. The most renowned instance of typing a situation by quoting Homer must be Scipio Aemilianus' comment on the destruction of Carthage. As he viewed the dying city, Scipio famously wept and quoted the words of Hector to Andromache in *Iliad* 6 –

> ἔσσεται ἦμαρ ὅτ᾽ ἄν ποτ᾽ ὀλώληι Ἴλιος ἱρὴ
> καὶ Πρίαμος καὶ λαὸς ἐϋμμελίω Πριάμοιο.
> (6.448–9)

There will be a day when holy Troy will perish, and Priam, and the people of Priam of the good ash-spear.

– and in doing so thought of the future of Rome.[25] Scipio's behaviour in this anecdote does a lot to explain why he came to be regarded as a hero of humanistic sensibilities. But it did not take such a momentous event to bring Homer to Roman lips. Homerisms came to mind casually as well, and with humorous effect. Cicero is our best source, who in his letters drops Homeric quotations freely. These range in tone from the purely ironic and jocular to sincere expressions of high-minded principle. For the latter sort, which are in a similar vein to that of Scipio's famous utterance, we may consult a letter to Atticus about the stance Cicero should adopt towards Caesar's first

of Hellenistic and Imperial culture and the effect of this mentality on the reception of Homer, see Zeitlin (2001) 208.

25 Appian, *Punic.* 132 = Polyb. 39.6. Other quotations of Homer on historic events: Plutarch, *Aem.* 28.8: 1.528–30; Polyb. 36.8.8: x.495 (Cato on Scipio); Diod. fr. 34 (35) 7.3: 1 .47 (Scipio Aemilianus on death of Ti. Gracchus); Cicero, *Att.* [illegible] 11.804–5 (quoting Sex. Pompeius); Val. Max. 1.5.7: 16.849 (cf. Plut. *Brutus* 24.2); Plut. *Brut.* 23.3: 6.429, 491; Plut. *Brut.* 34.4: 1.259; Suet. *Oct.* 65: 3.40.

agrarian law in 60 BC. After spelling out the advantages of supporting the law – better relations with both Pompeius and Caesar, a chance to make peace with former opponents and to ingratiate himself with the masses, all in all an opportunity to play the tranquil role of elder statesman – he declares that he will be consistent with his principles and not consult personal convenience by supporting the law, but will oppose it on patriotic grounds, because, in the words of Hector,

> εἷς οἰωνὸς ἄριστος, ἀμύνεσθαι περὶ πάτρης
> (12.243)
>
> One omen is best, to defend your country!

But Cicero might also make fun of the pretensions implied by such quotations. In a letter addressed to Caesar *imperator* (and therefore written in 45 BC), Cicero recommends a young man by the name of Precilius.[26] The letter refers to Cicero's obstinacy in opposing Caesar in the war with Pompeius, and cites young Precilius as one of the many who had in vain urged him to relent. This was clearly a delicate situation: even if Cicero and Caesar had achieved a superficial rapprochement, they were hardly now on easy or affectionate terms. How might Cicero acknowledge the political differences that had divided him from Caesar, but still establish enough of a bond that he could ask Caesar for a favour on behalf of this young man? The 'innovative' solution that he found was to lay on the Homer.[27] The letter is in fact a virtual cento of Homeric quotations, leavened by one of Euripides. By resorting to Homer, Cicero can avoid speaking too directly of his political differences with Caesar and emphasise the humane interests that the two great men of letters share. At the same time, the abundance of quotation is so over-the-top that one cannot read the letter without a smile. This too must have been part of Cicero's intent, to release tensions between himself and his correspondent not only by referring to shared cultural interests, but by doing so in a humorous way.

There are also what might be called burlesque quotations. These generally occur in Cicero's most intimate correspondence, the letters to Atticus. For example, in the wake of Caesar's assassination, Cicero writes to Atticus about the decision he faces about which side to join in the civil war that is approaching, and imagines that his friend will counsel neutrality. The words that he puts in Atticus' mouth are playfully adapted from Homer:

[26] *Fam.* 13.15 = 317 Shackleton Bailey.

[27] Innovative: '*genere novo sum litterarum ad te usus ut intellegeres non vulgarem esse commendationem*' (13.15.3).

οὔ τοι, τέκνον ἐμόν, δέδοται πολεμήϊα ἔργα;
ἀλλὰ σύ γ' ἱμερόεντα μετέρχεο ἔργα γάμοιο.
(5.428–9)

So, at least, reads the received text, in which Zeus counsels Aphrodite, who has been wounded by the mortal Diomedes, to stay clear of the battlefield. Cicero, however, 'emends' γάμοιο 'marriage' to λόγοιο 'language'. Shackleton Bailey well captures the effect in his translation,

My child, the works of war are not for thee,
but thy concern the works of *worded* [v.l. *wedded*] joy.

In a similar vein, Cicero frequently calls Clodia Metelli by the Homeric nickname βοῶπις.[28] In giving Clodia an epithet that in Homer is the exclusive property of Hera, Cicero no doubt means to scoff at this noble lady's imperious attitude. Because Hera was married to her own brother, Cicero may allude to gossip about Clodia's relationship with her brother, P. Clodius Pulcher, one of Cicero's greatest political enemies.[29]

One might object that Cicero was unusual in the range and frequency of his Homeric citations, but in fact this is almost surely not the case. We are exceptionally well informed about Cicero because we possess so much of his voluminous correspondence. But passages similar to those just discussed are to be found in the correspondences of Pliny and of Fronto and in the historiographical and biographical tradition as well. As for literature, the great works of epic poetry have been intensively studied from this point of view. At the other end of the spectrum, a work like the *Apocolocyntosis* ascribed to Seneca is but the most visible representative of a rich tradition of Homeric parody in the literary realm, one that corresponds to and exaggerates the informal banter found in Cicero's letters. This text makes use of epic formulas for ludicrously incongruous purposes, such as telling the time of day.[30] When Claudius arrives upon Olympus, Jupiter is informed that no one can understand the stranger, because he seems to speak neither Latin, nor Greek nor any other known language.[31] Jupiter therefore dispatches the well-travelled Hercules to investigate; and, uncertain where to begin, Hercules addresses Claudius in Homeric terms:

τίς πόθεν εἰς ἀνδρῶν; πόθι τοι πόλις ἠδὲ τοκῆες;
(1.170 etc.)

[28] *Att.* 2.12.2, 2.14.1, 2.22.5; [illegible]

[29] Reference to the gossip concerning incest at *Cael.* 32; cf. Catullus, 79.

[30] Seneca, *Apoc.* 2. [31] Seneca, *Apoc.* 5.

Claudius gaudet esse illic philologos homines, sperat futurum aliquem historiis suis locum. Itaque et ipse Homerico versu Caesarem se esse significans ait:

> Ἰλιόθεν με φέρων ἄνεμος Κικόνεσσι πέλασσεν
> (IX.39)

Erat autem sequens versus verior, aeque Homericus:

> . . . ἔνθα δ' ἐγὼ πόλιν ἔπραθον, ὤλεσα δ' αὐτούς
> (IX.40)

'Who in the world are you, what your city and who your parents?'
Claudius, delighted that there are literary people there, hopes that there will be some place for his histories. And so he too replies with a line of Homer by way of saying that he is a Caesar:
'A wind carrying me from Ilium drove me to the Ciconians.'
But the following verse was more accurate, and just as Homeric:
'There I sacked the city and killed the people.'

And in equating the Roman Senate with a Homeric *concilium deorum*, the *Apocolocyntosis* draws on a satiric tradition extending back at least as far as Gaius Lucilius in the second century BC.[32]

Men like Cicero, Pliny, Seneca and Lucilius quote Homer casually and sententiously, habitually and deliberately, often amusingly and always with effect, in a manner that suggests not superiority to, but fellowship with their readers and interlocutors. The picture that emerges from their practice is of an elite society that sees itself in Homeric terms, whether in ironic detachment or in commitment to high ideals. Such shared habits of mind were formed early in life. From what we know of Roman schools, Homer occupied a central place in the curriculum.[33] Horace has left a famous, if fragmentary, account of his own education. After primary school in Venusia with the sons of centurions, he went to Rome to learn the kind of things that were reserved for the sons of senators (*Serm.* 1.6.71–8). That meant Homer (*Epist.* 2.2.41–2). In Rome, young Horace's schoolmaster Orbilius apparently drummed Homer into his pupils almost literally, using both the Greek text and, in the case of the *Odyssey*, the classic translation of Livius Andronicus (*Epist.* 2.69–71).[34] Horace's vignettes agree with the professional educator's point

32 Seneca, *Apoc.* 8–11. A similar treatment of the *concilium deorum* was the subject of Lucilius' first book of satires. Cf. Ovid, *Met.* 1.163–252.

33 On Homer's place in Hellenistic education, see Marrou (1965) 246–7; Morgan (1998) 69–71, 195–15; for Rome specifically, cf. Bonner (1977) 213.

34 As a mark of his punishing tuition, Orbilius receives from Horace the (mock-Homeric?) epithet *plagosus:* 'Orbilius of the many blows' (*Epist.* 2.1.70).

of view as stated by Quintilian over a century later: 'The best principle is to begin by reading Homer and Virgil, even though one needs more mature judgement to appreciate their qualities. But there is time for that, since one will read these authors more than once.'[35]

In Horace's boyhood, Homer was paired with Livius. By Quintilian's time, Homer remained, but Virgil had supplanted Livius. What should we make of these pairings? They could suggest that Latin epic – first Livius, then Virgil – was more familiar and accessible than Greek and that it provided the context within which Roman students learned their Homer; but the converse is probably closer to the truth. Horace may have used texts like Livius' *Odusia* as a trot, but that would have exposed him to the consequences faced by a modern student who, when called upon to translate, speaks in a pidgin of undergraduate argot and Alexander Pope.[36] If, as Quintilian suggests, Virgil eventually replaced Livius in such settings, the *Aeneid* will not have been used to facilitate translation of Homer's Greek. The overt point of comparing Latin translations and adaptations to the original must have been to develop the student's facility for creative imitation of approved models and his connoisseurship in this important aesthetic domain. Both the cultural translations pioneered by Livius – invoking one of the Italian Camenae, for instance, instead of a Greek Muse – and the narrative transformations wrought on Homer's epics by Virgil will have provided excellent opportunities not only for refining the student's command of Greek and Latin, but also for drawing conclusions about the larger implications of studying Greek poetry on Italian soil.[37] How did Homer become, and why did he remain, such an important element in Roman education?

The answer to this question has a lot to do with class and social rank. Here we must bear in mind Horace's distinction between the education of centurions' sons and that of future senators. Easy familiarity with Homer was the mark of an expensive education, and those who had had one liked to sneer at frauds. But some knowledge of Homer appears to have circulated throughout Roman culture in quite casual forms. Even the illiterate might converse in quasi-Homeric expressions that had become proverbial. Of course, it can be difficult to determine whether a given reference to, say, Achilles is 'Homeric' in any particular way. In Plautus, for instance, the

35 *Ideoque optime institutum est ut ab Homero atque Vergilio lectio inciperet, quamquam ad intellegendas eorum virtutes firmiore iudicio opus est; sed huic rei superest tempus, neque enim semel legentur* (*Inst.* 1.8.5). Cf. the remarks of Morgan (1998) 96–9.

36 The essential point is made by Mariotti (1986) 14.

37 Camena: Livius, fr. 1. On the artistic and cultural issues involved in Livius' translation see Mariotti (1986) and Traina (1970).

insufferable Pyrgopolynices is repeatedly compared with Achilles, just as a clever slave like Pseudolus or Bacchides might be called a Ulysses.[38] Such references hardly depend on a close familiarity with Homer. And even when Plautus speaks of 'an *Iliad* of hate' – a phrase closely parallelled, as it happens, by Cicero – we move into the realm of proverbs that might well have circulated in general conversation even among the less well educated.[39]

How deeply such sayings penetrated into the social hierarchy is unclear: our sources, including those I have just cited, mainly represent the Hellenised literary culture rather than the lower, less literate strata of society. Still, literary representation takes it for granted that some generalised, very imperfect knowledge of Homer did exist among the uneducated and alleges that social climbers pretended to greater knowledge than they actually had. Trimalchio, the unbearable vulgarian immortalised by Petronius, tries to fake it, with hilarious results. After boasting of his Greek and Latin libraries, Trimalchio asks the *rhetoricus* Agamemnon whether he knows 'the story of Ulysses, how the Cyclops took off his thumb?'[40] He later brings on a band of 'Homeristae' and informs his guests that they are witnessing Homer's account of the war between Troy and – Tarentum![41]

These gaffes resemble certain odd features in Trimalchio's self-mythologisation, but here I want to focus on a specific point.[42] Not only is Trimalchio's grasp of Homer ludicrously weak, but he is so unsure of himself as well that he resorts to following the performance of his Homeristae with a libretto. Trimalchio's insecurity is well justified; but the poseur's reliance on such crutches is clearly a matter for ridicule, here and elsewhere. Seneca skewers a similar expedient adopted by one Calvisius Sabinus (suspected by some to be the living model for the fictitious Trimalchio). Calvisius, being very rich but lacking a polite education, wished to seem familiar with the Greek classics. Solution: he bought himself a *familia* of slaves, each one of whom had either Homer, or Hesiod, or one of the nine lyric poets by heart. For going to such lengths, he made himself the favourite target of Satellius Quadratus, who loved to expose the pretensions of the ignorant rich.[43] It is clear from such stories as these that knowledge of Homer was valued by the elite not merely as a context for appreciating Latin literature but as a mark

[38] Achilles: *Mil.* 61, 1,054, 1,289; Ulysses: *Pseud.* 1,063, 1,244; cf. *Bacch.* 949.

[39] Plautus: '*Ilias odiorum*', *Mil.* 743; Cicero: '*tanta malorum impendet Ilias*', *Att.* 8.11.3. Cf. Dem. *De fals. leg.* 148, Zenob. 4.43, Diogen. 5.26; Ovid, *Pont.* 2.7.34. See Leutsch-Schneidewin *Paroemiogr.* 2: 34; Otto (1890) *s.v.* 'Ilias'. The modern version of this proverb appears to be 'longer than *War and Peace*'.

[40] *Sat.* 48.7.

[41] *Sat.* 59.

[42] On Trimalchio's self-mythologisation, see *Sat.* 29–30.

[43] Seneca, *Epist.* 27.7.

of their social rank, and that this knowledge could not be counterfeited if one wished to be accepted by polite society.[44]

Snob appeal aside, Homer was more than a decorative element in Roman social life. The *Iliad* and *Odyssey* were revered as repositories of profound wisdom and as guides to proper behaviour. Not that many Romans were as naïve as Ion, the rhapsode of Plato's dialogue, who regarded Homer as an expert even on technical matters, such as strategy, horsemanship, and so forth. But where moral and ethical matters were concerned, Homer's prestige was immense. The clearest illustration of this reverence for Homer's ethical teachings is contained in the opening lines of Horace's epistle to Lollius Maximus:

> Troiani belli scriptorem, Maxime Lolli,
> Dum tu declamas Romae, Praeneste relegi.
> Qui quid sit pulchrum, quid turpe, quid utile, quid non,
> Planius ac melius Chrysippo et Crantore dicit.
>
> (*Epist.* 1.2.1–4)

> While you were declaiming at Rome, Lollius Maximus, I was at Praeneste reading the writer of the Trojan War, who says more plainly and better than Chrysippus and Crantor what is fair, what is base, what is useful and what is not.

There follows a précis of the *Iliad* and *Odyssey* in no more than twenty-five lines that sketches both poems as morality plays. The *Iliad* is described as an allegory of human passion getting the better of sound government: the rank and file suffer for the self-indulgence of their leaders. In the *Odyssey*, on the other hand, the hero is a paradigm of self-control. The Sirens and Circe stand for the worldly temptations that he must resist, and his men, who succumb to these temptations or who would do if not for their leader's stratagems, are set on the same level as the suitors and the Phaeacians, who live for pleasure. Both readings are tendentious, but consistent with the interpretive procedures that prevailed in Horace's day, and there is no reason to doubt that these sketches were meant to be broadly familiar to Horace's cultivated readership.[45] The *mise-en-scène* of the epistle is significant as well. Horace claims to have written this letter from Praeneste, which was traditionally

44 Cicero's Homerising might easily seem precious to a modern reader. Certainly the character Bloch in Proust's *Remembrance of Things Past,* who constantly refers to acquaintances as 'so-and-so of the shining helm' and 'brilliant, swift-footed such-and such', is open to the charge. But Bloch displays no evidence of having a sense of humour. It would be hard to make such a charge stick to Cicero.

45 On the long history of interpreting Homer allegorically see Buffière (1973), Lamberton (1986) 1–43; Lamberton and Keaney (1992), *passim*; Hardie (1986).

regarded as a foundation of Telegonus, son of Odysseus and Circe. Thus the Homeric content of the epistle resonates with the fact that it is sent from an Italian town that was founded by the son of one of Homer's two greatest heroes.

Why, then, did the Romans esteem Homer to this extent? What made those who mattered in the most powerful nation on earth adopt the foundational texts of an alien culture as a central element in their own aristocratic self-fashioning? Was it indeed the influence of Homer's great Roman imitators in the field of epic – Livius Andronicus, Naevius, Ennius, Virgil – that made it so important for elite Roman readers to gain an accurate knowledge of Homer in the original Greek? Or is this not to put matters the wrong way around? Is it not far more likely that the Roman epigoni found their audience so receptive because that audience was already familiar not merely with the text of the canonical *Iliad* and *Odyssey*, but with certain habits of interpreting those stories that had been practised on Italian soil for centuries before the specifically literary imitations that we know ever came into being? Significant here is not merely the extreme frequency with which Homer sprang to the lips of educated Romans, but particularly the fact that this was as likely or perhaps even more likely to happen in trivial and humorous contexts as compared with serious occasions. Such habits seem to imply a very long tradition – longer, perhaps, than the recorded history of Roman literature – of comparing aspects of contemporary life to Homeric paradigms. In fact, self-identification with the actions and characters depicted in Homer's epics and adoption of ideals embodied in those actions and characters, is characteristic not only of Roman but of other Italian elites as well.

Conclusion

To approach even the most familiar literary texts with this background in mind changes measurably our appreciation of their engagement with the Homeric poems. Epic poets like Livius, Ennius and Virgil are not to be seen as revolutionaries in the intensity of their engagement with Homeric material, nor should the history of that engagement be seen in purely literary terms. The kind of Homeric agon represented by the *Aeneid*, for example, has important forerunners not only in earlier Hellenistic and Roman epic, but in the compositions devised by unnamable Greek and Etruscan artisans and patrons centuries before. And the kinds of cultural comparisons implied by these monuments of literary and visual artistry were parallelled by the everyday behaviour of the Roman elite and of those who emulated them. In this sense, Homer was part of Roman culture from an early date, and he remained an important force throughout the classical period. Several other authors claimed for themselves or have had claimed for them the title of Roman Homer, but if we consider all the available evidence, it is clear that the Roman Homer was none other than Homer himself.

FURTHER READING

On Homer as the school not only of Hellas but of Rome, see Zeitlin (2001). Zeitlin's focus is on Greeks in the imperial period, but her important observations on the 'theatrical mentality' (a phrase borrowed from Pollitt (1986)) and on the behaviour of the Roman elite complement many of the points made in this chapter. Malkin (1998) situates Etruscan and Roman experience within the context of Greek settlement throughout the Mediterranean in the archaic period. Gruen (1992) presents a lucid and convincing analysis of Hellenism and Roman identity in the classical period. The literature on Homeric scenes in the visual arts is vast but not very well organised from a cultural–historical point of view. Essential reading includes Brilliant (1984). On the reception of the *Odyssey* in the visual arts, see Touchefeu-Meynier (1968); Andreae (1982); Andreae and Presicce (1996); Andreae (1999). The *Iliad* is less well served in general, but on the *tabulae Iliacae*, see Sadurska (1964). Literary material attesting Homer's presence in Roman elite culture is collected by Tolkhien (1897). Tolkhien's more analytical study *Homer und die römische Poesie* (1900) has itself been translated, updated, and equipped with an introduction and notes by Scaffai (1991). But the study of the relationship between Homer and the Roman epic poets has always been a major scholarly industry. On issues of translation, see Traina (1970). On poetic self-fashioning in the early period, see Suerbaum (1968a). Questions centering on religion and literary convention are surveyed by Feeney (1991). There are in addition many important studies of Homeric influence on individual Roman poets. On Livius Andronicus see Mariotti (1986); on Naevius, Mariotti (1955) and Barchiesi (1962). Ennius is very well served by Otto Skutsch's magisterial edition and commentary on the *Annales* (Skutsch (1985)); see also Brink (1952). Virgil looms especially large over this landscape. For the *Aeneid* the essential study remains Knauer (1964a) (English summary Knauer (1964b)). The system that Knauer explicates is open to interpretation from many points of view. Crucial contributions include Heinze (1915; English version 1993); Otis (1964); Barchiesi (1984); Hardie (1986). Homer also exerts a formative influence on the *Georgics*, largely through the procedures of ancient allegoresis: see Farrell (1991); Morgan (1999). For Statius, Valerius Flaccus and Silius Italicus see Juhnke (1972) with, however, the important modifications to Juhnke's approach suggested by Smolenaars (1994) xxvi–xlii. Homer's influence was felt in other poetic genres as well, particularly in elegy, but comprehensive general studies are lacking. The *Odyssey* is universally acknowledged as the ultimate model for the typical novelistic plot. On Petronius see Courtney (2001) ch. 6, 'The Voyage' and *passim*. On Apuleius see Harrison (1990); for further reading cf. Schlam and Finkelpearl (2000).

17

PENELOPE WILSON

Homer and English epic

The subject of this chapter – in keeping with its chronological place in this section – is the importance of Homer for English epic up to the end of the eighteenth century. Its rationale, however, is not solely diachronic: the starting point is rather a widely accepted premise that between what goes before and what comes after there is a fault-line in the nature of the availability of Homer to English literary consciousness. A critical event can be readily identified, in the publication of F. A. Wolf's *Prolegomena to Homer* of 1795. This work itself is the product of a period of change and questioning: the eighteenth century saw a steady growth in historical, topographical and antiquarian interest in the ancient world. In relation to Homer, Robert Wood had provided one of the most influential landmarks in his investigation, based on travels undertaken in the early 1750s, of Homer's own time and culture, *An Essay on the Original Genius of Homer* (1769).[1] Wolf, however, is definitive:

> The Homer that we hold in our hands now is not the one who flourished in the mouths of the Greeks of his own day, but one variously altered, interpolated, corrected, and emended from the times of Solon down to those of the Alexandrians. Learned and clever men have long felt their way to this conclusion by using various scattered bits of evidence; but now the voices of all periods joined together bear witness, and history speaks.[2]

The interests of classical scholarship and literary criticism rarely, if ever, keep precise step: a primitive and even 'patched together' Homer is a presence in English letters long before 1795, and the image of Homer as the supreme poetic ancestor prevails, for those who chose or choose to view him thus, long after. Homer – inevitably, as a focal point of ancient–modern controversies and of a range of aesthetic debates about simplicity, originality and the

[1] On the growth of the historical approach and on Wood, see Foerster (1947) *passim*, and Simonsuuri (1979) 133–42.

[2] Wolf (1985) 209.

heroic – is not a simple value in the period here under discussion. By the end of it, however, the ground is laid for the separation of a newly historicised and pre-literate 'Homer' from his text and its authority, and for a significant challenge to the possibility of a direct engagement with a single author as source: Homer becomes as emphatically a question as an authority. With this context in mind, the questions asked in this chapter are about the availability of Homer before this point for 'epic' creativity in English, and they will be explored in particular through a consideration of the two unquestionably creative Homeric readings of the period – those of Milton in *Paradise Lost* and Pope in his translation of the *Iliad*.

Another function of this chapter, before the focus is brought to bear on this specific argument, is to offer a broader characterisation of the place of Homer in English epic up to the end of the eighteenth century. It might first be pointed out that there is a latent paradox in the subject itself. A primary requirement of epic since its first theorisations has been that it should have a serious significance for its own age and nation. The neo-classical version of the premise that epic should have a serious moral purpose led Dryden not only to conclude that all succeeding poets ought rather to imitate Virgil than Homer (whose hero Achilles is seen as flawed by extremes of passion and revenge), but further – when contemplating his own epic project – to seek specifically an English story, one 'neither too far distant from the present age, nor too near approaching it'.[3] An English epic may draw strength from analogy with the epics of the past, but it must also typically render them anachronistic. Its relation to earlier examples is energetically revisionary. For E. M. W. Tillyard fifty years ago, 'English epic' is a qualitative rather than formal entity, the canon composed of works with a national or choric significance (*Piers Plowman*, *The Faerie Queene*, *Paradise Lost*, Bunyan's *Holy War*, Pope's *Iliad* and Gibbon's *Decline and Fall*).[4] What is characteristic of these greater works is also visible in the lesser, in the mostly forgotten 'epic' hinterland with which British poetry of this period abounds.[5] English epic, whether qualitatively or quantitatively defined, has only limited contact with Homer: many epic endeavours have a Latinate rather than

[3] Dryden (1962) 1.191; 2.186. [4] Tillyard (1954).

[5] Writers of epic poems include Michael Drayton, Samuel Daniel, Abraham Cowley, Richard Blackmore and Samuel Glover. Hugh Blair in his lecture on epic poetry (Lecture 42) makes a case against what he calls 'the pedantry of Criticism' for the acceptance of a wide range of such poems into the epic canon along with the *Iliad* and the *Aeneid*, 'though some of them approach much nearer than others, to the perfection of these celebrated Works. They are, undoubtedly, all Epic; that is, poetical recitals of great adventures; which is all that is meant by this denomination of Poetry' (Blair (1783) 2.407–9).

Homeric fuelling, and nearly all involve a resistance to what might be seen as mere antiquarianism. The search for an appropriate and sufficient subject is a key element of epic endeavour. The several incompatibilities of classical epic with a true 'English' epic design seem to make themselves manifest in the eight-line *cul de sac* of Pope's late fragment 'Brutus', with the poet's plea to be 'snatched'

> . . . . to thy holy hill of spotless Bay,
> My Countrys Poet, to record her Fame,

followed only by a silence which constitutes an ironic and involuntary counterpart to the silence at the end of Book 4 of the *Dunciad*.[6] Fielding's semi-serious construction of a classical epic genealogy for the English novel at almost exactly the same time in the 'Preface' to *Joseph Andrews* perhaps primarily serves to point up the discontinuities and departures of the new form.[7]

The more general importance of Homer for English readers up to the end of the eighteenth century has been well explored by scholars in recent decades, and new technologies now offer new ways of quantifying his presence in the world of the printed book.[8] Thanks to the electronic resources of the *ESTC*, we can say with a new certainty that up to the end of the eighteenth century Homer comes in, in terms of English 'editions' (including translations), first of Greek and fifth of all classical writers (after Ovid, Horace, Cicero and Virgil, and just before Aesop and Xenophon); and that by the same sort of measure the *Iliad* is more than twice as popular as the *Odyssey*. A search of the English poetry database of *Literature Online* (*http://lion.chadwyck.co.uk/*) suggests that even excluding Pope there are more references to Homer before 1800 than to any other classical poet except Horace. As with all classical authors, the eighteenth century sees a significant increase in the availability of the *Iliad* and the *Odyssey* to the English reader, and in particular to English readers previously excluded by class or gender from access to the classics. The count of editions of Pope's Homer alone is startling evidence of the degree to which the translations that served Pope himself so well financially

[6] Pope, 'Fragment of Brutus an epic', in Pope (1940–69) 6.404.

[7] On the relations of classical epic to the eighteenth-century novel see, e.g. Maresca (1974), Mace (1996) 61–76.

[8] General studies include Clarke (1981), King (1987), Simonsuuri (1979), Stanford (1963), Foerster (1947). The most important electronic resource for the study of the classical tradition in English is *ESTC: English Short-Title Catalogue* (1981–), online version, produced by the British Library and *ESTC*/North America (http://eureka.rlg.ac.uk/cgi-bin/zgate2.prod).

were to become a staple item for provincial, especially Scottish, booksellers and printers.[9]

Despite the availability of earlier translations like those of Arthur Hall (1581), Chapman (1598–1615), John Ogilby (1660–9) or Thomas Hobbes (1675–6), 'Homer' before the eighteenth-century colonisation of the classics was a more composite and more uncertain entity. Troy was Homer's terrain, and a magnet for local 'Homeric' emotion both for visitors and in the imagination, but Troy in European and English literature is not always or even primarily Homeric. The *Iliad* and the *Odyssey* deal with two episodes falling before and after the fall of Troy – the wrath of Achilles, and the homecoming of Odysseus. The fuller story of Troy, from the marriage of Peleus and Thetis and the judgment of Paris to the death of Achilles, the Trojan horse and the returns of the various heroes to their homelands, is elsewhere, and the tradition feeding into the version of Troy known to writers and readers in the Renaissance – and beyond – has many later classical and post-classical threads. Chaucer's apt vision is of 'gret Omer' with a number of others – Dares, Tytus [Dictys], 'Lollius', Guido and Geoffrey of Monmouth – all together 'besy for to bere up Troye' (*The House of Fame*, 1,464–80). Among the most influential rival accounts were the two allegedly 'eye-witness' memoirs of the war by 'Dictys the Cretan' and 'Dares the Phrygian', offering invitingly novelistic detail and verisimilitude. A new love emphasis is introduced, in Achilles' love for Polyxena, setting the scene for the Ovidian developments of Benoît de Sainte-Maure's twelfth-century *Roman de Troie* and the introduction of Troilus' romance with Briseida, later the Cressida of Chaucer and Shakespeare. From its various medieval versions the Troy story moves to Lydgate's *Troy Book* and Caxton's *Recuyell of the Histories of Troye* (1475) – the first book printed in the English language, and an important source for Shakespeare's *Troilus and Cressida*.[10] Chapman's translation of seven books of the *Iliad* had been published in 1598, some three or four years before the production of the play. But *Troilus and Cressida* is a 'Trojan war' play rather than a Homeric one, one which builds on an awareness of the *Iliad* and its heroic mode – an awareness in

[9] Of eighty-seven pre-1800 editions of Pope's *Iliad* and *Odyssey* listed in the *ESTC* twenty-three were published in Edinburgh and a further nine in Glasgow (as well as two in Aberdeen). Pope's version was anthologised in William Holwell's *The Beauties of Homer* in 1775; Henry William Tytler as late as 1793 compared every line of the *Iliad* with Pope's translation to put himself in 'a congenial train' for translating Callimachus (see *Critical Review*, January 1793, 59–65); and Gilbert Wakefield issued a new edition of Pope's *Iliad* and *Odyssey* in 1796.

[10] [illegible] Stanford (1963) 146–58.

which burlesque is perhaps the primary feature – but revels in the eclecticism of the Greek and Trojan compound rather than suggesting any wish to draw on Homer himself as a significant challenge to it.

In the 1614 dedication to the *Odyssey*, Chapman invited Robert Carr, earl of Somerset, to the patronage of 'Homer's English life', presenting his English versions of the *Iliad* and the *Odyssey* as together offering a complete and balanced exploration of what heroism might be:

> In one, Predominant Perturbation; in the other, over-ruling Wisedome; in one, the Bodie's fervour and fashion of outward Fortitude to all possible height of Heroicall Action; in the other, the Mind's inward, constant and unconquerd Empire, unbroken, unalterd with any most insolent and tyrannous infliction.[11]

Directly through example, or indirectly through allegory, Homer here represents not only the source of epic poetry but also mastery of all useful knowledge. What may not be immediately apparent to a modern reader is the degree to which – despite his fame and the many ancient testimonies to it marshalled by Chapman himself – Homer was, and was to remain, in need of patronage as a worthy epic authority. The stability of the crowded Homeric pillar in Chaucer's *House of Fame* (1,477–9) is threatened by the stresses of envy ('Oon seyde that Omer made lyes, | Feynynge in hys poetries, | And was to Grekes favorable'), and the history of the Homeric wars of detraction and defence from antiquity to the eighteenth century has been well documented by Howard Clarke and others.[12] In seventeenth-century France Homer became the primary target of the supposedly progressive 'modern' faction anxious to rid themselves of allegiance to the classical past in general, but the manners of both gods and heroes in the poems were in any case unsurprisingly vulnerable on a number of counts to the proprieties of seventeenth-century neo-classicism and religion. Travesty and burlesque abound in English responses to Homer and translations of Homer.[13] Even among the advocates of the 'ancients' aesthetically Homer was not secure, given the strength of the championship of Virgil and the representation of the *Aeneid* as the perfection of epic form. The octogenarian Thomas Hobbes will go on to defend Homer specifically against Virgil in his preface 'Concerning the vertues of an heroique poem', but a curious light is shed on what might be called the consumer profile by the summary of events incorporated (perhaps

[11] Nicoll (1956) 2.3–4. On Chapman see Lord (1956), Sowerby (1992).

[12] Clarke (1981) 106–55; Patey (1997); Weinbrot (1993) 193–236, 296–307. On the prevalence of pro-Trojan feeling see Spencer (1954), esp. 8–12.

[13] Cf., e.g. Thomas Tooly, *Homer Travestie: being a new translation of that great poet. With a critical preface and learned notes. Shewing how this translation excells Chapman, Hobbes, Ogilby, Dryden, Pope, and all other pretenders* (1720).

by the bookseller) into the title page of Hobbes' first Homeric offering in 1674: *The travels of Ulysses; wherein is related how he got from the Ciconians and Lotophagians, where his men eat forgetfulness. Coming to the land of the Cyclops, Polyphemus eat six of his men. Having with difficulty got from him, Aeolus gave him a wind ty'd in a leather sack. How Circe turn'd his men to boars; and how the Lestrygon giants eat his men like fishes. Also what converse he had with the ghosts in Hell; and at his return, how Scylla eat six of his men at one mouthful. How he escaped the charming Syrens; and falling on the Suns isle, the dreadful effects of it, &c. With many other passages, strange and wonderful. Translated out of Greek by Mr Hobbes of Malmesbury, author of the Leviathan.*

It is against this contested and various context that I want to look more closely at the two specific examples of Milton and Pope as Homeric readers. It has become a necessary device in studies of Milton simply to incorporate acknowledgement of the accumulating body of work on the dense compound of reading and recollection that makes up Milton's epic strain.[14] Some works attempt exhaustive trackings of classical reference, some offer new hierarchies of influence within the classical tradition, and some argue that classical influences have in various ways been over-estimated. The issue of Milton's relation to Homer brings into question, as many critics have recognised, the very nature of allusion, and with it the difficulty of bridging the gaps in 'fitness' to read between Milton himself as a seventeenth-century polymath, his variously educated contemporaries, and the readers of an age like our own in which that learning has been displaced in favour of other things. Milton could read Greek with ease, and as his earliest published remarks on his poetic ambitions make clear (in *The Reason of Church Government*, 1642), he was fully immersed in an older and more eclectic European tradition which fed into his own rousing brand of literary patriotism:

> I apply'd my selfe to . . . fix all the industry and art I could unite to the adorning of my native tongue; not to make verbal curiosities the end, that were a toylsom vanity, but to be an interpreter & relater of the best and sagest things among mine own Citizens throughout this Iland in the mother dialect. That what the greatest and choycest wits of Athens, Rome, or modern Italy, and those Hebrews of old did for their country, I in my proportion with this over and above of being a Christian, might doe for mine; not caring to be nam'd abroad, though perhaps I could attaine to that, but content with these British Ilands as

14 See, e.g. Highet (1949), Harding (1962), Steadman (1967), Mueller (1969), Blessington (1979), DuRocher (1985), Lewalski (1985), Martindale (1986) and Burrow (1993).

> my world, whose fortune hath hitherto bin, that if the Athenians, as some say, made their small deeds great and renowned by their eloquent writers, *England* hath had her noble atchievements made small by the unskilfull handling of monks and mechanicks.[15]

All Milton's 'industry and art' as revealed twenty-five years later in the publication of *Paradise Lost* is clearly a tall order for any reader or even any scholar to match, then or now. There is however one simpler overarching pattern which effectively contains almost any degree of awareness of or sensitivity to the texture of allusion in the poem. As Michael's immediately post-lapsarian tutorial to Adam makes manifest, the action of *Paradise Lost* establishes itself as a pre-condition of all other examples of the heroic or epic within the history of mankind. Adam (himself still, or already, inclined to look forward to a good conventional fight between the Son and the serpent at 12.384–5) is looking forward, not back, to an age in which 'Might only shall be admir'd | And Valor and Heroic Virtue call'd' (11.689–90). Throughout the poem Milton resolutely refuses the condition of 'following after': the wit of this densely composite work is to assert its own primacy over the *disiecta membra* of which it is composed. References and allusions – however explicitly invoked or hidden, however easily recognised or far-fetched – are thereby transformed into fore-shadowings, ironic typologies, echo-chambers of the future rather than the past. This paradoxical but powerfully evocative effect both ironises and in its inclusiveness sanctions the allusion-hunting industry which has flourished ever since Patrick Hume's *Annotations* of 1695 and Addison's *Spectator* essays of 1712; and it inevitably throws its colouring over the presence of Homer as of the other 'greatest and choicest wits' in the poem.

Perhaps the most striking Homeric allusion in *Paradise Lost* is the evocation as a parallel for Satan's journey through Chaos of the wanderings of Odysseus, although the dialogue with the *Iliad* – as a narrative of the fatal consequences of error culminating in a version of reconciliation – is in terms of the poem's structures arguably the more consistent. Rhetorically, the relation with the Homeric poems is constructed through complex but controlled processes of *contaminatio* (the mixing of several traditions in one), *retractatio* or revisionary handling, and overt comparison, where the axis of allusion is always as much that of discrimination as of similarity. In Book 9 of *Paradise Lost*, for example, there are three explicit references to

[15] 'The reason of church-government urg'd against prelaty', in Milton (1953–82) 1.811–12. Fletcher (1956–61) offers a useful and comprehensive account of the educational background, although his account of Milton's Greek reading relies on the attribution to Milton (no longer accepted) of copious marginal annotations in a 1620 edition of Pindar. See also Parker (1996).

Homer's *Odyssey*, all suggesting a negative calibration of comparability: in the invocation, where the just rebuke and judgment of Jehovah is asserted to be 'not less but more heroic' than 'Neptune's ire . . . that so long | Perplex'd the Greek'; in the garden of Eden, 'spot more delicious' than the gardens of Alcinous; and in relation to Eve herself, as an innocent Circe, attended by 'more duteous' beasts. Seen from one side the trope is a relatively simple one of augmentation, with the primacy of Milton's subject constantly asserted, whether as prototype or superior replacement: as seen from the other it becomes what Puttenham calls the 'disabler', with the classical world invoked always as a paler, paradoxically secondary, imitation. These moments where the *Odyssey* surfaces – or perhaps rather, is held under – in explicit reference are held in a kind of tension with a more diffuse and uncertain network of refraction, where Satan 'like a black mist low creeping' (9.180) is suddenly suggestive not only of Thetis in the *Iliad* (1.359) but also of Odysseus swathed in Athene's protective mist (VI.15), and Eve in her garden is like Nausicaa with her washing (VI.85–98) as well as like Patroclus in fatal confrontation, in *Iliad* 16, with a foe larger than had been imagined. In this frame of reference, Odysseus' notorious interest in the *Odyssey* in where his next meal was coming from offers a mundane counterpoint not only to the reality of the temptation of taste but to the whole emphasis throughout Book 9 on the need for food – a need whose perils will also be exemplified in Homeric history by the Lotos-eaters, the cattle of the Sun and Circe.

In a surprisingly literal sense *Paradise Lost* becomes in effect a primer for reading Homer – one as thoroughly revisionary as Blake's later reading of Milton himself or any later 'readings against the grain'. In this light, the reader's own active engagement with and reassessment of the allusive qualities of the poem act as an empirical demonstration of the secondary and subordinate nature of whatever reserves may be conjured up of pagan learning and commentary. Milton argues elsewhere[16] that no learning is necessary to expound the truths of scripture: here, in *Paradise Lost*, he brings the whole of his creativity to bear in a complex poetic mechanism of intellectual challenge generating – ultimately, as its most triumphant outcome – the recognition and acceptance of moral defeat. Alexander Pope – a man with his own strong Scriblerian views on the abuses of commentators' commentary, and one who in the *Essay on Criticism* (127–8) had recommended 'the Mantuan Muse' as the best comment on Homer – was one reader who found it natural to use Milton as well as Virgil in this role. On Hera's seduction of Zeus in *Iliad* 14, for example, he devotes a whole note to Milton's various imitations of 'the

[16] See, e.g. *Considerations Touching the Likeliest Means to Remove Hirelings out of the Church* (1659).

several beautiful parts of this episode': in particular, he notes, 'that which seems in Homer an impious fiction, becomes a moral lesson in *Milton*; since he makes that lascivious rage of the passion the immediate effect of the sin of our first parents after the fall'. Pope's note does not stop here, with the bald statement: unapologetically, he quotes in his note the whole passage from Book 9 of *Paradise Lost*, forcing the revisionary Miltonic filter on to Homer's eighteenth-century readers at the same time as elevating the beauty of both passages through the juxtaposition.[17]

The allusive mode of *Paradise Lost* operates as a series of tests or challenges thrown out to winnow the audience down to the 'few' who are truly 'fit' to hear. Even if the thrust is ultimately a simplifying rather than an esoteric one, it is of course arguable that – in relation to Homer, for example – only those with a sufficient pre-existing engagement with Homeric epic can experience the full revisionary paradox enacted through reading. An *absence* of learning becomes a readerly equivalent of the untested innocence rejected in *Areopagitica* as 'a fugitive and cloistered virtue, unexercised and unbreathed'. Pope's 'epic' achievement, by contrast, is a popularising one, intent both on rescuing Homer from the depradations and irrelevancies of scholars and critics, and establishing the Homeric poems at the centre of a new literary market-place. The achievement of his processing of Homer is all the more impressive in view of the fact that this was a market better attuned to mock-heroic and to the sceptical positions of modernism than to automatic veneration of the monuments of the past. Homer holds a key place in any battle of the ancients and the moderns, and Pope's Homer is at one level a strikingly successful engagement in that ongoing controversy.[18] Pope was by no means an uncritical impresario. Although the hyperbolic images of his 'Preface' to Homer – figuring Homer as 'a wild paradise', a chariot-wheel setting itself on fire, 'a powerful star, which in the violence of its course, drew all things within its vortex' – may strike today's readers as little short of adulatory, the preface itself was seen by some of the partisans of the ancients as dangerously attuned to the modern side. Pope's annotations show him constantly adjusting between the greatness he perceives in 'Homer's' poetic spirit and the things in the poems which are plainly, or ought to be, unacceptable to the modern age.[19] But for Pope it is clear that the relevance of the Homeric poems for the modern age far outweighed these difficulties of adjustment. This conviction is bodied forth not only in the detail of the arguments but in the whole strategy of dissemination: the processing of the

[17] Pope (1996) 694–6. [18] See esp. Patey (1997), Weinbrot (1993) 193–236, 296–307.

[19] See, e.g. his criticism of Macrobius and the '*Je ne sçay quoy*' in the 'Observations on the second book', Pope (1996) 129; also Weinbrot (1993) 296–303.

Greek text into verse which over thirty-three thousand lines of heroic couplet establishes itself as a poetic lexicon for the eighteenth century;[20] the way in which the commentary buttonholes all sorts of readers beyond those normally to be expected for a Greek poem, and especially female readers;[21] and the importance of the marketing of the work itself, with the building up of a subscription list with a glittering array of noble and other worthy subscribers to the point where the list can itself be seen as a 'satisfactory piece of vanity' for Pope to transmit to posterity.[22] Modern advertising techniques would have little to teach Pope about selling an epic experience, but at a more instinctive level too Pope is often most engaged with his text and his commentary when he is responding to the sense that others have been there before him, that reading Homer is an experience which accrues value from being shared, and from having been shared across the ages. A gallery of earlier readers accompany him through the 'Observations' – commentators like Eustathius and Madame Dacier ('the Bishop and the Lady' in Pope's mischievous formulation), great figures of the past like Alexander the Great, Pythagoras, Plutarch, and above all the poets like Virgil, Tasso and Milton, where citation of parallel passages becomes, as in the example quoted above, less a matter of source study than one of dual critical appreciation. Pope's Homer has fallen victim to the strength of critical prejudice in favour of 'original' works, and there is room for much more investigation of the primary importance of his Homeric enterprise for eighteenth-century poetry and criticism. In what follows my emphasis is on the *Iliad* rather than the collaborative *Odyssey*, and on taking the whole production together – neither as a poem (pretty or otherwise) in itself, nor as a piece of criticism in itself, but as a composite reading and recreation of Homer.

Regardless of the acknowledged strength of Homer's powers of invention and poetic ornament, a necessary condition of his defence for Pope and his contemporaries was the identification of a proper and serious heroic purpose for the poems, one fit to withstand the burlesque or mock-heroic impulse which Pope was himself so excellently qualified to understand. For Pope, following a tradition expressed for him as for Dryden most influentially by the rather wooden neo-classicism of René le Bossu (1631–89), the *Iliad* is a nationalist and civic text, 'the principal design' of which (as Pope notes in considering the character of Diomedes as the spotlight falls on his prowess in the fifth book) is 'to shew, that the greatest personal qualities and

[20] Cf. Coleridge's view in *Biographia Literaria* that the Homer translations had laid the foundations of eighteenth-century poetic diction.

[21] See Thomas (1990), Williams (1993).

[22] Pope, Letter to Caryll, 19 March 1714. See also Foxon (1991).

forces are of no effect when union is wanting among the chief rulers, and that nothing can avail 'till they are reconciled so as to act in concert' (Book 5, n.1).[23] Dry as this might sound as a summary of the *raison d'être* of the poem, Pope made it much more than a ritual neo-classical gesture. Naturally, Achilles presents a problematic figure as hero in this respect. Instead of the communal loyalties which fuel the spirit of a Diomedes, Achilles' own native aggression is controlled uniquely by his sense of himself, and so far does he seem from sharing human sympathies that his closest friend Patroclus speculates (16.33–5) that rocks and tempestuous seas gave him birth rather than the tenderness of love. His solipsism becomes more emphatic in Pope. Early in Book 16 Pope's Achilles indulges in a rejection of the notion of higher external influences upon his behaviour (such as Jove, or oracles) in a supreme assertion of egotism, suggestive of such other individualists as Shakespeare's Edmund and Iago, or Milton's Satan:

> My Wrongs, my Wrongs, my constant Thought engage,
> Those, my sole Oracles, inspire my Rage . . .
> I made him Tyrant; gave him Pow'r to wrong
> Ev'n me . . .
> 'Tis time our Fury should relent at last:
> I fix'd its Date; the day I wish'd appears.[24]

And he finishes his speech with a wish for the universal destruction of the rest of the Greeks as well as the Trojans – a passage warmly defended against its would-be athetisers by Pope, who marks his interest by drawing a strong Shakespearean parallel with Northumberland's reaction to the death of Hotspur.[25] In terms of the conflict between individuality and co-operation seen by Le Bossu at the poem's heart, Achilles and his opposite number on the Trojan side, Hector, offer Pope a textbook contrast. In a poem exposing the ill effects of discord, Hector has all the qualities tending to a preservation of unity: he stands as a 'character of valour unruffled by rage and anger, uniting his people by his prudence and example'. 'The motive of all his actions' is love of his country, together with affection towards his parents and kindred, including his wife and son. He is perhaps the acme of successful interpersonality – though not quite in the modern sense of Pope's nice phrase, 'Hector appears in every Battel the Life and Soul of his Party'.[26]

[23] Pope (1996) 259. Le Bossu's *Traité du poème épique* was published in Paris in 1675 and translated into English in 1695. Translated excerpts were printed (as 'A general view of the epic poem and of the *Iliad* and *Odyssey*') with the first volume of Pope's *Odyssey* (Pope (1940–69) 9.3–24).

[24] Pope (1996) 750. [25] *Henry IV Part II*, I.i.153–60: Pope (1996) 781.

[26] Note on Book 3, 53: Pope (1996) 155–6.

Homer's account of Hector's last battle, and Achilles' pursuit of him round the walls of Troy is read by Pope as an emblem of this contrast: Hector is running away towards the walls, so that his friends may help him, while Achilles, constantly turning him from the city towards the plain, makes a sign to the Greek troops not to intervene, insisting on single combat.[27] The passage on which I shall focus here is Pope's version of the end of Hector's soliloquy before the Scaean gate as he weighs up the possibilities of retreat, parley or combat with Achilles. It comes early in the twenty-second book of the *Iliad*, a book which Pope identifies as one of the most 'over-mastering' in its dialectic of the sublime and the sentimental: 'And indeed thro' the whole Book this wonderful Contrast and Opposition of the *Moving* and the *Terrible*, is perpetually kept up, each heightening the other: I can't find Words to express how so great Beauties affect me.'[28] The passage (22.126–8) is obscure in the Greek, some proverbial usage probably hidden in its expression. Pope gives a literal version: 'There is no talking with Achilles, from an Oak, or from a Rock, as a young Man and a Maiden talk together', and also a paraphrase: 'There is no conversing with this implacable Enemy in the Rage of Battel; as when sauntring People talk at leisure to one another on the Road, or when young Men and Women meet in a Field.'[29] It is an extraordinarily moving 'beauty' of exactly the kind Pope has pointed to, Hector's mind, as he ('like a coiled serpent') awaits the gleaming rage of the onrushing Achilles, suddenly reverting to a pastoral peacetime scene. Fleetingly, before the inevitable choice of glory over safety, Hector seems to be envisaging the possibility that he and Achilles might drop out of the domain of epic confrontation – not just formally or ritualistically, with exchange of gifts, as do Glaucus and Diomedes in Book 6, but into another world altogether where they might casually and simply be friends.

> We greet not here, as Man conversing Man
> Met at an Oak, or journeying o'er a Plain;
> No Season now for calm familiar Talk,
> Like Youths and Maidens in an Evening Walk:
> War is our business.[30]

[27] Note on Book 22, 269: Pope (1996) 1,037–8.
[28] Note on Book 22, 37: Pope (1996) 1,030.
[29] Note on Book 22, 167: Pope (1996) 1,032–3.
[30] Book 22, 167–72: Pope (1996) 1,016. The quality of Pope's achievement may be suggested by a comparison with John Ogilby's version of the same passage. 'He'le not be mov'd at all with Stories vain | Of Okes and Rocks, fond Tales which entertain | Credulous Virgins and admiring Youth | Who swallow things impossible for Truth.'

Behind Pope's Hector here – a man who might understand the social pleasures beautifully embedded in the word 'sauntring' in the paraphrase – stands Milton taking breath at the beginning of Book 9 of *Paradise Lost* for the cataclysmic scene (and Homer's Hector himself behind Milton, who goes on within the next ten lines to allude to this same Homeric episode):

> No more of talk where Man or angel guest
> With man, as with his friend, familiar used
> To sit indulgent . . .
> I now must change
> These notes to tragic.

At moments like this the density of Pope's Homeric tapestry is completely satisfying, weaving together an interpretation of the concerns of the poem with its later influence and with Pope's own refractive creativity. It is an oddity of literary history that in giving voice so consummately in some ways to the 'group-consciousness of an age'[31] Pope's version of Homer quickly becomes a trigger for its own stylistic rejection, and for a movement variously back to the Greek (for those who could manage it), to the literal, or to Chapman.[32] Let Homer's readers think, urges Pope in his 'Preface', that 'they are growing acquainted with nations and people that are now no more; that they are stepping almost three thousand years back into the remotest antiquity': but in a sense Pope brought Homer too close, and that was not, ultimately, what the next age wanted, with its appetite for nostalgia and estrangement. Pope did more, of course, than turn Homer into a speaker of eighteenth-century poetic diction: his erasing of stylistic difference is only one aspect of a larger campaign to secure recognition for Homer as above all the greatest of fellow poets. In projecting forward acceptance of this premise he was ultimately far more successful, to the point where one might see his Homeric contribution as partially at least a powerful pre-emptive strike against the distancing effect of the new sense of historical difference. Thomas Parnell's 'Essay on the life, writings and learning of Homer', prefixed to Pope's *Iliad*, opens with a vision of literary influence as in itself a kind of friendship.

> There is something in the Mind of Man, which goes beyond bare Curiosity, and even carries us on to a Shadow of Friendship, with those great Genius's whom we have known to excell in former Ages. Nor will it appear less to any one, who considers how much it partakes of the Nature of Friendship; how it compounds itself of an Admiration rais'd by what we meet

[31] The phrase is from Tillyard (1958) 15. [32] See Webb in this volume p. 297.

> with concerning them; a Tendency to be further acquainted with them, by gathering every Circumstance of their Lives; a kind of Complacency in their Company.[33]

In terms of the developments in Homeric scholarship and criticism outlined at the beginning of this chapter, what is striking about Pope's creative response to Homer is that, sophisticated (and far from complacent) as it is, it is predicated absolutely, through interpretation as well as annotation, on the notion of a single shaping poetic mind. Despite all Pope's indications of an unbridgeable gap between himself and Homer's greatness, we are more aware of a sense of relationship than of historical or cultural distance – a sense that is underlined in many of his letters about the processes of the translation as well as in the lovely image, in the note on the death of Patroclus (16.1032), whereby he figures himself as playing Sancho Panza to Homer's Don Quixote. Pope's transfusion of Homeric theme, characters, customs and events into English is matched in significance by a transfusion almost into the flesh of poetic quality and personality. Homer, I have suggested, had often before this been a more provisional and uncertain figure, and for Milton too he had been a generic rather than an individual prototype of post-lapsarian epic and its various interpreters. Before the end of the eighteenth century the development of new historical interests would bring about significant changes in the perception of Homer – through Anthony Blackwell's *Enquiry into the Life and Writings of Homer* (1735), analysing Homer's genius as a product of particular human circumstances; through the challenge of Ossian in the 1760s and 1770s as not only a national British bard but one at once more primitive and less barbaric than Homer; and perhaps most significantly through the conclusions about the oral nature of the poems on which Wolf was to build his analytical approach in the *Prolegomena*.[34] It would, however, be a mistake to assume a simple teleological narrative here. As Wolf himself pointed out, the question he had raised about Homer was not new. Comparable ideas had been expressed not only in France by Charles Perrault and by the abbé d'Aubignac, but also in England, and in English, by Richard Bentley.[35] Curiously, there is a contribution in July 1725 to *Applebee's Journal*, possibly by Daniel Defoe, in which an attack on Pope's subterfuge over the collaborative nature of his *Odyssey* is enlivened with just such an analogy with Homer himself – as an old blind ballad singer securing the collaboration

33 Pope (1940–69) 7.26.

34 See esp. Simonsuuri (1979) 99–142. For an extended discussion of Homer and Ossian, see the *Occasional Thoughts on the Study and Character of Classical Authors* by John Gordon, archdeacon of Lincoln, published anonymously in 1762.

35 Wolf (1985) 116–18 n. 84. See Bentley (1713).

of less eminent wits in order to sell his ballads 'still in his own Name, as if they had been own'.[36] It is interesting to consider the degree to which Pope, in his commitment to a Homer characterised above all by the consistency of individual poetic spirit and fire, may or may not have been able to see the writing on the wall.

FURTHER READING

Wide-ranging accounts of the reception of Homer are to be found in Clarke (1981) and Stanford (1963). More detailed discussion of Homer's presence in particular periods is to be found in King (1987), Burrow (1993), Foerster (1947), Simonsuuri (1979), and Weinbrot (1993). See also the following: on Chapman's Homer, Lord (1956); on Milton, Blessington (1979) and Martindale (1986); and on Pope, Mason (1972) and C.Williams (1993).

[36] Lee (1869) 3.409–12.

18

TIMOTHY WEBB

Homer and the Romantics

The authority of 'old' Homer: a new range of admiring responses

Responses to Homer during the 'Romantic' age (roughly, 1770–1830) were largely positive yet the emphases were often subtly different from those of the previous period and sometimes registered challenge or difficulty as well as easy acceptance. Many writers were prepared to acknowledge that Homer, or 'Homer', was endowed with a special authority which, like that of Shakespeare, gained in force from the absence of biographical detail. Homer was an originator, an original genius, the great poetic father (according, among others, to Godwin, Coleridge and Lamb). The worlds of the *Iliad*, the *Odyssey* (and, for some readers, the *Hymns*) were vividly realised yet almost 'unimaginably different' from those which had developed in Western Europe in the late eighteenth and early nineteenth centuries. Homer's achievement was often unquestioned but it could be daunting and untouchable. This complex of reactions was given expression by Robert Southey in July 1797 when he wrote: 'With Homer and Milton no future, indeed no other, poems can be compared. The age of the one and the subject of the other preclude it, independant of their unequalled and perhaps *unequalable* merit.'[1] Phrases such as 'old Homer' (used, for example, by Keats and Hazlitt) signalled that the Greek poet, who was still conveniently compressed into one individual by most readers, was endowed with the wisdom and insight achieved by experience: in artistic representations he is never youthful, unlike Apollo, the god with special jurisdiction over poetic affairs. The absence of biographical fact, and the generalising force of early busts and heads, allowed in time for freighted descriptions like Keats's 'deep-brow'd Homer',[2] which suggests both the furrowed forehead of maturity and the public marks of profound contemplation. Homer's blindness (celebrated by Keats in the sonnet 'To Homer') was another sign of his apartness and his prophetic insight

[1] Southey (1965) I.137. [2] 'On first looking into Chapman's Homer', l. 6.

2. Angelica Kauffman, *Penelope Invoking Minerva's Aid for the Safe Return of Telemachus*

and a model of creative interiority for later periods. The formulation 'old Homer' (by a happy extension, Hazlitt also wrote of Homer's translator as 'old Chapman')[3] combines affectionate recognition and the acknowledgment of poetic paternity with an awareness that the gulf of history necessarily separated contemporary admirers from their venerated and venerable Greek ancestor. If Homer was primary, he was also, in a number of senses, primitive,

[3] Hazlitt (1930–4) 6.247.

3. Angelica Kauffman, *Penelope Weeping Over the Bow of Ulysses*

and the register of Romantic encounters is partly a record of establishing a balance, or a viable equilibrium, between these two polarities.

Tributes to Homer's special presiding presence were widespread and sometimes perfunctory, but his work and reputation also attracted celebrations from diligent followers, from scholars, and from a large number of the most creative figures of the age. Some examples were more directly influential than others (prints, in particular, were easily and tangibly imported) but the European dimension should not be neglected. A suggestive example is that of Angelica Kauffman (1741–1807), the Swiss-born artist who spent fifteen years in England, became a founder member of the Royal Academy of Arts in 1768 and was unusually attracted by the role of Penelope in Homeric narrative (Plates 2–3). Another, even more resonant case is that of the young Johann Wilhelm von Goethe, which may have been more representative than directly influential in the first place but which vividly illustrates the force of the Homeric and especially of a Homer who, it seemed, had been freshly discovered. Goethe and his German contemporaries had been enlivened and enlightened by this momentous intellectual event. Many years later Goethe gave this rapturous account in *Dichtung und Wahrheit*:

> Happy is ever that literary epoch, when great works of the past surface again and are added to the agenda, for it is then that they produce a new effect. For us, Homer's sun rose again, and just as was required by the age . . . No longer did we see in those poems a strained and bloated heroic world, but rather the reflected truth of a primordial present, and we tried to draw this to ourselves as much as possible.[4]

Goethe's experience of this re-rising sun was affected by many factors, including the researches of Scottish and English travellers, connoisseurs, antiquarians, pioneering anthropologists and early archaeologists. This shared impetus in turn reflected back on the second renaissance of Homer in Britain since this cultural and intellectual phenomenon was European in scope, even if the momentum was largely generated by a small number of countries.

English interest and admiration was certainly intense. The political philosopher and novelist William Godwin, who had become a publisher of children's books under the name of Edward Baldwin, advised Charles Lamb whose *The Adventures of Ulysses* he was to bring out later in 1808: 'The Preface ought I think to tell what Homer was – the Father of poetry, the eldest of historians, the collector & recorder of all that was then known, the parent of continuous narration, of imagery, of dramatic character, of dramatic dialogue, of a whole having beginning, middle & end.'[5] Benjamin Robert Haydon, the idiosyncratic and ambitious historical painter who was a friend of Keats and who crusaded for the recognition of the 'Elgin Marbles' in England, recurrently celebrated the achievements of Homer. Having provided his own account of the action of *Iliad* 22.25–176, he concluded: 'Nothing can exceed this.' Homer's treatment of the character of Achilles 'awes one into silence'. On 14 September 1808 he had even admitted that he was using Homer (in translation) as an inspiration to his own artistic activities: 'Read Homer, in English, to stir up my fancy, that I may conceive and execute my Hero's head with vigour.'[6] A third suggestive example is provided by William Hazlitt. In one of his *Lectures on the English Poets* (both delivered and published in 1818) Hazlitt characterised Homer's attributes:

> Homer's poetry is the heroic: it is full of life and action: it is bright as the day, strong as a river. In the vigour of his intellect, he grapples with all the objects of nature, and enters into all the relations of social life. He saw many countries, and the manners of many men; and he has brought them all together in his poem.

[4] Cited in Most (1989a) 54. For Homer's reception in Germany see e.g. Finsler (1912), Marchand (1996).

[5] C. Lamb and M. A. Lamb (1975–8) 2.83.

[6] Quotations respectively Haydon (1960–3) 1.171, 171, 18.

This description appears to allow for the *Odyssey* (especially in the final sentence quoted which seems to equate Homer with Odysseus) but it is predominantly informed by a knowledge of the *Iliad* which Hazlitt evokes in some detail before concluding by celebrating Homer's physicality and the tangibility of his verse: 'The multitude of things in Homer is wonderful; their splendour, their truth, their force, and variety. His poetry is, like his religion, the poetry of number and form: he describes the bodies as well as the souls of men.'[7]

Yet another instance is afforded by Percy Bysshe Shelley who was keenly devoted to the study of ancient Greek literature. In his pioneering essay 'On the manners of the antient Greeks' (written in 1818 as a supplement to his translation of Plato's *Symposium* but not published in his own lifetime) Shelley declared: 'as a poet, Homer must be acknowledged to excel Shakespeare in the truth, the harmony, the sustained grandeur, the satisfying completeness of his images, their exact fitness to that to which they belong'.[8] Again, in 1821 when Shelley wrote *A Defence of Poetry* Homer was granted a canonical and originating status in the history of European poetry: 'The poems of Homer and his contemporaries were the delight of infant Greece; they were the elements of that social system which is the column upon which all succeeding civilization has reposed.' In keeping with the larger designs of his argument about the moral and social significance of poetry, Shelley assumed that the *Iliad* and the *Odyssey* both captured a social reality and, in turn, exercised their own effect on Homer's audience (this idealising of the poet's imaginative impact recreates both public performance and the more solitary engagement with a text which is usually involved in reading).[9]

The ambivalent attractions of the *Iliad*

Homer (or 'Homer') was largely represented by two epic poems but the impact of the *Odyssey* on writers, though undeniable and in some ways pervasive, is often difficult to chart in convincing detail, and it is still the *Iliad* which features most frequently in contemporary responses. Yet the *Iliad* presented an apparent obstacle to the appreciation of Homer since it unmistakeably focused on the operations of war with whatever variety, especially in its closing books. With the passage of time, such difficulties and discrepancies became even more noticeable and caused more anxiety and alienation among readers, who sometimes considered the *Iliad* morally questionable and even anachronistic in a period dominated by the Napoleonic Wars. At the height of the French Revolution, John Flaxman had responded to these

[7] Hazlitt (1930–4) 5.16. [8] Notopoulos (1949) 405. [9] Reiman and Fraistat (2002) 516.

4a. Thomas Piroli (after Flaxman), *The Fight for the Body of Patroclus*

4b. Thomas Piroli (after Flaxman), *Thetis Bringing the Armour to Achilles*

elements which balanced or countered the more obviously violent elements in the Homeric epics (see Plates 4–5). David Irwin has calculated that eighteen out of his twenty-eight illustrations to the *Odyssey* (1793, engraved by Piroli) were devoted to 'gentle scenes' in the first edition. Naturally, the *Iliad* (also 1793, also engraved by Piroli) made different claims, but even here the thirty-four illustrations in the first edition were 'divided . . . equally between tranquil and violent scenes' and of the five plates added in 1805 only one involved 'any violence'. Irwin claims: 'In choosing his scenes from Homer,

5a. Thomas Piroli (after Flaxman), *Penelope Surprised by Suitors*

5b. Thomas Piroli (after Flaxman), *Ulysses at the Table of Circe*

Flaxman showed a bias both in his choice of subjects and in his treatment of them. Although he did not avoid the more passionate and horrific moments in Homer's lines, Flaxman tended to minimise them.'[10] Such choices can be attributed partly to timidity, partly (as Irwin suggests) to the demands of compositional variation within the volume, and partly to a contemporary shift towards the apparently less challenging morals of the *Odyssey*. As Henry Boyd, the translator (cited by Irwin) wrote in 1785: 'we can go along with the resentment of Ulysses, because it is just, but our feelings must tell us that Achilles carried his resentment to a savage length, a length where we cannot follow him'.[11]

Another symptomatic case is that of Robert Southey, who was awarded a government pension in 1807 and was appointed Poet-Laureate in 1813, the year in which he published his best-selling *Life of Nelson*. Yet in spite of his public record, Southey had always been suspicious of the imperatives of war. From an early stage in his career he had sensed the danger of a Homeric model and had preferred the *Odyssey* to the *Iliad* for reasons which clearly suggest his own impatience and the growing irrelevance of the heroic ethic: 'The judgement must applaud the well-digested plan and splendid execution of the Iliad, but the heart always bears testimony to the merit of the Odyssey: it is the poem of nature, and its personages inspire love rather than command admiration.'[12] In the original preface to *Joan of Arc* (1793), Southey made another statement which does not mention Homer but is obviously directed at him and the tradition which he originated:

> I have avoided what seems useless and wearying in other poems, and my readers will find no descriptions of armour, no muster-rolls, no geographical catalogues, lion, tiger, bull, bear and boar similes, Phoebuses or Auroras. And where in battle I have particularised the death of an individual, it is not I hope like the common lists of killed and wounded.[13]

Here Southey seems anxious both to avoid the Homeric legacy and to distance himself from the cold presentations of daily newspaper reportage ('common lists of killed and wounded'). Many years later, he wrote to an old friend suggesting that important changes in taste had taken place which necessarily affected attitudes to Homer:

> We admire Homer deservedly (and undeservedly too) . . . but if Homer were living now [1814], he would write very differently. Book after book of butchery, however skilfuly performed is unsuitable to the European state of mind at

[10] Irwin (1979) 69–71. [11] Irwin (1979) 71.
[12] Southey (1829) 2. [13] Southey (1829) 2.

> present, and the raw head and bloody-bone-monster of the *Odyssey* are not better. In this age Homer would address himself more to our feelings and reflecting faculties.[14]

The specific example Southey mentions here is taken from the *Odyssey*, so both the heroic imagination and the epic are necessarily compromised, but the larger criticism is obviously directed at the *Iliad* (where a reader would certainly find 'book after book of butchery').

Yet, for all these recognitions and resistances, many discriminating readers still admired the *Iliad* more than the *Odyssey*, and the figure of Achilles still exercised a fierce imaginative attraction. For example, William Cowper noted that the *Odyssey* was 'a poem of a gentler character' but he conceded that the *Iliad* represented a higher level of achievement.[15] Again, Shelley was a strong critic of the militaristic ethos and its consequences and, both ideologically and temperamentally, may have preferred those elements in the Homeric canon which allowed room for the pastoral; yet, from a relatively early stage, he expressed a particular admiration for the achievement of the *Iliad*. So, on 6 July 1817, he wrote to his friend Thomas Jefferson Hogg:

> I have [been] reading little else but Homer. I am now in the 23rd book; you can imagine, the wonders of poetry which I have enjoyed in the five preceding books. Indeed this part of the Iliad, the Patrocleiad, seems to me to surpass all other portions of the Iliad, as that production as a whole surpasses any other single production of the human mind. Familiarity with Homer increases our admiration and astonishment – I can never believe that the Odyssey is a work of the same author.[16]

John Keats, too, seems to have responded to this element in Homer, even if briefly. In 'I stood tip-toe upon a little hill' he envisages a bright and clear evening when 'men of health were of unusual cheer, | Stepping like Homer at the trumpet's call' (216–17); such a version of Homer as briskly committed to the imperatives of battle (which may be conflated with the claims of the poetic struggle) does not seem out of place among the other details of his poem. Coleridge, who was finely responsive to the range of Homeric achievement, also acknowledged that one of the effects of its influence may have been on military behaviour: 'to it perhaps the bravest of our soldiery might attribute their heroic deeds'.[17]

[14] Southey (1965) 2.105. [15] Cowper ([illegible]) [illegible] [16] Shelley ([illegible]) [illegible]
[17] Coleridge (1987) 1.287 (as reported by John Payne Collier).

6. Henry Fuseli, *Achilles Grasps at the Shade of Patroclus*

Another strong reaction to Homer's warlike propensities was offered by the Swiss artist Henry Fuseli (1741–1825) who, like Haydon but in a strikingly different way, was fearlessly outspoken and highly distinctive in his opinions and especially in his art. Sporadically, but with a peculiar intensity, Fuseli illustrated scenes from the *Iliad* and the *Odyssey* between 1765–9 and 1819–22, returning to the Homeric subject on several occasions. Some years before Haydon, Fuseli (who had made his permanent home in England since 1779 and had eventually become Professor of Painting and then Keeper at the Royal Academy) claimed that the genius of war blazes through the *Iliad*, a conclusion partly illustrated by the intensity of his own drawings of the naked Achilles sacrificing his hair at the funeral pyre of Patroclus (1800–5) and of Achilles grasping at the shade of Patroclus (*c.* 1810; both pictures in the Zurich Kunsthaus).[18] William Hazlitt, himself an unfulfilled artist, who complained that 'Homer only sung of battles' remembered Fuseli's claim when he wrote in July 1827: 'Longinus complains of the want of interest in the *Odyssey*, because it does not, like the *Iliad*, treat of war. The very complaint that we make against the latter is that it treats of nothing else; or that, as Fuseli expresses it, every thing is seen "through the blaze of war".'[19] Yet, for all his objections, it was the same Hazlitt who had presented Homer's virtues in *Lectures on the English Poets* in a way which seemed to associate many of them directly with their appearance in the *Iliad* and which hinted at no reservations.

[18] Here Plates 6–7. See Fuseli (1975) 75–81. For a comprehensive catalogue, including illustrations, see Schiff (1973).

[19] Hazlitt (1930–4) 17.207 (see also 5.66 and 16.337).

7. Henry Fuseli, *Achilles Sacrifices his Hair on the Funeral Pyre of Patroclus*

> He describes his heroes going to battle with a prodigality of life, arising from an exuberance of animal spirits: we see them before us, their number, and their order of battle, poured out upon the plain 'all plumed like estriches, like eagles newly bathed, wanton as goats, wild as young bulls, youthful as May, and gorgeous as the sun at midsummer,' covered with glittering armour, with dust and blood; while the Gods quaff their nectar in golden cups, or mingle in the fray; and the old men assembled on the walls of Troy rise up with reverence as Helen passes them.[20]

The almost unbroken momentum of the prose and the incorporation here of a sizable, if slightly misremembered or creatively misinterpreted, quotation might easily conceal the fact that Hazlitt's appreciation of Homer embraces Shakespeare's *Henry IV* without specifically alerting the reader and in a way which suggests or assumes an imaginative continuity. This apparently unquestioned conjunction of Homer and Shakespeare is particularly interesting if one considers the review of August Wilhelm von Schlegel which Hazlitt had published in February 1816. This extensive account takes the very same passage from Shakespeare (in this case, from 'all plumed' to 'young bulls') and contrasts it with characteristic Homeric description. Shakespeare's description, says Hazlitt, is 'too bold, figurative, and profuse of dazzling images, for the mild equable tone of classical poetry, which never loses sight of the object in the illustration'.[21] The very passage which Hazlitt himself was to use in his later lecture to imply an intimate likeness between Homer and Shakespeare, especially in the presentation of war, here serves as text (or pretext) both for correcting Schlegel and for exploring essential differences between 'classical' and 'Romantic' styles.

Yet Hazlitt's admiration was conditional and partial. While his recognition of Homer's virtues was positive, his anxieties pointed to larger reservations expressed or experienced by a number of his contemporaries. A particularly rich example of this ambivalence can be found in the work of Byron who was both a severe critic of contemporary war and the militaristic ethos and, in his own special way, a fighter for freedom. Byron's divided allegiances come to a head in those books of *Don Juan* in which his 'true' and 'unflattering Muse' provides a detailed account, analysis and demystification of an extended military episode which is based on the Siege of Ismail. Among other sources, Byron looks towards Homeric epic and specifically the *Iliad*, which he invokes on a number of occasions. Looking back on Canto 8, he claims that it is '*Epic*, if plain truth should prove no bar; | For I have drawn much less with a long bow | Than my forerunners.'[22] Reference to drawing with

[20] Hazlitt (1930–4) 5.15–16. [21] Hazlitt (1930–4) 16.62.

[22] *Don Juan* 8.1,101–3; text cited from Byron (1986).

a long bow may have become almost a cliché, or a routine phrasal reaction, but in this particular context one may easily detect Homeric resonances. On other occasions, he leaves no room for doubt that both he and his subject are in competition with the *Iliad*: so he records 'Troy | Saw nothing like the scene around', asks himself 'Am I | Describing Priam's, Peleus', or Jove's son?' and invokes the 'sad family of Hector'.[23]

The Byronic account of battle leaves space for such intermittent and self-conscious gesturing towards the achievement of Homer and towards the epic tradition. Byron also seems to express some cultural anxiety in his suggestion that a more sophisticated technology of warfare may have improved the efficiency of the war machine and increased the number of fatalities but had also made things more difficult for the modern poet.

> Oh, thou eternal Homer! who couldst charm
>   All ears, though long; all ages, though so short,
> By merely wielding with poetic arm,
>   Arms to which men will never more resort,
> Unless gun-powder should be found to harm
>   Much less than is the hope of every Court,
> Which now is leagued young Freedom to annoy;
> But they will not find Liberty a Troy: –
>
> Oh, thou eternal Homer! I have now
>   To paint a siege, wherein more men were slain,
> With deadlier engines and a speedier blow,
>   Than in thy Greek gazette of that campaign;
> And yet, like all men else, I must allow,
>   To vie with thee would be about as vain
> As for a brook to cope with Ocean's flood;
> But still we Moderns equal you in blood;
>
> If not in poetry, at least in fact,
>   And fact is truth, the grand desideratum![24]

Here again we find Byron translating into the Homeric mode, this time not the events of the Siege of Ismail but the pattern of contemporary European politics after the establishment of the Holy Alliance. Yet even if Homeric weaponry has an archaic charm and the ordnance at the disposal of modern governments is far more effective and damaging, Byron has a wryly ironical warning for tyrannical over-reachers: 'they will not find Liberty a Troy'.

Byron's insistence on 'truth, the grand desideratum' is essentially a moral imperative but it also has significant implications for his choice of poetic

[23] *Don Juan* 8.963–4, 837–8, 1,123. [24] *Don Juan* 7.625–42.

language. So he considers the question of a style which is appropriate to the treatment of modern warfare:

> The work of Glory still went on
>   In preparations for a cannonade
> As terrible as that of Ilion,
>   If Homer had found mortars ready made;
> But now, instead of slaying Priam's son,
>   We only can but talk of escalade,
> Bombs, drums, guns, bastions, batteries, bayonets, bullets,
> Hard words, which stick in the soft Muses' gullets.[25]

Here the invocation of the Homeric example might seem to suggest a sense of loss just as the 'Hard words, which stick in the soft Muses' gullets' might seem to indicate a yearning for the sugared diction of lyric poetry. Certainly, Byron allows the language of war to establish its impact on the stanza: 'Bombs, drums, guns, bastions, batteries, bayonets, bullets' signal their presence by the intrusion of seven heavy stresses and because the line is allowed to expand noticeably beyond the metrical norm. One senses, though, that Byron is offering more than an exercise in mimetic dexterity and that the verse invites us to take pleasure in this collection of sharp particularities and the energetic clustering of 'hard words'. Byron's respect for Homeric precedent is complicated by his own revulsion from war which he sees as a primary concern of the *Iliad* in particular; he seems to be fascinated by the very phenomena which he wishes to reject.

Other contemporaries were less concessive and less prepared to recognise merit in Homer. For instance, William Blake was sometimes prepared to acknowledge the special status of Homer as a visionary poet and even to support 'Visionary Men' against a state system which found it convenient to classify them as 'Mad Men'; but in denouncing the poetry of Homer and Virgil, and particularly the uses which were made of them, he asserted: 'The Classics! It is the Classics, & not Goths nor Monks, that Desolate Europe with Wars.'[26] According to Blake's conception of a warlike state, 'It will Rob & Plunder & accumulate into one place, & Translate & Copy & Buy & Sell & Criticise, but not Make.'[27] The verb 'Translate' is particularly pointed here but the connections of Blake's list as a whole suggest that what is involved is a whole cultural system which uses every opportunity, especially the processes of commerce and trade, to impose its own values. Blake's resentment is directed at a system validated and sustained by the ethos of war,

[25] *Don Juan* 7.617–24. [26] Blake (1966) 777–8. [27] Blake (1966) 778.

which he specifically associates with the values promoted by the study of the classics, and in which Homer featured significantly. Ironically, Blake himself was by nature combative as is recurrently demonstrated by the subjects and the manner of his own verse; yet his objective was to replace the merely militaristic imperialism of the Greeks and Romans with a more enlightened system of 'intellectual war'. As the Preface to *Milton* shows, there is also a fierce independence which rejects not only the militaristic code of the classical epics ('the silly Greek & Latin slaves of the Sword') but the very notion of necessary reliance on a tradition: 'We do not want either Greek or Roman Models if we are but just & true to our own Imaginations.'[28]

This awkward relationship with classical models and the desire to reject their values and their influence links Blake with the majority of his male contemporaries who knew nothing of Greek or Latin. Perhaps it is for a variety of these reasons that, although Homer left a significant impress on a number of male writers in the Romantic period, he seems to have been almost entirely ignored by the women. Anna Barbauld, Charlotte Smith, Felicia Hemans and Mary Robinson scarcely mention him, except briefly to excuse themselves from engaging with his influence. Mary Shelley (widely read daughter of Wollstonecraft and Godwin and wife of Percy Bysshe) once confessed with some pride to a woman friend that she could now read sixty lines of the *Odyssey* in the original;[29] but Homer plays no part in her own fiction or in the emergent genre of the novel (though its relevance had once exercised Henry Fielding). In fact, the *Iliad* is invoked in the Preface to *Frankenstein* (1817) which claims for itself a distinguished set of precedents for preserving 'the elementary principles of human nature'; but although Mary Shelley had read Pope's translation in 1815 the reference is due not to her but to her husband, who actually wrote the Preface and whose own enthusiasm for Homer's poem was particularly strong at this point, as evidenced in his introduction to *Laon and Cythna*.

The case for the irrelevance of Homer was put with great persuasive force by Germaine de Staël in *De la littérature considérée dans ses rapports avec les institutions sociales* which was published in 1800. First, de Staël argued for the limited value of Greek heroism, which privileged the physical. Secondly, she conceded the literary virtues of Homer and other Greek poets which were based on immediacy and openness to experience:

> Homère et les poètes grecs ont été remarquables par la splendeur et par la variété des images, mais non par les réflexions approfondies de l'esprit . . . La métaphysique, l'art de généraliser les idées, a de beaucoup hâté la marche de l'esprit humain, mais, en abrégeant la route, elle a pu quelquefois la dépouiller

[28] Blake (1966) 480. [29] Shelley (1980) 155.

> de ses brillans aspects. Tous les objets se présentent un à un aux regards d'Homère; il ne choisit pas toujours avec sévérité, mais il peint toujours avec intérêt.[30]

This account ascribes to Homer a capacity to record every object in a sequence which allows for the uniqueness of the individual unit ('un à un') rather than a more comprehensive and ordering vision. Yet this very freshness and this paratactic concentration on the force and charm of the individual unit or object was also a function of Homer's point in history since it necessarily deprived him of those deeper, if more abstract, considerations which were produced by the passage of time. In particular, human progress had produced a different distribution of values which had shifted towards a recognition of the importance of the inner world, the abstract, and especially of women's experience. As de Staël put it: 'Les Grecs font aussi, relativement à nous, beaucoup de fautes dans leur manière de parler des femmes.'[31]

According to her interpretation, the *Odyssey* illustrated very tellingly this unfortunate bias of Greek culture: 'Les fils même respectoient à peine leur mère. Télémaque ordonne à Pénélope de garder le silence; et Pénélope sort, pénétrée d'admiration pour sa sagesse.'[32] At the heart of Homer's epic, which for many illustrated the charming and stable virtues of domesticity, she discovered a revealing silence which demonstrated an unexamined bias towards the patriarchal (a modern term de Staël herself would not have used but whose implications she seems to have anticipated). Had de Staël's criticism been directed at the *Iliad*, it would have been unsurprisingly in keeping with her critique of Greek heroism; her choice of the *Odyssey* is much less obvious but indicates that for women readers in particular the shortcomings of Homer and Homeric values were not confined to the 'bloody tale' of the *Iliad*.

The challenges of translation and the rediscovery of George Chapman

Perhaps the most notable Homeric translation of this phase, which is in other ways so original and so highly productive, is Shelley's version of the *Homeric Hymn to Mercury* which he made in July 1820 in a constructively recreational (and perhaps recreative) spirit. This lively translation, which is animated by Shelley's own belief in the joyfulness of ancient Greece (it is, he claimed, 'infinitely comical'), is strikingly contrasted to his declared allegiance to Homeric epic and especially to the *Iliad*.[33] Yet this shift of emphasis is symptomatic. Like his friends and contemporaries Thomas Love Peacock

[30] De Staël (1959) 1.54–5. The thought strikingly anticipates Perry (1937).

[31] De Staël (1959) 1.72. [32] De Staël (1959) 1.59. [33] Shelley (1964) 2.218.

and Leigh Hunt (both of whom translated from the *Hymns* though Hunt also attempted several passages from the *Iliad*), Shelley's taste and temperament may have drawn him to such charming mythologies. One also suspects a reluctance to engage directly with the painful intensities of the epic. And yet the equations are complicated. Shelley claimed that Greek was 'the only sure remedy for diseases of the mind'[34] yet his middle-length poem 'The Witch of Atlas' (written 1820 in the same *ottava rima* as the Homeric translation) shows that even the apparently visionary or imaginative can often reflect sharply, if obliquely, on the problems of contemporary society. Shelley generously recognised that in *Don Juan* Byron had followed his repeated advice to write 'something wholly new & relative to the age'.[35] His own imaginative modesty, or timidity, may have discouraged him from undertaking such an enterprise himself, yet both his translation of Plato's *Symposium* and his repossession of Aeschylus' cycle of Prometheus plays indicate that his interest in classical Greece was often informed by a strong sense of social relevance. It is, at the least, suggestive that the 'Homer' which he chose to make available to contemporaries was not the epic poet of travel and of war but one who had lightly and amusingly indicated the sustaining pleasures of an alternative mythology. An interesting comparison can be made with Giacomo Leopardi, although the poets were unaware of each other. In 1816 Leopardi had translated the first book of the *Odyssey* and the beginning of the second into Italian and had promised, in an accompanying essay, that he would do more if his compatriots approved. Leopardi did not continue with this translation, but his Homeric efforts were transferred to the *Batrachomyomachia* (or *The Battle of the Frogs and Mice*) which he translated three times (1815, 1821–2, 1826) and which also formed the basis for his own continuation, the *Paralipomeni della Batracomiomachia*.[36]

The objectives of translation, whether stated or merely implied, are often complex and need to be examined in terms of a potential readership. Pope's translation was probably intended to reach the Greekless as both the congenial style and the explanatory essays and notes indicate, but it was also intended to be read by those who were privileged enough to know the language and perhaps Homer's original, as is shown by the frequent use of Greek in the notes. By the Romantic period, that is from about 1770 onwards, the sense of this division was no less acute. The most notable example of the Greekless reader, perhaps, is that of John Keats. His sonnet 'On first looking into Chapman's Homer' (written in October 1816) acknowledges with particular force the opportunities accorded to well-intentioned ignorance.

[34] Shelley (1964) 2.309. [35] Shelley (1964) 2.323.
[36] Leopardi (1987) 205–310; see also 515–16 (essay); 517–35 (*Odyssey*).

Unquestionably, it is a tribute to the powers of Homer but it is also a celebration of the power of translation which sometimes can carry the force of discovery itself:

Much have I travell'd in the realms of gold,
   And many goodly states and kingdoms seen;
   Round many western islands have I been
Which bards in fealty to Apollo hold.
Oft of one wide expanse had I been told
   That deep-brow'd Homer ruled as his demesne;
   Yet did I never breathe its pure serene
Till I heard Chapman speak out loud and bold:
Then felt I like some watcher of the skies
   When a new planet swims into his ken;
Or like stout Cortez when with eagle eyes
   He star'd at the Pacific – and all his men
Look'd at each other with a wild surmise –
Silent, upon a peak in Darien.[37]

The circumstances connected with this sonnet are well known and do not need further rehearsal. What Keats seems to commemorate and to celebrate here is a recognition both of Homer and of Chapman, or rather of Homer through Chapman. For once, translator and the object of translation (or in technical terms, the target text) are intimately and indissolubly connected. The poem pays homage to Homer but the memory it recreates is of hearing 'Chapman speak out loud and bold', an experience which provides the poet with access to a new level of literary consciousness. The title reminds Keats' readers that this is a poem about reading but the final line of the octet insists on the oral, or the aural. Chapman's sonorous line speaks both for itself and for Homer so that at this vital point we can hear both poets together and recognise also the voice of Charles Cowden Clarke, who effected this memorable introduction. Keats was particularly susceptible to the effects of sound. On 27 April 1818 he told John Hamilton Reynolds: 'I long to feast upon old Homer . . . if you understood Greek, and would read me passages, now and then, explaining their meaning,'twould be, from its mistiness, perhaps a greater luxury than reading the thing one's self.'[38] In this relationship, the role of listener does not imply passivity so much as the opportunity for imaginative and associational interpretation. 'Yet did I never breathe its pure serene' wrote Keats finally, but only after he had tried 'Yet could I never tell what men could mean', and then, 'Yet could I never judge what Men could

[37] Keats (1982) 34. [38] Keats (1958a) 1.274.

mean'.[39] The received version avoids the petulance of its predecessors and presents this new experience more in terms of positives achieved than in terms of uncomprehending exclusion. Whatever anxieties this sonnet might repress, and however awkward Keats may have felt elsewhere about attempting to recreate the language of the gods too late and in an unpropitious time, these lines appear to suggest empowerment rather than disablement. With Chapman's help, the poet is given lungs to breathe a rarefied atmosphere. Chapman is not so much occluding Homer or drawing attention to Keats' inadequacy as turning translation into a virtue.

The sonnet makes use of Keats' reading about the journeys and voyages of exploration. The opening reference to 'the realms of gold' may be related to the standard praise of Homer and his work as 'treasure' which can be found, for instance, in Chapman's introduction. More obviously, though, the poem centres its images of discovery on the search for El Dorado and the penetration of South America: this focus is confirmed by the mention of Cortez while the concluding 'peak in Darien' looks back to the 'realms of gold'. All of this contains another, larger, metaphor which envisages Homer as the ruler of a capacious demesne ('one wide expanse'). The presiding poet is 'deep-brow'd', which indicates appropriate thoughtfulness but which also looks forward to the desire Homer inspires (according to the sonnet 'To Homer' which was written in 1818) to 'visit dolphin-coral in deep seas', where profundity is imaged in terms of a dimension which extends invitingly downwards to the ocean-bed. There is, at least, a suggestive correspondence here with Chapman's claim in his dedication to the *Odyssey* that 'he that writes by any beame of Truth | Must dive as deep as he past shallow youth', and again that the search is strenuous and challenging: 'Truth dwels in Gulphs, whose Deepes hide shades so rich | That Night sits muffl'd there in clouds of pitch'.[40] Keats did not approach Homer so moralistically or allegorically as Chapman, nor did he interrogate the text in pursuit of Homer's hidden 'Mysteries'; yet the two styles of response have an interesting consonance.[41]

Keats' acknowledgment of Homer/Chapman or Chapman's Homer speaks with special eloquence for those who were linguistically dispossessed. The choice of Chapman also represents a distinctive shift in taste which for some writers meant the discovery of the unrecognised strengths of a much earlier English literature and which usually involved the rejection of Pope who was most obviously associated with his own version of the *Iliad*. This emphasis accords neatly with Blake's epigram, which Hazlitt will not have known. Most readers and writers during this period were highly critical of Pope's

[39] Keats (1958b) 45. [40] 'To the . . . earle of Somerset', lines 163–4.
[41] For an account of Chapman see Burrow (1993) 201–33.

transformation of Homer and did not think it for the better. As Blake put it, with malicious and ironical force: 'Hayley on his Toilette seeing the sope, | Says. "Homer is very much improv'd by Pope".'[42]

Resistance to Pope is exemplified by the ways in which one passage in particular had been selected for critical analysis. This was Homer's description of the campfires of the Greeks the night before battle, which leads into the simile of the moon and stars (8.685–708 in Pope's translation). Pope told his readers: 'This comparison is inferior to none in *Homer*. It is the most beautiful Nightpiece that can be found in Poetry.' Although his note offers some scholarly purchase, Pope is concerned to indicate that, although he is aware of the concerns of scholarship, poetry has its own superior allegiances: 'I see no Necessity why the Moon may not be said to be bright, tho' it is not in the full. A Poet is not obliged to speak with the Exactness of Philosophy, but with the Liberty of Poetry.'[43] Whether Wordsworth was aware of Pope's notes or Coleridge's 1812 lecture is not clear but in his *Essay, Supplementary to the Preface* (1815) he selects this passage as the focus of his attack on a poetic diction which is dangerously distanced from the objects it describes: 'A blind man, in the habit of attending accurately to descriptions casually dropped from the lips of those around him, might easily depict these appearances with more truth.' Neither the liberty of poetry nor an attention to its genius seems to spare Pope whose lines are 'throughout false and contradictory'. According to his own account in *Biographia Literaria* Coleridge, who regarded Pope's translation as 'the main source of our pseudo-poetic diction', analysed Pope's lines in a lecture (probably of 27 January 1812) with an effect on the audience which was 'sudden and evident'.[44] Famously, Wordsworth had told Walter Scott in January 1808: 'It will require yet half a century completely to carry off the poison of Pope's Homer.'[45] Now he complains that Pope's lines 'still retain their hold upon public estimation': in fact, he argues, 'there is not a passage of descriptive poetry, which at this day finds so many and such ardent admirers'.[46] Embarrassingly, Wordsworth himself had once been one of those admirers since, as Robert Griffin and Lawrence Lipking have argued, Wordsworth was much concerned with Pope, and 'A night-piece' is related in suggestive ways to the very passage he singled out for critical attention.[47] Perhaps the only serious defence of Pope in the face of such attacks was made by Byron, notably in a letter of 30 October 1815 to Leigh Hunt:

[42] Blake (1966) 555. [43] Pope (1967) 728.

[44] Coleridge (1983) 1.39–40. [45] W. Wordsworth and D. Wordsworth (1969) 191.

[46] Wordsworth (1974) 3.73–4. [47] See Griffin (1995) esp. 91.

> . . . it is no translation I know – but it is not such *false* description as asserted – I have read it on the spot – there is a burst – and a lightness – and a glow – about the night in the Troad – which makes the 'planets vivid' – and the 'pole glowing' the moon is – at least the sky is clearness itself – and I know no more appropriate expression for the expansion of such a heaven – over the scene – the plain – the sea – the sky – Ida – the Hellespont – Simois – Scamander – and the isles – than that of a 'flood of Glory'.[48]

Characteristically, Byron draws upon his personal knowledge and a sense of place to defend Pope even though, as Byron knew, Pope himself had never visited Greece. Perhaps in delayed response to Byron's letter and to the larger controversy to which it contributed, Leigh Hunt published his own version of these lines in the *Examiner* in June 1816 when readers were told that the lines were 'literally translated from Homer'.

The rediscovery of Chapman was partly animated by the recognition that he had captured much more of the essence of Homer than Pope because of the greater flexibility of his lines. This seemed to apply even in the case of the *Odyssey* which Chapman translated into rhyming couplets but which still seemed closer to the heroic mode and the 'beyond-seas' manner of Homer than the polite and polished formalities of Pope. Chapman went much further in the fourteeners of his *Iliad* yet, in spite of the metaphysical complexities of his writing which hardly reproduced the admired 'simplicity' of Homer, responses to his work were strongly positive. It was Chapman's version which Lamb used as the basis for *The Adventures of Ulysses*. Lamb's letters provide some suggestive glosses both on his admiration for Chapman (and Homer) and his reservations about other translators. His views are expressed with particular force in a response to Godwin's proposal that he modify certain shocking elements in his own book since 'We live in squeamish days' and Godwin is afraid of 'excluding the female sex from among your readers'.[49] Lamb defends nearly all of his emphases, referring not so much to his own preferences as to the nature of Homer's original. 'If you want a book which is not occasionally to *shock*, you should not have thought of a Tale which was so full of Anthropophagi & monsters. I cannot alter those things without enervating the Book, I will not alter them if the penalty should be that you & all the London Booksellers should refuse it.'[50] He does not say so to Godwin (who also admired Chapman) but one of his reasons for preferring Chapman to Pope is that Chapman's version is much more responsive to the fierce and primitive element, to what Hazlitt called Homer's 'rough work': 'What I seem to miss [in the translation by

[48] Byron (1975) 324–5. [49] C. Lamb and M. A. Lamb (1975–8) 2.278.
[50] C. Lamb and M. A. Lamb (1975–8) 2.279.

Charles Lloyd the Elder], and what certainly everybody misses in Pope, is a certain savage-like plainness of speaking in Achilles – a sort of indelicacy – the heroes in Homer are not half civilised, they utter all the cruel, all the selfish, all the *mean thoughts* even of their nature, which it is the fashion of our great men to keep in.' Lloyd's fundamental decency and his civilising faculty might disqualify him as an effective translator: 'your principles and turn of mind would, I have no doubt, lead you to *civilise* his phrases, and sometimes to *half christen* them'.[51] This acute analysis indicates very clearly why Pope was so generally regarded as inadequate; it also helps to suggest some of the reasons why Chapman, by happy contrast, came to be so widely admired.

Chapman's virtues were recognised by a number of the most original creative writers. Keats celebrated his translation in the famous sonnet and both Blake and Shelley had their own copies. Perhaps the most eloquent tribute was paid by Coleridge, both a school contemporary and a friend of Lamb, who may have been the first to interest him in Chapman's Homer. In April 1808 Coleridge sent to Sara Hutchinson a copy of Chapman's translation with an accompanying letter in which he analyses Chapman's attributes with passionate and revealing insight:

> Chapman I have sent in order that you might read the Odyssey | the Iliad is fine but less equal in the Translation as well as less interesting in itself. What is stupidly said of Shakespere is really true & appropriate of Chapman – 'mighty faults counterpoised by mighty Beauties.' Excepting his quaint epithets . . . it has no look, no air, of a translation. It is as truly an Original poem as the Faery Queen – it will give you small Idea of Homer; tho' yet a far truer one than from Pope's *Epigrams* or Cowper's cumbersome most anti-homeric *Miltoniad* – for Chapman writes & feels a Poet – as Homer might have written had he lived in England in the reign of Queen Elizabeth.[52]

This is an exceptional tribute to the poetic powers of a great translation. With one reservation, Coleridge rejoices in Chapman's linguistic exuberance (Lamb had identified in him an '*endless Egression of phrases*', selecting as a description of this attribute an unusual word which Chapman himself had used).[53] At the centre of the tribute is Coleridge's recognition that even this 'exquisite Poem' is an imperfect translation of the original, perhaps because translations must be imperfect if they are to be readable and are not usually readable if they aim for strict correctness. Chapman's version will give its reader 'small idea of Homer' but it is still, in more essential ways, 'far truer' than the versions of Pope and Cowper. The informing presence of Homer was

[51] C. and M. A. Lamb (1975–8) 3.17. [52] Coleridge (1984) 1.119–20.
[53] C. Lamb and M. A. Lamb (1975–8) 2.82.

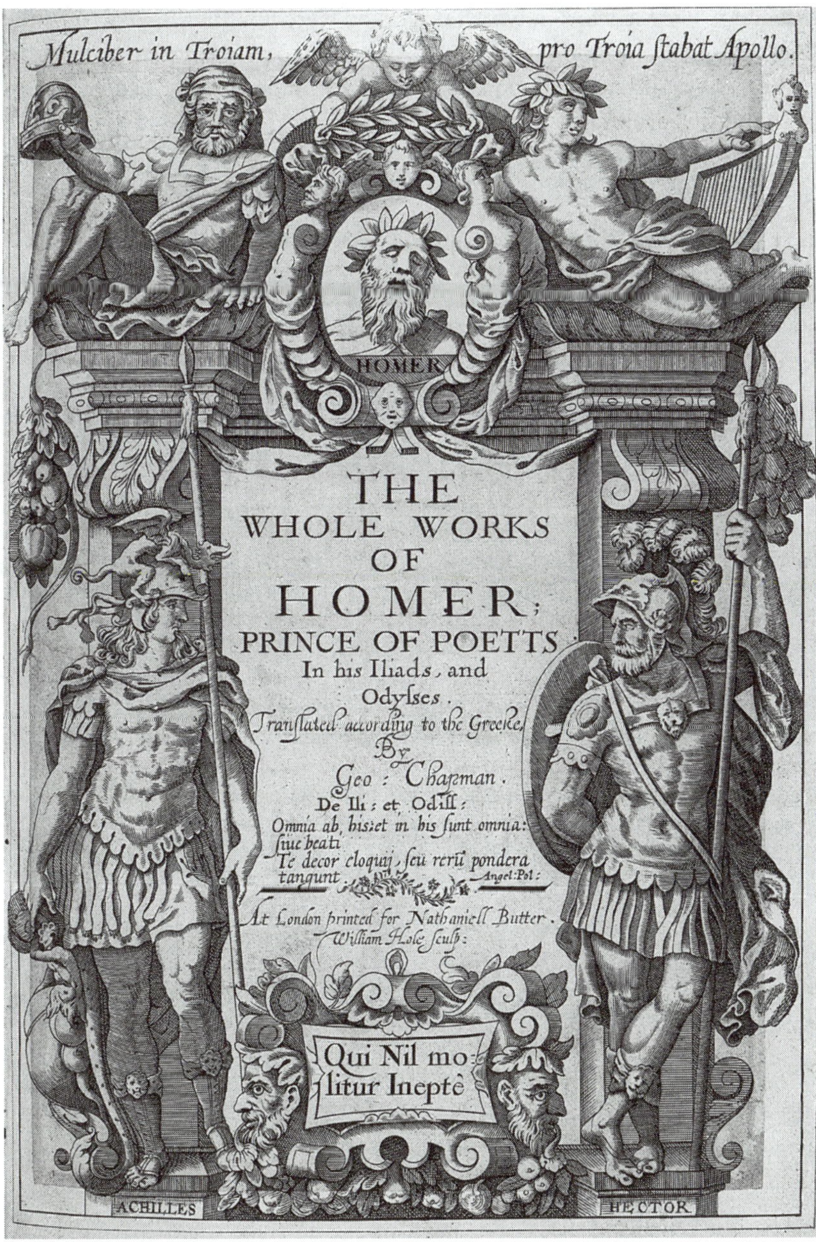

8. 'The Whole Works of Homer: Prince of Poets', title page from Chapman's translation of Homer's *Iliad*

undeniable but the ways in which it worked were not always easy to define. That one of its most eloquent praises should involve a translation which is both effective and ineffective in conveying the import of the original seems satisfyingly appropriate.

FURTHER READING

There have been relatively few sustained analyses of those translations of Homer which attracted most attention during the Romantic period. A useful introductory account can be found in Foerster (1947); some indicative extracts and commentary can also be found in Webb (1982). Still perhaps the fullest analysis of Chapman's practice can be found in Lord (1956) though, as the title indicates, this study concentrates on only one part of Chapman's achievement. A more recent, but frustratingly brief, reading can be found in Chapter 7 of Burrow (1993), pp. 200–33. Readers may also consult Sühnel (1958). The most detailed account of Pope's versions can be found in vols. 7–10 of the Twickenham Edition of Pope, edited by M. Mack, whose general introductions and annotations provide much valuable material. Pope (and Goethe) are suggestively placed in Most (1989a). For Romantic responses to Homer, preliminary guidance can be found in Webb (1993); from a feminist perspective, briefly though suggestively, in Lefkowitz (1981a); from a more specific angle, in Webb (1976), which includes a discussion of Shelley's versions of the Homeric Hymns; and in Aske (1985).

From an artistic perspective, a reader might begin with the standard account in Honour (1968), which offers some suggestive indications of the assumptions and standard practice from which the Romantic versions emerged. For a rather different view, which concentrates on travelling and on Philhellenic contexts, there is Tsigakou (1981). For accounts of individual artists, see Irwin (1979), Symmons (1984), Schiff (1973), second volume devoted exclusively to plates; Schiff and Viotto (1977), Roworth (1992).

19

VANDA ZAJKO

Homer and *Ulysses*

In the opening episode of Joyce's *Ulysses* the memory of noisy horseplay between undergraduates disrupts a conversation between Stephen Dedalus and his co-tenant Buck Mulligan.[1] The sound floats out of an open window and startles the tranquillity of an Oxford quadrangle, even as the moment of recall disrupts the narrative. Into the remembered scene a deaf gardener enters, aproned and 'masked with Matthew Arnold's face'. Unable to hear the shouts of the students he pushes his mower over the 'sombre lawn' concentrating on his task intently. Before the students continue their conversation a single broken line intrudes consisting of the phrases 'To ourselves', 'new paganism' and 'omphalos'. This fragmented line, which might be said to express a parodic mantra of modernist concerns, serves to ensure that issues of identity, Hellenism and the return to the primitive remain firmly to the front of the reader's mind even as Stephen's attention is drawn back to the prosaic question of the behaviour of his lodger.

So what are we to make of Arnold's cameo appearance at this early stage of the novel? It is interesting that the main commentators on Joyce have nothing to say about it. But for anyone reading the text with an eye to the relationship between Homer and modernity, the evocation of one of the nineteenth century's most illustrious interpreters of Homer cannot fail to invite speculation about this particular figuration of the relationship between an ancient Greek literary text, one of the traditional landscapes of classical learning, and the cacophony of the modern. As is invariably the case in *Ulysses* the moment is fleeting, the image tantalising and the potential for fanciful engagement huge. Why is the masked figure a gardener? Is it significant that he is cutting a lawn, tidying and preserving the college rather than planting something new? Does the fact that he is aproned draw attention to his servile status? What is it specifically that he is unable to hear? We shall

[1] Joyce (1922) 7. References to *Ulysses* throughout are to the Penguin Twentieth-Century Classics edition (1992).

return to these questions at the end of the chapter as Joyce returns to the Arnold image in the episode subtitled Circe.[2]

Arnold's three public lectures entitled *On Translating Homer*, originally delivered to Oxford undergraduates, were published in 1861 and were widely disseminated. They constituted a bold attempt to take hold of what is distinctive about Homer and develop a language in which to talk about it. One thing is clear from reading these lectures: for Arnold the Homeric is the *Iliad*. Not only are the vast majority of his superlative examples of Homer's style taken from the *Iliad* but he also focuses on the *Iliad* in his discussions of earlier translations and on Achilles at the expense of any other hero. For the modernists, on the other hand, Homer was the *Odyssey*. There are different ways of explaining this switch of attention from one poem to the other. An account that emphasises external events suggests that the experience of the First World War brought with it such widespread disillusionment with the association of conflict and the heroic that a recognition of a different kind of hero in Odysseus was welcomed.[3] Stanford outlines another reason for change in a literary tradition when he stresses the role of identification of artist with hero:

> This consists in each creative author's personal reaction to the traditional personality of a mythical hero, the give and take between his own temperament and the figure which he has discovered in the earlier tradition . . . For the writer it can be a means of self-discovery, self-encouragement, and self-realisation. For the mythical hero who is the partner of this imaginative empathy, the effect may be an entirely new mutation in his evolution. When an author's thoughts and feelings merge into the traditional symbol, his imagination can make a sudden mythopoeic leap beyond the slow tide of normal literary development: then, quite unpredictably, a new conception of an ancient hero, a new major figure in the annals of European literature, may spring into life.[4]

This works very well as an explanation for Ulysses' fascination for Joyce, whose self-imposed exile may have been, in the words of Eco 'at first, only an imaginary act of intellectual distancing, an affirmation of spiritual independence, a literary device for the purpose of forging his own personal and artistic identity'.[5] The absorption of the wandering, homesick Odysseus into the artist's persona contrasts vividly with Arnold's 'preoccupation with the

[2] I am very grateful to Bob Fowler, Aleka Lianeri and Charles Martindale for their comments on this piece. I would particularly like to thank Liz Prettejohn for her enormous generosity in helping me get started.

[3] This is of course a belated explanation. Joyce was working on *Ulysses* throughout the period of the war and his fascination with Ulysses is reputed to have begun at school.

[4] Stanford (1963) 5–6. [5] Eco and Santoro-Brienza (1998) 53.

fortifying qualities of epic'[6] and signifies a fascination with the blurring of boundaries between the external and internal which the novel *Ulysses* develops. Stanford's description of this process also throws out a challenge to us as we struggle to clarify what different periods have recognised as Homer: our own processes of self-realisation make it impossible for us to be wholly outside of the operations we describe.

I stated above that it could be argued that the shift from the *Iliad* to the *Odyssey* is a feature of modernist literary production. The only example I have given so far is Joyce, and this raises the question of how the stature of Joyce influences our understanding of what we designate as the modernist period as a whole. In common with every act of literary periodisation, the identification of a group of texts or a group of authors as 'modernist' is also an act of myth-making which functions to organise potential relationships between literary works. It promotes certain moments and certain texts as emblematic, as holding the key to the interpretation of others, and diminishes the importance of the rest. Of course any such act leaves the way open for those with a revisionist agenda to create new literary histories by arguing that rival texts define a literary period more potently.[7] In the case of modernism, there is the additional vexed question of the relationship between the terms 'modernism' and 'modernity', the use of the former inevitably invoking some notion of the latter. As we shall see below it is possible to regard the moments of realism in Joyce as celebrating the contemporary and so to regard the modernity invoked by his writing as exhilarating and liberatory. But some critics prefer to emphasise the distrustful and resentful attitude of self-styled modernists towards their changing world. As Tony Pinkney comments on their work: 'The greyer that world becomes, the more luridly its own apocalyptic rhetoric reads – to the point where T. S. Eliot sees in his secretary's supper of baked beans in *The Waste Land* ("lays out food in tins") a terminal threat to a Great Tradition that has come down to us

[6] Anderson (1965) 85.

[7] An obvious and important revisionist literary history is the one that focuses upon women writers of the period. It is fascinating that, rather than focus on the *Odyssey*, female modernists tended to turn to the *Iliad* and 'lyricise' or 'feminise' its content, which was traditionally regarded as more masculine than that of the *Odyssey*. I would speculate that one reason for this was that the resistance the *Iliad* offered was part of their inspiration as they consciously worked to undermine warlike aggression and epic ambition. H. D.'s *Helen in Egypt* is the most well-known example and there is a discussion of H. D.'s relation to Homer in Gregory (1997) 173–8. But there is huge scope for more work in this area. An interesting text in which Homer is criticised as responsible for 'an ever-ancient story' about Troy which 'for almost three thousand years, has urged surrender to the fascinations of ruin' is Laura Riding's novel *A Trojan Ending*, which is set mainly in Troy. For a discussion of this novel particularly as it relates to Graves' *The White Goddess* see Hoberman (1997) 57–72.

from Homer. Modernism and modernity are by now mortal antagonists, not blood brothers.'[8]

When we construct a story about the connections between Homer and the literature produced in the early decades of the last century, it is not only a story about relationships between literary texts but also about relationships between literary texts and those other kinds of texts that we interpret more readily under the heading of politics or culture. The self-conscious experimentation with form and content that has become a defining feature of modernist art can be regarded as either 'enactive' or 'reactive' depending on how we choose to characterise these other relationships in terms of their attitude towards the innovations of the present.[9] A fascination with the so-called everyday is not sufficient in itself to establish that a text seeks to emphasise its estrangement from its predecessors or to denigrate modernity. And it is something that we might argue much modernist writing shares with Homer.

It is perfectly possible to construct alternative narratives of the period which are not dominated by *Ulysses*. However, to ignore Joyce completely would seem perverse given the provocation contained in the title of his major work. Together with the size of the self-conscious 'epic', the title insists that we consider the *Odyssey* as an intertext for the novel. And this must lead us to consider why Joyce undertook to 'return' to Homer at all. In his famous review of *Ulysses* Eliot appears to argue that Joyce uses the mythic underpinning of the Homeric text to dignify the modern world of Dublin he depicts. In words which are often cited he describes the mythical method as being 'simply a way of controlling, of ordering, of giving a shape and significance to the immense panorama of futility and anarchy which is contemporary history'.[10] He goes on to claim that its value is as 'a step

[8] Williams (1989) 5.

[9] I owe this formulation to Tony Pinkney in his editorial introduction to Williams (1989) 6.

[10] This review was first published in *The Dial* (New York, November 1923) and can be found in Eliot (1975). It is worth quoting the relevant paragraph in full since I shall be referring to it later: 'In using the myth, in manipulating a continuous parallel between contemporaneity and antiquity, Mr Joyce is pursuing a method which others must pursue after him. They will not be imitators, any more than the scientist who uses the discoveries of an Einstein in pursuing his own independent, further investigations. It is simply a way of controlling, of ordering, of giving a shape and significance to the immense panorama of futility and anarchy which is contemporary history. It is a method already adumbrated by Mr Yeats, and of the need I believe Mr Yeats to have been the first contemporary to be conscious. It is a method for which the horoscope is auspicious. Psychology (such as it is, and whether our reaction to it be comic or serious), ethnology, and The Golden Bough have concurred to make possible what was impossible even a few years ago. Instead of narrative method, we may now use the

towards making the modern world possible for art'. In a version of the same kind of argument Eagleton suggests that modernism's return to myth is a highly conservative move.[11] For him, the modernists' preoccupation with an ancient and underlying structure is at odds with their fascination with the chaos of a rapidly changing world. It is also at odds with the conception of the subject of modernity as fragmented and profoundly unknowable. A regrettable effect of the mythological underpinning of art is, for Eagleton, the naturalisation of the contemporary world, which makes it appear that human beings can have little impact upon it.

Eliot's review appears in 1923, shortly after the first publication of *Ulysses*, and represents an early attempt to give a public account of modernism's self-conscious experimentation. Eagleton's comments come from a book published some seventy years later and form part of an exploration of the category of the aesthetic in modern European thought. The two critics' relation to Joyce is differently constituted in terms both of their historical positioning and the aims of their projects. What is interesting is that even from their different perspectives there is agreement that the function of the *Odyssey* is to organise and tame the tumult of the contemporary. But it is not at all clear that when a reader is introduced, for example, to Leopold and Molly Bloom in the fourth section of the novel she would necessarily make sense of their relationship in terms of that between Odysseus and Calypso, were it not for the Odyssean chapter headings made public in the 1930 edition. To insist on such a subordination of the Dublin couple may have the effect of making the sensual surface of the text seem trivial and the structural device a conceit. Eagleton himself comments that any such symbolic system carries within it the forces of its own deconstruction:

> If a day in Dublin can be made meaningful through its allegorical alliance with a classical text, could not the same equally be done for a day in Barnsley or the Bronx? The textual strategies which invest a particular time or place with unwonted centrality, ridding it of its randomness and contingency, do so only to return the whole of that contingency to it. In this sense the compliment Joyce pays to Ireland, in inscribing it so unforgettably on the international map, is of a distinctly backhanded kind. To privilege any particular experience, you must refer it to a structure which is always elsewhere; but this equivalencing of the two realms in question is enough to rob both of them of their distinctiveness.[12]

mythical method. It is, I seriously believe, a step towards making the modern world possible for art, toward that order and form which Mr Adlington so desires. And only those who have won their own discipline in secret and without aid, in a world which offers very little assistance to that end, can be of any use in furthering this advance.'

[11] Eagleton (1990) 316–25. [12] Eagleton (1990) 320.

If we resist the idea that Joyce returns to Homer in order to lend authority to modernity, is it possible to figure the relation of Homer to Joyce in a more dynamic way? And might we relate this then to the question of why the *Odyssey* has become a more important text than the *Iliad*? Ezra Pound writing in *The Dial* in 1922 describes the relation of *Ulysses* to the *Odyssey* differently from Eliot:

> Telemachus, Circe, the rest of the Odyssean company, the noisy cave of Aeolus gradually place themselves in the mind of the reader, rapidly or less rapidly according as he is familiar or unfamiliar with Homer. These correspondences are part of Joyce's mediaevalism and are chiefly his own affair, a scaffold, a means of construction, justified by the result, and justifiable by it only. The result is a triumph in form, in balance, a main schema, with continuous inweaving and arabesque.[13]

For Pound the value of the earlier text is primarily for the author. A classically educated reader might rush to form associations between Joyce's characters and those of Homer, but appreciation of the novel is not dependent on the process and the associations are dispensable. In the same review Pound draws attention to possible resonances between *Ulysses* and Dante, Flaubert, Sterne, Swift and Henry James. He also comments on the 'uncensored meditations' of the last episode with its Freudian flavour and on the details of Dublin architecture that occur on every page. Different readers, he seems to be suggesting, will gain satisfaction from the process of recognition at different moments, and no one reader can possess all the information, which would enable him automatically to dominate the others. It is from within this Poundian tradition of Joyce criticism that Derek Etteridge writes over half a century later:

> Every reader of *Ulysses* or *Finnegans Wake* contextualises the work differently, producing a different text and a different reading experience. The reader who does not have access to, or any interest in, the learned tomes produced by the Joyce industry and has not internalised the cultural encyclopaedia constantly raided by Joyce is not thereby an inferior interpreter, failing in the face of an elite cultural product, but one reader among millions, just as capable as any other – in principle – of careful and responsive attention to the words, and the understanding and enjoyment that follows, though always differently, from such attention.[14]

[13] This review of *Ulysses* formed the author's 'Paris letter' to *The Dial*, New York (June 1922). It can be found in Eliot (1954).

[14] Etteridge (2000) 33.

Homer, then, can be seen as providing Joyce with one intertext amongst many rather than with the underlying structure of the novel. Given that both the Eliotic and the Poundian traditions are available to critics seeking to explore the relation between the two, why has Eliot's definition of the mythic method dominated their discussions so decisively? One reason may be that the publication of Joyce's own Homeric chapter headings in Stuart Gilbert's book *James Joyce's Ulysses* in 1930 seems to support the idea that knowledge of the *Odyssey* is necessary to any reading of it. Another reason may be that, such is the complexity of *Ulysses*, any formulation that appears to offer itself as the key to its interpretation has been seized upon with avidity. But the interpreters of Eliot's review have tended to simplify his comments, whilst the impact of the Homeric chapter headings has been evaluated for the most part without reference to Joyce's interest in experimentation with content and frame. An analogy can be drawn here between the chapter headings and the footnotes to *The Waste Land*, reputedly added by Eliot as the result of a request by the publishers that he find something more to fill up some pages.

It has long been recognised that the value of these footnotes for understanding the poem is minimal, if what we mean by understanding in this context is the identification and explanation of references in the poem. Sometimes the notes do indeed give references to other texts in what we tend to think of as a relatively straightforward way, but many of them appear to be more wayward and capricious, and the reader has to work hard to try to pin down the sense of irony which she has a suspicion might be operating. If we compare Eliot's introduction to the notes with the paragraph describing the mythical method (above, n. 10), we can see that they might be read as a similar kind of explanatory statement.

> Not only the title, but the plan and a good deal of the incidental symbolism of the poem were suggested by Miss Jessie L. Weston's book on the Grail legend: From Ritual to Romance (Cambridge). Indeed, so deeply am I indebted, Miss Weston's book will elucidate the difficulties of the poem much better than my notes can do; and recommend it (apart from the great interest of the book itself) to any who think such elucidation of the poem worth the trouble. To another work of anthropology I am indebted in general, one which has influenced our generation profoundly; I mean The Golden Bough; I have used especially the two volumes Adonis, Attis, Osiris. Anyone who is acquainted with these works will immediately recognise in the poem certain references to vegetation ceremonies.[15]

But how many people today would read this introduction as the final word on how to 'elucidate' *The Waste Land*? A comparison of the two paragraphs

[15] Included in Eliot (1974) 80.

should at the very least draw our attention to the way in which Eliot in 1922 is acutely aware of likely readerly responses to the dense texture of his work and of the role played by para-textual devices in shaping them. Even if we only go so far as to accept the possibility that the same might be said of Joyce, we should concede that his chapter headings have the potential to raise as many questions as they resolve. It is however possible to offer readings of both passages of Eliot which allow for a pervasive irony but which also perceive them as contributing towards a modernist theory of art. The issue at stake is one of form: what techniques are available to combine the ancient and modern in order to produce a work of art? It is an issue that preoccupies Pound as well as Eliot and Joyce, and in the case of all three writers it is partly by responding to Homer that they work it through.[16]

In 1923 Pound revised the opening sections of his epic work *The Cantos* so that it began with his own translation of Andreas Divus' 1538 Latin version of the opening eighty-five lines of *Odyssey XI*. It has been argued that this revision was in part a response to *Ulysses* which he had read in chapter form and had reviewed for *The Dial* in one of his 'Paris letters'. One of the fascinations of Homer and particularly of the *Odyssey* for Pound was its novelistic quality. In his earlier essay 'Translators of Greek' he had commended the Divus translation for its simplicity, saying that a crib of its sort 'may make just the difference of permitting a man to read fast enough to get the swing and mood of the subject, instead of losing both in a dictionary'.[17] In the same essay he commented favourably on Homer's 'authentic cadence of speech; the absolute conviction that the words used, let us say by Achilles to the "dog-faced" chicken-hearted Agamemnon, are in the actual swing of words spoken'.[18] When it comes to writing about *Ulysses* he particularly admires the ways in which Joyce's characters 'not only speak their own language, but [they] think their own language' and praises the way that the variegation of dialects 'allows Joyce to present his matter, his tones of mind, very rapidly'.[19] Pound constructs a literary history for *Ulysses* which begins with Homer and which emphasises continuity within a prose-writing tradition. The Homer that he recognises in Joyce encourages him to search for ways to utilise colloquial and idiomatic modes of expression and to figure the modern poet as an Odyssean adventurer experimenting with form.

[16] In an earlier draft of *The Waste Land* that Eliot sent to Pound for comment the 'Death by Water' section was much longer and more explicitly inspired by Canto XXVI of Dante's *Inferno* and by Tennyson's 'Ulysses'. Although Pound recommended that much of the section should be cut, it is clear from this earlier version that Phlebas the Phoenician constitutes Eliot's Odysseus.

[17] Included in Pound (1935) 143–4. [18] Pound (1935) 127. [19] In Eliot (1954) 404.

When writing his review of *Ulysses* Pound faced the problem of how adequately to represent its capaciousness. '*Ulysses*', he complains, 'contains 732 double-sized pages, that is to say it is about the size of four ordinary novels, and even a list of its various points of interest would probably exceed my allotted space.'[20] Size is certainly one element in the response of modernist writers to the challenge of producing an epic in the modern world. In the case of Joyce, Stanford suggests that this is an attempt to rival what he calls the 'comprehensiveness' of Homer, who alone of his predecessors within the epic cycle presented 'the whole man' rather than just one or a selected group of his roles.[21] Arnold endeavoured to illustrate what was Homeric about Homer by giving synecdochical examples, and any attempt to illustrate what might be Homeric about Joyce will partly rely on a similar strategy. The passage I have selected below is taken from the seventeenth episode of the novel which is subtitled 'Ithaca'. In this episode Stephen and Bloom walk together back to Bloom's house and, since he has forgotten his key, Bloom climbs over the railings and enters the house by the scullery door. He then lights a fire and fills the kettle at the sink. The whole episode consists of a series of questions and answers that vary in length and rhetorical sophistication. The question posed in this instance is 'What in water did Bloom, waterlover, drawer of water, watercarrier returning to the range, admire?'

> Its universality: its democratic equality and constancy to its nature in seeking its own level: its vastness in the ocean of Mercator's projection: its unplumbed profundity in the Sundam trench of the Pacific exceeding 8,000 fathoms: the restlessness of its waves and surface particles visiting in turn all points of its seaboard: the independence of its units: the variability of states of sea: its hydrostatic quiescence in calm: its hydrokinetic turgidity in neap and spring tides: its subsidence after devastation: its sterility in the circumpolar icecaps, arctic and antarctic: its climatic and commercial significance: its preponderance of 3 to 1 over the dry land of the globe: its indisputable hegemony extending in square leagues over all the region below the subequatorial tropic of Capricorn: the multisecular stability of its primeval basin: its luteofulvous bed: its capacity to dissolve and hold in solution all soluble substances including millions of tons of the most precious metals: its slow erosions of peninsulas and downwardtending promontories: its alluvial deposits: its weight and volume and density: its imperturbability in lagoons and highland tarns: its gradation of colours in the torrid and temperate and frigid zones: its vehicular ramifications in continental lakecontained streams and confluent oceanflowing rivers with their tributaries and transoceanic currents: gulf-stream, north and south equatorial courses: its

[20] In Eliot (1954) 407. [21] Stanford (1963) 211.

> violence in seaquakes, waterspouts, artesian wells, eruptions, torrents, eddies, freshets, spates, groundswells, watersheds, waterpartings, geysers, cataracts, whirlpools, maelstroms, inundations, deluges, cloudbursts . . .[22]

The passage continues for about another half page in an exuberantly mimetic outpouring of words and ideas associated with water. For some readers the idea that Joyce's attitude to modernity is one of cynicism and distaste is implausible precisely because his fastidious dramatisation of everyday activities and objects makes them seem so remarkable and challenges easy categorisations. It is impossible to restrict this passage to being either a lyrical description of what is essentially a prosaic act or as a slightly nerdish treatment of poetic subject-matter, although it can be read as both. For Joyce the turning on of a tap is a miracle of modern engineering, and it also inspires the poet. The modern world he recognises is possible for art without the need for Homer. But how then, might we use the term 'Homeric' and, more particularly, the term 'Odyssean' to describe the passage?

One way might be to examine the archival notebooks and look for specific references to the Homeric poems which subsequently found their way into Joyce's fiction.[23] This involves playing a game of literary detection and negotiating a position between the two extremes of philological and intertextual fundamentalism as formulated by Stephen Hinds.[24] Alternatively we might locate an analogy at the level of character or plot, and point to an equivalence between Odysseus and Bloom, Telemachus and Stephen and Bloom's house and Ithaca, whilst simultaneously acknowledging that none of them is restricted to one Homeric role.[25] On a more thematic level we might decide that the conflation of Stephen and Bloom, the artist and intellectual and the sensuous man of the world, echoes the coming together of father and son in *Odyssey* XXII to overcome the suitors. On this view it would be significant that the harmony between the two constitutes a non-violent means

[22] Joyce (1922) 783–4.

[23] The standard reference is Schork (1998).

[24] Hinds (1998) 47–51. Philological fundamentalism here describes the kind of allusion spotting that depends upon being able to argue for some degree of authorial intention. So e.g. if we found a reference in the notebooks equating Bloom's house with Eumaeus' hut we might argue that Joyce intended this passage to refer to Book XIV. Intertextual fundamentalism, on the other hand, describes the kind of procedure which emphasises the reader's role in creating an allusion. So e.g. the humble domestic realia of the Joyce passage might lead us to think of the hut in XIV and so we might identify a connection between the two passages.

[25] An interesting example of this kind of criticism is Doherty (1990) who argues that the delayed character development of Penelope is mirrored by the same narrative device in Ulysses which keeps Molly chiefly characterised by the comments and reactions of others until the last episode of the novel.

of confronting worldly rivals.[26] Or if we prioritise the passage's form we might see the list of scholastic information as a mock-heroic treatment of a scene in Homer such as the description of Agamemnon's sceptre in *Iliad* 2.101–9. Yet another way of proceeding would be to think about the passage meta-poetically in the context of Hellenistic comparisons of Homer to Oceanus.[27] We might then make something of 'Roundwood reservoir in county Wicklow'[28] as a modern image of poetic inspiration.

When confronted with these numerous interpretative possibilities we could decide that it is the many-wiled novel itself which is truly Odyssean. Boitani's comments about the *Odyssey* might then be read as comments about *Ulysses*: [It] 'is prodigal with "excessive" and contradictory information, raising questions it refuses to answer – excesses and gaps which creative and philosophical interpretation rushes to explain and fill.'[29] *Ulysses* itself creates an *Odyssey* which it mimics, parodies and alludes to[30] and, just as we can read *Ulysses* looking for traces of the *Odyssey*, so we can read the *Odyssey* and discover the influence of Joyce. For if we find ourselves mesmerised by Joyce's account of turning on a faucet we might be inclined to re-evaluate passages of Homer, such as descriptions of the preparation and eating of a meal or the beaching of a ship, which previously we had regarded as being of negligible literary merit. Not everyone has agreed that Joyce transfigures the mundane. In *Time and Western Man* Wyndham Lewis decries Joyce's detailing of everyday objects, and suggests that reading *Ulysses* might make the reader long to be in another place:

> Much as you may cherish the merely physical enthusiasm that expresses itself in this stupendous outpouring of *matter*, or *stuff*, you wish, on the spot, to be transported to some more abstract region for a time, where the dates of

[26] The integration of the two is emphasised by the combination of their names as 'Bloom Stoom' and 'Stephen Blephen'. Joyce (1922) 798.

[27] See the discussion on lines 105–11 of Callimachus, *Hymn to Apollo* edited by Williams (1978) and the relevant appendix 98–9.

[28] This is the source of the water which pours out of the faucet. Joyce (1922) 782.

[29] Boitani (1994) 10.

[30] So Eliot in 'Tradition and the individual talent', 15: 'what happens when a new work of art is created is something that happens simultaneously to all the works of art which preceded it. The existing monuments form an ideal order among themselves, which is modified by the introduction of the new (the really new) work of art among them. The existing order is complete before the new work arrives; for order to persist after the supervention of novelty, the *whole* existing order must be, if ever so slightly, altered; and so the relations, proportions, values of each work of art toward the whole are readjusted; and this is conformity between the old and the new. Whoever has approved this idea of order, of the form of European, of English literature will not find it preposterous that the past should be altered by the present as much as the present is directed by the past.'

> various toothpastes, the brewery and laundry receipts, the growing pile of punched 'bus-tickets, the growing holes in the baby's socks and the darn that repairs them, assume less importance. It is your impulse perhaps quickly to get your mind where there is nothing but air and rock, however inhospitable and featureless, and a little timeless, too.[31]

The nostalgic opposition of modernity to a more austere and more sparsely inhabited antiquity is typical of one kind of response to contemporary clutter.[32] But, as we have seen, Joyce's narrative delights in the twentieth century and does not juxtapose the ancient and the modern only to reinforce the differences between them.

In his book *The Tradition of Return* Jeffery Perl links the subject matter of the *Odyssey* to an exploration of how the uses of the word 'return' might be utilised in the construction of literary history. 'Odyssean nostos', he argues, is complex: 'it is a return to something old but also a new beginning; it is a meeting of oldest and newest, yet it is in addition the seemly conclusion of an unbroken continuum.'[33] Joyce's return to Homer might well be described in just such a way. One of the things which makes Homer irresistible to the modernists is that he is the earliest, someone to whom it is impossible to be prior. Yet in *Ulysses* there is a sense in which the earliest and the latest coalesce so that Homer is also someone whom it is impossible to get beyond. In the episode entitled 'Circe' the mask of Matthew Arnold reappears, only this time it covers the faces of two figures that haunt the imagination of the intoxicated Stephen. The Siamese twins, Phillip Sober and Phillip Drunk, described as 'two Oxford dons with lawnmowers' appear framed in a window and engage in a conversation that the reader assumes is going on in Stephen's head, the former exhorting moderation, the latter musing extravagantly upon intellectual aspiration.[34] During the course of the novel Arnold has not become irrelevant, but what he represents has multiplied and diversified. Classicism and modernity are not held apart from each other but are rather locked into a mutually defining embrace. Without the modern we could not recognise the classical, just as when Odysseus first lands on Ithaca he does not recognise that he is home. But the modern also depends on the classical to show it what it might be. The return to the ancient world is modernism's defining moment.

FURTHER READING

For a highly readable general introduction to modernist literature which is interestingly organised by theme (time, space etc.) see Stevenson (1992). An engaging series

[31] Lewis (1975) 104. [32] In this sense *Ulysses* becomes a great, big, baggy Victorian novel.
[33] Perl (1984) 18. [34] Joyce (1922) 635.

of connected essays on the whole Joycean corpus is Etteridge (2000). An accessible yet provocative book which deals with modernism's reputation for being 'difficult' is Leonard Diepeveen, *The Difficulties of Modernism* (Routledge 2003). Good on H.D. is Gregory (1997). And of course Eliot's edition of Pound's literary essays is indispensable, as is Eliot's own essay 'Tradition and the individual talent'. Tomlinson's (1983) collection of essays contains some incisive discussion of both Pound and Eliot. Kenner's (1978) *Joyce's Voices* is a classic.

20

JAMES I. PORTER

Homer: the history of an idea

Why Homer?

The *Iliad* and the *Odyssey* have been required reading in Western culture from its first beginnings, despite the complete mystery surrounding the circumstances of their date and authorship, and despite their obvious flaws and blemishes – the repetitions, inconsistencies and irregularities which have led to their impeachment as products of a single mind.[1] All of the uncertainties about Homer and his poems notwithstanding, their place in the cultural imagination in the West has been unrivalled. Indeed, as secular texts with no pretensions to revealed truth and yet conferred with nearly Biblical stature, their status in world literature is unique.[2] How can we account for their standing, and especially for their enduring attraction? Whatever the answer, approaching the question will involve confronting the monumentality of the two poems – less their quality as great works of literature than their role as cultural icons, as signifiers of value, and as landmarks in the evolving relationship between literature and culture. To look at Homer in this way is to consider his place – the very idea of Homer – in the culture wars of antiquity and modernity. But it is also to do more, for a perspective such as this is an invitation to study the intellectual and cultural history of value. And given his idealised role in our culture, Homer is an ideal place to begin such an inquiry.

Any discussion like this must needs be selective and, inevitably, reductive. My own treatment will be limited to a selection of developments mainly within the English- and German-speaking worlds from around 1800, starting with a glance back at predecessors in antiquity, where the patterns for

[1] We might as well ask with Murray (1934) 242, 'Now why is it that the *Iliad* is a good poem when it has so many of the characteristics of a bad one?'

[2] The point is well made by Burkert (1987) 43; cf. Nietzsche (1988) 8.78; Graziosi (2002) 1–2. Virgil enjoyed a similar status in the Latin Middle Ages and into the Renaissance; see Comparetti (1997), Curtius (1953), and Vogt-Spira (2003).

Homer's modern reception were first set. Threading through these reflections will be three recurrent themes: first, the persistent reading of Homer as a classical, and not pre-classical, author; second, the elements of disavowal that go into the construction and sustaining of Homer's ever-imaginary identity;[3] and third, the utter mystery of Homer, his unreachability, and above all the insolubility of his definition. 'Homer', by which we may understand the meaning and value of the poet and his poems, is the product of a particular kind of fascination, and by the same token these have been a compulsive and productive source of culture in the West since antiquity. Despite the recently voiced worry that contemporary classical scholarship has itself mystified Homer and killed him in the process, it has to be acknowledged that Homer was never in fact a stable entity from which a sure base of culture and learning could flow. (In Greek *homerizein*, 'to Homerize', after all can mean 'to lie'.[4]) Whether he is made to stand for the sanctity of the Classical Tradition itself or for any of its transmitted ideals, Homer cannot have existed prior to the debates about him and independently of them. Indeed, one suspects that with Homer the ancients and moderns have made a rather telling choice of object for contention, one that ceaselessly *authorises* the imaginative work of culture. Culture is not just an arena of contestation. It is a deviously calculating and self-enabling thing. Homer, we can safely say, has been 'good to think with', from the earliest appearances of his name right through to the culture and scholarship of the recent past. Nor does the fascination with Homer show any signs of abating, as the recent, massive exhibition in Germany, 'Troy – Dream and Reality', attests, not to mention the book you are now reading.[5]

Still, there must be more to the fascination with Homer than this. Surely other relics of antiquity are equally mysterious and unfathomable, though nowhere near as compelling, as Homer. So alongside our overview of Homer's reception I want to add a further speculation, namely that Homer is, and probably always was from his baptismal naming, an idea of something that remains permanently lost to culture – whether this be a Heroic Age, an ideal of unattainable poetic excellence, or a vague sense of some irretrievably lost past. It was only natural that Homer, the narrator of Troy, should become inseparably linked to the violent destruction of Troy. That

[3] See Mannoni (1969) on the logic of (fetishistic) disavowal, which in the case of Homer would run: 'I know very well that Homer never existed (he is a myth or fiction or a collective identity, not a historical person), but I will treat him as if he did exist nonetheless.'

[4] ὁμρίδδειν· ψεύδεσθαι Hsch. Cf. Arist. *Poet.* 24.1460a18–19: 'Homer most of all has taught the rest of the poets how to lie.'

[5] See the catalogue volume *Troia: Traum und Wirklichkeit* 2001, and the archived web-site: *http://www.troia.de/*. See also Michael Wood's BBC production (1985) and book (1998).

destruction was complete, and the memory of this loss was traumatic for the ancient world – and, in different ways, remained this for the modern world. So let us first consider briefly how Troy might have functioned as a trauma for Greece – not in a clinical sense, but in an imaginary sense, one that works through the artifices of cultural memory – and then take up Homer's connection to this memory, which (all speculations aside) is an integral element of Homer's reception.[6] Then we can turn to some of the implications these questions have had for modernity.

Homer in antiquity

Troy had two connotations in antiquity. It was known either as Homer had described it – as a vital, flourishing civilisation, albeit one pitched on the brink of disaster – or as it appeared in dim memory and on the ground, by reference to its *aphanismos*, or obliteration.[7] Troy's sacking was first mythologically and then conventionally the start of Greek history, the ground zero of relative dating within human time (indeed, it was tied to the unrepealable division between mortal and immortal time), and so history began, oddly but canonically and symbolically, in an obliteration.[8] There is a lesson to be learned here, and it was frequently drawn. The orator Lycurgus could warn the Athenians in 331 BCE, in the direst of tones, of a fate similar to Troy's, involving brutal betrayal, destruction and desolation.[9] The identification of Greece with the Trojan perspective is striking, but not unparalleled (and it was encouraged by the epics).[10] Troy for Lucan, centuries later, was

6 On the poetics of cultural memory, see Assmann (2000).

7 Homer is our first reference to this obliteration. Cf. Strab. 13.1.41–2; Eust. 459.22, 690.4, 889.8, 1,549.31, 1,694.29; Anon. in *Rhet. Gr.* 3.158.5 Spengel; Meyer (1877) 106.

8 See Hes. *Op.* 90–173e; [Hes.] *Ehoeae* fr. 204 M–W; *Cypria* fr. 1 Allen (= Schol. A *Il.* 1.5); Eur. *El.* 1,282–3, etc.; Kullmann (1955) and (1956); Scodel (1982); and n. 14 below on Arist. fr. 162 Rose. Though not the first datable event for the chronographers (the Marmor Parium lists 1581 as the first date in Greek history), the sack of Troy was nonetheless a standard device for marking the start of history, given Homer's primacy as a historical witness (one who often presents himself as a virtual eyewitness) and the symbolic charge of the event. Taking Homer as the first reliable historical source, Eratosthenes and Apollodorus scientifically eliminated all unverifiable sources (legends and myths, all understood as prehistory) and began their chronographies with the fall of Troy (1184/3 BC; *FGrHist* 241 F1, 244 F61); cf. Diod. Sic. 1.5.1. This symbolic view of history had implications for later poets; see Feeney (1999) and Mazzoli (2001).

9 *Leocr.* 62.

10 Greeks of the Troad vied in a civic competition for the Trojan past, while mainland Greeks variously remembered Trojan heroes and Trojan kinship, perhaps the most bizarre case of all being the tomb cult of Hector in Boeotian Thebes. See Erskine (2001) 93–127.

a paradoxical *lieu de mémoire*, a place where 'even the ruins have perished (*etiam periere ruinae*)'.[11] In between stretched a long tradition of intense literary and artistic engagements with the destruction of Troy, but it was Homer, not other poets, whose name was soldered to the catastrophic memory of Troy.[12] Together they became a fixed point around which Greece's idea of itself would take form.[13] It is ironic, or simply telling, that the Greek sense of identity formed itself around a possible fiction.

Representing a loss that could not be confirmed but only imagined, the historicity of the Trojan War could be doubted, at least in its details if not as a whole.[14] As if by attraction, Homer was himself often felt to be as grand and distant as Troy, and it was only inevitable that he should assume mythic proportions. One anecdote, probably Hellenistic in origin, relates how Homer's poems suffered near-total destruction due to fire, floods, and earthquakes, as though Homer were not a text but a place.[15] No other ancient author – and few places – enjoyed this kind of catastrophic fame.[16] The survival of Homer's poems, it was felt, was in ways too good to be true. How real, in fact, *was* Homer? Though never conceded to be a fiction during antiquity, Homer was in fact treated as both real and fictional at the same time: his historicity was etched around the borders with transcendental hues. Consequently, Homer became more than real – he became surreal.

Throughout antiquity Homer was a controversial entity, as much a myth as a person, but always a legend (the son of a river, of one of the Muses and Apollo, or of divine poets, and claimed by various places, he died unable to solve a children's riddle or from the debility of old age), and

[11] Luc. 9.969. Cf. Catull. 68.89–90; Ov. *Met.* 15.424.

[12] E. Vermeule (1986), C. Vermeule (1995), Anderson (1997), Erskine (2001). There were, to be sure, independent traditions about the sack of Troy, especially before the sixth century, both in art and in poetry (see Snodgrass (1998), Burgess (2001)). After that date, independence was likelier to signal dissent from the authority of the increasingly canonical Homeric poems.

[13] One need only consider the northern Parthenon frieze in Athens, with its decorative motifs from the *Iliad*. For later appropriations, see Zeitlin (2001).

[14] Stesich. fr. 15 Page; Herod 2.113–20 and Eur. *Hel.* (doubting the abduction of Helen); Thuc. 1.10.3 (Homer embellishes); and, e.g. Dio Chrys. *Or.* 11 (rewriting the Trojan War yet again). Cf. Aristotle's comment (followed by the scholia) on the Achaean wall by the ships, which he says never existed, because 'the poet who created it [viz., made it up] (πλάσας) obliterated it (ἠφάνισεν)' (fr. 162 Rose = Strab. 13.1.36). A parallel with the Trojan wall is hard not to draw: see *Il.* 7.451–3; Schol. bT *Il.* 7.445 and 12.3–35; and Scodel (1982).

[15] Schol. in Dion. Thrac. 29.16–30.24 Hilgard; cf. Cic. *De Orat.* 3.137; Paus. 7.26.13; *Anth. Pal.* 11.442 = [Plut.] *Vit. Hom.* [illegible] Allen.

[16] We do occasionally hear of lesser places, some of them mentioned by Homer, that have vanished, e.g. at Strab. 8.8.2 or Paus. 10.33.8.

ultimately a potent symbol, an idea, and a prize.[17] Just to challenge, criticise, or even rewrite Homer was another way of confirming his ultimate prestige. Moreover, if, as is likely, Homer's name was added to 'his' poems as an afterthought, retroactively, possibly once they became fixed as texts, it seems equally likely that this is when the contests over his identity were launched.[18] That is, Homer became uncertain – literally lost to memory – the moment he was named and found. In any event, slowly the Greeks began the work of framing, and variously laying claim to, a monumental Homer.[19] In this enterprise they were building on the tendencies to revere, monumentalise and idealise the heroic past which were the norm in the archaic period even prior to the creation of the Homeric poems, as the Dark Age hero-cults around Bronze Age sites and the inevitable existence of epic poetry before Homer suggest.[20] The modern reception of Homer took its cue from here.

To turn to Homer was (and still is) to search for past meanings, a desire that is palpable in the poetic memory of the epics themselves: they, too, are backward-facing. That memory may be differently characterised. But there is no denying that the uncertain question and meaning of 'Homer' – Homer's location in the cultural present – was the source of anxieties and debates throughout the whole of antiquity, which gave rise to a veritable Homer-industry not much different from our own. The monstrous but now lost work in thirty volumes by Demetrius of Scepsis in the Troad (mid-second century BCE) is a case in point. Devoted at least in part to establishing the true location of Troy, this polemical and proudly local work was a commentary on a mere sixty-two lines from the Catalogue of the Ships (2.816 ff.).[21] The fury

[17] Cf. *Certamen Homeri et Hesiodi* (ed. West (2003)), *passim*; and *Anth. Pal.* 2.715, a series of epigrams that confess Homer's origins to be 'unknown', while Homer is a godlike hero beyond earthly location. Further, Allen (1924) 11–4. See Schwartz (1940) 4: 'Homer' is a kind of 'patent'.

[18] Cf. Welcker (1865) 1.120; Nagy (1996a) 21; West (1997a) 622; West (1999); Graziosi (2002) 48. The dates of Homer's invention are unknown, but the mid- to late sixth century is a good candidate. Further puzzlement surrounds Homer's very name, as it did in antiquity (West (1999) 366).

[19] The culmination is perhaps to be found in ps.-Plutarch's compendious *Life of Homer*. See West (1999) and Graziosi (2002) covering developments down to the end of the fifth century; for later developments, see Mehmel (1955), Buffière (1956), Kindstrand (1973), Lamberton (1986), and Lamberton and Keaney (1992).

[20] See Coldstream (1976), Snodgrass (1981) 18, 21, 68–78; Humphreys (1981), Vermeule (1986), Crielaard (1995), 266–73; Antonaccio (1998), Boardman (2002), Osborne in this volume.

[21] Strab. 13.1.45.

of Demetrius' historicism is telling (no doubt of different things).[22] But it is only one exaggerated instance of a widespread tendency with roots in ancient legends and lore and in the earliest rationalisations of Homer. Philology itself, which arose early on out of the need to make sense of Homer's often obscure and troubling poems (starting with word-glosses), is but a symptom of this larger process, which could be driven by the pleasures of invention and often evinces a high degree of self-reflexivity.[23] From Hesiod to the Second Sophistic, the ancients do seem to have generated a good deal of their culture around the mere hypothesis, and puzzle, of Homer.[24]

The modern idea of Homer

The permanent loss that Homer embodied was felt more acutely as time went on, as Homer came to stand for the lost splendour of antiquity itself. But it was the particular achievement of modernity to name Homer finally as the idea that he always had been. Nietzsche provocatively summed up the modern problem in his inaugural lecture at Basel from 1869: in Homer 'has a person been made out of a concept (*Begriff*) or a concept out of a person?'[25] But it was Giambattista Vico who first articulated the view, in his *Scienza nuova seconda* (1730), that Homer was not a person but an idea (*un'idea*) created by the Greeks (though believed in by them).[26] The denial of Homer's historicity is for Vico tied to a denial of the historicity of the Trojan War as one more fiction from antiquity ('it never in the world took place'), but this doesn't prevent Homer from being somehow more *real* than Troy. Troy after all has vanished, while Homer's poems have not.[27] But this can't be right. After all, the Trojan War is no less 'a famous epoch in history' for its never having happened.[28] And so, in the last analysis both Homer and Troy have to be equally *real*. Not willing to let go of Homer entirely, unlike some of his French predecessors from the Quarrel of the Ancients and the Moderns (such as d'Aubignac, who dismissed Homer's existence altogether in 1670),[29] Vico here is playing out the logic of disavowal that would typify Homer's reception

[22] One of his motives would undoubtedly have been to resolve the question whether Aeneas' descendants ruled the Troad after the fall of Troy, and if so, where (Scepsis was Demetrius' preference) and for how long (see Strab. 13.1.52, and 13.1.42 on Hellanicus, which could point to a debate already in the fifth century; cf. Pfeiffer (1968) 250).

[23] See Pfeiffer (1968) Index, *s.v.* γλῶσσαι; Porter (1992) on Homeric scholia and their interpretive licences; and, e.g. Lucian, *Ver. Hist.* 2.20, mocking the tradition and its desire to 'really know' the truth about Homer.

[24] Cf. Nietzsche ([illegible]) [illegible]. [25] Nietzsche ([illegible]) [illegible]. [26] Vico (1948) 289 (§873).

[27] Vico (1948) 289 (§873). [28] Vico (1948) 289 (§873). [29] D'Aubignac (1925).

for centuries to come, and which runs: 'Homer was the best poet ever, but he never existed (and here are the proofs for both claims – his poems).'[30] Vico's simpler hypothesis, anticipating F. A. Wolf by half a century, is better known: it is that Homer's poems were the final product of a long tradition of oral composition and compilation.[31] But his sinuous, uncertain logic, which is the logic of the MacGuffin (an impossible, nonexistent and empty object the effects of which are nonetheless real), is equally an anticipation of Wolf and of the analytical tendency (see below) – and very likely of most readers of Homer today.[32] Thomas De Quincey nicely caught this logic in a wry moment of his essay 'Homer and the Homeridae' (1841): 'Some say, "there never was such a person as Homer." "No such person as Homer! On the contrary," say others, "there were scores."'[33]

Homer, historicity and classicism

It is tempting to say that one of the greatest achievements of modern thinking about Homer was its rediscovery, in the eighteenth century, of the historicity of Homer's texts and his world. But this is only half of the story. For once it dawned on modernity that it might be possible to locate Homer in space and time, and in a way that antiquity never could, it remained to come to grips with this realisation. Locating the by now thoroughly idealised Homer had innumerable implications, and not all of them were desirable. Archaeology eventually held out the promise of a solution, but this in turn created further dilemmas and no solutions. Reinserting the encumbered Homer of tradition into history was an arduous affair. Much of the progress (if that is the correct word) was made reluctantly, and often with as much backtracking as advances. To return to the language from which we set out, we might say that the traumatic loss that was embodied by Homer in classical antiquity became the traumatic prospect of Homer's possible *recovery* in the modern world. Formerly a comfortable notion, for instance an icon of naive genius of the kind that Goethe and Schiller could romanticise, Homer – the very idea of him – suddenly became problematic, threatening and consequently a source of fresh anxieties. In this new uncertainty was encapsulated the whole

[30] Cf. Vico (1948) 281 (§823): even Vico's claim that Homer is an idea ('*un poeta d'idea*' and '*un'idea*') is evasively hedged by the desire to 'affirm him *per la metà*', half-way.

[31] Vico (1948) 285–8 (§§850–72).

[32] See Hitchcock in Truffaut (1967) 98–100, on the MacGuffin; further Žižek (1989) 184. On Vico and the logic of belief, see further Said (1985) 361.

[33] De Quincey (2001) 18.

of modernity's relationship to the classical past, and so too its own historical self-image.

Coming face to face with Homer the historical reality was painful, because it brought with it a 'feeling of estrangement' of the sort that Freud experienced when he stood for the first time among the ruins of the Acropolis: could all this really exist?[34] Indeed, as J. P. Mahaffy (1876) recognised upon going through a similar experience of his own, no monument in the Western cultural imagination could 'sustain the burden of such greatness', and disappointment was bound to ensue.[35] Homer in the modern age had much the same status as the Acropolis – as would, eventually, Troy. A monument in his own right, Homer bore an uncomfortable relation to historical reality. His reality was both affirmed and denied by classicism, both desired and unwanted, as was the case with all classical ideals. But Homer was a special case that stretched classicism to its limits. As a consequence, Homer occupied an uneasy place apart in the modern classicising paradigm, and the strains showed. He came too early to be compared with the fully developed classicism of Phidias and Sophocles, but given his paradigmatic role even in the fifth century Homer's classicism could not be denied.[36] In some ways prototypically classical (balanced, perfect and grandly noble), in others Homer could be felt to be both more and less classical than the classical authors of the fifth century – more authentically and more pristinely classical, if also representing a simpler, more naive and less developed (not to say primitive) form of classicism. To the humanist way of thinking, from Winckelmann and Humboldt to Jebb and beyond, Homer could give a picture of the essence of the human mind ('for it is here that the seeds of the true Greek character actually lie'), while the details of Homeric psychology could be left unexplored – in part, for fear of what might be discovered there.[37]

Eager to leave Homer standing in the protective haze of noble simplicity, exponents of classicism were warding off the opposed extreme, which finds in Homer a prehistoric childlikeness that is more naive than even children can be. (A caricature of this view was developed by Bruno Snell in *The Discovery of the Mind* (1946; tr. 1953).[38]) These are not really opposed

34 Freud (1964).

35 Mahaffy (1876) 81: 'the truth does not answer to [one's] desire'; Meyer (1877) 51–2, expressing a similar disappointment about Troy.

36 Cf. Strab. 8.3.30.

37 Winckelmann: Kraus (1935) and Schadewaldt (1941); Humboldt (1961–81) 2.22 (quotation); Jebb (1902) 38.

38 A [illegible] apply to Snell in that Homeric Greeks are recognisably unified selves just like us (Williams (1993)).

views, but are merely two faces of a single coin.[39] Both tendencies derive from the Romantic but classicising paradigm of Homeric mentality, which gives rise to two mutually incompatible pictures: the view of the Homeric individual as something either less or more than a whole person, that is, either an imperfectly formed and undeveloped version of the self (a superseded instance of the self) or a lost ideal of the self (a self that could never again be known or had). And behind these two views lies the ambivalent construction of the ancient Greek in relation to the modern self. The realisation of either fantasy promised to bring with it incalculable terrors. And with the onset of archaeology, thanks to the energies of Heinrich Schliemann at Mycenae, Tiryns and above all at the symbolically laden Troy, that promise finally seemed to be about to be made good. But not if others could stop him first.

Troy and the preclassical past: Jebb, Schliemann and Nietzsche

Richard Claverhouse Jebb, the leading classicist in the English-speaking world and the future editor of Sophocles, was among Schliemann's fiercest opponents.[40] What business did he have getting involved? Various issues were in play: a boundary dispute between professionals and amateurs; a contest between disciplines (the study of material culture and physical remains as opposed to the study of literary culture and ideas);[41] a clash between idealism and materialism (the new religion of the nineteenth century);[42] and finally, after so many millennia, a palpable confrontation with the Homeric past. Classicism felt endangered.[43] But there was more. Which past was properly speaking Homer's? Schliemann's digs probed into archaic Greece, pushing the horizon of modern contact with classical antiquity into the furthest reaches of the Bronze Age, well beyond what anyone gazing at the Elgin marbles, which were hung in the British Museum in 1817, could imagine. In search of Homer, Schliemann unwittingly pushed past him altogether. Nietzsche's resort to a preclassical and at times 'pre-Homeric' era, replete with a terrifying psychological profile of its inhabitants, while anything but straightforward, had much the same effect: Homer was too tame for his tastes, too Apolline and 'cheerful', and so not sufficiently strange, brutal and

39 Fränkel (1962) 75–93, while implicitly refuting Snell, ultimately shares Snell's Romantic prejudices about the Homeric mind. Similarly, for all their differences, Lukács (1971), Bakhtin (1981), and Auerbach (1953).

40 See, generally, Traill (1995).

41 See Marchand (1996). Jebb's resistance is complicated by the fact that he also strongly supported the founding of British archaeological schools in Athens and Rome.

42 See Frank Calvert to Schliemann in 1873, cit. by Allen (1999) 156–7; Lang (1906) 1–14.

43 See Beard (2002) 18–20 and 155–73, on a parallel case (the Elgin Marbles); and below.

threatening – even if the image to which Nietzsche objects was that of a thoroughly classicised Homer, which is to say more a product of modernity than of antiquity.[44] Wilamowitz fiercely attacked Nietzsche in 1872 for his lack of historicism, but this is to miss the point.

All criticisms notwithstanding, the discoveries of Nietzsche and Schliemann served to underline two deficiencies. First, the age of Homer, be this Homer's own (what we today call the archaic age) or that of his epic world, had no place in the existing histories of Greece: it was all wrapped in a timeless gauze, lacking any real definition, and felt to be vaguely 'classical'.[45] Second, preclassical Greece lacked not only a history but a way of conceiving it at all: there was no adequate picture of preclassical art available, and none of religion either. Nietzsche's *The Birth of Tragedy* (1872) and then later on, in conscious echo, Pater's *Greek Studies* (1895) began the work of establishing something like a preclassical aesthetics for the age of Homer and earlier. They also illustrated how difficult it was to wean any aesthetic appreciation of the Greek past from the classical models. Both thinkers frequently treaded the line of archaic romanticism, which came to be a new vogue and a modern cult of sorts, replacing an earlier era's aesthetic paganism, though in many respects indistinguishable from it.[46]

But it was Schliemann beyond anyone else who presented to the modern world the spectre of a Homer *redivivus*: now Homer would be shown to have been not a phantom but a material reality, as solid as the foundations of a rediscovered Troy. Asiatic by birth, would he even be recognisably *Greek* any longer?[47] The British cultivated a tendency, rare among Europeans, to Orientalise Homer with a certain forthright gusto, from Robert Wood in the mid-eighteenth century, who gleefully conducted a kind of Homeric ethnography on modern-day Bedouins, to De Quincey in the mid-nineteenth, who briefly wondered aloud whether Homer's name, otherwise unattested in early Greek, wasn't Arabic or Hebrew in origin: '(sinking the aspiration) it may

44 Porter (2000b) 246–7 ('*das vor-Homerische*') and Porter (2000a) ('the Dionysian'). Paley would agree in part. See Paley (1871) 365 on 'treachery, brutality, and debauchery [that] marked to a great extent the same characters in the [more] ancient epics' (quoted with horror in Lang (1875) 588).

45 A study like Finley's *The World of Odysseus* (1965; 1st edn 1954) was unimaginable throughout most of the nineteenth century; see Most (1989c) and Morris (1997).

46 Pater (1911) 209; Joël (1905) and (1906).

47 A genuine worry. Cf. Wilamowitz-Moellendorff (1884) 415–16 and contrast Jebb: 'The Greek character . . . subtle like that of Asiatics, but more manly' (King's College Library, ref. [illegible], after the notes kindly lent to me by Chris Stray). Helbig [illegible] outwardly Asiatic, intellectually Homeric characters are 'genuinely (*echt*) Hellenic' (Helbig (1884) 318–19).

have been *Omar*'.[48] This fantasy of a deformed classicism was an ancient one, even older than Lucian (whose Homer reveals himself to be a Babylonian boasting the name of Tigranes),[49] but it was consistently repelled, as it was by Gladstone for whom Homer, the author of 'the immortal poems', must be European.[50] How Schliemann imagined Homer is unclear. Most likely he approved of the racialising portrait by Karl Blind, which he included as an appendix to *Troja* in 1884, and which had a long pedigree in Germany. Appealing to Virchow's cranial anthropology, Blind certified that the Trojans were of Teutonic stock, Aryan, 'blue-eyed, red-haired . . . martial, musical, Bacchic, and philosophical'.[51] Forensic and racial results aside, what Schliemann unearthed was both excitingly and frighteningly strange, and Jebb, like others, would have none of it.[52] He disputed Schliemann's methods and challenged his findings. At the formal centre of the dispute was the location of ancient Troy: Hisarlık according to Schliemann, Pınarbaşı according to Jebb. Mahaffy, backing Schliemann, would align Jebb with 'those who are playing Demetrius' part', and by the strangest of inversions the nineteenth century found itself thrown back into the mid-second century BCE.[53]

But unlike Demetrius, Jebb was ultimately unconcerned with the location of ancient Troy. He wanted to dispute the location of *Homer's* Troy. Jebb held that Troy of the *Iliad* and *Odyssey* was a work of the fancy, a pure poetic invention by Homer.[54] And to prove his point he would play the classicising card that trumped all others: sublimation, by claiming that 'it is in taking a bird's-eye view from a height, not in looking around one on the

48 De Quincey (2001) 21. Little did De Quincey know that the name *(H)omaros* is attested in third-century BCE Aetolian and Cretan inscriptions (West (1999) 366; Wilamowitz-Moellendorff (1916) 372), although see Croese (1704) for the suggestion that Homer was a Jew; West (1997a) 622 n. 122.

49 Lucian, *Ver. Hist.* 2.20. Cf. Dio Chrys. *Or.* 36. Earlier, the epigrammatist Meleager had made Homer a Syrian (Ath. 157b), while others made him an Egyptian; cf. Allen (1924) 32 (facing table); West (1997a) 622 n. 121.

50 Gladstone (1876) 72; (1858) 1.1; (1869) 288.

51 In Schliemann and Sayce (1884) 353 and 357–60; cf. Virchow, in Schliemann (1880) 511; further, Morris (1997) 111–12.

52 Cf. Meyer (1877) 57–63 esp. 56: 'Altogether, the human figures [depicted on the finds] are scarcely recognizable', and quoting von Sybel (1875) on their 'childish' quality (p. 57). Further, Wilamowitz-Moellendorff (1884) 415–16 (expressed in terms of his own 'horror').

53 Mahaffy (1882) 78; cf. Jebb (1881) 34. The *Saturday Review* of 28 January 1882 went a step further and dubbed the exchange 'the new Trojan War'.

54 Jebb (1883a) 155; cf. Jebb (1880), (1882) 201 and (1884). Similarly, Grote (1859–65) 1.321–22, 334; Meyer (1877), and more recently, Finley (1965), Burkert (1995b) and Raaflaub (1997). Schliemann, for his part, wouldn't budge (Schliemann (1880) 517), though he knew better (Schliemann in Deuel (1977) 210; cf. Gladstone (1857) 23) – a classic case of disavowal (cf. Jebb (1880) 269).

level, that the comprehensive truth of Homeric topography is most vividly grasped. Homer is as his own Zeus or his own Poseidon, not as one of the mortals warring on the lower ground.'[55] While patently designed to keep archaeology at arm's length from the Homeric poems, this move of reducing the poet to the vanishing point of his gaze as it frames the reality of the poems – to their objectified sovereign consciousness – was a well-rehearsed element of the classical tradition, from Mme Dacier to Wood, Goethe, Hegel and Coleridge.[56] As Coleridge succinctly put it, 'There is no subjectivity whatever in the Homeric poetry.'[57] Its later expression is to be found in the Romantic literary theory of the epic from the next century, in the writings of Lukács, Auerbach and Bakhtin. Evidently, the problem for classicism was not reducing the personality of Homer to a notional existence (to the idea of his poems), but eliminating this idea from the poems altogether.[58] To that extent, the Homeric question was of no real consequence to classicism, while the exponents of historicism fondly (or furtively) clung to their classicism.

Homer and classical philology

A case in point is Friedrich August Wolf, the founder of modern *Altertumswissenschaft.* Applying equal doses of scepticism and historical reasoning, and drawing on the latest evidence (the recently published Venetian scholia to Homer) and on methods imported from Biblical scholarship, Wolf set the tone of modern inquiry into the classics with a short and iconoclastic essay, the *Prolegomena ad Homerum* (1795), in which he argued that the Homeric texts had a long history of emergence that had yet to be told, and that they were largely not the work of Homer.[59] The *Prolegomena* enjoyed a *succès de scandale* that lasted well into the next century, not least because of the indecision it embodied, only some of which was rhetorically staged.[60] Wolf's hesitations were genuine, but they were also complex. Homer, Wolf reasoned, must have been a simple and illiterate bard, but in the end he remains an unknowable cipher. Meanwhile, the monumentality of the

[55] Jebb (1883b) 520.

[56] Dacier (1711), cit. DeJean (1997) 105; Goethe and Schiller, 'Epische und dramatische Dichtung' (1797); Wood (1775), Hegel (1975) 1.298 and 1,048–9; Coleridge (1990). Jebb's image, and the philhellenism, are an inheritance. For a close parallel, see Philostr. *VA* 4.7.

[57] Coleridge (1990) 2.88; cf. 1.130.

[58] 'The unity of the *Iliad* was all that mattered; the personality of Homer seemed to be a mere annex of this' (Wilamowitz-Moellendorff (1884) 403); cf. Gladstone (1858) 1.22.

[59] See Introduction to Wolf (1985) and Grafton (1981).

[60] See Jebb (1902) 109–10 and Lang (1906) 7–8 on Wolf's marked ambivalences. For Bérard (1917), the scandal is still fresh. Further, Porter (2000b) 69–81.

Homeric poems, though undeniable even for Wolf, is nonetheless a mirage, the source of which can never be fully retraced: they are a paradoxical kind of monument, a sublime object, about which it can be said, along with Lucan, that 'even the ruins have perished' – they exist only in our minds.[61] Instantly, the timeless Homer of popular and literary imagination became an object of scientific historical analysis and of damning critique, albeit on a somewhat irrational basis: Wolf was at bottom an intuitionist whose touchstone was his philological *sensus* ('feeling'), while his science was an *ars nesciendi*, or 'art of ignorance'. If the perplexities of Wolf's stance tended to be repeated rather than confronted by later generations (Nietzsche's inaugural lecture is a notable exception), it was nonetheless his historicist approach that swept the field. Henceforth, the Homeric texts themselves began to appear as something like an archaeological site, with layers of history built into them in a palpable stratigraphy: the disparate effects of multiple compositional layers (some, including Jebb, would actually call them 'strata') and the intrusive hands of editors could all be felt in the poems.

The temptation was to separate out these layers of accretion – indeed, just to detect them was already to prise them apart – with the result that Homer and his texts slowly unravelled, even if there was still something sublime about this heap of threads. Foucault's question, 'What is an Author?' here found an early anticipation. No longer a unitary author of unified texts, Homer was at the extreme rather a discursive effect, the function of institutional apparatuses and practices that had developed over time.[62] The 'Homer' of the classical philologists was only the latest transformation in the chain. Indeed, by the end of the century the 'analysed' Homer was such a commonplace that it had percolated into popular consciousness. In 1897 the novelist and essayist Samuel Butler published his curious, half-satirical and half-whimsically serious study aimed at the late-Victorian public, *The Authoress of the Odyssey*, in which he argued that the *Odyssey* was written by a woman who, 'young, self-willed, and unmarried', had never left her modest home in Sicily and who strongly disagreed with Homer's portrayal of the second sex. Though critical of 'the Wolfian heresy', Butler claimed with considerable confidence to be able to detect, *inter alia*, traces of 'two distinct poems [in the *Odyssey*], with widely different aims', which had been 'cobbled' together and 'united into a single work, not unskillfully, but still not so skillfully as to conceal a change of scheme'.[63] The remark could have easily come from a work like Wilamowitz's *Homerische Untersuchungen*.[64]

[61] Wolf (1985) 47 and 209; and e.g. Gladstone (1857) 29.

[62] Porter (2000b) 63–9; Graziosi (2002) 13–18.

[63] Butler (1922) 252.

[64] E.g. Wilamowitz-Moellendorff (1884) 228–9.

But how different, in fact, was the rest of Butler's reasoning from that of the philologists? Butler's self-styled 'subversive' intervention in the debates of the big boys at Oxbridge, with his privileging of the tumbledown *Odyssey* over the manly *Iliad* and his cavalier manipulation of the evidence (while strictly playing by the rules that sanctioned this very manipulation), deserves to be recognised as a watershed of sorts in the history of classical scholarship, despite the stony silence his book received, and continues to receive, from professing classicists.[65] *The Authoress of the Odyssey* is at the very least an extreme symptom of the age.

No longer a matter of the historicity of Homer and his world alone, it was the historicity and the frail contingency of an entire set of disciplines that was being brought into the public glare through philological inquiry and its various spin-offs. As Homer, the new disciplinary object, was being put to the test (and not least of all to the test of gender-bending), so too were the disciplines that sought to encompass him. A certain debasement of Homer was perhaps inevitable. At one extreme, folding Homer back into history was felt as a loss: 'We can no longer see the heroic age as the writers of the literary period in Greece beheld it – a golden distance in the history of their race, a beautiful mysterious background of law and religion. Far more remote in point of time, we yet discern the Homeric epoch more closely and minutely.' So a wistful Andrew Lang could write in 1875.[66] At another extreme, Homer could be read as a light, comic author who excelled in a lowly genre, as the Assyriologist and classicist A. H. Sayce declared him to be in 1883: 'The Iliad [seems to me to breathe] the spirit of Aristophanes. . . . To me the general tone of the Iliad sounds like that of Don Quixote' in its mockery of vanished Greek pieties.[67] This seems in retrospect to be just what Butler later set out to prove. Indeed, for Butler *humour* and *Homer* were practically one word.[68] Both kinds of response doubtless came from a frustration, and exhaustion, with the dry and fruitless Homeric question (recall De Quincey's delightful squib, 'Homer and the Homeridae'), even if the Homeric *problem*, properly speaking, persisted. But above all, as the century wore on one fact

[65] Exceptions are Farrington (1929) (uncritically), and now Whitmarsh (2002) and Beard (forthcoming).

[66] Lang (1875) 575 addressing the historicising and analytical streams of Homeric criticism (and singling out F. A. Paley of Cambridge).

[67] Sayce (1883) 37–8, and cf. Mure (1854) 1.396–7, 405, 412 and 510–12; Wright (1864) 1; Newman (n. 72 below). On the novelisation of Homer in the nineteenth century, see Jenkyns (1980) 208–10; Shaffer (1988) 187. In contrast, Bakhtin (1981) would cling to the Romantic Homer, walling him off from the novel's modernity.

[68] See Butler, 'The humour of Homer' (Butler (1923)). Butler's colloquial prose translations of Homer in 1898 and 1900 are part of the same process.

was growing clear: from classical philology to archaeology, but also in their popular precursors and by-products (Romanticising travel writing, visual art, popular literature, educational reform and even moral hygienic discourse), Homer was manifestly becoming part of the modern culture industry.[69] By now firmly located centuries away from the stories he sang, Homer had become its alienated witness, and in his alienation he now stood closer to us.[70] But just how close do we want to get to Homer?

On (not) translating Homer: Arnold, Newman and Parry

That question was tacitly at the centre of Matthew Arnold's Victorian quarrel, from 1860–1, with Francis W. Newman over the latter's translation of the *Iliad* (1856). The debate raises vital issues about translating the classics, but also about the destiny of British letters, which even before Chapman and Pope had made translating Homer into a national pastime.[71] Newman took the position that the task of the translator is to render the strangeness of Greek relative to English. Adopting the old English lyrical ballad form and an antiquated Saxon diction (his translation is accompanied, like a schoolbook, by a glossary), Newman's 'historical' rendering creates, or else recreates, the effect of a historical alienation. Only, this alienation is tempered by a familiarising analogy: Homer must sound as antiquated in translation as Robert Burns' English sounds to us, because that is how Homer's Greek must have sounded to Sophocles. Oddly, Newman's Homer, whom he deems crude and simple (if not 'barbaric' and 'disgusting and horrible occasionally'), is to be filtered through a classicising lens; but through that lens he will appear hoarily antique and decidedly unclassical.[72]

Arnold finds all of this barbaric (Newman's translation *is* fairly horrendous), and he takes up a position that is even more radically alienating than Newman's, but also ultimately more classicising. Arnold's premise is

[69] Shaffer (1988), Jenkyns (1980); cf. Gladstone (1857), Kingsley (1880), Arnold (below).

[70] Cf. Vermeule (1986) 84 and 86, confronting the long-standing view that 'the poet of the *Iliad* was more like us, civilized, warm, wise, rational and fair', in contrast to the bloodier and more brutish pre-epic past.

[71] Over twenty-five new translations of Homer, some of them in hexameters, had appeared between 1800 and 1860 (and sixty-four more appeared up to 1900 (Foster (1918)), further prompting a fair amount of speculation at the time about why it was so difficult to pack the English language into Greek hexameters, let alone Homer into English – a nice classical dilemma (not entirely unknown to the Germans; cf. Wolf (1869)). See Wright (1864), Cayley (1862–3) and (1877), Blackie (1861), Lang (1891), Venuti (1995), Steiner (1996) and in this volume; Prins (forthcoming).

[72] Newman (1856) iv, xv–xvi; Newman (1861) 73; cf. 14, 48, 56, 59, 86, 95 etc.

that Homer is forever historically and aesthetically lost to us ('we cannot possibly tell *how* the *Iliad* "affected its natural hearers"', not even in the fifth century[73]), and so the next best thing is to strike a compromise. The object of the translator is to recreate the '*feeling* which to read the original gives' informed and poetically sensitive modern scholars: 'they are the only tribunal in this matter'.[74] Accordingly, Arnold's translation, done up in authentic hexameters (and demonstrated *exempli gratia* in the lectures), will be a kind of simulacrum, not of the original poems, but of the *experience* of reading Homer's Greek *at the university today*. Arnold's solution is fundamentally a pedagogical one, and it suits both his liberal politics and his take on the social mission of English criticism.[75] Classics is dying as a field – indeed, '*the Greeks are dead*'[76] – but literacy is rising. The untutored, Greekless reader is to be treated to a surrogate experience of the classics, and on a scale never previously seen. But what she will receive (will learn to understand and even *hear*) is no longer Homer, but rather his monumentality: for Homer is to be presented not as a classroom text, but 'as the most important poetical monument existing'.[77]

Two Victorian arguments about how not to translate Homer, but also, as it turns out, about Homer's untranslatability.[78] For all their unbridgeable differences, the two critics concur in their belief that the meanings of Homer's individual words are all too frequently opaque, which is to say lost and irrecoverable. But whereas Newman seeks to capture the strangeness of words whose meaning may have vanished, Arnold perceives no obstacles to a translator, for whom nothing in Homer is so opaque as to lie beyond capture. For Arnold, a reader's practised enjoyment will annul all philological scruples: 'poetically he feels clearly about the word, although philologically he may not'.[79] With this gesture, Arnold is not standing outside of philology. Quite the contrary, he is re-enacting a conventional ambivalence of modern Homeric scholarship since Wolf, an ambivalence that (as we have seen) was driven by diverging aesthetic and philological impulses. Let us dwell a while longer on the opacity – the loss and lack of meaning and sense – that joins these two impulses before they turn into philological doubt and distance or into aesthetic pleasure and an illusory contact with the past, as we turn now to a twentieth-century reenactment of this victorian controversy.

73 Arnold (1960) 98, 100.

74 Arnold (1960) 99; italics added.

75 See Baldick (1983), Eagleton (1996).

76 Arnold (1960) 99; italics added.

77 Arnold (1960) 97.

78 Both sides of the debate are interestingly anticipated in De Quincey (2001) 48–51.

79 Arnold (1960) 10[illegible] Similarly, De Quincey (2001) [illegible]. In contrast, Murray (1934) 245 would find Homer's language to be inscrutable at its most ancient core.

Milman Parry's discovery of oral formulaic composition changed the face of Homeric studies even more dramatically than Wolf had.[80] Parry, a Romantic, but also a hard-headed statistician, gives the sense that with his work one can glimpse the oldest and indelible layers of the Homeric tradition, practically its unconscious memory and poetics. The poet (whom Parry conventionally dubs 'Homer') is here a spokesman of the rhapsodic tradition that preceded him, virtually its unconscious product. How much of this tradition is Homer actually aware of? Does he even *understand* what he sings? Parry stares down this last question in an article from 1928.[81] There he isolates to his satisfaction a category of words whose meaning is obscure to Homer and his audience. Oddly, the starting point is made up by phrases whose meaning is obscure, if not utterly opaque, to *ourselves*. But why should these words be unknown to Homer and his audience? One pressing reason is the need to preserve intact the Homeric hypothesis itself: the datability of Homer is founded on the absolute undatability of some of his language. Homer must come after the tradition, and he must be ignorant of some of what preceded him. He must be a poet of memory without complete access to what he remembers.[82]

Parry's axioms require that Homer must 'blindly accept a large number of words concerning whose meaning he was completely ignorant'.[83] Blindly, but not without effect, for it is possible to recover from epic poetry an 'aesthetics of traditional style', and especially from those places where linguistic fossilisation is most concentrated, the traditional noun–epithet combinations. 'Vague', if not altogether opaque, fixed epithets are not 'attentively' used or heard. Being a mere incidence of sound, their effect is one of 'rapidity'.[84] They are both familiar, from their repeated occurrences, and strange. Their uses tend to be 'irrational' and ultimately connotative: the auditor '*feel[s]* in them only an element which ennobles the heroic style'.[85] Indeed, they confirm in their archaic quality the very antiquity and epic distance of the poetry itself. Like Homer, the auditor 'is fully alive to their sense, but scarcely heedful of their meaning', and so on.[86]

Here, or already, Parry's theory has begun to sound strangely familiar, at once Arnoldian and Newmanian – not surprisingly, given that Parry cites Arnold's essay in a handful of places and knows it well.[87] A section of his

80 See Fowler (this volume).

81 'The Homeric gloss: a study in word-sense', in Parry (1971) 240–50.

82 Parry (1971) 245, 22; for a confirmation, see Leumann (1950). 83 Parry (1971) 248.

84 The term is originally Arnold's: Parry (1971) 428; Arnold (1960) 153, 183, 207 etc.

85 Parry (1971) 250; italics added. 86 Parry (1971) 250.

87 Parry (1971) 428 (and 172, 250, 306 etc.) sides with Arnold, but agrees with Newman's recourse to Anglo-Saxon analogies (p. 367). Epithets, strangely repeated, were a primary

doctoral thesis from 1928 even asks, 'Can the fixed epithet be translated?' and the answer is, predictably, No (and it doesn't need to be).[88] Nor is this all. Obscure or opaque epithets, far from being an aberrant moment of the epic experience, are for Parry symbolic of that experience as a whole: here the auditor listens with as it were a third ear, feeling more than hearing what is sung. In effect, these are words that have ceased to signify and instead have become what they always were: music.[89] So understood, oral poetry, with its appeal to the unanalysable (the 'distant and wondrous', the effects of feeling and sound) and its ideological attractions (nobility, heroic ethos and grandeur), folds back into the conventional ideology of the classical ideal.[90] The quality of the sound and voice of epic diction, in its essential aesthetic 'unity', is instrumental in producing what we might call an 'epic-effect'.[91] One of these effects is Homer himself: the *voice* of Homer that somehow, despite the intervening layers of mediation, can be directly heard by us today.[92] A questionable Homer, to be sure, but it *is* what Parry's answer to the Homeric question is ultimately all about: the poems do finally have a 'unity', but this unity can be discovered only once we have grasped 'Homer's idea of style and poetic form', that is, once we correctly adjust our idea of Homer.[93] Philology, the science of antiquity, has once again sanctioned itself with an appeal to traditional aesthetic ideology. Here it has historicised, we might say, that ideology, by rooting it in an experience that is both our own and definitionally Greek. An ideal scientific object in every sense of the word, Homer is nothing other than the modern idea of what is ancient about antiquity – a thought we can feel, or imagine we feel, but can never really know.[94]

Conclusion: Homer and culture

Questions about Homer's translatability crystallise several concerns, none of which is exclusively modern. At issue, in a most basic sense, is how we can

obstacle to modern comprehensions of Homer and therefore a sensitive issue. Cf. Hegel (1975) 2.1,002–3.

88 Parry (1971) 171; cf. 126–7.

89 Parry (1971) 374–5.

90 Parry (1971) 127, 251–3; cf. 319–24, 331–3, 374. For Parry's Phidian and Winceklmannian biases, see Parry (1971) xxiv–xxv, 127, 417, 424–5, 427, 431.

91 Parry (1971) 128.

92 Hearing the South Slavic bards sing, 'one . . . has the overwhelming feeling that, in some way, he is hearing Homer' (Parry (1971) 378).

93 Parry (1971) 269.

94 See further García (2001) and Kahane (2004) on Parry and then-contemporary scientific inquiry.

communicate with the past. And standing behind this is the question whether Homer's Greeks are in any way like ourselves. Pressed to the extreme, these issues raise the problem of Homer's intelligibility today: can we even *understand* the Homeric mind?[95] At stake, behind everything, is nothing less than our self-definition.

On the other hand, Homer has always been compelling not only for what he is but also for what came before him. This is his abyssal attraction. And yet modern interpreters of Homer seem to have been increasingly drawn into Homer's past and its opacities, which exercised a powerful if hidden fascination even at the very height of classicism.[96] The most obvious instance, after Nietzsche, comes in the study of Greek mythology and religion. From Grote and Gladstone to the Cambridge Ritualists and Gilbert Murray, the world of Homer threw long, dark shadows on a violent prehistory that was felt to have been more or less purged from the poems but to be legible in them.[97] It would take the horrors of two world wars for the darker implications of these *fin de siècle* approaches to be realised more immediately in the poems themselves, above all in the disenchanted readings produced by Simone Weil (1940–1) and by Horkheimer and Adorno (1947).[98] The Vietnam experience led to a further reinterpretation.[99]

Homer's poems contain and imply much violence, but this violence has been dealt with in different ways. Is violence part of their attraction, or is there a comfort to be had in rejecting its allures, especially through disidentification and disavowal? Was classicism guilty of transfiguring the violence in Homer or of secretly nourishing a fascination with it? Are Homer's readers drawn to the clarity of his poems or to their opacity, which represents a violence of another kind (a violence, say, of sense and meaning)? To read Homer is to be involved, willy-nilly, in questions such as these. But to ask such questions in an open and explicit way is to begin the work of cultural understanding.[100]

[95] See, most recently, Clarke (1999) and Williams (2000).

[96] See Karl Philipp Moritz's influential *Götterlehre* (1791) in Moritz (1981), vol. 2, with Porter (2000b) 395–6 n. 90.

[97] Nietzsche (1967) [1872]; Grote (1859–65) 1.13; Gladstone (1858) 2.1–23; Murray (1934) 120–45 and 266–7; on Murray and the Cambridge Ritualists, see Fowler (1991) and Schlesier (1994).

[98] See Murray (1934) 27 straining to 'humanize' Homer, and contrast Weil (1953); Horkheimer and Adorno (1971) 72 n. 61, critical of philhellenism's complacencies; and Auerbach (1953), written on the eve of the Second World War.

[99] Shay (1994). See now also Buchan, forthcoming.

[100] This chapter further develop Porter (2002).

FURTHER READING

For discussion of Homer's identity and the uses of Homer in antiquity see Mehmel (1955), Burkert (1987), West (1999) and Graziosi (2002) (down to the fourth century BCE); Buffière (1956) and Lamberton and Keaney (1992) (on philosophers, literary critics and grammarians down to the Byzantine era); Kindstrand (1973) and Zeitlin (2001) (the Second Sophistic); Lamberton (1986) (Neoplatonics); Erskine (2001) (Troy in the ancient historical imagination); Snodgrass (1998), Burgess (2001) and Boardman (2002) (art and material culture); Allen (1924), Jacoby (1933) and Schwartz (1940) are a mine of primary information. On later reception, see Finsler (1912), Hepp (1968), Myres (1958), Clarke (1981), Wood (1998), Létoublon *et al.* (1999) and *Troia: Traum und Wirklichkeit* (2001) (surveys); Grafton in Lamberton and Keaney (1992) and Grafton (1997) 135–83 (Renaissance readers); Vogt-Spira (2003) (early modern period); Simonsuuri (1979) (eighteenth century); Jenkyns (1980) and Turner (1981) (Victorian era). For further reading on archaeology and the Homeric question, see the contributions of Osborne and Fowler respectively in this volume.

21

LORNA HARDWICK

'Shards and suckers': contemporary receptions of Homer

On 12 April 1989 in the Main House of the Düsseldorf Theatre a staged version of Homer's *Iliad* had its première. *Die Ilias des Homer* was a co-production between the Düsseldorf Schauspielhaus and the Schauspiel Essen. It was presented in two parts, each lasting two and a half hours, directed by Hansgünther Heyme and Hanns-Dietrich Schmidt, based on the translation into German by the Homer scholar Wolfgang Schadewaldt (1900–74) who had completed work on the project shortly before his death.[1] A proposal to make the version into a television production to be shown in the early evening in order to attract a young audience to Homer had foundered for financial reasons.

Alongside his research, Schadewaldt also worked extensively on translations, many of which were published in the later stages of his career and some of which were staged.[2] In 1958 he had published a prose translation of the *Odyssey* so the *Iliad* translation both completed his translation of Homer and linked to his staged translations of Greek drama. Schadewaldt also published works on the history of German culture, especially on the relationship between classicism and Romanticism, including *Goethe-Studien: Natur und Altertum* (1963). The 1989 stage production was therefore notable for bringing together scholarly translation and theatre practice, for its purpose of presenting Homer to a new audience and for its claim for Homer as a seminal influence in European cultural history. This last aspect of the project was developed in the production's Programme, which was itself a major document of cultural history and of Homeric reception and ran to 168 pages. It

[1] Schadewaldt had held chairs of Classical Philology at the Universities of Königsberg, Freiburg i.Br., Leipzig, Berlin (from 1941) and Tübingen (from 1950).

[2] These included *König Ödipus* (1952), *Antigone* (1965 and 1970), *Aias* (1967), *Der Ödipus des Sophokles* (1968 – a reworking of Sophocles' two Oedipus plays), *Die Sieben gegen Theben* (1970), *Die Bakchen des Euripides/Die Frösche des Aristophanes* (1973), *Die Frauen von Trachis* (1976).

not only set out on the left-hand page the full text of the performance with line by line cross references to the Homeric text but also included on the right-hand facing pages a commentary and selections from the literature of antiquity and modern Europe, together with photographs of art works and of the performance itself.

I began with this example of a huge work of Homer reception because it actually foreshadows many of the issues with which I shall be concerned in this chapter. These include the relationship between different specialisms in the presentation of Homer to a modern audience (for instance those of academics, translators, adaptors, poets, theatre practitioners) and the relationship of their work as a whole to their treatment of Homer. Also vital is the way in which Homer has provided a basis for aesthetic innovation and critical debate both within antiquity and subsequently. The German production also reflects the paradox that while Homer reception has generated a major strand in literature and art, familiarity with the Homeric texts themselves is no longer a central part of education or culture (even 'high' culture) and that there is therefore a changing balance between tradition and modernity in communication with new readers and audiences. Thus when compared with the receptions discussed in this chapter it helps to highlight the cultural shifts currently taking place.

I propose to explore these issues by focusing on a small group of modern receptions of Homer and setting out the main aspects of their relationship to Homeric epic and to the general points set out above. The scope of the German reception I described also provides a salutary reminder of the limited scope of a study like this one, which concentrates on contemporary receptions in one language only. However, I shall show that the European cultural tradition is only one of the strands in Homer reception – new ones are developing. I shall be confining attention to work published or performed in the last third of the twentieth century or beginning of the twenty-first. This presents particular problems since it is arguably too soon to make judgments about longer term trends, let alone identify watersheds in recent reception. However, there is some merit in recording perceptions of 'a moment in time' and in trying to identify key points of convergence and divergence between modern works and Homer and between the modern works themselves in their response to Homer. I shall assume without arguing it that there is often a fruitful correspondence between key debates in Homeric scholarship and the literary and dramatic analysis involved in modern reception studies. In particular, issues such as oral culture, social values, refiguration of mythology, gender studies, the presentation of war and violence and the poetic techniques of Homeric epic (such as the use of epithets, similes and embedded and focalised narrative) recur both in Homer criticism and in reception analysis.[3] The chapter is divided into three sections, followed by some tentative conclusions. The sections are: 'Performance poetry'; 'Homer on the stage'; 'Poetic refigurations of Homer'. It will quickly become apparent that the sections are to a high degree interdependent.

Performance poetry

Homeric epic was created for performance and for 'touring' to a variety of audiences.[4] Modern receptions have developed this aspect in several different directions. Homeric epic has once more been recognised for its story-telling qualities and versions have been made for public performances for young people.[5] The stories associated with figures in Homer have also inspired dramatic monologues, notably by Carol Ann Duffy who has re-examined Homeric and mythological paradigms from the perspective of the female participants, including 'Mrs Tiresias', Penelope and Circe.[6] Duffy's poems add an edge of dark humour to the exploration of silenced voices and marginalised figures in Greek literature developed in the nineteenth-century variations on the dramatic monologue form by proto-feminist writers such as Augusta Webster and Amy Levy.[7]

In new works such as Elizabeth Cook's prose poem *Achilles*, Homer is a major source, together with fragments from the epic cycle, drama and representations of myth in vase painting.[8] *Achilles* has been read in theatres and at literary festivals and, featuring the classical actor Greg Hicks, won a Fringe First award at the Edinburgh Festival in 2001. The work is divided into three sections. The first is 'Two rivers' which begins with Odysseus' encounter with Achilles in the Underworld and uses a combination of focalised narrative and sharp dialogue to lay bare Achilles' psychology. This is followed by a series

[3] For an overview of the current situation of scholarly debates see other contributors in this volume and de Jong (1999) esp. vol. 3.

[4] For discussion of the evidence concerning ancient epic in performance and recitation, see Taplin (1992), Thomas (1995) and Nagy (1996b).

[5] For instance Hugh Lupton and Daniel Morden have adapted both the *Iliad* and the *Odyssey* for two-hour story-telling sessions held at various venues in 2001–2, including a sell-out session at the Edinburgh Book Festival in 2002.

[6] Duffy (1999).

[7] For discussion of the literary innovation and radical social criticism of Webster and Levy see Hardwick (2000a).

[8] Published text in Cook (2001). Homeric sources and the epic cycle were included in Barton (2000), which was further adapted in the Royal Shakespeare Company's production directed by Peter Hall. For discussion of the play cycle as an anthology of ancient material, see Hardwick (2001).

of flashbacks to the death of Patroclus and Priam's supplication for the body of Hector – 'Imagine: the mighty Priam crouched before you like a child' (p. 44). The second section 'Gone' explores the death of Achilles and the responses of Thetis and Helen. It also contains an eviscerating sequence on the sack of Troy which sets in parallel the atrocities inflicted by and on the unnamed and those perpetrated by the famous on the famous – 'There are only so many parts you can slice or hack from a man or a woman' (p. 81). Cook's method is to avoid anachronism since she considers that what makes ancient stories 'of the present' is a combination of physiology and chemistry which generate emotions enabling moderns to have a rapport with the ancients.[9] Another aspect of her approach which is particularly important for reception studies is her treatment of the influence of the figure of Achilles on later poetry, specifically addressed in the third section 'Relay'. This sets out Keats' reflection on the impact of the image of Achilles on his mental state and on his poetry. Using the dynamic present tense, Cook communicates the effect on Keats of his reading of Chapman's Homer and his sense of his own affinity with Achilles.

Probably the most influential performances of poetry in Homer reception are those of the work of Christopher Logue.[10] *Kings* has been presented on BBC Radio 3 and in the theatre by Alan Howard at the National Theatre, September 1992, and by Peter Florence at the Ledbury Poetry Festival in 1999. *War Music* was toured in the USA in 2001 and 2002 by the New York based company Verse Theater Manhattan, with a UK tour in for 2003 (the company had previously also presented *Kings*). In September 2001 Verse Theater Manhattan was forced to suspend its (all-female) performance of *War Music* at the Wings Theater after the September 11 attack on the nearby World Trade Center but subsequently additional performances were held in aid of the Red Cross relief fund. The popular reaction to the performances raises very interesting questions about the ambivalent resonances of a piece based on violence and the culture of revenge.[11]

Logue is not a translator as such. His works are described as 'Accounts', which implies an almost documentary approach (intensified by his use of cinematic techniques). He does not know Greek and has worked from a number of translations/versions including Chapman (1611), Pope (1720), Lord Derby (1865), A. T. Murray (1924) and E. V. Rieu (1950).[12] He regards poetic and

9 Source: Cook's discussion with the audience following her reading at the Edinburgh Book Festival, 12 August 2002.

10 Published texts: Logue (1981), Logue (1992), Logue (1996), Logue (1999).

11 For an example, see Stuttaford (2002): 'a shout across time – Logue's work is steeped in the past but unafraid of the present'.

12 Logue (1981) 7.

popular versions as better raw material for his work than translations made by scholars such as R. L. Lattimore (*Iliad* (1951), *Odyssey* (1965)), Robert Fitzgerald (*Odyssey* (1961), *Iliad* (1974)) or Robert Fagles (*Iliad* (1990), *Odyssey* (1997)).[13] Logue's work is characterised by his stress on the need to capture 'brilliant moments' and 'luminous detail'. In this he follows Ezra Pound's belief that a poem has underlying energies that go beyond the language in which it was written and which must be communicated in the 'translation'.

In terms of Homeric reception, two aspects of Logue's work are crucial. The first is that he has focused on what may be termed the naked spine that joins the episodes in the *Iliad*. The subject-matter is brutal (600 lines in *War Music* devoted to mass violence with a section heading 'GBH');[14] the diction is direct and demythologising ('Cuntstruck Agamemnon', *Kings* 19); the narrative voice is openly directive not focalising or multivocal, sometimes appearing in the text as a film director's instruction ('Reverse the shot. Go close. Hear Agamemnon', *Kings* 16); the ruthless unquestioned exploitation of women and the rank and file is never concealed; the idea of reciprocity, so sensitively shaded by Cook and Longley in their responses to *Iliad* 24, is reduced to a coarse material exchange.[15] Logue's Homer is stripped of the debate, empathy and compassion which form a contrast and challenge to the raw violence and exercise of power. Logue exposes the unpalatable aspects of the culture represented in Homer, the effects of which the ancient epic mitigates by the emotional and moral sensitivity of Books 6 (Hector and Andromache at Troy), 9 (the debate about privilege and obligation) and 24 (the retrieval of Hector's body by Priam). Thus Logue is a major example of how modern receivers confront the unacceptable in Homer (compare Walcott and Oswald in the next section).

The second significant aspect of Logue's work is the critical debate it has provoked on the interpretation of Homer and on Homer's lasting effect as a cultural icon. Logue has been variously described as a near genius (by George Steiner) and as a vulgar sensationalist (by Bernard Knox). Both judgments implicitly pay tribute to the power of Logue's poetry. He has not only challenged established norms in Homer 'translation' and adaptation but also in interpretation. He has brought to the surface aspects of Homer which have

[13] For examination of the paradoxes in this apparent polarity, see Underwood (1998) ch. 6, and for discussion of the conventions and changes in the evaluative criteria applied to translations of classical texts, see Hardwick (2000b) ch. 1.

[14] Grievous bodily harm (GBH) is a term used as a charge in the British criminal justice system.

[15] These aspects are discussed further in Hardwick (2000b) ch. 3.

sometimes been marginalised, or worse have been given a kind of respectability and authority by the poetic force of other parts of the poem. Yet he also seems obsessed with violence. The only way to come to a judgment about these issues is to read Homer and to read Logue.

Homer on the stage

Transposition across genres is a major feature of modern receptions. Some commentators have identified Homer as the creator of drama before theatre was invented.[16] Exploration of Homer's dramatic potential was one aspect of his importance for the Athenian tragedians in the fifth century BCE (along with the creative refiguration of figures from epic and mythology). Dramatisations of Homer have resituated the triangular relationship between Homer, classical drama and modern appropriations and two from the late twentieth century provide particularly acute contrasts in the selection and representation of figures and episodes from Homer. They also demonstrate that Homer can no longer be regarded as a pillar of any one cultural tradition.

Peter Oswald's verse translation of parts of Homer's *Odyssey* was performed as a play by the Gate Theatre Company in 1999.[17] It was premièred as *The Odyssey* at Chipping Norton Theatre, Oxfordshire, on 20 September 1999, directed by Martin Wylde and designed by Roger Butlin. The play transferred to the Gate Theatre, London, on 20 October 1999 and subsequently toured in the UK. Neither the author nor the director was a classicist and they consulted a number of translations, both literal and free before agreeing to take Richmond Lattimore's translation as the basis for the adaptation.[18] The programme notes for the production described Homer's epic as 'the most famous life journey in western culture'. The version focused on Odysseus' return to Ithaca and emphasised the self-discovery that accompanied his re-integration into his homeland. According to Martin Wylde, the director, 'the power of the sea and the fantastic journey was a metaphor for the psychological journey Odysseus undergoes on his return . . . In rehearsals we looked a great deal at post-traumatic stress disorder; how this expresses itself and can be come to terms with'.[19] The relationships between the sea

[16] For example, Rieu (1950) in the introduction to his translation of Homer's *Iliad* (Rieu (1966) xiii).

[17] Published text Oswald (1999).

[18] Source: Martin Wylde (director), interview November 1999 for The Open University Research Project on The Reception of the Texts and Images of Ancient Greece in Late-Twentieth-Century Drama and Poetry.

[19] Source: Martin Wylde (director), see n. 18 above.

and Odysseus' psychological trauma were brought together in the design and staging of the production, which opened with Odysseus lying as if dead on the seashore. The actors remained on stage all the time when not directly participating in the action. Some functioned as a Chorus, wearing half-masks. They expressed 'the voices inside Odysseus' head; the dead from his past that haunted him' (Wylde). The addition of a Chorus helped the production to communicate some aspects of the complex time-schemes in Homer, including flashbacks, narrative loops and echoes of past experience.

The production gained from the close integration of the set and lighting design and the spoken text, which was verbally dense, had a strong rhythm which drove the action forward while leaving room for delicate and allusive half-rhymes. It assumed an audience sensitive to notions of psychological suffering and trauma and one focused on the experience of a single individual rather than that of a society. Odysseus' re-establishment as head of the household was largely expressed in terms of the healing of his mind. In the recognition scene with Penelope he responded when at last she spoke his name –

So often in the past it would have been
death to have heard my name.
Now it is life . . . And so I cast off No One
And watch him sink into the deepening
Of the sea's eye. And now I stand unguarded.
Loved and exposed, as you remember me.
(Scene 9, p. 61)

However, the impact of the homecoming was lessened because of the diminution of the role of Penelope. She had no loom, no *kleos* of her own and so her banishment to the upper room presented no reversal of situation (surprising for a production which was in many ways sensitive to gendered double standards). This, together with the fact that the killing of the suitors was represented by percussion and darkness followed by Telemachus' report of their death and that the killing of the maids and the fumigation of the polluted house were totally omitted, meant that the audience was not challenged by a clash between Homeric and modern social and moral values.[20]

Exploration of the psychological trauma of Odysseus was also a factor in the major stage production of Homer, Derek Walcott's *The Odyssey: A Stage*

[20] For discussion of the authorial and narrative types of audience involvement and the values of this production see Hardwick (2000b) ch. 7. The production is documented on the database of the Open University Reception of Classical Texts Research Project at *http://www2.open.ac.uk/ClassicalStudies/GreekPlays*.

Version.[21] The play was first performed by the Royal Shakespeare Company at The Other Place, Stratford-upon-Avon, on 2 July 1992, directed by Gregory Doran and designed by Michael Pavelka. It subsequently transferred to The Pit, Barbican, London, on 22 June 1993.[22] The play was also staged in Denmark at the Aarhus Theater Scala from 23 September – 5 November 1994 as *Odysseen af Derek Walcott efter Homer*, translated into Danish by Bo Green Jensen and directed by Hans Rosenquist. It had a dramatised reading in Port of Spain by the Trinidad Theatre Workshop (with which Walcott had long-standing connections during his career as dramatist and director) and was read in New York at the Young Men's Hebrew Association. It was also performed in Washington D.C. from 30 September – 6 November at the Arena stage, directed by Douglas Wager, where it was criticised by reviewers for its spectacular stage effects which were thought to detract from the words.[23] The paradox reveals a tension between Walcott's repeated insistence on the remobilisation of poetry in modern drama[24] and his equal insistence on the vitality and physicality of theatre and its relationship to Caribbean art forms such as Carnival (see Plate 9). It has been his wish to perform the play on a Caribbean beach but as yet this has not taken place.[25]

Walcott's stage version differed from that of Oswald in three important regards. First, there was a strong narrative voice presented by the blind blues singer Billy Blue (see Plate 10). Just as the Homeric bard Demodocus sang the adventures of heroes within the *Odyssey* so Billy Blue was the symbol of the relationship between diaspora and artistic invention; the point was explicitly made that 'The sea speaks the same language round the world's shores' (Act II, Scene iv, p. 122). Billy Blue represented both the travelling bard of ancient Greece and the shaping voice of twentieth-century black consciousness, carrying the memory of the past, alluding to slavery and diaspora but also creating its own language and resonances, 'someone who contains a history of the race . . . someone who sings ballads, the preserves of the cultural

[21] Published text Walcott (1993b).

[22] Documentation of the production is included on the Database of the Open University Reception of Classical Texts Research Project at *http://www2.open.ac.uk/ClassicalStudies/GreekPlays*.

[23] For discussion of the background to these productions and their relationships to other aspects of Walcott's work, see King (2000) ch. 31.

[24] Notably in the Poetry Book Society Ronald Duncan Lecture, London 1990.

[25] Walcott quoted in Burnett (1992). A one-man *Odyssey* was, however, performed on Pittenweem Beach in Fife by John Taylor in August 2000 as part of the Pittenweem Arts Festival, having transferred from the Crawford Arts Centre in St Andrews. See Taylor (2003).

9. Circe's Carnival scene with the banquet of the pigs, *The Odyssey: A Stage Version* (Royal Shakespeare Company, 1992)

memory'.[26] Thus the narrative of the poem vocalised interplay between past and present and between cultural traditions.

Second, Walcott's play, in keeping fairly close to the outline of events in the *Odyssey*, invited comparison between Homeric episodes and modern equivalences.[27] This presented some problems in the rehearsal process, notably in the treatment of the Cyclops episode. The Cyclops episode is a turning point in both Homer's *Odyssey* and Walcott's. In IX.105–566 the poet develops a structure of polarities in which a received folk-tale is reworked in a context of self-conscious Hellenism that sets out cultural, social and moral boundaries between the way of life of the Cyclopes and the Greeks. In Walcott, too, the assumed experience and ideology of the audience are incorporated

[26] Derek Walcott in an interview with Lorna Hardwick excerpted in Video II, 'Truth imagination and value', in *Homer Poetry and Society*, Milton Keynes, BBC/Open University Production, 1992. The role of Billy Blue has also been likened to that of an Egyptian praise singer. Burnett (2001) 281 discusses the theme of Egyptian wisdom in the play.

[27] Some episodes were omitted (e.g. the Oxen of the Sun) and others such as the Lotus Eaters referred to only briefly. Calypso was absorbed into the figure of Circe (see Plate 9).

10. Blind Billy Blue, the jazz-playing bard, *The Odyssey: A Stage Version* (Royal Shakespeare Company, 1992)

in the play. The Cyclops is presented as an Orwellian tyrant, characterised by the Eye, who reduces people to things and consumes them. In the early drafts of the script the Eye was an Orwellian style television spying on people's movements. In the RSC Stratford-upon-Avon production the Eye was a periscope-like attachment to the grotesque figure of the Cyclops. Links between ancient and modern spheres of reference were pointed up in the wordplay of the Martial Chorus

> To Die for the Eye is best, it's the greatest joy
> *Dulce et decorum est pro patria mori*
> There is no I after the eye, no more history
> (Act I, Scene vii, p. 60)

Other resonances were redolent of Eastern Europe and the episode was elaborated to include allusions to the Ceaucescu regime in Romania and the junta of the Greek colonels.[28] The director of the production, Gregory Doran, thought that these contemporary political allusions were already outdated (since the Berlin Wall has been demolished) and that the analogy between the Cyclops and the police state of Orwell's novel *1984* (1949) was overdone. He did, however, note that the symbol of the Iraqi secret service was a giant's eye. The disagreement showed how a translation to the stage can be just as vulnerable as a translation to the page in the danger it runs that apparently vibrant contemporary allusions can actually date very quickly.[29]

The third significant contrast in the cultural orientation and construction of correspondences in the Walcott and Oswald versions was the aftermath of Odysseus' homecoming – the slaughter of the suitors, hanging of the maids and fumigation of the house. In Oswald the victory over the situation was represented by a *coup de théâtre* and the rest omitted. In Walcott, the role of Penelope became decisive at this point (in contrast to Homer). She actually prevented the hanging of the maid and accused Odysseus of turning the house into an abattoir (Act II, Scene vi, p. 153).[30]

The reasons for Walcott's radical change were complex. He did not want Penelope to behave as though she were 'a sort of marble statue' although he asserted, 'it's not because of feminism and all that stuff'.[31] However, he did want the play to recognise that Penelope had to have some say in the process of her re-domestication. It was also significant that the maid, Melantho, was played by a black actress and the role doubled with Nausicaa. The

[28] For discussion see Hardwick (1997).

[29] For documentation of the history of the production of various disagreements between Walcott and Doran see King (2000) ch. 20 esp. 534–6.

[30] The Homeric hanging of the abused serving-women has attained the status of a topos in twentieth-century feminist consciousness; see Hardwick (2000b) ch. 7, 120–5 for discussion of the significance of Walcott's staging of 'Penelope's wrath' in comparison with the treatments of the episode by Peter Reading, Michael Longley and Atwood (1987).

[31] Source: Interview, 1992 (n. 26 above). Marble statues were a pervasive image in the play representing both Penelope and ancient culture as passive objects of material value only.

text made explicit the corruption of innocence. Walcott's other reasons for changing the episode were the impact of a *performed* (rather than a recited) hanging and concern for the image of his hero. Just as it was plausible in Homer for Penelope to retire to the upper room (XXI.350–8) and for the maids to be hung (XXII.446–72), so it was plausible in Walcott's version for Penelope to insist and Odysseus to agree that there should be no hanging. Throughout the play the audience had been implicitly asked to authenticate a complex interaction of commonalities and differences between Homer and modern culture – in the figure of the Blues singer, in the representation of the Cyclops as a totalitarian monster. Now they had to authenticate correspondences between Penelope-of-the-loom as an intelligent woman of *kleos* and the assertion of female humanitarianism. Just as the poet of the *Odyssey* had to observe cultural norms and reposition Penelope back in the upper chamber, so the translation from epic to drama and from *koine* Mediterranean culture to Atlantic Caribbean, created a new cultural site with norms to be observed. Thus Walcott's play provided a radical challenge to traditional Westernised expectations of Homer and also recognised that the changed cultural horizons of modern audiences required not just a politics but also an aesthetics of plausibility in Homeric reception.

Poetic refigurations of Homer

Walcott's long poem *Omeros* is somewhat paradoxical in Homer reception since it is both part of the tradition of classical poetry in English and also breaks radically with its main concerns.[32] Walcott has denied both that the poem is, in the strict sense, an epic and also that it involves direct parallels with the *Iliad* or the *Odyssey*.[33] However, in its scope and structure the poem could be described as an epic. It is constructed round interlocking layers of meaning; it is permeated with allusions to Homer, Virgil and Dante and the rhyme scheme resembles the *terza rima* used by Dante in *The Divine Comedy*. The most important implications for Homer reception are Walcott's creative adaptation of Homeric poetic techniques, especially his use of the simile (both the short simile and the structural) and his adaptation of the paradigmatic episode. Also significant are his transplantation of classical names and allusions into a Caribbean context in a way that frees Homer from narrow association with Western European cultural traditions and allows

32 Walcott (1990).

33 Source: Interviews in the *New York Times*, 9 October 1990, and *Poetry Please*, BBC Radio 4, 20 October 1990.

fresh encounter with a decolonised culture, which uses a variety of linguistic idioms, including Creole.

Walcott's use of the simile is the main mechanism for transplantation into different geographical, cultural and political contexts and especially for pointing up double-edged references. Names, relationships and situations familiar from Homer also bring with them reminders of enforced diaspora and a plantation culture which replaced the African names of its slaves with classical ones. Helen, a beautiful waitress, is not only the 'cause' of a quarrel between the fishermen Achille and Hektor but also the prize for which the athletes compete in the informal games of Book 1.VI. 1 (p. 73). And in the same manner, empires contended for the islands of the Caribbean, where Walcott's own island of St Lucia was known as the Helen of the Caribbean.

Another embedded simile is the wound on the leg of Walcott's character Philoctete. In the *Iliad* (2.718–23) Philoctetes' wound is caused by the bite of the water snake. Philoctete's wound is caused by a rusty anchor. In *Omeros*, as in Seamus Heaney's play *The Cure at Troy*, the wound becomes a metaphor for the anguished history and strife of a community.[34] The anchor which is the source of Philoctete's wound is left by the ships of conquerors and slavers, its rust spreading infection at a touch. The wound also represents the pain and alienation from the community that Philoctete shares with the narrator, the anonymous 'I' of the poem. The narrator's 'cure' is activated at two levels, the first being his recovery from a love affair with Circe, who nearly deluded him into thinking that he was a pig. The episode is, like Odysseus' sojourn in *Odyssey* X, a part of his progress towards self-awareness. The narrator comes to see that History in the imperialist form taught to the islanders was like Circe in that it charmed them into accepting oppression and exploitation.[35]

Thus Homeric echoes have a major shaping role in Walcott's exploration of affliction, its causes and its cures. He uses Homer and receptions of Homer in later epic to intensify critical perceptions of the past and yet to proclaim the need in the present to be liberated from the past. A key example is the *katabasis* sequence, modelled on the descents to the Underworld in the *Odyssey* and the *Aeneid*. In epic convention a visitor to the Underworld is guided into an examination of the past and through this achieves wisdom for the present and the future. In *Omeros* Book 3.XXV–XXVIII Walcott adapts this paradigm when Achille, suffering from sun-stroke, makes a metaphorical

[34] Published text Heaney (1990).

[35] For detailed discussion of Walcott's use of the simile in *Omeros*, see Hardwick (2000b) ch. 6, 'Walcott's Philoctete: imaging the post-colonial condition'; for anti-imperialist associations of Walcott's work see Ramazani (1997), Terada (1992) and Hardwick (2004).

journey back to his African roots, to the village of his ancestors, where his 'father' has forgotten the name he gave him (just as Anticleia did not recognise her son in *Odyssey* XI). Achille also witnesses the abduction of his ancestors by slave raiders and knows what their future holds. His reaction parallels the frenzy of Achilles in *Iliad* 21 after the death of Patroclus but his rescue attempt is ended when he is caught by the heel 'in a cord of thorned vine'.

The rest of the episode relates more to Dante than directly to Homer in its presentation of the Middle Passage as a purgatory of suffering. 'But they crossed, they survived. There is the epical splendour' (Book 3.XXVIII. 1, p. 149). Nostalgia for the past is replaced by the vitality of the present and for a future which contains and is informed by the past but is not dominated by it. In this way, new epic is built from the fragments and shards of ancient epic.[36] The fragments offer the opportunity for new creations. And, so far as Walcott's work is concerned, the Homeric poems had to be fragments, diasporic texts removed from *their* roots, in order for this refiguration to take place.

Michael Longley has made lyric, not epic, a major medium for Homer reception. Longley, who was born in Belfast, read classics at Trinity College Dublin and in his work uses Homer not simply as a cultural referent but as an integral voice in dialogue between past and present, friend and enemy, public and private. Longley's reflection on the continuing poetic presence of Homer is encapsulated in the short poem 'Homer's Octopus' in which poetry is

Like Homer's octopus
Yanked out of its hidey-hole, suckers
Full of tiny stones, except that the stones
Are precious stones or semi-precious stones[37]

These suckers of Homer's octopus fulfil two main functions in Longley's poetry. First, they are carriers of images and situations – simple and compelling, focusing the reader's attention on the details of form. Second, the 'stones' that they bring are used to trigger recognition of affinities between ancient and modern and to illuminate both. Yet, as the last line of the octopus poem suggests, Longley's poetic technique also undermines easy generalisations and eschews naive parallelism.

Another feature of his approach to Homer is the use of translation, often close. This is particularly striking in 'The Horses'. This poem of eleven lines

36 See further Walcott (1993a).

37 Longley (1995) 45; cf. *Od.* V.432–5.

responds to an implied question concerning a contemporary debate about setting up a memorial

For all the horses butchered on the battlefield,
Shell-shocked, tripping up over their own intestines,
Drowning in the mud

The analogy between the horses and the soldiers of the First World War is clear.[38] Longley then inverts chronology by suggesting that 'the best war memorial is in Homer', recalling the mourning of Patroclus' immortal horses in *Iliad* 17.423–45 and using this to turn the focus to the death of the human. The poem ends with the direct inclusion of lines that follow closely the prose translation of E.V. Rieu.[39] The horses are

Immovable as a tombstone . . .
Because they are still in mourning for Patroclus
Their charioteer, their shiny manes bedraggled
Under the yoke pads on either side of the yoke.[40]

The poem reveals many aspects of Longley's reception technique – selection of a potent image, reversal of expected similes and analogies, inversion of chronology, use of implied questions, a closure in an apparently minor key.

Much of Longley's response to Homer is based on the *Odyssey*, focusing on the themes of homecoming and social and personal relationships. Early poems such as 'Circe' and 'Nausicaa'[41] relate these figures to the rhythms and idioms associated with the sea but in the later volume *Gorse Fires*[42] the emphasis moves to the interaction between Homeric episodes and the experience of the poet, expressed through a contemplative narrative voice. These poems explore different facets of Homeric recognition scenes. In 'Eurycleia' the episode from *Odyssey* XIX (361–475) is described in lines which follow closely those of Homer (lines 388–91)

But Odysseus shifted out of the firelight, afraid
She might notice his scar, the key to his identity
A wound a boar inflicted years back

[38] The suffering of soldiers in and after war is a recurrent theme in Longley's work. See 'Wounds', which juxtaposes incidents in the slaughter of the Ulster Division on the Somme with incidents in the contemporary slaughter in the North of Ireland (in Longley (1973)) and 'A poppy' which relates the death of an Ulster soldier to *Iliad* 8.306–8, 'An image in Homer picks out the individual | Tommy and the dough boy in his doughboy helmet' (Longley (1998)).

[39] Rieu (1950), (1966).

[40] *Times Literary Supplement* (21 January 2000); Longley (2000) 29.

[41] Longley (1991b) 32 and 33.

[42] Longley (1991b).

The narrative voice seeds the reference to identity, which is developed in the second part of the poem. The poet likens himself to Odysseus, falling in love with the wrong woman who alone remembers the dense undergrowth

> Where in a compost of dead leaves the boar conceals
> Its bristling spine and fire-red eyes and white tusks.

The implication is that the boar is still menacing. Although the origins of the incident are forgotten, it has permanently marked the identity of the speaker. The lines have been taken to refer to the scars of conflict in the North of Ireland – 'this Northern Irish poet adverts to the ambiguities and violence of Odysseus' homecoming as an "allegory" of the Belfast condition'.[43] However, as always with Longley the analogy has many layers and brings associations of loss of memory of the origins of the scar (leaving a hint of shame and regret) and of the complexity of human experience.

In the same volume, two companion pieces 'Anticleia' and 'Laertes' explore a recognition scene between parent and child. 'Laertes' is based on the encounter between Odysseus and his father in *Odyssey* XXIV, showing how recognition comes not through explanation or revelation of Odysseus' scar (omitted by Longley) but through the asking of questions which awaken memory.

Thus Longley uses the Homeric recognition scenes as sites for the investigation of the human situation and as triggers for exploration of resonances with contemporary public and private experience. This involves a concept of recognition which challenges the reader to make a leap of imagination rather than simply to accept what is told.

In Longley's subsequent collection *The Ghost Orchid*, he explores the darker side of Homer by focusing on the *Iliad*.[44] In *Gorse Fires* he had already addressed the issue of Homeric violence in 'The butchers' in which readers' revulsion at the events surrounding Odysseus' homecoming is built up by a graphic account. That poem contains a typical Longley reversed simile in which Hermes 'like a clergyman waves a supernatural baton'. In 'The helmet' he recreates a view of the scene in which Hector plays with his son Astyanax (6.466 ff.). The 'wean' is terrified by Hector's bronze armour and the horse-hair crest on the helmet. Everyone laughs as Hector takes off his helmet to cradle the child. The scene of domestic bliss is then dissolved by the bitterly laconic closing line, when Hector

> Prayed that his son might grow up bloodier than him.
> (p. 38)

43 Editorial comment in Steiner (1996) 337.

44 Longley (1995).

This dark gloss on the Homeric values which the *Iliad* makes explicit in the concept of the son's emulation of the father picks up the line at 6.481 when Hector hopes that his son will one day 'bring home the blooded spoils and delight the heart of his mother' (in Lattimore's translation). Longley's closure subverts the mood of domesticity built up in the preceding lines of his poem and is an important aspect of his poetics of reception. Together with his use of the recognition scene (*anagnorisis*), this reversal of the reader's expectation (*peripeteia*) is a telling dramatic technique, transplanted into lyric and providing, together with the reverse simile and disruption of timescale, an experience for the readers which unsettles any sense of ease in the impact of Homeric parallels. The effect is intensified in what is perhaps Longley's best-known Homeric reception, 'Ceasefire' (*The Ghost Orchid* 39). The poem draws on the episode in *Iliad* 24 in which Priam journeys to the Greek camp to supplicate Achilles for the return of the body of Hector. Longley follows the Homeric chronology closely with one notable exception. He describes Achilles' response to Priam and the meal of mutual reconciliation but the poem ends rather than begins with a close translation of Homer's description of Priam's initial action:

> I get down on my knees and do what must be done
> And kiss Achilles' hand, the killer of my son.

The rhyme scheme emphasises the self-contained nature of this action. It is not assimilated into the behaviour pattern and attitudes set out in the earlier lines of the poem and as the title of the poem emphasises, the whole episode only marked an intermission in a long and cruel war. Homer's and Longley's audiences know that the war will resume and that Achilles and Priam are to die. The resonances for the modern equivalent, the truce that had been negotiated in the Troubles in the North of Ireland, remain dark.[45]

It is Longley's response to Homer which provides crucial points of insight, tension and sometimes reversal in the contemporary resonances of his poetry. His selection of episodes, his unexpected closures, his reworked timescales and his use of very close translation are all factors in the centrality of *anagnorisis* and *peripeteia* in his receptions. Like his contemporary and friend Seamus Heaney, Longley explores through reception of classical texts the relationships not just between past and present, public and private, but also between the conflicting demands of Irish cultural politics.[46]

[45] For more detailed discussion of reception of Homeric poetics and values in poetry concerned with modern wars, see Hardwick (2000b) ch. 3.

[46] Heaney's classical work is not considered here as it is more Latinate and Virgilian than Homeric in its emphasis and his play *The Cure at Troy* (1990) derives more closely from

My final question is whether, given the very recent creation of the Homer receptions discussed in this chapter, it is possible to draw any provisional conclusions about general trends or cultural shifts. On the basis of the evidence discussed here it is possible to point to two main developments:

(1) Homer has been uncoupled from a position at the centre of western cultural hegemony (this is also true to a high degree of Greek drama). The reasons for this are two-fold. First, reception studies have enabled more nuanced distinctions to be made between the ancient texts and values and the forms and contexts in which they have subsequently been appropriated. Second, the most important modern poets and dramatists refiguring classical material in English draw on more than one cultural tradition (Harrison, Heaney, Hughes, Lochhead, Longley, Walcott). All make extensive use of classical referents and their adaptations are therefore never univocal but create a forum for critical energy and insight.
(2) Since Homer is now regarded less as a cultural model and more as a source of rich diversity in poetry and experience, the aspects of the *Iliad* and the *Odyssey* which have been selected for exploration and refiguration provide a significant insight into contemporary concerns. The relationship between classical knowledge and creative reception is also diverse. In particular, the way in which some aspects of Homer have been made more prominent and others have been marginalised, rejected or changed provides an often explicit commentary on both contemporary and ancient social and aesthetic values. Homeric paradigms are a vehicle for translation into other times and cultures but the ways in which they are adapted or refined are also indicators of cultural transitions. These receptions are not reverent. They provide a critical perspective not just on contemporary society but also on the values represented in Homer.

Taken together, these points suggest that Homer is and will continue to be a catalyst but not a model in the creation of new work in poetry and drama[47].

FURTHER READING

The best way to follow up the issues raised in this chapter is to read some of the translations and adaptations based on Homer and compare them with the Homeric episodes and poetics on which they draw. A good starting point is the collection of

Sophocles' tragedy than from Homer. See Hardwick (2000b) ch. 5. I hope to address Heaney's use of classical referents in a forthcoming article 'Heaney's classical ground'.

47 Special thanks for help and constructive criticism to Sonja Cameron, David Fitzpatrick, Carol Gillespie, Naoko Yamagata.

Steiner (1996). For individual authors, try Cook (2001), Logue (1999) and (2003), Longley (1991a), (1995) and (1998); Oswald (1999), Walcott (1990) and (1993b). There is further discussion of some of these modern texts in Lorna Hardwick (2000) and (2003). Homeric poetry in performance is increasingly on the programme at book and literary festivals. For discussion of the epic and oral tradition see Taplin (1992) and for an introduction to influential Homeric translations Underwood (1998).

22

GEORGE STEINER

Homer in English translation

Our *Iliad* and *Odyssey* begin as acts of translation. The background to the *Iliad* is that of possibly archaic orality. The transfer into writing implies translation in both the generic and the more technical sense. The world of the rhapsode and the bard, of the singer of ancient tales, many-layered, open to personal and local variations, is not that of the writer. The relation of text to audience – literally to the listener – is altogether different from that of writer to reader. Perforce, we have no knowledge of the epic of Troy, of the heroic and clan-sagas which went into its assemblage, prior to 'Homer'. What is manifest, however, is the process of linguistic adjustment and semantic stylisation. The idiom of the *Iliad* as we know it is a composite artifice in which vestiges of archaic forms and dialects still surface. The redactor has translated, not always with absolute confidence or understanding, from diverse lexical–grammatical materials. Here also there is translation.

Persistently and, at moments, critically, the *Odyssey* draws on its predecessor. It presumes knowledge of the *Iliad*. Though the point cannot be proved, it would seem that the *Odyssey*, the earliest and perhaps greatest of novels in the Western legacy, was set down in writing by a master's hand. The complex sensibility at work – consider only the manifold perspectives, the haunting *mise en abîme* of the Demodocus episodes in Book VIII – almost necessitates a unifying vision and script. 'Translation' in this instance is a question of moral and aesthetic revaluation, of a transfer into what is already, in some respects, 'modernity'. There is a more than playful paradox to Borges' finding that the *Odyssey* comes after Joyce's *Ulysses*.

We do not know precisely how or when the Homeric epics, now in their canonic form, reached Rome. The process must have been gradual and fragmentary. What we do have is an *Ilias Latina* (perhaps the last of numerous translations) which abridges its Homeric source to 1,070 hexameters. Long ascribed to Silius Italicus, it is now thought by a number of scholars to be the work of one Baebius Italicus composed, very possibly, during the reign of Nero. Whatever their authorship or precise date, the lines

Iram pande mihi Pelidae, Diva, superbi,
Tristia quae miseris iniecit funera Grais
Atque animas fortes heroum tradidit Orco
Latrantumque dedit rostris volumcrumque trahendos
Illorum exsangues, inhumatis ossibus, artus.

signal the beginning of a long and rich story. From imperial Latin, Homer will branch out into a prodigality of tongues.

Of all literary works, excluding the Bible from this rubric, the *Iliad* and the *Odyssey* are the most frequently translated. In several European languages, such translations are classics in their own right. We need only consider Johann Heinrich Voss's German version, Pope's *Iliad* or, to give a modern example, Philippe Jaccottet's *L'Odyssée* of 1982. Complete or selective renderings of the two epics, sometimes based on intermediate translations where direct access to the Greek is lacking, run into the hundreds. No listing so far available is anywhere near exhaustive. In continental Europe, in the Anglo-American sphere, new 'Homers' appear almost annually.

Homer's entrance into European awareness forms an intricate chapter, not all of which is altogether clear. The *Iliad* and *Odyssey* were, so far as we have evidence, totally unknown to Western Europe in the Middle Ages. Yet the 'matter of Troy' was, next to the meteoric saga of Alexander the Great, the most popular of topics for romances founded on classical sources. The Troy-legend derived from two brief prose narratives assigned to Dictys Cretensis of the fourth century AD and Dares the Phrygian of the sixth. From this meagre font, Benoît de Sainte-More distilled a Norman-French *Roman de Troie* running to thirty thousand verses (*c.* 1155–60).

A *Seege of Troye* of some two thousand lines was probably composed in the north-east midlands at the start of the fourteenth century. In about 1400, a cleric issued the *Laud Troy Book* comprising some eighteen thousand verses of narrative. The manuscript of Lydgate's *Troy Book*, adapted from the Latin prose of Guido della Colonna, dates from 1412 to 1420 and incorporates what seems to have been a previous Scottish version. 'Gestes' of the destruction of Troy and of Odysseus' homecoming and death (usually at the hands of his son Telegonus) are numerous throughout medieval vernacular literatures in both verse and prose. They do not, to be sure, constitute 'translations' of Homer in any substantive sense. But a concept of Homer's primordial stature and of certain motifs in his work became disseminated, often in ways which are still opaque to us, across European culture.

A matchless articulation of this *translatio* is to be found in Dante. Not only does Dante place Homer among the begetters and sovereigns of poetry – *quegli è Omero poeta sovrano* – but his own account of Odysseus' last and fatal voyage (*Inferno* XXVI) captures elements of the *Odyssey* at so central a level as to rival (surpass?) their ancient precedent. If indeed he knew nothing of the Greek original, Dante's clairvoyant genius intuited, discerned the Homeric presence in the *Aeneid*. It is Virgil's Homer which guides his insight. We, in turn, are heirs to this refraction, to an *Iliad* and *Odyssey* mirrored in Augustan Latin and a *vulgaris eloquentia*.

The engagement with Homer of the English languages and of Anglo-American sensibilities is unparalleled. There is since the late sixteenth century hardly a generation in the English-speaking world which has not produced its 'Homers'. This production spans virtually every genre and theory of literature. It comprises not only an unbroken sequence of complete or partial translations dating back to the 1560s, but every conceivable mode of imitation, adaptation, parody and transference into drama, fiction and even musical forms both grave and humorous. Again, no inventory can hope to be complete. The reasons for this incessant abundance of the Homeric cannot be readily summarised. Deep impulses and mechanisms of identification, at once individual and collective, are operative (Shelley's 'We are all Greeks'). That Caxton's translation from the French of a *Recuyell of the Historyes of Troy*, printed in Bruges in 1474 or 1475, should be the very first printed book in English is a wholly emblematic fact. As is the publication, in the United Kingdom and the United States, of a dozen new versions of the *Iliad* and the *Odyssey* since the end of the Second World War.

Competent access to Homeric Greek came only very slowly. Early English 'Homers' derive from Latin, French and Italian intermediaries, such as Boccaccio. Indeed, certain striking translations from the two epics have, to this day, been achieved by poets with no direct knowledge of Greek. No less than Ezra Pound's *Cathay*, Christopher Logue's readings of the *Iliad* pose the psychological enigma of brilliant formal and hermeneutic appropriations at second hand. 'Homer' enters English literature via two masterpieces of indirection. Chaucer's *Troylus and Criseyde*, patterned on Boccaccio and completed in *c.* 1385, strikes that high note of desolation and cruelty proper to the *Iliad* but conjoins it with a merriment (Pandarus) and sardonic realism peculiarly English. Shakespeare's possible acquaintance with Homer (via Arthur Halls' partial translation from the French, via Chapman's 1598 *Seuen Bookes of the Iliades*?) remains open to debate. Probably composed in late 1602, *Troilus and Cressida* is an unnerving masterpiece. The slaying of Hector in Scene viii of Act v –

> The dragon wing of night ore-spreads the earth
> And stickler-like the Armies separate –

is, together with Chaucer, the first of the imaginative metamorphoses which will incorporate the Homeric world into the marrow, as it were, of English (and via Henryson's 'Testament of Cresseid') Scottish poetic consciousness.

It is with Chapman's *Iliads* and *Odysses* of 1598 to 1615 that the long march of actual translation enters into force. This, famously, is the version at which Keats took an inspired if cursory look. Just how much ancient Greek could Chapman make out? We do not know. What counts are not only his own strengths as a poet and playwright, but his explicit resolve 'With Poesie to open Poesie'. At his best, Chapman hears and conveys the dark music of the original. The Beggar strings the great bow:

Then twang'd he up the string,
That as a Swallow in the aire doth sing
With no continu's tune, but (pausing still)
Twinkes out her scatter'd voice in accents shrill –
So sharp the string sung when he gave it touch.

It is Chapman, moreover, who will capture in a way representative of the Anglo-Saxon experience, the surge and toss of the great Homeric seas, those seascapes and tempests instinctive to Robert Fitzgerald as they are to Derek Walcott:

The billowes' rage was; which scap't backe, so fast
The rocke repulst it, that it reft his hold,
Sucking him from it, and farre back he rould.

Dryden's temper was thoroughly Latinate and Virgilian. He strove for *civilitas* and the poise of reason. Hence his gloss on the *Iliad*'s 'moral': to urge concord among confederate states when 'engaged in a war with a mighty monarch'. Dryden purposed a version of the Homeric epic 'such as would have been composed by the original author were he alive now and writing in English'. All he was able to complete was a highly praised rendition of Book I in the *Fables Ancient and Modern* of 1700. The rest consists of fragments. Of these, Hector's adieu to Andromache, in which Dryden's sense of Virgilian pathos unfolds, comes close to magic:

I see, I see thee, in that fatal hour,
Subjected to the victor's cruel power;
Led hence a slave to some insulting sword,
Forlorn and trembling at a foreign lord;
A spectacle in Argos, at the loom,
Gracing with Trojan fights a Grecian room. . . .

where Dryden makes of Hector's prophetic sorrow a thoroughly Homeric anticipation of Penelope at her weaving.

A constellation of partial translations followed, including an excerpt from Book 24 showing a masterly, if somewhat unexpected, side of Congreve's powers. But all roads now led to Pope's 'Proposals for subscription' issued in 1713. The six volumes, the *Odyssey* being largely collaborative, were completed in 1720. It is a neglected truism that Pope's *Iliad* is and remains after Milton the foremost heroic epic in the language. To dismiss it, as did the Romantics, to ignore it as do the moderns, is to exhibit tone-deafness to the virtuosities and perceptions of a translator of the first order. The text itself, furthermore, is augmented by critical and philological commentaries characteristic of Pope's lasting contributions to poetics and the craft of interpretation.

Pope drew freely on his predecessors (including Chapman for whom he professed a certain lofty disdain). Dryden's fragments and the French of Mme Dacier were much in his mind. But Pope's 'Homer' is intensely his own. His epics are indispensable 'histories' of the ancient world whose historical, military and political verities are made undying art. This conception of 'the ultimate master of poetic invention' induces Pope to attenuate, even to elide what he judges to be gross or primitive in Homeric theology and in certain episodes of the war at Troy. In counterpart, Pope amplifies and elaborates on what he feels to be the pictorial elements in Homer's aesthetics, as well as on the morally sententious. Pope knew nothing of modern insights into the formulaic construction of Homer's narrative, but his resolve to generalise, to make typological much that might have seemed individual and idiosyncratic in the original does come near to being itself formulaic. This effect is reinforced by Pope's adherence to the heroic couplet, a form which both 'rounds' and sections into paragraphs. The varieties Pope elicits from this commanding format, the prodigality of local tonalities, repay close study.

The Preface is an arresting document. It evokes Homer's 'wild Paradise' – a tag which bridges the distance between Milton and Blake. Homer's creativity is that of 'a powerful Star, which in the Violence of its Course, drew all things within its *Vortex*'. Comparisons are invited with the sublime simplicities and concisions of Holy Scripture. Anticipating Matthew Arnold's celebrated programme for the translator, Pope aims to keep alive 'that Spirit and Fire' which are Homer's distinctive glory. Homer's was 'a Soul capable of ranging over the whole Creation with an intellectual View', where 'intellectual' is, in the early Enlightenment context, and with no possible reference to Vico, a challenging claim.

Only extensive quotation could provide a fair impression of Pope's *Iliad* and its annotations. I have, elsewhere, tried to give a representative sample (cf. *Homer in English* (1996)). Here, almost absurdly, a single extract must suffice. It comes from Book 11 and the near-encounter of Hector and Ajax:

> But partial *Jove*, espousing *Hector*'s Part,
> Shot heav'n-bred Horror thro the *Grecian*'s Heart;
> Confus'd, unnerv'd in *Hector*'s Presence grown,
> Amaz'd he stood, with Terrors not his own.
> O'er his broad Back his moony Shield he threw,
> And glaring round, by tardy steps withdrew.
> Thus the grim Lion his Retreat maintains,
> Beset with watchful Dogs, and shouting Swains,
> Repuls'd by Numbers from the nightly Stalls,
> Tho' Rage impells him, and tho' Hunger calls. . . .

There is utter mastery in the compaction of the third line as there is in 'with Terrors not his own' – a dissociation prepared for by 'Confus'd, unnerv'd'. And though difficult to analyse, there is a Virgilian Homer, so instrumental in Pope, in 'the nightly Stalls'.

Pope was acquainted with Thomas Hobbes' version of the *Iliad* and the *Odyssey*, the first instalment of which, Books IX–XII of the *Travels of Ulysses*, had appeared in 1673. Tradition has it that Hobbes turned to this task when embittered by the apparent failure of *Leviathan*. The sombre philosopher was no poet. His rendition of the piercing of the Cyclops' eye verges on the comical:

> But I myself erecting, with my hand
>   Twirled the bar about, with motion nimble,
> As joiners with a tring below do stand
>   To give a piercing motion with a wimble . . .

But Hobbes' compendious preface, with its uncompromising observations on Homeric politics and warfare, is well worth reading, as are the analytic summaries with which he precedes and characterises successive books. These contain aphorisms of Tacitean, if not Homeric, style.

Successive 'Homers' now come 'after Pope'. James Macpherson's *Iliad* of 1773 is unreadable but significant in its attempt to forge (perhaps the *mot juste*) an 'epic prose', Biblical and formulaic, in which to convey Homer's voice. T. E. Lawrence will proceed in Ossian's wake. William Cowper works deliberately *contra* Pope. He is persuaded that there are deep-lying analogies between the Homeric and the Miltonic visions of gods and men. He deplores Pope's persistent striving for sublimity, finding in many Homeric scenes the domesticity and minuteness of the Flemish painters. Cowper's own nightmares give poignancy to his understanding of Odysseus' longing. Whatever Circe's beauty, the wanderer thirsts for

> My home, and languish daily to return.
> But should some god amid the sable deep
> Dash me again into a wreck, my soul
> Shall bear *that* also; for, by practice taught,
> I have learn'd patience, having much endured
> By tempest and in battle both. Come then
> This evil also ! I am well prepared.

Issued in 1791, Cowper's Homer argues that the two epics are 'written always to the eye'. This is an original, if unconvincing, axiom possibly founded on Cowper's collaboration with Fuseli. Graphic representations and illustrations of the *Iliad* and the *Odyssey*, such as those of Flaxman, now enter the lineage of Homeric reception in Anglo-American culture.

Having experienced success with his *Tales from Shakespeare* of 1807, Charles Lamb, the year after, produced a prose re-telling of the adventures of Odysseus closely dependent on Chapman. A failure in its time, this oddity has been all but forgotten (the text is not easy to turn up). But Lamb is, at moments, himself, and his voice unmistakable: 'Then great Circe spake, and gave order, that there should be no more sadness among them. For as yet they fared like men that are exiles from their country, and if a gleam of mirth shot among them, it was suddenly quenched with the thought of their helpless and homeless condition.' A child could do worse than find his first *Odyssey* in Lamb's keeping.

The nineteenth century sharpened the dialectical tension between philology and poetics, between a scholarly and a literary ideal of translation. This tension is implicit in Bentley's notorious dismissal of Pope's *Iliad*, but becomes acute in the light of Friedrich August Wolf's *Prolegomena ad Homerum* of 1795 and the evolution of Indo-Germanic linguistics and text-criticism. An awareness of archaeological evidence, moreover, is entering its pre-modern phase. A proper understanding of the Homeric epics now solicits a scholarly awareness of the relevant problems of idiom, historical context and executive form. Such insight is only rarely accessible to the poet–translator, let alone to the amateur. Reciprocally, the Homeric scholar will either avoid translation altogether – why should he make use of it? – or provide learned paraphrase. The consequence will be a host of uneasy hybrids, of more or less philologically fraught interlinears which will be crowned by the *Iliad* of Lang, Leaf and Myers, indispensable to generations of school-boys and general readers. The inherent conflict is unresolved to this day.

This does not signify that poets and non-academic lovers of the classical world abstained from Homer. On the contrary. Keats' two great sonnets (1817–18) on 'deep-brow'd Homer' and his 'dolphin-coral' seas are among the stellar, if tangential responses in the language. Shelley's versions of the so-called *Homeric Hymns*, composed in 1818, represent the authority not only of a major poet but of an ardent and often acute practitioner of ancient Greek. Interestingly, Shelley's reading points back to the Neoplatonic tenor of certain Renaissance and baroque interpretations of Homer 'the sage' and even, perhaps, the custodian of esoteric, Orphic science. When the moon is down

> The beam-invested steeds whose necks on high
> Curve back, she drives to a remoter sky
> A western Crescent, borne impetuously.
> Then is made full the circle of her light. . . .

Having, in the 1832 collection of his poems, published two of the best-loved variations on themes from Homer, 'The Lotos-eaters' and 'Ulysses', Tennyson briefly tried his hand at actual translation. He chose Achilles at the trench (*Iliad* 18.202–31. 'Full-maned horses' recoil in terror, and charioteers are astounded

> To see the dread, unweariable fire
> That always o'er the great Peleion's head,
> Burn'd, for the bright-eyed goddess made it burn.

J. G. Lockhart's hexameter rendering of *Iliad* 24 was published in 1846. It exercised considerable influence. Numerous attempts to translate Homer into hexameters or syllabic or quantitative verse will ensue. William Maginn's *Homeric Ballads* of 1850, in which the epic singer is given the register of a blind Irish minstrel, mocked the new pedantries.

The extent of Victorian interest in matters Homeric can be gauged from William Gladstone's four tomes of studies on Homer and the age of Homer as well as from the general attention elicited by the debate between F. W. Newman and Matthew Arnold. Newman's *Iliad* appeared in 1856. It is couched in a 'more or less antiquated idiom' replete with echoes from Anglo-Saxon. The verse is alliterative:

> 'Achilles, image of the gods! thy proper sire remember,
> Who on the deadly steps of Eld far on, like me, is carried.
> And haply him the dwellers-round with many an outrage harry,
> Nor standeth any by his side to ward annoy and ruin.

The result is often close to illegibility. But Newman's concept is suggestive. He aims to communicate the archaic strangeness and remoteness of the original, '*the more foreign it may happen to be*'. This perspective and the reading of the *Iliad* as a bardic saga not wholly unrelated to *Beowulf*, will have its later adepts.

Arnold's devastating critique came in his celebrated lectures *On Translating Homer* (1861). These lectures retain their incisive authority. So do the criteria postulated by a great literary critic: 'eminent rapidity'; 'eminent plainness and directness in both vocabulary and syntax', 'eminent plainness in matter and ideas'; 'eminent nobility'. Would that Arnold's own samples of such a translation – he confessed to not being poetically qualified – demonstrated these admirable ideals: hearing the derision of her captors, Andromache will suffer grief redoubled

> At the want of a man like me, to save thee from bondage.
> But let me be dead, and the earth be mounded above me,
> Ere I hear thy cries, and thy captivity told of.

If Thomas Starling Northgate's dramatic blank verse and indiscriminate archaicism seems to follow on Newman, P. S. Worsley's sprightly *Odyssey* in Spenserian stanzas earned Arnold's praise.

James Inglis Cochrane's *Iliad* of 1867 fully adopts Arnold's preference for hexameters. At moments, the driven beat reminds one of Longfellow. North American versions now begin to matter. W. Cullen Bryant was a Boston brahmin, a scholar–poet and esteemed man of letters. His *Odyssey* was published in the United States in 1873. It shows Arnoldian 'rapidity' and a strength all its own. Penelope prays to Diana:

> I would that thou wouldst send into my heart
> A shaft to take my life, or that a storm
> Would seize and hurl me through the paths of air,
> And cast me into ocean's restless streams,
> As once a storm, descending, swept away
> The daughters born to Pandarus. . . .

That echo of Dante in the third line is finely judged.

The Butcher and Lang prose-translation of the *Odyssey* issued in 1879 was immensely influential. It continued in print across generations. Almost overlooked is the contentious programme on which it is built. The translators argue that the English of the Authorized Version 'seems as nearly analagous to the Epic Greek, as anything our tongue can offer'. In its way, this conviction echoed the suppositions expressed by the Cambridge divine Zachary

Bogan in his *Homerus Hebraizon* of 1658, a tract which may, by meandering means, have reached Joyce when he made Odysseus into Leopold Bloom. Bogan argues that Odysseus and the epic derive from Hebrew sources. Even today the Lang–Leaf–Myers *Iliad* of 1882 has not completely lost its appeal. It is the bridge into the modern period.

Limitations on space do not allow me anything but the most summary and selective look at the years between William Morris' part Tennysonian, part 'socialist' *Odyssey* of 1887 and the close of the millennium. The multiplicity of British and American 'Homers' is near to bewildering. It enlists many of the ranking poets, but also outsiders such as T. E. Lawrence and theoreticians of literature such as I. A. Richards. We find the Homeric epics rendered into verse, into prose and into diverse combinations of both (as in Robert Graves' *The Anger of Achilles, Homer's Iliad* of 1959). Some translators draw as near as they dare to the rigours of an interlinear format, abreast with the latest philological and text-critical findings. Others, such as Richmond Lattimore in the 1950s and 1960s are at once distinguished classicists and poets in their own right. Yet others exercise extreme freedom (licence?) in their interpretations and representations of Homer. This wealth of options is, throughout modernity, under pressure from the uses of Homeric material, of Homeric references by the masters, such as D. H. Lawrence, W. H. Auden and, supremely, Joyce. Texts such as Auden's 'Shield of Achilles', Ezra Pound's *Cantos* or Joyce's *Ulysses* greatly influence, be it subliminally, both readers and translators of the *Iliad* and the *Odyssey*. As, henceforth, will Derek Walcott's *Omeros*. What remains arresting, and not totally explicable, is the readiness of publishers to commission and print new 'Homers' on both sides of the Atlantic. Kitto follows immediately on Rieu, Robert Fitzgerald on Lattimore, Fagles on Fitzgerald, Mandelbaum on Fagles, Martin Hammond on Mandelbaum.

Fascinatingly, the focus has varied. The First World War brought a wave of involvement with the *Iliad*. The disaster at the Dardanelles could be construed all too readily in the light of the Trojan War. In turn, the global impact of Joyce's *Ulysses* together with the fate of the displaced, of the exiled, of the unhoused during and after the Second World War, redirected sensibility towards the *Odyssey*. The humane sorrows, the compassion in that text were felt to be in tune with a smitten age. Frequently, however, the translator will venture on and publish a complete 'Homer', even including the hymns.

In the preface to his pseudonymous translation of the *Odyssey* (1932), T. E. Lawrence finds Homer to have been ignorant of combat and 'very bookish, this house-bred man'. In contrast, also to all previous translators, Colonel Lawrence has 'hunted wild boars and watched wild lions, sailed the

Aegean (and sailed ships), bent bows, lived with pastoral peoples, woven textiles, built boats and killed many men'. These attainments, listed in a letter to Bruce Rogers who designed the handsome book, more than compensate, argues Lawrence, for any lacunae in his scholarship and knowledge of ancient Greek. Unfortunately, they do not quicken into life a cadenced prose largely indebted to Doughty's *Arabia Deserta* and often cribbed from George Herbert Palmer's version of 1920, itself conceived in the model of 'church chant or Wagner's recitative'. Lawrence does, however, make an influential proposal when he qualifies the *Odyssey* as 'the first novel of Europe'.

This is very clearly what E. V. Rieu had in mind when he produced his *Odyssey* in 1946 and his *Iliad* in 1950. Intended as 'easy reading for those who are unfamiliar with the Greek world', issued in Penguin format, Rieu's Homer was read by hundreds of thousands new to the two epics (revised, the *Odyssey* maintains its popularity). The prose is swift and plain. The spirit is indeed that of fiction giving not only the Sirens but what is enigmatic or lyric in the original 'a wide berth'. Legend has it that a good many grateful readers assumed E. V. Rieu to have been the author of the travails of Odysseus and begged him to *orthograph* their dog-eared copies accordingly.

H. D. F. Kitto followed suit, bringing to a 'prosaic' ideal his scholarly authority. But the poets riposted, affirming that any prose rendering of Homer is virtually a contradiction in terms. Robert Fitzgerald's *Odyssey* (1961) is a major feat of poetic insight and scruple. Time and again, the translation is in shaping dialogue with the original. In the Underworld, Odysseus has spoken to Achilles:

> Now other souls of mournful dead stood by,
> each with his troubled questioning, but one
> remained alone, apart: the son of Télamon,
> Aîas it was – the great shade burning still
> because I had won favour on the beachhead
> in rivalry over Akhilleus' arms.

Or consider Odysseus' prognostication of his fated end:

> Then death will drift upon me
> from seaward, mild as air, mild as your hand,
> in my well-tended weariness of age,
> contented folk around me on our island.
> He said all this must come.

Poet also speaks to poet, though in metaphrase rather than translation, when Walcott evokes Odysseus' galley:

On its tired shadow
the prow turns slowly, uncertain of its aim.
He peels his sunburnt skin in maps of grey parchment

which he scrolls absently between finger and thumb.
The crew stare like statues at that feigned detachment
whose heart, in its ribs, thuds like the galley-slaves' drum.

If 'translation' extends, as Roman Jakobson would have it, to 'transmutation', to the metamorphosis of an original text into other media, any survey of Homer's persistent presence would want to consider musical and operatic treatments, the stage, film, the radio-play, television and the comic book. Berlioz's *Les Troyens*, Tippett's *King Priam*, Dallapiccola's *Ulisse* are masterpieces of their own kind. As are graphic presentments of Homeric motifs in the paintings of Turner. Comic-book versions of the *Odyssey* have reached out to millions. The puppet-theatre and ballet have enlisted Homer and our repertoire of laughter would be poorer without Offenbach's Menelaus and *Belle Hélène*. Themes out of Homer, often quite specific, modulate into the space-wars and intergalactic voyages of science-fiction. Here also there is 'translation', and the catalogue would be interminable.

With the eclipse of the classics in our schooling, with the increasing relegation of any ease in Homeric Greek to the mandarin and specialised scholar, translation proper and its hybrid off-shoots must prevail. The vast majority of those who come to the *Iliad* and the *Odyssey* as 'when a new planet swims into their ken', will do so by courtesy of the translator. His task becomes ever more crucial and difficult. As even elementary references to and out of ancient mythology tend to become esoteric, the temptations of internalised explication and commentary grow drastic. The translator expands on the sovereign concision of the Homeric texts in order to explain, to clarify, to guide his otherwise bewildered readers. Much of recent translation is, against its better instincts, as it were, inflationary. Footnotes, such as Pope used with masterly largesse, discourage a twenty-first-century public. Set high on these stilts, the poetry tends to retreat. Robert Fagles' translations of both epics during the 1990s, popularised by their transfer to CD-ROM, show that compromise is still achievable. But the tension is unmistakable.

Like Pound and Robert Lowell before him, Christopher Logue wrestled with Homer lacking ancient Greek. His *Patrocleia* (1962), his *Pax* (1967) in imitation of the *Iliad* may, indeed, touch the limits of the inadmissible. Such is their wild freedom. I cannot but feel that 'Homer' would have thrilled to Logue's reading of Achilles' chariot as the hero leaves to avenge fallen Patroclus:

Soothing the perfect horses; watching his driver cinch,
shake out the reins, fold, lay them across the rail;
dapple and white the horses are, perfect they are,
sneezing to clear their cool black muzzles.
He mounts.
  The chariot's basket dips. The whip
fires in between the horses' ears,
and as in dreams or at Cape Kennedy they rise,
slowly it seems, their chests like royals, yet,
behind them in a double plume the sand curls up
a yellow canopy,
is barely dented by their flying hooves
and wheels that barely touch the world,
and the wind slams shut behind them.

Nor is it any scholar, however indispensable, and philologist or textual critic, however observant, who has come nearest to defining the force of Homer in our consciousness. It is Logue the poet when he tells of the light from Achilles' helmet 'screaming across three thousand years'.

So long as that light is to be heard, the translator has his humble but commanding task.

FURTHER READING

Apart from the fuller treatment in Steiner (1996), the reader may usefully consult Brower (1959), Steiner (1998), and Eco (2000).

DATELINE

This table gives a selection of significant dates in the background, composition, and reception of Homer's poems. Some dates, especially those BC, are necessarily approximate.

BC	
1500–1200	Age of the great Mycenaean Bronze Age palaces
1184	Traditional date of the fall of Troy
1000	Burials in the apsidal building at Lefkandi, Euboea
770	Earliest evidence of the Greek alphabet
730	'Nestor's cup'
700–675	Homer: *Iliad*, *Odyssey*
700–500	Epics of the *Cycle* composed
675–650	Hesiod: *Theogony, Works and Days*
610	Sappho of Mytilene active
530	Hipparchus, son of Peisistratus, said to have brought Homer's poems to Athens
525/4–456/5	Aeschylus of Athens
498–446	Pindar of Thebes' dated poems
496–406	Sophocles of Athens
485–406	Euripides of Athens
450–386	Aristophanes of Athens
429–347	Plato of Athens
335–22	Aristotle of Stagira and Athens, lectures on *Poetics*
284	Zenodotus of Ephesus first head of Alexandrian library
280–240	Heyday of Alexandrian literature: Callimachus of Cyrene, Theocritus of Cos, Apollonius of Rhodes
240–207	Lucius Livius Andronicus active; translates *Odyssey* into Latin
216–144	Aristarchus of Samothrace, greatest Homeric scholar of antiquity

169	Quintus Ennius, *Annals*
19	Virgil, *Aeneid*
AD	
50	'Longinus', *On the Sublime*
95	Quintilian, *Institutes of Oratory*
300	Heliodorus, *Ethiopian Story*
1475	William Caxton, *Recuyell of the Historyes of Troye*, first printed book in English
1488	First printed edition of Greek text of Homer
1598–1615	George Chapman's translations
1674	John Milton, *Paradise Lost*
1715	Alexander Pope's translation of the *Iliad*
1726	Alexander Pope's translation of the *Odyssey*
1774	Johann Wolfgang von Goethe, *The Sorrows of Young Werther*
1788	Publication of the scholia to Homer in MS 'A' of the *Iliad*
1795	Friedrich August Wolf, *Prolegomena ad Homerum*
1816	John Keats, 'On first looking into Chapman's Homer'
1824	Lord Byron, *Don Juan*
1861	Matthew Arnold, 'On translating Homer'
1869	Friedrich Nietzsche, 'Homer and classical scholarship'
1870	Heinrich Schliemann begins excavations at Hisarlık (Troy)
1919	T. S. Eliot, 'Tradition and the individual talent'
1922	James Joyce, *Ulysses*
1928	Milman Parry, *L'Épithète traditionnelle dans Homère*
1981	Christopher Logue, *War Music*
1990	Derek Walcott, *Omeros*
2001	Elizabeth Cook, *Achilles*

WORKS CITED

Adkins, A. W. (1960) *Merit and Responsibility. A Study in Greek Values*. Oxford

Albright, D. (2000) *Untwisting the Serpent: Modernism in Music, Literature and Other Arts*. Chicago

Alden, M. (2000) *Homer Beside Himself. Para-Narratives in the Iliad*. Oxford

Alexiou, M. (2002) *The Ritual Lament in Greek Tradition*, 2nd edn. Lanham, Md.

Allen, A. (1993) *The Fragments of Mimnermus*. Stuttgart

Allen, S. H. (1999) *Finding the Walls of Troy: Frank Calvert and Heinrich Schliemann at Hisarlik*. Berkeley and London

Allen, T. W. (1924) *Homer: The Origins and the Transmission*. Oxford

Alles, G. D. (1990) 'Wrath and persuasion: the *Iliad* and its contexts', *Journal of Religion* 70: 167–88

Andersen, Ø. (1990) 'The making of the past in the *Iliad*', *Harvard Studies in Classical Philology* 93: 25–45

(1998) 'Allusion and the audience of Homer', in M. Païsi-Apostolopoulou, ed. *Homerica. Proceedings of the 8th International Symposium on the* Odyssey *(1–5 September 1996)*, 137–49. Ithaca, Greece

Andersen, Ø. and Dickie, M., eds. (1995) *Homer's World: Fiction, Tradition, Reality*. Papers from the Norwegian Institute at Athens 3. Bergen

Anderson, M. J. (1997) *The Fall of Troy in Early Greek Poetry and Art*. Oxford

Anderson, W. S. (1958) 'Calypso and Elysium', *Classical Journal* 54: 2–11, repr. in Taylor (1963) 73–86

Anderson, W. (1965) *Matthew Arnold and the Classical Tradition*. Ann Arbor, Mich.

Andreae, B. (1962) 'Der Zyklus der Odysseefresken im Vatikan', *Rheinisches Museum für Philologie* 69: 106–17

(1982) *Odysseus: Archäologie des europäischen Menschenbildes*. Frankfurt

(1999) *Odysseus: Mythos und Erinnerung*. Mainz am Rhein

Andreae, B. and Presicce, C. P. (1996) *Ulisse: Il mito e la memoria*. Rome

Antonaccio, C. (1998) 'The archaeology of ancestors', in C. Dougherty and L. Kurke, eds. *Cultural Poetics in Archaic Greece: Cult, Performance, Politics*, 46–70. Cambridge

Apthorp, M. J. (1980) *The Manuscript Evidence for Interpolation in Homer*. Heidelberg

Arend, W. (1933) *Die typischen Scenen bei Homer*. Berlin

Armstrong, J. I. (1958) 'The arming motif in the *Iliad*', *American Journal of Philology* 79: 337–54

Arnold, M. (1896) *On Translating Homer*, 2nd edn. London
(1960) 'On translating Homer', in R. H. Super, ed. *Complete Prose Works*, vol. 1, 97–216. Ann Arbor (orig. edn 1861)
Arthur, M. B. [M. A. Katz] (1973) 'Early Greece and the origins of western attitudes toward women', *Arethusa* 6: 7–58
(1998) 'Daughters of Demeter', in R. Bridenthal, S. Stuard and M. Wiesener, eds. *Becoming Visible: Women in European History*, 3rd edn. Boston
Aske, M. (1985) *Keats and Hellenism: An Essay*. Cambridge
Assmann, J. (2000) *Religion und kulturelles Gedächtnis: Zehn Studien*. Munich
Attridge, D. (2000) *Joyce Effects*. Cambridge
Atwood, M. (1987) *The Handmaid's Tale*. London
Auerbach, E. (1953) *Mimesis*, tr. W. Trask. Princeton
Austin, N. (1966) 'The function of digressions in the *Iliad*', *Greek, Roman and Byzantine Studies* 7: 295–312
(1975) *Archery at the Dark of the Moon: Poetic Problems in Homer's Odyssey*. Berkeley
Bailey, J. and Ivanova, T., trs. (1998) *An Anthology of Russian Folk Epics*. Armonk, N.Y.
Bakhtin, M. M. (1981) *The Dialogic Imagination*, tr. C. Emerson and M. Holquist. Austin, Tex.
Bakker, E. J. (1988) *Linguistics and Formulas in Homer*. Amsterdam
(1990) 'Homeric discourse and enjambement: a cognitive approach', *Transactions of the American Philological Association* 120: 1–21
(1997) *Poetry in speech: orality and Homeric discourse*. Ithaca, N.Y.
Bakker, E. J. and Fabricotti, F. (1991) 'Peripheral and nuclear semantics in Homeric diction: the case of dative expressions for "spear"', *Mnemosyne* 44: 63–84
Baldick, C. (1983) *The Social Mission of English Criticism, 1848–1932*. Oxford
Bannert, H. (1978) 'Zur Vogelgestalt der Götter bei Homer', *Wiener Studien* 91: 29–42
Barchiesi, A. (1984) *La traccia del modello: effetti omerici nella narrazione virgiliana*. Pisa
Barchiesi, M. (1962) *Nevio epico: Storia, interpretazione, edizione critica dei frammenti del primo epos latino*. Padua
Barton, J. (2000) *Tantalus*. London
Bassett, S. E. (1926) 'The so-called emphatic position of the runover word in the Homeric hexameter', *Transactions of the American Philological Association* 57: 116–48
(1938) *The Poetry of Homer*. Berkeley
Beard, M. (2002) *The Parthenon*. London
(forthcoming) 'Why Homer was a woman'
Beissinger, M., Tylus, J. and Wofford, S., eds. (1999) *Epic Traditions in the Contemporary World: The Poetics of Community*. Berkeley and Los Angeles
Belcher, S. (1999) *Epic Traditions of Africa*. Bloomington
Bennet, J. (1996) 'Homer and the Bronze Age', in Morris and Powell (1997) 511–33
Bentley, R. (1713) *Remarks upon a Late Discourse of Free-Thinking*. London
[illegible], V. (191[illegible]) *Un [illegible] de la science allemande [illegible]* Paris
Bergren, A. (1980) 'Helen's web: time and tableau in the *Iliad*', *Helios* 7: 19–34

(1981) 'Helen's good drug: *Odyssey* IV 1–305', in S. Krésic, ed. *Contemporary Literary Hermeneutics and Interpretation of Classical Texts*, 201–14. Ottawa

(1983) 'Language and the female in early Greek thought', *Arethusa* 16: 69–95

Bernabé, A. (1987) *Poetarum Epicorum Graecorum: Testimonia et Fragmenta*, pt 1. Leipzig

Bernstein, G., ed. (1985) *Ezra Pound Among the Poets*. Chicago

Bertolín Cebrián, R. (forthcoming) *Singing the Dead: A Model of Epic Evolution*

Bethe, E. (1914) *Homer* 1: *Die Ilias*. Leipzig

Bevington, D., ed. (1998) *Troilus and Cressida*. The Arden Shakespeare, 3rd ser. Walton-on-Thames

Bidart, F. (1997) *Desire*. New York

Biebuyck, D. and Mateene, K. C., eds. and trs. (1969) *The Mwindo Epic from the Banyanga (Congo Republic)*. Berkeley and Los Angeles

Bing, P. (1988) *The Well-Read Muse. Present and Past in Callimachus and the Hellenistic Poets*. Göttingen

Bjork, R. E. and Niles, J. D., eds. (1997) *A Beowulf Handbook*. Lincoln

Black, M. (1962) *Models and Metaphors: Studies in Language and Philosophy*. Ithaca, N.Y.

Blackburn, S., *et al.* (1989) *Oral Epics in India*. Berkeley and Los Angeles

Blackie, J. S. (1861) 'Homer and his translators', *Macmillan's Magazine* 4: 268–80

Blair, H. (1783) *Lectures on Rhetoric and Belles Lettres*, 3 vols. Edinburgh

Blake, W. (1966) *The Complete Writings of William Blake*, ed. G. Keynes. London, New York and Toronto

Blankenhagn, P. H. von (1963) 'The Odyssey frieze', *Rheinisches Museum für Philologie* 70: 100–46

Blech, M. (1982) *Studien zum Kranz bei den Griechen*. Berlin and New York

Blessington, F. C. (1979) *'Paradise Lost' and the Classical Epic*. Boston and London

Boardman, J. (2002) *The Archaeology of Nostalgia: How the Greeks Re-Created Their Mythical Past*. London

Boedeker, D. and Sider, D., eds. (2001) *The New Simonides: Contexts of Praise and Desire*. New York

Boehringer, D. (2001) *Heroenkulte in Griechenland von der geometrischen bis zur klassischen Zeit*. Klio Beiträge zur alten Geschichte, 3. Berlin

Boitani, P. (1994) *The Shadow of Ulysses*. Oxford

Bonner, S. F. (1977) *Education in Ancient Rome*. Berkeley

Bowie, E. (1970) 'Greeks and their past in the Second Sophistic', *Past and Present* 46: 3–41

Bowra, C. M. (1930) *Tradition and Design in the Iliad*. Oxford

(1961) *Heroic Poetry*, 2nd edn. London

Branch, M. (1994) 'The invention of a national epic', in M. Branch and C. Hawkesworth, eds. *The Uses of Tradition: A Comparative Enquiry into the Nature, Uses and Functions of Oral Poetry in the Balkans, the Baltic, and Africa*, 195–212. London and Helsinki

Brault, G. R., ed. (1978a) *The Song of Roland: An Analytical Edition*, 2 vols. University Park, Penn.

(1978b) 'The French Chansons de Geste', in Oinas (1978) 193–215

Bravo, B. (2001) 'Un frammento della *Piccola Iliade* (P.Oxy. 2510), lo stilo narrativo tardo-arcaico, i racconti su Achille immortale', *Quaderni urbinati di cultura classica* 67.1: 49–114

Bremer, J. M., de Jong, I. J. F. and Kalff, J., eds. (1987) *Homer: Beyond Oral Poetry*. Amsterdam

Brilliant, R. (1984) *Visual Narratives: Storytelling in Etruscan and Roman Art*. Ithaca

Brink, C. O. (1972) 'Ennius and the Hellenistic worship of Homer', *American Journal of Philology* 93: 547–67

(1985) *English Classical Scholarship. Historical Reflections on Bentley, Porson and Housman*. Oxford

Brower, R. A., ed. (1959) *On Translation*. Cambridge, Mass.

Buffière, F. (1956) *Les mythes d'Homère et la pensée Grecque*. Paris (2nd edn. 1973)

Burgess, J. S. (1996) 'The non-Homeric *Cypria*', *Transactions of the American Philological Association* 126: 77–99

(2001) *The Tradition of the Trojan War in Homer and the Epic Cycle*. Baltimore and London

Burkert, W. (1960) 'Das Lied von Ares und Aphrodite', *Rheinisches Museum für Philologie* 103: 30–44, repr. in Burkert (2001) 105–16, tr. in Wright and Jones (1997) 249–62

(1972) 'Die Leistung eines Kreophylos: Kreophyleer, Homeriden und die archaische Heraklesepik', *Museum Helveticum* 29: 74–85 = Burkert (2001) 138–49

(1985) *Greek Religion*, tr. J. Raffan. Cambridge, Mass.

(1987) 'The making of Homer in the sixth century B.C.: rhapsodes versus Stesichoros', in D. von Bothmer, ed. *Papers on the Amasis Painter and his World*, 43–62. Malibu, New York and London = Burkert (2001) 198–217 = Cairns (2001) 92–116

(1992) *The Orientalising Revolution: Near Eastern Influences on Greek Culture in the Early Iron Age*. Cambridge, Mass.

(1995a) '*Irrevocabile verbum*: Spuren mündlichen Erzählens in der Odyssee', in U. Brunold-Bigler and H. Bausinger, eds. *Hören – Sagen – Lesen – Lernen. Bausteine zu einer Geschichte der kommunikativen Kultur. Festschrift für Rudolf Schenda zum 65. Geburtstag*, 147–58. Bern = Burkert (2001) 117–26

(1995b) 'Lydia between East and West, or, how to date the Trojan War: a study in Herodotus', in Carter and Morris (1995) 139–48, repr. in Burkert (2001) 218–32

(2001) *Kleine Schriften*, I: *Homerica*, ed. C. Riedweg. Göttingen

Burnett, P. (1992) 'Walcott's spell binding dreams', *Caribbean Times* (7 July)

(2001) *Derek Walcott: Politics and Poetics*. Gainesville

Burrow, C. (1993) *Epic Romance: Homer to Milton*. Oxford

Butler, J. (1990) *Gender Trouble: Feminism and the Subversion of Identity*. New York

Butler, S. (1922) *The Authoress of the Odyssey: Where and When She Wrote, Who She Was, the Use She Made of the Iliad, and How the Poem Grew under Her Hands*, 2nd edn. London (1st edn 1897)

(1923) [1892] 'The humour of Homer', in H. F. Jones and A. T. Bartholomew, eds. *The Shrewsbury Edition of the Works of Samuel Butler*, vol. 19, 239–71. London

Byre, C. (1988) 'Penelope and the suitors before Odysseus', *American Journal of Philology* 109: 159–73

Byron, Lord (1975) *Byron's Letters and Journals*, vol. IV, ed. L. A. Marchand. London
(1986) *The Complete Poetical Works*, vol. V: *Don Juan*, ed. J. J. McGann. Oxford
Cairns, D. L. (1993a) *Aidos*. Oxford
(1993b) 'Affronts and quarrels in the *Iliad*', *Papers of the Leeds International Latin Seminar* 7: 155–67
ed. (2001), *Oxford Readings in Homer's Iliad*. Oxford
Calhoun, G. M. (1933) 'Homeric repetitions', *University of California Publications in Classical Philology* 12: 1–26
(1962) 'Polity and society (i) The Homeric picture', in Wace Stubbings (1962) 431–52
Cambitoglou, A. *et al.* (1971) *Zagora I*. Sydney
(1988) *Zagora II*. Athens
Campbell, M. (1981) *Echoes and Imitations of Early Epic in Apollonius Rhodius*. Leiden
Cantarella, R. (1926) 'Imitazioni e reminiscenze omeriche in Sofocle, secondo la critica antica', *Rivista Indo-Greco-Italica di Filologia-Lingua-Antichità* 10: 84–95
Carpenter, R. (1946) *Folk Tale, Fiction and Saga in the Homeric Epics*. Berkeley
Carspecken, J. F. (1952) 'Apollonius Rhodius and the Homeric epic', *Yale Classical Studies* 13: 33–143
Carter, J. B. and Morris, S. P., eds. (1995) *The Ages of Homer: A Tribute to Emily Townsend Vermeule*. Austin
Cassio, A. C. (2002) 'Early editions of the Greek epics and Homeric textual criticism in the sixth and fifth centuries BC', in Montanari and Ascheri (2002) 105–36
Càssola, F. (1975) *Inni omerici*. Milan
Cavell, S. (1981) *Pursuits of Happiness: The Hollywood Comedy of Remarriage*. Cambridge, Mass.
Cayley, C. B. (1862–3) 'Remarks and experiments on English hexameters', *Transactions of the Philological Society* 67–85
(1877) *The Iliad of Homer. Homometrically Translated*. London
Chantraine, P. (1968–80) *Dictionnaire étymologique de la langue grecque*. Paris
Cheng, V. and Martin, T., eds. (1992) *Joyce in Context*. Cambridge
Chogjin (1997) 'Mongolian oral epic poetry: an overview', *Oral Tradition* 12: 322–36
Chogjin and Foley, J. M. (2002) 'The challenge of comparative oral epic' (in Chinese), *Mongolian Studies*
Clark, M. (1997) *Out of Line. Homeric Composition Beyond the Hexameter*. Lanham, Boulder, New York and Oxford
Clarke, H. W. (1981) *Homer's Readers: A Historical Introduction to the Iliad and the Odyssey*. Newark, London and Toronto
Clarke, M. (1995a) 'The wisdom of Thales and the problem of the word *hieros*', *Classical Quarterly* 45: 296–317
(1995b) 'Between lions and men: images of the hero in the *Iliad*', *Greek, Roman and Byzantine Studies* 136: 137–59
(1999) *Flesh and Spirit in the Songs of Homer: A Study of Words and Myths*. Oxford
Clay, J. S. (1983) *The Wrath of Athena: Gods and Men in the* Odyssey. Princeton
(1984) 'Homeric ΑΧΡΕΙΟΝ', *American Journal of Philology* 105: 73–6
(1989) *The Politics of Olympus*. Princeton

(1997) 'The Homeric Hymns', in Morris and Powell (1997) 489–507

(2002) 'Dying is hard to do', *Colby Quarterly* 38.1: 7–16

(2003) *Hesiod's Cosmos*. Cambridge

Coffey, M. (1957) 'The function of the Homeric simile', *American Journal of Philology* 78: 113–32

Cohen, B., ed. (1995) *The Distaff Side: Representing the Female in Homer's Odyssey*. Oxford

Coldstream, J. N. (1976) 'Hero-cults in the age of Homer', *Journal of Hellenic Studies* 96: 7–17

(1977) *Geometric Greece*. London (2nd edn 2003)

(1983) 'Gift exchange in the eighth century', in Hägg (1983) 201–6

Coleridge, S. T. (1983) *Biographia Literaria, or, Biographical Sketches of My Literary Life and Opinions*, ed. J. Engell and W. J. Bate, 2 vols. London and Princeton

(1984) *Marginalia*, vol. II: *Camden to Hutton*, ed. George Whalley. Princeton

(1987) *Lectures, 1808–1819, On Literature*, ed. R. A. Foakes. Princeton and London

(1990) *Table Talk. Recorded by Henry Nelson Coleridge (and John Taylor Coleridge)*, ed. C. Woodring, 2 vols. London and Princeton

Colonna, G. (1973–4) 'Nomi etruschi di vasi', *Archeologia Classica* 25–6: 132–50

Comparetti, D. (1997) *Vergil in the Middle Ages*, tr. E. F. M. Benecke, with a new introduction by J. M. Ziolkowski. Princeton (orig. edn 1885)

Connelly, B. (1986) *Arab Folk Epic and Identity*. Berkeley and Los Angeles

Considine, P. (1985) 'The Indo-European origins of Greek *menis*', *Transactions of the American Philosophical Society* 144–76

Conticello, B., Andreae, B. and Bol, P. C. (1974) 'Die Skulpturen von Sperlonga,' *Antike Plastik* 14

Cook, E. (2001) *Achilles*. London

Courtney, E. (2001) *A Companion to Petronius*. Oxford

Cowper, W. (1979–86) *The Letters and Prose Writings of William Cowper*, ed. J. King and C. Ryskamp, 5 vols. Oxford

Crane, G. (1988) *Calypso: Backgrounds and Conventions of the Odyssey*. Frankfurt

Cribiore, R. (2001) *Gymnastics of the Mind*. Princeton

Crielaard, J. P. (1995) 'Homer, history and archaeology: some remarks on the date of the Homeric world', in Crielaard, ed. *Homeric Questions: Essays in Philology, Ancient History and Archaeology*, including the Papers of a Conference Organized by the Netherlands Institute at Athens, 15 May 1993, 201–88. Amsterdam

(2002) 'Past or present? Epic poetry, aristocratic self-representation and the concept of time in the eighth and seventh centuries BC', in Montanari and Ascheri (2002) 239–95

Croese, G. (1704) *Omeros Ebraios, sive, Historia Hebraeorum ab Homero: Hebraicis Nominibus ac Sententiis Conscripta in Odyssea & Iliade*. Dordrecht

Crotty, K. (1994) *The Poetics of Supplication: Homer's Iliad and Odyssey*. Ithaca, N.Y.

Crouwel, J. (1981) *Chariots and Other Means of Land Transport in Bronze Age Greece*. Amsterdam

Crudden, M. J., tr. and comm. (2001) *The Homeric Hymns*. Oxford

Curtius, E. R. (1953) *European Literature and the Latin Middle Ages*, tr. W. R. Trask. New York

Danek, G. (1988) *Studien zur Dolonie*. Vienna

(1998) *Epos und Zitat. Studien zu den Quellen der Odyssee. Wiener Studien Beiheft* 22. Vienna

(2002) 'Traditional referentiality and Homeric intertextuality', in Montanari and Ascheri (2002) 3–19

d'Aubignac, François-Hédelin (1925) *Conjectures académiques, ou, Dissertation sur l'Iliade*, ed. V. Magnien. Paris (orig. edn 1670)

Davidson, J. (1999–2000) 'Euripides, Homer and Sophocles', *Illinois Classical Studies* 24/5: 117–28

Davies, M. (2001) *The Epic Cycle*, 2nd edn. Bristol

Davison, J. A. (1962) 'The Homeric question', in Wace and Stubbings (1962) 234–65

(1968) *From Archilochus to Pindar*. London

De Quincey, T. (2001) [1841] 'Homer and the Homeridae', in G. Lindop, ed. *The Works of Thomas de Quincey*, vol. 13, 1–63. London

DeJean, J. E. (1997) *Ancients against Moderns: Culture Wars and the Making of a Fin de Siècle*. Chicago

Derrida, J. (1972) *Marges de la philosophie*. Paris

Detienne, M. and Vernant, J.-P. (1978) *Cunning Intelligence in Greek Culture and Society*, tr. J. Lloyd. Hassocks

Deuel, L. (1977) *Memoirs of Heinrich Schliemann: A Documentary Portrait Drawn from His Autobiographical Writings, Letters, and Excavation Reports*. New York

Di Benedetto, V. (1994) *Nel laboratorio di Omero*. Turin

Dickinson, O. T. P. K. (1994) *The Aegean Bronze Age*. Cambridge

Dimock, G. (1956) 'The name of Odysseus', *Hudson Review* 9: 52–70

Dirlmeier, F. (1967) *Die Vogelgestalt homerischer Götter*. Heidelberg

Dodds, E. R. (1951) *The Greeks and the Irrational*. Berkeley and Los Angeles

Doherty, L. (1990) 'Joyce's Penelope and Homer's: feminist reconsiderations', *Classical and Modern Literature* 10: 343–49

(1995) *Siren Songs: Gender, Audiences and Narrators in the Odyssey*. Ann Arbor

Donlan, W. (1980) *The Aristocratic Ideal in Ancient Greece: Attitudes of Superiority from Homer to the End of the Fifth Century B.C.* Lawrence, Kans.

(1993) 'Dueling with gifts in the *Iliad*: as the audience saw it', *Colby Quarterly* 29.3: 155–72

(1997) 'The Homeric economy', in Morris and Powell (1997) 649–67

Dowden, K. (1989) *Death and the Maiden: Girls' Initiation Rites in Greek Mythology*. London

(1992) *The Uses of Greek Mythology*. London

(1996a) 'Heliodoros: serious intentions', *Classical Quarterly* 46: 267–85

(1996b) 'Homer's sense of text', *Journal of Hellenic Studies* 116: 47–61

Dryden, J. (1962) *Of Dramatic Poesy and Other Critical Essays*, ed. G. Watson. London

DuBois, P. (1988) *Sowing the Body. Psychoanalysis and Ancient Representations of Women*. Chicago

DuBois, T. A. (1995) *Finnish Folk Poetry and the Kalevala*. New York

Dué, C. (2002) *Homeric Variations on a Lament by Briseis*. Lanham, Md.
Duffy, C. A. (1999) *The World's Wife*. London
Duggan, J. J. (1973) *The Song of Roland: Formulaic Style and Poetic Craft*. Berkeley
Dumézil, G. (1970) *The Destiny of the Warrior*, Eng. tr. Chicago
Durante, M. (1968) 'Untersuchungen zur Vorgeschichte der griechischen Dichtersprache', in Schmitt (1968) 291–323
(1971–4) *Sulla preistoria della tradizione poetica greca*, 2 vols. Rome
DuRocher, R. (1985) *Milton and Ovid*. Ithaca, N.Y. and London
Eagleton, T. (1990) *The Ideology of the Aesthetic*. Oxford
(1996) *The Function of Criticism: From* the Spectator *to Post-Structuralism*. London
Easterling, P. E. (1985) 'Anachronism in Greek tragedy', *Journal of Hellenic Studies* 105: 1–10
(1991) 'Men's κλέος and women's γόος: female voices in the *Iliad*', *Journal of Modern Greek Studies* 9: 45–51
ed. (1997) *The Cambridge Companion to Greek Tragedy*. Cambridge
Easterling, P. E. *et al.*, eds. (2000) *Theatre Ancient and Modern*. Milton Keynes, and electronically at *http://www.open.ac.uk/Arts/CC99/*
Eco, U. and Santoro-Brienza, L. (1998) *Talking of Joyce*. Dublin
Eco, U. (2000) *Experiences in Translation*, tr. A. McEwen. Toronto
Edwards, A. T. (1985) *Achilles in the* Odyssey = *Beiträge zur klass. Phil.* Heft 171. Meisenheim
Edwards, G. P. (1971) *The Language of Hesiod in its Traditional Context*. Oxford
Edwards, M. W. (1966) 'Some features of Homeric craftsmanship', *Transactions of the American Philological Association* 97: 115–79
(1975) 'Type-scenes and Homeric hospitality', *Transactions of the American Philological Association* 105: 51–72
(1980) 'Convention and individuality in *Iliad* 1', *Harvard Studies in Classical Philology* 84: 1–28
(1986) 'Homer and oral tradition: the formula, part I', *Oral Tradition* 1: 171–230
(1987) *Homer, Poet of the Iliad*. Baltimore
(1988) 'Homer and oral tradition: the formula, part II', *Oral Tradition* 3: 11–60
(1991) *The Iliad: A Commentary,* v: *Books 17–20,* Cambridge
(1992) 'Homer and oral tradition: the type-scene', *Oral Tradition* 7: 283–330
Effe, B. (1975) '"Personale" Erzählweisen in der Erzählliteratur der Antike', *Poetica* 7: 135–57
Eliot, T. S., ed. (1954) *Literary Essays of Ezra Pound*. London
(1974) *Collected Poems 1909–1962*, 2nd edn. London
(1975) 'Tradition and the individual talent', in F. Kermode, ed. *Selected Prose of T. S. Eliot*, 37–44. London
Elton, W. R. (2000) *Shakespeare's Troilus and Cressida and the Inns of Court Revels*. Aldershot
Emlyn-Jones, C. (1992) 'The Homeric gods: poetry, belief and authority', in C. Emlyn-Jones, L. Hardwick, J. Purkis, eds. *Homer: Readings and Images*. London
Erbse, H. (1972) *Beiträge zum Verständnis der Odyssee*. Berlin
(1980) 'Homerische Götter in Vogelgestalt', *Hermes* 108: 259–74
(1986) *Untersuchungen zur Funktion der Götter in homerischen Epos*. Berlin

Erskine, A. (2001) *Troy between Greece and Rome: Local Tradition and Imperial Power*. Oxford and New York

Etteridge, D. (2000) *Joyce Effects*. Cambridge

Evans, S. (2001) *Hymn and Epic: A Study of their Interplay in Homer and the Homeric Hymns*. Turku

Fantuzzi, M. and Hunter, R. (2002) *Muse e modelli. La poesia ellenistica da Alessandro Magno ad Augusto*. Rome and Bari. Engl. tr. (2004) *Tradition and Innovation in Hellenistic Poetry*. Cambridge

Farrell, J. (1991) *Vergil's Georgics and the Traditions of Ancient Epic*. New York

Farrington, B. (1929) *Samuel Butler and the Odyssey*. London

Feeney, D. C. (1983) 'The taciturnity of Aeneas', *Classical Quarterly* 23: 204–19

(1991) *The Gods in Epic: Poets and Critics of the Classical Tradition*. Oxford

(1999) '*Mea tempora*: patterning of time in the *Metamorphoses*', in S. Hinds, P. R. Hardie and A. Barchiesi, eds. *Ovidian Transformations: Essays on the Metamorphoses and Its Reception*, 13–30. Cambridge

Felson (= Felson-Rubin), N. (1987) 'Penelope's perspective: character from plot', in Bremer *et al.* (1996) 61–83, expanded in Schein (1996) 163–83

(1994) *Regarding Penelope: From Character to Poetics*. Princeton

Fenik, B. (1968) *Typical Battle Scenes in the Iliad: Studies in the Narrative Technique of Homeric Battle Description*. Hermes Einzelschrift 21. Wiesbaden

(1974) *Studies in the Odyssey*. Hermes Einzelschrift 30. Wiesbaden

(1978) 'Stylization and variety: four monologues in the *Iliad*', in Fenik, ed. *Homer. Tradition and Invention*, 68–90. Leiden

Ferrari, G. (2002) *Figures of Speech*. Chicago

Fingerle, A. (1939) *Typik der homerischen Reden*. Munich

Finkelberg, M. (1990) 'A creative oral poet and the Muse', *American Journal of Philology* 111: 293–303

(1998) *The Birth of Literary Fiction in Ancient Greece*. Oxford

(2000) 'The *Cypria*, the *Iliad* and the problem of multiformity in oral and written tradition', *Classical Philology* 95: 1–11

Finley, M. I. (1954) *The World of Odysseus*. London

(1957) 'Homer and Mycenae: property and tenure', *Historia* 6: 133–59, repr. in Finley (1982) *Economy and Society in Ancient Greece*, ed. B. D. Shaw and R. P. Saller, 213–32. London

(1965) *The World of Odysseus*, rev. edn. New York

Finnegan, R. (1992) *Oral Poetry: Its Nature, Significance, and Social Context*. Bloomington (orig. edn. Cambridge 1977)

Finsler, G. (1912) *Homer in der Neuzeit von Dante bis Goethe: Italien, Frankreich, England, Deutschland*. Leipzig

Fitzgerald, R., tr. (1961) *Homer, The Odyssey*. New York

Fletcher, H. F. (1956–61) *The Intellectual Development of John Milton*, 2 vols. Urbana, Ill.

Flueckiger-Guggenheim, D. (1983) *Göttliche Gäste: die Einkehr von Göttern und Heroen in der griechischen Mythologie*. Bern and New York

Foerster, D. M. (1947) *Homer in English Criticism: the Historical Approach in the Eighteenth Century*. New Haven

Foley, H. P. (1978) '"Reverse similes" and sex roles in the *Odyssey*', *Arethusa* 11: 7–26

(2001) 'Virgins, wives and mothers: Penelope as paradigm', in *Female Acts in Greek Tragedy*, 109–44. Princeton

Foley, J. M. (1985) *Oral-Formulaic Theory and Research: An Introduction and Annotated Bibliography*. New York [available with updates online at *www.oraltradition.org*]

(1986) *Oral Tradition in Literature: Interpretation in Context*. Columbia, Miss.

(1988) *The Theory of Oral Composition: History and Methodology*. Bloomington [repr. (1992)]

(1990) *Traditional Oral Epic: The Odyssey, Beowulf, and the South Slavic Return Song*. Berkeley and Los Angeles [repr. (1993)]

(1991) *Immanent Art: From Structure to Meaning in Traditional Oral Epic*. Bloomington

(1995) *The Singer of Tales in Performance*. Bloomington

(1997) 'Oral tradition and its implications', in Morris and Powell (1997) 146–73

(1998) 'Individual poet and epic tradition: Homer as legendary singer', *Arethusa* 31: 149–78

(1999a) *Homer's Traditional Art*. University Park, Penn.

(1999b) 'Epic cycles and epic traditions', in J. N. Kazazis and A. Rengakos, eds. *Euphrosyne: Studies in Ancient Epic and Its Legacy in Honor of Dimitris N. Maronitis*, 99–108. Stuttgart

(2002a) *How to Read an Oral Poem*. Urbana

(2002b) 'How genres leak in traditional verse', in M. Amodio and K. O'Brien O'Keeffe, eds. *Unlocking the Wordhord: Anglo-Saxon Studies in Memory of Edward B. Irving, Jr.*, 76–108. Toronto

Ford, A. (1992) *Homer. The Poetry of the Past*. Ithaca and London

(1997) 'Epic as genre', in Morris and Powell (1997) 396–414.

(2002) *The Origins of Criticism*. Princeton

Foster, F. M. K. (1918) *English Translations from the Greek: A Bibliographical Survey*. New York

Foucault, M. (1985). *The History of Sexuality*, vol. II: *The Uses of Pleasure*, tr. R. Hurley. New York

Fowler, R. (1983) 'On not knowing Greek: the classics and the woman of letters', *Classical Journal* 78: 337–49

(1999) 'Moments and metamorphoses: Virginia Woolf's Greece', *Comparative Literature* 51: 217–42

Fowler, R. L. (1987a) *The Nature of Early Greek Lyric: Three Preliminary Studies*. Toronto

(1987b) 'The rhetoric of desperation', *Harvard Studies in Classical Philology* 91: 5–38.

(1991) 'Gilbert Murray: four (five) stages of Greek religion', in W. M. Calder III, ed. *The Cambridge Ritualists Reconsidered*, Proceedings of the First Oldfather Conference, Held on the Campus of the University of Illinois at Urbana-Champaign, 27–30 April 1989, 79–95. Atlanta

Fox, J. J., ed. (1988) *To Speak in Pairs: Essays on the Ritual Languages of Eastern Indonesia*. Cambridge

Foxhall, L. (1998) 'Cargoes of the heart's desire: the character of trace in the archaic Mediterranean world', in N. Fisher and H. van Wees, eds. *Archaic Greece. New Approaches and New Evidence*, 295–309. London
Foxon, D. F. (1991) *Pope and the Early Eighteenth-Century Book Trade*. Oxford
Frame, D. (1978) *The Myth of Return in Early Greek Epic*. New Haven
Fränkel, H. (1921) *Die homerischen Gleichnisse*. Göttingen
(1926) 'Der kallimachische und der homerische Hexameter', *Gött Nachr.*: 197–229
(1962) *Dichtung und Philosophie des frühen Griechentums*, 2nd edn. Munich
Freud, S. (1964) 'A disturbance of memory on the Acropolis', in *Standard Edition of the Complete Works of Sigmund Freud*, vol. XXII, 239–48. London
Friedrich, R. (2000) 'Homeric enjambement and orality', *Hermes* 128: 1–19
Friedrich, W.-H. (1956) *Verwundung und Tod in der Ilias*. Göttingen
Fuseli, H. (1975) *Henry Fuseli 1741–1825*. London
Fusillo, M. (1989) *Il romanzo greco*. Venice [= *Naissance du roman*, Paris 1991]
García, J. F. (2001) 'Milman Parry and A. L. Kroeber: Americanist anthropology and the oral Homer', *Oral Tradition* 16: 58–84
Garland, R. (1981) 'The causation of death in the *Iliad*', *Bulletin of the Institute of Classical Studies* 28: 43–60
Garner, R. (1990) *From Homer to Tragedy: The Art of Allusion in Greek Poetry*. London
Garvie, A. F. (1994) *Homer: Odyssey Books VI–VIII*. Cambridge
Gaskin, R. (1990) 'Do Homeric heroes make real decisions?', *Classical Quarterly* 40: 1–15
Geddes, A. G. (1984) 'Who's who in Homeric society?', *Classical Quarterly* 34: 17–36
Genette, G. (1982) *Palimpsestes: la littérature au second degré*. Paris
George, A. R. (1999) *The Epic of Gilgamesh*. London
(2003) *The Babylonian Gilgamesh Epic*, 2 vols. Oxford
Gerrig, R. J. (1989) 'Suspense in the absence of uncertainty', *Journal of Memory and Language* 28: 633–48
Giacomelli (= Carson), A. (1980) 'Aphrodite and after', *Phoenix* 34: 1–19
Gill, C. (1996) *Personality in Greek Epic, Tragedy and Philosophy*. Oxford
Giovannini, A. (1969) *Etudes historiques sur les origines du catalogue des vaisseaux*. Bern
Gladstone, W. E. (1857) 'On the place of Homer in classical education and in historical inquiry', in *Oxford Essays*, 1–56. Oxford
(1858) *Studies on Homer and the Homeric Age*, 3 vols. Oxford
(1869) *Juventus Mundi: The Gods and Men of the Heroic Age*. Boston
(1876) *Homeric Synchronism: An Enquiry into the Time and Place of Homer*. New York
Glück, L. (1996) *Meadowlands*. Hopewell, N.J.
Goldhill, S. (1986) *Reading Greek Tragedy*. Cambridge
(1991) *The Poet's Voice: Essays on Poetics and Greek Literature*. Cambridge
(2002) *The Invention of Prose*. Oxford
Goldman, E. (1970) [1911] 'The traffic in women', repr. in A. K. Shulman, ed. *The Traffic in Women and Other Essays on Feminism*. New York

Goldman, J., Kolocotroni, V. and Taxidou, O., eds. *Modernism: An Anthology of Sources and Documents*. Edinburgh
Goody, J. (1977) *The Domestication of the Savage Mind*. Cambridge
(2000) *The Power of Written Tradition*. Washington
Goold, G. P. (1977) 'The nature of Homeric composition', *Illinois Classical Studies* 2: 1–34
Gould, J. (2001) *Myth, Ritual, Memory, and Exchange: Essays in Greek Literature and Culture*. Oxford
Grafton, A. (1981) 'Prolegomenon to Friedrich August Wolf', *Journal of the Warburg and Courtauld Institutes* 44: 101–29
(1997) *Commerce with the Classics: Ancient Books and Renaissance Readers*. Ann Arbor
Graziosi, B. (2002) *Inventing Homer: the Early Reception of Epic*. Cambridge and New York
Graziosi, B. and Haubold, J. (2003) 'Homeric masculinity: ἠνορέη and ἀγηνορίη', *Journal of Hellenic Studies* 123: 60–76
Gregory, E. (1997) *H.D. and Hellenism*. Cambridge
Griffin, J. (1977) 'The Epic Cycle and the uniqueness of Homer', *Journal of Hellenic Studies* 97: 39–53 (= Cairns (2001) 365–84)
(1980) *Homer on Life and Death*. Oxford
(1986a) 'Heroic and unheroic ideas in Homer', in J. Boardman and C. Vaphopoulou-Richardson, eds. *Chios. A conference at the Homereion in Chios, 1984*, 3–13. Oxford
(1986b) 'Words and speakers in Homer', *Journal of Hellenic Studies* 106: 36–57
(1995) *Homer: Iliad IX*. Oxford
(2003) *Homer: The Odyssey*, 2nd edn. Cambridge
Griffin, J. and Hammond, M. (1982) 'Critical appreciation: Homer, *Iliad* 1.1–52', *Greece and Rome* 29: 126–42. Repr. in McAuslan and Walcot (1998) 65–82
Griffin, R. J. (1995) *Wordsworth's Pope: A Study in Literary Historiography*. Cambridge
Grote, G. (1859–65) *History of Greece*, 12 vols. New York
Gruen, E. S. (1992) *Culture and National Identity in Republican Rome*. Ithaca
Gudeman, A. (1934) *Aristoteles* Περὶ ποιητικῆς. Berlin and Leipzig
H. D. [H. Doolittle] (1961) *Helen in Egypt*. New York
Hägg, R., ed. (1983) *The Greek Renaissance of the Eighth Century B.C.* Stockholm
Hägg, T., ed. (1999) 'Dividing Homer', *Symbolae Osloenses* 74: 5–91
Haing, D. and Welo, E. (2001) 'The proto-hexameter hypothesis: perspectives for further research', *Symbolae Osloenses* 76: 130–6
Hainsworth, J. B. (1968) *The Flexibility of the Homeric Formula*. Oxford
(1988) 'The epic dialect', in Heubeck, West and Hainsworth (1988) 24–32
(1989) ed. *Traditions of Heroic and Epic Poetry*, vol. 2, *Characteristics and Techniques*, London, 1989
(1993) *The Iliad: A Commentary*, vol. III: *Books 9–12*. Cambridge
Hale, T. A. (1998) *Griots and Griottes: Masters of Words and Music*. Bloomington
Hall, E. (1996) *Aeschylus, Persians*. Warminster
Hall, E., Macintosh, F. and Wrigley, A., eds. (2004) *Dionysus since '69*. Oxford
Halperin, D. M. (1983) *Before Pastoral: Theocritus and the Ancient Tradition of Bucolic Poetry*. New Haven and London

Halperin, D., Winkler, J. J. and Zeitlin, F. I., eds. (1990) *Before Sexuality: The Construction of Erotic Experience in the Ancient Greek World*. Princeton

Halverson, J. (1985) 'Social order in the *Odyssey*', *Hermes* 113: 129–45

Hardie, P. R. (1985) 'Imago mundi: cosmological and ideological aspects of the shield of Achilles', *Journal of Hellenic Studies* 105: 11–31

(1986) *Vergil's Aeneid: Cosmos and Imperium*. Oxford

(1993) *The Epic Successors of Virgil*. Cambridge

(2002) *Ovid's Poetics of Illusion*. Cambridge

Harding, D. P. (1962) *The Club of Hercules: Studies in the Classical Background of Paradise Lost*. Urbana, Ill.

Hardwick, L. (1997) 'Reception as simile: the poetics of reversal in Homer and Derek Walcott', *International Journal of Classical Tradition* 3: 326–38

(2000a) 'Theatres of the mind: Greek tragedy in women's writings in English in the nineteenth century', in Easterling *et al.* (2000) 68–81

(2000b) *Translating Words, Translating Cultures*. London

(2001) '*Tantalus* staged: anthology, narrative and the audience', *Didaskalia* 5.2 (*www.didaskalia.net*)

(2003) *Reception Studies*. New Surveys in the Classics 33. Oxford

(2004) 'Greek drama and anti-colonialism: decolonising classics', in Hall, Macintosh and Wrigley (2004) 219–42

Harris, J. (1982) '*Beowulf* in literary history', *Pacific Coast Philology* 17: 16–23, repr. in R. D. Fulk, ed. *Interpretations of Beowulf: A Critical Anthology* (1991), 235–41. Bloomington

Harrison, S. J. (1990) 'Some Odyssean scenes in Apuleius' *Metamorphoses*', *Materiali e discussioni per l'analisi dei testi classici* 25: 193–201

Harvilahti, L. (1994) 'Epic poetry cultures and the use of formula technique: some problems of definition', in M. Branch and C. Hawkesworth, eds. *The Uses of Tradition: A Comparative Enquiry into the Nature, Uses and Functions of Oral Poetry in the Balkans, the Baltic, and Africa*, 165–76. London and Helsinki

Haslam, M. (1997) 'Homeric papyri and transmission of the text', in Morris and Powell (1997) 55–100

Hatto, A. T., ed. (1980) *Traditions of Heroic and Epic Poetry*, 2 vols. London

(1999) *The Mohave Heroic Epic of Inyo-kutavêre*. Folklore Fellows Communications 269. Helsinki

Haubold, J. (2000) *Homer's People: Epic Poetry and Social Formation*. Cambridge

(2002) 'Greek epic: a Near Eastern genre?', *Proceedings of the Cambridge Philological Society* 48: 1–32

Haug, D. and Welo, E. (2001) 'The proto-hexameter hypothesis: perspectives for further research', *Symbolae Osloenses* 76: 130–6

Hausmann, U. (1959) *Hellenistische Reliefbecher aus attischen und böotischen Werkstätten*. Stuttgart

Havelock, E. (1982) *The Literate Revolution and its Cultural Consequences*. Princeton

(1986) *The Muses Learn to Write: Reflections on Orality and Literacy from Antiquity to the Present*. New Haven

Hawkes, T. (1972) *Metaphor*. London

Hawley, R. and Levick, B., eds. (1995) *Women in Antiquity: New Assessments*. London and New York

Haydon, B. R. (1960–3) *The Diary of Benjamin Robert Haydon*, ed. W. B. Pope, 5 vols. Cambridge, Mass.

Hazlitt, W. (1930–4) *The Complete Works of William Hazlitt*, ed. P. P. Howe, 21 vols. London and Toronto

Heaney, S. (1990) *The Cure at Troy: After Sophocles*. London

Hegel, G. W. F. (1975) [1820–29] *Hegel's Aesthetics: Lectures on Fine Art*, tr. T. M. Knox, 2 vols. Oxford

Heiden, B. (1996) 'The three movements of the *Iliad*', *Greek, Roman and Byzantine Studies* 37: 5–22

(2000a) 'The placement of "book divisions" in the *Odyssey*', *Classical Philology* 95: 247–59

(2000b) 'Narrative discontinuity and segment marking at *Iliad* 3/4, 7/8, 10/11 and *Odyssey* 4/5, 17/18, and 23/24', *Classica et Mediaevalia* 51: 5–16

(2000c) 'Major systems of thematic resonance in the *Iliad*', *Symbolae Osloenses* 75: 34–55

Heinze, R. (1915) *Vergils epische Technik*, 3rd edn. Leipzig and Berlin

(1993) *Virgil's Epic Technique*, trs. H. and D. Harvey and F. Robertson. Berkeley

Heissig, W., ed. (1987) *Fragen der mongolischen Heldendichtung*, vol. 4. Wiesbaden

Helbig, W. (1884) *Das Homerische Epos aus den Denkmälern Erläutert*, 2nd edn. Leipzig

Hepp, N. (1968) *Homère en France au XVIIe siècle*. Bibliothèque Française et Romane, série C, études littéraires 18. Paris

Herington, J. (1985) *Poetry into Drama: Early Tragedy and the Greek Poetic Tradition*. Berkeley

Hershkowitz, D. (1998) *The Madness of Epic*. Oxford

Herter, H. (1929) 'Kallimachos und Homer. Ein Beitrag zur Interpretation des Hymnos auf Artemis', in *Xenia Bonnensia* (Bonn) 50–105 [= *Kleine Schriften* (Munich 1975) 371–416]

Hesse, E., ed. (1969) *New Approaches to Ezra Pound*. London

Heubeck, A. (1974) *Die homerische Frage*. Darmstadt

(1979) *Schrift. Archaeologia Homerica. Die Denkmäler und das frühgriechische Epos* Bd. 3 Kap. 10. Göttingen

Heubeck, A., West, S. and Hainsworth, J. B., eds. (1988) *A Commentary on Homer's Odyssey*, vol. I: *Books I–VIII*. Oxford

Heubeck, A. *et al.*, eds. (1988–92) *A Commentary on Homer's Odyssey*, 3 vols. Oxford

Heyne, C. G. (1802) *Homeri Carmina cum brevi annotatione*. Leipzig

Higbie, C. (1990) *Measure and Music: Enjambment and Sentence Structure in the Iliad*. Oxford

Highet, G. (1949) *The Classical Tradition: Greek and Roman Influences on Western Literature*. Oxford

Hinds, S. (1998) *Allusion and Intertext*. Cambridge

Hobbs, A. (2000) *Plato and the Hero*. Cambridge

Hoberman, R. (1997) *Gendering Classicism: The Ancient World in Twentieth-Century Women's Historical Fiction*. New York

Hoekstra, A. (1969) *The Sub-Epic Stage of the Formulaic Tradition*. Amsterdam

Hölkeskamp, K.-J. (2002) 'Ptolis and *agore*. Homer and the archaeology of the city-state', in Montanari and Ascheri (2002) 297–342.

Holmberg, I. (1998) 'The creation of the ancient Greek epic cycle', *Oral Tradition* 13: 456–78

Hölscher, U. (1967) 'Die Atridensage in der Odyssee', in H. Singer and B. von Wiese, eds. *Festschrift für Richard Alewyn*, 1–16. Cologne

(1988) *Die Odyssee: Epos zwischen Märchen und Roman*. Munich (2nd edn. 1989)

Holst-Warhaft, G. (1992) *Dangerous Voices. Women's Laments and Greek Literature*. London and New York

Holton, M. and Mihailovich, V. D., trs. (1997) *Songs of the Serbian People: From the Collections of Vuk Karadžić*. Pittsburgh

Honko, L. (1998) *Textualising the Siri Epic*. Folklore Fellows Communications 264. Helsinki

Honko, L. *et al.*, eds. and trs. (1998a) *The Siri Epic as Performed by Gopala Naika*, pt 1. Folklore Fellows Communications 265. Helsinki

(1998b) *The Siri Epic as Performed by Gopala Naika*. pt 2. Folklore Fellows Communications 266. Helsinki

Honko, L. and Honko, A. (2000) 'Variation and textuality in oral epics: a South Indian instance', in L. Honko, ed. *Thick Corpus, Organic Variation, and Textuality in Oral Tradition*, 351–72. Helsinki

Honour, H. (1968) *Neo-classicism*. London

Hope Simpson, R. and Lazenby, J. (1970) *The Catalogue of Ships in Homer's Iliad*. Oxford

Hopkinson, N. (1994) 'Nonnus and Homer', in N. Hopkinson, ed. *Studies in the Dionysiaca of Nonnus*, 9–42. Cambridge

Horkheimer, M. and Adorno, A. (1971) *Dialektik der Aufklärung: Philosophische Fragmente*. Frankfurt am Main

Horrocks, G. C. (1980) 'The antiquity of the Greek epic tradition: some new evidence', *Proceedings of the Cambridge Philological Society* n.s. 26: 1–11

(1997) 'Homer's dialect', in Morris and Powell (1997) 193–217

Horsfall, N. (1979) 'Stesichorus at Bovillae', *Journal of Hellenic Studies* 99: 26–48

Horsley, G. (2000) 'Homer in Pisidia: aspects of the history of Greek education in a remote Roman province', *Antichthon* 34: 46–81

Howes, G. E. (1895) 'Homeric quotations in Plato and Aristotle', *Harvard Studies in Classical Philology* 6: 153–237

Hubbard, T. (2003) *Homosexuality in Greece and Rome: A Textbook of Documents*. Berkeley and Los Angeles

Humboldt, W. (1961–81) *Werke in fünf Bänden*, eds. A. Flitner and K. Giel, 5 vols. Stuttgart

Humphreys, S. C. (1981) 'Death and time', in S. C. Humphreys and Helen King, eds. *Mortality and Immortality: The Anthropology and Archaeology of Death*, 261–83. London and New York

Hunter, R. (1996) 'Callimachus swings (frr. 178 and 43 Pf.)', *Ramus* 25: 17–26

(1998) 'The *Aithiopika* of Heliodorus: beyond interpretation?', in R. Hunter, ed. *Studies in Heliodorus*, 40–59. Cambridge

(1999) *Theocritus. A Selection*. Cambridge

(2000) 'The politics of Plutarch's *Comparison of Aristophanes and Menander*', in S. Gödde and T. Heinze, eds. *Skenika. Beiträge zum antiken Theater und seiner Rezeption*, 267–76. Darmstadt

(2003) *Theocritus. Encomium of Ptolemy Philadelphus*. Berkeley

Hymes, D. (1975) 'Breakthrough into performance', in *Folklore: Performance and Communication*, 11–74. The Hague. Repr. with 'Appendix' and 'Postscript' in Hymes (1981) *'In vain I tried to tell you': Essays in Native American Ethnopoetics*, 79–141. Philadelphia

Immerwahr, S. A. (1990) *Aegean Painting in the Bronze Age*. Philadelphia

Irwin, D. (1979) *John Flaxman 1775–1826: Sculptor, Illustrator, Designer*. London

Irwin, E. (2000) 'The epic situation and the politics of exhortation: political uses of poetic tradition in archaic Greek poetry', Ph.D. diss. Cambridge University

Isager, S. (1998) 'The pride of Halikarnassos', *Zeitschrift für Papyrologie und Epigraphik* 123: 1–23

Ismond, P. (2001) *Abandoning Dead Metaphors: The Caribbean Phase of Derek Walcott's Poetry*. Barbados

Jacoby, F. (1933) 'Homerisches', *Hermes* 68: 1–50

Jacopi, G. (1958) *I ritrovamenti dell' Antro detto 'di Tiberio' a Sperlonga*. Rome

(1967) *Grotto of Tiberius and the National Archaeological Museum, Sperlonga*. Rome

Janko, R. (1982) *Homer, Hesiod and the Hymns: Diachronic Development in Epic Diction*. Cambridge

(1990) 'The *Iliad* and its editors: dictation and redaction', *Classical Antiquity* 9: 326–34

(1992a) *The Iliad: A Commentary* IV*: Books 13–16*. Cambridge

(1992b) 'L'*Iliade* fra dettatura e redazione', *Studi italiani di filologia classica*, 3rd ser., 85: 833–43

(1994) review of H. van Thiel, *Homeri Odyssea*, *Gnomon* 66: 289–95

(1998) 'The Homeric poems as oral dictated texts', *Classical Quarterly* 48: 1–13

Jansen, A. (2001) 'Chariots on the roads of Mycenae', *Mouseion* 1: 103–10

Jeanmaire, H. (1975) *Couroi et courètes*. New York

Jebb, R. C. (1880) review of H. Schliemann, *Ilios: The City and Country of the Trojans*, in *Edinburgh Review* (April) 152: 264–79

(1881) 'Homeric and Hellenic Ilium', *Journal of Hellenic Studies* 2: 7–43

(1882) 'I. The ruins at Hissarlik. II. Their relation to the Iliad', *Journal of Hellenic Studies* 3: 185–217

(1883a) 'The ruins of Hissarlik', *Journal of Hellenic Studies* 4: 147–55

(1883b) 'A tour in the Troad', *Fortnightly Review*, n.s. 33: 514–29

(1884) 'Homeric Troy', *Fortnightly Review*, n.s. 35: 433–52

(1902) *Homer: An Introduction to the Iliad and the Odyssey*, 6th edn. Boston

Jenkyns, R. (1980) *The Victorians and Ancient Greece*. Oxford

Jensen, M. S. (1980) *The Homeric Question and the Oral-Formulaic Theory*. Copenhagen

Joël, K. (1905) *Nietzsche und die Romantik*. Jena and Leipzig

(1906) *Der Ursprung der Naturphilosophie aus dem Geiste der Mystik. Mit Anhang: Archaische Romantik*. Jena

Johnson, J. W. (1980) 'Yes, Virginia, there is an epic in Africa', *Review of African Literatures* 11: 308–26

(1992) *The Epic of Son-Jara: A West African Tradition*. Text by Fa-Digi Sisòkò. Bloomington (orig. edn 1986)

Johnson, J. W. *et al.* (1997) *Oral Epics from Africa: Vibrant Voices from a Vast Continent*. Bloomington

Jones, P. V. (1997) 'Introduction', in Wright and Jones (1997) 1–46
Jong, I. J. F. de (1987) *Narrators and Focalizers: The Presentation of the Story in the Iliad*. Amsterdam
ed. (1999) *Homer: Critical Assessments*, 4 vols. London and New York
(2001) *A Narratological Commentary on the Odyssey*. Cambridge
Joyce, J. (1922) *Ulysses*. London
Juhnke, H. (1972) *Homerisches in römischer Epik der flavischen Zeit*. Munich
Kahane, A. (1994) *The Interpretation of Order: A Study in the Poetics of Homeric Repetition*. Oxford
(2004) *Diachronic Dialogues: Continuity and Authority in Homer and the Homeric tradition*. Lanham, Md.
Kaiser, E. (1964) 'Odyssee-Szenen als Topoi', *Museum Helveticum* 21: 109–36, 197–224
Kakridis, J. T. (1970) 'Dichterische Gestalten und wirkliche Menschen bei Homer', *Das Altertum und jedes neue Gute* = Festschrift W. Schadewaldt, 51–64. Stuttgart
(1971) *Homer Revisited*. Lund
Katz, M. A. [= M. B. Arthur] (1981) 'The divided world of *Iliad* VI', in H. P. Foley, ed. *Reflections of Women in Antiquity*, 19–44. New York
(1991) *Penelope's Renown. Meaning and Indeterminacy in the Odyssey*. Princeton
Kay, M. W. (1995) *The Index of the Milman Parry Collection, 1933–1935: Heroic Songs, Conversations, and Stories*. New York
Kearns, E. (1982) 'The return of Odysseus: a Homeric theoxeny', *Classical Quarterly* 32: 2–8
Keats, J. (1958a) *The Letters of John Keats 1814–1821*, ed. H. E. Rollins, 2 vols. Cambridge, Mass.
(1958b) *The Poetical Works of John Keats*, ed. H. W. Garrod, 2nd edn. Oxford
(1982) *Complete Poems*, ed. J. Stillinger. Cambridge, Mass., and London
Kemp-Lindemann, D. (1975) *Darstellung des Achilleus in griechischer und römischer Kunst*. Munich
Kenner, H. (1978) *Joyce's Voices*. London
(1987) *Ulysses*, rev. edn. Baltimore
Kim, J. (2000) *The Theme of Pity in the Iliad. Oral Style and the Unity of the Iliad*. Lanham, Md.
Kindstrand, J. F. (1973) *Homer in der zweiten Sophistik*. Uppsala and Stockholm
King, B. (2000) *Derek Walcott: A Caribbean Life*. Oxford
(2001) 'Briseis and the impossible marriages of the *Iliad*', paper presented at the annual meeting of the APA, Philadelphia
King, H. (1998) *Hippocrates' Woman. Reading the Female Body in Ancient Greece*. London and New York
King, K. C. (1987) *Achilles. Paradigms of the War Hero from Homer to the Middle Ages*. Berkeley and London
Kingsley, C. (1880) 'Nausicaa in London, or, The lower education of women?', in *Sanitary and Social Lectures and Essays*, 107–27. London
Kirk, G. S. (1962) *The Songs of Homer*. London
(1966) 'Studies in some technical aspects of Homeric style', *Yale Classical Studies* 20: 73–152

(1985) 'The epic tradition after Homer and Hesiod', in P. E. Easterling and B. M. W. Knox, eds. *Cambridge History of Greek Literature*, ch. 4. Cambridge (= ch. 3 of the pbk partial reprint, *Early Greek Poetry*. Cambridge 1989)

(1990) *The Iliad: A Commentary*, II: *Books 5–8*. Cambridge

Kirk, G. *et al.* (1985–93) *The Iliad: A Commentary*, 6 vols. Cambridge

Knauer, G. N. (1964a) *Die Aeneis und Homer*. Göttingen

(1964b) 'Vergil's *Aeneid* and Homer', *Greek, Roman and Byzantine Studies* 5: 61–84

Knight, V. (1995) *The Renewal of Epic. Responses to Homer in the Argonautica of Apollonius*. Leiden

Knox, B. M. W. (1964) *The Heroic Temper*. Berkeley

Köhnken, A. (1991) 'Die Narbe des Odysseus', in J. Latacz, ed. *Homer: Die Dichtung und ihre Deutung*, 101–14. Darmstadt

Kraus, K. (1935) *Winckelmann und Homer, mit Benutzung der Hamburger Homer-Ausschreibungen Winckelmanns*. Berlin

Krischer, T. (1971) *Formale Konventionen der homerischen Epik*. Zetemata 56. Munich

Kullmann, W. (1955) 'Ein vorhomerisches Motiv im Iliasproömium', *Philologus* 99: 167–92

(1956) 'Zur ΔΙΟΣ ΒΟΥΛΗ des Iliasproömiums', *Philologus* 101: 132–3

(1960) *Die Quellen der Ilias. Hermes* Einzelschrift 14. Wiesbaden

(1992) 'Gods and men in the *Iliad* and *Odyssey*', in W. Kullmann, *Homerische Motive: Beiträge zur Entstehung, Eigenart und Wirkung von Ilias und Odyssee*, ed. R. J. Muller, 243–63. Stuttgart [= *Harvard Studies in Classical Philology* 89 (1985) 1–23]

Kullmann, W. and Reichel, M., eds. (1990) *Der Übergang von der Mündlichkeit zur Literatur bei den Griechen*. ScriptOralia 30. Tübingen

Labarbe, J. (1949) *L'Homère de Platon*. Liège

Laffineur, R., ed. (1987) *Thanatos. Les coutumes funéraires en Egée à l'Age du Bronze*. Liège

Lamb, C. and Lamb, M. A. (1975–8) *The Letters of Charles and Mary Anne Lamb*, ed. E. W. Marrs Jr, 3 vols. Ithaca and London

Lamberton, R. (1986) *Homer the Theologian: Neoplatonist Allegorical Reading and the Growth of the Epic Tradition*. Berkeley and London (pbk edn. 1989)

(1992) 'The Neoplatonists and the spiritualization of Homer', in Lamberton and Keaney (1992) 115–33

Lamberton, R. and Keaney, J. J. (1992) *Homer's Ancient Readers: The Hermeneutics of Greek Epic's Earliest Exegetes*. Princeton

Lang, A. (1875) 'Homer and his recent critics', *Fortnightly Review*, n.s. 17: 575–89

(1891) 'Homer and the study of Greek', in *Essays in Little*, 77–92. New York

(1906) *Homer and His Age*. London and New York

Lang, M. (1975) 'Reason and purpose in Homeric prayers', *Classical World* 68: 309–14

(1989) 'Unreal conditions in Homeric narrative,' *Greek, Roman and Byzantine Studies* 30: 5–26

Latacz, J. (1977) *Kampfparänese, Kampfdarstellung und Kampfwirklichkeit in der Ilias, bei Kallinos und Tyrtaeus*. Munich

(1996) *Homer. His Art and his World*, tr. J. P. Holoka. Ann Arbor

(2001) *Troia und Homer. Der Weg zur Lösung eines alten Rätsels*. Munich and Berlin

(2002) 'Response: Latacz on Kullmann *Gnomon* 73 (2001) 657–63', *Bryn Mawr Classical Review* 2002.02.15

Lateiner, D. (1995) *Sardonic Smile: Nonverbal Behavior in Homeric Epic*. Ann Arbor

(1997) 'Homeric prayer', in B. Heiden, ed. *The Iliad and its Contexts. Arethusa* 30: 241–72

(2002) 'Pouring bloody drops (*Iliad* 16.459): the grief of Zeus', *Colby Quarterly* 38.1: 42–61

Leaf, W. (1960) *The Iliad, edited, with Apparatus Criticus, Prolegomena, Notes and Appendices*, 2nd. edn. Vol. I, *Books I–XII*, vol. II, *Books XIII–XXIV*. Amsterdam (Reprinted from 1900–02 edn. London)

Leduc, C. (1992) 'Marriage in ancient Greece', in P. Schmitt-Pantel, ed. *A History of Women, 1: From Ancient Goddesses to Christian Saints*, 235–94. Cambridge, Mass.

Lee, D. J. N. (1964) *The Similes of the Iliad and the Odyssey Compared*. Melbourne

Lee, W., ed. (1869) *Daniel Defoe: His Life, and Recently Discovered Writings*, 3 vols. London

Lefkowitz, M. (1981a). *Heroines and Hysterics*. London

(1981b) *The Lives of the Greek Poets*. London

Leopardi, G. (1987) *Poesie e Prose*, vol. 1, ed. M. A. Rigoni. Milan

Lesky, A. (1961) *Göttliche und menschliche Motivation im homerischen Epos*. Heidelberg

(1967) 'Homeros', *Real-Encyclopädie der classischen Altertumswissenschaft* Suppbd. XI. 687–846

Létoublon, F., Volpilhac-Auger, C. and Sangsue, D., eds. (1999) *Homère en France après la Querelle, 1715–1900: Actes du Colloque de Grenoble, 23–25 Octobre 1995, Université Stendhal-Grenoble 3*. Champion-Varia 32. Paris

Leumann, M. (1950) *Homerische Wörter*. Schweizerische Beiträge zur Altertumswissenschaft, Heft 3. Basel

Levine, J. M. (1991) *The Battle of the Books: History and Literature in the Augustan Age*. Ithaca

Lévi-Strauss, C. (1969) *The Elementary Structures of Kinship* (*Les structures élémentaires de la parenté*), eds. and trs. J. H. Bell, J. R. von Sturmer and R. Needham, 2nd edn. London

Lewalski, B. K. (1985) *Paradise Lost and the Rhetoric of Literary Forms*. Princeton

Lewis, W. (1975) *Enemy Salvoes: Selected Literary Criticism*. London

Lloyd-Jones, H. (1981) 'Remarks on the Homeric question', in H. Lloyd-Jones, V. Pearl and B. Worden, eds. *History and Imagination: Essays in Honour of H. R. Trevor-Roper*, 15–29. London (= Lloyd-Jones (1989) 3–20)

(1983) *The Justice of Zeus*, 2nd edn. Berkeley and Los Angeles

(1989) *Greek Epic, Lyric, and Tragedy: The Academic Papers of Sir Hugh Lloyd-Jones*. Oxford

(1999) 'The pride of Halicarnassus', *Zeitschrift für Papyrologie und Epigraphik* 124: 1–14

Logue, C. (1981) *War Music: An Account of Books 16 to 19 of Homer's Iliad*. London

(1992) *Kings: An Account of Books 1 and 2 of Homer's Iliad*. London

(1996) *The Husbands: An Account of Books 3 and 4 of Homer's Iliad*. London
(1999) *Logue's Homer: War Music*. London
(2003) *All Day Permanent Red*. London
Lohmann, D. (1970) *Die Komposition der Reden in der Ilias*. Berlin
Longley, M. (1973) *An Exploded View*. London
(1991a) *Gorse Fires*. London
(1991b) *Poems 1963–1983*, 2nd edn. London
(1995) *The Ghost Orchid*. London
(1998) *Broken Dishes*. Belfast
(2000) *The Weather in Japan*. London
Lonsdale, S. H. (1990) *Creatures of Speech: Lion, Herding, and Hunting Similes in the Iliad*. Stuttgart
Loraux, N. (1977) 'La belle mort Spartiate', *Ktêma* 2: 105–20
(1987) 'Le lien de la division', *Le Cahier du collège international de philosophie* 4: 101–24
(1990) *Les mères en deuil*. Paris
(1993) *The Children of Athena: Athenian Ideas about Citizenship and the Division between the Sexes*, tr. C. Levine. Princeton
(1995) *The Experiences of Tiresias* (English edn). Princeton
Lord, A. B. (1948) 'Homer and Huso III: enjambement in Greek and South Slavic heroic song', *Transactions of the American Philological Association* 79: 113–24
(1951) 'Composition by theme in Homer and South Slavic epos', *Transactions of the American Philological Association* 82: 71–80
(1991) *Epic Singers and Oral Tradition*. Ithaca and London
(1995) *The Singer Resumes the Tale*. Ithaca and London
(2000) *The Singer of Tales*. 2nd edn, ed. S. Mitchell and G. Nagy. Cambridge, Mass. (original edn 1960)
Lord, G. deF. (1956) *Homeric Renaissance: The Odyssey of George Chapman*. London
Louden, B. (1993) 'Pivotal contrafactuals in Homeric epic', *Classical Antiquity* 12.2: 181–98
(1999) *The Odyssey: Structure, Narration, and Meaning*. Baltimore
Lowe, N. (2000) *The Classical Plot and the Invention of Western Narrative*. Cambridge
Lowenstam, S. (1992) 'The uses of vase-depictions in Homeric studies', *Transactions of the American Philological Association* 12 (1992) 165–98
(1993) *The Scepter and the Spear: Studies on Forms of Repetition in the Homeric Poems*. Lanham, Md.
(1997) 'Talking vases: the relationship between the Homeric poems and archaic representations of epic myth', *Transactions of the American Philological Association* 127: 21–76
Lukács, G. (1971) *Die Theorie des Romans: Ein geschichtsphilosophischer Versuch über die Formen der Grossen Epik*. Neuwied (orig. edn 1920)
Lynn-George, M. (1988) *Epos: Word and Narrative in the Iliad*. London
Maas, P. (1962) *Greek Metre*, tr. H. Lloyd-Jones. Oxford
Mace, N. A. (1996) *Henry Fielding's Novels and the Classical Tradition*. Newark
Mackay, E. A., ed. (1999) *Signs of Orality. The Oral Tradition and its Influence in the Greek and Roman World*. Leiden and Boston

Macleod, C. W. (1982) *Homer: Iliad xxiv*. Cambridge
(1983) 'Homer on poetry and the poetry of Homer', in O. Taplin, ed. *Collected Essays*, 1–15. Oxford (= Cairns (2001) 294–310)
Magoun, F. P. (1953) 'The oral-formulaic character of Anglo-Saxon narrative poetry', *Speculum* 28: 446–67 (repr. in R. D. Fulk, ed. *Interpretations of Beowulf* (Bloomington 1991)
Mahaffy, J. P. (1876) *Rambles and Studies in Greece*. London (repr. Washington D. C. 1973)
(1882) 'The site and antiquity of the Hellenic Ilion', *Journal of Hellenic Studies* 3: 69–80
Malkin, I. (1998) *The Returns of Odysseus: Colonization and Ethnicity*. Berkeley
Mannoni, O. (1969) 'Je sais bien, mais quand-même . . .', in *Clefs pour l'imaginaire, ou, L'autre scène*, 9–33. Paris
Marchand, S. L. (1996) *Down from Olympus: Archaeology and Philhellenism in Germany, 1750–1970*. Princeton
Maresca, T. E. (1974) *Epic to Novel*. Columbus
Marg, W. (1957) *Homer über die Dichtung*. Münster
Marincola, J. (1997) 'Odysseus and the historians', *Histos* 1 [*http:www.dur.ac.uk/Classics/histos*]
Mariotti, S. (1955) *Il 'Bellum Punicum' e l'arte di Nevio*. Rome
(1986) *Livio Andronico e la traduzione artistica*, rev. edn. Urbino
Marrou, H. I. (1965) *Histoire de l'éducation dans l'antiquité*, 6th edn. Paris
Martin, R. P. (1989) *The Language of Heroes: Speech and Performance in the Iliad*. Ithaca
(1997) 'Similes and performance', in E. Bakker and A. Kahane, eds. *Written Voices, Spoken Signs: Tradition, Performance, and the Epic Text*, 138–66. Cambridge, Mass.
Martindale, C. (1986) *John Milton and the Transformation of Ancient Epic*. London and Sydney
(1996) 'Ruins of Rome: T. S. Eliot and the presence of the past', *Arion*, n.s. 3: 102–40
Mason, H. A. (1972) *To Homer through Pope: An Introduction to Homer's Iliad and Pope's Translation*. London
Mauss, M. (1954) *The Gift: Forms and Functions of Exchange in Archaic Societies*, tr. I. Cunnison. London
Mayer, K. (1996) 'Helen and the *Dios boulē*', *American Journal of Philology* 117: 1–15
Mazzoli, G. (2001) 'Quali preistorie? Catullo, Lucrezio', in G. Cajani and D. Lanza, eds. *L'antico degli Antichi*, 133–52. Rome
McAuslan, I. and Walcot, P., eds. (1998) *Homer*. *Greece and Rome* Studies 4. Oxford
McCarthy, W. B. (2001) 'Oral theory and epic studies', *Choice* 39. 1 (September): 61–75
McClure, L. K., ed. (2002) *Sexuality and Gender in the Classical World, Part 1: Greece*. Oxford
McLuhan, M. (1965) *The Gutenberg Galaxy*. Toronto
Meer, L. B. van der (1977–8) 'Etruscan urns from Voletta: studies on mythological representations', *Bulletin Antieke Beschaving* 52/53: 57–131
Mehmel, F. (1955) 'Homer und die Griechen', *Antike und Abendland* 4: 16–41

Merkelbach, R. (1952) 'Die Pisistratische Redaktion der homerischen Gedichte', *Rheinisches Museum für Philologie* 95: 23–77 (repr. in Merkelbach (1969), 239–62)
(1969) *Untersuchungen zur Odyssee* (2nd edn Munich)
Merkelbach, R. and Stauber, J. (1998) *Steinepigramme aus dem griechischen Osten*, vol. 1. Stuttgart and Leipzig
Meyer, E. (1877) *Geschichte von Troas*. Leipzig
Michelakis, P. (2002) *Achilles in Greek Tragedy*. Cambridge
Mickey, K. (1981) 'Dialect consciousness and literary language: an example from ancient Greek', *Transactions of the American Philosophical Society* 35 66
Miller, D. A. (2000) *The Epic Hero*. Baltimore
Milton, J. (1953–82) *Complete Prose Works*, ed. D. M. Wolfe, 8 vols. New Haven and London
Minchin, E. (2001) *Homer and the Resources of Memory*. Oxford
Monro, D. B., ed. (1901) *Homer's Odyssey, Books XIII–XXIV*. Oxford
Monsacré, H. (1984) *Les larmes d'Achille: les héros, la femme et la souffrance dans la poésie d' Homère*. Paris
Montanari, F. (2002) 'Alexandrian Homeric philology: the form of the *ekdosis* and the *variae lectiones*', in M. Reichel and A. Rengakos, eds. *EPEA PTEROENTA: Beiträge zur Homerforschung. Festschrift für Wolfgang Kullmann*, 119–40. Stuttgart
Montanari, F. and Ascheri, P., eds. (2002) *Omero tremila anni dopo*. Rome
Montiglio, S. (2000) 'Wandering philosophers in classical Greece', *Journal of Hellenic Studies* 120: 86–105
Mooij, J. J. A. (1976) *A Study of Metaphor*. Amsterdam
Moret, J.-M. (1975) *L'Ilioupersis dans la céramique italiote: les mythes et leur expression figurée au IVe siecle*. Bibliotheca Helvetica Romana 14. Rome
Morgan, K. (2000) *Myth and Philosophy from the Presocratics to Plato*. Cambridge
Morgan, L. (1999) *Patterns of Redemption in Virgil's Georgics*. Cambridge
Morgan T. (1998) *Literate Education in the Hellenistic and Roman Worlds*. Cambridge
Moritz, K. P. (1981) *Werke*, ed. H. Günther, 3 vols. Frankfurt am Main
Morris, I. (1986) 'The use and abuse of Homer', *Classical Antiquity* 5: 81–138 (= Cairns (2001) 57–91)
(1987) *Burial and Ancient Society: The Rise of the Greek City-State*. Cambridge
(1997) 'Periodization and the heroes: inventing a Dark Age', in M. Golden and P. Toohey, eds. *Inventing Ancient Culture: Historicism, Periodization and the Ancient World*, 96–131. London and New York
(2000) *Archaeology as Cultural History*. Oxford
Morris, I. and Powell, B., eds. (1997) *A New Companion to Homer*. Leiden (= *Mnemosyne* Suppl. 163)
Morris, S. (1997) 'Homer and the Near East', in Morris and Powell (1997) 599–623
Morrison, J. V. (1992a) 'Alternatives to epic tradition: Homer's challenges in the *Iliad*', *Transactions of the American Philological Association* 122: 61–71
(1992b) *Homeric Misdirection*. Ann Arbor
(1999) 'Homeric darkness: patterns and manipulation of death scenes in the *Iliad*', *Hermes* 127.2: 129–44

Most, Glenn (1989a) 'The second Homeric Renaissance: allegoresis and genius in early modern politics', in P. Murray, ed. *Genius: The History of an Idea*, 54–75. Oxford and New York

(1989b) 'The structure and function of Odysseus' Apologoi', *Transactions of the American Philological Association* 119: 15–30

(1989c) 'Zur Archäologie der Archaik', *Antike und Abendland* 35: 1–23

(1993) 'Hesiod and the textualization of personal temporality', in G. Arrighetti and F. Montanari, eds. *La componente autobiografica nella poesia greca e latina fra realtà e artificio letterario*, 73–92. Pisa

(1997) 'Hesiod's myth of the five (or three or four) races', *Proceedings of the Cambridge Philological Society* 43: 104–27

Moulton, C. (1977) *Similes in the Homeric Poems*. Göttingen

Mueller, M. (1969) '*Paradise Lost* and the *Iliad*', *Classical Literature Studies* 6: 292–316

Muellner, L. (1990) 'The simile of the cranes and pygmies: a study of Homeric metaphor', *Harvard Studies in Classical Philology* 93: 59–101

(1996) *The Anger of Achilles: Mēnis in Greek Epic*. Ithaca

Mühll, P. von der, ed. (1962) *Homeri Odyssea*, 3rd edn. Stuttgart

Mure, W. (1854) *A Critical History of the Language and Literature of Antient Greece*, 2nd edn, 5 vols. London

Murnaghan, S. (1987) *Disguise and Recognition in the* Odyssey. Princeton

(1995) 'The plan of Athena', in Cohen (1995) 70–1

Murray, G. (1934) *The Rise of the Greek Epic*, 4th edn. Oxford (repr. 1960)

Murray, O. (1982) 'Symposium and *Männerbund*', in P. Oliva and A. Frolikóvá, eds. *Concilium Eirene* 16.1: 47–52. Prague

Myres, J. L. (1932) 'The last book of the *Iliad*', *Journal of Hellenic Studies* 52: 264–96

(1958) *Homer and His Critics*, ed. D. Gray. London

Nagler, M. N. (1967) 'Toward a generative view of the oral formula', *Transactions of the American Philological Association* 98: 269–311

(1974) *Spontaneity and Tradition: A Study in the Oral Art of Homer*. Berkeley, Los Angeles and London

(1996) 'Dread goddesses revisited', in Schein (1996) 141–61

Nagy, G. (1974) *Comparative Studies in Greek and Indic Meter*. Cambridge, Mass.

(1979) *The Best of the Achaeans: Concepts of the Hero in Archaic Greek Poetry*. Baltimore (2nd edn 1999)

(1990) *Pindar's Homer. The Lyric Possession of an Epic Past*. Baltimore and London

(1992a) 'Homeric questions', *Transactions of the American Philological Association* 122: 17–60

(1992b) 'Mythological exemplum in Homer', in R. Hexter and D. Selden, eds. *Innovations of Antiquity*, 311–31. London

(1996a) *Homeric Questions*. Austin

(1996b) *Poetry as Performance: Homer and Beyond*. Cambridge

(1997) 'Homeric scholia', in Morris and Powell (1997) 101–22

(1998a) 'Aristarchean questions', *Bryn Mawr Classical Review* 07.14

(1998b) 'Is there an etymology for the dactylic hexameter?', in J. Jasanoff, H. C. Melchert, and L. Oliver, eds. *Mír Curad: Studies in Honor of Calvert Watkins*, 495–508. Innsbruck

(1999) 'Homer and Plato at the Panathenaia: synchronic and diachronic perspectives', in T. M. Falkner, N. Felson, D. Konstan, eds. *Contextualizing Classics. Ideology, Performance, Dialogue. Essays in Honor of John J. Peradotto*, 123–50. Lanham, Boulder and New York

Nelson, S. A. (1998) *God and the Land: The Metaphysics of Farming in Hesiod and Vergil*. New York and Oxford

Nesselrath, H.-G. (1992) *Ungeschehenes Geschehen. 'Beinahe-Episoden' im griechischen und römischen Epos von Homer bis zur Spätantike*. Stuttgart and Leipzig

Newman, F. W. (1856) *The Iliad of Homer, Faithfully Translated into Unrhymed English*. London

(1861) *Homeric Translation in Theory and Practice: A Reply to Matthew Arnold, Esq., Professor of Poetry, Oxford*. London

Newton, R. (1987) 'Odysseus and Hephaestus in the *Odyssey*', *Classical Journal* 83: 12–20

Niane, D. T. (1989) *Sundiata: An Epic of Old Mali*. London

Nicoll, A., ed. (1956) *Chapman's Homer, with Introduction, Notes and Commentary*, 2 vols. New York

Nietzsche, F. W. (1967) *The Birth of Tragedy, and the Case of Wagner*, tr. Walter Kaufmann. New York

(1982) 'Homer und die Klassische Philologie', in G. Colli and M. Montinari, eds. *Friedrich Nietzsche: Werke. Kritische Gesamtausgabe*, vol. 2.1 *Philologische Schriften 1867–1873*, 247–69. Berlin

(1988) *Friedrich Nietzsche, Sämtliche Werke. Kritische Studienausgabe*, 2nd edn, eds. G. Colli and M. Montinari, 15 vols. Berlin

Niles, J. D. (1999) *Homo Narrans: The Poetics and Anthropology of Oral Literature*. Philadelphia

Nilsson, M. P. (1932) *The Mycenaean Origin of Greek Mythology*. Berkeley, Los Angeles and London

Notopoulos, J. A. (1949) *The Platonism of Shelley: A Study of Platonism and the Poetic Mind*. Durham, N.C.

Nowottny, W. (1962) *The Language Poets Use*. London

Oinas, F. J., ed. (1978) *Heroic Epic and Saga: An Introduction to the World's Great Folk Epics*. Bloomington

O'Keeffe, K. O'B. (1990) *Visible Song: Transitional Literacy in Old English Verse*. Cambridge

Okpewho, I. (1975) *The Epic in Africa: Toward a Poetics of the Oral Performance*. New York

(1992) *African Oral Literature: Backgrounds, Character, and Continuity*. Bloomington

Olson, S. D. (1989a) '*Odyssey* 9: guile, force and the subversive poetics of desire', *Arethusa* 22: 135–45

(1989b) 'The stories of Helen and Menelaus (*Odyssey* 4.240–89) and the return of Odysseus', *American Journal of Philology* 110: 387–94

(1990) 'The stories of Agamemnon in Homer's *Odyssey*', *Transactions of the American Philological Association* 120: 57–71

Olson, D. (1995) *Blood and Iron: Stories and Storytelling in Homer's Odyssey*. *Mnem*. Suppl. 148. Leiden

O' Neill, E., Jr (1942) 'The localization of metrical word-types in the Greek hexameter', *Yale Classical Studies* 8: 103–78
Ong, W. (1982) *Orality and Literacy: The Technologizing of the Word*. London
Ortony, A., ed. (1993) *Metaphor and Thought*, 2nd edn. Cambridge
Osborne, R. (1996) *Greece in the Making, 1200–479 B.C.* London
(1998) *Archaic and Classical Greek Art*. Oxford
Oswald, P. (1999) *Odysseus*. London
Otis, B. (1964) *Virgil: A Study in Civilized Poetry*. Oxford
Otterlo, W. A. van (1944) *Untersuchungen über Begriff . . . der griechischenRingkomposition, Mededeel. der kon. Ned. Ak.* Nieuwe Reeks, Deel 7, no. 3. Amsterdam
Otto, A. (1890) *Die Sprichwörter und sprichwörtlichen Redensarten der Römer*. Leipzig
Owen, E. T. (1946) *The Story of the Iliad*. Toronto
Padel, R. (1992) *In and Out of the Mind: Greek Images of the Tragic Self*. Princeton
(1995) *Whom Gods Destroy: Elements of Greek and Tragic Madness*. Princeton
Paganelli, L. (1979) *Echi storico-politici nel 'Ciclope' Euripideo*. Padua
Page, D. L. (1955) *The Homeric Odyssey*. Oxford
(1973) *Folktales in Homer's Odyssey*. Cambridge, Mass.
Paley, F. A. (1871) 'On the comparatively late date and composite character of our *Iliad* and *Odyssey*', *Transactions of the Cambridge Philosophical Society* 11: 360–86
Palmer, L. R. (1962) 'The language of Homer', ch. 4 of Wace and Stubbings (1962)
(1980) *The Greek Language*. London
Papadopoulos, J. K. (1996) review of Andersen and Dickie (1995), *Bryn Mawr Classical Review* 96.5.2
Parker, W. R. (1996) *Milton: A Biography*, 2nd edn, rev. G. Campbell. Oxford
Parks, W. (1990) *Verbal Duelling in Heroic Narrative*. Princeton
Parry, A. A. (1973) *Blameless Aegisthus: A Study of* ΑΜΥΜΩΝ *and Other Epithets in Homer*. Amsterdam
Parry, A. M. (1956) 'The language of Achilles', *Transactions of the American Philological Association* 87: 1–7
(1966) 'Have we Homer's *Iliad*?', *Yale Classical Studies* 20: 175–216 (= Parry (1989) 104–40)
(1971) 'Introduction', in M. Parry (1971) ix–lxii (= Parry (1989) 195–264)
(1989) *The Language of Achilles and Other Papers*. Oxford
Parry, M. (1971) *The Making of Homeric Verse: The Collected Papers of Milman Parry*, ed. A. Parry. Oxford
Pater, W. (1911) *Greek Studies: A Series of Essays*. London (orig. edn 1895)
Patey, D. L. (1997) 'Ancients and moderns', in *The Eighteenth Century*, vol. IV in H. B. Nisbet and C. Rawson, eds. *The Cambridge History of Literary Criticism*, 32–71. Cambridge
Peabody, B. (1975) *The Winged Word: A Study in the Technique of Ancient Greek Oral Composition as Seen Principally through Hesiod's 'Works and Days'*. Albany
Pedrick, V. (1988) 'The hospitality of noble women in the *Odyssey*', *Helios* 15: 85–101
Pelliccia, H. (1995) *Mind, Body and Speech in Homer and Pindar*. Hypomnemata 107. Göttingen

(2003) 'Two points about rhapsodes', in M. Finkelberg and G. Stroumsa, eds. *Homer, the Bible, and Beyond: Literary and Religious Canons in the Ancient World*, 97–116. Leiden

Peradotto, J. (1990) *Man in the Middle Voice: Name and Narration in the Odyssey*. Princeton

Perl, J. (1984) *The Tradition of Return*. Princeton

Perry, B. E. (1937) 'The early Greek capacity for viewing things separately', *Transactions of the American Philological Association* 68: 403–27

Perysinakis, I. N. (1992) 'Sophocles' *Philoctetes* and the Homeric epics', *Dodona* 21: 79–120

Pfeiffer, R. (1968) *History of Classical Scholarship from the Beginnings to the End of the Hellenistic Age*. Oxford

(1976) *History of Classical Scholarship from 1300 to 1850*. Oxford

Pinkwart, D. (1965a) *Das Relief des Archelaos von Priene und die 'Musen des Philiskos'*. Kallmünz

(1965b) 'Das Relief des Archelaos von Priene', *Antike Plastik* 4: 55–65

Polignac, F. de (1995) *Cults, Territory and the Origins of the Greek City-State*, Eng. tr. Chicago

Pollitt, J. J. (1986) *Art in the Hellenistic Age*. Cambridge

Pope, A. (1940–69) *The Twickenham Edition of the Poems of Alexander Pope*, various eds., 11 vols. London and New Haven

(1967) *The Illiad Books I–IX*, ed. M. Mack. London and New Haven

(1996) *The Iliad of Homer*, ed. S. Shankman. London

Popham, M., Calligas, P. G. and Sackett L. H., eds. (1993) (with J. J. Coulton and H. W. Catling), *Lefkandi II: the Protogeometric Building at Toumba. Pt. 2: The Excavation, Architecture and Finds*. London

Porter, D. H. (1972–3) 'Violent juxtaposition in the similes of the *Iliad*', *Classical Journal* 68: 11–21

Porter, H. N. (1951) 'The early Greek hexameter', *Yale Classical Studies* 12: 1–63

Porter, J. I. (1992) 'Hermeneutic lines and circles: Aristarchus and Crates on Homeric exegesis', in Lamberton and Keaney (1992) 67–114

(2000a) *The Invention of Dionysus: An Essay on the Birth of Tragedy.* Stanford

(2000b) *Nietzsche and the Philology of the Future*. Stanford

(2002) 'Homer: The Very Idea', *Arion* 10.2: 57–86

Pound, E. (1935) *Making It New*. New Haven

(1987) *The Cantos*, 4th edn. London

Powell, B. (1991) *Homer and the Origins of the Greek Alphabet*. Cambridge

(1997) 'Homer and writing', in Morris and Powell (1997) 3–32

(2002) *Writing and the Origins of the Greek Alphabet*. Cambridge

Prins, Y. (forthcoming) 'Nineteenth-century Homers and the hexameter mania', in S. Berman and M. Wood, eds. *Nation/Language and the Ethics of Translation*. Princeton

Pucci, P. (1987) *Odysseus Polutropos. Intertextual Readings in the Odyssey and the Iliad*. Ithaca and London

(1998) *The Song of the Sirens*. Lanham, Boulder, New York and Oxford

(2002) 'Theology and poetics in the *Iliad*', *Arethusa* 35: 17–34

Puhvel, J. (1956) 'Greek ΑΝΑΞ', *Zeitschrift für Vergleichende Sprachforschung* 73: 202–22

(1987) *Comparative Mythology*. Baltimore and London
Pulleyn, S. (1997) *Prayer in Greek Religion*. Oxford
Qviller, B. (1981) 'The dynamics of the Homeric society' *Symbolae Osloenses* 56: 109–55
Raaflaub, K. A. (1993) 'Homer to Solon. The rise of the polis', in M. H. Hansen, ed. *The Ancient Greek City-State*, 41–105. Copenhagen
(1997) 'Homer, the Trojan War, and history', in D. D. Boedeker and K. A. Raaflaub, eds. *The World of Troy: Homer, Schliemann, and the Treasures of Priam*, 75–97. Washington D.C.
Rabel, R. (1997) *Plot and Point of View in the Iliad*. Ann Arbor
Rainey, L. (1999) *Institutions of Modernism: Literary Elites and Public Culture*. Yale
Ramazani, J. (1997) 'The wound of history: Walcott's *Omeros* and the post-colonial poetics of affliction', *Publications of the Modern Language Association of America* 112.3 (May): 405–15
Ramsey, J. W. (1970) 'The provenance of Troilus and Cressida', *Shakespeare Quarterly* 21: 223–40
Raven, D. S. (1962) *Greek Metre: An Introduction*. London
Reading, P. (1994) *'Homeric' Last Poems*. London
Reardon, B. P., ed. (1989) *Collected Ancient Greek Novels*. Berkeley, Los Angeles and London
Reden, S. von, and Goldhill, S. (1999) 'Plato and the performance of dialogue', in S. Goldhill and R. Osborne, eds. *Performance Culture and Athenian Democracy*, 257–89. Cambridge
Redfield, J. M. (1975) *Nature and Culture in the Iliad: The Tragedy of Hector*. Chicago and London
Rehak, P., ed. (1995) *The Role of the Ruler in the Prehistoric Aegean*. Liège
Reichl, K. (1992) *Turkic Oral Epic Poetry: Traditions, Forms, Poetic Structures*. Albert Bates Lord Studies in Oral Tradition 7. New York
(2000) *Singing the Past: Turkic and Medieval Heroic Poetry*. Ithaca
(2001) *Das usbekische Heldenepos Alpomish: Einführung, Text, Übersetzung*. Turcologica 48. Wiesbaden
Reiman, D. H. and Fraistat, N., eds. (2002) *Shelley's Poetry and Prose*, 2nd edn. New York and London
Reinhardt, K. (1961) *Die Ilias und ihr Dichter*, ed. U. Hölscher. Göttingen
(1996) 'The adventures in the *Odyssey*', tr. H. Flower, in Schein (1996) 63–132
Rengakos, A. (1992) 'Homerische Wörter bei Kallimachos', *Zeitschrift für Papyrologie und Epigraphik* 94: 21–47
(1993) *Der Homertext und die hellenistischen Dichter*. Stuttgart
(1994) *Apollonios Rhodios und die antike Homererklärung*. Munich
(1998) 'Zur Zeitstruktur der Odyssee', *Wiener Studien* 111: 45–66
(2002) 'The Hellenistic poets as Homeric critics', in Montanari and Ascheri (2002) 143–57
Reynolds, D. F. (1995) *Heroic Poets, Poetic Heroes: The Ethnography of Performance in an Arabic Oral Epic Tradition*. Ithaca
Richardson, N. J. (1975) 'Homeric professors in the age of the sophists', *Proceedings of the Cambridge Philological Society* 21: 65–81
(1993) *The Iliad: A Commentary*, VI: *Books 21–24*. Cambridge

Richardson, S. (1990) *The Homeric Narrator*. Nashville

Richman, P., ed. (1991) *Many Ramayanas: The Diversity of a Narrative Tradition in South Asia*. Berkeley and Los Angeles

Ricoeur, P. (1975) *La métaphore vive*. Paris

Ridgway, B. (1990) *Hellenistic Sculpture*, vol. 1. Bristol

Riding, L. (1937) *A Trojan Ending*. London

Rieu, E. V., trs. (1950) *The Iliad*. Harmondsworth (2nd edn 1966)

Rissman, L. (1983) *Love as War: Homeric Allusion in the Poetry of Sappho*. Königstein

Robert, C. (1890) *Homerische Becher*. Berlin

Rosaldo, M. Z. and Lamphere, L., eds. (1974) *Women, Culture, and Society*. Palo Alto

Rose, P. W. (1997) 'Ideology in the *Iliad: polis, basileus, theoi*', *Arethusa* 30: 151–99

Rosenmeyer, P. (1997) 'Her master's voice: Sappho's dialogue with Homer' *Materiali e discussioni* 39: 123–49

Rossi, L. E. (1971) 'Il *Ciclope* di Euripide come κῶμος mancato', *Maia* 23: 10–38

(1978) 'I poemi omerici come testimonianza di poesia orale', in R. B. Bandinelli, ed. *Storia e Civiltà dei Greci*, 1.1: *Origini e sviluppo della città. Il medioevo greco*, 73–147. Milan

(1997) 'Esiodo, *Le Opere e i Giorni*: un nuovo tentativo di analisi', in F. Montanari and S. Pittaluga, eds. *Posthomerica* 1, 7–22 Genoa

(1999) 'La méthode philologique de Jean Baptiste Gaspard d'Ansse de Villoison et le *Venetus Marcianus* A', in Létoublon, Volpilhac-Auger and Sangsue (1999) 51–61

Rothe, C. (1910) *Die Ilias als Dichtung*. Paderborn

Roworth, W. W., ed. (1992) *Angelica Kauffman: A Continental Artist in Georgian England*. Brighton

Rubin, G. (1975) 'The traffic in women: notes on the "political economy" of sex', in R. R. Reiter, ed. *Toward an Anthropology of Women*, 157–210. New York

Ruijgh, C. J. (1957) *L'élément achéen dans la langue épique*. Assen

Russell, D. A. (1964) *Longinus: On the Sublime*. Oxford

Russo, J. (1963) 'A closer look at Homeric formulas', *Transactions of the American Philological Association* 94: 235–47

(1966) 'The structural formula in Homeric verse', *Yale Classical Studies* 20: 219–40

(1968) 'Homer against his tradition', *Arion* 7.2: 275–95

(1982) 'Interview and aftermath: dream, fantasy, and intuition in *Odyssey* 19 and 20', *American Journal of Philology* 103: 4–18

(1997) 'The formula', in Morris and Powell (1997) 238–60

Rutherford, I. (2001) *Pindar's Paeans: A Reading of the Fragments with a Survey of the Genre*. Oxford

Rutherford, R. (1982) 'Tragic form and feeling in the *Iliad*', *Journal of Hellenic Studies* 102: 145–60

(1986) 'The philosophy of the *Odyssey*', *Journal of Hellenic Studies* 106: 145–62

(1991–3) 'From the *Iliad* to the *Odyssey*', *Bulletin of the Institute of Classical Studies* 38: 37–54

(1992) ed. *Homer, Odyssey, Books* XIX *and* XX. Cambridge

(1996) *Homer*. Greece and Rome New Surveys in the Classics 26. Oxford
Sacks, R. (1987) *The Traditional Phrase in Homer: Two Studies in Form, Meaning and Interpretation*, 45–62. Columbia Studies in the Classical Tradition 14. Leiden
(1996) 'Odysseus traditions and the *telos* of the *Odyssey*', American Philological Association talk, New York
Sadurska, A. (1964) *Les tables Iliaques*. Warsaw
Said, E. W. (1985) *Beginnings: Intention and Method*. New York
Saïd, S. (1979) 'Les crimes des prétendants, la maison d'Ulysse, et les festins de l'Odyssée', in S. Saïd *et al.*, eds. *Études de littérature ancienne*. Paris
Sale, M. (2001) 'The oral-formulaic theory today', in J. Watson, ed. *Speaking Volumes: Orality and Literacy in the Greek and Roman World*, 53–80. Leiden
Sale, W. M. (1987) 'The formularity of the place phrases in the *Iliad*', *Transactions of the American Philological Association* 117: 21–50
(1989) 'The Trojans, statistics, and Milman Parry', *Greek, Roman and Byzantine Studies* 30: 341–410
(1994) 'The government of Troy: politics in the *Iliad*', *Greek, Roman and Byzantine Studies* 35: 5–102
Sandy, G. N. (1982) 'Characterization and philosophical decor in Heliodorus' *Aethiopica*', *Transactions of the American Philosophical Association* 112: 141–67
Saussure, F. de. (1969) *Course in General Linguistics*. New York (orig. edn 1915)
Sayce, A. H. (1883) 'The Age of Homer', *Journal of Philosophy* 12: 36–42
Scaffai, M. (1991) *Omero e la poesia latina*. Bologna
Schadewaldt, W. (1941) *Winckelmann und Homer*. Leipziger Universitätsreden 6. Leipzig (= *Hellas und Hesperien* (Zurich and Stuttgart 1960 600–36)
(1943) *Iliasstudien*. 2nd edn. Leipzig (repr. Darmstadt 1966)
(1944) *Von Homers Welt und Werk*. Leipzig
(1975) *Der Aufbau der Ilias*. Frankfurt
Schefold, K. (1952) *Pompejanische Malerei: Sinn und Ideengeschichte*. Basel
(1975) *Wort und Bild*. Basel
Schein, S. (1984) *The Mortal Hero: An Introduction to Homer's Iliad*. Berkeley
(1996) *Reading the Odyssey: Selected Interpretive Essays*. Princeton
(2002) 'Mythological allusion in the *Odyssey*', in Montanari and Ascheri (2002) 85–101
Schiff, G. (1973) *Johann Heinrich Füssli 1741–1825*. Zurich
Schiff, G. and Viotto, P. (1977) *L'opera completa di Füssli*. Milan
Schlam, C. and Finkelpearl, E. (2000) 'A review of scholarship on Apuleius' *Metamorphoses*, 1970–1998', *Lustrum* 42: 211–13
Schlesier, R. (1994) *Kulte, Mythen und Gelehrte: Anthropologie der Antike seit 1800*. Frankfurt am Main
Schliemann, H. (1880) *Ilios: The City and Country of the Trojans. The Results of Researches and Discoveries on the Site of Troy and through the Troad in the Years 1871-72-73-78-79. Including an Autobiography of the Author.* London (repr. New York 1976)
Schliemann, H. and Sayce, A. H. (1884) *Troja. Results of the Latest Researches and Discoveries on the Site of Homer's Troy and on the Heroic Tumuli and Other Sites, Made in the Year 1882. And a Narrative of a Journey in the Troad in 1881.* New York

Schmid, W. and Stählin, O. (1929) *Geschichte der griechischen Literatur* 1. München

Schmitt, R. (1967) *Dichtung und Dichtersprache in indogermanischer Zeit*. Wiesbaden

(1968) *Indogermanische Dichtersprache*. Wege der Forschung 165. Darmstadt

(1973) *Indogermanische Dichtersprache und Namengebung*. Innsbrucker Beiträge zur Sprachwissenschaft 10. Innsbruck

(1977) *Einführung in die griechischen Dialekte*. Darmstadt

Schnapp-Gourbeillon, A. (1981) *Lions, héros, masques: les représentations de l'animal chez Homère*. Paris

Schofield, M. (1986) '*Euboulia* in the *Iliad*', *Classical Quarterly* 36: 6–31

Schork, R. J. (1998) *Greek and Hellenic Culture in Joyce*. Florida

SCHS (1953–80) *Serbocroatian Heroic Songs* (*Srpskohrvatske junačke pjesme*). Cambridge, Mass. and Belgrade

Schwabl, H. (1990) 'Was lehrt mündliche Epik für Homer?', in Kullmann and Reichel (1990) 65–109

Schwartz, E. (1940) 'Der Name "Homeros"', *Hermes* 75: 1–10

Scodel, R. (1982) 'The Achaean wall and the myth of destruction', *Harvard Studies in Classical Philology* 86: 33–50

(1989) 'The word of Achilles', *Classical Philology* 84: 91–9

(1992) 'Inscription, absence and memory: epic and early epitaph', *Studi italiani di filologia classica* 85: 57–76

(1997) 'Pseudo-intimacy and the prior knowledge of the Homeric audience', *Arethusa* 30: 201–17

(1998) 'Bardic performance and oral tradition in Homer', *American Journal of Philology* 119: 171–94

(2001) 'Poetic authority and oral tradition in Hesiod and Pindar', in Watson (2001) 109–37

(2002) *Listening to Homer. Tradition, Narrative, and Audience*. Ann Arbor

Scott, J. A. (1911) 'Repeated verses in Homer', *American Journal of Philology*, 313–21

Scully, S. (1984) 'The language of Achilles: the ὀχθήσας formula', *Transactions of the American Philological Association* 114: 11–27

(1990) *Homer and the Sacred City*. Ithaca, N.Y.

Seaford, R. (1984) *Euripides, Cyclops*. Oxford

(1994) *Reciprocity and Ritual: Homer and Tragedy in the Developing City-State*. Oxford

Segal, C. (1971a) 'Andromache's *anagnorisis*', *Harvard Studies in Classical Philology* 75: 33–57

(1971b) *The Theme of the Mutilation of the Corpse in the Iliad*. Leiden

(1994) *Singers, Heroes and Gods in the Odyssey*. Ithaca

Selden, D. (1998) 'Alibis', *Classical Antiquity* 17: 289–412

Shaffer, E. S. (1988) *Erewhons of the Eye: Samuel Butler as Painter, Photographer, and Art Critic*. London

Shay, J. (1994) *Achilles in Vietnam: Combat Trauma and the Undoing of Character*. New York and Toronto

Shelley, M. Wollstonecraft (1980) *The Letters of Mary Wollstonecraft Shelley*, vol. 1, ed. B. T. Bennett. Baltimore and London

Shelley, P. B. (1964) *The Letters of Percy Bysshe Shelley*, ed. F. L. Jones, 2 vols. Oxford

Sheppard, J. T. (1922) *The Pattern of the Iliad*. London

Sherratt, E. S. (1990) '"Reading the texts": archaeology and the Homeric question', *Antiquity* 64: 807–24
Shewan, A. (1913) 'Does the *Odyssey* imitate the *Iliad*?', *Classical Quarterly*, 234–42
Shewring, W. (1980) tr. *Homer, The Odyssey*. Oxford
Shipp, G. P. (1972) *Studies in the Language of Homer*, 2nd edn. Cambridge
Shive, D. (1987) *Naming Achilles*. Oxford
Silk, M. S. (1974) *Interaction in Poetic Imagery with Special Reference to Early Greek Poetry*. Cambridge
(1988) 'Pathos in Aristophanes', *Bulletin of the Institute of Classical Studies* 34: 78–111
(2003) 'Metaphor and metonymy: Aristotle, Jakobson, Ricoeur, and others', in G. R. Boys-Stones, ed. *Metaphor, Allegory, and the Classical Tradition*, 115–47. Oxford
(2004) *Homer, The Iliad*, 2nd edn. Cambridge
Simonsuuri, K. (1979) *Homer's Original Genius: Eighteenth-Century Notions of the Early Greek Epic (1688–1798)*. Cambridge and New York
Sinn, U. (1979) *Die homerischen Becher: hellenistische Reliefkeramik aus Makedonien*. Berlin
Sinos, D. (1980) *Achilles, Patroklos and Meaning of Philos*. Innsbruck
Skutsch, O. (1985) *The Annals of Quintus Ennius*. Oxford
Slatkin, L. (1988) 'Les amis mortels: les injures sur le champ de bataille', tr. N. Loraux, *L'écrit du temps* 19: 119–32
(1991) *The Power of Thetis: Allusion and Interpretation in the Iliad*. Berkeley and Los Angeles
(1996) 'Composition by theme and the *metis* of the *Odyssey*', in Schein (1996) 23–37
(2006) *The Power of Thetis and selected essays*. Washington, D. C. and Cambridge, MA
Sloane, T. O., ed. (2001) *Encyclopedia of Rhetoric*. Oxford
Sluiter, I. (1999) 'Commentaries and the didactic tradition', in G. W. Most, ed. *Commentaries – Kommentare*, 173–205. Göttingen
Smith, J. D., ed. and trs. (1991) *The Epic of Pabuji: A Study, Transcription, and Translation*. Cambridge
Smolenaars, J. J. L. (1994) *Statius, Thebaid VII, A Commentary*. Leiden
Snell, B. (1953) *The Discovery of the Mind*, tr. T. G. Rosenmeyer. Oxford (orig. German edn 1946)
Snipes, K. (1988) 'Literary interpretation in the Homeric scholia: the similes of the *Iliad*', *American Journal of Philology* 109: 196–222
Snodgrass, A. M. (1971) *The Dark Age of Greece*. Edinburgh (2nd edn 2000)
(1974) 'An historical Homeric society?', *Journal of Hellenic Studies* 94: 114–25
(1980) *Archaic Greece: The Age of Experiment*. Berkeley
(1998) *Homer and the Artists: Text and Picture in Early Greek Art*. Cambridge
Solmsen, F. (1986) 'Aeneas founded Rome with Odysseus', *Harvard Studies in Classical Philology* 90: 93–110
Sotiriou, M. (1998) *Pindarus Homericus. Homer-Rezeption in Pindars Epinikien*. Göttingen
Sourvinou-Inwood, C. (1995) *Reading Greek Death*. Oxford

(1997) 'The Hesiodic myth of the five races and the tolerance of plurality in Greek mythology', in O. Palagia, ed. *Greek Offerings: Essays on Greek Art in Honour of John Boardman*, 1–21. Oxford

Southey, R. (1829) *The Poetical Works of Robert Southey.* Paris

(1965) *New Letters of Robert Southey*, ed. K. Curry, 2 vols. New York and London

Sowerby, R. (1992) 'Chapman's discovery of Homer', *Translation and Literature* 1: 26–51

Spencer, T. (1954) *Fair Greece Sad Relic: Literary Philhellenism from Shakespeare to Byron.* London

Spinazzola, V. (1953) *Pompei alla luce degli scavi nuovi di Via dell'Abbondanza.* Rome

Stadter, P. (1997) 'Herodotus and the North Carolina oral narrative tradition', *Histos* 1 *(http://www.dur.ac.uk/Classics/histos/1997/stadter.html)*

Staël, G. de (1959) *De la littérature considérée dans ses rapports avec les institutions sociales*, ed. P. van Tieghem, 2 vols. Geneva and Paris

Stanford, W. B. (1939) *Ambiguity in Greek Literature.* Oxford

(1958–9) ed. *Homer, Odyssey*, 2 vols. London

(1963) *The Ulysses Theme.* Oxford

Stanley, K. (1993) *The Shield of Homer. Narrative Structure in the Iliad.* Princeton

Steadman, J. (1967) *Milton and the Renaissance Hero.* Oxford

Steiner, G., ed. (1996) *Homer in English*, with the assistance of A. Dykman. London

(1998) *After Babel: Aspects of Translation*, 3rd edn. Oxford

Stella, L. A. (1978) *Tradizione micenea e poesia dell'Iliade.* Rome

Sternberg, M. (1978). *Expositional Modes and Temporal Ordering in Fiction.* Baltimore

Stevens, H. and Howlett, C., eds. (2000) *Modernist Sexualities.* Manchester

Stevenson, R. (1992) *Modernist Fiction.* Hemel Hempstead

Stewart, A. (1997) *Art, Desire, and the Body in Ancient Greece.* Cambridge and New York

Stokes, M. C. (1997) *Plato: Apology of Socrates.* Warminster

Strasburger, H. (1972) 'Homer und die Geschichtsschreibung', *Sitz. Heidelberg* (= *Studien zur alten Geschichte*, 2: 1,057–97. Hildesheim and New York 1982)

Stuttaford, A. (2002) 'Ode to Troy: the *Iliad* in Lower Manhattan', *National Review Online*: March 21

Suerbaum, W. (1968a) *Untersuchungen zur Selbstdarstellung älterer römischen Dichter: Livius Andronicus, Naevius, Ennius.* Hildesheim

(1968b) 'Die Ich-Erzählungen des Odysseus', *Poetica* 1: 150–77

Sühnel, R. (1958) *Homer und die englische Humanität: Chapmans und Popes Übersetzungskunst im Rahmen der humanistichen Tradition.* Tübingen

Sullivan, S. D. (1988) *Psychological Activity in Homer: A Study of Phren.* Ottawa

Suzuki, M. (1989) *Metamorphoses of Helen: Authority, Difference, and the Epic.* Ithaca, N.Y.

Sybel, L. von (1875) *Ueber Schliemann's Troja: Vortrag.* Marburg

Symmons, S. (1984) *Flaxman and Europe: The Outline Illustrations and their Influence.* New York

Tandy, D. W. and Neale, W. C. (1996) *Hesiod's Works and Days: A Translation and Commentary for the Social Sciences.* Berkeley

Taplin, O. P. (1980) 'The shield of Achilleus within the *Iliad*', *Greece and Rome* 27: 1–21 (repr. in McAuslan and Walcot (1998), 96–115)
(1983) 'Tragedy and trugedy', *Classical Quarterly* 33: 331–3
(1992). *Homeric Soundings. The Shaping of the Iliad*. Oxford
Tate, T. (1998) *Modernism, History and the First World War*. Manchester
Taylor, C., ed. (1963) *Essays on the Odyssey: Selected Modern Criticism*. Bloomington
Taylor, J. (2003) 'Performing *The Odyssey* – a practitioner's view', in L. Hardwick and C. Gillespie, eds. *The Role of Greek Drama and Poetry in Crossing and Redefining Cultural Boundaries*, 34–42. Milton Keynes
Telò, M. (1999) 'Eliodoro e la critica omerica antica', *Studi italiani di filologia classica* 92: 71–87
Terada, R. (1992) *Derek Walcott's Poetry: American Mimicry*. Boston
Thalmann, W. G. (1984) *Conventions of Form and Thought in Early Greek Epic Poetry*. Baltimore
(1988) 'Thersites: comedy, scapegoats, and heroic ideology in the *Iliad*', *Transactions of the American Philological Association* 118: 1–28
(1998) *The Swineherd and the Bow. Representations of Class in the Odyssey*. Ithaca N.Y.
van Thiel, H. (1991) *Homeri Odyssea*. Hildesheim
Thomas, C. (1990) 'Pope's *Iliad* and the contemporary context of his "Appeals to the Ladies"', *Eighteenth Century Life* 14(2): 1–17
Thomas, R. (1995) 'The place of the poet in Archaic society', in A. Powell, ed. *The Greek World*, 106–17. London and New York
(1998) '"Melodious tears": sepulchral epigram and generic mobility', in M. A. Harder, R. F. Regtuit and G. C. Wakker, eds. *Genre in Hellenistic Poetry*, 205–23. Groningen
(2000) *Herodotus in Context*. Cambridge
Thornton, A. (1984) *Homer's Iliad: its Composition and the Motif of Supplication*. Göttingen
Tilley, C. (1999) *Metaphor and Material Culture*. Oxford
Tillyard, E. M. W. (1954) *The English Epic and its Background*. London
(1958) *The Epic Strain in the English Novel*. London
Tolkhien, J. (1897) 'De Homeri auctoritate in cotidiana Romanorum vita', *Jahrbücher für classische Philologie* Suppl. 23. Leipzig
(1900) *Homer und die römische Poesie*. Leipzig
(1991) *Omero e la poesia latina*, tr. M. Scaffai. Bologna
Tomlinson, C. (1983) *Poetry and Metamorphosis*. Cambridge
Touchefeu-Meynier, O. (1968) *Thèmes odysséens dans l'art antique*. Paris
Traill, D. A. (1995) *Schliemann of Troy: Treasure and Deceit*. New York
Traina, A. (1970) *Vortit barbare: Le traduzioni poetiche da Livio Andronico a Cicerone*. Rome
Troia: Traum und Wirklichkeit. Begleitband zur Ausstellung 'Troia – Traum und Wirklichkeit' (2001). Darmstadt
Truffaut, F. (1967) *Hitchcock*, with the collaboration of H. G. Scott. New York
Tsagarakis, O. (1977) *Nature and Background of Major Conceptions of Divine Power in Homer*. Amsterdam

Tsigakou, F.-M. (1981) *The Rediscovery of Greece: Travellers and Painters in the Romantic Era*. London

Turner, F. M. (1981) *The Greek Heritage in Victorian Britain*. New Haven

(1997) 'The Homeric question', in Morris and Powell (1997) 123–45

Ullmann, S. (1975) *Précis de sémantique française*. Bern

Underwood, S. (1998) *English Translators of Homer*. London

Van Nortwick, T. (1979) 'Penelope and Nausicaa', *Transactions of the American Philological Association* 109: 269–76

Venuti, L. (1995) *The Translator's Invisibility: A History of Translation*. London and New York

Vermeule, C. (1995) 'Neon Ilion and Ilium novum: kings, soldiers, citizens, and tourists at classical Troy', in Carter and Morris (1995) 467–82

Vermeule, E. (1979) *Aspects of Death in Early Greek Art and Poetry*. Berkeley and Los Angeles

(1986) 'Priam's castle blazing: a thousand years of Trojan memories', in J. L. Angel and M. J. Mellink, eds. *Troy and the Trojan War: A Symposium Held at Bryn Mawr College, October 1984*, 77–92, Bryn Mawr

Vernant, J.-P. (1968) *Problèmes de la guerre en Grèce ancienne*. Paris

(1982) 'La belle mort et le cadavre outragé', in G. Gnoli and J. P. Vernant, eds. *La mort, les morts dans les sociétés anciennes*, 45–76. Cambridge and Paris

(1983) *Myth and Thought among the Greeks* (tr. from French orig. 1965). London

(1991) 'A "beautiful death" and the disfigured corpse in Homeric epic', in *Mortals and Immortals: Collected Essays*, 50–74. Princeton

(1996) 'The refusal of Odysseus', in Schein (1996) 185–9

Veyne, P. (1988) *Did the Greeks Believe in their Myths?* tr. P. Wissing. Chicago and London

Vico, G. (1948) *The New Science of Giambattista Vico: Translated from the Third Ed. (1744)* ed. and trs. T. G. Bergin and M. H. Fisch. Ithaca

Viscogliosi, A. (1996) '*Antra Cyclopis:* osservazioni su una tipologia di *coenatio*', in Andreae and Presicce (1996) 252–69

Visser, E. (1988) 'Formulae or single words? Towards a new theory on Homeric verse making', *Würzb Jahrb. f.d. Altertumsw. Neue Folge*. 14: 21–37

(1997) *Homers Katalog der Schiffe*. Stuttgart

Vivante, P. (1982) *The Epithets of Homer: A Study in Poetic Values*. New Haven and London

Vogt-Spira, G. (2003) 'Warum Vergil Statt Homer? Der frühneuzeitliche Vorzugsstreit zwischen Homer und Vergil im Spannungsfeld von Autorität und Historisierung', *Poetica* 35: 323–44

Wace, A. J. B. and Stubbings, F. H., eds. (1962) *A Companion to Homer*. London and New York

Wackernagel, J. (1916) *Sprachliche Untersuchungen zu Homer*. Göttingen

Wade-Gery, H. T. (1958) *Essays in Greek History*. Oxford

Walcott, D. (1990) *Omeros*. London and Boston

(1993a) *The Antilles: Fragments of Epic Memory: The Nobel Lecture*. New York

(1993b) *The Odyssey: A Stage Version*. London

Watkins, C. (1995) *How to Kill a Dragon: Aspects of Indo-European Poetics*. New York and Oxford

Watson, J., ed. (2001) *Speaking Volumes: Orality and Literacy in the Greek and Roman World*. Leiden, Boston and Cologne

Webb, T. (1976) *The Violet in the Crucible: Shelley and Translation*. Oxford

(1982) *English Romantic Hellenism, 1700–1824*. Manchester

(1993) 'Romantic Hellenism', in Stuart Curran, ed. *The Cambridge Companion to British Romanticism*, 148–76. Cambridge

Weber-Lehmann, C. (1995) 'Polyphem in der Unterwelt? Zur Tomba dell'Orco II in Tarquinia', *Rheinisches Museum für Philologie* 102: 71–100

Webster, T. B. L. (1962) Revision of Pickard-Cambridge, A. W. *Dithyramb, Tragedy and Comedy*. Oxford

Wees, H. van (1992) *Status Warriors: War, Violence and Society in Homer and History*. Amsterdam

(1997) 'Homeric warfare', in Morris and Powell (1997) 668–93

Weil, S. (1953) 'L'*Iliade*, ou la poème de la force', in *La Source grecque*, 11–42. Paris

(1999) 'The *Iliad* or the poem of force' (tr. from French original of 1940–1), in I. J. F. de Jong, ed. *Homer: Critical Assessments*, vol. III, 66–90. London

Weinbrot, H. D. (1993) *Britannia's Issue: The Rise of British Literature from Dryden to Ossian*. Cambridge

Weitzmann, K. (1959) *Ancient Book Illumination*. Cambridge, Mass.

(1970) *Illustrations in Roll and Codex*, 2nd edn. Princeton

Welcker, F. G. (1865) *Der Epische Cyclus, oder die Homerischen Dichter*, 2nd edn, 2 vols. Bonn

West, M. L. (1966) *Hesiod: Theogony*. Oxford

(1978) *Hesiod: Works and Days*. Oxford

(1982) *Greek Metre*. Oxford

(1987) *Introduction to Greek Metre*. Oxford

(1988) 'The rise of the Greek epic', *Journal of Hellenic Studies* 108: 151–72

(1990) 'Archaische Heldendichtung: Singen und Schreiben', in Kullmann and Reichel (1990) 33–50

(1992a) *Ancient Greek Music*. Oxford

(1992b) 'The descent of the Greek epic: a reply', *Journal of Hellenic Studies* 112: 173–5

(1995) 'The date of the *Iliad*', *Museum Helveticum* 52: 203–19

(1997a) *The East Face of Helicon: West Asiatic elements in Greek Poetry and Myth*. Oxford

(1997b) 'Homer's metre', in Morris and Powell (1997) 218–37

(1998–2000) *Homerus: Ilias*. Stuttgart, Munich and Leipzig

(1999) 'The invention of Homer', *Classical Quarterly* 49: 364–82

(2000) 'The gardens of Alcinous and the oral dictated text theory', *Acta Ant. Hung.* 40: 479–88

(2001) *Studies in the Text and Transmission of the Iliad*. Munich and Leipzig

(2002) '"Eumelus": a Corinthian epic cycle', *Journal of Hellenic Studies* 122: 109–32

(2003) *Homeric Hymns, Homeric Apocrypha, Lives of Homer*, Loeb Classical Library. Cambridge, Mass.

West, S. (1967) *The Ptolemaic Papyri of Homer*. Papyrologica Colonensia 3. Cologne and Opladen

(1988) 'The transmission of the text', in Heubeck *et al.* (1988–92) 1.33–48
(1989) 'Laertes revisited', *Proceedings of the Cambridge Philological Society* n.s. 35: 113–43
Wetzel, W. (1965) *De Euripidis fabula satyrica, quae Cyclops inscribitur, cum Homerico comparata exemplo*. Wiesbaden
Whallon, W. (1969) *Formula, Character, and Context: Studies in Homeric, Old English, and Old Testament Poetry*. Washington, D.C.
Whitley, J. (1991) 'Social diversity in Dark Age Greece', *Annual of the British School at Athens* 86: 341–65
(2001) *The Archaeology of Ancient Greece*. Cambridge
Whitman, C. (1958) *Homer and the Heroic Tradition*. Cambridge, Mass.
(1964) *Aristophanes and the Comic Hero*. Cambridge, Mass.
Whitmarsh, T. (1998) 'The birth of a prodigy: Heliodorus and the genealogy of Hellenism', in R. Hunter, ed. *Studies in Heliodorus* 93–124. Cambridge
(2002) 'What Samuel Butler saw: classics, authorship and cultural authority in late Victorian England', *Proceedings of the Cambridge Philological Society* 48: 66–86
Wilamowitz-Moellendorff, U. von (1884) *Homerische Untersuchungen*. Berlin
(1916) *Die Ilias und Homer*. Berlin
Willcock, M. M. (1964) 'Mythological paradeigms in the *Iliad*', *Classical Quarterly* 14: 141–54 (= Cairns (2001) 435–55)
(1970) 'Aspects of the gods of the *Iliad*', *Bulletin of the Institute of Classical Studies* 17: 1–10 (repr. in Wright (1978) 58–69)
(1997) 'Neoanalysis', in Morris and Powell (1997) 174–89
Williams, B. (1993) *Shame and Necessity*. Berkeley
(2000) 'Understanding Homer: literature, history and ideal anthropology', in N. Roughley, ed. *Being Humans: Anthropological Universality and Particularity in Transdisciplinary Perspectives*, 224–32. Berlin and New York
Williams, C. (1993) *Pope, Homer and Manliness: Some Aspects of Eighteenth Century Classical Learning*. London
Williams, F. (1978) *Callimachus. Hymn to Apollo*. Oxford
Williams, R. (1989) *The Politics of Modernism*. London
Wilson, D. (1999) 'Symbolic violence in the *Iliad* book 9', *Classical World* 93.2: 131–47
(2002) *Ransom, Revenge, and Heroic Identity in the Iliad*. Cambridge
Winkler, J. (1982) 'The mendacity of Kalasiris and the narrative strategy of Heliodoros' *Aithiopika*', *Yale Classical Studies* 27: 93–158
(1990) *The Constraints of Desire: The Anthropology of Sex and Gender in Ancient Greece*. New York
Winterbottom, M. (1989). 'Speaking of the gods', *Greece and Rome* 36: 33–41
Wohl, V. (1993) 'Standing by the stathmos: the creation of sexual ideology in the *Odyssey*', *Arethusa* 26: 19–50
(1998) *Intimate Commerce: Exchange, Gender, and Subjectivity in Greek Tragedy*. Austin, Tex.
Wolf, F. A. (1869) 'Ist Homer auch Übersetzbar?', in *Kleine Schriften in lateinischer und deutscher Sprache*, 2 vols. II: 620–43. Halle
(1985) *Prolegomena to Homer*, trs. A. Grafton, G. W. Most and J. E. G. Zetzel. Princeton (orig. edn 1795)

Wood, M. (1985) *In Search of the Trojan War*. British Broadcasting Corporation Television Service. Films Incorporated, Wilmette, Il.
(1998) *In Search of the Trojan War*, rev. edn. Berkeley and Los Angeles
Wood, R. (1769) *An Essay on the Original Genius of Homer*. London
(1775) *An Essay on the Original Genius & Writing of Homer. With a Comparative View of the Ancient & Present State of the Troade*, rev. edn. London (orig. edn 1767)
Woodhouse, W. J. (1969) *The Composition of Homer's Odyssey*. Oxford (orig. edn 1930)
Wordsworth, W. (1974) *The Prose Works of William Wordsworth*, eds. W. J. B. Owen and J. W. Smyser, 3 vols. Oxford
Wordsworth, W. and Wordsworth, D. (1969) *The Letters of William and Dorothy Wordsworth*, vol. 2, *The Middle Years, Part 1, 1806–1811*, ed. E. de Selincourt, 2nd edn, rev. M. Moorman. Oxford
Worman, N. (2001) 'This voice which is not one: Helen's verbal guises in Homeric epics', in A. Lardinois and L. McClure, eds. *Making Silence Speak: Women's Voices in Greek Literature and Society*, 19–37. Princeton
Wright, G. M. and Jones, P. V., trs. (1997) *Homer: German Scholarship in Translation*. Oxford
Wright, I. C. (1864) *A Letter to the Dean of Canterbury, on the Homeric Lectures of Matthew Arnold*. London and Cambridge
Wright, J., ed. (1978) *Essays on the Iliad: Selected Modern Criticism*. Bloomington and London
Yamagata, N. (1994) *Homeric Morality. Mnemosyne* Suppl. 131. Leiden
Yang E. (1998) 'A comparative study of the singing styles of Mongolian and Tibetan geser/gesar artists', *Oral Tradition* 13: 422–34
Zanker, G. (1994) *The Heart of Achilles: Characterization and Ethics in the Iliad*. Ann Arbor
Zeitlin, F. (1996) 'Figuring fidelity in Homer's *Odyssey*', in *Playing the Other: Gender and Society in Classical Greek Literature*, 19–52. Chicago
(2001) 'Visions and revisions of Homer', in S. Goldhill, ed. *Being Greek under Rome: Cultural Identity, the Second Sophistic, and the Development of Empire*, 195–266. Cambridge and New York
Žižek, S. (1989) *The Sublime Object of Ideology*. London and New York

INDEX OF PASSAGES DISCUSSED

GENERAL INDEX

CAMBRIDGE COMPANIONS TO LITERATURE

Period and thematic

The Cambridge Companion to Greek Tragedy
edited by P. E. Easterling

The Cambridge Companion to Old English Literature
edited by Malcolm Godden and Michael Lapidge

The Cambridge Companion to Medieval Women's Writing
edited by Carolyn Dinshaw and David Wallace

The Cambridge Companion to Medieval Romance
edited by Roberta L. Krueger

The Cambridge Companion to Medieval English Theatre
edited by Richard Beadle

The Cambridge Companion to English Renaissance Drama, second edition
edited by A. R. Braunmuller and Michael Hattaway

The Cambridge Companion to Renaissance Humanism
edited by Jill Kraye

The Cambridge Companion to English Poetry, Donne to Marvell
edited by Thomas N. Corns

The Cambridge Companion to English Literature, 1500–1600
edited by Arthur F. Kinney

The Cambridge Companion to English Literature, 1650–1740
edited by Steven N. Zwicker

The Cambridge Companion to Writing of the English Revolution
edited by N. H. Keeble

The Cambridge Companion to English Restoration Theatre
edited by Deborah C. Payne Fisk

The Cambridge Companion to British Romanticism
edited by Stuart Curran

The Cambridge Companion to Eighteenth-Century Poetry
edited by John Sitter

The Cambridge Companion to the Eighteenth-Century Novel
edited by John Richetti

The Cambridge Companion to Gothic Fiction
edited by Jerrold E. Hogle

The Cambridge Companion to Victorian Poetry
edited by Joseph Bristow

The Cambridge Companion to the Victorian Novel
edited by Deirdre David

The Cambridge Companion to Crime Fiction
edited by Martin Priestman

The Cambridge Companion to Science Fiction
edited by Edward James and Farah Mendlesohn

The Cambridge Companion to Travel Writing
edited by Peter Hulme and Tim Youngs

The Cambridge Companion to American Realism and Naturalism
edited by Donald Pizer

The Cambridge Companion to Nineteenth-Century American Women's Writing
edited by Dale M. Bauer and Philip Gould

The Cambridge Companion to the Classic Russian Novel
edited by Malcolm V. Jones and Robin Feuer Miller

The Cambridge Companion to the French Novel: from 1800 to the Present
edited by Timothy Unwin

The Cambridge Companion to the Spanish Novel: from 1600 to the Present
edited by Harriet Turner and Adelaida López de Martínez

The Cambridge Companion to the Italian Novel
edited by Peter Bondanella and Andrea Ciccarelli

The Cambridge Companion to the Modern German Novel
edited by Graham Bartram

The Cambridge Companion to Jewish American Literature
edited by Hana Wirth-Nesher and Michael P. Kramer

The Cambridge Companion to the African American Novel
edited by Maryemma Graham

The Cambridge Companion to Contemporary Irish Poetry
edited by Matthew Campbell

The Cambridge Companion to Modernism
edited by Michael Levenson

The Cambridge Companion to Postmodernism
edited by Steven Connor

The Cambridge Companion to Australian Literature
edited by Elizabeth Webby

The Cambridge Companion to American Women Playwrights
edited by Brenda Murphy

The Cambridge Companion to Modern British Women Playwrights
edited by Elaine Aston and Janelle Reinelt

The Cambridge Companion to Twentieth-Century Irish Drama
edited by Shaun Richards

European authors

The Cambridge Companion to Homer
edited by Robert Fowler

The Cambridge Companion to Virgil
edited by Charles Martindale

The Cambridge Companion to Ovid
edited by Philip Hardie

The Cambridge Companion to St Paul edited by James D. G. Dunn

The Cambridge Companion to Dante
edited by Rachel Jacoff

The Cambridge Companion to Cervantes
edited by Anthony J. Cascardi

The Cambridge Companion to Goethe
edited by Lesley Sharpe

The Cambridge Companion to Dostoevskii
edited by W. J. Leatherbarrow

The Cambridge Companion to Tolstoy
edited by Donna Tussing Orwin

The Cambridge Companion to Chekhov
edited by Vera Gottlieb and Paul Allain

The Cambridge Companion to Ibsen
edited by James McFarlane

The Cambridge Companion to Proust
edited by Richard Bales

The Cambridge Companion to Thomas Mann
edited by Ritchie Robertson

The Cambridge Companion to Kafka
edited by Julian Preece

The Cambridge Companion to Brecht
edited by Peter Thomson and Glendyr Sacks

The Cambridge Companion to Walter Benjamin
edited by David S. Ferris

The Cambridge Companion to Lacan
edited by Jean-Michel Rabaté

UK authors

The Cambridge Companion to Chaucer, second edition
edited by Piero Boitani and Jill Mann

The Cambridge Companion to Shakespeare
edited by Margareta de Grazia and Stanley Wells

The Cambridge Companion to Shakespeare on Film
edited by Russell Jackson

The Cambridge Companion to Shakespearean Comedy
edited by Alexander Leggatt

The Cambridge Companion to Shakespeare on Stage
edited by Stanley Wells and Sarah Stanton

The Cambridge Companion to Shakespeare's History Plays
edited by Michael Hattaway

The Cambridge Companion to Shakespearean Tragedy
edited by Claire McEachern

The Cambridge Companion to Spenser
edited by Andrew Hadfield

The Cambridge Companion to John Dryden
edited by Steven N. Zwicker

The Cambridge Companion to Ben Jonson
edited by Richard Harp and Stanley Stewart

The Cambridge Companion to Milton, second edition
edited by Dennis Danielson

The Cambridge Companion to Samuel Johnson
edited by Greg Clingham

The Cambridge Companion to Jonathan Swift
edited by Christopher Fox

The Cambridge Companion to Mary Wollstonecraft
edited by Claudia L. Johnson

The Cambridge Companion to William Blake
edited by Morris Eaves

The Cambridge Companion to Wordsworth
edited by Stephen Gill

The Cambridge Companion to Coleridge
edited by Lucy Newlyn

The Cambridge Companion to Keats
edited by Susan J. Wolfson

The Cambridge Companion to Mary Shelley
edited by Esther Schor

The Cambridge Companion to Jane Austen
edited by Edward Copeland and Juliet McMaster

The Cambridge Companion to the Brontës
edited by Heather Glen

The Cambridge Companion to Charles Dickens
edited by John O. Jordan

The Cambridge Companion to George Eliot
edited by George Levine

The Cambridge Companion to Thomas Hardy
edited by Dale Kramer

The Cambridge Companion to Oscar Wilde
edited by Peter Raby

The Cambridge Companion to George Bernard Shaw
edited by Christopher Innes

The Cambridge Companion to Joseph Conrad
edited by J. H. Stape

The Cambridge Companion to D. H. Lawrence
edited by Anne Fernihough

The Cambridge Companion to Virginia Woolf
edited by Sue Roe and Susan Sellers

The Cambridge Companion to James Joyce, second edition
edited by Derek Attridge

The Cambridge Companion to T. S. Eliot
edited by A. David Moody

The Cambridge Companion to Ezra Pound
edited by Ira B. Nadel

The Cambridge Companion to Beckett
edited by John Pilling

The Cambridge Companion to Harold Pinter
edited by Peter Raby

The Cambridge Companion to Tom Stoppard
edited by Katherine E. Kelly

The Cambridge Companion to David Mament
edited by Christopher Bigsby

US authors

The Cambridge Companion to Herman Melville
edited by Robert S. Levine

The Cambridge Companion to Nathaniel Hawthorne
edited by Richard Millington

The Cambridge Companion to Theodore Dreiser
edited by Leonard Cassuto and Claire Virginia Eby

The Cambridge Companion to Edith Wharton
edited by Millicent Bell

The Cambridge Companion to Henry James
edited by Jonathan Freedman

The Cambridge Companion to Walt Whitman
edited by Ezra Greenspan

The Cambridge Companion to Ralph Waldo Emerson
edited by Joel Porte and Saundra Morris

The Cambridge Companion to Henry David Thoreau
edited by Joel Myerson

The Cambridge Companion to Mark Twain
edited by Forrest G. Robinson

The Cambridge Companion to Edgar Allan Poe
edited by Kevin J. Hayes

The Cambridge Companion to Emily Dickinson
edited by Wendy Martin

The Cambridge Companion to William Faulkner
edited by Philip M. Weinstein

The Cambridge Companion to Ernest Hemingway
edited by Scott Donaldson

The Cambridge Companion to F. Scott Fitzgerald
edited by Ruth Prigozy

The Cambridge Companion to Robert Frost
edited by Robert Faggen

The Cambridge Companion to Eugene O'Neill
edited by Michael Manheim

The Cambridge Companion to Tennessee Williams
edited by Matthew C. Roudané

The Cambridge Companion to Arthur Miller
edited by Christopher Bigsby

The Cambridge Companion to Sam Shepard
edited by Matthew C. Roudané

CAMBRIDGE COMPANIONS TO CULTURE

The Cambridge Companion to Modern German Culture
edited by Eva Kolinsky and Wilfried van der Will

The Cambridge Companion to Modern Russian Culture
edited by Nicholas Rzhevsky

The Cambridge Companion to Modern Spanish Culture
edited by David T. Gies

The Cambridge Companion to Modern Italian Culture
edited by Zygmunt G. Baranski and Rebecca J. West

The Cambridge Companion to Modern French Culture
edited by Nicholas Hewitt

The Cambridge Companion to Modern Latin American Culture
edited by John King